The Middle East in the World Economy

1800–1914

To Margaret

The Middle East
in the World Economy
1800-1914

Roger Owen

I.B. Tauris & Co Ltd
Publishers
London · New York

Reprinted in 2002 by
I. B. Tauris & Co. Ltd
6 Salem Road
London W2 4BU

175 Fifth Avenue
New York
NY 10010
www.ibtauris.com

In the United States of America
and Canada distributed by
Palgrave Macmillan
a division of St. Martin's Press
175 Fifth Avenue
New York
NY 10010

First published in 1981 by Methuen & Co Ltd, London and New York
Copyright © 1981, 1993, 2002 by Roger Owen

A CIP record for this book is available from the British Library

A full CIP record is available from the Library of Congress

ISBN 1-85043-658-4

Produced by Bookchase (UK) Ltd
Printed and bound in Great Britain by Biddles Ltd, www.biddles.co.uk

Contents

Preface   ix

A note on transliteration   xii

A note on weights, measures and currency   xiii

List of abbreviations   xiv

List of tables   xvi

List of maps   xix

Introduction to the Second Edition   xxi

Introduction: The Middle East economy in the period of so-called 'decline', 1500–1800   1
    The Middle East economy during the first three Ottoman centuries   2
    The structure of Ottoman administration and the appropriation of the surplus from agriculture, the craft industry and trade   10

1 *The Middle East economy in 1800*   24
    Rural economic activity   25
    Urban economic activity   45
    Regional and international trade   50
    Conclusion   56

2 *The economic consequences of the age of reforms, 1800–1850*   57
    The Ottoman reforms   58
    Egypt   64
    The Syrian provinces   76
    The Iraqi provinces   82

3 *The expansion of trade with Europe, 1800–1850*   83
    The expansion of trade between the Middle East and Europe   84
    The institutional support for the expansion of European trade   88
    The economic effects of the expansion of trade with Europe   91

4   *The Ottoman road to bankruptcy and the Anatolian economy,*
    1850–1881   100
    The growth of the Ottoman public debt, 1854–75   100
    Bankruptcy and after, 1875–81   108
    Foreign trade : the irregular growth of agricultural exports to Europe   110
    The state and the Anatolian economy   116

5   *Egypt, 1850–1882 : from foreign borrowing to bankruptcy and*
    occupation   122
    The growth of the public debt : the financial policies of Abbas, Said
       and Ismail   122
    Egypt and its creditors : the financial arrangements of 1876–80 and
       their consequences   130
    The agricultural sector of the economy   135
    Industry   148

6   *The provinces of Greater Syria, 1850–1880 : the economic and*
    social tensions of the 1850s and their consequences   153
    Beirut and Mount Lebanon   154
    The Syrian interior   167
    Palestine   173

7   *The Iraqi provinces, 1850–1880*   180
    The development of Iraq's sea-borne trade   180
    Ottoman policy towards the agricultural sector   183

8   *Anatolia and Istanbul, 1881–1914*   189
    The pattern of foreign financial control   191
    The agricultural sector   200
    Industry and mining   209
    Trade and payments   213

9   *The Egyptian economy, 1882–1914*   216
    The pattern of British control over the Egyptian economy   220
    The agricultural sector   226
    Industry, commerce and banking   233
    Trade and payments   240

10 *Mount Lebanon, Syria and Palestine, 1880–1914*   244
    Mount Lebanon and Beirut   249
    The Syrian interior   253
    Palestine   264

11 *The Iraqi provinces, 1880–1914*   273
    Transport and trade   274
    Agriculture and government policy towards the land   279
    Industry   285

12   *A century of economic growth and transformation : conclusion*   287

Notes   294

Bibliography of references cited   346

Index   371

Preface

Anyone attempting to write about the nineteenth-century economic history of the Middle East is at once brought face to face with a number of difficult problems. One is the question of defining the region itself. In recent years many historical works have tended to see the Middle East in large terms and as comprising a group of lands running all the way from Persia in the east to Egypt (or perhaps even Morocco) in the west, and from Turkey in the north to the Sudan in the south. But this is to produce a region which is much too vast and various for general analysis. It also encourages the imposition of a misleading homogeneity and spurious historical particularity based on unifying definitions couched in either religious/cultural or geographical/climatic terms. Thus for some the Middle East is a region inhabited primarily by Muslims; for others it is an arid, desert band of territory in which economic and political organization is determined by the need to control access to water. In either case, analysis of historical change relies heavily on those few defining factors which are supposed to give the Middle East its unity to the neglect of those many features which it shares with other parts of the non-European world.

For my purpose I propose to deal with a much smaller geographical unit. As far as the present work is concerned, the Middle East is taken to mean the region comprising present-day Turkey (that is Anatolia and the Istanbul district), Egypt, Iraq and what is sometimes called Greater Syria (the area which now includes Syria, Lebanon, Israel and Jordan). This has the advantage of focusing on lands which, at the beginning of the nineteenth century, were all part of the Ottoman Empire, which all possessed roughly similar economic structures and which all underwent roughly similar processes of transformation as the century progressed. It has an additional advantage in that it allows the region to be split up into provinces or groups of provinces for the purpose of historical treatment, that is, into entities which, if not single markets in the strict economic sense, at least possessed enough of a common political and administrative structure to allow them to be regarded as a single unit.

A second problem stems from the lack of specialist studies on many important aspects of Middle Eastern economic life. In spite of the work of writers like Charles Issawi, André Raymond, Dominique Chevalier,

ix

Muhammad Salman Hasan, Halil Inalcik and others there are still a great many yawning gaps in present-day knowledge of the region's history. To speak very generally, the study of the economic history of the Middle East — Egypt apart — remains underdeveloped compared with that of many other parts of the non-European world. More so than elsewhere, much of what is being written about the region has to be regarded as introductory or only provisional.

A final problem, not surprisingly, concerns the scarcity of reliable statistics. This is not to say that figures do not exist for all kinds of activity, rather that they can easily appear as what Emmanuel Le Roy Ladurie has called a *mirage chiffré* enticing the economic historian into believing that he is able to know, or to quantify, much more than he safely can.[1] Before using any set of figures a vital preliminary is to ask how they might have been collected. Here, for example, is the British Consul, Dennis, at Izmir in 1883 explaining how he went about estimating the value of the city's imports and exports for report to Britain:

> In drawing up the following notices of the trade and commerce of Smyrna for the last five years . . . I have had to depend wholly on such information as I could obtain from private sources, seeing that no statistics are published by the Government or obtainable from the customs house. In such a case it is evident that the figures cannot lay strict claim to accuracy, either as regards the value or of the quantities . . . of the merchandise shipped or landed. The figures, therefore, given in the subjoined tables, can be regarded only as approximate to the truth but with what margin of deficit in each particular instance it is beyond my power to hazard a conjecture. (CR (UK), Smyrna, 1877–81, PP, 1883, LXXIII, 329)

With such warnings in hand it is vital to get away from a state of mind which sees any figure, however unreliable, as better than none at all. It is also necessary to admit that, with the exception of some of the statistics collected during the British occupation of Egypt after 1882 or some relating to the economic activities of specific institutions like banks and railways, there are none for the nineteenth-century Middle East which will bear the weight of anything more than the simplest methods of analysis.

For all these reasons I cannot pretend that what is offered here is a comprehensive, systematic survey of the subject. It is more like a collection of essays organized round two major themes. The first is the uneven impact on various parts of the Middle East economy of two sets of stimuli: the centralizing policies of the rulers of Egypt and the Ottoman Empire and the growing commercial, financial, and finally political penetration of the region by an expanding Europe. The second is the belief that the nature of this impact can only be properly understood by an examination of a complex set of interactions between outside influences and local economic and social forms. In all this it is my hope that what is being revealed is seen not simply as dead history but as the early stages of a process which continues to have an enormous effect in shaping the structures of present-day Middle Eastern economies.

The book has been so long in the writing that I have, inevitably, incurred more than usually large debts to numerous friends, colleagues and students with whom I have either discussed many of the topics presented here or from whose written works I have learned much. I hope that they will forgive me if I simply list their names: Talal Asad, Terry Burke, Yaacov Firestone, Muhammad Salman Hasan, Bent Hansen, Albert Hourani, Robert Hunter, Huri Islamoğlu, Rick Joseph, Çaglar Keydar, Robert Mabro, Donald Quataert, Samir Radwan, André Raymond, Paul Saba, Linda Schatkowski-Schilcher, Alexander Schölch, Yahya Tezel and Sami Zubaida. I would also like to give special mention to Charles Issawi whose pioneering works on the economic history of the Middle East have been a constant source of encouragement.

Roger Owen   *Oxford, Autumn 1979*

A note on transliteration

The system of transliterating Arabic and Turkish words and proper names has been kept as simple as possible. No diacritical marks have been used in the text and only *ayns* and *hamzas* in the references. Where Arabic or Turkish terms can be found in the *Shorter Oxford Dictionary* (e.g. feddan, agha) this spelling has been used. Otherwise they have been transliterated according to the system employed in Wehr's *Dictionary* and (for Turkish) by the one used by the *International Journal of Middle Eastern Studies*. Where the same term is transliterated differently in Turkish and Arabic (for example *vakf/waqf*) the Turkish term has been given first. Place-names which can be found in the *Oxford Regional Economic Atlas: The Middle East and North Africa* (2nd edn, Oxford, 1964) have been given in this form. The remainder have been given, where possible, in the form in which they appear in official government maps or lists of place-names of the inter-war period.

A note on weights, measures and currency

The situation with regard to Middle Eastern weights and measures in the nineteenth century is one of the greatest complexity. Both varied greatly from area to area and from one period to the next. Even after both the Ottoman and Egyptian governments had attempted to introduce the metric system in the second half of the century there was only a limited improvement, as a contemporary report noted of rural Iraq: 'Almost every village has its own standard stones, no two of which are exactly alike; and the merchants of the towns and cities buy with one system of weights and measures and sell with another and smaller system.'* In these circumstances it would be misleading to provide a precise set of equivalents for the *ardabb*, cantar, *kilé* and *oke*, the main units used in measuring the volume of agricultural produce, and I have simply defined these anew on each occasion I have used them. The same applies to European measures like the 'bale' which also varied from time to time and crop to crop.

Measures of land area were equally unstandardized. However, as the majority of the references to these come from the end of the nineteenth century I have felt able to use the following equivalents:

1 feddan = 1.038 acres

1 dunum (Palestine) = 1000 square metres (or about ¼ acre)

As far as European measures are concerned 1 hectare = 2.471 acres.

Units of currency present another difficult problem. A bewildering variety of coins were in use in the Middle East throughout the period, and in most cases their relative values were constantly changing. As a rule I have provided a sterling equivalent. But as far as the Turkish gold pound and the Egyptian pound were concerned I have assumed the following value throughout:

£T (gold) = 100 kuruş/piastres = £0.909

£E = 100 piastres = £1. 0s. 6d.

For further discussion see C. Issawi, ed., *The Economic History of the Middle East, 1800–1914* (Chicago, 1966), 517–24; E. R. J. Owen, *Cotton and the Egyptian Economy 1820–1914* (Oxford, 1969), 381–5.

* W. H. Hall (ed.), *Reconstruction in Turkey* (n.p., 1918), 241.

List of abbreviations

AA	Austrian Archives (Consular Reports from Egypt, copies of which were found in the Abdin Palace, Cairo)
AAS	*African and Asian Studies*
AF	*L'Asie Française*
AJSLL	*American Journal of Semitic Languages and Literature*
AO	*Archivum Ottomanicum*
ASQ	*Arab Studies Quarterly*
BEO	*Bulletin d'Etudes Orientales*
BIE	*Bulletin de l'Institut égyptien*
BJS	*British Journal of Sociology*
BSOAS	*Bulletin of the School of Oriental and African Studies*
BUSAE	*Bulletin d'Union syndicale des Agriculteurs d'Egypte*
CHI	*Cambridge History of Islam*
CO	Colonial Office (London)
CR	*Commercial Report*
CSJ	*Cairo Scientific Journal*
CSSH	*Comparative Studies in Society and History*
DE¹ and *DE²*	*Description de l'Egypte*, 1st and 2nd edns (Paris)
EC	*L'Egypte Contemporaine*
EHR	*The Economic History Review*
ES	*Economy and Society*
FO	Foreign Office (London)
HJ	*Historical Journal*
HP	*Hekekyan Papers* (British Museum)
IBRD	International Bank for Reconstruction and Development
IEJ	*Israeli Exploration Journal*
IJMES	*International Journal of Middle East Studies*
ISS	Institute of Social Studies (The Hague)
JA	*Journal Asiatique*
JCA	*Journal of Contemporary Asia*
JCAS	*Journal of the Central Asian Society*
JESHO	*Journal of the Economic and Social History of the Orient*
JMH	*Journal of Modern History*
JEH	*Journal of Economic History*

JPOS	*Journal of the Palestine Oriental Society*
JPS	*Journal of Peasant Studies*
MEJ	*Middle East Journal*
MES	*Middle Eastern Studies*
MIE	*Mémoires presentés à l'Institut égyptien*
MTIE	*Mémoires et Travaux originaux presentés et lus à l'Institut égyptien*
NLR	*New Left Review* (London)
PDA	Public Debt Administration
PEF	Palestine Exploration Fund (London)
PP	*Parliamentary Papers* (Accounts and Papers) (London)
PRO	Public Record Office (London)
QR	*Quarterly Review*
RC	*Receuil Consulaire* (Brussels)
RDM	*Revue des Deux Mondes*
REI	*Revue des Etudes Islamiques*
RH	*Revue Historique*
RHC	*Revue d'Histoire des Colonies*
RI	*Revue d'Islam*
RMM	*Revue de Monde Musulman*
RO	*Revue de l'Orient*
ROMES	*Review of Middle East Studies*
SAPP	*St. Antony's Private Papers*
SH	*Scripta Hierosolymitana*
SRO	Scottish Record Office (Edinburgh)
UK IO	India Office (London)
WI	*Die Welt des Islams*

List of tables

1 English and French imports from the Middle East during the seventeenth and eighteenth centuries *6*
2 French imports of Levant cotton during the eighteenth century *7*
3 Estimates of the cost of production, value and profit of various Egyptian crops − *c.*1800 *31*
4 Estimates of the volume and value of Egyptian cotton exports, 1821−49 *67*
5 Importance of the land tax and of profits from cotton in total Egyptian government revenues, 1821−38 *68*
6 British exports to the eastern Mediterranean, 1814−50 *85*
7 British exports of cotton goods to the eastern Mediterranean, 1824−50 *85*
8 French trade with the eastern Mediterranean, 1790−1856 *87*
9 Estimates of the numbers of looms at work in Aleppo and Damascus, 1825−60 *94*
10 Estimates of the value of trade between Egypt and Syria/Palestine and various European and Middle Eastern sources, 1836−9 *96*
11 The nationality and tonnage of shipping arriving at various Mediterranean and Black Sea ports in the 1840s *97*
12 Ottoman foreign loans, 1854−79 *104*
13 Ottoman revenues and expenditure, 1860/1−1880/1 *106*
14 Estimates of the value of the principal agricultural exports from Izmir, 1863−79 *111*
15 Estimates of the export of Anatolian cotton by volume, 1860−79 *112*
16 Estimates of the value of the sea-borne trade of Izmir, Trabzon and Mersin, 1850−79 *114*
17 The production of silk thread in the Bursa district, 1850−79 *115*
18 Estimates of Egyptian government revenues and expenditures, 1852−79 *124*
19 Egypt's foreign loans, 1862−73 *127*
20 Estimates of the area of *kharajïya* and *ushurïya* land in Egypt, 1863−77 *130*
21 Estimates of the amount of money spent on Egyptian public works *131*

·22 Export of Egypt's principal crops, 1850–79 *136*
23 The Egyptian industrial sector in 1873 *149*
24 Egypt's import of selected manufactured goods via Alexandria, 1866–79 *150*
25 Egypt's trade in sugar, 1863–80 (Alexandria only) *151*
26 The value of silk exports from Beirut and the price of Lebanese cocoons, 1850–9 *155*
27 Syrian silk production, 1861–80 *156*
28 British exports of cotton goods to Syria/Palestine, 1852–72 *160*
29 Estimates of the value of Beirut's sea-borne trade, 1850–78 *161*
30 Exports of cereals from ports on the Syria/Palestine coast *168*
31 Estimates of the number of textile looms at work in the main Syrian towns, 1861–79 *172*
32 Estimates of the sea-borne trade of Jaffa, 1850–81 *176*
33 Estimates of the volume of agricultural exports from Jaffa, Haifa and Acre, 1857–80 *177*
34 The growth in Iraq's foreign trade, 1864–80 *182*
35 Turkey's foreign trade, 1880–1913 *191*
36 Revenues ceded to the Ottoman PDA, 1882/3–1912/13 *193*
37 The Ottoman Empire's revenues and expenditures, 1887/8–1911/12 *197*
38 The proportion of land devoted to crops of various types in the provinces and sanjaks of Anatolia, 1909/10 *200*
39 The value and volume of some of Izmir's major agricultural exports, 1880–1912 *201*
40 Exports of cereals from Anatolia, 1881–1911 *202*
41 The production and export of tobacco, silk and cotton from certain districts of Anatolia, 1881–1914 *203*
42 Changes in the average annual price of major Anatolian crops at Istanbul, 1881–1908 *204*
43 The proportion of agricultural land in Anatolia held in properties of various sizes, 1909/10 *207*
44 The Turkish industrial censuses of 1915 and 1921 *210*
45 The production of minerals in Anatolia, 1909–10 *213*
46 The amount paid by the Ottoman government in kilometric guarantees to foreign railway companies *214*
47 Egypt's population and cultivated land, 1882–1917 *217*
48 The distribution of Egypt's agricultural land in properties of various sizes, 1894–1913 *218*
49 Areas devoted to seven major Egyptian crops, 1886/7 and 1893/4–1912/13 *218*
50 Egyptian government revenues and expenditures, 1881–1913 *223*
51 Egyptian agricultural production: quantity indexes of major field

crops and all field crops, 1887–1914 *227*

52 The distribution of Egyptian medium and small landed property into plots of various sizes in 1913 *229*

53 The state of indebtedness of Egyptian owners of 5 feddans or less, by province, 1913 *232*

54 Paid-up capital and debentures of companies operating in Egypt showing amount held abroad and amount held in Egypt, 1883–1914 *234*

55 Companies in the Egyptian modern industrial sector, 1901 and 1911 *236*

56 Workers in the Egyptian industrial and craft-industrial sector, 1897, 1907 and 1917 *240*

57 Egypt's foreign trade, 1885–1913 *241*

58 Egypt's balance of payments, 1884–1914 *242*

59 Ottoman census figures for the populations of the three provinces of Aleppo, Beirut and Damascus and the *mutasarriflik* of Jerusalem, 1885–1914 *244*

60 Goods traffic carried on the Syrian railways, 1899–1911 *246*

61 Estimates of the trade at Syria/Palestine's seven principal ports (Iskanderun, Latakia, Tripoli, Beirut, Acre/Haifa, Jaffa and Gaza), 1883 to 1913 *247*

62 Estimates of the composition of exports at Syria/Palestine's seven principal ports, 1883 to 1913 *247*

63 Eastern Mediterranean sea-borne trade: the trade of Iskanderun, Beirut and Jaffa with Egypt and Turkey, 1910–12 *248*

64 Production of Syrian silk, 1880–1913 *250*

65 Volume and price of Beirut's exports of silk thread and value of Syria/Palestine's silk exports, 1881–1913 *250*

66 Estimates of the volume of exports of certain important agricultural products from Syrian/Palestinian ports, 1881 to 1913 *260*

67 Estimates of the numbers of looms and textile workers in Syria's major towns, 1890–1912 *261*

68 The foreign trade of Palestine, 1883–1913 *265*

69 The value of Iraq's sea-borne trade, 1880–1913 *275*

70 The volume and price of Iraq's principal sea-borne exports, 1880–1913 *275*

List of maps

1 The Middle East: major geographical and climatic features *27*
2 Middle Eastern caravan routes *48*
3 The provinces of Egypt and the Ottoman Empire in Asia at the end of
   the nineteenth century *190*
4 Middle Eastern railway systems, *c*.1914 *288*

Introduction to the Second Edition

Although the first edition of this book was published in 1981, the bulk of it was written in the late 1970s. It was obviously very much a product of that time, written with reference to the themes and historical debates concerning Third World economic transformation which then seemed to me most relevant. Nevertheless I believe that its primary aim, which was to provide a succinct outline of the major changes taking place in the Middle East economy during the nineteenth century, is still achieved. In particular, I remain satisfied with the main outlines of the periodization I then adopted, with my analysis of the dynamic behind the growth of the official debt and with my tentative explorations of some of the processes which opened up the region to world trade, for example that of the spinning of Lebanese silk.

What issues would I address if I were now to try to write the same book all over again? The answers to this question fall into two groups. The first consists of those areas in the original work which were subject to significant criticism or misunderstanding at the time. The second involves consideration of the many pieces of research into recent Middle Eastern economic history which have come out in the dozen years since its original publication.

As far as the conceptual apparatus of the original book is concerned, some readers expressed criticism of my failure to define what I meant by the term 'world economy', while others suggested that I should have begun my account in 1750, rather than 1800, as the moment when global forces began to have an impact on the local economies in a systematic way. Concerning the first point, I would certainly have to plead guilty. Then as now I conceived of the world economy as simply a catch-all phrase indicating a bundle of different features, not as a single coherent object to be precisely defined and then used as a single explanation for complex processes. If I did have any one central dynamic in mind, I think it should more usefully have been described as an expanding European capitalism, driven by relentless competition and always ready to call upon its own government to use its power to improve its advantage overseas.[1] But I should have made this more clear.

By the same token, I also remain happy with my choice of 1800 as a starting point. This is not to say that no important changes took place before then but, as I tried to show in my first Introduction, these were largely part of a local dynamic which was influenced only in fits and starts by outside forces, none of which had the power to maintain significant pressure for long. What changed at the end of the eighteenth century was the twin impact of the French (political) Revolution and the British (industrial) Revolution which set in train processes which were consistent, irreversible and largely beyond the control of Middle Eastern merchants and entrepreneurs or Middle Eastern regimes.

A third criticism concerned my sceptical attitude to most nineteenth-century statistics. I had thought that I had made my views clear in my original Preface but apparently I had not. What I meant to assert was not that such statistics did not exist in plenty in Middle Eastern and other archives (they do), but only that the economic historian needed to be extremely conscious of the way that they had been collected and of what reality they could be supposed to represent. In particular, I believe that they should only be aggregated to allow measurement of larger and more abstract entities, like national price indices or national product, with great care, and they should be accompanied by a warning as to the wide margin of possible error. Here, as perhaps elsewhere, it was the historian in me talking to the economist.

Lastly, a number of reviewers took me to task for my treatment of figures for population and population growth. In some cases I chose badly from data then available: for example, a better estimate of the population of Istanbul at the beginning of the nineteenth century would be 360,000.[2] In other cases I was unable to benefit from important recent research, notably Justin McCarthy's careful tabulations of the Ottoman records, complemented by his vital observation that all such so-called 'censuses' were no more than an attempt to produce aggregates from existing, but almost always incomplete, registers.[3] All this stands in marked contradistinction to the type of enumeration carried out in Egypt from 1882 onwards, which is the only pre-First World War Middle Eastern example of what McCarthy calls the 'modern' census, in which an attempt is made to count every single person residing within a particular country on a particular day. I would also want to stress that what McCarthy's research provides, *inter alia*, is further proof of Issawi's argument, which I followed, that for most of the Middle East (as I define it) the nineteenth century was a time of significant demographic expansion.[4]

Apart from population, the other area of Middle Eastern economic history which received most attention in the 1980s was that of land, land ownership and the balance between large and small agricultural units. I remain content with what I wrote about the 1858 Ottoman Land Law, although I should certainly have observed that much of the continuing debate as to its exact interpretation depends on an assumption that the modern notion of legislative intent can be applied backwards to the Ottoman officials of that time. If not, as I believe to be the case, there is no point in arguing about what the law really intended – which could not be a practical issue as it was never tested in the courts – but only about how it was understood and interpreted by those who had to put it into effect.

Where I did make an important mistake was in my general assumption that the build-up of large estates, so prominent a feature in Egypt and the Fertile Crescent, also applied to Anatolia itself. Here, recent work by Aricanli and others has proved beyond doubt that the Ottoman officials were extremely adept at maintaining the existence of small and medium-sized properties in all the Anatolian provinces except those in the east.[5] I also take note of Gerber's argument that, in the Jerusalem district at least, peasants showed no inclination to have their properties registered in the name of a local notable or strongman, something which every writer since Warriner has supposed.[6] But I keep an open mind as to whether this was the case in the Iraqi and Syrian provinces as well.

Fortunately for my own work, I was able to refer to Firestone's imaginative attempts to account for the origins and then subsequent development of the system of joint land ownership known as *mushaa*. Since then, however, he has returned to the subject one last time in an article which does much to illuminate the legal position of such holdings under both Ottoman and Islamic law.[7] Here I find his argument for defining *mushaa* as a species of co-ownership, not communal ownership, compelling. I would also like to underline the refinements which this last article brings to his earlier distinction between two types of *mushaa* – 'fixed share' and 'open-ended' – depending on the way in which rights of ownership, and thus access, were allocated. Further useful progress in the understanding of this difficult subject has been made in the Transjordanian context by Munday.[8]

A last contribution to the discussions about land ownership and land use of which I would certainly have wanted to take account is Shafir's groundbreaking analysis of the dynamics of Jewish–Arab relations in Palestine before 1914.[9] This benefits greatly from his view that Jewish settlement activity encountered much the same conditions as those to be found in other sites of white settler colonialism and responded to them in many of the same ways, for example by relegating local agricultural labour to an inferior status. Not the least of the virtues of such an approach is that it opens up Middle Eastern economic and social history to perspectives tried and tested with respect to other, analogous, regions of the non-European world.

The remainder of the important research published in recent years can be divided roughly into two parts. The first builds on approaches already set out in the standard works, collating information about Middle Eastern trade, for example, or finding the figures necessary to create new indices for agricultural output or the prices of important commodities.[10] Under the same rubric I would include the interesting studies of urban development, of the growth of port cities and of the changing role of minorities.[11] To this should be added the creative attempts by Kasaba and others to show how these same studies can throw new light on the dynamics contained within the new relationships which European capitalism came to establish with certain local groups and certain specific forms of local economic activity.[12]

The other growth area in the 1980s was the use of local court records – both administrative and legal – for the study of nineteenth-century economic and social change. This is difficult work, but when patiently conducted can be used to make sense of such vital distinctions as those between ownership or control of landed property and rights of access. It can also be used to fill in many of the gaps in existing analyses by providing rich data about economic practices at village or district level.[13] Last, but by no means least, such records can be employed to illuminate the lives of many groups previously hidden from the economic historian's attention, notably women and the urban poor.[14]

The study of court records has two additional points in its favour. The first is the way in which it has tended to be conducted as a cooperative enterprise by groups of scholars under the overall direction of a leading expert such as Abdul-Karim Rafeq when he was teaching at the University of Damascus or Adnan Bakhit during his days at the University of Jordan in Amman.[15] Another such centre can be found at the Lebanese University in Beirut. Second, centres like these have also provided some of the very few sites for regular cooperation between Arab and foreign economic and social historians.[16]

What the last decade and a half has not produced in great number is works of synthesis or those which open up a whole new field for research. Among the very few examples of the former I would cite Charles Issawi's *An Economic History of the Middle East and North Africa* and Asim al-Disuqi's *Nahw fahm misr al-iqtisadi al-ijtima'i*.[17] As for the latter, two of the most interesting are Haim Gerber's provocative, but only partially convincing, *The Social Origins of the Modern Middle East* and Timothy Mitchell's innovative *Colonising Egypt*, both of which provide great encouragement to those looking for new points of entry for the study of nineteenth-century economic history.[18]

In general, this has not been a good time for grand theory. However, we are now beginning to see examples of those works which reflect the enormous changes that have taken place in the academic orthodoxies concerning long-term economic development ushered in by the international debt crisis of the 1970s and, more recently, the collapse of the Soviet model. A good example of a study which looks at economic transformation in terms of its growth performance measured almost exclusively in statistical terms is Bent Hansen's *The Political Economy of*

Poverty, Equity and Growth: Egypt and Turkey, which had its origins in a programme of comparative analysis promoted by the World Bank.[19] Another, more controversial, approach is that offered by Robert Vitalis in his *Power, Wealth and Industry: The Rise and Fall of the ʿAbbud Pasha Group and Egypt's Business Oligopoly*, which though focused primarily on the post-1922 period does use nineteenth-century material to launch a revisionist examination of the orthodoxies underlying most of what has been written about Egyptian economic development over the past fifty years.[20] Such works will certainly do much to enliven scholarly interest in the field in years to come.

Roger Owen
Oxford, March 1993

Notes

1. I find the best analysis of the relation between capitalist expansion overseas and the state to be P. J. Cain and A. G. Hopkins, 'Gentlemanly capitalism and British expansion overseas', 1 and 2, *Economic History Review*, XXXIX, 4, 501–25 and XL, 1, 1–26.

2. Pointed out by Gad G. Gilbar in a review which appeared belatedly in *Middle Eastern Studies*, 24, 4 (Oct. 1988), 502. He himself cites H. Inalcik's article, 'Istanbul' in *Encyclopaedia of Islam*, EI², IV, 244.

3. Justin McCarthy, *The Arab World, Turkey and the Balkans (1878–1914): A Handbook of Historical Statistics* (Boston, Mass., 1982) and *The Population of Palestine: Population Statistics of the Late Ottoman Period and the Mandate* (New York, 1990). See also, Kamal Karpat, *Ottoman Population: Demographic and Social Characteristics* (Madison, 1985).

4. McCarthy, *Population of Palestine*, 2–4; and Charles Issawi, *The Economic History of the Middle East 1800–1914: A Book of Readings* (Chicago, 1966), 17.

5. For example, Tosun Aricanli, 'Agrarian relations in Turkey: A historical sketch' in Alan Richards, ed., *Food, States and Peasants: Analyses of the Agrarian Question in the Middle East* (Boulder, Colorado, 1986), 25 and 'Property, land and labor in nineteenth century Anatolia' in Caglar Keyder and Faruk Tabak, eds., *Landholding and Commercial Agriculture in the Middle East* (Albany, 1991), 123–33. See also, Haim Gerber, *The Social Origins of the Modern Middle East* (Boulder, Colorado, and London, 1987), 85.

6. Gerber, *The Social Origins of the Modern Middle East*, 76–7.

7. Yaʿakov Firestone, 'The land-equalizing mushaʿ village: a reassess-

ment' in Gad G. Gilbar, ed., *Ottoman Palestine 1800–1914* (Leiden, 1990), 91–129.

8. Martha Munday's analysis of *mushaa* has yet to be published. For an example of another aspect of her ground-breaking studies of land tenure in Ottoman Transjordan see, 'Shareholders and the state: representing the village in the late 19th century land registers of the Southern Hawran' in Thomas Philipp, ed., *The Syrian Land in the 18th and 19th Century: The Common and the Specific in Historical Experience*, Berliner Islamstudien, Band 5 (Stuttgart, 1992).

9. Gershon Shafir, *Land, Labor and the Origins of the Israeli–Palestinian Conflict 1882–1914* (Cambridge, 1989), particularly Chapters 1 and 3.

10. For example, Sevket Pamuk, *The Ottoman Empire and European Capitalism, 1820–1913: Trade, Investment and Production* (Cambridge, 1987).

11. For example, Leila T. Fawaz, *Merchants and Migrants in Nineteenth Century Beirut* (London and Cambridge, Mass., 1983); Robert Ilbert, *Heliopolis: Le Caire 1905–1927: Genèse d'une ville* (Paris, 1981); and Thomas Philipp, *The Syrians in Egypt, 1725–1975*, Berliner Islamstudien, Band 3 (Stuttgart, 1985).

12. Caglar Keyder, 'Bureaucracy and bourgeoisie: reform and revolution in the age of imperialism', *Review*, XI, 2 (Spring 1988), 151–65; Bruce Masters, 'The 1850 events in Aleppo: an aftershock of Syria's incorporation into the world capitalist system', *International Journal of Middle East Studies*, 22, 1 (Feb. 1990), 3–20; and Donald Quataert, *Social Disintegration and Popular Resistance in the Ottoman Empire, 1881–1908: Reactions to European Economic Penetration*, New York University Studies in Near Eastern Civilization, No. 9 (New York and London, 1983).

13. For example, Kenneth M. Cuno, *The Pasha's Peasants: Land, Society and Economy in Lower Egypt, 1740–1858* (Cambridge, 1993); and James A. Reilly, 'Status groups and propertyholding in the Damascus hinterland 1828–1889', *International Journal of Middle East Studies*, 21, 2 (Nov. 1989), 517–39.

14. For example, Ehud R. Toledano, *State and Society in Mid-Nineteenth Century Egypt* (Cambridge, 1990), particularly Part II; Judith R. Tucker, *Women in Nineteenth-Century Egypt* (Cambridge, 1985).

15. To give just one example from the Bakhit group, see Akram al-Ramini, *Nablus fi-l qarn al-Tasiᶜ ᶜashar* (Amman, 1979).

16. See for example the various conferences on the Bilad al-Sham, especially the one organized at the University of Damascus in 1987, the proceedings of which were published in 2 volumes by the Kuliya al-Adab of the University (nd).

17. Issawi (London, 1982); Disuqi (Cairo, 1981).

18. Gerber (see Note 5 above); and Mitchell (Cambridge, 1988).

19. Hansen (Oxford, 1991).

20. Vitalis's work is yet to be published (1993) but see an extract in R. B. Vitalis, 'On the theory and practice of compradors: the role of 'Abbud Pasha in the Egyptian political economy', *International Journal of Middle East Studies*, 22, 3 (Aug. 1990), 291–315.

Introduction: The Middle East economy in the period of so-called 'decline', 1500–1800

Among historians of the Middle East the conventional view is that the period 1500 to 1800 is to be seen as one of declining economic activity. This view clearly has its origin in the belief that Islamic civilization itself – the traditional unit of study for such historians – reached its zenith some time in the early Middle Ages and thereafter entered a centuries-long era of diminishing vitality. Initially this alleged decline was described mainly in cultural and, to some extent, political terms. With the publication of Gibb and Bowen's influential *Islamic Society and the West*, however, historians began to give it a more economic and social content, characterizing it as a period of falling population, reduced trade, stagnant craft production and impoverished agriculture.[1]

The problem with this approach is that it rests on only the flimsiest basis in fact. Although much support can be found for it in the reports of the eighteenth-century European travellers or in the works of contemporary Turkish and Arab chroniclers – for whom the past was generally more glorious than the present – there is little, if any, statistical confirmation.[2] To take only one of the most basic indices necessary to analyse economic performance, all efforts to produce even a series of well-informed guesses as to the size of the Middle Eastern population before the nineteenth century have proved totally unsatisfactory.[3] Again, with the limited exception of the work done on the Ottoman tax registers for Anatolia in the sixteenth, for Palestine in the sixteenth and eighteenth centuries, and for Egypt during the whole Ottoman period, nothing is known about the vital relationships between the size of population, cultivated area, and agricultural production.[4] Figures for the volume of intra-regional trade and for the output of the craft industry are similarly lacking; and yet without such information no proper evaluation of changes in the total volume of economic activity is possible.

If this were not bad enough other features make it worse. One is the tendency to generalize and to assume that the economies in every part of the Middle East were subject to the same pressures and thus were moving in the same general direction. Another is the failure of almost all writers on the subject to make clear whether what they are talking about is 'decline' in absolute terms or *vis-à-vis* an expanding Europe. Given the rapid emergence of commercial capitalism in England, France, Holland and

1

elsewhere from the seventeenth century onwards it would be quite easy to envisage a limited growth in certain sectors of the Middle East economy which still left it less well able to compete with the new developments in European trade and industry. This last point is the more important as the same writers generally seem to work on the assumption that the economic impact of Europe only really began to be felt in the Middle East after about 1800, whereas in an uneven and disjointed way some such impact is apparent throughout the whole period under discussion. Finally, the issue is further bedevilled by its involvement in the sterile debate surrounding another much written about problem: the attempt to explain why capitalist industrialization never took place in the Middle East.[5]

Attempts to provide an explanation for the alleged economic decline are equally unsatisfactory. One argument often resorted to is the supposedly anti-capitalist, anti-progressive character of the Islamic religion or, in some formulations, the Islamic state.[6] Military rule or the organization of the so-called 'Islamic city' have also been put forward as reasons for lack of advance on the grounds that neither provided a protective environment in which merchants and entrepreneurs could flourish.[7] Another, equally fallacious, argument is the assertion that there was a diminution in the Middle East's international commerce following the discovery of the Cape route to India, something which is supposed, in Lewis's words, to have left Turkey and its Arab provinces 'in a stagnant backwater through which the life-giving stream of world trade no longer flowed'.[8]

Simplistic explanations of this type can be challenged individually, either on the grounds that the facts used to support them are incorrect − trade across the Middle East did not dry up in the way Lewis suggests − or that they could not possibly have worked in the way in which they are supposed to have.[9] But a more constructive approach, and one which does not simply seek to refute a fallacious proposition in its own terms, is to combine a critical attitude to the facts as presented with the employment of an alternative method which can be used to provide a systematic and coherent account of the available evidence. In what follows I will adopt a practice of this latter type, beginning with a discussion of the main trends within the economies of the various parts of the Middle East region, where these can be discerned, before going on to attempt to elucidate some of the principal relationships that obtained between the organization of economic activity in the three major spheres of agriculture, handicraft production and commerce, and then to examine the method of appropriating and distributing the surplus derived from them.

The Middle East economy during the first three Ottoman centuries

There is some evidence for a belief that the Ottomans conquered lands still recovering from a period of economic dislocation which might well have begun as long ago as the fearful visitation of the Black Death (both the bubonic and the pulmonary plagues) in 1347−9 with its dreadful decimation of the Egyptian and Syrian population.[10] Whether this is true or not there can be little doubt that the immediate impact of the extension of Ottoman rule to the Arab regions at the eastern end of the Mediterranean was a century or so of significant expansion. It is not difficult to see why. The agricultural sector − which contained within it many areas long devoted to the production of cash crops for the market − benefited directly from Ottoman concern for rural security, from the repair of the systems of irrigation and from the institution of a more regular and efficient system of tax collection. Again, the incorporation of the Arab lands into a single empire removed a whole series of barriers to intra-regional trade, while the Ottomans were active in putting down piracy and in encouraging overland commerce by building caravanserais, digging wells and establishing garrisons at strategic points along major routes.[11] Many of the same influences were also at work in the newly captured areas of Anatolia.[12]

Detailed studies of the Ottoman administrative records for Anatolia, southern Syria and Egypt support these general conclusions. As far as the first of these is concerned Barkan and Cook have shown that there is good reason to suppose that the population rose by a considerable extent during the sixteenth century, perhaps by as much as 40 per cent.[13] This can almost certainly be taken to imply that there was an accompanying expansion of agricultural output as the increase in the rural labour force allowed new land to be brought into cultivation until supplies of cultivable land began to run out in some areas towards the end of the century.[14] Further incentive to increase output came from the rapid rise in the population of Istanbul and other cities and the continuous advance in European cereal prices which provided a basis for a flourishing − though, from the state's point of view, illegal − export of Anatolian grain.[15] Lewis's researches in the Ottoman registers for southern Syria (Palestine) reveal a similar picture of economic expansion. There, too, the population was increasing, at least until mid-century, with a corresponding advance in agricultural output and tax revenue.[16] Finally, in Egypt, Shaw has found evidence of the same kind of revival. Rural security was improved; peasants who had fled their fields were persuaded to return; the system of irrigation was repaired and extended.[17] To this must be added the evidence put forward by Lane that Egypt suffered only momentarily from Portugal's efforts to establish a spice monopoly in the Indian ocean. Figures from Portuguese and Venetian sources show that the transit trade in pepper was as large in the 1560s as it had been in the late fifteenth century; and that it was not until the first decades of the seventeenth century that this lucrative trade was much reduced.[18]

The only exceptions to this general pattern of economic revival would seem to have been those relatively inaccessible regions of coastal Syria, for example Mount Lebanon, and of Iraq which the Ottomans were never able to penetrate with any success or where it was necessary for them to come to terms with the existing local rulers.[19] The rich province of Basra, for example, always proved difficult to control and was rarely subject to Ottoman authority for more than short periods of time. Its neighbour to the north, Baghdad, suffered repeated invasions from Persia until the final recapture of the city by the Turks in 1638. However, the evidence concerning the economic conditions in such areas is inconclusive and it is possible that some of them may have enjoyed a temporary benefit from such region-wide improvements as the increase in the volume of international trade.[20]

But if, parts of Iraq and Syria excepted, the sixteenth century was one of widespread economic revival, can the conventional assumptions concerning comprehensive Middle Eastern economic decline be applied to the seventeenth and eighteenth centuries? Unfortunately the quality of the Ottoman records for this period is very much poorer and any attempt to answer the question must rely on fragmentary pieces of evidence. In almost every case, it will have to be admitted that the available data is insufficient to support any general conclusion about overall changes in the level of economic activity.

To begin with Egypt: here as elsewhere in the Middle East there is some reason to believe that, due to the return of regular visitations of the plague, the population was at best stationary and may well have been declining. According to Raymond, Cairo suffered at least eight visitations in the seventeenth century and another five in the eighteenth, many of which, in his opinion, may have killed off between a third and a half of the city's population.[21] Given such repeated disasters it is unlikely that the population would have had time to recover from one attack before another struck. As for the major economic indicators, for all Shaw's detailed work on the Ottoman tax registers the only figures he can find which give any guide to movements in agricultural production are those for the volume of taxes collected in kind in Upper Egypt between 1670–1 and 1765–6: these show just a small diminution in the amount of cereals delivered.[22] To this can be added the assumption that there must have been a certain increase in agricultural productivity as a result of the introduction of a new and more prolific crop, *durra* or American maize, some time in the seventeenth century.[23] By the end of the next century, according to Girard of the French Expedition, it had become the staple diet of peasants throughout Upper Egypt.[24] For the rest, descriptions of agricultural life consist almost entirely of references to the sufferings of the peasants, rising taxation and the abandonment of villages, without being able to show that this had any direct effect on the volume of output.[25] It may have done, but there is no way of proving it.

The need to be wary of the general assumption that a combination of increasing political disorder and rising taxation lead inevitably to a decline in economic activity is also shown by Raymond's work on Cairo during the Ottoman period. In particular he is able to show how, once the transit trade in eastern spices had been reduced to a trickle in the early seventeenth century, Egypt's merchants were able to transfer their attention to another equally lucrative commodity: coffee from Mocha in the Yemen. He also shows, again contrary to received opinion, that this trade was little affected by the political faction fighting of the eighteenth century and that, as far as the total value of merchants' fortunes were concerned, it remained more or less constant from the beginning of the century to the end.[26] On the other hand, there is his evidence that the craft sector, and particularly the textile manufacturers, were under increasing pressure during the same period from the growing competition from imported European cloth, both in Egypt itself and in some of Egypt's traditional export markets.[27]

The only other area of the Middle East on which an equal amount of research has been done is Palestine. Here two types of approach have been used. One is that of the historical geographer, Hütteroth, who compared the pattern of village settlement in the central districts (but not those north of Jenin or south of Jaffa) as revealed in the Ottoman tax registers for the 1580s with that shown on the first detailed maps of Palestine produced by the Palestine Exploration Fund three hundred years later.[28] His conclusion is a simple one: while there was undoubtedly a great continuity of settled life in mountainous regions like those of Jabal Nablus, elsewhere a large number of villages, and even small towns, were abandoned by their inhabitants between the latter parts of the sixteenth and nineteenth centuries. Hütteroth further observes that the majority of the abandoned villages were on sites which were difficult to defend from attack, either on the plain or on the lower slopes of the mountains which face the desert to the south and east of Jerusalem and Hebron.[29] The result was that much of what was potentially the most fertile land in southern Palestine passed out of cultivation. The inhabitants of the 'safer' mountain villages no longer dared to till fields at any distance from their homes; sizeable areas along the coastal plain reverted to swamp around which malaria and other diseases posed additional hazards.[30]

The cause of this phenomenon is more difficult to pin down. At first sight it might seem that Hütteroth's findings provide powerful support for the conventional assumption − to be found, among other places, in Gibb and Bowen's *Islamic Society and the West* − that agricultural activity in eighteenth-century Syria was much reduced as a result of the growing inability of the Ottomans to maintain rural security and, in particular, to cope with the problems posed by the arrival in the North Syrian desert of new tribal groups like the Anaza which, by upsetting the existing delicate balance between beduin nomads and scarce resources, forced the existing tribes to prey more directly on the settled population working the land along the desert fringe.[31] Such explanations, however, raise two problems, the one peculiar to Palestine, the other general. To take the general first, a number of writers have begun to challenge the use of the beduin as a multi-purpose explanation for rural economic decline.[32] And while of necessity many of their own counter-assertions cannot be conclusively proved they do at least demonstrate that the relationship between nomads, semi-nomads and the settled population was very much more complex than the traditional arguments allow. Among many other things they raise the question of whether beduin pressure might be not the cause of a decrease in economic activity but itself the consequence of some prior decrease which left a vacuum into which nomadic elements were drawn. Then, as far as Palestine itself was concerned, arguments based on nomadic-inspired disturbance have to confront the problem that in both the northern districts and the southern ones between Jaffa and Gaza the inhabitants of the plains

Table 1   English and French imports from the Middle East during the seventeenth and eighteenth centuries (annual averages)

	England (£)*	France (thousands of livres)*				
	Total	Egypt	Saida Acre Jaffa Tripoli	Aleppo	Izmir	Total
1621, 1630, 1634	249,000					
1633, 1669	421,000					
1671–5		1870	965	882	2080	5797
1686–1700		2225	1235	736	2332	6528
1699–1701	314,000					
1711–15		3520	2278	924	2135	8857
1717–21		2494	3256	1179	2306	9235
1722–4	356,000					
1724–8		1560	2224	1582	1806	7712
1736–40		2017	3373	1666	1949	9005
1750–4		2532	3702	2078	5089	13,401
1752–4	152,000					
1765–9		2889	3138	2578	9606	18,211
1773–7		3172	1965	2293	9142	16,572
1785–9		2863	1810	3517	14,221	22,411

* From 1726 onwards £1 = 24 livres (approx).

Sources: (England) Davis, 'English imports from the Middle East' in Cook, Studies, 202.
(France) G. Rambert (ed.), Histoire du commerce de Marseilles, V, Le Levant by R. Paris (Paris, 1957), 370, 393n, 403n, 415n, 447n.

seem to have found ways and means of protecting themselves from the worst effects of beduin incursions. In the north, for example, as Cohen demonstrates, far from there being a decline in agricultural production under the powerful rule of Zahir al-Umar (d. 1775) and Ahmad Jazzar Pasha (d. 1804) there may well have been an increase, stimulated by the lucrative sale of crops like cotton to the European merchants on the coast.[33]

Table 2   French imports of Levant cotton during the eighteenth century (annual averages)

		a By value (thousands of livres)				
		1700−02	1717−21	1736−40	1750−4	1785−9
Syria (excluding Palestine and Aleppo)		95			1134	69
Aleppo		56			95.5	339
Izmir		22			1621	6923
		b By weight (quintals)*				
All ports	raw	4316	18,944	30,789	52,550	95,979
	spun	16,946	15,607	14,889	13,853	10,805

* 1 quintal = 100 kg.

Source: Rambert (ed.), v (Le Levant), 407n, 416, 448n, 511n.

No work of an equivalent type has been carried out on northern Syria during the seventeenth and eighteenth centuries and the figures showing a continuous advance in the value of French imports from Aleppo (Tables 1 and 2) do not necessarily imply any concomitant rise in local agricultural production, as some of this trade represented goods, such as Persian silk, which simply passed through the city in transit.[34] Otherwise the only safe assumption to make is that as a result of visitations of the plague as regular as those at Cairo − Aleppo had five attacks between 1719 and 1760−2, Damascus four between 1691−2 and 1731−2 − it is likely that Syria's urban population remained at least constant, and may well have declined.[35]

Information about conditions in Anatolia is just as scanty. Here most work has concentrated on the price inflation of the late sixteenth century and the effect this may have had in encouraging the widespread rural uprisings of the early seventeenth century known as the Celali revolt, as well as in bringing about changes in the whole system of local administration.[36] Nevertheless, although historians like Inalcik have argued cogently that the economic crisis of the late sixteenth century had an enormous impact on the organization of government (to be discussed on p. 12ff.), its long-term effect on the Anatolian economy is impossible to discern, given the almost complete lack of reliable data.[37] A general impression that the rural population may well have diminished between 1600 and 1800, that large numbers of villages were abandoned, that agricultural production probably declined, is no substitute for hard statistical evidence. Such things may well have happened, but as yet there is no proof. For the rest all that exists is some unsatisfactory information concerning a falling-off of Turkish craft activity in the late sixteenth and seventeenth centuries. As Barkan notes, the production of silk cloth in Bursa (Brussa) and mohair woollens in Ankara fell away dramatically towards the end of the sixteenth century, once Europeans began to weave similar textiles and no longer needed to import them from Turkey.[38] Another important craft activity in which production declined, this time in the seventeenth century, was that of the pottery and tiles produced at Iznik and Kütahya, perhaps because, as Carswell suggests, they no longer had the market provided by an expanding court and by the energetic construction of mosques and other public buildings during the early Ottoman period.[39] Once again, though data of this type may be enough to provide a hint as to a general trend, it is hardly enough to provide conclusive proof. The same caution has to be applied to the figures which indicate that there was a considerable increase both in the volume and value of primary products exported from Izmir (Smyrna) during the course of the eighteenth century (Table 1) and in the amount of money invested in tax-farms connected with customs duties on foreign trade.[40] This could be a reflection of a rise in agricultural production. It could equally well be a sign either of an increase in the amount of cash crops brought to the city from other parts of Anatolia or of a decrease in the volume of local products utilized in its workshops; there is no way of being sure.

When so little is known about a period, when conditions varied so much from one part of the region to another, no simple evaluation of economic performance is possible. All that can be said with any certainty is that the argument for a general contraction of agricultural output, of craft activity and of trade remains to be proved. In some areas, notably the central districts of Palestine, such a decline may well have taken place; in others, such as northern Palestine during the first half of the eighteenth century and the Izmir district of western Anatolia during the second, there could have been something of an upsurge in rural production stimulated by European purchases of local cotton. In the present state of knowledge it is impossible to say more.

If there is no proof of a general decline during the seventeenth and eighteenth centuries it is still certainly true that there was a significant shift in the balance of economic power between the Middle East and the nation states of western Europe. One important aspect of this shift was the change in the pattern of sea-borne trade both in the Mediterranean and the Indian Ocean. During the sixteenth century a major feature of Middle Eastern commerce was the transit of Asian pepper, spices and silk, most of it destined, at least in the first instance, for Venice. But during the first decades of the seventeenth century the spice trade was almost completely rerouted round the Cape of Good Hope while the pre-eminence of the Venetians in the Mediterranean was successfully challenged by the Dutch (briefly), and then by the British and the French, with their faster, better armed ships.[41] The result was the establishment of a new pattern of international trade characterized by the sale of European manufactured goods, notably woollen cloth, in exchange for Middle Eastern primary commodities for which there was a growing demand (Table 2). The only major exception to this was the export of silk and cotton thread, but even here the Levant products were so coarse that in Britain their use was confined to the cheaper end of the market.[42] Levant silks could not be used on the new Italian silk-throwing machines introduced into England in the early eighteenth century, while by 1780 Levant cottons were restricted to the manufacture of candlewicks and fustians.[43] There was a wider use of them in France.

The effect of this new pattern of trade on the Middle Eastern economy was localized, irregular and uneven. In some areas the production of cash crops was stimulated by increasing European demand, much to the profit of local merchants, and more importantly, tax-farmers. In others, a sudden decline in demand, whether due to a change in taste or technique (e.g. the diminished use of Turkish mohair for buttons in western Europe during the eighteenth century) or to competition from cheaper sources of supply (e.g. West Indian coffee) forced local producers either to find a new outlet or to plant their fields with any alternative crop they could find.

The effect on the Middle Eastern craft industry was similarly uneven. The most obvious dislocations were caused in certain major centres of textile production, where producers began to suffer from European competition at least as early as the mid-eighteenth century. In Egypt it seems to have been the woollens from France which posed the major threat. As the Danish traveller, Hasselquist, noted of Cairo, the French merchants there made particular efforts to discover what types and colours the local inhabitants preferred, sending samples back to France to have them copied.[44] Elsewhere, in Iraq, it was the import of cloth from British India which made the greatest inroad into domestic production.[45] But the direct effects of European and Indian competition were not the only problems faced by Middle Eastern industry. On occasions, a sudden increase in British or French demand for cotton or silk meant that all the existing stocks were exported leaving local craftsmen with little or nothing to work on. Just as important was the growth of a European pattern of consumption among the ruling élite during the Ottoman centuries. The import of Bohemian glass – much of it especially produced for the Turkish market – the Swiss watch – according to the Baron de Tott the proud possession of many

Istanbul Muslims — even the cult of the tulip, all speak of a move towards a quasi-European life style involving a neglect of traditional products and, just as significant, the beginnings of that still prevalent assumption that anything of European manufacture was automatically better than anything local.[46] Finally, in the sphere of currency it has been forcefully argued by Raymond that it was the use of European coins by European merchants and their local allies which was a powerful factor inhibiting Ottoman efforts to stabilize their own system of coinage, leaving it subject to marked shifts in value.[47]

Nevertheless, significant though such developments were to become during the high tide of European economic penetration of the Middle East in the nineteenth century, their importance in the earlier period should not be exaggerated. They affected only some aspects of economic activity in some areas, and then often only for a short space of time. Meanwhile, the resilience of many sectors of the Middle Eastern economy sometimes made it possible to find alternative sources of wealth to replace those which had been lost, for example the seventeenth-century growth in the trade in Yemeni coffee as a substitute for the income lost from spices. As yet, the development of capitalist industry in Europe and the creation of commercial and financial links between Britain and France and the Mediterranean had still not developed sufficiently far to produce a progressive, irreversible transformation of the Middle East economy. This had to wait until the nineteenth century.

The structure of Ottoman administration and the appropriation of the surplus from agriculture, the craft industry and trade

Having discussed some of the questions related to the growth, or otherwise, of production during the first three Ottoman centuries it is now important to turn to an examination of certain basic relationships which underlay the pattern of economic activity. To begin with a large generalization: the Ottoman government in Arab provinces was primarily concerned with the task of maintaining military preparedness, preserving urban and rural security, and raising revenue. To carry out these tasks it relied, initially, on a small group of officials, most of whom were either Turks or slaves like the *kapıkulları* in Anatolia or the Mamluks in Egypt and the Fertile Crescent, the majority of whom had received military training. In areas where Ottoman authority was weak or exercised only irregularly, such as parts of Syria and Iraq, it was necessary to use the services of local chieftains and shaikhs, who alone had the power to maintain order and to collect the taxes.

As for the actual sources of revenue, in the majority of areas the land was far and away the most important. Ownership remained with the state, which allowed the peasant population to work the fields, either individually or communally, in exchange for the payment of a regular tax (the *miri*).[48] In theory, the *miri* consisted of a fixed proportion of total output (generally a tenth), but in reality the amount of tax actually taken depended on the power of the tax-collector and his relationship with both government and peasants. It is this factor which allows the use of the word 'surplus' to describe the amount taken in tax for it is arguable that the nature of the power relations involved was usually such that the *miri*, as well as a number of other dues (market taxes, the taxes on animals, the war tax in Anatolia, etc.) represented all, or almost all, of what the peasants produced over and above what they needed to feed and clothe themselves and to maintain production.[49] The other two major sources of revenue, craft activity and commerce, will be analysed later in this section.

During the first Ottoman century the system of administration established in the rural areas varied according to the weight given to military as opposed to financial considerations. In Anatolia itself, where it was necessary to strike a balance between maintaining the war-making potential of a predominantly Turkish Muslim population and the raising of revenue, part of the land was awarded as *timars* or *ziamets* (usually translated as fiefs) to *sipahis* (cavalrymen) who were expected to use the taxes they collected in order to maintain local security as well as, in time of war, to provide a contingent of troops for service in the Ottoman army.[50] Given the close association between many *sipahis* and the peasant population they helped to administer, and the profitable opportunities which often existed for selling agricultural products at a price higher than that fixed by the state, it is not surprising to learn that some of them began to cultivate part of their fief on their own account.[51] Much of the remainder of the land was either kept as Imperial estates known as *has/khass* – in which case its revenues were collected either by salaried officials (*emins*) or tax-farmers (*multezims/multazims* or *mukataçis/muqatajis*) – or used to provide financial support for senior administrators like the provincial governors (*beylerbeys*) or the *sanjakbeys* who looked after sub-divisions of a province.[52] Lastly, some agricultural estates were established as *vakfs/waqfs*, the revenues from which were either used for the upkeep of some mosque or other religious institution or, in the case of those that had been created illegally, for the profit of the family concerned.[53] According to a source quoted by Gibb and Bowen, the distribution of land in a typical sanjak might have been: half as *timars* and *ziamets*, one-fifth as *khass*, one-fifth as *waqf*, with the remainder set aside to provide revenues for a variety of government establishments like the fortresses along the frontier.[54]

In Egypt, on the other hand, where the province was garrisoned by a few thousand Turkish troops organized in *ojaks* (corps) and where the local Egyptian population was not called on to fight in the sultan's wars, the

Ottomans' primary concern was to maximize revenue from the land. This they attempted to do in the sixteenth century by collecting the *miri* directly, using *emins* who were paid a regular salary.[55] The situation in Syria was more ambiguous. Here efforts to raise revenue had to be balanced by the fact that parts of the provinces were only tenuously under Ottoman control, as well as the need to maintain a considerable force of *sipahis* in order to protect the settled population from beduin raids and to act as an escort for the pilgrimage caravan from Damascus to Mecca.[56] There was thus a considerable variety of systems of rural administration, including *timars* and *ziamets*, Imperial estates where the taxes were collected by *emins* or *multazims*, and whole areas like Mount Lebanon, the Bekaa valley and parts of the lands across the Jordan river which were placed under local governors who received an annual salary in exchange for delivering a fixed sum in taxes.[57] As for the Iraqi provinces, Ottoman control was too uncertain to allow any fixed pattern of rural administration so that the collection of land tax, most of which was used to maintain the Turkish garrisons, was probably left to the local governors to do as best they could: the sources are too inadequate to be more specific.

The patterns of land administration and surplus appropriation just described began to undergo a significant modification towards the end of the sixteenth century with the extension of the area subject to tax-farms (*mukataas/muqataas* or *iltizams*) where the right to collect the taxes was auctioned by the government in advance. The main reason for this develop- ment was clearly the Ottoman government's need to augment the revenues it obtained from the land in order to finance the increasingly costly standing army in which the central role of the *sipahi* cavalry was giving way more and more to that of the regular corps of musket-bearing foot-soldiers (the Janissaries and others).[58] Another force also at work, at least in Anatolia, was pressure from merchants, courtiers and others for the right to administer rural land in order to be able to profit from the rising price of the wheat and other cereals either exported (illegally) to Europe or used to provision Istanbul.[59] The result was that many *timars* and *ziamets* were converted to tax farms as their *sipahis* died, retired, or were simply expelled. Elsewhere, on the Imperial estates or in Egypt and parts of Syria, the same need for larger government revenue led to the replacement of most of the *emins* by tax-farmers.[60]

The new system of tax-farming possessed five main features. First, the fact that the *mukatajis* or *multazims* were either men of authority and influence with command over troops or men who had to be given access to such troops simply to allow them to collect the *miri* from an unwilling peasant population meant that there was a continual tension between the central government and its agents: the tax-farmers had to be given enough power to allow them to do their job but not so much that they became strong enough to defy government regulations, to increase the rate of taxation, and to hold back a significant proportion of the rural surplus for their own use. This tension could be contained when the central and provincial governments were strong, but once they began to weaken this rapidly had a cumulative effect. Tax-farmers would keep back more and more of what they owed to the Treasury, using the money to augment their own power. Meanwhile, the government, deprived of the funds it needed to maintain its own forces, grew steadily weaker. In such a situation an increase in the illegal creation of *waqfs* ensured a further reduction in the government's share of revenue.[61]

Second, once the system of tax-farming had been introduced on a large scale, there was a tendency for some officials to build up their own personal military organizations specifically for the purpose of competing with others, and with the government, for control over the rural surplus through the acquisition of *iltizams*. A significant proportion of the land tax was thus diverted for the purpose of recruiting and arming retainers, building up networks of clients and engaging in the type of conspicuous consumption calculated to impress the government, rival tax-farmers and the tax-paying population alike. The result was a fierce competition for access to rural economic wealth, a competition which itself ensured that much of that wealth was invested in unproductive strife. The method of competition for access to the surplus thus came largely to determine the way in which the surplus was spent.

Third, the system by which would-be tax-farmers had to pay a certain portion of the value of their *iltizam* before obtaining possession automatically increased the importance of those groups within the society with money to lend. These might be the bankers and money-changers of Istanbul and the major Turkish towns or the merchants, *alims* (religious officials), or wealthy administrators elsewhere.[62] As Urquhart described their function in the early nineteenth century, potential office-holders in Anatolia had to bind themselves to a 'capitalist' who apart from providing them with the necessary advance also furnished them with arms and horses for a 10 per cent commission. Urquhart further noted that such men were also useful in disposing of any of the harvest collected in kind.[63]

Fourth, as with the *sipahis* in the sixteenth century, there was a tendency for some tax-farmers in some places to enter the process of production more directly, lending money to the peasants and interesting themselves in the sale of their crops for their own additional profit.[64] The precondition for this development remained the existence of a market for such crops, either in some local town, or, depending on movements in regional or European demand, further afield. In some instances the initial impulse might come from the fact that, under some systems of tax-farming (for example in Egypt), the *multazim* was given a portion of the land for his own use with the right to put his fields into cultivation using a corvée of local peasants.[65] In others, the tax-farmer might begin by speculating with that part of the surplus which he collected in kind or by taking advantage of the fact that he was often the only source of the working capital required by peasant agriculturalists or those who processed crops like flax or rice.[66] But, for whatever reason, the desire of some tax-farmers to obtain extra profits from their own or their peasants' fields — and even to reorganize village production along more lucrative lines — represents a significant modification of the conventional assumption that in the Orient the state and its agents left the cultivators alone to grow whatever they chose in whatever way they chose.

Fifth, and finally, though in such a system the proportion of the surplus taken by the *multazim* was decided mainly in terms of the balance of political and economic power between him and the population of his tax-farm, two other factors were also important. One stemmed from his need to exercise his control by means of local agents who had their own interests to promote and protect. The other was the fact that the whole process remained subject to a set of rules and regulations supervised by the *qadis* (judges) and their courts designed to place limits on the tax-farmer's use of his power. Though very difficult to enforce, such rules were still sometimes referred to in peasant complaints of unjust taxation.[67] How much of a constraint they actually imposed cannot possibly be discovered but it is at least arguable that they had some force at least as a result of the fact that they had their origins in the same fount of religio-legal authority which legitimized the tax-farmers' own rights to collect taxes on the sultan's behalf. If he wished to be obeyed by the peasants without question his position as a representative of the ruler himself was clearly a useful asset.

The processes just described can be seen at work in both Anatolia and Egypt during the seventeenth and eighteenth centuries. In the former the extension of the area in which taxes were collected by tax-farmers was accompanied by a series of important changes in the system of rural administration.[68] Put in the most simple terms, these began when the central government was forced to increase the power of its provincial governors in order to enable them to combat the Celali rebels and to re-impose rural order. The governors then used this new power to build up their own wealth at the expense of the state with the result that the state, in turn, attempted to regain control of the situation by encouraging the emergence of a countervailing force represented by the *ayans* (usually translated as notables), a new rural group formed out of a mixture of well-to-do *kapıkulları*, *alims* (or *ulama*), merchants and leading craftsmen. However, by the eighteenth century, it was the *ayans* themselves who were able to use their new official positions to increase their own share of local revenues — notably the land tax, the collection of which they now largely dominated through their control over the system of awarding tax-farms and over the type of commercial transactions to be allowed in the major market towns.[69]

One result was a fierce struggle between members of prominent local families for the key positions within the administration. 'To this end,' to quote Inalcik, 'they not only resorted to intrigue, bribery, and the use of force, but also formed factions of supporters and even sought alliances with bandits, *derebeys* (rebels) and tribal chiefs.'[70] But even when one family was successful and managed to hold a particular post over several generations they had no option but to continue to use a large part of their resources to maintain a force strong enough to deter potential rivals. The enhancement of prestige through the consumption of luxury goods and lavish expenditure on display was also an important prop of power and the households of Anatolia's leading *ayans* have been described as 'small replicas' of the Sultan's palace at Istanbul.[71] Hence much of the surplus from rural Anatolia remained in the hands of local dynasts, the central treasury was starved of funds, and government efforts to repair the situation were rendered useless by the lack of the money necessary to maintain a standing army large and powerful enough to reimpose its authority. The introduction of a new system of awarding *iltizams* for life (known as *malikanes*) at the end of the seventeenth century and the grant of whole sanjaks, or even provinces, as tax-farms, sometimes on an hereditary basis, further aggravated the situation.[72] So too did the extensive creation of large estates, either as a result of the simple seizure of peasant plots or the establishment of a private (and illegal) *vakf*.[73]

Measures of this kind greatly facilitated the maintenance of continuous control by notable families over large tracts of land, a situation some of them sought to put to additional advantage by profiting from the sale of the agricultural products they collected as tax. Such was certainly the case in a number of districts round the coast where the power of the *ayans* could also be used to take advantage of European demand by circumventing the government regulations forbidding the private sale or export of many of the principal crops. Some of the features of this situation were well described by the Baron de Tott at the end of the eighteenth century:

The riches of some persons of large property maintain, in the environs of Smyrna (Izmir), a system of independence the progress of which increases every day. They rely principally on the power of money and this power is irresistible. It is likewise to be remarked that the efforts made by the Porte for some years to destroy one of these Aghas has less terrified the rest than shown the weakness of the despot.[74]

As elsewhere in the Middle East, power brought wealth and wealth power.

Much the same processes were at work in Egypt during the same period. First, as a result of the mutinies of the various *ojaks* in the last decade of the sixteenth century – part of the Empire-wide response to the diminution of military salaries in real terms as a result of the price-inflation — the Ottoman provincial administration was no longer strong enough to assert regular control over the collection of the land tax by government officials and was encouraged to substitute a system of tax-farming by Mamluks, *ojak* officers and others with enough power and authority to do the job. A second stage soon followed. This was the creation by some of the more powerful Mamluks and officers of personal military organizations specifically for the purpose of competing with one another and with the government for control of the surplus, both urban and rural, a process which was well under way by the mid-seventeenth century.[75] The wealth from the tax-farms was then used to support Mamluk military households (*baits*) or similar organiza-tions; new Mamluks were purchased from abroad; the loyalty of networks of clients was obtained by a combination of threats, patronage and largesse.[76] Once a power base of such a kind was established it could be used to coerce the Ottoman governor into awarding more and more tax-farms; it could also be used to deter rivals and to overawe the tax-payers. The result, as in Anatolia, was a fierce competition for access to Egypt's economic wealth, a competition which set one Mamluk house, one military corps, against another, egged on, in many cases, by the Ottoman governor who had no other means of maintaining any sort of control other than by a never-ending process of seeking to divide and rule. Hence the descriptions given by the Egyptian historian, al-Jabarti, of the Mamluk houses as military head-quarters containing the arms and ammunition, the permanent corps of retainers, the luxurious fittings, which the process of constant competition required.[77] Hence too the regular assertion of military prowess, the frequent clashes between rival bands, and the repeated attempts of one house to destroy a rival, either to pre-empt an attack or simply to seize its wealth. It is little wonder, as Ayalon observes of al-Jabarti's history, that the death of a Mamluk in his bed was a sufficiently rare event for it to be specially recorded.[78]

Intra-Mamluk rivalries became even more intense during the eighteenth century when some of an élite formed by a coalition of leading Mamluks with senior *ojak* officers finally seized most of what was left of the power of the Ottoman governor, gaining access to the funds of the Central Treasury as well as the machinery for awarding tax-farms. Finding that the great power of the *multazims* had reduced the flow of taxes almost to a trickle, the new rulers were forced to try to find the money to maintain themselves in power by any means they could, a process which was bitterly resisted by their rivals.[79]

Meanwhile, during the same century, two other important processes were also set in train. The first was the increasing frequency with which native-born Egyptians, not just Mamluks and Turks, began to obtain rural tax-farms.[80] Thus, at about the time members of the Mamluk/*ojak* hierarchy finally took over the machinery of government, they lost the monopoly they had previously exercised over the award of Egypt's rural *iltizams*. Paradoxical as it might seem, there may even have been a connection between the two events. But whereas the conventional approach would stress the fact that the Mamluks, as foreigners, were anxious to obtain the support of leading Egyptian intermediaries, it is at least worth raising the possibility that it was another manifestation of those links which any system of tax-farming must create between an élite which is allowed to bid for farms and those local merchants and others with cash and the commercial connections needed to market that part of the surplus raised in kind. Certainly the temptation to intensify such links must have grown during the eighteenth century as the increasing numbers of exactions and forced loans encouraged richer members of the urban population to look for means of diversifying their investments.[81]

Second, there is evidence that, once again, a number of tax-farmers were involving themselves directly in the process of agricultural production. The reports of the French Expedition mention Mamluks who were concerned with the management of sugar refineries at Girga, providing land and animals for the production of the necessary cane.[82] In addition, in the provinces of Lower and Middle Egypt (north of Minya) many *multazims* were still cultivating a portion of their tax-farm (the part known as *usya*) for their own profit, using the (usually unpaid) labour of peasants dependent upon them.[83] Such an involvement clearly altered the nature of the relationship between tax-collector and tax-payer. One sign of this is contained in al-Jabarti's account of the way in which Shaikh al-Sharkawi sought to protect his peasants from being ruined by huge tax-demands by lending them the money himself.[84] This determination to protect his own investment in the land was only a symptom of a much more deep-rooted change; for some *multazims* at least, their appropriation of the surplus was now as much by means of the economic exploitation of the rural population as it was by sheer political coercion.[85]

The situation with regard to the appropriation of the rural surplus in Syria was both more complicated and more various. For one thing, the *sipahi* system continued more or less unimpaired throughout the period, at least as far as the province of Damascus was concerned.[86] For the rest, the land subject to some kind of tax-farming (whether awarded for a short period or, after the end of the seventeenth century, as a *malikane*) was controlled by a great variety of different persons and groups ranging from members of the Ottoman administration to *alims*, merchants, Janissaries, and, in the districts far from towns, beduin shaikhs.[87] As elsewhere, tax-farms were generally awarded only to people with wealth and influence who could be used to build up a local power at the expense of the Ottoman government. The rise of the famous Azm family is a case in point. The money they obtained from the award of the *malikane* of Homs and Hama was used to purchase the support they needed in Istanbul to obtain a series of appointments as governor of Damascus.[88]

The award of a tax-farm could be obtained in a variety of ways: simple purchase, the exercise of influence, or the use of political pressure. Just as important, as in Egypt and Anatolia, certain persons and groups deliberately organized bands of supporters for the particular purpose of coercing the provincial administration into allowing them to build up wealth and power by means of access to the rural surplus. This was especially the case in the two major cities of Aleppo and Damascus where control over the cereal crop collected as tax in kind in the surrounding countryside could be used to create artificial shortages, thus forcing up the price at which it was finally sold. In Aleppo the major struggle for such control took place between officials within the Ottoman administration, the Janissaries, and a cohesive social group known as the Ashraf, composed of men who owed their position to their descent, or alleged descent, from the Prophet Muhammad. Both Janissaries and Ashraf were organized along military lines under leaders who created households of supporters similar to those of the *ayan* in Anatolia.[89] A similar struggle took place in Damascus, although in this case between two rival military corps, the *yerliyya* (locally-recruited Janissaries) and the *kapıkulları* (Imperial Janissaries) and the provisional administration – which for part of the eighteenth century was in the hands of the Azm family.[90] Of these groups, the *yerliyya* were particularly well-placed to control the city's grain supply through their close links with the merchants of the Damascus Maidan who organized the purchase and transport of wheat and barley from the Hauran, the richest grain-growing area in southern Syria.[91]

Whether or not the regular attempts to create a 'corner' in cereals by monopolizing the grain collected in taxes led members of some of these groups to interfere more directly in the actual process of production is less clear. Certainly the opportunity existed, while evidence of something that might be called an 'economic' relationship between tax-farmers and peasants is provided by the many examples of merchants and *multazims* (in Aleppo as well as Damascus) who advanced money to the cultivators whose crops they either purchased or collected as tax.[92] It may also be that the regular income which families like the Azms obtained from the sale of wheat, barley and sheep persuaded them to encourage their production more directly.[93]

Urban control over the rural surplus was less easy in the other areas of Syria, Mount Lebanon and Palestine, where lack of Ottoman power in the seventeenth and eighteenth centuries made it even more necessary to come to terms with the local families which alone had the means of collecting the taxes. In Lebanon there existed the nearest thing in the Arab provinces to a territorially-based class of notables in which the *muqatajis* (hereditary tax-farmers) were established in particular districts of the Mountain, owing allegiance to an Ottoman-recognized Emir and tax-farmer-in-chief but otherwise being left to manage their fiefs in any way they chose, provided only that they surrendered a fixed portion of the taxes each year and supplied a contingent of armed supporters whenever required.[94] The fact that each *muqataji* was resident in his district allowed the development of a complex series of duties and obligations on the part of the local peasant population, including the provision of certain services and the payment of a wide variety of dues and 'gifts', the whole system enforced by his superior power. It also permitted a closer identification with the agricultural life of the district. *Muqatajis* had their own private holdings of land which they usually sublet to landless peasants on the basis of a crop-sharing agreement.[95] In general, it can probably be assumed that a resident lord would be more anxious than an absentee one to attempt to increase his own revenue by stimulating agricultural production through the provision of loans and the development of trade.

As elsewhere, the bulk of the surplus was used to maintain large households, to indulge in ostentatious consumption and to support the bands of armed men necessary to protect the interests of the *muqataji*, to overawe the tax-paying population, and to vie with their neighbours for control over profitable trade routes, for disputed villages or even, before the Shihab family established its paramountcy after 1711, for the right to rule over the whole Mountain. Meanwhile, sons and other relatives would build up their own strength in order to challenge the position of the head of the family, such disputes often being supported by the Emir or the nearest Ottoman governor for their own purposes. When asked by David Urquhart in the mid-nineteenth century how he and his class spent their money, one of the Druze Emirs replied, 'We spend it on injuring one another.'[96]

In Palestine, too, local men of power were often able to establish themselves in particular districts, but with greater difficulty. In the north at least, by the end of the seventeenth century, the practice of granting *ziamets* and *timars* had almost entirely ceased and the bulk of the land was parcelled out in *iltizams* or, increasingly, in *malikanes*.[97] These were vied for by the leaders of important families, each anxious to persuade the Ottoman authorities that they were too powerful to be ignored when it came to the collection of taxes. The most successful were the Zaidanis of the Galilee region who, during the first half of the eighteenth century, were able to extend their control over tax-farms throughout almost the whole of northern Palestine, reaching their peak under Zahir al-Umar who extended the family's rule as far as Acre on the coast. Although profiting from the fact that their right to collect taxes was recognized by the Ottomans, they were often strong enough to withhold a large part of what they had raised.[98]

In addition, as Cohen notes, Zahir's regime had two important features. First, as tax-farmer-in-chief he was in a position to allot the sub-farms under his control to his sons and other relatives. This led to a great deal of intra-family fighting, of a somewhat theatrical kind designed more to demonstrate the possession of local power than to annihilate competitors.[99] Second, the ascendancy of the whole family rested in large measure on their ability to profit from the competition between British and French merchants for the cotton of the Galilee region for which there was a growing European demand. This they did by persuading such merchants to pay them money in advance against future delivery of the crop. It is to be supposed that the bulk of the cotton (and other products) which they supplied came from the taxes paid to them in kind.[100] Whether or not they also bought cotton, cultivated it on their own account, or attempted to reorganize the pattern of peasant production is not known.

Zahir's overthrow in 1775 and the rise of the Acre-based regime of Ahmad Jazzar Pasha over northern Palestine is another illustration of two of the basic processes which were then in train in many areas of the Middle East. One was that, for all the Ottoman government's anxiety to overthrow Zahir and to regain control of Palestinian revenue, it was nevertheless forced into choosing a successor strong enough to ensure that these revenues were regularly and efficiently collected. This at once allowed Jazzar scope to build up his own power and to challenge Ottoman authority in a number of ways, even though, according to Cohen, he was very much more reliable than Zahir when it came to handing over the taxes he owed to the Central Treasury.[101] Second, like other local rulers, Jazzar was able to use his position to attempt to maximize his returns from agriculture and trade. However, he went considerably further than most: first breaking the monopoly of the French merchants at Acre over the export of primary commodities and then establishing monopolies of his own over the purchase and sale of cotton, cereals and other products.[102]

In central and southern Palestine, on the other hand, access to the rural surplus continued to be disputed between a variety of different centres of power; for example the fief holders who controlled the more than three hundred *ziamets* and *timars* in the area, local strongmen, and the shaikhs of tribes and other nomadic groups – all with their bands of armed followers.[103] The Ottoman authorities made some effort to ensure that some portion of the taxes reached them by trying to manipulate the award of *iltizams*, but with little success.

A somewhat different situation was to be found in the Iraqi provinces of Baghdad, Basra and Mosul. The fact that they were on the Persian 'frontier' and subject to repeated Persian attacks, the fact that they stood astride rich and important trade routes, meant that from an Ottoman point of view it was better to have strong local governors than compliant ones. For this reason both Baghdad and Basra were classified as *salyane* provinces in which the *wali* (governor) was paid a yearly salary out of revenues as well as being allowed, himself, to sublet much of the business of tax-collection to local agents.[104] In the capital cities such arrangements usually gave the governors sufficient strength to resist the challenge of rivals whether from inside their household or without; in the countryside power to give or to withhold tax-farms provided some kind of leverage over the tribal shaikhs who controlled much of the land.[105] Much the same process also took place during the seventeenth century in the northern province of Mosul, where control over the urban and rural economy was allowed by the Ottomans to pass into the hands, first of a number of local families, then of just one, the Jalilis, who were able virtually to monopolize the office of *wali* from the 1730s onwards.[106] As in the case of the Mamluk rulers of Baghdad, one way in which challenges from potential rivals were contained was by a successful manipulation of the right of access to the surplus of a small but extremely fertile agricultural hinterland.[107]

Much less is known about the division of the urban surplus in the Middle East, the greater part of which was appropriated by means of taxes, duties or simply forced 'protection' imposed on those engaged in craft activity or trade, and it is only possible to talk in generalities.[108] In the case of the craft industry the major administrative instrument was the power exercised by the guilds or corporations (*esnaf/asnaf*) to which most artisans had to belong, combined with close supervision of the urban markets.[109] In the case of trade the major instrument was the award of the right to collect customs dues, both internally and at the frontier, augmented, in so far as this trade consisted of agricultural products raised as taxes and destined to supply the towns with food and raw materials, by the issue of permissions (*tezkeres*) allowing particular individuals to participate in their transport and sale. But again as in the rural areas, the power to tax and to control urban economic activity tended to pass into the hands of town-based groups which grew strong enough to keep an increasing share of the surplus for themselves. Furthermore, over time, members of such groups began to develop some identity with the economic interests of those they taxed and controlled, for example, some of the merchants who obtained customs-farms or the Janissaries who enrolled themselves in craft corporations. This does not seem, however, to have led to any reorganization of the activity in question along more productive lines nor, as far as can be seen, to any diminution of tax demands. Indeed, in some cities like Cairo, competition between rival groups for access to the urban as well as the rural surplus, and the growing impoverishment of the Central Treasury, may well have led to an increase in irregular demands such as *avanias* and enforced protection (*himaya*) during the eighteenth century. In a very tentative set of calculations (based on the assumption that urban tax-farmers were able to collect something like five to six times the annual purchase price of their farm) Raymond suggests that shortly before the French Expedition a sum of between 400 and 500 million *paras** was being appropriated from the economically-active population in Egypt's capital, roughly the same amount as that taken from the entire agricultural sector.[110]

It would be wrong, however, to draw too close a parallel between the mechanisms for controlling and taxing trade and those relating to the craft industry. Throughout the Ottoman period merchants were left much freer to accumulate wealth without interference. Their activities were not circumscribed by the type of rules and regulations which the corporations imposed on the crafts. In many cases they were able to ensure that control over the customs-farms was exercised by men of commerce like themselves.[111] In addition they were able to profit (as well as to protect themselves from irregular exactions) by their association with the government in the transportation and marketing of much of the rural surplus. In addition, the richer merchants (*tujjar*) engaged in international trade came to benefit more and more from their role in providing credit for tax-farmers. Such links were further strengthened by the fact that such merchants also imported the luxury goods from both east and west which the governing élite required.

The craftsmen, on the other hand, were subject to much tighter government control and lost more of their surplus in the process. Apart from the rules imposed by the shaikhs over their own corporations, there was also the supervision exercised by such officials as the *muhtasib* (who was responsible for regulating prices and for monitoring the exchange of goods in most markets). In the Arab provinces, and in many of the Anatolian towns, there was fierce competition for the urban tax-farms which allowed control over the craft sector by many of the same groups which were also vying for access to the rural surplus.

In these circumstances it was not surprising that the underlying conflict of interest between the merchants and their allies on the one hand, and the craftsmen on the other sometimes possessed something of a class character. Tension had always existed, based, as Inalcik suggests, on the craftsmen's reliance on the merchants for raw materials and, in some cases, for a market outlet for their goods.[112] By the eighteenth century it must certainly have been exacerbated by the new relationship established between the *tujjar* and the ruling élite as well as by the fact that many of the merchants were becoming more closely identified with the European consuls and traders who provided a bridgehead for foreign competition in cloth and

* The value of the *para* depreciated throughout the Ottoman period. In 1773 there was an exchange rate of some 18 *paras* to the French franc, in 1798 this had gone down to 28.5 *paras* a franc. On the basis of the latter rate Raymond's calculation of the urban surplus would have been roughly the equivalent of 14 to 17 million francs.

other articles. Meanwhile, the economic links which bound merchant and craftsmen may well have diminished through time. Whereas in sixteenth-century Bursa (in Anatolia) merchants themselves organized the production of some wares for which there was a strong external demand, in eighteenth-century Cairo there is no evidence that any of the wealthy *tujjar* invested anything in the craft sector other than in the construction of workshops for rent.[113] For all these reasons the conflict of interest between craftsmen and merchants may well have formed one ingredient of the regular outbursts of popular opposition to the policies of government and ruling élite which took place in Istanbul and many of the cities of the Arab provinces in the seventeenth and eighteenth centuries.[114]

The system just described, and in particular the central importance attached to the use of coercion by the state or a military élite to collect the surplus, has led a number of writers to identify it with the Asiatic mode of production examined by Marx and others.[115] However, this is to raise a host of difficulties. To state my own position as clearly as possible. First, I do not believe that the concept of a mode of production has been sufficiently well-elaborated in the literature to provide more than general guidance to the analysis of pre-capitalist social formations. As usually understood it reduces the number of key relationships at the centre of the social process to only two or three. It does not and cannot account for changes in these relationships; and in the hands of a number of writers it has produced the further assumption that phenomena which do not fit into the basic pattern can be treated by means of the somewhat arbitrary creation of extra, or supplementary, modes of production to be articulated in some unspecified way, with the major mode. Just as important, the use of the concept tends to encourage the belief that the political economist knows more about the complex processes at issue than he possibly can. Second, as far as the Middle East itself is concerned, the concept of the Asiatic mode cannot be reconciled with such central features of my own analysis as the inbuilt tension between the state and its servants over the distribution of the surplus and the possibility that the control which the right to tax involved could lead on to direct intervention in the process of production itself.

For these reasons it seems best simply to leave the system of relationships which I have attempted to outline without name or without seeking to define it in terms of a single or mixed mode of production and to proceed with the task of examining the process by which, during the nineteenth century, it was transformed by influences deriving from two great revolutions: the French and the Industrial. But it is necessary first to take a more detailed look at the economy of the Middle East as it existed at the moment when this process first began.

1 The Middle East economy in 1800

Any study of the state of the Middle East economy at the beginning of the nineteenth century must suffer from one major disadvantage: the almost complete absence of reliable statistics. This can be seen with special clarity in the case of attempts to calculate the population of regions or towns. With the exception of Egypt (in 1897 and 1907) no reliable census was taken in any Middle Eastern country before 1914. Instead, such estimates as exist were based on badly kept tax-registers, on the guesses of local residents, or on such simple expedients as an attempt to count the number of houses in a particular town or the numbers of men attending Friday prayers in the principal mosque.[1] And if this was the best that could be done for the towns how much more imprecise must have been the occasional guess as to the population of the countryside? In these circumstances the best that can be done is to suggest that, subject to a very wide margin of error, Anatolia and the Arab provinces of the Empire may have contained some 11 to 12 million inhabitants in 1800, of whom roughly 6.5 million may have lived in Anatolia itself (excluding Istanbul), 3.85 million in Egypt, and between 1 and 1.5 million each in Iraq and Greater Syria — including perhaps 300,000 in Mount Lebanon and the immediate environs.[2]

In each region the great majority of the population must certainly have lived in the rural areas. Of the remainder, a sizeable proportion was to be found in towns of over 10,000 inhabitants. According to Issawi perhaps 10 per cent of Egypt's population lived in Cairo, Asyut, Mahalla, Tanta, Rosetta, Damietta and Alexandria, 20 per cent of Syria's in Damascus, Aleppo, Homs, Hama, Jerusalem and Tripoli and 15 per cent of Iraq's in Baghdad, Mosul, Hillah and Basra.[3] At the same time Anatolia was served by one huge city, Istanbul, with a population of up to 750,000, as well as Izmir (about 100,000), Bursa (50,000 or more) and many other important centres like Erzurum, Konya and Ankara.[4]

To the extent that such figures can be trusted they reveal a high degree of urbanization, at least by contemporary European standards. Part of the explanation of this phenomenon must probably be sought in the function of the Middle Eastern town as a place of refuge for the surrounding agricultural population at times when rural life became particularly difficult as a result of nomadic incursions or the demands of the tax-collector.[5] There were also the periodic famines when food was more easy to obtain in the administrative centre of a province where the governor had an obvious interest in maintaining the flow of provisions in order to prevent popular riots and commotions.[6] In some cases the newcomers might disperse again once the danger was over; in others they remained where they were, whether finding employment within the walls or continuing to work on farms and gardens outside.[7] Without this regular inward movement it is unlikely that the towns could have maintained their level of population at a time when epidemics and disease were rampant.[8] As a member of the French Expedition put it: 'malgré tant de sobriété, malgré la fecondité des femmes, et la salubrité du climat, il est fait que l'Egypte, et singulièrement le Kaire, dévore la population.'[9]

The flow of migrants was not all one way, however. Just as cultivators might be driven to seek refuge in a town so too, at times of plague or other catastrophe, town-dwellers might be driven out to find safety in the country-side.[10]

For the rest, the best that can be said with safety is that in the Middle East, as in any other pre-industrial society, the level of population was constrained by three inter-related influences: the high mortality rates and low life expectancy, debilitating disease, and sudden major fluctuations due to wars, famines and epidemics. Contemporary estimates throw light on only the last two of these features. As far as epidemics were concerned, Panzac's work on eighteenth-century Izmir suggests that in particularly bad attacks of plague a Middle Eastern city could lose as much as a third of its population.[11] Debilitating diseases were also rampant, as can be be seen from the French Expedition's study of ophthalmia in Cairo which suggested that one in every three Egyptians was one-eyed and one in ten totally blind.[12] For mortality and life expectancy, the only guide is provided by the first vital statistics established for Egypt and Palestine during the 1920s. These give death rates of 26.2 per 1000 for the former and 28 per 1000 for the Muslim inhabitants of the latter, as compared with 12.3 per 1000 for England during the same period.[13] As for life expectancy, the first Egyptian natural life tables produced in the 1930s estimated that the average male Egyptian could expect to live only until the age of thirty-one, roughly the same span as that of a late thirteenth-century Englishman.[14] Another way of making the same point is to return to the figures for Palestine and Egypt in the 1920s which suggest that only one in four Muslim Palestinians and one in three Egyptians reached the age of twenty, as opposed to nearly three out of four men born in England.[15] There seems every reason to suppose that conditions were even worse a hundred years earlier.

Rural economic activity

The study of the agricultural conditions in any area must inevitably begin with the study of its geography. It is the facts of geography — above all the nature of the terrain, climate and water resources — which largely determine what crops can be grown and, to a lesser extent, where they can be marketed.[16] They also help to determine where people live. In 1800 in many areas of the Middle East the inhabitants had to balance their need for water and cultivable land with their need to protect themselves from attack by finding refuge in mountains or other inaccessible places. Again, in any particular year it was the amount of rainfall or the height of a great river like the Nile which exercised a major influence over the size of the cultivated area over yields, and consequently over the volume of production. All could vary greatly: according to Hirsch — writing of the early twentieth century — the yield of Turkish wheat in a bad year can be as little as a quarter of that in a good one.[17] The same was also true of the pastoral sector of the rural economy: large numbers of the sheep and goats raised in the northern part of the region were liable to be killed in a bad winter as a result of the cold or of the snow and ice which prevented them from finding grass, while in dry summers, when food was scarce, many animals had to be slaughtered for their meat.

From the facts of climate and weather much else followed. On the volume of the harvest and the well-being of the animal population depended the amount of taxes collected in the rural sector, the level of agricultural exports — and thus of imports — the volume of raw materials available for working up by craftsmen, and the size of the market for many locally manufactured goods. An accurate set of annual rainfall statistics — which does not exist — would thus do much to provide a reliable index to year-to-year changes in the health of the Middle East economy.[18]

It follows that a study of Middle Eastern agriculture in 1800 ought to start with a glance at two types of map: a relief map of the region and a map showing the average amount of rainfall (Map 1). In the case of the latter the vital line is that which marks the boundary of the areas which have an average of 10 inches or more of rain a year, for this is the minimum amount required to grow a single cereal crop. In the Middle East this line begins on the coast near Jaffa/Tel Aviv, moves inland and then northwards up to the Mediterranean coast — but about 75 miles inland, skirts the northern extremity of the Syrian desert and then curves south east along the Tigris river to the Gulf. The only land south and east of this line where cultivation was possible on any scale in 1800 was that along the two great river systems of Egypt and Iraq. Elsewhere all must have remained barren except for small patches around the occasional well or in wadis which held some of the run-off from a winter storm. Inside the 10-inch rainfall line, on the other hand, the fact that most of the rain falls in the first few months of the year allowed at least one winter crop to be grown in the inland districts of Syria near the desert, in Central Anatolia, and in the mountainous regions of north-east Iraq, while the higher annual precipitation among the Mediterranean and Black Sea coasts of Anatolia generally permitted cultivation all the year round.

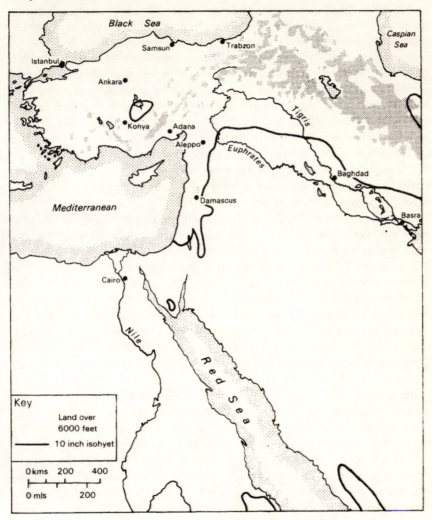

1 The Middle East: major geographical and climatic features

A glance at a relief map is also necessary. Here the most important features are the flat, low-lying valleys of the Nile, the Tigris and the Euphrates, the two parallel mountain chains running north/south through coastal Syria, the great Syrian desert and, in Anatolia, the contrast between the high central plateau and the narrow fringe of fertile coastline in the south round Adana and Antalya, in the east round Izmir and Bursa, and in the north along most of the Black Sea coast. Each of these features had a significant effect on the economic life of the region.

In the case of the flat river valleys, complicated systems of irrigation had long been in existence to allow water to be taken to fields at some distance from the rivers themselves. Again, transport by boat was cheap and relatively easy. Elsewhere, however, the problem of moving bulky agricultural goods was very much more difficult and costly, the more so as there were few all-weather roads and, with the exception of northern Iraq and, perhaps, parts of Anatolia, no use of carts or other wheeled vehicles.[19] In mountainous areas in particular it was only profitable to transport cereals and other food crops more than 20 or 30 miles at times of exceptionally high prices. And although, as Bulliett argues, the use of animals had some advantages over the wheel in the pre-modern Middle East, it was not until the construction of the first metalled roads from the mid-nineteenth century onwards that many inland districts were able to export more than a small proportion of their agricultural surplus.[20]

But if the mountain ranges made movement a problem they had the one great advantage that they provided security from outside attack. Whereas most of the villagers of Egypt, south and central Iraq, the coastal plain of Palestine and the land in Syria along the edge of the desert lay right open to the incursion of beduin, Turkoman or other nomadic tribesmen, the inhabitants of the Nablus district of northern Palestine, of Mount Lebanon or of the Jabal Druze in southern Syria could defend their homes and fields with relative ease.[21] Such considerations were of enormous importance at a time when the Ottoman authorities were unable to provide the basic security which any agriculturalist requires if he is to increase his input of labour and capital to increase production.

After these few introductory remarks it is now possible to return to the pattern of agricultural activity as it existed round the year 1800. As far as Anatolia was concerned there was a vital distinction between the type of agriculture practised on the coastal plain and that on the central plateau.[22] In the case of the former, the fact that it possessed the important advantages of good soil, reasonable annual rainfall and relatively easy transport allowed the cultivation of a wide variety of crops including cotton, figs, grapes and tobacco, the greater part of which was exported to Europe or to the Arab provinces of the Empire.[23] The central plateau, on the other hand, suffered from a very much harsher climate with long, vigorous winters (often with as much as three months of snow), hot summers, and a low annual rainfall. As a rule its cultivators concentrated their attention on crops like wheat and barley which were grown by dry farming methods and which produced only enough for their own requirements, for animal fodder, and for the demands of the tax-collector.[24] Cash crops were largely confined to the opium which the traveller, Richard Wood, found growing north of Antalya in the 1830s and the small quantities of fruit, vegetables and cotton grown in irrigated gardens round the larger towns.[25] There were also a number of export crops which grew more or less wild: yellow berries and madder roots used in dyeing and valonia (from oak-apple cups) employed in tanning. Finally, most of the cultivators of the Central Anatolian plateau raised some sheep, cattle, mules and horses in excess of their own needs. This activity became the more important towards the east as the cultivation of field crops became increasingly difficult. Great flocks of sheep were owned by the villagers of the Trabzon region, for instance, the animals spending the summer grazing on the hills and the cold winters down in the valleys. Further to the east again, Turkomans and Kurds bred horses and mules in the high mountains. They also raised sheep and goats for their wool and their mohair, which was spun in the local villages and then sold in the towns for export. The best known yarn was that from the goats of the Ankara (Angora) district which had found a steady market in England and France from at least as early as the seventeenth century.[26]

As far as geography and climate were concerned, Syria, like Anatolia, can be divided into two regions – at least if you exclude the desert. Along the coast there is a mild winter climate and sufficient rainfall (between 20 and 40 inches a year) to allow the cultivation of such crops as cereals, vegetables, tobacco, olives, citrus fruits and even cotton without irrigation.[27] But inland, as soon as you get over the two mountain ranges and up on to the high plateau on which Damascus and Aleppo stand, the amount of rain diminishes to an annual average of only 10 to 20 inches, as it also does in the cultivated areas of southern and eastern Palestine. In these districts cereals could be grown by dry farming methods, being sown in October and November just before the winter rains, but some system of irrigation was required for the cultivation of fruit, vegetables or cotton, most of which require water during the summer months. The most famous of these systems, known as the *ghuta*, provided water for the densely packed gardens around Damascus itself.[28]

As to the crops actually cultivated in 1800, wheat was grown almost everywhere throughout Syria, while other cereals like maize and sorghum (both confusingly known as *durra* in Arabic) were grown only in certain areas like Mount Lebanon and northern Palestine. One district of particular importance was the fertile plain in southern Syria known as the Hauran which generally produced enough good quality wheat and barley to allow a flourishing export trade. In addition, there was also a considerable degree of specialization in the cultivation of particular cash crops. Tobacco had been grown in the Latakia district since the seventeenth century when so great had been the demand, particularly from Egypt, that its production had spread rapidly. To the south, the tobacco from the hills behind Sur (Tyre) was sold mostly in Damascus. Meanwhile, cotton was sown in a number of areas, notably around Saida (Sidon) on the Lebanese coast and the Nablus district of northern Palestine. There it was generally spun locally and either sold as thread in the larger towns or exported to France. Other cash crops included olive oil (Beirut and the coastal districts to the south), indigo (the Beisan valley in Palestine), rice (the Hula district of Syria) and grapes (the Druze villages of Mount Lebanon).

But in spite of all this specialization it would seem that there was only one area where the process had been taken so far that the inhabitants had ceased to produce enough food to support themselves: Mount Lebanon. There, so much of the scarce agricultural land was devoted to the cultivation of the mulberry trees necessary to provide the leaves for feeding silkworms that there was no room on the narrow hillside terraces to grow all the cereals or to pasture all the cattle which self-sufficiency would have required.[29] Hence part of the profits from silk were used to buy rice from Egypt, cereals from Rosetta and the Hauran, and the sheep which were brought each year to the market town of Zahle in the Bekaa valley by Kurdish shepherds.

Agricultural conditions in the river valleys to the south and east of Syria were different again. Egypt, in Heroditus's famous phrase, remained 'the gift of the Nile'. Then, as now, cultivation was confined to a narrow strip of land running either side of the great river from Aswan to a point just north of Cairo where the Nile divided in two to form the Delta, an area shaped like an equilateral triangle with sides of about 100 miles in length and containing (in 1800) approximately 2 million feddans (acres) of cultivated land.[30] Rainfall throughout the country averaged less than 10 inches a year and agriculture depended almost exclusively on the overflow of the Nile between August and November each year when the land was covered with water held in vast basins until the fall in the level of the river allowed the flood to return. After a minimum of preparation a winter crop of cereals or, to a lesser extent, of flax, *birsim* (clover), tobacco or opium was sown and then harvested in the spring, four or five months later.[31] Most of the land remained fallow for the rest of the year, until the next flood, but there were some areas close to the Nile where it was possible to obtain sufficient summer water by means of lifting devices like the *saqiya* (a wheel with pots attached to it) or the *shaduf* (a bucket which was swung down into the river on the end of a long pole) to permit the cultivation of sugar, short-staple cotton, henna, sesame and ground nuts. Rice too could be grown during the summer months in flooded fields between the Nile and Lake Manzala and around Rosetta in the north of the Delta. Summer crops yielded a very much higher profit than winter ones.[32] On the other hand, they also required very much more labour and capital (see Table 3). It was necessary to keep them well irrigated at a time of year when the river was at its lowest; sowing and weeding had to be carried out with special care; all such crops generally required some kind of processing before delivery to the merchants.[33]

Table 3 Estimates of the cost of production, value and profit of various Egyptian crops – c. 1800 (based on a plot of 10 feddans)

Crop	Cost of production pataques-medins*	Gross value pataques-medins	Net profit pataques-medins
Winter			
Wheat (without extra irrigation)	52–74	200–20	146–36
(with extra irrigation)	133–54	241–75	108–21
Beans	35–55	162–11	126–46
Barley (without extra irrigation)	28–14	85–49	57–35
(with extra irrigation)	94–51	139–42	44–81
Summer			
Indigo	961–12	1504–00	542–78
Rice (grown with wheat)	940–00	1202–00	260–00
Cotton (short staple)	374–10	534–00	159–80
Sugar	839–04	2010–00	1170–86

* A *pataque* was a unit of account. In 1774 it was worth 90 *paras* (roughly 5 francs). There were 90 *medins* to a *para* (Raymond, *Artisans et commerçants*, 26–40; E. R. J. Owen, *Cotton and the Egyptian Economy 1820–1914* (Oxford, 1969), 383–4).

Source: Girard, 'Mémoire' *DE*[2], 187ff.

According to an estimate made by members of the French Expedition perhaps 250,000 to 500,000 feddans in the Delta, as well as a small amount of land in Middle and Upper Egypt, was placed under summer crops.[34] And it is here, in the first instance, that we should look for products which were specially grown for sale on the market. But it should also be noted that even those who grew only a winter crop may often have sold at least part of their harvest, either to pay that part of their tax burden which was levied in cash or in order to meet their own consumption needs. Such activity was facilitated by the fact that transport in Egypt was both cheaper and easier than in Anatolia and Syria. No part of Upper Egypt was more than a few miles away from the Nile, while in Lower Egypt there was a well developed system of navigation along both branches of the river as well as a large number of canals.

In Iraq too the agriculture practised over a large part of the country was dependent on the water obtained from a major river. Only in the hilly area in the north, roughly north-east of a line running from Mosul and Kirkuk to Khanaqin on the Persian frontier, was there sufficient rain to allow the cultivation of winter crops, mostly cereals, or a few summer crops like

cotton or tobacco around wells and springs.[35] Cultivation in the remainder
of the country was almost exclusively confined to patches of land along the
Tigris and Euphrates as well as along some of the east–west canals which
connected the two rivers just below Baghdad.[36] Cereals were grown in the
northern part of this area, while to the south peasant cultivators belonging
to tribal confederations like the Muntafiq and the Bani Lam were able to
use water from both rivers and canals to grow winter crops like wheat and
barley and summer crops like rice. Finally, in the marshy district formed by
the confluence of the Tigris and Euphrates near Basra there was the world's
largest concentration of date palms.

But if agriculture in much of Iraq, like that in Egypt, was almost completely dependent on water from a large river, there the similarity ends.
Unlike the Nile, the Tigris and Euphrates posed enormous problems for the
cultivators along their banks. Owing to the short distance between their
source and the alluvial plain their flood waters, swollen by winter rain and
snow, reached Baghdad in April and May (not in the autumn as in Egypt),
too late to irrigate the winter crop but just in time to destroy it by in-
undating any unprotected fields. Moreover, as a result of their swift descent
from the northern mountains, the Iraqi rivers were constantly carving new
channels for themselves, scouring out one place while leaving another silted
up and without water.[37] Proper management was further handicapped by
the fact that there were huge variations in the amount of water passing
through them from one year, as well as one season, to another.[38] For all
these reasons navigation also presented considerable difficulty, made worse
by the fact that, unlike in Egypt, the prevailing wind blew from the north in
the same direction as the current, making it very easy to float down-river
but extremely difficult to return. Whereas large Egyptian boats could be
propelled slowly southwards by the Mediterranean breeze, conditions in
Iraq dictated that it took four or five times as long to make the journey from
Basra to Baghdad than it did to travel in the opposite direction. Perhaps the
only advantage Iraqi cultivators possessed was that the multiplicity of old
river channels allowed water to be stored without great difficulty during the
summer months by the simple expedient of damming them up with rolls of
reed matting reinforced with branches and mud, a practice which, as
Fernea has shown, could be managed by the peasants themselves without
any need to rely on the assistance of the government and its officials.[39] No
figures exist which show the proportion of summer to winter crops grown on
irrigated land between Baghdad and Basra at the beginning of the nineteenth century, but according to the World Bank Mission which visited Iraq
in 1951 there was then still only sufficient water to grow summer crops over
an area a quarter of the size devoted to winter ones.[40] It would seem reasonable to suppose that 150 years earlier this proportion was very much
smaller.

Just as important as the question of what was produced in the Middle East in 1800 is the question of how it was produced, by whom, and under what conditions. But this, in turn, involves a preliminary discussion of the systems of land tenure and tax collection, for it was these systems which, as much as geography and climate, defined the context in which agriculturalists were forced to operate.

It need hardly be pointed out that the subject of Middle Eastern land tenure is one of overwhelming complexity. Not only did particular methods of allocating land, each with its own particular terminology, vary from province to province, and even from district to district; but also there seems often to have been little connection between a system as it existed in theory or in law and what actually happened in practice. In the Middle East, as elsewhere, the attempt to create or define new forms of rural property was generally the work of men living in the towns. Whether or not they were successful depended on a whole host of conditions, among them the extent to which they had power to control events in the countryside and the skill with which they related their innovations to traditional or customary practice, most of which were rarely fulfilled. The result was often total confusion, a situation in which town and country spoke entirely different languages.

Bearing all this in mind a few generalizations are still possible. First, according to both Islamic law and Ottoman practice the greater part of the cultivated land in the Middle East was classified as *miri*, that is as belonging to the state, the only exception to this being some lands held in absolute freehold (*mulk*).[41] At the beginning of the nineteenth century, however, *mulk* land in the rural areas was still almost exclusively confined to village property on which buildings had been erected or to orchards, gardens and vineyards. Secondly, as far as the *miri* land contained in the tax or cadastral registers was concerned, individuals, or in some cases communities, were able to establish a variety of different rights over it, although always stopping short of full legal ownership. It would be helpful to look at the process by which these rights were established at two levels: at the level of those who controlled the land and collected the taxes and at the level of those who actually cultivated it.

At the first level members of various groups were able to use the powers granted to them by the Ottoman government to obtain a more permanent control over the lands assigned to them. One method was to ensure that the tax-farm was granted for life or, if possible, made hereditary within a particular family.[42] Another method of establishing permanent control over an estate was to convert it into a *waqf*, ensuring that the profits were used not for the upkeep of some mosque or other religious institution but for the family of the founder. Although *waqf* land could not legally be sold or mortgaged like real private property, the right to the use of its products could be leased or inherited.[43] Even more important, the estate in question was safe from seizure either by private creditors or by the state. Finally, *waqf* land may, in some instances, have been either subject to lower taxes or have been left completely free, although evidence about this is contradictory.[44] The creation of family *waqfs* was most common in Anatolia and Egypt. In the latter, for example, the historian al-Jabarti estimated that up to a fifth of all the agricultural land had been converted in this way.[45]

Once such permanent rights had been established it was then possible to put the land to some profit. In Mount Lebanon there is evidence of *muqatajis* selling that part of their *iqtas*, known as *uhdas* (farms), which had been originally assigned to them for their own use.[46] Elsewhere, in Egypt for instance, there is occasional mention of the collection of rent.[47] But how these rights had been established over time, and what they really amounted to in law, is uncertain.

To turn now to the second level, that of the peasant cultivators, here too there were many areas in which the rights to the usufruct of particular pieces of land were well established. In Anatolia, Lower Egypt and parts of Syria these rights (known as *tasarruf* − use) allowed a peasant to cultivate a plot during his lifetime, to alienate it temporarily to another cultivator, or to pass it to his sons (and sometimes to some other member of his family).[48] In addition, in the districts round Damascus at least, peasants seem to have been able to sell the *tasarruf* to a person from another village, while in Mount Lebanon, where usufructory rights seem to have developed into what was very close to private ownership, some peasant cultivators were able to buy land from their *muqatajis*.[49]

To what extent given rights were actually respected in practice is less clear; but there are a number of reasons to suppose that they usually were. For one thing they provided the *multazim* or *muqataji* with an assured tax income, as it was the *tasarruf* holders who paid the major share of rural imposts.[50] For another, it is not likely to have been in the interests of the tax-farmer or his local agents to take over a usufructory right for themselves if this meant that they had to find someone else to cultivate the plot in question for wages or on a crop-sharing basis. Land, of itself, did not have any value except in those few areas where the regular production of a marketable crop allowed cash rents to be charged; what mattered was the ability to appropriate an already existing surplus. Peasants probably received additional protection for their rights in those many districts where there were considerable reserves of cultivable land remaining uncultivated for lack of men to work them.

Elsewhere, in parts of Upper Egypt, in southern Syria and in the irrigated areas of Iraq, the emergence of individual or family rights was inhibited either by a communal system of land ownership, or the regular redistribution of fields among the local population, or both. In Iraq the river-irrigated land was controlled by tribes, or in some cases confederations of tribes like the Muntafiq on the Lower Euphrates, which included both nomads and peasant agriculturalists.[51] Each tribal group had its own *dira* or area which it customarily occupied, part of which would be cultivated each year as water, labour and animal power permitted. Due to the fact that the rivers did not flood in a regular way and were constantly shifting their channels, the land placed under cultivation could well move considerably over time. As for the fields themselves, some of them might be allocated to the shaikh who used the produce to support himself and the tribal guesthouse (*mudif*). Alternatively he might simply receive a share of the total harvest. The remainder of the land was controlled by *sirkals* or sub-chiefs who, in turn, might work part of it themselves, dividing the rest into plots to be tilled by the peasant members of the tribe. How this sytem actually worked in practice at the beginning of the nineteenth century is impossible to say. But by mid-century, if not earlier, there was an observable tendency for some shaikhs and tribesmen to develop prescriptive rights (known as *lazma*) to individual plots of land.[52]

In Palestine and parts of southern Syria land was also held in common and subject to redistribution among the villagers. But, once again, this particular system (known as *mushaa*) is one about which too little is known to be categoric. As it existed a little later in the century the land was divided into parcels, or collections of parcels, which were then divided between the different members of the local community at regular intervals.[53] Unfortunately nothing is known about the way the shares were allocated among the cultivators or their relationship, if any, to the size of the plots. While it is interesting to speculate that the system might have had its origins in the days when nomadic tribes took up settled agriculture, this provides no clue as to the way it developed nor to its interaction with the distribution of power either inside the village or without.[54] Land was also subject to redistribution among members of the peasant communities in Upper Egypt, but for different reasons. The system of irrigation involving the flooding of large basins of land made it difficult to establish regular boundaries and the cultivable land was allocated annually after the flood according to the labour and animal power which each cultivator possessed.[55]

A general description of the system of taxation is equally difficult, for here too the written rules and regulations bore little relation to actual practice. In theory each cultivator's major liability was a land tax amounting to anywhere between 10 per cent and 50 per cent of his annual production, or a similar tax on his animals.[56] Even if this proportion was still being adhered to at the end of the eighteenth century there were also a whole host of extra dues, many of which had been added or augmented over time. In Egypt these included the *faiz* and the *barrani* (which belonged to the *multazim*), the *kushufiyah* (which went to the provincial governor and his agents) and the *mudaf* (a general surcharge) all of which must certainly have exceeded the *miri*, or ordinary land tax, by a considerable amount.[57] In addition, that part of the harvest which was not taken by the collector himself was at the mercy of his agents (who often quartered themselves in the villages for long periods at harvest-time) of local shaikhs and headmen, and of merchants who had been given the right to purchase all that remained of a particular crop. Further losses were suffered in areas where the bulk of the taxes were collected in kind from the rule that the crop could not be harvested until it was measured, a method designed to prevent the peasants from hiding part of it and (in Anatolia at least) from the insistence that it be transported to the nearest town at the peasant's expense. As al-Jabarti noted at the time, it seems likely that little was left to the cultivator beyond his own consumption needs.[58] According to Tallien of the French Expedition, more than two-thirds of the Egyptian harvest was taken in tax.[59] Meanwhile, the situation in the tribal areas beyond the reach of the Ottoman government is probably best summed up by the following observation by Muhammad Agha, a Kurdish chieftain:

I allow the peasants to cultivate my estate, as they may find it convenient, and I take from them my due, which is the zakat or a tenth of the whole, and as much more as I can squeeze out of them by any means, and on any pretext.[60]

In these circumstances, if a cultivator was able to keep a little more than he needed to sustain himself and his family and animals and to use as seed for the next year's planting, it was less the result of any small protection that he might receive from custom or the law than of his own skill at avoiding some of the demands made on him, of a fortunate geographical location, or the interest which a particular tax-collector or his agents might have in not pushing his peasants too far. The reports of European travellers in the region give examples of all three kinds. The most obvious weapon was simply to hide part of the harvest. Almost all the Kurdish villages visited by Richard Wood contained deep, carefully concealed holes for storing grain out of sight of both chieftain and robbers.[61] In other areas, like Egypt, where the collector had agents inside the local community, it was probably easier to sell a part of the crop and then to hide the coins. Again, some peasants received additional protection from the fact that they lived at a distance from the nearest town or from their ability to add to the cost of collection in various ways. In southern Syria, where taxes were collected from local shaikhs and peasants alike during an annual armed expedition organized by the governor of Damascus (known as the *daura*), it might simply be a question of hiding until the troops had gone by.[62] In Egypt, too, distance from the capital city was a great advantage. Schulkowski of the French Expedition suggested that one of the reasons why the fields he found in a district 80 miles from Cairo looked so prosperous was that the *multazims* stood to gain more by allowing the peasants to pay some of what they owed, peacefully, than by going to the trouble and expense of sending an armed force against them.[63] In Iraq, tribesmen often protected themselves from government tax-collecting expeditions by cutting the dykes along the canals and surrounding themselves by flooded fields.[64] Finally, in the last resort there was always revolt, or the threat of revolt.[65] A third set of factors which also served to protect some peasants from over-excessive demands was the network of relationships which might tie them to landlord, usurer or merchant. In each case there was an obvious interest in allowing cultivators to prosper sufficiently to be able to pay their rents, to produce marketable crops, or to meet their debts.[66]

Taxes and dues were paid in either cash or kind, or a combination of the two. According to Inalcik the Anatolian land-tax was collected in kind – he has described how the cultivators had to place their threshed grain in eight piles for the collector to choose one – while many of the extra duties (perhaps amounting to a half of the total receipts) were levied in coins.[67] In parts of Syria and Palestine and in Upper Egypt the main land-tax was also taken in kind, but in Lower Egypt and the Hauran peasants seem to have had to pay a portion of what was due in cash.[68] As for the *multazims*, they might forward taxes collected in kind to the Central Treasury, as they were supposed to do in Upper Egypt, or they might have to sell what they had raised in order to meet their obligation to pay the government only in coin.[69]

In all cases the question of how the taxes were actually paid is an important one. To the extent that the peasants (and by the same argument, the *multazims*) had to find the money to pay what they owed, they had to take care to produce a marketable crop. This, in turn, brought them within the sphere of market forces, encouraging them to organize production according to considerations of relative prices and of demand, extending their use of coins, and, in many cases, forcing them to borrow what they could not raise themselves from merchants, usurers, or even the *multazim* himself. For all these reasons it would be useful to have more information on the subject, but even categorical statements by contemporary observers about how taxes were actually collected must be suspect, for it would seem likely that the proportion demanded in cash must have varied considerably, not only from one district to another, but also from one period of time to another, according to the availability of market outlets for crops and the collectors' own calculations as to how best to increase their own profit. The best that can be done is to assert simply that, in most areas, at least some part of the range of taxes and dues which the peasants were forced to pay must have been demanded in coin.

What is more sure is that however peasants were made to surrender the bulk of the surplus, they got little in return. In most areas neither the government nor its agents offered the agricultural population any protection, and the most that could be expected was that the local shaikh or chieftain would preserve his own villagers from the rapacity of rival chieftains.[70] Travel was hazardous, roads and bridges were in bad repair and central control of the irrigation system in the great river valleys was either completely abandoned (as in Iraq) or exercised only irregularly, as in Egypt, where much of the money assigned to the task was simply appropriated by the provincial governors and their agents.[71] That the agricultural population was able to survive, or even occasionally to prosper, was due largely to the ability of members of small communities to work together and to protect themselves. In Lower Egypt and in the hill districts of Palestine the villages were often more like fortresses with strong walls and narrow entrances.[72] In the Egyptian Delta and on the Tigris north of Baghdad those working away from home found additional protection in high, windowless towers built near their fields into which they could retire if danger threatened.[73] Otherwise, if active defence was impossible, cultivators might pay money to the beduin to look after them or to leave them in peace.[74] Finally, if all else failed, peasants might be forced into a more peripatetic existence, like the inhabitants of the Hauran who could only protect themselves against the exactions of both government and nomad alike by constant movement from one district to another or, as a last resort, taking temporary refuge (with their families and animals) among a local beduin tribe until conditions improved.[75]

As a result of all these stratagems the lot of the Middle Eastern peasant population could not have been quite as bad as many writers have attempted to prove.[76] If it had, it is difficult to see how agriculture could have continued to be practised at all, let alone to produce enough food for the oversize towns, enough materials for the local craft industry, and enough extra to sustain a low level of exports. Nevertheless, this was not a situation which permitted any accumulation of capital in the agricultural sector nor any regular increase in production. This had to wait until the beginnings of the transformation of the Middle East economy in the nineteenth century.

Having made these preliminary points it is now possible to discuss the actual practice of agriculture itself. Here it is important to begin by stressing the fact that in the Middle East in 1800, the cultivation of the soil was almost exclusively the working of peasant families, farming small plots of land and using only the most simple tools.* Although a certain number of landless labourers seem to have existed in most areas, they could hardly

---

* There is a large literature on what types of agriculturalists ought properly to be called peasants.[77] For the purpose of this present work I propose to ignore the difficulties posed by the use of the term and to call all settled cultivators in the Middle East peasants (*fellaheen*). There is also a considerable problem about the definition of what might have constituted a 'family' at this same period. Not surprisingly there is no information about how peasants grouped themselves into households. Nevertheless it can be suggested that, in logic at least, there must have

have provided more than a limited addition to the regular workforce, with the possible exception of districts like those in Mount Lebanon where their numbers were augmented by cultivators whose own plots were too small to provide them with full-time employment.[79] If the family was the main production unit it was also the main unit of consumption, devoting most of its energies to growing enough food to feed its members and its animals and to meet the demands of the tax-collector, leaving little over for sale or exchange.

Techniques remained simple. The majority of tools and implements in use had to be related to the level of mechanical skills to be found at village level. They had to be constructed and repaired locally and utilized by uneducated men. In addition, they had to be pushed and pulled by what were often weak, half-starved animals. This is not to say, however, that such implements were necessarily as inefficient as their European critics often maintained. Travellers always had harsh things to say about the Egyptian plough, no more than two small pieces of sharpened wood at right angles to each other, the longer piece connected to a yoke, which was so light that it only scratched the surface of the soil. But this was to ignore the fact that, in a country where the water table was so near the surface, deep ploughing inevitably turned up salts which were harmful to soil fertility.[80] Similarly in Palestine or Mount Lebanon it was generally necessary for a peasant to be able to carry his plough up and down the steep hill-terraces.[81]

There is no doubt, however, that it was these same tools which helped to keep productivity at a low level. In the Trabzon district cultivators had to choose between a scratch plough which hardly penetrated the dry ground and a heavy Byzantine-type one which was difficult to pull. Elsewhere in Anatolia the fact that there was only a very short ploughing season (between the onset of the winter rains which moistened the soil enough to allow it to be tilled and the first frosts after which sowing was impossible) severely limited the amount of ground which any one peasant could work with the inefficient implement at his disposal.[82] To take another example, the small crude sickle in general use throughout the Middle East could cut off only the ears (not the whole stem) of standing wheat or barley.[83] Meanwhile, in Egypt, the use of badly-made wooden cogs on water lifting devices like the *saqiya* produced a great deal of unnecessary friction, making the mechanism heavy to turn, while the *nauraj* (or bullock-drawn chair used in threshing) tended to leave the grains covered in dirt.[84]

Not surprisingly, many criticisms can be made of other agricultural

been considerable pressures to include as many actual or potential labourers as possible under one roof. This follows from the obvious difficulty of maintaining a stable adult workforce over time sufficient to plough and to harvest even quite a small plot of land when life expectancy was so low and disease so rampant.[78] This was as true of the great estates and *waqf* properties (where a portion of the land was either let to peasants or farmed in co-operation with them) as it was of the field subject to a communal system of ownership in Syria and Lower Iraq.

techniques. Crops tended to be planted at the time of year decreed by custom rather than science. Fertilizers were rarely used, particularly in treeless districts where animal manure was needed for fuel, with the result that in Anatolia it was necessary to maintain the fertility of the soil by the wasteful process of leaving fields fallow for two years out of three.[85] In many other areas, for example, in Kurdistan, land was left fallow every other year for the same reason.[86] Only in Egypt was some attention paid to maintaining the fertility of the soil. There, pigeon guano was used on village gardens while the nitrogen-rich earth to be found on the sides of abandoned towns (known as *khum* from the mounds where it was found) was often spread over those fields which had not been inundated by the annual flood.[87] Harvesting, too, was carelessly done, often leaving the crop damaged or dirty and difficult to process, as in the case of Palestinian olives which were badly bruised as a result of being shaken from their trees, rather than picked. More generally, techniques tended to remain the same, generation after generation, peasants being naturally unwilling to risk any change which might threaten their precarious existence.

As to the type of crops which were grown, there is no doubt that the greater part of the cultivated area of the Middle East was devoted to the winter cereals required for subsistence, for feeding the animals and for taxes. Such crops were usually planted in late autumn and harvested in spring or early summer. In the rain-fed areas the field would then be left fallow, but in the irrigated areas of Egypt and Lower Iraq another crop might be put in just before or just after the main cereal one. As a rule the seed was sown broadcast and there was no weeding or harrowing. Little working capital was required for agriculture of this type − simply a plough with an animal to draw it, and a sickle − and, such as it was, could be provided as part of some crop-sharing agreement with the holder of the *timar* or *iltizam* or, in Syria, by a merchant or usurer living in the nearest town.[88] According to Burckhardt, in the latter type of arrangement the peasant might receive the tools he needed, and have the land-tax paid for him, in return for two-thirds of the harvest.[89] In addition to the major cereals, small quantities of sesame, maize and sorghum, tobacco, beans and water melons were also grown during the winter months in some areas.[90]

The majority of summer crops required more working capital and a greater degree of care and attention. The working capital came from a variety of sources. In the districts round Damietta, for example, where the cultivation of ten feddans of land with rice was estimated by Girard to require twelve oxen and two ploughs as well as three water-wheels (each of which had to be replaced every five years) and a machine for threshing, the necessary advance was provided by usurers from the town at what seems the very low rate of 10 per cent a year.[91] Meanwhile, in Upper Egypt, the peasants who grew sugar near Girga obtained money to buy the animals they needed from the Mamluk beys who owned the local sugar factories.[92] Another source of credit was the foreign merchants resident in the coastal towns. In the district round Saida it was French traders who advanced money to the cotton-growing peasants until their expulsion by Jazzar in 1790.[93]

In addition to a discussion of crops and credit, peasant agricultural activity must also be understood in terms of the organization of the village and of its relationship to the wider world. Almost all the settled cultivators in the Middle East lived in such communities, for obvious reasons. Villages provided a degree of protection for their inhabitants as well as the possibility of co-operation with others in such vital tasks as harvesting, processing cash crops, or in maintaining major works of irrigation. Again, the concentration of agriculturalists in villages allowed a minimal amount of specialization in the production of non-agricultural products like clothes, pots and a few items of furniture, activities which also opened up the possibility of alternative means of employment for peasants and their wives when times were hard. Finally, a village community could often support a shaikh or some other religiously-trained man who, apart from his role as a teacher, could also be used to settle the inevitable disputes about inheritance or the boundaries of particular plots of land.

Nevertheless, in spite of the degree of self-sufficiency which the organization of village life allowed, it cannot be argued, as many have tried to do, that the village must be seen as an 'independent community', almost completely isolated from the economic and political arrangements of the society of which it formed a part.[94] For one thing no group of peasant agriculturalists could escape from their obligation to pay taxes and dues, either to a government-appointed collector or to some powerful local figure. Second, as already noted, many peasants were dependent on outsiders for working capital while others must certainly have required more credit than their own community could provide to finance feasts and weddings. Third, there was often a considerable degree of local specialization, with particular villages producing particular kinds of food, vegetables or handicrafts which were traded widely throughout the district.[95] In addition, few communities were completely self-sufficient when it came to the manufacture of a variety of goods like spears and guns or metal cooking pots. For all these reasons villages which regularly practised pure subsistence must have been very rare, although some might occasionally have been forced to adopt such a pattern when times were particularly hard. The remainder, which must certainly have included the overwhelming majority of peasant communities, were firmly locked into a 'centralised network of domination', to use Shanin's phrase, linking political and cultural dependence with exploitation by tax-farmers, state and town.[96]

The extent to which links of this kind brought the Middle Eastern village into market relations with the wider economy is a question of central importance. Unfortunately it can only be answered in the most general terms. While there is a relatively large amount of information about the organization of international trade, especially with Europe, little has been written about the petty commerce carried on within districts. There are also difficult conceptual problems which, even in an African context where much more work has been done, have not yet been satisfactorily resolved.[97] Perhaps the only safe assertion to make is that, for most areas of the Middle East, the overwhelming proportion of agricultural goods traded consisted of products either taken directly as taxes or sold by the peasants in order to raise the cash needed to pay given taxes. In both cases the collector (and his associated banker) and, to some extent, the merchant stood between the producer and market forces, reducing the effect of changes in price or demand in influencing peasant decisions about what crops to grow and in what quantity. Some were given permission to buy up all of a particular crop from the peasants of a particular district, using their monopoly position to force down prices; others, like the Frenchman d'Arvieux based at Saida, were able to obtain the cheap silk and other products at the beginning of the harvest from cultivators who urgently need the money to meet their tax demands.[98] Activities of this kind sustained a widespread network of markets and systems of transport which allowed goods collected in tax to be distributed throughout the Ottoman Empire, and sometimes beyond.

For an examination of the sale of the remainder of the surplus in order to meet needs which could not be catered for at village level, or simply to make money, a useful analytical tool is Hopkins's distinction between short and long distance trade.[99] The former is characterized by the exchange of goods in regular local markets and results from the different production strategies of the different peasant households and from variations in natural and human resources endowments which allow the development of complementary specializations within quite small areas. It may also involve some buying and selling within the continuous markets to be found in towns, where the larger population and more varied forms of economic activity create a wider demand for local agricultural products. In both cases competition among those who engage in the trade is fierce, as there are hardly any barriers to entry. Just as important, the geographical extent of such trade is restricted to a few miles − perhaps no more than ten − round the principal marketplace. As a result, although Hopkins does not make the point, most agricultural goods are brought for sale by the cultivators themselves, transport costs are high, and there are obvious limits to the degree by which the prices of foodstuffs can be reduced in order to increase demand. Long distance trade, on the other hand, is organized and financed by specialist merchants and is a way of gaining access to a much larger market.

The observations of members of the French Expedition to Egypt provide some support for Hopkins's method of analysis. Throughout the country there were regular local markets to which the peasants brought a variety of agricultural produce, for example the one at Isna in Upper Egypt where the cultivators (and nomads) of the district sold their cereals, butter, cheese, oxen, sheep and chickens.[100] The effect of these markets on the practice of peasant agriculture is less clear. While many cultivators must certainly have taken care to produce some goods for which there was a local demand, it would seem likely that this activity was no more than ancillary to their main concern with growing enough food for their own nourishment and for taxes. By the same token the effect of changes in price on the decision to plant more or less of a cash crop must have been limited. Where market forces did have any role to play was in the production of goods which entered longer distance trade. These would be financed, purchased and processed by merchants whose knowledge of prices and of changes in demand would be reflected in pressure on the peasant cultivators to organize production in the light of market conditions. Part of the rice grown in Lower Egypt was exported to the Greek islands, to Anatolia and to Mount Lebanon, while much of the short-staple cotton was bought up by urban merchants for resale to local or foreign weavers.[101] Again, as an example of the way in which some cultivators were responsive to the needs of the market, there is Girard's assertion that the area placed under flax in the Delta depended on whether its export was possible, and thus whether the price would be a good one.[102] More generally, it would seem that, throughout the Middle East, it was the areas where summer cash crops were grown which were the most likely to have been affected by the pressure of the market, whether Lower Egypt, Mount Lebanon, or the Anatolian coast.

It would be wrong, however, to confine a description of Middle Eastern agriculture in 1800 merely to the cultivation of the soil by settled communities of peasants. Equally important in many areas was the raising of horses, mules and camels for transport, cattle for use as draft animals and for their meat, and sheep and goats for their hair, wool and skin. Activities of this type covered a wide spectrum. At one end there were the ordinary villagers who spend most of their time cultivating their fields and who devoted little time to their animals; at the other groups like the marsh dwellers of southern Iraq who obtained the greater part of their income from their buffaloes, or the beduin who had no fixed homes and who wandered through the desert for most of the year with their flocks, only returning to the fringes of the cultivated area during the driest months to trade. In between there were many kinds of nomads, members of tribes who obtained most of their livelihood from the possession of large numbers of sheep, goats and horses and whose seasonal migration depended entirely on the need to find pasture all the year round.[103]

In seeking to analyse the role played by the raising of animals in the Middle East three important questions can be asked. First, to what extent did the income of a particular community or group depend on its herds or flocks? As far as the bulk of the settled population was concerned it relied chiefly on its crops for its needs and raised animals only as a source of power, of milk and meat, or, in the last resort, as a form of insurance against the failure of the harvest. On the other hand there were few groups of nomads who depended entirely on their animals for food and clothing as well as a source of extra income from the fees they received from the caravans they guided, or from the booty they obtained in raids.[104] In all this there were perhaps only two examples of pure specialization: the carriers who used their own animals to transport goods, and the shepherds who tended other people's animals for cash.[105]

Second, in so far as the groups which obtained the bulk of their income from animals were concerned, it is necessary to ask whether or not they were able to produce a marketable surplus. To judge from the evidence of European travellers many Middle Eastern pastoralists were well able to do just this. In some cases specialization in animal production was clearly taken so far that the nomads in question made no effort to grow the food or to produce all of the clothing they required, relying on the fact that the towns and cities provided a ready market for their meat and wool. According to Burckhardt, the Kurds brought 20,000 to 30,000 sheep into Syria every year, the great majority of which were sold either in Aleppo and Damascus or in Mount Lebanon.[106] Similarly, the Turkomans who wintered on the Amq plain in northern Syria provided Aleppo and its surrounding villages with sheep as well as wool, butter, cheese and carpets in exchange for cloth, dyes, guns, and small amounts of coffee, sweets and jewellery.[107] In other areas most nomadic groups must certainly have produced a sufficient surplus to allow some trade with the villages they passed on their regular migrations.

Third, whatever the relations between the nomads and the settled population, it is important to ask if some at least of their transactions were not carried out in cash rather than by means of barter. This would certainly seem to have been the case with some of the numerous transactions carried out between the inhabitants of Aleppo and visiting Turkomen, Kurds and beduin.[108] More generally, it would seem reasonable to assume that it would have been very difficult for groups which had such a limited variety of resources at their command and a much wider variety of needs not to have carried some coins with them. As Barth's study of present-day South Persia demonstrates, there are occasions on which it is necessary for nomads to sell animals in bulk in one place and then to use the proceeds to purchase small quantities of goods in several others.[109] It is for reasons such as this that it is essential to consider nomadic groups not as independent economic entities but as part of the wider regional economy.[110]

Urban economic activity

Towns and cities have multiple economic roles: industrial, commercial, administrative. In the Middle East one of the most important involved their place at the centre of the agricultural life of their region. With the exception of Istanbul, all the major cities of Anatolia, Syria, Egypt and Iraq lay at the edge of districts of rich, cultivable land for which they served as a market, a source of credit and a centre of government. Indeed, so intimate was the connection with the rural hinterland that it is certainly wrong to think of the city as belonging to a different economic or political order.[111] For one thing, in most parts of the Middle East the groups which vied with one another for control of the rural tax-farms were urban based. Again, as already noted, much of the credit required for the cultivation of both summer and winter crops came from urban merchants and *multazims*, while the large towns were an important market for locally produced food and raw materials as well as a source of the goods which peasants and nomads could not make for themselves. In both cases it was the cities which obtained the bulk of the rural surplus, whether by the direct use of force or by the manipulation of their monopoly position with regard to the provision of working capital and the purchase of crops.

The Middle Eastern city had other roles as well. One of the most important was its function as a centre of industrial production. To oversimplify greatly, two types of goods were produced. First, there were the goods required to satisfy the every-day needs of the urban population itself, for example textiles, furniture and pottery. Such goods were also manufactured in many of the villages as well and, in this case, the only distinction between town and country is that the former contained *suqs* (bazaars) with a greater concentration of artisans and their shops.[112] European travellers like Burckhardt and Buckingham who passed through Syria and Palestine during the first decades of the nineteenth century, or like Wood and Olivier whose journeys took them across Anatolia and northern Iraq, all noted that practically every urban centre through which they passed contained workshops making cotton and woollen goods and other textiles, as well as numerous dyeing establishments. Many also supported bakers, millers, saddlers, carpenters, blacksmiths, coppersmiths, in addition to glass-making plants, tanneries, lime kilns and brick works.[113] The same was also true of the main Egyptian towns.[114]

Second, most of the larger towns tended to specialize in the production of a number of articles which required more capital and a greater degree of craftsmanship and skill. Of these perhaps the best known historically were the muslins from Mosul and the damask from Damascus, both of which had taken their name from these same cities. But they also included the fine silks and cotton stuffs (often with gold and silver thread) of Aleppo, the olive oil soap from Nablus, the embroidered cloth from Majdal, the glass from Hebron, and the linen woven in Damietta. Such products were sufficiently well known to be traded over a wide area. Most of Nablus's soap was sent to Egypt, many of Damietta's linen napkins were exported to Anatolia, while the fine textiles from Damascus and Aleppo were sold throughout the Middle Eastern world.[115]

Urban industry was generally organized on a house basis. According to the Turkish traveller Celebi, who visited Cairo in the mid-seventeenth century, the average number of men employed in each workshop was three and a half.[116] The capital was owned by the master and consisted of no more than the house itself (if this was not rented), some simple and not very valuable tools, and the working or circulatory capital tied up in raw materials and a few finished articles. It generally passed from father to son. In addition, most of the important towns contained some larger establishments such as tanneries and textile works. Girard, in the *Description de l'Egypte*, mentions linen factories at Damietta, Mansura, Samanud and Cairo.[117] Similarly, in Aleppo, Russell notes that there existed some large textile manufactories with many looms under one roof.[118] It may well be, however, that it was just as common for the different parts of these same industrial processes to be carried out in different workshops in different parts of the city, as was certainly the case of the manufacture of the small caps known as *shashiyas* in eighteenth-century Tunisia.[119] It was also true of textile production in mid-nineteenth-century Damascus when the separate processes of reeling, twisting and dyeing the thread, attaching it to looms and then weaving, though organized by a single entrepreneur, were carried out in separate locales.[120] In all such cases the main purpose seems to have been to reduce risks and to limit the need to pay and to maintain a regular labour force which might have little to do when demand was slack.

As a general rule the standard of technique was low compared with that of western Europe.[121] It is true that the Turkish naval and military arsenals were still able to imitate most of the ships and weapons employed by their European enemies.[122] It is also true that certain groups of craftsmen, like the weavers, continued to produce articles of a very high quality. On the other hand, manufacturers had not begun the transition from the employment of men and animals to turn their machines to the use of water or wind. Again, as Russell pointed out, the majority of tools were so crude that it was virtually impossible to reproduce fine European work.[123] What was just as important was the low level of mechanical skill — well illustrated by the fact that Volney was unable to find anyone in Cairo to repair his watch — and the fact that there was no tradition of industrial innovation and discovery.[124]

The barriers in the way of progress were various. One was the organization of industry itself, with artisans divided up into corporations or guilds consisting of masters and apprentices under a shaikh.[125] Although the main purpose of this system was almost certainly to facilitate government control over an important section of the urban population, it could also be used by the guild members themselves to impose strict regulations on the exercise of their trade. Entry was restricted because apprentices had to attach themselves to masters, and only a master could open a workshop; competition was made virtually impossible by the practice of fixing uniform prices.[126] Again, as Marx noted of European guilds, the fact that masters could only employ a limited number of workers in their own shop and were prevented from employing men in other crafts excluded any attempt to capitalize on the further development of the division of labour.[127] Such a system could have helped to maintain standards of craftsmanship over the centuries. But the fact is that it also reinforced a situation in which incomes were more or less equal, in which the old controlled the young, and in which competition could hardly exist, all of which must have acted as a powerful brake on development.

Institutional factors were not the only problem faced by the Middle Eastern craft industry in the early nineteenth century. One was the difficulty of obtaining money to invest in expanded production. Neither the workshop nor the few tools owned by the master were realizable assets while in Egypt at least it seems to have been unusual, if not unheard of, for merchants and others with money to invest in the industrial sector.[128] A second factor was the limited size of the local market for most goods, made worse in some areas by European competition. This not only acted to discourage expansion but also led craftsmen to produce only on demand and not for stock.[129]

A third important role played by the Middle Eastern city was concerned with local, regional and international trade. Each of the major cities of Anatolia, Syria, Iraq and Egypt lay at the intersection of a number of important routes along which goods were carried across the region (see Map 2). Aleppo, for example, received European goods from the ports of Latakia and Iskandarun/Alexandretta while the products of India and Persia reached it by the regular caravans from Iraq and those from Africa and Arabia by other caravans travelling northwards through Palestine and Syria. Istanbul, Izmir, Diyarbakir, Damascus, Baghdad, Basra and Cairo occupied similar positions across north-south and east-west routes. Meanwhile, it was in these same large cities that long distance trade was planned, organized and financed. There lived the camel masters who led the great trans-desert caravans, there the merchants who specialized in buying and selling the commodities produced in the different regions of the world. Lastly, Middle Eastern cities were important markets for the luxury goods which because of the high cost of transport then formed a large part of

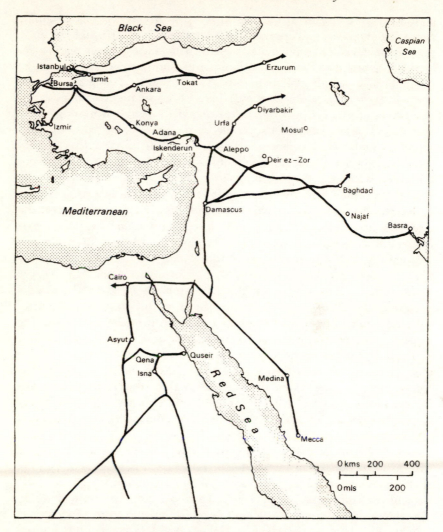

2 Middle Eastern caravan routes

international trade, containing as they did the residences of almost all the
rich men of the area. Not only did such men buy expensive foreign goods
like furs, cloth and weapons for their own use but also for the members of
their households as well. As Hasselquist noted of the import of fine, thin
French cloth into Cairo in the eighteenth century, the greatest part of it was
sold at the festival at Bairam 'when everyone who can afford it must have a
new set of clothes' and when 'the grandees and the rich men have to clothe

their servants'.[130] The same was true of the purchase of British woollens in Istanbul.[131] Then, as for many centuries before, the consumption pattern of the ruling élite and its allies was heavily weighted towards foreign imports.

The only Middle Eastern city about which anything is known in detail is Cairo. Thanks to the reports of the members of the French Expedition and to the work of Raymond and Shaw in the Ottoman archives it is possible to form some picture of the organization of its economic activity in the late eighteenth century, even if many gaps remain. In 1798 it was a city of some 250,000 to 300,000 inhabitants, with its adult male population divided roughly as follows: Mamluks, soldiers in *ojaks*, and other members of the Turkish ruling group – 12,000; 'propriétaires', *ulama* – 6,000; merchants, artisans and others engaged in economic activity – just over 80,000.[132] Of these the majority lived and worked within the boundaries of the old Fatimid capital of al-Qahira, to the north of the citadel. There, as in any other pre-industrial city, a warren of narrow streets made transport difficult, confining the warehousing and sale of bulk goods to markets either outside or just inside the gates. The more specialized crafts, however, were carried on in the middle of the Fatimid enclave, many of them along the one central thoroughfare which linked the northern gates with those in the south. The maze of streets, some of them blocked off to form dead ends, also helped to create a system of quarters (*hara*), in which the inhabitants could group themselves together for defence or mutual support.[133]

As for the economically active population, according to French estimates about a quarter were craftsmen and another tenth or so merchants and retailers.[134] Of the latter, perhaps a quarter again were engaged in some aspect of textile production with a small proportion employed in wood and leather work, food processing, and other types of manufacture.[135] Workshops were small and generally contained no more than a master and two or three apprentices. But there were also a few large establishments like the tanneries, which employed several hundred workers, and the houses for dyeing cloth, with thirty or forty. Capital was very limited. According to Raymond's analysis of the wills of nine silk weavers between 1688 and 1751, the average value of material in stock was only 974 *paras* (under £40).[136] The value of the tools and of the working premises itself was also small. Commerce too was characterized by limited financial resources. Again according to Raymond, the wills of the smaller merchants, like the craftsmen, showed that they generally possessed only small quantities of stock.[137]

The only group with large amounts of capital at its disposal was that of the merchants engaged in the international trade in coffee and textiles. Whereas the average value of the wills of 154 craftsmen studied by Raymond for the period 1776–98 was 29,644 *paras* and that of 205 small merchants (excluding those involved with coffee, spices and textiles) was 32,924 *paras*, 143 big merchants left an average of 249,319 *paras*.[138] It is also interesting to note that the bulk of the capital left by the coffee and textile merchants had either been kept liquid (whether in coin, loans or coffee itself) or invested in rural tax-farms: only a small proportion was tied up in ships or shops and other commercial premises.[139]

Control over the activities of both merchants and craftsmen was exercised in two types of way. One was by means of the corporation or guild. According to Raymond there were at least seventy-four craft corporations in Cairo in 1801 and at least sixty-five for merchants.[140] In some cases, workers engaged in the same economic activity were grouped within different corporations. In 1801, for example, there were five corporations of dyers and eight of wool merchants in Cairo.[141] This probably reflects the fact that the separate corporations were needed to control activities taking place in different parts of the city.[142]

The other instrument of control was the urban tax-farm. Of these the most important was the *hisba* or system of market regulation controlled by the official known as the *muhtasib*. As originally conceived it was the duty of the *muhtasib* to supervise the provisioning of a major city with food as well as to regulate the prices of foodstuffs and the weights and measures used in their sale.[143] But in Cairo at least, the office had passed into the hands of the Mamluk emirs, and was used by them as a method of exploiting a wider section of the urban population than that simply engaged in supplying or processing food.[144] In addition, a whole host of other urban tax-farms allowed members of the ruling group to levy duties on particular corporations or particular economic activities while additional farms were regularly created by those in power, whether as a kind of enforced protection over some urban group or other or as an extra duty levied on a specific type of economic transaction.

Given the relative ease with which even taxes and dues could be extracted the question must once again arise of how Cairo's craftsmen and merchants were able to maintain any kind of economic activity when competition for their surplus was so intense. As before, this can probably be explained in part by the links which connected them to those who oppressed them. In the case of the craftsmen, for example, their enrolment in one of the *ojaks* was roughly equivalent to a peasant's becoming a member of a nomadic tribe. Others paid various types of 'protection' in order to safeguard themselves from greater demands.[145] In the last resort, as Raymond has also described, there was nothing for it but for the lower strata of the urban population to riot, to strike, or simply to threaten to do so.[146] The numerous disturbances in late-eighteenth-century Cairo against new taxes, higher prices, or further depreciation of the coinage were a regular reminder to those in power not to press too hard, whether the demonstrators succeeded in their immediate objective or not.

Regional and international trade

Middle Eastern trade in 1800 can conveniently be divided into three types:

trade with countries outside the region, intra-regional and local trade. Of these, the last has already been considered in the sections on the rural and urban economy and only the first two types will be discussed here. International trade at this time was largely a matter of the import and, often, the re-export of goods from Europe in the west, Persia, India and the East Indies in the east, and Africa and the Arabian Peninsula in the south.[147] As far as those from Europe were concerned the main ports of entry were Istanbul, Izmir and Alexandria, although a limited volume also passed through the small, badly protected harbours on the Syrian coast – Alexandretta, Latakia, Tripoli, Beirut, Sidon and Acre, as well as Basra in southern Iraq. In addition, there was a substantial import of European products overland either through the Balkans or by way of the Danube or the region between the Black and the Caspian seas. Trade consisted almost exclusively of an exchange of the purchase of manufactured goods (mostly textiles) and so-called 'colonial' goods (mostly West Indian coffee and sugar) in exchange for Middle Eastern raw materials like cotton, silk and wool, the only major exception being the export of small quantities of Syrian cotton thread and cloth to France. More details about this commerce will be given in Chapter 3.

Goods from the south and east reached the Middle East overland through Baghdad and Cairo or by sea through Basra or the Red Sea. Among other products Basra received Indian textiles, sugar, spices, indigo, ginger and rice, sugar and spices from the East Indies, and coffee, incense, gums and resin from Arabia.[148] In addition, both Basra and Baghdad imported silk, wool, skins, textiles, tobacco, fruit, carpets and drugs from Persia. Apart from some horses, dates and textiles the Iraqi provinces produced little to offer in exchange and a large part of the goods from the east were almost immediately re-exported. Thus the role of Baghdad and Basra is best seen as that of distribution centres for eastern (particularly Indian) products on their way to Arabia, Kurdistan, Armenia, Anatolia and Syria.[149]

Egypt was another province where the transit trade was of particular importance. Yearly caravans from Darfur and Sennar in the eastern Sudan brought ivory, hides, skins, gum, ostrich feathers, gold dust and natron to Cairo in exchange for European or Indian goods. Meanwhile, trade with North Africa included the import of honey, butter, tarbushes, Moroccan slippers, woollen shawls and cloaks in return for locally produced linen and cotton, and coffee and spices from India and Arabia. As for the Red Sea ports, which according to Raymond's estimates accounted for half of Egypt's total imports, the most important items included coffee from the Yemen, gums and incense from south Arabia and Indian goods which were exchanged for Egyptian cereals and textiles and for European manufactures. Some of Egypt's imports from Africa and the east were consumed locally, others re-exported to Syria, Anatolia and Europe.[150] Finally, to turn to Turkey, the main imports from Europe were manufactured goods — notably woollen cloths — and colonial products like West Indian coffee. Meanwhile, from Persia and India came silks, satins, muslins and carpets. The main exports were either local raw materials like cotton and wool or the re-export of the large quantities of Persian silk shipped across Anatolia from Tabriz.[151]

As for the second type of commerce, that of trade within the region, here the flow of goods seems to have been governed by two different, though related, factors. First, there was a regular pattern of exchange involving the manufactured and semi-manufactured products, the food and raw materials, which were the specialities of each particular area. Second, there was a more irregular pattern which depended very largely on the appearance of shortages in one or other part of the region as a result of a bad harvest or a natural disaster like a plague or earthquake. An examination of Egypt's trade with Syria and Anatolia at the end of the eighteenth century reveals examples of both types of pattern. To Syria, Egypt sent foodstuffs like rice, beans and wheat, the volume of which depended on the relative size of the harvest of the cereal crop in each country. It also sent relatively stable amounts of sugar, dates, flax, indigo, hides, and fabrics of cotton, linen and silk. In return Egypt obtained regular supplies of dyestuffs, olive oil, soap, fruit, tobacco and silk yarn as well as, in bad years, sufficient Syrian cotton to make up for any shortfall in the local crop.[152] At this same period exports to Anatolia included rice, wheat, flax, dates, skins, cotton and linen, and re-exports of Sudanese and Indian goods which were exchanged for textiles, dried fruits, furs, wood and arms. There was also a considerable trade in slaves between Rosetta and Istanbul, black slaves from Africa being sent to Turkey in return for white slaves from Russia and the Balkans.[153]

Unfortunately few figures exist which would allow any comparison between the importance of trade of different types and only one point can be established with any degree of certainty. This is that in the case of Egypt trade with Europe represented only a small proportion of the value of its total external trade.[154] In the 1750s, for example, the goods exported to Syria were estimated at between £500,000 and £800,000 compared with those worth only £100,000 sent to France.[155] Again, in 1776, the Abbé Reynal calculated that Egypt's trade with Europe (both imports and exports) was worth 13,000,000 francs as opposed to trade with Turkey worth 67,500,000 francs.[156]* Trécourt's estimates of the value of Egypt's sea-borne trade in 1783 tell the same story: whereas goods exchanged with Europe were put at nearly 14,000,000 livres, those with the rest of the Ottoman Empire were estimated at over 43,000,000 livres and those with Jedda at nearly 34,000,000.[157]† As to Syria and Anatolia, it would also seem

* From 1726 onwards, 24 livres = £(sterling)1.
† 1 livre = 1 franc.

reasonable to assume that intra-regional trade played a much more important role than trade with Europe.

Goods shipped by sea across the eastern end of the Mediterranean were carried either in locally owned boats (most Turkish or Greek) or in European coasting vessels.[158] One of the great advantages of the latter was that they were generally safer and less likely to suffer pirate attack.[159] In 1798, according to Girard, there were at least a hundred French vessels on cabotage in the Levant.[160] In the Persian Gulf and Indian Ocean, on the other hand, the dates and horses exported from Basra were shipped in boats of 60 tons, known as 'bagloes', owned by Arabs or Indians.[161]

Goods being taken overland were carried in river boats or by animals. In Egypt, imported articles arriving at Alexandria were generally taken round the coast in small boats to Rosetta and then shipped down the Nile to Bulaq, the port of Cairo. Similarly, goods landed at Quseir on the Red Sea coast were first transported by camel to Qena and then by river to the capital. In each case there was considerable danger from river pirates. Meanwhile, in Iraq, cargoes reaching Basra by sea were sent north to Baghdad along the Tigris or the Euphrates according to the season. In general the former was the preferred route between March and November. But after then the current often became too strong and the Euphrates was used instead, goods being transferred to camels and donkeys at Hillah for the last twenty miles of the journey.[162] The boats in use could carry 20 to 50 tons and took something like thirty to forty days to make the journey upstream to Baghdad, compared with only seven or eight days for the return trip. Duty was paid to the various beduin tribes along the way. As in Egypt, there was considerable risk from pirates and other robbers and in many cases all the vessels going north gathered together at Basra to form a convoy for their own protection.[163] A second type of craft was used for goods being sent from Mosul to Baghdad down the Tigris. These were known as *kalaks* and consisted of no more than a platform of planks placed on a number of goatskins which had been inflated and tied together with reeds. Once at Baghdad the crews sold the skins and the wood and returned north by road, just as their ancestors had done in the days of Heroditus.[164]

The major Middle Eastern caravan routes are shown on the map on page 48. They included, among others, the main east—west routes across the Syrian desert, the great silk routes between Isfahan and Izmir, and the routes of the caravans bringing African goods to Cairo. Caravans were organized one or more times a year according to the amount of traffic and the degree of safety. Those terminating at the Mediterranean needed to arrive at roughly the same time each year so that ships could wait for them without delay.[165] Those crossing the desert were more likely to be organized in winter when climatic conditions were easier. In the late eighteenth century two or three caravans a year passed between Damascus and

Baghdad, while in the early nineteenth it is reported that four caravans left Aleppo annually for the principal towns of Iraq and Anatolia and two for Persia via Baghdad.[166] Such caravans might include up to several thousand camels, although the average was probably close to 1500, of which only a fifth would be in load.[167] Each camel could carry something like 500 to 700 lbs, roughly equivalent to the capacity of three to five horses, and the total value of the merchandise could be as high as 10,000,000 or 11,000,000 francs.[168] Movement was slow and even in good conditions few caravans managed more than 25 miles a day. Thus it took something like 25 to 30 days to cross the Syrian desert from Aleppo to Baghdad direct, and about 45 days by way of the town of Diyarbakir in eastern Anatolia. To the west, the journey from Aleppo to Istanbul took 40 days.[169] Dues paid to the beduin and others in order to ensure safe passage formed a substantial part of the cost. According to Masson, in the seventeenth century a camel load of silk could be sent from Isfahan to Izmir for 40 piastres, but to this would have to be added 122 piastres for duties along the route and another 46 piastres at Izmir itself.[170]

In addition to the ordinary caravans much trade was conducted by means of the annual pilgrim caravans from North Africa to the Red Sea via Cairo and from Damascus to Mecca, the latter containing something like 15,000 camels in the 1820s.[171] Many merchants joined such caravans for the protection they offered while, as Gibb and Bowen notes:

The connection between the Pilgrimage to Mecca and petty commerce has always been very close in Islam. Practically all the pilgrims chaffered their way to and from the Hijaz. Starting out with the merchandise of their native countries, they sold most of these on the journey and with the proceeds they purchased at Mecca the spices, pearls and coffee of Arabia and the muslin, shawls and pepper imported from India and disposed of these on their way home.[172]

The transport of goods over shorter distances presented more problems. There were no regular caravans between Aleppo and the port of Latakia or between Damascus and the coastal towns of Saida and Beirut. Thus merchants were frequently attacked and those who wished to pass in safety usually had to pay high tolls to men from the tribes and villages along the way.[173] As a result costs were particularly high as can be seen from a report sent to the British Foreign Office in 1848 which calculated that it was no more expensive to send goods from Damascus to Iraq by caravan across the desert than it was to send them the 70 or 80 miles to the coast.[174]

To turn to the merchants themselves, it would seem that particular types of trade were often under the control of particular groups. This was obviously the case of trade with Europe which was very largely conducted by Europeans, albeit with the important assistance of local intermediaries. But it was also true of the Persian silk trade and much of the movement of goods in and out of Aleppo and Baghdad which was organized by Armenians who made good use of their links with their communities in London, Amsterdam, Isfahan and India as well as throughout the Middle East.[175] Muslim Turks controlled the commerce across the Black Sea which had been closed to European shipping until the very end of the eighteenth century.[176] As for Egypt, trade with the Sudan and the Red Sea was largely conducted by local merchants while that with Syria was the work of two hundred or so Syrians domiciled at Damietta.[177]

Different groups of merchants operated under quite different conditions. The Europeans, for example, were tightly organized in commercial 'factories' protected by the Capitulations and by their trading companies (such as the Levant Company) and their consuls, with very little contact with the local population. Few Englishmen or Frenchmen working in the Middle East knew Arabic or Turkish or any of the other local languages while their isolation was further reinforced by fear of the plague and by the fact that there were a number of ports and cities where Europeans lived in quite considerable fear of local hostility.[178] This was particularly true of Egypt during the last decades of the Mamluk regime where the Christian merchants were subject to numerous attacks as well as repeated *avanias* by a government desperately searching for new sources of revenue.[179] Even in the cities of Anatolia and northern Syria, where foreign merchants were very much better tolerated, there were occasional anti-European outbursts like the riot in Izmir in 1763 in which no European house was left standing.[180]

In these circumstances it was inevitable that great reliance should be placed on local intermediaries, usually Christians or Jews, who spoke Arabic and Turkish, who were familiar with Middle Eastern commercial practices and who had their own ways and means of recovering loans made to shopkeepers or cultivators. In return such intermediaries were often given or sold a *barat* placing them under the protection of a European consulate and allowing them to benefit from the privilege of paying the same low customs duties as Europeans.[181] Later, when many European merchants were forced to retire from the eastern Mediterranean at the end of the eighteenth century as a result of local hostility, a decline in trade, or the effects of the Napoleonic wars, their places were often taken by their former agents and protégés who, in some cases, also took over the name and trading connections of their former employees as well.[182]

Trade among Ottoman or Persian subjects was organized in a very different way. For one thing there was no legal or administrative framework provided by the government within which to operate and, as far as possible, local merchants seem to have relied on their own resources to manage their affairs. It was for this reason that trade was conducted, where possible, between members of the same community or, more advantageously, between members of the same family. This encouraged trust. It also allowed the use of communal or family relations to put pressure on recalcitrant debtors. Again, in a number of ports merchants seem to have established informal commercial tribunals to settle disputes between them. These were quite independent of the government which, in general, they were anxious to keep at arm's length lest its officials learn too much about the size of their fortunes or their methods of business. As Fontanier described the situation in Basra in the early part of the nineteenth century:

when discussions arise between merchants, they appeal to their fellow tradesmen and abide by their decisions. To go before the Cadi would be the equivalent of shutting up shop. It is desirable also to avoid as much as possible any intimacy with the government, or those in authority, as no confidence is placed in anyone who appears to be their friend.[183]

Due to a persistent shortage of coin much trade was conducted for credit or on a barter basis; but there were also many occasions on which purchases were made in cash. One good example of this is contained in an East India Company report on Basra in the eighteenth century which noted that many rich merchants had come there from Istanbul, Damascus, Aleppo, Urfa, Diyarbakir, Mosul, Mardin and Baghdad 'with large sums of money in order to obtain goods arriving from India'.[184]

Conclusion

If a single word is needed to describe the general state of the Middle East economy as it existed in this period it would have to be 'stagnant' — whether in terms of income and investment, techniques and methods or organization, or simple levels of population. On the other hand, throughout the region there were considerable resources of under-utilized and easily cultivable land which required only minimal attention to questions of security, better transport and, in some districts, improvements in the system of irrigation to put them to productive use. But this had to wait for the profound changes which were to take place in the first decades of the nineteenth century: the reassertion of central government control over the rural areas, the sudden and mysterious disappearance of the plague and, most important of all, the multiplication of the commercial links which were to bind the Middle East to the expanding industrial economies of western Europe.

2 The economic consequences of the age of reforms, 1800–1850

At the end of the eighteenth century the growing political and economic power of western Europe found expression in two great revolutions: the French and the Industrial. Their effect on the Middle East was profound. The one encouraged a series of reforms by the rulers of both the Ottoman Empire and the semi-independent province of Egypt designed to allow them to withstand the increasingly dangerous threat of political and military intervention by Britain and the continental powers, the other produced a huge increase in trade which began the complete transformation of the region's economy. Although the two developments must be seen as part of a single general process, for the purposes of analysis they will be examined separately in this and the next chapter.

To begin with the political and military threat posed by the operations of the European armies during the Napoleonic wars: this had the effect of stimulating the rulers of Egypt and Turkey to create new military organizations based on conscription rather than the use of mercenaries, equipped with modern weapons and trained according to the most modern tactics. But such policies, in turn, required large sums of money and led, inexorably, to an attempt to increase the revenues which the governments obtained from a variety of sources, the most important of which was the tax placed on the land and its produce, then largely controlled by the tax-farmers and the 'owners' of agricultural *waqfs*. The result was a collision between the central administration, on the one hand, and the derebeys, ayans, Mamluks and *ulama* with some power on the other. Within a few decades the control of the old local ruling élite was greatly reduced and rural security, a vital ingredient for any economic progress, much improved.

But there were other consequences as well. New armies required a new type of officer and a new type of technician; the attempt to reassert the control of the central government over distant provinces and to maximize tax revenues required new forms of administrative organization. Educational missions were sent to Europe; specialized departments of government began to be created; and, particularly in Egypt, the state attempted to augment its military potential by developing the country's agricultural and industrial potential. In the event, however, the major effect of the reforms was entirely the opposite of what was originally intended. Instead of making these states more independent of Britain, France and Russia they made them more dependent, instead of allowing them to control the process of European economic penetration it made the whole process of penetration a great deal more easy.

The Ottoman reforms

The first serious effort to modernize the Ottoman army was made by the Sultan Selim III (1789–1807). Realizing that it would be useless to attempt to institute reforms affecting existing military corps like the Janissaries, which had their own vested interests to preserve, he decided to create entirely new ones. The first men for the Sultan's *Nizam-ı Cedid*, or New Order, were recruited in the 1790s and by 1806 their number had reached nearly 25,000.[1] The navy too was not ignored: changes in the system of administration in the dockyards allowed the introduction of a programme of construction which between 1789 and 1798 saw the launching of forty-five major fighting ships, the largest a vessel of 122 cannons with a crew of 1200.[2] However, these early efforts to build up a modern military machine and the measures which it was necessary to take to pay for it aroused great opposition. Selim III himself was deposed in 1807, and though one of his successors, Mahmoud II (1808–39) made a brief effort to continue his work, the experiment was brought to a sharp halt by the disturbances of 1808.[3] An almost continuous series of campaigns against rebellions in the Balkans, in Arabia, and in Greece followed and it was not until 1826, when many of the Janissaries had been killed after a mutiny and their corps disbanded, that the policy of military reform could proceed. By 1828 the Sultan's new army contained 75,000 regular troops.[4] Foreign officers were employed to train his men and a military academy opened in 1834.

Meanwhile, having come to the conclusion that a successful reform of the army required changes in other areas of Ottoman administration, the Sultan and some of his advisers began to reorganize the system of government as well as to extend its control by re-asserting the power of Istanbul over the provinces. Once under way this process developed its own momentum, pushed on by the bureaucrats themselves; government offices were no longer given as tax-farms or fiefs; a system of regular appointments, promotion and pensions was introduced; day-to-day control of policies by the Grand Vizier and other ministers was institutionalized.[5] The scope for reform was further enlarged by the proclamation of the *Hatt-ı Şerif* (or Imperial edict) of Gulhane of November 1839, a few months after Mahmoud's death. Though issued at a time of great crisis and in an effort to obtain British support in the face of the threatened invasion of Anatolia by the army of Muhammad Ali of Egypt, it was also a serious attempt to draw up a comprehensive programme for future reform in a variety of different fields, including the military (the introduction of a regular system of conscription) and the administrative (the abolition of tax-farming).[6]

The general history of the movement for Ottoman reform, and some analysis of the groups which directed its path, has been given by a number of writers and need not be discussed yet again.[7] What is more important in this present context is an examination of the economic consequences of the reforms and, in particular, their effect on control of the land and other major sources of revenue, as well as the way in which they helped to establish a framework for European commercial and, later, financial penetration of the Ottoman Empire.

The first and most obvious implication of military reform was the need to increase government income. Here Selim III's efforts to maximize the amounts raised from the land tax (in Anatolia the tithe or *ushr*) are of special importance. To this end a new Treasury — the *Irad-ı Cedid* — was created in 1793, side by side with the old Treasury, to which was assigned control over all the tax-farms formerly controlled by the latter.[8] In theory, the New Treasury was supposed only to take over a farm when the existing contract ran out. It was also supposed to hand over to the Old Treasury a sum equal to the price previously paid by private individuals for the purchase of such farms as it took over. But in each case these provisions seem to have been increasingly ignored. By 1793 the chief of the *Irad-ı Cedid* had seized over 400 fiefs from tax-farmers, using his own agents to collect their revenues, most of which he kept for the New Treasury. Later, from 1804 to Selim's deposition in 1807, came efforts to transform what was left of the whole *timar* system so as to provide a firm financial base for the *Nizam*. As a result more and more fiefs were seized and turned over to salaried government officials.[9]

The significance of this attempt to reform the system of rural tax-collection can be seen in two ways. The first is to compare the size of Ottoman public revenue with that of the nation states of western Europe. Estimates of the former vary — Stratford Canning put it at £2,250,000 in the early 1800s, Thornton at £3,750,000 — but it was clearly a very long way short of the average British figure of £16,800,000 for the years 1787–90.[10] A second is to look at the major sources of Ottoman taxes and dues: the tithe itself, the *kharaj* or poll tax imposed on adult non-Muslims, the poll tax on the urban population, the external tariff and the duties on the internal movement of goods, the excise duties on certain commodities subject to state monopolies such as gunpowder, snuff and wine, and the annual tribute from the provinces of Moldavia, Wallachia and Egypt.[11] Of these, the tithe was the only one susceptible to any large increase. To raise the level of the tributes would be to run the risk of sparking off fresh revolts, while there was an obvious limit to the amount which could be levied on individual Ottoman subjects, whether Muslim or not. A little more money could be raised from the duties on imports and exports by replacing the customs-farmers by government officials but here the scope for major improvement was limited by the fact that the tariffs on European goods were fixed at a low rate by Capitulatory Treaty or commercial convention. The tithe on agricultural produce or animals, on the other hand, was known to produce large sums, although the bulk of these remained in the hands of officials and tax-farmers. Some idea of the magnitude of the amount involved can be gained from Thornton's calculation that while around £20,000,000 was being squeezed from the peasants by the collectors, only a small proportion of this sum was being passed on to the Treasury.[12] It followed that if the state was to try to maximize its own receipts it had either to institute a system of direct collection by government agents or to find ways and means of forcing the tax-farmers to disgorge more of their profit. In addition, more money might well be raised by a duty on the produce of agricultural *vakfs*, hitherto mostly untaxed.

Reforms along these lines were first attempted by Selim III, and then revived by Mahmoud II. But in each case they were largely unsuccessful. It is true that Mahmoud made a number of improvements in the system of financial administration and that he was able to regain control over important sources of revenue like the hereditary pashaliks of Trabzon, Erzerum and Van.[13] He also instituted the census of 1831, designed as a prelude to the introduction of more efficient methods of tax-collection and conscription.[14] Against this, the gains from the abolition of the remaining *timars* (in 1831) was largely nullified by the decision to auction them to a new set of tax-farmers while at the same time compensating their former administrators with a pension.[15] Later, with the Imperial Rescript of 1839, a more serious attempt was made to abolish tax-farming throughout the Empire — only for it to founder in the early 1840s as the result of the opposition of those groups that stood to lose their former privileges and the failure to create an alternative system of collecting by trustworthy local agents.[16] In spite of the appointment of new central government officials and the establishment of local councils to help in the assessment of what ought to be paid, the position of those persons and groups who had previously managed to appropriate a considerable part of the rural surplus was largely unchanged. In the south-eastern region of Cilicia, for example, the two officials sent from Istanbul — the Governor and the Treasurer — had so little power and so few troops at their disposal that they were forced to ally themselves with one or other of the factions which formed within the Adana council.[17] And it was the same in many other parts of Anatolia. As Ziya Paşa, a leading reformer, summed up the position:

Though the privileges of the ayans, the control of the Janissaries and bad practices such as placing government agents into governorships have been abolished on paper by the Blessed Tanzimat, in the provinces the feudal lords still flourish but under different names now, one group of them consisting of the foreign consuls and the other of influential and rich local people such as council members and other urban notables.[18]

Efforts to obtain access to the revenues obtained by private individuals and religious foundations from *vakf* property were almost equally unsuccessful. A Directorate, then a Ministry, of Waqfs was created under Mahmoud II with the aim of centralizing the collection of such revenues, spending only what was necessary for the upkeep of the religious buildings and other foundations concerned and passing on the rest to the Treasury. But in practice there was no fiscal advantage to the state: the members of the *ulama* and others who controlled the new administration managed to pay out more for the upkeep of the properties they controlled than they were able to collect in income.[19]

Failure to obtain any large increase in the revenue obtained from the land forced the government to search for alternative sources of income. One possibility seemed to be the duties on internal and external trade. In the aftermath of the war with Russia in the early 1830s, for instance, rates paid on the movement within the Empire of certain goods like wool, Bursa silk and grain were raised from 5 to 21 per cent.[20] Although such measures produced some temporary relief their effect was limited by the fact that it was still not possible to staff the customs posts with government officials rather than auctioning them to farmers.[21] Equally important was the fact that any effort made to raise the duties on articles traded by Europeans at once produced fierce protests. This can be seen with special force during the negotiations carried on in 1837 for the renewal of the Anglo-Turkish Commercial Convention of 1820. Even though the Ottoman government was desperately anxious to raise the duties paid by British merchants, it lacked sufficient political power to obtain more than an agreement to allow the tariff on imports to be increased from 3 to 5 per cent *ad valorem*, and even this was in exchange for a large reduction in the rates paid by such merchants on the internal movement of goods.[22] Later Ottoman efforts to modify the terms of the new Commercial Convention in the interests of obtaining greater revenue all came to nothing in the face of strong British pressure.[23] Attempts to raise the level of the *kharaj* tax paid by non-Muslims ran into similar difficulties and, in the end, the government was reduced to such financially dangerous experiments as the issue of short-term bonds (*kaimé*), begun in 1841 in order to be able to pay the war indemnity to the Russians.[24] The problems which soon followed from the almost unlimited sale of such paper are yet another illustration of the consequences of Ottoman failure to reform the system of rural tax-collection. Thus, even though there was a small increase in government revenue during the first half of the nineteenth century this was insufficient to pay for the cost of reforms as well as repeated wars. During the late 1830s, for example, the army was absorbing 70 per cent of total revenues, and even then many of the troops were left unpaid.[25] In these circumstances some kind of government loan soon became an absolute necessity; but here too the failure to maximize the revenues obtained from the land had unfortunate long-term consequences for it ensured that the administration would be unable to maintain the interest payment on its ever mounting debt.

But all this lay in the future, and will be discussed at length in Chapter 4. For the time being what is important is a brief examination of some of the other economic consequences of the era of reforms. One of the most significant was the government's positive role in attempting to encourage the development of industry and agriculture. In the case of the former the stimulus seems to have come, once again, from military necessity. The further modernization of the army was an integral part of the policies ushered in by the *Hatt-ı Şerif* and in 1843 regulations were passed providing for a regular system of recruitment for a fixed term of years. At the same time it was laid down that five separate armies would be created – two based at Istanbul, a third in the Balkans, a fourth in Anatolia and a fifth in Syria – each of which was to be responsible for its own conscription based on a lottery involving the names of all adult Muslim males.[26]

It is certainly no coincidence that these moves were accompanied by an ambitious programme of constructing new factories designed to provide the troops with uniforms and equipment.[27] A spinning mill, a tannery and the Tophane cannon foundry and Dolmabahce musket works already existed, the last two converted from animal to steam power in the late 1830s. To these were added several more foundries, iron works and textiles factories, a number of them located in a new industrial 'park' just to the west of Istanbul. Most of the machinery, some of the very latest design, was imported. Skilled foremen and craftsmen were recruited in Europe and a local labour force of 5000 assembled. Meanwhile, efforts were made to ensure that the new factories were assured of a regular supply of raw materials, whether wool, cotton or copper, and the whole programme was placed under the control of a man, Ohannes Dadian, who had been involved with various state manufacturing enterprises since he had started work in the government powder mill in 1813.[28] Nevertheless, in spite of the fact that the factories had a protected market in the Ottoman army few of them were kept in production after the end of the 1840s. The reasons for this are not entirely clear but it would seem that, in the first instance, it was a political decision based on the fact that the upkeep of the factories, their provision with imported raw materials to supplement shortfalls in local supply, and the high cost of the foreign technicians – who were paid twice the average wage in their home countries – was considered to be more than the government could afford. Other difficulties were mentioned by contemporary observers – among them the general lack of managerial experience, bureaucratic interference and the discontent of the local labour force – but many of these are the kinds of problems which face any newly industrializing country and it is possible that some of them could have been overcome if more time had been allowed. As it is, at least four government textile factories continued in operation up to the First World War, making tarbushes and cloth for army uniforms on the old machines.[29] Unlike Muhammad Ali's very much more ambitious programme of factory building (to be examined in the next section) the Turkish experiment was not impossibly far beyond the Empire's technical capacities; and while it would be absurd to suggest that the system of mills and foundries as originally planned could have constituted the basis for an Ottoman 'industrial revolution' it might have developed in such a way as to have reduced the necessity of importing such large quantities of equipment.[30] With the first foreign loans of the 1850s came the first big purchases of foreign arms.

The attempt by the Ottoman government to stimulate the development of agriculture by direct intervention was similarly unsuccessful. The report of a high-level commission charged with recommending ways and means of increasing production was not acted upon while the Agricultural School, founded on an Imperial farm in 1847, was obviously on too small a scale to have had any effect on the techniques employed by the millions of peasant cultivators.[31] Early efforts to encourage agriculture by regularizing the system of land holding were also ineffective. One reason for this was that the Ottoman government did not have the administrative resources to carry out the registration of all title deeds, as envisaged in the law of 1847. Just as important was the fact that the aims of the reformers themselves were contradictory. On the one hand they wished to provide cultivators with that security of tenure without which, so it was thought, no one would be willing to work hard to accumulate wealth. But, on the other, they were even more anxious to reassert government control over large areas of land which, though officially belonging to the state, had passed more or less completely into private hands. Thus, whereas the first aim required a move in the direction of the establishment of a system of private property in land, the second involved the opposite step of re-emphasizing state ownership of all land classed as *miri*.[32] This contradiction was to remain at the centre of Ottoman efforts to regulate the system of property rights throughout the nineteenth century.

In the end, far and away the most important contribution made by the Ottoman reformers to the growth of Turkish agricultural production was the overthrow of many of the more powerful lords of the valleys, ayans and hereditary pashas, and the re-establishment of state control over much of the coastal region and some but by no means all of the Central Anatolian plateau. It took ten years (1837–47) to complete the pacification of Turkish

Kurdistan and by 1850 there were still many areas, for example the rich Cilician plain and its surrounding mountains in the south-east, which remained almost completely beyond the Sultan's jurisdiction.[33] But if security could be guaranteed in a particular district then merchants and peasants were usually quick to take advantage of rising European demand for their products by increasing the cultivation of cash crops like cotton and opium and the output of animal products like wool.[34] The consequent increase in Anatolian exports will be examined in Chapter 3.

Egypt

If military reform in Turkey was the result of a growing recognition of the increasing disparity of power with Europe, that in Egypt stemmed just as much from an effort to build up an army strong enough to wrest independence from the Ottomans themselves. This process can be said to have begun in the mid-eighteenth century with the rule of the Mamluk leader, Ali Bey al-Kabir (d. 1773) whose attempts, first to strengthen his hold over the central administration in Cairo, then to extend his influence throughout Egypt and beyond, required the employment of mercenaries on a much larger scale than ever before. His expeditions against the beduin in Middle and Upper Egypt and, even more, his invasions of the Hijaz and Yemen in 1770 and Syria in 1771 involved armies of anything up to 60,000 men, while his second expedition to Syria in 1775 consisted not only of many thousands of soldiers but also a train of artillery commanded by an Englishman called Robinson.[35]

Efforts to find the resources to pay for forces of this size took a number of forms. Apart from outright refusal to pay the Tribute required by the Ottomans or various subterfuges to whittle it down – a policy which led to the brief reoccupation of the country by Turkish forces in 1786 – three of these were of particular importance. First, attempts were made to raise the amount of money obtained from foreign trade, culminating, in the last years of Mamluk rule, in a takeover of the whole customs administration by Murad and Ibrahim Beys (1779–98), who then ran it with their own agents at the ports.[36] Second, the later Mamluk leaders increased the numbers of government monopolies on the sale of agricultural and other produce.[37] Third, and most important of all from Ali Bey onwards they began to evict *multazims* from their tax-farms and to seize their estates, which were then managed by their own supporters. Access to a larger share of the rural surplus was, as they must have begun to realize, the key to the whole financial situation. According to estimates made by members of the French Expedition for the year 1798/9, some three-quarters of the total government receipts of four million francs came from the tax on land. And yet such was the power of the *multazims* that in some villages this represented only a little over a fifth of the amount actually taken from the cultivators, the remainder being retained by the collectors themselves.[38] Hence, as in Anatolia, if the government were to be able to establish a system of direct collection using its own agents it could increase its revenues many times.

For reasons of this kind, a more comprehensive programme of establishing state control over the land was attempted by the French during their three years of occupation, 1798–1801, while a similar policy was also attempted by the Ottoman governor sent to Egypt by Selim III after the French withdrawal.[39] In each case the new rulers of Egypt were overthrown before they had time to institute an improved system of collection and it was left to Muhammad Ali (1805–49), faced with the need to find money for his own mercenary army, to undertake a comprehensive reform along these lines between 1812 and 1814. Following his massacre of many of the Mamluks in 1811, which at one blow removed the most powerful body of opposition to such a move, he confiscated all the *iltizams* in Upper Egypt in 1812 and in Lower Egypt in 1814, reasserting the state's right of ownership of *miri* land and transferring the tax income from it to the Cairo Treasury.[40] Pensions were paid to some of those whose tax-farms had been appropriated but, unlike in Anatolia, the sums involved were quite small in proportion to the overall increase in revenue. A similar policy was followed with agricultural *waqfs*: within a few years the greater part of this land had also been confiscated by the state, as those who previously controlled it were unable to provide the many proofs of legal ownership demanded of them. Finally, Muhammad Ali took great care to tighten his grip on the administrative apparatus itself to ensure that the agents entrusted with the collection of the taxes could be relied upon to deliver what was owed. This could be done more easily in Egypt than in Anatolia for not only was there a corps of experienced Coptic clerks to run the new system but also Muhammad Ali was able to use the services of the village shaikhs whose combination of local power and long tradition of subservience to external authority made them ideal agents of the central government.[41] By these means Muhammad Ali gain control over the major source of Egyptian revenue and, on the evidence of the few budgets published during his reign, it is easy to see that the land tax remained the mainstay of his financial system, usually supplying at least half of total receipts (Table 5).

A second source of revenue utilized by Egypt's new ruler was the income which could be made from the export of agricultural products. In particular Muhammad Ali was able to make large profits by selling Egyptian cereals to the British armies fighting the French during the Napoleonic wars and then to Britain and the continent in the immediate post-war food shortage. This was accompanied by an increasing degree of state control, culminating in 1811 in his prohibition of private trade in grain, ensuring for himself the monopoly of the collection and the foreign sale of the entire

Upper Egyptian cereal crop.[42] Other agricultural monopolies followed. In 1812 it was rice production in the Delta, in 1815 sugar in Upper Egypt, and in 1816 the system was extended to cover most of the country's cash crops including sesame, indigo, short-staple cotton and hemp as well as wheat, barley and beans.[43] Each was purchased at a price fixed well below the free market level; private transactions were forbidden; the government's monopoly of supply allowed it to dictate the terms on which the harvest was sold to the merchants.

In this way Muhammad Ali began the process of trying to establish a system of economic management designed to ensure that the government was able to appropriate the bulk of the rural surplus. No longer was it necessary to rely simply on the hand-to-mouth expedients that had characterized the first years of his rule: the forced loans, the new types of taxes which al-Jabarti describes so vividly.[44] Control of the land now allowed him to push the possibilities inherent in the institution of the government monopoly to their limits, combining regulation, price fixing and taxation by state officials with energetic participation in the economic activity in question. Not only did Muhammad Ali and his servants act as middleman and merchant in a host of transactions, they also stepped in to try and re-organize production on a more profitable basis. Unlike all his predecessors Egypt's ruler was quick to see that revenues could be further increased by efforts designed to develop the country's agricultural wealth. A co-ordinated effort was made to repair and improve the entire system of irrigation, using a corvée of peasant labour — in effect an extra tax on the cultivating population. The Mahmudiya canal was re-excavated to provide a quick method of moving goods from the western branch of the Nile to Alexandria and a host of other canals straightened and deepened to provide the fields with a regular supply of water, both summer and winter.[45] Summer canals had to be dug deeper than winter ones in order to be able to take off water from the Nile when it was at its lowest.

The ruler was also active in promoting the introduction of new crops and new techniques. One example of this was the way in which, in an (unsuccessful) effort to revive the Egyptian silk industry, 500 Syrians were brought to the Wadi Tumilat in the east of the Delta and provided with the tools and animals necessary to cultivate the mulberry trees which were planted there.[46] The most important symbol of Muhammad Ali's concern with agricultural improvement, however, was the rapidity with which he grasped the commercial implications of the chance discovery in a Cairo garden of a new type of long-staple cotton.[47] * After the success of some early experiments in its cultivation, Muhammad Ali was able to use the machinery of agricultural administration he had built up in the provinces

---

* Long-staple cotton is cotton with fibres of 1.75 inches and over in length: the cotton grown in Egypt before 1820 was of short or medium staple.

Table 4   Estimates of the volume and value of Egyptian cotton exports, 1821–49 (annual averages)

	Volume (cantars)[1]	Value (£E)[2]
1821–5	124,252	
1825–9	186,641	
1830–4	180,610	
1835–9	228,939	780,933
1840–4	195,653	393,450
1845–9	236,392	427,347

Source: Owen, *Cotton*, Tables 1 and 5 (with misprint for cotton volume in 1823 corrected to 159,426 quintals).

Notes:

1 I have reworked the original figures to give cantars of 94 lb.
2 Strictly speaking the Egyptian pound (£E) was not introduced before 1885 but a number of sources use it for units of 100 piastres (Pt. 100) before that date. According to Muhammad Ali's monetary tariff of 1835, £1 (sterling) = Pt. 97.5, making an Egyptian pound worth a little more than a pound sterling.

to cause the new crop (now known as Mako after the owner of the garden in which it was first noticed, or Jumel after its French discoverer) to be grown on an extensive scale. Tracts of land were allocated to its production in areas of the Delta which had easy access to summer water. New *saqiyas* were erected and dikes constructed. Animals were sold to the peasants on credit, seed provided and cotton gins and presses manufactured and distributed among the villages. Furthermore, when a sudden decline in quality convinced Muhammad Ali of the need to instruct the peasants more systematically in the correct method of cultivation, he brought experts from Syria and Anatolia, each of whom was assigned a number of villages in which the cultivators were placed completely under his control.[48]

The success of these measures can be seen from the rapid increase in the volume of cotton exported (see Table 4) as well as from the fact that the quality of Mako/Jumel was sufficiently high to find a ready market in Lancashire and other European spinning and weaving centres. Again, from a financial point of view it provided the funds for a second large expansion of the army based on the conscription of native Egyptian peasants: there were several years in the 1820s when the profits from cotton reached £600,000 to £700,000, between two-thirds to three-quarters as much as the land tax (Table 5). Mako/Jumel had the additional advantage that it could be sold in advance to foreign merchants in Alexandria, a practice which could be employed to ensure a steady flow of receipts thus mitigating the problem posed for the government of any agricultural country by the fact that the principal source of revenue, the land tax, is only available in a lump sum once or twice a year at harvest time.[49]

Seen in wider perspective, Muhammad Ali's introduction of long-staple

Table 5 Importance of the land tax and of profits from cotton in total Egyptian government
revenues, 1821−38 (millions of francs)

	Land tax	Cotton profits	Total revenue
1821	26.46		48.03
1826			100.00
1829	19.40		
1830[1]	36.16		77.97
1833 (1)			76.00
1833 (2)	28.13		62.78
1834	35.13 (1834/5)	4.96	77.85 (1834/5)
1835	40.00 (1835/6)	17.14	76.61
1836		19.21	
1837		10.32	
1838		12.49	90.00

Source: Owen, *Cotton,* Tables 2 and 4.

Note: 1 Figures for 1830 converted at a rate of £1 = 25 francs.

cotton was a brutal though successful way of exploiting Egypt's underdeveloped resources of labour and land. Previously, as noted in Chapter 1,
the greater part of the cultivated area had been devoted to winter crops and
had thus remained idle through the summer months. The same applied to
the men who worked it, while the women and children of the villages were
hardly seen in the fields. All this changed with the coming of Mako/Jumel:
new systems of rotation were developed to accommodate a crop which was
planted in the spring and picked in the autumn; peasants now laboured
most of the year round while their wives and children joined them at harvest
time when their particular skill at picking the bolls from the cotton plants
was much in demand. In addition, during the few remaining slack months
these same peasants were required to work in the corvée gangs, cleaning out
the mud deposited by the slow-moving waters in the existing deep-level
summer canals, and digging new ones.[50]

Most foreign observers agreed that the agricultural population could not
have been persuaded to undertake all this extra labour without coercion, and
this must have been generally true.[51] According to several twentieth-century
estimates cotton requires about twice the number of man-days per feddan as
wheat, quite apart from the work of the women and children needed for
picking.[52] In addition, during the rule of Muhammad Ali peasants were
expected to gin their own cotton crop − another time-consuming activity −
if they could not afford to pay someone else to do it.[53] That all this was necessary at a time when the tax rate was high and when there was heavy recruitment for the army and navy and for the ruler's factories is enough to explain
the regular reports of cultivators fleeing their villages and being forcibly
returned by troops.[54] Nevertheless, there is some evidence that, during the
first few years of Jumel's cultivation, the prices paid to peasants were

sufficient to persuade them that the extra effort was worth their while. As Drovetti, the French Consul-General, put it in 1825, when the agricultural population saw how much the new cotton trees could produce and that the pasha was willing to pay them 175 piastres (roughly £1.75) for a cantar of good quality, they worked even harder than before to ensure the success of the new crop.[55] * If the Frenchman was right, this is a good example of the adaptability of the Middle Eastern peasant population and their quick response to market opportunity.

With the introduction of long-staple cotton the link between military expenditure and changes in the system of taxation and administrative control becomes less easy to discern. During the 1820s Muhammad Ali's system of economic management of the agricultural sector began to have a momentum and logic of its own. The same point can also be made concerning Muhammad Ali's construction of modern, European-style factories. Although most of his first establishments, like the arsenals at Cairo and Bulaq, were designed specially to produce guns, ships and munitions, and although part of the product of the first textile mills was used to supply the army with uniforms, by the 1820s the system as a whole had the more general aim of making the entire country virtually independent of foreign manufactured goods.[57]

Muhammad Ali's interest in a programme of import substitution seems to have begun at least as early as 1814, but it was not until 1816 that he established his first textile factory in the Kuronfish quarter of the Fatimid city of old Cairo.[58] Machines were brought from Europe and skilled workers recruited from France, Italy and elsewhere. It would seem that his intention was to manufacture velvets and other silk products, perhaps using the cocoons he planned to produce in the Wadi Tumilat. At about the same time, according to al-Jabarti, he also moved to monopolize urban textile production, closing down the existing workshops and forcing the craftsmen to work either at Kuronfish or at other smaller establishments.[59] The next year he extended his control to village production, instructing his officials to buy up all the cloth and thread manufactured by the peasants: the cloth for sale to merchants at a profit, the thread for use in his own workshops. As an additional precaution against private transactions all textiles bought by the government were marked with a special stamp and orders were given that anyone found with unmarked cloth should be punished.

Within a short time Muhammad Ali became dissatisfied with the quality of the silk produced at Kuronfish and in 1816 the factory was converted to cotton spinning and weaving, as the first stage of an ambitious new

---

* The weight of the cantar changed during Muhammad Ali's reign. In the early 1820s it was usually estimated at about 122.25 lbs; but after 1836/7 most authors treat it as weighing anywhere between 94 and 99 lbs. According to the *Statistique de l'Egypte* of 1873 (p. 2) it was then fixed at 44.5458 kilograms or just under 99 lbs.[56]

programme of textile manufacturing. A second factory, known as Malta —
from the origin of part of its early workforce — was built at Bulaq, the port
of Cairo, to be followed by three more, also in or near Cairo, in 1820, as well
as a bleaching and print works known as Mabyadea (Mubayyida).[60] Pleased
with their success, Muhammad Ali then ordered the construction of
another 14 factories in Lower Egypt (1821–6) and 9 in Upper Egypt
(1827–8).[61] Two more factories in the Cairo area brought the grand total to
30 by the early 1830s, although whether they were all actually put into
operation it is impossible to say.[62] With the exception of a few machines
brought from Europe to serve as models, all the remaining equipment were
constructed (albeit with imported lathes and tools) by Egyptian carpenters,
smiths and turners under the general supervision of Jumel, the manager of
the Malta complex.[63] Estimates of their number must be accepted with
caution but according to Fahmy there were a total of 1381 mule jennies
(each with some 180 to 220 spindles), 1124 carding machines and 1750
looms.[64] Again it is not clear if they were all put into use.[65] In almost every
case the jennies were turned by bullocks and other cattle but during the
1820s three factories were equipped with steam engines imported from
England.[66] Given an estimated average of 500 workers per plant the total
labour force may have been as high as 12 to 15,000.[67]

The Englishman, St John, who visited Egypt in the early 1830s has left a
graphic description of the system as it existed in those days. Spinning was
mainly carried out in the provincial mills where the raw cotton was beaten,
carded and then spun into yarn. Most of the yarn was then put loosely into
bags and carried by camel to Cairo, but a part of it was sometimes retained
to be woven on handlooms or paid to the operatives in lieu of wages. None
of the mills which St John visited were working to full capacity, either
because some of the machines were worn out or because of shortages of
labour. Moreover, according to his estimates, some 50 per cent of the raw
material was wasted as a result of carelessness. St John's evaluation of
the quality of the finished product was equally gloomy: in his opinion
'the value of the article, when spun [was] inferior to cotton in its natural
state'.[68]

At their peak, in the mid-1830s, Muhammad Ali's factories seem to have
been consuming something like a fifth or a sixth of the Egyptian cotton
harvest.[69] Out of this the mills produced enough thread to meet the
country's demands with some left over for export.[70] Factory-spun cotton was
then woven into cloth and bleached, printed or dyed in other government
establishments. Although there is no satisfactory estimate for the amount of
cloth produced it seems very unlikely that it could have reached anything like
Fahmy's figure of two million 'pics' a year if a 'pic' was the equivalent of an
English 'piece'.[71] A more reasonable upper limit, based on Hekekyan's assertion that one of the better mills was producing 50,000 pieces a year, would be a

maximum of 400,000 pieces.[72] Unlike the case of thread this was certainly not enough to meet all domestic needs. Figures from various foreign sources would seem to show that imports of cotton cloth were increasing during the 1830s, an indication that the national market was too large for the capacity of Egypt's looms.[73] Some of Egypt's output was used by the armed forces, some was sold to local retailers and merchants, and a small quantity sent abroad.[74] When sold cheaply enough Egyptian muslins seem to have been able to compete with imports from India while, according to Col. Campbell, the British Consul-General, locally made 'indiennes' (a small handkerchief-size piece) took away some of the market from the rival British product.[75] It seems likely, however, that factory-produced textiles were often sold well below their cost price, either to get rid of them, or, in some cases, because the rudimentary system of accounting employed did not allow Muhammad Ali to calculate how expensive they really were.[76]

Apart from the cotton spinning and weaving mills, three other types of state factory were constructed during the Muhammad Ali period. The first and most successful were those directly connected with the production of military equipment. A large arsenal built within the Cairo Citadel in 1815–16 was employing 400 men in the mid-1820s and turning out cannons, swords and munitions, as well as muskets at the rate of 1600 a month.[77] Their quality was rated highly by French experts.[78] Later a second arsenal was built at Cairo, with others at Bulaq, Rosetta and Alexandria, all of which manufactured boats as well as arms.[79] Of these, the complex of foundries, workshops and ship-building yards at Alexandria was the largest. Towards the end of the 1830s it is said to have employed 4000 workers and is credited with the production of twenty-two naval vessels including nine warships with over a hundred guns.[80] Other military factories included those for making gunpowder and at least six saltpetre works.[81] Although Egypt continued to purchase ships, arms and munitions abroad, local production was certainly sufficient to reduce the military import bill by a large amount.

The other two types of factories were concerned with the manufacture of textiles like wool, silk and linen, and the processing of agricultural produce – including at least three sugar refineries, nine indigo works, rice mills and tanneries. Unfortunately too little is known about this activity to allow any general statements about either the volume or the quality of output. In at least one case, the tarbush factory built at Fouah on the Nile in 1825, production at the rate of 24,000 hats a month must have been sufficient to meet all military demand, with a product which was at least the equal of that of the well established manufactures in Tunisia.[82] Large quantities of good quality linen were also produced but in this case many of the 30,000 or so looms remained in private hands (though working under licence) and it is likely that only a small proportion of total output came from government establishments.[83]

Altogether Muhammad Ali's factories (including the cotton mills) employed some 30,000 to 40,000 workers during the 1830s, some of them women and children. Power was provided by the workers themselves, by perhaps 3000 animals, and, at the most, by seven or eight steam engines.[84] Had the system been allowed to develop there are some who suppose that it could have permitted Egypt to follow England and France closely along the path of early-nineteenth-century industrialization.[85] But this is to ignore the enormous problems faced by the ruler of a small country with a narrow local market, no coal, wood or workable iron, and none of the accumulated technical or entrepreneurial resources of western Europe. Indeed, even to characterize Muhammad Ali's programme of factory construction as 'in-dustrialization' is to beg all kinds of questions given the very limited use of power-driven machines.[86] Moreover, in Egypt, unlike Britain and France, it was the government itself, not a class of local entrepreneurs, which was attempting to develop the factory system, an activity which would have severely taxed the resources of much better organized administrations. This can be seen clearly from Muhammad Ali's efforts to co-ordinate activities from Cairo, establishing production targets, trying to remove bottlenecks, and seeking to ensure that plant was used at something like its proper capacity. The stream of letters he sent to factory managers trying to get them to act according to the methods of supervision copied directly from Europe and often accompanied by blood-curdling threats of punishment was unlikely to succeed, the more so as the people he chose to put in charge of his factories were not the young men sent to Europe for technical training but, as a rule, members of what was still fundamentally a Turkish/Mamluk military élite.[87] Hekekyan's description of Latif Bey, the Inspector of Factories in 1843, who preferred the manual operation of machines to the use of steam or bullock power, requires no further comment.[88] What would certainly have worked much better would have been a less ambitious scheme centred on the production of military material, an activity which, as in Anatolia, was within the competence of an urban labour force supervised by Europeans or European-trained engineers. As it was, not only did the unwieldy factory system require far more resources of skill and enterprise than the country possessed but there is also no sign that the standard of management or of workmanship improved over time: according to Hekekyan's account, it may even have diminished.[89]

By the late 1830s the difficulties of administering the factories were only part of the wider problem of attempting to use what was still basically an Ottoman system of administration to exercise the most minute supervision of almost every aspect of the economic activity of a resentful population. In spite of an on-going attempt to establish a more formal set of administrative institutions culminating in the creation of a mixture of councils and supervisory departments in 1837, in spite of the efforts to train potential administrators in government schools or on educational missions abroad, government still consisted largely of the direct exercise of power by Muhammad Ali, members of his family and household and members of the Turkish military élite. The ruler himself was the lynchpin of the whole process, occupied continually with the supervision of state affairs, either through his Privy Council or through the use of personal orders and directives and regular tours of inspection in the provinces.[90] As the scope of government activity continued to expand, this over-centralized method of administration proved more and more difficult to maintain. It also came to be increasingly vulnerable to external pressure, both economic and political. By 1837 the occupation of Syria with a huge army of nearly 100,000 men, the enmity of the Ottoman government and its powerful ally the British, and the extent to which Egypt's finances were bound up with the movement of the price of cotton in the world market all combined to produce a sense of crisis and the beginning of a policy of economic retrenchment and administrative decentralization which was to mark the last decade of Muhammad Ali's rule.

Although it is difficult to be sure, what seems to have triggered off the process was the sudden fall in cotton prices during the downturn in the international business cycle in 1836–7. This led Muhammad Ali to hold the Egyptian cotton crop off the market for several months in the hope of a rise, further exacerbating an already difficult financial situation.[91] The fact that many of the foreign merchant houses at Alexandria on which the ruler relied for credit were forced into bankruptcy only made things worse. In these difficult circumstances Muhammad Ali instituted a major reversal of policy, handing back large tracts of land to the control of members of his family, senior officers and others. This process was formalized by a decree of March 1840 (just after the return of the army from Syria) which, according to Artin, compelled high officials, army officers and others who had grown rich in the wars to accept estates made up of village land (known in Egypt as *uhdas*) to pay its tax arrears and to guarantee its tax liabilities in future.[92] The new proprietors, *mutaahids*, were expected to continue government policy towards agriculture, providing the peasants under their control with working capital and collecting all the harvest from them for sale to the government. In return they received a part of the *uhda* for their own use — Hamont states that this was a half — and the right to work it with a corvée of peasant labour.[93] In addition much of the best land in the Delta was given to members of Muhammad Ali's family in *jiftliks* or private estates which they were able to exploit for their own profit. According to Hekekyan these royal estates amounted to something like 675,000 feddans by 1846.[94] Together with the *uhdas*, which may have amounted to another

1.2 million feddans, they must have constituted almost all the cultivated land in Lower Egypt.[95]

The aim of this policy was threefold: to make up for a temporary shortfall of tax revenue and to reduce the cost of rural administration while at the same time preserving the system of monopolies which allowed the government to appropriate the bulk of the rural surplus. Unfortunately, from Muhammad Ali's point of view, it also contained a basic contradiction: he was handing over day-to-day control of the agricultural sector to people who had an obvious interest in circumventing the regulations banning private sales if they could make more money by selling their crops directly to the merchants in excess of the fixed government price. This applied not only to the *mutaahids*, many of whom had been forced more or less to bankrupt themselves in order to pay off village tax-arrears, but also to those members of the royal family like Ibrahim and Said who were anxious to develop the agricultural potential of their estates as well as a third group, the village shaikhs, who had been able to use their powerful position as chief government agent in the village to build up sizeable properties of their own.[96] What made matters even more difficult for the ruler was that both *mutaahids* and shaikhs were intensely hostile to the privileged position enjoyed by the *jiftliks* which were not only given favourable treatment when it came to the distribution of water or the construction of new public works but were also able to take workers and animals away from the lands of their less powerful neighbours.[97] The result was an open condemnation of the ruler's policies during a direct confrontation between Muhammad Ali and the shaikhs in 1844, followed by some years of what Hekekyan called a species of rural revolt in which it became increasingly difficult for the government to collect the rural taxes.[98] In these circumstances Muhammad Ali's ability to withstand the intense foreign pressure designed to get him to abolish his agricultural monopolies simply crumbled away. One sign of this was the appearance of foreign merchants at Delta markets in the mid-1840s.[99] Another was the order officially closing the government crop storage warehouses in Lower Egypt in 1848.[100]

The consequences of the breakdown of Muhammad Ali's system of rural control were of the greatest importance. First, the government was deprived of considerable revenues. From then on rulers had to rely almost exclusively on the land tax and the customs, supplemented where possible by the income they could obtain from their own private estates. The temptation to expand the size of these estates was thus greatly enhanced. Second, even though Abbas Pasha (1849–54), Muhammad Ali's successor, tried briefly to re-institute government control over the collection and sale of certain major crops, Egypt's international position had become too weak to allow this to be continued for long in the face of foreign opposition; and from then on the country's peasant cultivators were drawn into more and more intimate contact with the merchants, usurers, ginners and others who were the intermediaries between them and the world market. Third, there is an important sense in which the policy of granting *uhdas* and *jiftliks* paved the way for the creation of the great agricultural estates of the second half of the nineteenth century. While it is true that Abbas appropriated many of the *uhdas* (perhaps as many as three-quarters) and some of the *jiftliks*, this was only to donate them to others of the Egyptian élite more directly beholden to him.[101]

The crisis of the late 1830s and the policy of retrenchment and administrative decentralization of the 1840s also had an important role to play in the gradual abandonment of many of Muhammad Ali's factories. While the conventional explanation of this policy focuses on the imposition on Egypt of the terms of the Anglo-Turkish commercial convention of 1838 (which banned all monopolies and preserved a low tariff of 5 per cent on Ottoman imports) and of the Treaty of London (which limited the size of the army to 18,000 men) the reality is more complex.[102] To begin with there is the question of chronology. Not only is there evidence that Muhammad Ali extended his 1837 programme of retrenchment to the factories as well (by letting some of them to private individuals) a year before the signing of the Commercial Convention, but it is also a fact that he continued to talk about building new plants and reorganizing the old until well into the 1840s.[103] Only in April 1845 did he admit to Hekekyan that his 'mania' for industry had been a failure.[104] Even then there is no sign that he acted quickly to close factories, and as late as 1856 there were still at least four weaving mills, one worked by steam, making cloth for military uniforms.[105]

A second difficulty with the use of the Commercial Convention as the major determinant is that Muhammad Ali had never needed a high external tariff to protect his domestic market. In the case of textiles, for instance, the greater proportion of finished output was either passed on to the armed forces or sold, sometimes forcibly, to local merchants. There is no reason to suppose that this type of administrative protection need have been any the less efficacious in the early 1840s even if, over time, the progressive reduction in the size of his army would have meant a serious diminution in military demand. All that can be deduced from the increase in the import of English cottons during the 1840s is that Muhammad Ali's ability to enforce the purchase of his own cloth must have declined with the general relaxation of central control. Only in the case of the military factories themselves is it possible to link their reduction in output directly to defeat in Syria and the Treaty of London. In spite of the addition of a dry dock to the Alexandria arsenal the workforce there was down to 1000 in 1844.[106]

Probably the key question is whether most of the factories would not have had to close sooner or later whatever the circumstance. Certainly there is much evidence that the aim of producing textiles which could compete in price with British or French imports was as far away from realization in the 1840s as it had been earlier, if not further. More immediately, at this same time Muhammad Ali was faced with two very difficult problems. First, the machinery in the cotton mills, which even when originally built had not been of very high quality, was now in a state of great dilapidation and needed to be replaced, obviously at some cost.[107] Second, the failure to maintain Egypt's few steam engines, and the terrible cattle murrain of 1843 which had carried off most of the country's bullocks posed the problem of power for the factories in a particularly sharp form. Once again the only satisfactory solution would have necessitated the expenditure of large sums of money.[108] Perhaps for the first time in history, a ruler well-embarked on a programme of import substitution had discovered that such policies often lead to an increase rather than a reduction in the need for imports. Although there is no direct evidence of how Muhammad Ali himself viewed the problem there is no doubt that in the end he must have decided that the cost of re-equipping his factories was more than he could contemplate.

It only remains to take a brief glance at the impact of Muhammad Ali's policies on Egyptian handicraft production. There is no doubt that the initial attempt to establish a complete government monopoly of textile manufacture and the forcible recruitment of many spinners and weavers into government factories must have had an enormously disruptive effect on organization and output.[109] Thus, whatever his motives, it could well be argued that the net effect of Muhammad Ali's policies was actually to pave the way for the domination of the domestic market by European manufacturers from the 1840s onwards as a result of the actual destruction of any local competition. Nevertheless, the situation does not seem to have been quite as bad as some contemporary European reports would suggest. For one thing there were a number of workers who used the training they had received in the government factories to set up on their own once those establishments had been closed down.[110] For another, in Egypt as elsewhere, local craftsmen showed themselves to be reasonably adept at standing up to the great tide of foreign textile imports (which in Egypt began in the 1840s) by finding new markets for their own goods or by producing new types of product which the Europeans found difficult to imitate (see p. 94).[111] For all these reasons some local handicraft production was able to survive, and by the early 1870s a government survey gives the number of Egyptian textile workers as over 28,000, roughly three times Raymond's estimate for eighteenth-century Cairo.[112]

The Syrian provinces

It was not until after their conquest by Muhammad Ali's troops in 1831/2 that the Syrian provinces of the Ottoman Empire felt the full impact of the era of reforms in Egypt and Turkey. Previously, in the late 1820s, Mahmoud II had made a number of attempts to bring the north under more effective government control and had also tried to abolish such *timars* as still existed in the Aleppo district. But in each case he and his officials had lacked sufficient power to impose their will on the large cities of the interior or on the virtually independent chieftains who controlled the greater part of the mountainous areas as well as the desert margin to the east. Again, every attempt by the Ottoman pashas of Damascus or Aleppo to increase taxes or to extend their control was thwarted by popular opposition, often promoted by social groups like the urban notables or the Janissaries who believed that their interests would be threatened by any growth of central government power.[113] Meanwhile, in southern Syria and Palestine the regimes of semi-independent rulers like those of Jazzar Pasha and Abdullah Pasha (1818–31) at Acre had themselves to continue to face the perennial problem of raising sufficient revenue to support the mercenary armies on which their power depended.[114] Jazzar had instituted a system of monopolies by which he sought to ensure that he alone benefited from commerce of all kinds. He had also cultivated land on his own account. But, unlike Muhammad Ali, who may have begun by copying a number of his methods, he remained content to farm out the revenues from the land and the customs to the highest bidder.[115]

The Egyptian invasion produced a radical change in the situation. For the first time for many hundreds of years the whole of Greater Syria was placed under one central administrative authority: the Egyptian governor at Damascus. Again, there was a systematic attempt to use the large standing army to subdue the power of the autonomous and semi-autonomous chieftains and to introduce some measure of order and security throughout the whole area. Efforts were made to disarm the inhabitants of Mount Lebanon and Palestine; many of the beduin tribes were cowed into submission; the power of the rulers of mountain communities like the Alawites of the Jabal Ansariyeh was broken.[116] In spite of a number of serious anti-Egyptian revolts this policy was sufficiently successful to allow Ibrahim Pasha, Muhammad Ali's eldest son, to introduce the same type of economic policies that his father had instituted in Egypt.

Inevitably, Ibrahim's primary concern was to find enough money to pay for an army which by 1836 was variously estimated at between 40,000 and 60,000 men and which, by 1839, may have numbered 90,000.[117] To this end new taxes were imposed, notably the *ferdé*, a capitation tax on all adult males, which by 1836 was producing a third of total revenue.[118] At the same time the yield from existing taxes was increased by raising the rates at which they were levied and by more efficient administration. Although it proved impossible to institute a system of direct collection by government agents, tax-farms were now auctioned for a very much larger sum. Moreover, in districts like some of those of Mount Lebanon where the Druze *muqatajis* had fled, the government was able to appropriate many of the special dues previously paid to those who controlled the land.[119] In addition, the growth in foreign trade which accompanied the establishment of the Egyptian administration also meant an increase in customs revenue. In 1836, for example, the Damascus customs was being farmed at three times its 1830 price.[120]

For all the success of these measures, however, the Egyptians were never able to raise enough revenue in Syria to pay for the cost of their own occupation. Administrative practices varied too much from one area to another to allow the introduction and execution of a coherent taxation policy. The Egyptians were also handicapped by the fact that there was no Syrian equivalent of their own village shaikh, someone with semi-official status who could be used by the government to supervise the collection of a land tax.[121] Equally important, they were prevented by international pressure from making use of one of their most successful domestic revenue raising devices: the government monopoly over a major agricultural export. Although they bought and sold at least one year's Syrian silk crop soon after the invasion, this led to such strong protests from the British, anxious at all costs to prevent the extension of Muhammad Ali's monopolies to Syria, that the attempt was abandoned in 1835.[122] Thereafter, Ibrahim had to be content with the much less lucrative business of monopolizing only those goods which were traded internally and which were not exported.[123]

From the point of view of the growth of the Syrian economy, however, the fact that the Egyptians were unable to cover the costs of their occupation was of very much less importance than the mere effect of their presence on agriculture and commerce. Once again the key to the whole situation was the establishment of order. By 1836, in the opinion of a number of British consuls, Ibrahim's troops had made travel very much more secure, not only inside the Syrian provinces but also along the desert caravan routes.[124] Furthermore, the Egyptians were able to use their power to give greater protection to members of Christian and Jewish minorities engaged in industry and commerce, as well as to foreign merchants anxious to establish themselves in the towns of the interior. It was only after the Egyptian invasion, for example, that a British consul was able to take up residence in Damascus. Although permission had been obtained from the Ottoman government before 1832 the man appointed had been unable to enter the city because of the hostility of the local population.[125] As for the rural areas, as always the establishment of greater security allowed the peasants to return to abandoned villages and, once again, to cultivate fields at some distance from their homes.

The economic policies of the new administration were also important.

Following Egyptian practice, successful efforts were made to settle members of beduin tribes along the Euphrates, in southern Palestine, along the Jordan Valley and elsewhere, by granting them land and by allowing them immunity from taxation for a number of years.[126] Local peasants, too, were given similar concessions if they returned to long-abandoned fields; in some cases they were also given the seeds and implements they required. Again, Ibrahim himself cultivated large tracts of land on his own account, as well as making his officers do the same, particularly in the grain and cotton growing districts of northern Syria.[127] Further stimulus to the growth of agricultural production was given by the introduction of new crops and efforts to improve the quality of the old, by the provision of government loans and of tools and equipment to cultivators, and by Ibrahim's direct orders that more vines, olive and mulberry trees should be planted.[128] In addition, various small duties were abolished on the movement of products, such as the *octroi* imposed on crops brought to market in the towns.[129] It has also been asserted that the mere presence of a large army itself acted as a spur to an increase in output.[130] It would be more reasonable, however, to regard it as something of a mixed blessing: on the one hand, apart from the security which it provided, it also constituted a large market for produce of all kinds; on the other, soldiers regularly provisioned themselves with crops and animals for which they paid little or nothing while the practice of conscripting many thousands of local people (often with their animals) either for service with the army or for corvée work on roads and fortifications was a steady drain on a population which was already too small to cultivate all the available land.[131]

But, corvée and conscription notwithstanding, it seems certain that the Egyptian occupation led to a considerable increase in agricultural output, and thus of trade. This can be seen from a number of different indicators. First, many contemporary reports speak of a considerable extension of the land devoted to the cultivation of mulberry trees. In 1836, the British Consul-General at Beirut wrote that the mulberry plantations in his district had increased by a quarter since the invasion, while four years later the English MP, John Bowring, asserted that 37,000 new trees had been planted on Egyptian orders at Tripoli, Beirut and Saida.[132] One result was the sizeable increase in the export of silk which, according to Bowring, advanced from 582 bales in 1833 to 1760 bales in 1836.[133] Contemporary reports speak of the cotton area in Syria being doubled during the Egyptian occupation and of cereal production in the Latakia district increasing by the same amount.[134] Second, there is much evidence to indicate that there was a considerable extension of the area of cultivated land in the Bekaa valley, in the Marj ibu Amir (Plain of Esdraelon) in northern Palestine, in the districts south of Jerusalem and, above all, in the Aleppo district where, according to a British consular report, Ibrahim was responsible for

repopulating 170 villages.[135] Third, such figures as do exist point to a significant rise in the volume and value of Syrian trade during the Egyptian
period. In Beirut, for example, the arrival of Ibrahim's army and the subsequent opening up of Damascus to European commerce led to an immediate
increase in the numbers of incoming ships, from 256 in 1830 to 500 during
the first nine months of 1833.[136] Exports from the town doubled in value
between 1833 and 1838 while imports went up by something like a half.[137]
Some of the other ports on the Syrian coast may have suffered from competition by Beirut, but this was not true of Iskandarun, one of the three
harbours at which goods were trans-shipped to and from Aleppo, where the
numbers of British vessels using the harbour increased by 100 per cent
between 1833 and 1837.[138]

With the retreat of the Egyptians in 1840 and the return of the Syrian
provinces to Ottoman government much of the drive towards a more
centralized system of administration was lost. Even though the incoming
Turkish officials attempted to extend their control over the whole of the
region and to subject it to the main policies outlined in the *Hatt-ı Şerif* of
Gulhane they had neither the military nor financial power nor the regular
support from Istanbul to be able to effect such an ambitious programme.[139]
In addition, they had to contend with the first signs of active European
intervention in Ottoman provincial affairs, notably in Lebanon where
efforts to bring the Mountain under direct Turkish administration were
thwarted by pressure from the British, French and other governments,
leading to the establishment of a more local system of administration based
on the recognition of the existence of two separate communities: the
Maronite and the Druze.[140]

In these circumstances the governors of the three Syrian provinces soon
found themselves in the familiar vicious circle in which they did not have
enough money to maintain a large enough army of troops and not enough
troops to collect more than a small part of the potential revenue. An
obvious symptom of this unhappy situation was their inability to utilize the
new fiscal institutions created by Ibrahim to their own advantage. They
failed to make proper use of the tax registers drawn up by the Egyptians;
they also failed to exercise the same high degree of control over the tax-
farmers.[141] After a brief and unsuccessful attempt in 1841 to introduce the
same system of direct collection which had been attempted in Anatolia they
were soon forced to return to traditional methods, selling *iltizams* to
wealthy townspeople or granting them to the same type of local chieftain –
whether the shaikhs of southern Palestine or those Druze *muqatajis* who had
returned to their estates following the Egyptian retreat – who had commanded the rural surplus ten years earlier.[142] In spite of the regulation
forbidding government officials to bid for tax-farms they were often able to
obtain them in the name of some local 'man of straw' using their power to

ensure that they paid a lower than average price.[143] More importantly, the councils which the Ottomans had established in the major towns soon became the vehicle for a new élite of notables (drawn like the ayans of eighteenth-century Anatolia from members of the old ruling families, the *ulama*, rich merchants, officers in the Ottoman army and others) who were able to use them to secure many of the richer *iltizams* for themselves, again at very much less than they were worth.[144] The result, inevitably, was a considerable loss of revenue: according to Ma'oz, during the 1840s and 1850s the Ottoman governors of Syria were only able to collect half the income which the Egyptians had raised in the 1830s.[145]

Other results followed. For one thing there was never enough money to employ sufficient troops to maintain the degree of security in the rural areas which Ibrahim had achieved. According to contemporary chronicles, Palestine seems to have lapsed into the general condition of disorder from which the Egyptians had rescued it.[146] In Jabal Nablus, for instance, new families like the Abd al-Hadis had gained enough power during the Egyptian period to challenge the older groups, often bringing in their peasant clients and beduin allies for those largely ritual trials of strength designed to improve their position as tax-collectors and surplus appropriators.[146] Conditions in other areas were little better. Meanwhile, the Ottoman governors continued to create more trouble for themselves by mistaken tactics. They set one family against another, encouraging competition for important posts within the local administration. In the rural areas they preferred to abandon Ibrahim's policy of encouraging nomad settlement for the more traditional strategy of harrying the tribesmen into submission where they could; and trying to set one faction against another where they could not.[147] Such policies could only have one consequence. Travel at once became more hazardous – in 1842 the British consul at Aleppo wrote that no road out of the town was perfectly safe, while all along Syria's eastern border with the desert there was yet another contraction of the cultivated area as many of the villages established or re-settled under the Egyptians were rapidly abandoned.[148] In 1843, Wood at Damascus estimated that of the 100 villages which had existed in the Hauran a few years earlier three-quarters were now without population.[149] It was a similar story around Aleppo and in the south, along the Jordan river.[150]

These were not circumstances in which agriculture, or the commerce and trade based upon it, could have been expected to flourish. But the evidence is too weak to be certain. While the production of certain cash crops in certain districts certainly expanded, while the value of trade passing through ports such as Beirut undoubtedly increased, there were many areas, particularly in the interior, where productive activity must have been in decline.[151] It is just as difficult to evaluate the effects on the economy of the rapid period of economic and social transformation ushered in by the

Egyptian occupation, the Ottoman return, and the concomitant opening up of Greater Syria to European trade. One obvious symptom was the increasing tension between various classes and groups within the society, tension which found its first overt expression in the popular revolts which broke out in all the major cities of the interior between 1850 and 1860 and the various armed conflicts in Mount Lebanon during the same period. Underlying such outbursts was a complex alteration in the relative power and economic strength of many groups within the society which will be analysed in detail in Chapter 6.

The Iraqi provinces

The one area of the Middle East which was largely exempt from the effect of government-inspired reforms before mid-century were the provinces of Iraq. It is true that the last of the semi-independent Mamluk pashas of Baghdad, Daud (1817–31), was able to augment the strength of his own position for some years by increasing revenues, incorporating the local Janissaries into his regular army and curbing the power of the Resident of the British East India Company.[152] It is also true that the Ottomans themselves succeeded in regaining control of the major provincial centres as a result of military expeditions sent against Daud himself, against the Jalili pashas of Mosul in 1833 and against the major Kurdish chieftains between 1837 and 1847.[153] Nevertheless, in spite of such successes the Ottomans were not able to build up sufficient power to maintain regular control over more than a small portion of the rural countryside. This was particularly the case with the lands lying between the Tigris and the Euphrates south of Baghdad where, if anything, they were less successful in asserting their authority than their Mamluk predecessors. There were frequent tribal revolts, taxes were collected only with the greatest difficulty and, in general, conditions were such that even reforms of the limited type introduced in Anatolia and Syria were impossible. As a result, what little economic change did take place in the first half of the nineteenth century was almost entirely in response to a small increase in trade with Europe, Arabia and India. This forms part of the subject of Chapters 3 and 7. Only with the arrival of a series of energetic governors in the 1850s and 1860s can the Iraqi provinces be said to have entered the age of reforms.

3 The expansion of trade with Europe, 1800–1850

At the same time that Muhammad Ali and the Turkish sultans were beginning their programmes of military reform, fundamental changes were also taking place in the nature of trade between the Middle East and Europe. As it existed during the eighteenth century the main characteristics of this trade can be summarized briefly under four heads. First, well over half the sea-borne trade was controlled by the French merchants of Marseilles.* In some parts of the region, notably the Syrian coast where in 1789 they possessed nearly twenty houses in the principal ports, the French were virtually the only European residents.[1] Second, French commercial predominance was based largely on the export of a woollen cloth which was lighter, thinner, softer and in general more suitable to Middle Eastern use than that manufactured in England or elsewhere. Although the rich of Istanbul and other major cities continued to purchase the more high-priced English woollens, mostly from Gloucestershire, the trade at the cheaper end of the market was mainly in French hands.[2] The French had the additional advantage that their manufacturers provided a steady market for most of the primary products then exported from the Middle East, especially short-staple cotton.[3] Third, while French trade with the majority of Levant ports continued to increase throughout the eighteenth century, that of the other European nations, the British in particular was definitely in decline from at least as early as 1740 (see Table 1). Fourth, and finally, the relative importance of the Middle East in west European trade was falling steadily as new markets and new sources of supply were developed in the Americas, India and elsewhere.

This pattern was changed out of all recognition by the Napoleonic wars and the first stages of the Industrial Revolution in Britain. For one thing French trade in the Mediterranean was almost entirely destroyed, first by the restrictions imposed on exports by the Convention in 1793, then by command of the sea exercised by the British fleet after the Battle of the Nile (1798) and by the way in which the French merchants living in Istanbul, Izmir, and along the Syrian coast were either imprisoned or forced to flee as soon as their country commenced hostilities against the Ottoman Empire,

* The overland trade through the Balkans or the Danube provinces has had to be excluded for lack of information.

losing most of their assets in the process.[4] This at once provided a perfect opening for the British, for not only was French merchant shipping banished from the Mediterranean but that of Napoleon's allies, the Dutch, the Austrians and the Italians, as well. Again, the introduction of the French Emperor's 'Continental System' placed a very high premium on any British goods which could be smuggled into Europe via Turkey and the Danube provinces. Trade was also promoted by the need to provision the British garrisons at Malta and Gibraltar and, more importantly, Wellington's army fighting in Spain. Lastly, the British were able to profit from their position as allies of the Ottomans against the French to obtain the abolition of certain restrictions on their trade. It was during the Napoleonic wars that the Levant Company realized its long-sought aim of obtaining permission for its ships to enter the Black Sea.[5] It was also at this time that British vessels began to use the safer eastern harbour at Alexandria, previously reserved for Ottoman craft; while the exigencies of war virtually put an end to the traditional Ottoman restrictions placed on the export of Middle Eastern cereals outside the Empire.[6]

All this, however, was only a prelude to the opening up of the Middle East as a market for ever increasing output of British manufactured goods during the first decades of the nineteenth century.

The expansion of trade between the Middle East and Europe

The role of the Middle East as a market for British exports was of the greatest importance. On the one hand, the volume of factory-produced goods was increasing at an enormous rate: in the case of cotton textiles from some £10 million at the beginnings of the wars with France to some £30 million at the end.[7] On the other, the struggle with Napoleon severely reduced the possibility of selling these goods in Europe. The Mediterranean seemed one of the most promising alternatives; and it was there, as in other parts of the world, that British cottons, so much lighter, cheaper and more brightly coloured than their competitors', were the main instruments of British commercial expansion. By 1816, the first year of peace, British exports to the Levant were valued at £300,000, of which nearly £190,000 were cotton goods of one kind or another. Two years later, at the peak of the post-war boom, the value of these exports had increased to £800,000, including cottons worth £550,000.[8] However, in the conditions which then existed this was more than the market could bear and for the next two decades British exports averaged only between £500,000 and £600,000 with cottons providing something like 70 per cent of the total. There were then years of further rapid expansion — stimulated by a continuous decline in price — until by 1845–9 exports to the Middle East had reached an average of over £3,000,000 a year (three-quarters of which were articles of cotton) (Tables 6, 7). By this same period, according to another calculation, Turkey, Egypt and Africa provided 14 per cent of the world market for British cotton piece goods.[9]

Table 6   British exports to the eastern Mediterranean, 1814–50
(£ – declared values) (annual averages)

	Turkey*	Syria/Palestine	Egypt
1814	153,903		
1815–19	460,661		
1820–4	566,315		
1825–6	600,543		
1827–9	428,655		49,377
1830–4	1,036,166		130,138
1835	1,331,669		269,225
1836–9	1,466,569	119,753	200,844
1840–4	1,564,447	441,107	237,444
1845–9	2,350,184	382,219	494,824
1850	2,515,821	303,254	648,801

* Definitions of the territorial area of Turkey vary from source to source. In addition, until 1827 it included Egypt and until 1836 Syria/Palestine.

Table 7   British exports of cotton goods to the eastern Mediterranean, 1824–50
(£ – declared values) (annual averages)

	Turkey*	Syria/Palestine	Egypt
1824	567,112		
1825–6	465,761		
1827–9	326,497		27,939
1830–4	824,576		81,968
1835	1,062,781		131,672
1836–9	1,199,943	112,155	198,120
1840–4	1,365,657[1]	430,194	179,328[1]
1845–9	1,833,197	358,456	307,114
1850	1,975,059	271,457	354,427

* Definitions of the territorial area of Turkey vary from source to source. In addition, until 1827 it included Egypt and until 1836 Syria/Palestine.

Sources: Wood, *Levant Company*, 194.
J. Marshall, *A Digest of all the Accounts Relating to the Population, Production, Revenues ... of the United Kingdom and Ireland* (London, 1833), 135.
PP, 1842, xxxix. 135.136, 181; 1844, xlvi, 124–5, 135; 1852, li, 490–3.
Macgregor, *Commercial Statistics*, ii, 71 and v, Supplement 2, 102–4.

Note: 1 Excludes 1841.

Throughout the half century, 1800–50, the great bulk of British trade was with the ports of Anatolia where Istanbul and, to a lesser extent, Izmir were major markets as well as distribution centres. Istanbul, with a population of perhaps 750,000, was far and away the largest city in the eastern Mediterranean, as well as an important point of trans-shipment for goods destined for the towns along the Black Sea coast like Trabzon or for caravans setting out for the interior of Anatolia, Iraq and Syria. Izmir, on the other hand, besides being an entrepôt for the Asian trade was also a major source of the raw materials which British merchants purchased in exchange for manufactures, notably dyestuffs (valonia, yellow berries), silk, cotton and wool. The other main source of industrial raw materials in the Middle East was Egypt, with its long-staple cotton, but, unlike Anatolia, it did not become an important market for British goods until after Muhammad Ali's monopoly system had been brought to an end in the 1840s. As for the Syrian coast, there was no direct trade with Britain until the 1830s, although before then it must have received some British manufactured goods via an Anatolian port.[10] From this decade onwards, however, there was a steady expansion in the export of cotton goods to Beirut, most of which were then forwarded into the interior for sale in Aleppo, Damascus and the cities of Iraq. Later, in the 1840s, British ships also began taking on cereals from the Palestinian ports of Jaffa and Gaza.[11] Nevertheless, at mid-century neither the Syrian nor the Egyptian market had yet begun to challenge the Turkish in importance and the latter continued to absorb over 75 per cent of all British exports to the Middle East (see Tables 6, 7).

Britain's main commercial rivals in the eastern Mediterranean from the 1830s onwards were the French and the Austrians. Although all figures must necessarily be viewed with caution it would seem that the total value of the sea-borne trade of these two countries with the Middle East was just under £2,000,000 (compared with Britain's £2,500,000) in 1840/1 and about £3,500,000 (as compared with Britain's £6–6,500,000) at the end of the same decade.[12] In the case of Austria, however, these figures exclude the important overland trade which in the early 1840s may have been worth another £2,000,000.[13]

France took a number of years to re-establish its links with the eastern Mediterranean broken by the Napoleonic wars and it was not until the 1840s that the value of its trade with the Middle East regained its prerevolutionary level (see Table 8). French merchants were slow to return to the Levant; those who did were handicapped by the fact that, in the aftermath of defeat, their government had had no option but to allow them to operate under conditions in which they paid very much higher duties than the merchants of other nations.[14] Nevertheless, once France's own industrial revolution began in earnest the Middle East became increasingly important as a source of raw materials, notably silk and cotton, for its new factories. As a result, imports from Turkey (and Greece) nearly tripled between 1832–5 and 1843–5. Exports remained sluggish, however, and hardly increased at all by value until the end of the 1840s.[15] During the 1830s the bulk of French trade was with Izmir, but this soon came to be rivalled by that with Beirut

Table 8   French trade with the eastern Mediterranean, 1790–1856
(annual averages in millions of francs)

	Turkey*		Syria/Palestine		Egypt	
	Exports	Imports	Exports	Imports	Exports	Imports
Pre-1791	32.0	38.0				
1816–17	11.0	12.5				
1827	13.9	23.2				
1832–5	17.1[1]	18.7			3.1	4.1
1836–8			4.0[2]	3.8[2]	7.5[2]	7.2[2]
1840	13.3	26.2				
1841–4	23.7[1]	46.6[1]			5.0	11.6
1847–56	29.1	51.8			6.4	13.1

* Geographical definitions of Turkey vary from source to source.

Sources: De la Ferronays (Alexandria) 28 Feb. 1829 in G. Douin (ed.), L'Egypte de 1828 à 1830 (Rome, 1935), 339.
G. R. Porter, The Progress of the Nation (London, 1847), Section II, ch. 3.
PP, 1844, XLVI, 783, 785.
Block, Statistique, 291–2.

Notes:
1 Includes Greece.
2 Converted from £ at the rate of £1 = 25f.

and Alexandria from which France obtained increasing quantities of silk and long-staple cotton.

Details of Austria's commerce with the Middle East are more difficult to discover and there is good reason to regard the figures for both sea-borne and overland trade with some scepticism. It should also be noted that many of the goods transported from Trieste to the eastern Mediterranean by the large number of Austrian vessels engaged in the carrying trade were of Swiss, French and German origin. As in the case of the British and the French, the bulk of Austria's trade was with Izmir and Istanbul.[16] But commercial links with the Black Sea ports were also important, while there was a significant import of Egyptian cotton through Trieste in the 1840s.[17]

It is difficult to form even the crudest estimate of the growth of total European trade with the Middle East during the first half of the nineteenth century but it was certainly large. In the case of Britain, for instance, the value of goods (both imports and exports) exchanged with the Levant increased from an annual average of between £200,000 and £300,000 during the first stage of the Napoleonic wars to £5,500,000 in 1845–9, while the French advance was from 70 million francs (£2,800,000) in 1791 to roughly 90,000,000 francs (£3,600,000) in 1840–4 and 100,000,000 francs (£4,000,000) in the early 1850s (see Table 8). In addition, the commerce of Russia, Belgium and Holland, the United States, Italy, Austria and other industrializing countries also grew by a substantial amount. Given the fact that the price of most manufactured goods was falling during this period, the increase in European trade in volume terms was correspondingly larger.

The institutional support for the expansion of European trade

Such a great expansion of trade could not have taken place without other developments of much importance. To begin with there was the sharp increase in the numbers of European merchants resident in the major Middle Eastern ports. In Alexandria, for example, the number of European commercial houses more than tripled between 1822 and 1840, from 14 to 44.[18] In other ports, notably those on the Syrian coast, there was a rapid emergence of a number of local firms, also with their own links with Europe.[19] Again, in either case, as it was the usual practice to purchase local crops in cash while selling imported manufactured goods on credit, these new merchants had to provide themselves with considerable funds. According to one Izmir resident, quoted in McCulloch's *Dictionary of Commerce*, anyone desirous of setting himself up in trade there required an initial capital of £20,000 'to do any good'.[20] A regular credit link with a European banking house was equally important, the more so as interest rates on borrowed money were usually very much lower in Britain and France than in the Middle East itself.[21]

Another necessity was the establishment of links with the local retailers who actually sold the imported goods in their shops as well as providing useful information about the tastes of their customers. With their assistance European merchants were often able to increase sales by copying Egyptian or Syrian designs or by adapting their wares to the particular requirements of particular areas.[22] Contact between European merchants and retailers was usually effected through the role of local intermediaries whose knowledge of the language, the market and of Middle Eastern commercial practices was vital when it came to finding retail outlets, attempting to enforce contracts or collecting debts.[23] Such intermediaries were also necessary in order to do business with the large cities of the interior where, for a combination of political and economic reasons, European merchants often found it difficult to establish themselves with any great success. This was particularly true of Aleppo and Damascus. According to Bowring's 'Report on Syria' there were only four British merchant houses in the former city in the late 1830s as against 110 local establishments (30 owned by Christians, 70 by Muslims and 10 by Jews) which retailed European goods.[24] As for Damascus, of the five British houses which had established themselves in 1842 not one managed to survive until 1849.[25] Meanwhile, when it came to the purchase of Middle Eastern goods local intermediaries were just as important. As Chevalier correctly notes, it was the merchant money-lenders of Syria who were the 'hinge' between the world market and large-scale commerce and banking on the one hand and small-scale peasant and artisan production on the other.[26] It was such men who, very largely, administered the exchange between the capitalist economies of Western

Europe and the pre-capitalist economies of the Middle East, using either their own existing capital resources or money obtained from Europeans to generate the credit required to expand local trade and to purchase local commodities.[27]

Finally, as far as British trade in particular was concerned, the increase in the numbers of merchants resident in the Middle East and the creation of new markets was greatly facilitated by the abolition, in 1825, of the monopoly exercised by the Levant Company. Not only did this open up the commerce of the eastern Mediterranean to a wider circle of merchants, it also transferred responsibility for the appointment and payment of many British consular representatives from Company to government.[28] One consequence among many was that the Foreign Office and the Board of Trade were now able to place men in ports and towns like Trabzon and Damascus where the Levant Company had been unable or unwilling to penetrate.[29] Furthermore, once the transfer was complete, the British Government, through its consular representatives, was in a much better position to support the various campaigns of protest begun by British merchants against Egyptian and Ottoman officials who, in their opinion, acted to prevent the free exercise of trade. Another example of the same trend was the removal of the monopoly exercised, admittedly with decreasing rigour, over French trade with the Middle East by the merchants of the port of Marseilles.[30]

A second factor of great importance in encouraging the expansion of European commerce was the developments which were taking place in the sphere of transport. One was the steady fall in ocean rates during the first half of the century. A second was the establishment of regular steamship routes between Egypt and the Levant from 1835 onwards.[31] Although the early steam vessels were too small and too few in number to carry more than a small fraction of the total trade, their arrival in the eastern Mediterranean brought several advantages. They were faster than sailing ships and also more reliable as they were much less affected by the hazards of contrary winds and sudden storms. For these reasons they were able to provide a quick and reliable method of transporting the coins and bullion necessary to finance the European trade and, more importantly, to meet the trade deficit run by certain areas of the Middle East with Europe before 1850. They also allowed merchants to travel more easily from one port to another in search of new markets, a facility which was undoubtedly of the greatest importance in opening up the Black Sea and Syrian coasts to European trade. Later, as the capacity of the steamships improved they also began to make an increasingly important contribution to freight traffic and by the early 1850s were carrying as large a total weight of cargo as their sail-driven rivals.[32] Transport along the region's great rivers was also much improved during the first half of the nineteenth century. In Egypt, Muhammad Ali's reforms encouraged the use of boats to take goods first to Cairo, then down the Nile towards the Sudan; in Iraq, Chesney's expedition and the subsequent exploration work carried on by the East India Company demonstrated that it was possible to navigate the Tigris between Basra and Baghdad on a year-round basis.[33] Only on the land was there little or no improvement apart from the general increase in security. The Middle East still possessed few roads usable by wheeled vehicles while the high cost of animal transport remained a considerable deterrent to the increased carriage of bulk goods. In Syria, for example, merchants shipping grain from Hauran were often required to pay one sack of cereals to the camel-men for each sack transported to the coast.[34]

A third factor in the expansion of European trade with the region was the increasingly active role played by the British and French governments in support of the commercial interests of their own merchants.[35] Apart from the general attempt to push the rulers of Egypt and the Ottoman Empire in the direction of a comprehensive administrative reform — a policy which found its most complete expression in Palmerston's active intervention in the struggle between Muhammad Ali and Mahmoud II in 1839 — two particular problems were of special importance. One was the question of the control of commercial relations between European and Ottoman subjects. With the rapid extension of credit and the growing use of the system of purchase in advance to secure access to regular supplies of local raw materials for export, the inability of foreign merchants to enforce contracts or to find some uncomplicated method of dealing with the non-payment of debts other than by a direct appeal to the Ottoman authorities became ever more irksome and the subject of increasing complaint.[36] Another problem which was frequently mentioned in contemporary reports was that of the so-called 'fraudulent bankrupt', the local merchant who simply declared himself insolvent as a way of avoiding his creditors.[37] As the volume of European complaint increased, so too did the efforts of the consuls and the foreign governments they represented to persuade the Egyptians and Ottomans to institute a system of commercial courts designed to settle such vexatious questions in a regular and orderly way. The result was a process by which the first, informal, councils consisting mainly of local merchants were replaced by mixed tribunals with a much stronger European representation. Thus, in the Syrian towns, for example, the councils of local merchants established during the Egyptian occupation were reconstituted as European-dominated commercial tribunals in Beirut and Damascus in 1850 and in Aleppo in 1853.[38] Meanwhile, there was a similar pressure to conduct business according to the precepts of British or French commercial law culminating in the enacting of the Ottoman Commercial Code of 1850, based on French practice, and its widespread introduction throughout the Empire.[39]

Of all the obstacles the European merchants saw as standing in the way of the expansion of their trade, two in particular came to assume overriding importance. One was the Egyptian and Ottoman policy of encouraging the monopoly of the purchase, sale, and even export of a variety of Middle Eastern agricultural products. The other was the existence of a large number of internal duties on the movement of goods within the region. Both together were blamed not only for the restraints they imposed on trade but also, just as important, for standing in the way of the sale of local crops to foreign merchants and thus reducing the Middle East's ability to pay for its imports.[40] Another aspect of the same complaint was the financial loss experienced by many British ships bringing manufactured goods out to the Levant as a result of their inability to find a return cargo or of their having to sail up and down the coast searching for a full load. This problem was particularly acute in Syria where, according to Boislecomte, there was never enough produce to be found at any one port to fill even a single vessel.[41] Bowring drew attention to the same situation several years later: in 1836 he reported that only 6 of the 14 ships bringing European goods to Iskandarun had been able to find a return cargo.[42] If only foreign merchants could bypass the local monopolies and make direct contact with the peasants, so it was argued, Syrian agricultural production would at once increase.

Government support for this argument was quickly won and in 1838 Palmerston was able to use Ottoman dependence on British military and political support to ensure that the renegotiated Anglo-Turkish Commercial Convention contained clauses outlawing the use of monopolies throughout the Empire and severely reducing the level of internal duties.[43] That this was the main aim of British policy is clear: as far as the tariff on United Kingdom exports to the Middle East was concerned the Foreign Secretary allowed it to be raised from 3 to 5 per cent, while Turkish produce sold to British merchants was still to be taxed at the relatively high rate of 12 per cent. The renewal of the French, the Russian and other commercial conventions over the next few years took place on the same terms.[44] There then followed a prolonged battle to make sure that the new regulations were properly enforced. British consuls throughout the Empire were required to submit regular reports on the matter while a fierce international campaign was conducted to force Muhammad Ali to allow the same regulations to be introduced into Egypt.[45] The result, in the end, was a clear victory for the European merchants: they secured the uninterrupted access to the Middle Eastern harvest they wanted; any future attempts by the rulers of Turkey and Egypt to control the sale of particular products were soon defeated.[46]

The economic effects of the expansion of trade with Europe

The major effect of the European commercial penetration of the Middle

East during the first half of the nineteenth century was to bring certain sections of the region's economy within the scope of the world economic system. This can be seen with some clarity in the way in which, from the 1820s onwards, an increasing number of districts were directly affected by fluctuations in the European business cycle, their level of agricultural and commercial activity being immediately influenced by movements in the international price of commodities or changes in the availability of bank credit.[47] It can also be seen, a little less clearly, in the general transformation of basic economic relationships consequent on the spread of monetary transactions, the enlargement of the scope for capital accumulation, and the growing involvement of peasants and artisans in the sphere of exchange. It is important to stress, however, that this was a very uneven process. While a few areas, notably those around the fast growing coastal cities like Alexandria or Izmir, were rapidly subject to powerful economic influences from Europe, others, like the central Anatolian plateau or the mountains of north-east Iraq, remained little affected until much later in the century. It is equally important not to telescope developments and to imagine that the different stages of the process of transformation took place more rapidly than they did.[48]

One of the most immediate consequences of the opening up of the Middle East to European trade was the stimulus given to the production of certain cash crops, notably cotton in Egypt, silk and cotton in Syria and Mount Lebanon, fruit and wool in Anatolia, as well as cereals in almost every district within easy reach of the coast. Unfortunately, however, it is almost impossible to give any idea of the magnitude of the increase or of the extent of agricultural land affected. The only figures which exist are those for the export of particular crops; but even these are suspect and also disguise the fact that an increase in foreign sales must sometimes have represented simply a diversion of a finite local supply from the domestic to the European market. Nevertheless, contemporary reports leave the impression of a number of areas in which the pull of the European market was able to produce a very rapid increase in output in a very short time.[49]

Equally difficult problems attend the attempt to trace the economic and social effects of this expansion of cash crop production. It is easy enough to hypothesize that it must have been accompanied by such obvious features as an increase in agricultural specialization, the introduction of new systems of rent and the wider use of seasonal wage labour. It is equally easy to find isolated examples of all these phenomena.[50] What is lacking, however, is evidence of how widespread such practices were or how they developed and intensified over time. For these reasons it is probably better to delay treatment of the subject until those later chapters which deal with similar and better documented processes later in the century.

The growth of commerce with Europe had more identifiable effects on

Middle Eastern industry. This was particularly the case with the local production of threads and textiles. Between 1824 and 1850 British exports of cotton manufactured goods to Turkey, Egypt and Syria/Palestine increased from an annual average of around £500,000 in the mid-1820s to £1,500,000 in 1836–9 and £2,500,000 in 1845–9 (Table 7). Of these the great bulk consisted of what were termed either 'plain or white' goods or 'printed and dyed' goods. In 1842, for example, there were over 50,000,000 yards of the former and 27,500,000 yards of the latter, enough to provide about four yards for every inhabitant of the region, man, woman and child.[51] With imports of this magnitude (and the figures just given exclude the large sales of French, Austrian and other textiles) the impact on local production was certainly considerable. Faced with this avalanche of cheap European fabrics, protected by only the most minimal of tariffs, it is not surprising that many Middle Eastern spinners, weavers and dyers were forced out of business. Others suffered greatly from the fact that it became more difficult to find local supplies of cotton and silk either as a result of falling production or of competition for their purchase by foreign buyers.[52] For all these reasons most European observers writing in the 1830s and 1840s were happily predicting the complete destruction of the Middle Eastern textile industry – if it had not already happened. According to McCulloch, most of the Turkish establishments manufacturing textiles had 'given up'.[53] According to the British Consul-General in Beirut, Moore, weaving in Syria was almost completely 'annihilated'.[54] Such statements were repeated over and over again.

Nevertheless, for all the weight of travellers' tales and official reports the evidence is too impressionistic and too contradictory to allow any proper estimate of the extent of the damage. As Chevalier points out, most Europeans were so certain that the Middle East textile industry was just about to disappear that they usually angled their account to prove that this was actually so.[55] And yet, as he is also able to demonstrate, the Syrian industry at least was remarkably resilient and continued to find ways and means of defending itself against its foreign rivals.[56] Contemporary estimates of the numbers of looms at work in Damascus and Aleppo, which are usually used selectively to show that textile production was declining, can be employed in exactly the opposite way to show that any temporary decrease was almost immediately followed by a revival (see Table 9). Or, to take another piece of evidence, in 1855, just after the end of the period under discussion, Allepan craftsmen were still said to have produced nearly £700,000 worth of textiles of all kinds.[57] Similarly, most writers on Egypt and Anatolia admit that village cloth production continued there throughout the century.[58]

Why was this so? How was it that in many parts of the Middle East textile production was able to protect itself against the effects of foreign competition? A number of factors would seem important. First, the whole

Table 9   Estimates of the numbers of looms at work in Aleppo and Damascus, 1825–60

	Aleppo	Damascus
1825	12,000[1]	
1829	5600–6000[2]	
1838	4000[2]	
1845	1500[3]	1000[3]
1850	10,000[4]	
1855	5560[5]	
1856	5500[6]	4000[7]
1859	10,000[6]	3436[4]
1860		2000[7]

Sources:
1 De Bocage, 'Notice sur la carte', 242.
2 Bowring, 'Report on Syria', 318.
3 French consular figures in Chevalier, 'Western Development', 214.
4 J. L. Farley, *Turkey* (London, 1866), 199, 212.
5 *CR* (UK) Aleppo, 1855, *PP*, 1856, LVII, 266.
6 British consular figures in Ma'oz, *Ottoman Reform*, 179.
7 French consular figures in Joseph, 'Material Origins', 111.

question of the influence of European textiles has to be seen in the context of a steady increase in the size of the Middle Eastern market. Once again figures are almost entirely lacking, but it seems safe to suggest that in areas like Egypt and Mount Lebanon there was a substantial growth in population during the second quarter of the century. Elsewhere, in parts of Syria and Anatolia, the gradual establishment of rural security coupled with the sudden disappearance of the plague may have allowed something of the same increase.[59] Quite simply there were many more people to be clothed.

Second, for all the efforts of European manufacturers to copy local patterns and local styles a large number of fabrics could not be imitated by machines, for example Turkish muslins or the cloth made in Syria from a mixture of silk and gold and silver threads.[60] As Ferdinand de Lesseps was to write in August 1850 (when still French Consul at Aleppo):

Les habitants préfèrent les tissus de soie et coton ou soie et or que se fabriquent en grande quantité dans le pays et dans Alep fait un grand commerce avec tout l'interieur où ils sont tres appréciés.[61]

Again, if Europeans were able to copy local designs, the same process was always possible in reverse.[62] In all this Middle Eastern weavers were aided by the fact that, in some areas, they had been able to reorganize production in a few central locations, thus taking advantage of a number of small economies of scale: this was certainly the case with the manufacture of silk cloth in Mount Lebanon which soon began to be centralized in such towns as Dair al-Qamar where the weavers were soon to install foreign-built Jacquard looms.[63] They were also able to profit from the use of imported European thread, which was cheaper and of better quality than the local product.[64] This can easily be seen from the growing volume of exports of British twists and yarns to the Middle East. Between 1831 and 1850, for example, Turkish and Syrian imports of these threads rose from just over 1,700,000 lb to nearly 6,350,000 lb.[65] Some idea of the amount of cloth produced as a result of this thread can be obtained from MacGregor's assertion that it required only 12 oz of it to weave one 'piece'.[66] Finally, the extensive use of imported 'white cloth' suggests that it provided employment for a considerable number of Middle Eastern dyers.[67]

A few general conclusions are possible about the effects of European competition. Perhaps the safest is that the widespread use of imported twists and yarns must certainly have had a devastating effect on Middle Eastern spinners. In Turkey, for instance, where according to Urquhart the local yarn was unequal in strength, uneven in weaving and easily liable to break, its replacement by foreign imports removed an important source of livelihood for large numbers of villagers, many of them women and children.[68] In Mount Lebanon the construction of the first European-type spinning mills must have had a similar effect on those who spun silk by hand with the traditional *hilali*.[69] Second, as far as the weavers were concerned, the figures for the import of British thread suggest that local producers were able to retain a small share of the expanding local market as a result of limited reorganization. Once again the chief sufferers were probably village craftsmen (except in districts like those of central Anatolia where they derived some protection from the fact that the movement of goods was difficult and expensive), as well as men who were unable to switch from the production of simple cotton goods, which bore the brunt of foreign competition, to more complex weaves.

With so few reliable statistics, the impact of the growing commerce between Europe and the eastern Mediterranean on the existing pattern of Middle Eastern trade is, if anything, even more difficult to analyse. The best that can be done is to make a number of general assertions supported, where possible, by such fragmentary pieces of evidence as can be found. The first of these assertions is that the increase in trade with Europe during the first half of the nineteenth century was almost certainly only one aspect of a more widespread increase in Middle Eastern trade based on a rising population and on greater economic specialization. In the case of Egypt, whereas the value of all exports from Alexandria in 1800 was estimated at just under £300,000, by the late 1830s exports to Levant ports alone (Palestine, Syria, Crete and Tarsus and Adana in Anatolia) averaged somewhere in the region of £1,500,000 a year.[70] One obvious result of this growth in intra-regional trade was the increasing opportunities it provided for local merchants and seamen in whose hands it largely remained. As can be seen from the figures in Table 10, the greater part of the sea-borne commerce of Egypt, Syria and southern Anatolia (measured by volume) consisted of the

Table 10   Estimates of the value of trade between Egypt and Syria/Palestine and various European and Middle Eastern sources, 1836–9 (£)*

A   *Sources of imports*

	Trieste	*Leghorn/ Genoa*	*Britain/ Malta*	*France*	*Ottoman Empire*
Egypt (Alexandria)					
1836	554,320	416,120	606,320	428,080	795,760
1837	348,240	169,880	445,960	178,480	748,320
1838	319,000	258,520	560,600	296,600	844,240
1839	187,760	199,880	585,400	195,360	591,640
Syria/Palestine					
1836	38,828	193,148[1]	333,792	183,804	250,504
1837	18,624	129,496[1]	284,932	144,428	219,196
1838	24,968	70,352[1]	398,412	153,168	359,732

B   *Destination of exports*

	Trieste	*Leghorn/ Genoa*	*Britain/ Malta*	*France*	*Ottoman Empire*
Egypt (Alexandria)					
1836	581,280	129,600	216,160	458,520	787,360
1837	374,160	55,640	256,720	215,960	537,680
1838	443,960	85,240	146,160	195,160	505,120
1839	230,160	77,160	227,800	148,240	445,640
Syria/Palestine					
1836	9224	86,484[1]	9540	176,136	197,272
1837	2468	63,784[1]	2984	105,768	152,364
1838	1984	47,444[1]	16,404	177,576	296,996

* These figures were collected from Ottoman officials by the various British consuls and should be viewed with great caution.

Source: PP, 1844, XLVI, 783, 785.

Note: 1 Leghorn only.

passage of commodities from one eastern Mediterranean port to another. Equally important, in most cases where records were kept for the year 1840/1 at least half the vessels involved in this commerce were Greek or Turkish (see Table 11). On the Palestine coast too (where no records were kept) the European consuls reported that coastal shipping consisted almost exclusively of what they called 'Arab' vessels.[71] Hence, although by 1850 European ships had begun to make substantial inroads into the local carrying trade – taking advantage of their larger size and their privilege of paying lower port dues than Ottoman vessels – it is unlikely that in absolute terms this led to any great diminution in local activity.[72] The fact that many Greek ships preferred to obtain the protection of one of the European powers and were thus classified as 'European' in the Turkish maritime statistics only serves to underline this point.[73]

Table 11 The nationality and tonnage of shipping arriving at various Mediterranean and Black Sea ports in the 1840s

	Izmir (1840)		Istanbul (1840)		Trabzon (1840)		Samsun (1850)	
	(no.)	(tons)	(no.)	(tons)	(no.)	(tons)	(no.)	(tons)
British	113	17,465	567		9	1825	44	36,783
Ionian	16	876						
Austrian	216	41,207	869		38	4538	39	18,662
French	40	5582						
Greek	515	30,675	2361		10	2179	2	550
Russian					24	2752	3	291
Turkish					105	18,375	48	42,692
Total (including others)	869	107,596	5630		189	34,220	148	99,768

	Iskanderun (Alexandretta) (1842)		Beirut (1841)		Alexandria (1840)	
	(no.)	(tons)	(no.)	(tons)	(no.)	(tons)
British	23	3203	35	5231	69	13,005
Austrian	2	318			48	9924
French	41	5921			38	7794
Tuscan	2	297			15	3185
Greek	13	1065	68	5576	21	1235
Turkish	23	780			1013	106,766
'Arab'	86	6570				

Sources: Macgregor, *Commercial Statistics*, II, 79.
Bailey, *British Policy*, pp. 95–7.
PP, 1844, XLVI, 784.
Suter (Kaissariah), 2 April 1851, FO 78/870.
Werry (Aleppo) 1 Feb. 1842, FO 78/539.

Nevertheless, for all the general growth in Middle Eastern commerce, the relative importance of the European sector was clearly increasing at a rapid rate. Already by 1836–8, according to the figures in Table 10, over half the value of the sea-borne trade of Egypt and Syria/Palestine was with Europe. The same trend can be seen with respect to the commercial activities of the cities of the interior. In the case of Damascus, for instance, Boislecomte calculated that whereas in 1825 the goods arriving from the east (mainly Baghdad) were worth twice as much as those from the Mediterranean coast, by 1833 this margin had shrunk to only 30 per cent.[74] One result, among many, was the beginning of a significant outflow of gold and specie to pay for that part of the trade with Europe which could not be financed by local exports.[75] This was particularly true of Anatolia and Syria, although whether the effects of this 'drain' were quite so bad as some writers, like Chevalier, have maintained is open to question.[76] For one thing, the unfavourable balance with Europe might well have been compensated, in part, by a surplus on trade with the countries to the east. For another, Chevalier's assumption that the outflow of specie produced a diminution in local monetary transactions is difficult to equate with the fact that, in Syria at least, there seems to have been quite a marked rise in prices during the 1840s.[77] But this is yet another area which has been far too little researched to allow categorical general statements.

Another feature of the same trend was the growing economic power of those coastal ports where the trade with Europe was concentrated: Alexandria, Beirut, Izmir, Trabzon and, to a lesser extent, Jaffa, Latakia and Iskandarun. By the 1840s such port cities, with the ever-expanding foreign population, their network of links with village retailers and peasant cultivators, had become major growth points within the region's economy. In Egypt, the increase in trade with Europe and, in particular, the export of long-staple cotton, had transformed Alexandria from the small, relatively unimportant town of 8000 inhabitants captured by the French in 1798 to a major international commercial centre with a population of 100,000 some fifty years later.[78] To the east, on the Syrian coast, the bulk of foreign business took place in Beirut which had rapidly overtaken Saida as a centre of trade. According to the French Consul-General, Guys, it owed its growing importance to its central position, to its harbour and, in the days before the Egyptian occupation, to the fact that merchants found it a relatively more secure place to live owing to the close proximity of the Mountain to which they could withdraw in times of trouble.[79] Estimates of the town's population show a rise from around 5 to 6000 in the 1820s to 30,000 in the early 1850s.[80] The third, and largest, east Mediterranean port city was Izmir with its excellent harbour and important commercial connections with the Anatolian hinterland. By 1850 its population had reached over 150,000.[81]

It was in such cities that trade was organized and credit provided. It was there that in the 1840s the first local banks were established, like the merchant houses of Pastré and Tozzizza at Alexandria.[82] They were also important as what Baran has called 'living spaces' for foreigners and wealthy Ottomans, centres of European commercial practice and European patterns of consumption.[83] Alexandria's first square of two-storey houses with glass windows was built by Muhammad Ali's son, Ibrahim Pasha, between 1835 and 1845, largely for the purpose of letting to foreigners.[84] Descriptions of contemporary Beirut speak of a great increase in the construction of a European type of accommodation in the 1840s, with 365 such dwellings being built in one boom year.[85]

If the major port-cities prospered, many of the older trading centres suffered a significant decline in commercial importance. By mid-century, for example, Damascus merchants wishing to use letters of credit had to obtain them from Beirut. By the same token, it was European merchants or local merchants who had managed to acquire either European protection or, later, European nationality who began to enjoy increasing economic advantage. Not only were they identified with the fastest growing section of the regional economy but they also paid less duty on the movement of their goods and were much better placed than their rivals to use the new commercial tribunals to secure redress of business injury. The result, in many places, was a decline in the importance of Muslim merchants. Whereas, according to Bowring, there was only one member of the local Christian commercial community of Beirut who had not managed to obtain foreign protection, he seems to assume that it was virtually impossible for Muslims to take the same step.[86] While Europeans often tended to exaggerate the extent of this process or, quite simply, to ignore or fail to notice the existence of non-Christian or non-Jewish traders, some of the evidence provided by the British and French consuls can probably be used as a rough guide to the growing disparities between the different religious sections of the Middle Eastern commercial community. Thus, according to consular lists of local Beiruti merchants who traded with Europe in 1826, only 6 out of 34 had names which would positively identify them as Muslims; by 1848 this number had shrunk to 3.[87] Muslim Turks and Egyptians also began to suffer from the same disabilities and to confine their activities more and more to trade with their own co-religionists in the interior.[88]

4 The Ottoman road to bankruptcy and the Anatolian economy, 1850–1881

During the year 1851 the Ottoman statesman, Reşid Paşa, signed an agreement with a British and a French bank for a state loan of 55 million francs.[1] This marked the beginning of a new era in Ottoman finance. Although Reşid's agreement was soon rejected by the Sultan, on the grounds that it would lead to too much foreign interference, the situation in which the Empire found itself at mid-century was such that a loan of some kind could hardly have been avoided.[2] On the one hand, the cost of maintaining an army large enough to ensure the survival of the state, and of constantly re-supplying it with modern weapons, could no longer be met out of local resources, the more so as the collapse of many of the local military factories and the rapid advance in European technology meant that more and more expensive equipment had to be imported from abroad. On the other, the short-term fiscal expedients necessary to bridge the gap between revenue and expenditure – such as the issue of *kaimé* and the depreciation of the currency, as well as the practice of leaving the wages of soldiers and officials unpaid for long periods – were sufficiently disruptive in themselves to lead the Ottoman reformers to seek alternative sources of funds.[3] If to this is added the fact that the 1850s saw the development of new European financial institutions designed to channel savings into investment abroad, it is easy to see how, in spite of all its fears, the Ottoman government soon embarked on a policy of regular foreign borrowing, one which in twenty years was to lead it to bankruptcy. In the circumstances a contemporary criticism of Reşid Paşa's first attempt to obtain a loan was particularly prophetic:

If this state borrows five piastres it will sink. For, if one loan is taken, there will be no end to it. It [the Ottoman State] will sink overwhelmed in debt.[4]

The growth of the Ottoman public debt 1854–75

The Ottoman government signed its first foreign loan agreement in 1854, soon after the start of the Crimean War, the obvious threat to the security of the Empire and the high cost of the military campaign against the Russians being enough to overcome the Sultan's fears of the danger of financial entanglement with Europe. The loan, which was supported, but not guaranteed, by the British government, was for a nominal sum of £3,815,800 (£T(gold)3,300,000).[5] But, as it was issued at 80, and as the Turks themselves had to bear the cost of the expenses connected with its flotation by the London house of Dent, Palmer and Co., the sum actually received only amounted to £T2,514,913.*[6] The interest was at 6 per cent; security was provided by the annual tribute from Egypt. In the event, however, the loan proved inadequate to meet the ever-increasing costs of the war – according to Du Velay these amounted to £11,200,000 between May 1853 and September 1855 – and a year later a new agreement was signed with Rothschilds of London.[7] For once the Ottomans were able to obtain really favourable terms: so anxious were the British and French governments to sustain the Turkish military effort against the Russians that they agreed to act as guarantors. This ensured enough public confidence to allow the loan to be issued at 102⅝ and to carry interest of only 4 per cent.[8]

Thereafter, during the next twenty years, the Ottoman government obtained thirteen more foreign loans, as a result of which, by the time the Empire had become bankrupt in 1875, it had amassed a total external debt of nearly £T242,000,000.[9] In addition, the same period also witnessed the accumulation of a large floating debt consisting of short-term bonds of several kinds.[10] The nature of the burden this imposed on Turkish finances can be seen from the fact that in 1874 over half of the regular budgetary expenditure was devoted to the service of the government's external debts.[11] How did the Ottomans come to find themselves in such a situation? What led them to borrow on such a large scale? The answer can be found by looking both at the international context and at the actual state of Turkish finances and of the Turkish economy.

To take the international context first, for Britain and France the decades of the 1850s and 1860s saw a period of rapid economic expansion unparalleled in their history. The trade figures provide a useful index. In Britain, for example, the value of exports doubled between 1848 and 1857 and then almost doubled again in the next twelve years; in France both imports and exports increased by nearly 100 per cent between 1852 and 1860.[12] What is equally important is the way in which expansion in Britain, and to a lesser extent in France, affected the economies of the rest of the world by means of a growing demand for raw materials. The Middle East offers a good example of this process. As far as both Anatolia and Egypt were concerned the movement began with the Crimean War, when the large sums

---

* It was regular practice to encourage investors to buy shares in foreign loans by issuing them below par. Thus, in the case of the first Ottoman loan, a subscriber would only have had to pay £4 for a bond worth £5. The Ottoman government, on the other hand, only received 80 per cent of the nominal sum but was deemed to have borrowed the full amount.

of money spent on provisions for the Allied armies were quickly reflected in an increase in exports and a growing demand for imports. Between 1853 and 1855 United Kingdom sales to Turkey rose from £2,500,000 to £6,600,000 and those to Egypt from £800,000 to £1,600,000.[13] Within these few years the region became as vitally important to British and French commerce as it had been in the seventeenth century.

Apart from the increase in overseas trade a second feature of mid-century economic expansion in Britain and France was the growth in foreign investment. Here, too, the Middle East had a significant role to play, particularly for the French, taking 3450 million francs or 23 per cent of that country's overseas lending between 1852 and 1881.[14] But just as important as the size of the sums invested was the change in the way in which the loans were made. Here the key development was the emergence, in France in the 1850s, in Britain in the 1860s, of new institutions for mobilizing domestic savings. Unlike the private banks which had previously monopolized the business of lending during the first half of the century, the Crédit Mobilier in Paris, and the credit and finance companies in London, were able to tap fresh sources of funds from a wider circle of investors. There was also a fundamental change of method. In France in particular the newcomers were at once forced to follow a less conservative path than the older banks, for their prestige and even their survival depended on their ability to effect 'spectacular promotions that promised rapid returns'.[15] Not all the new finance companies concentrated on foreign investment but for those that did many found the Middle East a particularly promising field. Apart from the considerable growth in trade with the region — of more importance to the British than to the French — there was the avowed determination of the rulers of both Egypt and Turkey to 'westernize' or 'Europeanize' their armies, their administrations, and to develop their economies on budgets which were clearly inadequate for the task. Moreover, the construction of systems of transport and irrigation and the investment in increased agricultural output throughout the Ottoman Empire seemed to require almost limitless sums of money, an important consideration at a time when the end of the British and French railway booms meant that there was a shortage of big schemes at home. For some, too, there was the lure of the high rates of interest allegedly charged by Middle Eastern money-lenders.[16] If, as reports seemed to indicate, local merchants and the proprietors of large estates were willing to borrow at rates of between 30 and 50 per cent a year why could not European companies arrange to lend them similar sums at half that rate and still make a large profit?[17]

For all the sums lent by the new British and French credit institutions to individual companies or banks established in the Middle East, far and away the most spectacular, as well as probably the most lucrative, venture was the government loan. It involved increasingly large amounts of money; it was easy to publicize; its flotation involved little risk and allowed the promoters to make easy profits from commissions and from their manipulation of the price of the bonds issued. For these and other reasons, in the 1860s and 1870s, a number of large institutions like the French Crédit Lyonnais, the Société Générale, and the Comptoir d'Escomte de Paris began to specialize more and more in the business of lending to Middle Eastern governments. It was they who thought up schemes likely to prove attractive to the Ottomans; they who perfected a well-tried mechanism for floating loans involving special announcements in the press and other promotional gimmicks; they who accustomed a large section of the investing public to the idea of purchasing 'Oriental' bonds.[18]

Apart from the London and Paris based credit companies a significant role in raising loans for Turkey and Egypt was also played by the European-controlled banks established in the Middle East itself. Of these the most important was the Ottoman Bank established at Istanbul in 1856 and re-organized as the Imperial Ottoman in 1863 with an especially privileged relationship with the Turkish government.[19] But others like the Anglo-Egyptian Bank (1864) in Egypt and the Crédit Général Ottoman (1869) in Istanbul were also active, either in the issue of public loans or in providing the governments with short term financial accommodation. In many cases one of the original aims of such institutions was given as encouraging the economic development of the region, but in reality it was soon discovered that the big profits were to be made in operations connected with state finance and little or no attention was paid to anything else.[20] The Imperial Ottoman is a good example: apart from its support for the schemes of a few European companies anxious to obtain concessions or contracts from the Ottoman government it too devoted most of its energy to public lending.[21] In this all the banks were further stimulated by their close involvement in the competition between rival European powers to extend their own economic and political influence within the Empire, by schemes of financial and administrative reform or of construction and development. Money, it goes without saying, was an important weapon in this struggle: whether it was given or withheld, the aim was generally to secure some particular advantage.[22] Finally, mention ought also to be made of the bankers of Galata, the local usurers and financiers who depended on the European banks for credit and who were also an important pressure group for greater and greater Ottoman borrowing.[23]

Such were the institutions which linked the Middle East with the money markets of Europe. By using their services the Ottoman administration could borrow almost as much as it wanted, but at a price. However hard it might bargain, however skilfully it might play off one institution against another, in the last resort, like any other would-be borrower, it was forced to accept what terms it could get in a competitive market. Apart from the general confidence, or lack of it, in the Empire's financial future, the willingness of European investors to purchase Turkish bonds depended on a whole host of factors — wars, rumours of wars, short-term movements in the price of previously issued stock — many of which were quite outside Ottoman control. As the cost of administration continued to rise it was not difficult for foreign bankers to use the government's urgent need for money to drive a harder and harder bargain. For all these reasons the terms on which Turkey was able to borrow became progressively less and less good: the favourable circumstances of the 1855 loan were never repeated and by 1874 the best that could be done was to obtain a last great issue of £T41,000,000 at 43.5 (of which the government received £T16,600,000) at a real rate of interest of 12.3 per cent.[24] Or, to look at the overall picture: of the total nominal sum borrowed between 1854 and 1874 (£T241,900,000) the Ottoman government only actually obtained just over half (£T127,570,000), most of which had to be repaid at real rates between 10 and 12 per cent.[25]

Table 12   Ottoman foreign loans, 1854–79 (£T,000)*

	Nominal amount of loan	Rate of issue (%)	Sum obtained Gross	Sum obtained Net**	Interest rate Nominal	Interest rate Actual
1854	3300	80.0	2640	2515	6	7.9
1855	5500	102.6	5644	5582	4	4.0
1858	3300	85.0	4180	3784	6	8.7
1859	2200	62.6	{	{		
1860	2241	62.5	1401	1356	6	9.8
1862	8800	68.0	5984	5665	6	9.4
1863	8800	71.0	6248	5480	6	9.7
1865a	6600	66.0	4356	4069	6	9.7
b	36,200	60 av	21,800	21,800	5	8.3
1869	24,444	54.0	13,200	12,711	6	11.5
1870	34,848	32.1	11,195	10,498	3	10.0
1871	6270	73.0	4577	4452	6	8.5
1872	5302	98.5	5222	5116	9	9.3
1873a	22,252	54 av	12,054	12,054	5	9.2
b	30,556	54.0	16,500	15,889	6	11.5
1874	41,000	40 av	16,600	16,600	5	12.3
1877	5500	52.0	2860	2860	5	9.6
1879	8725	100.0	8725	8725	5	5.0
Total	256,138		143,186	139,156		

* £T1 = £0.909 sterling.
** Net proceeds equal gross proceeds minus commissions paid to intermediary banks and the cost of issue.

Source: Tezel, 'Notes on the consolidated debt of the Ottoman Empire', Table 1.

Apart from an examination of the international context, analysis of the growth of Ottoman indebtedness must also focus attention on the internal financial situation. Four factors are of major importance. The first is the use to which the borrowed money was put. Here Tezel's calculations show that the greater part of what was actually received was used to pay the principal and interest on the debt itself. If the loans of 1877 and 1879 are also included, between 1854 and 1881 the Ottoman government paid out just over £T94,000,000 to its foreign creditors (£T21,000,000 in redemption of the principal, £T73,000,000 in interest) leaving only £T45,000,000 for other purposes.[26] How this last sum was spent is more difficult to discover. Contemporary European reports were full of stories of waste and extravagance, particularly by the Sultan Abdul-Aziz, but there is no doubt that the greater part of this sum must have been spent on the central administration and in particular on the army and navy.[27] By the time of the Russo-Turkish war of 1877–8 it has been estimated that the Ottomans had 75,000 soldiers armed with Henry-Martini and Snider rifles and heavy Krupp field guns, as well as the third largest navy in Europe (in terms of the number of ships and their firepower).[28] The cost of military campaigns against rebels within the Empire (for example in Crete in 1869) and foreign enemies like the Russians added further financial burdens. In these circumstances it was perhaps not surprising that little money was spent directly on works of economic improvement. Apart from the proceeds of the 1870 loan which was supposed to raise funds for Baron Hirsch's railway project across the Balkans, expenditure on public works remains limited even if the official figures probably do not take account of the activities of military expeditions sent to extend government control in districts in the east.

Second, given the pressures to increase expenditure stemming from the Empire's dangerously exposed military position, the only hope of maintaining interest payments on the debt was to increase revenue. This, in turn, depended either on a rise in the taxable capacity of the population as a result of general economic growth or on a combination of higher rates of taxation and more efficient methods of collection. In the event the regular increase in revenues throughout the first period of foreign borrowing (1854–74) must probably be ascribed almost equally to all of these processes. According to the figures contained in the various Ottoman budgets for these years, receipts from the tithe throughout the Empire increased by something like three times and those from the Customs and the animal tax by twice (see Table 13). Whether those taxes and dues collected in Anatolia increased in the same proportion it is impossible to say, but they may well have done. As far as agriculture was concerned the increase in exports noted in the next section, however uneven and irregular, must certainly have improved the taxable capacity of the rural population, as must the settlement of many hundreds of thousands of Muslim refugees from Russia and the well co-ordinated campaigns to pacify, administer and develop areas of Anatolia which had previously remained the preserve of nomadic tribes almost completely beyond the control of the central government.[29]

Table 13 Ottoman revenues and expenditure, 1860/1*–1880/1
(millions of kuruş/piastres)**

A *Revenues*

	Estimated revenues	Tithe	Animal tax	Customs duties	Salt tax	Tobacco tax
1860/1	1252					
1862/3	1661	434	88	283	75	93
1863/4	1505	413	90	250	63	60
1866/7	1607	401	145	191	128	71
1868/9	1713	567	157	200	68	52
1869/70	1730	534	163	197	80	52
1871/2	1920	654	203	215	82	83
1872/3	2064	750	208	215	82	53
1874/5	2481	700	221	208	83	150
1877/8	1973	675	179	148	84	111
1879/80	1429					
1880/1	1616					

B *Expenditures*

	Estimated expenditures	External debt[1]	Internal debt	Min. of Army	Min. of Navy	Imperial arsenal	Public works
1860/1	1476	92	132	491	98	32	
1862/3	1491	123	190	480	123	22	
1863/4	1485	176	261	414	105	19	
1866/7	1680	290	280	308	75	50	
1868/9	1701	290	1	360	84	50	3
1869/70	1679	290	1	380	75	75	5
1871/2	2277	620	1	385	83	50	10
1872/3	2140	651	1	345	80	48	7
1874/5	2513	784	1	415	100	90	11
1877/8	2947	991	1	300		80	3
1879/80	1524	82	285	481	61	91	
1880/1	1616	210	282	536	81	86	

* For the period before 1860/1, Ubicini gives estimates of revenues of £7,250,000 for 1853 and 1854 and estimates of expenditures of £6,932,080 and £7,371,280 respectively, quoted in R. R. Madden, *The Turkish Empire in its Relations with Christianity and Civilization* I (London, 1862), 534–6.

** 100 kuruş/piastres = £T1.

Note: 1 The figures for the sums spent on the repayment of the principal and interest on the external debt are significantly less than those to be found in Teẓel, 'Notes on the consolidated foreign debt of the Ottoman Empire', Table 2.

Sources: S. J. Shaw, 'The nineteenth-century Ottoman tax reforms and revenue system', *IJMES*, vi (1975), 451–2 and 'Ottoman expenditures and budgets in the late nineteenth and early twentieth centuries', *IJMES*, ix (1978), 374–7.

Nevertheless, for all these achievements, there were still great obstacles in the way of a more rapid growth of revenue. Throughout Anatolia the Ottomans continued to rely on tax-farmers to collect rural revenues.[30] A similar reliance on tax-farming probably accounts for the fact that there was so little increase in the size of the *verghi* (or poll tax).[31] At the same time no effort was made to exploit new sources of revenue or to end the anomaly

by which the inhabitants of Istanbul and its environs were exempt from
dues of almost every kind, while the Capitulations continued to present an
insurmountable barrier to the taxation of Europeans (or their protégés)
resident within the Empire.[32]

Third, given a situation in which expenditure continued to outrun
income the Ottomans were forced to use the receipts from foreign loans to
meet the deficit. They also left themselves with no alternative but to rely on
those same harmful methods of short-term finance which it was their
general intention to abolish. These involved loans, often raised at the last
minute, from the bankers of the Galata district, *havales* (short-dated paper)
issued by the Ministry of Marine, and a wide variety of bonds. All these
methods were equally unsatisfactory. The loans from the Galata bankers
involved the dangerous practice of servicing long-term loans by borrowing
short at high interest; they were also unreliable on account of the fact that
the bankers themselves could only find the money from larger, European
credit institutions and this was not always possible.[33] As for the short-term
bonds, their issue does not seem to have been subject to any central control,
each ministry handing them out to pay its own expenses as need arose. In
the meantime, because of the continuing budgetary deficit, every effort to
regularize the situation by using foreign money to liquidate the vast amount
of short-term paper came to nothing. To take only one example: although
the 1865 loan was used in a successful operation to fund all the floating
debt, continuing financial pressure meant that within a single year new
bonds had been issued by the various ministries to the value of 100,000,000
francs (£4,000,000).[34]

Fourth, and last, the position was made even more difficult by a system of
financial administration which was unable to cope with the rapidly multi-
plying demands placed upon it during the era of foreign borrowing. As a
British report of 1861 pointed out, although there existed an official with
the title of Minister of Finance, he had no responsibility for the general
financial position of the state and thus no opportunity to prepare a budget
or to ensure an overall balance between income and expenditure. Instead,
what happened was that the Sultan's ministers jointly agreed on the sum to
be allotted to each department of government without rendering any kind
of account to the Minister of Finance.[35] Other barriers to improving
financial management included the lack of control over the Sultan's private
expenditure – the Civil List was not the property of the state but remained
under the supervision of a separate ministry directly responsible to the ruler
– and the absence, until 1880, of any department of audit and account.
The lack of financial control in the rural areas was an added burden. In
some provincial towns, for instance, the taxes were not listed separately but
sold to the farmer *en masse* making it difficult, if not impossible, for the
Ministry of Finance to calculate the sums raised by any one of them.[36]

Efforts to reform the system did not lead to any major improvement. The first official budgets produced in the 1860s were no more than a set of rough estimates of revenue and expenditure made at the end of the fiscal year in question. Again, although other attempts were made to abolish the farming of certain rural taxes — for example, for several years in the early 1860s the tithe on the Trabzon district was collected by salaried officials — these experiments were soon given up when it was discovered that they had led to an actual loss of revenue.[37] Efforts to convert the *verghi* into a property, or income, tax were also quickly halted after the commissions appointed to make the necessary surveys had only managed to cover two or three areas.[38]

Whether more could have been achieved if the leading Turkish reformers, Fuad and Ali Paşas in particular, had applied themselves more consistently to the problem or if they had received more regular support from the Sultan is difficult to say. Certainly the problems they faced were enormous, given the underdeveloped state of the Ottoman bureaucracy, the uncertain control over many provincial administrations, and the numerous vested interests opposed to changes within the system of financial management. Nevertheless, the suspicion must remain that even the reformers themselves were not always completely serious, that their projects were often designed primarily to impress potential European donors. As an editorial in a local newspaper put it bluntly in September 1871 in a summary of the previous decade: 'Heretofore there was talk of reform, improvement and progress only when the state had a loan in view, only to forget all those beautiful intentions once the loan was received.'[39] Blaisdell's criticism goes even further: it is that it was the easy access to European credit itself which was largely responsible for preventing any major change in the system. So long as new loans could be raised at regular intervals there could be little urgency in efforts to maximize revenue or to reduce expenditure.[40] The British Foreign Secretary had made the same point in 1860. 'If no money is obtained by loan,' he wrote to the Ambassador in Istanbul, 'there may come a day of reform.'[41]

Bankruptcy and after, 1875–81

On 6 October 1875, the Ottoman government inserted an announcement in an Istanbul newspaper to the effect that in the presence of a budget deficit of £T5,000,000 it had decided to pay only half of the sums required to service the external debt in cash, making up the rest with a new issue of bonds.[42] This was tantamount to a formal declaration of bankruptcy. There then followed a short period during which the government tried to work out some alternative form of arrangement for paying its creditors; but these efforts were soon abandoned and in 1876 it stopped almost all cash payments entirely. Thus it was that Turkey joined the long list of nations (and American states) which, some time or other during the nineteenth century, had been unable to meet their commitments to their foreign creditors, a list which included Austria (five times), Holland, Spain (seven times), Greece (twice), Portugal (four times) and Russia, as well as every country in Latin America and the twelve southern states of the USA.[43]

That bankruptcy was inevitable, sooner or later, seems undeniable given the increasing proportion of current expenditure required simply to service the debt: if the figures contained in the various budgetary estimates for the years 1859/60 to 1874/5 can be trusted to provide a rough order of magnitude, the sum set aside to pay interest and amortization rose from nearly £1,000,000 (or just under 10 per cent of total expenditure) at the beginning of the 1860s to nearly £5,000,000 (33.3 per cent) at the end, and then to over £12,000,000 (nearly 60 per cent) in 1874.[44] Few, if any, countries could have continued to carry a burden of this size for long. But what seems to have precipitated the formal declaration of bankruptcy was the fall in tax revenues as a result of the series of disastrous harvests on the central Anatolian plateau from 1872 onwards combined with the need to finance a large-scale military expedition against rebels in the Balkans.[45]

The years 1876 to 1881 were occupied with a slow search for a general settlement. That it could not be reached sooner must be ascribed to a number of factors, among them the considerable time which it took for the European powers to co-ordinate their efforts on behalf of their own bond-holders and Ottoman determination to resist further foreign control over Turkish finances.[46] Divisions of interest among the various groups of bond-holders were also important; each loan had been issued subject to different conditions and it proved difficult to get all the parties concerned to agree on a common strategy. Some, like the holders of stock in the 1855 loan, had their interests guaranteed by the British and French governments; others, like those who had contributed to the 1854 and 1871 loans, were subject to a special convention of September 1877 by which the Ottomans agreed to resume payment of the interest due on just these two − although in the case of the 1871 loan at a slightly reduced rate.[47]

In the meantime, the Ottoman government, even though freed temporarily from the need to service the greater part of its debt, continued to run short of money. The campaigns against the Balkan rebels in 1875/6 and the war against Russia, 1877 to 1878, were followed, at the Congress of Berlin, by the surrender of some of the richest provinces of the Empire.[48] Elsewhere tax receipts continued at a low level as the effects of the famine in Anatolia and the huge loss of animal life in 1873−4 were compounded by the conscription of hundreds of thousands of peasant cultivators, by the relaxation of central control over distant areas as provincial garrisons were sent off to fight on the eastern front, and by the devastation of a wide tract of land during the Russian advance. Given these great difficulties there was nothing for it but to continue to rely heavily on the use of short-term bonds – according to Du Velay some £T16,000,000 were issued in 1876/7 – as well as one more foreign loan of £T5,500,000 (£T2,860,000 received) which was all its shaky foreign credit would allow.[49] Finally, in November 1879 it was able to come to an arrangement with various Istanbul bankers by which, in exchange for a further loan of £T8,725,000, the latter were themselves allowed to collect a number of local taxes set aside as security for its regular repayment.[50]

However, these were only short-term expedients and it was clear that, sooner rather than later, the government would have to reach a general agreement with its foreign creditors which would allow it to put its own financial house in order while, at the same time, giving it renewed access to the money markets of Europe. Political pressure from the powers was another important consideration. In 1878 a committee of bond-holders had attended the Congress of Berlin and obtained strong international support for their claims.[51] If this was not enough, in 1879 the British government sent a number of warships to the western approaches of the Dardanelles as a further reminder of its interest in a speedy settlement. Suitably encouraged, the Ottomans invited the representatives of the bond-holders to come to Istanbul and after prolonged negotiations an agreement was finally reached towards the end of 1881. With the publication of the terms of this agreement in the Decree of Muharram, in November of that year (to be described in Chapter 7) the period of acute financial difficulty was at an end, but only at the price of a very much greater degree of foreign financial control.[52]

Foreign trade : the irregular growth of agricultural exports to Europe

With the growth of the Ottoman external debt, foreign economic penetration of the Ottoman Empire was taken a stage further: from commercial to financial. Nevertheless, trade with Europe remained of great importance. During the period under discussion imports continued to rise at a steady rate, stimulated in many cases by the money borrowed from abroad. The purchase of foreign-made armaments is the best example of this process. By the mid-1870s the army contained 84 batteries of field guns and the navy 4 major warships, 8 frigates and 9 corvettes, almost all purchased in Europe.[53]

Against this rising tide of foreign imports there was also a significant growth in the production and export of certain Turkish agricultural crops, albeit of a very irregular and uneven kind. In almost every case the initial stimulus came from a sudden, sharp rise in the international price high enough to overcome the numerous barriers in the way of marketing Anatolian produce, notably the very high cost of transport. Even so, the districts mainly affected were those in the traditional exporting areas round

the coast. It was there that the majority of the high value industrial crops
were grown; there that the system of transport, though still unsatisfactory,
was best developed; there that the facilities for sale of the harvest and for the
provision of agricultural credit were most easily expanded. But some
districts of the central plateau must also have been influenced by the pull of
rising European prices for such products as wheat and barley, opium, wool
and mohair.

The period of sharp increase in European demand for Turkish produce
may be said to have begun with the repeal of the Corn Laws in England
which, by opening up the hitherto protected British market to foreign
cereals, led to a rapid growth in the import of Mediterranean wheat and
barley. This, however, was as nothing compared with the impact of the
Crimean War, when prices were driven up to great heights as a result of the
interruption of Russian grain shipments and the need to supply the Allied
armies fighting across the Black Sea. There followed a brief boom in
Turkish silk production in the late 1850s while the French worms were
being attacked by the disease *pébrine*, and then in the 1860s a vast increase
in cotton production for the European market brought about by the
reduction in American supplies during the Civil War. Other crops to be
temporarily affected by similar price rises were tobacco and grapes.

Table 14   Estimates of the value of the principal agricultural exports from Izmir, 1863–79
(annual averages in £,000,000)

	1863–4	*1865–70*	*1871–4*	*1875–9*
Cotton	1.471	0.899[1]	0.425	0.378
Wool	0.165	0.140[1]	0.192	0.459
Opium	0.709	0.568	0.675	0.486
Valonia	0.484	0.289	0.389	0.793
Tobacco			0.142	0.176
Raisins, figs and dried fruit	0.947	0.578	0.826	0.742
Cereals				0.272[2]

Source: British commercial reports and Quataert, 'Ottoman Reform'. 381.

Notes:
1 Excludes 1867.
2 Excludes 1875.

The area most directly influenced by the pull of the European market
was the coastal plain around Izmir and Aidin together with the rich lands in
the valleys of the Menderes and Gediz rivers flowing in from the East. Some
guide to the growth of output is provided by the increase in the value of
agricultural exports from Izmir itself, which rose from about £1,000,000 to
£2,000,000 during the 1850s and then doubled again during the 1860s (see
Table 14).[54] The crop to undergo the most dramatic advance was short-
staple cotton. Once the northern blockade of the southern American ports

Table 15 Estimates of the export of Anatolian cotton by volume, 1860–79 (bales*)

	Izmir	Mersin
1860	57,000	
1861	20,000	
1863	60,000	
1864	53–75,000	
1865	83,654	
1866	34,850	
1868	47,195	
1869	33,840	44,500
1870		17,600
1871	54,200	20,475
1872	55,100	23,175
1873	52,200	37,563
1874	57,430	14,800
1875	61,361	52,965
1876	75,073	33,375
1877	53,756	19,800
1878	34,980	14,785
1879	13,431	17,215

* The weight of a bale varied between 400 and 500 lb.

Sources: British and Belgian commercial reports; J. L. Farley, *The Resources of Turkey* (London, 1862), 58; Gould, 'Pashas and Brigands', 195 (figures converted as 1 bale = 400 lb).

became effective prices rose rapidly, from 250 to 300 piastres per quintal pre-war to between 700 and 1000 piastres per quintal in 1863 and perhaps as high as 1250 to 1300 piastres in 1864.[55] The result was a considerable extension of the area devoted to cotton and an increase in exports from something like between 5000 and 7000 bales in 1860 to a peak of over 80,000 bales in 1865 (see Table 15).[56] Some assistance came from the provincial government which distributed American and Egyptian seed and some agricultural implements, as well as allowing cultivators to grow cotton on waste land free of tax.[57] But for the most part the necessary infrastructure was created by Europeans and their local intermediaries. It was they who imported the gins and steam cleaning machines, they who erected the cotton presses, they who made arrangements to provide cultivators with working capital and to borrow the large amounts of gold coin necessary to buy the crop.[58] Others to profit from the situation were the district's merchants, many of them Greek or Armenian, who established themselves as retailers, money-lenders or purchasing agents in the villages of the interior.

Once the boom came to an end production fell away sharply but, as in Egypt, the area devoted to cotton remained very much higher than before the boom. Not only was it still a profitable proposition compared with most other alternatives but the existence of a network of agents and merchants also meant that many cultivators found themselves locked into a system by which the only way in which they could obtain the capital necessary to pay off their debts and to continue in agriculture was to go on growing the same marketable cash crop. Unlike Egypt, however, the end of the boom did not mean any falling off in the value of agricultural exports as a whole. Such was the variety of crops produced in the Izmir—Aydin area that any short-fall in one was generally made up by an increase in the demand for several of the others. As far as the 1870s were concerned the most important factors were the growth of American purchases of opium and the expanding market for valonia and for grapes and raisins, following the devastation wrought in the French vineyards by the disease phylloxera (see Table 14).

The production and export of such crops was further assisted by the construction of two European-owned railways. The first, built at a very slow rate between 1857 and 1866, connected Izmir to Aydin, a distance of 81 miles; while the second, also from Izmir, but started in 1864, reached Kasaba (62.5 miles) in 1866 and Alaşehir (another 47 miles) in 1872.[59] In spite of various early difficulties the effect on the local carrying trade was enormous and by the end of the 1860s the Kassaba line was said to have captured something like 90 per cent of the camel traffic coming down the Gediz valley while its rival had managed to take 50 per cent of the regular traffic to the south.[60] Once carriage rates had been reduced to a competitive level the speed, regularity and security of the goods trains encouraged most merchants to switch to the railways while both companies made every effort to generate more custom by establishing agencies in the towns just off the line where goods were collected and conveyed to the nearest station.[61] The effect on the transport of bulk agricultural goods was particularly important. Before the coming of the railways the high cost of carriage by camel meant there were definite limits to the area in which certain crops could be grown for export via Izmir. In the case of wheat, for example, it had never been possible to make a profit by selling anything produced at Uşak (only 100 miles away) for sale at the prices prevailing at the coast.[62] On the other hand, after the railways, and after the settlement of Circassian farmers from 1860s onwards, the districts beyond Uşak constituted the main cereal exporting region of Anatolia.

Apart from their role in encouraging agricultural production for export, the railways were also used as the spearhead of European economic penetration of the interior. By pushing the letter of the Capitulations to its limits the two companies made sure that they were left completely free in the management of their affairs, refusing even to recognize the jurisdiction of Turkish courts over any criminal matters connected with their operations.[63] At the same time Europeans resident in Izmir were quick to take advantage of the rise in land values along the railway routes to buy properties. They had already been doing this in the immediate vicinity of the town from at

The Middle East in the World Economy

Table 16 Estimates of the value of the sea-borne trade of Izmir, Trabzon and Mersin,
1850–79 (annual averages in millions of francs or £s)

	Izmir				Trabzon*		Mersin	
	Exports		Imports		Exports	Imports	Exports	Imports
	(francs)	(£)	(francs)	(£)	(francs)	(francs)	(francs)	(francs)
1850–4	34.4[1]		29.3		51.5	62.4		
1855–9	61.4		61.0		69.9[6]	78.7[6]		
1860–4	94.7[2]	3.53[5]	71.2[2]	2.92[5]	85.6[7]	94.4[7]		
1865–9	110.8[3]	3.58	51.7[3]	2.76	73.9[8]	47.8[8]		
1870–4	108.1[4]	4.19	105.0[4]	3.85	52.1[9]	65.7[9]	14.0	8.0
1875–9	102.3	4.11	91.3	3.66	31.7	36.2	14.9	13.6

* Includes transit trade with Persia.

Sources: Izmir – (francs) D. Georgiades, *Smyrne et l'Asia Mineure au point de vue economique et commerciale* (Paris, 1885), 188–9.
   (£) Madden, *Turkish Empire*, 538; J. L. Farley, *Banking in Turkey* (London, 1863), 20; Sir M. Stephenson, *Railways in Turkey* (London, 1859), 9; *CR* (Smyrna), 1872, *PP*, 1873, LXVII, 751–2 and 1877–81, *PP*, 1883, LXXIII, 334; McCulloch, *Dictionary*, 1st Supplement, ed. J. R. Reid (London, 1875), 89 and 2nd Supplement ed. J. R. Reid (London, 1877), 60.
Trabzon – C. Issawi, 'The Trabriz–Trabzon trade, 1830–1900: rise and decline of a route', *IJMES*, 1, 1 (Jan. 1970), 25. (These figures, taken from French consular sources, are generally higher than those produced by the Belgian consuls who may have excluded the silk trade.)
Mersin – Gould, 'Pasha and Brigands', 196.

Notes:
1 Excludes 1853; 2 Excludes 1861; 3 Excludes 1868/9; 4 Excludes 1870/1; 5 Excludes 1861/2;
   6 Excludes 1858; 7 Excludes 1863/4; 8 Excludes 1865; 9 Excludes 1871/2

least as early as the 1840s, often registering it in the name of an Ottoman subject to circumvent the legal prohibition on foreign ownership. Now they extended their purchases further inland, given added stimulus by the law of 1867 which extended rights over landed property to Europeans and others with Capitulatory privileges. It has been estimated that by the end of the 1860s a third of the agricultural land around Izmir belonged to Europeans: by 1878 half of it was owned by forty-one British merchants.[64]

As elsewhere in the Ottoman Empire, few foreigners actually worked their new estates. The majority preferred to employ a system of share-cropping – combined with pressure on the cultivators to produce specific export crops or, where this was possible, cash rents[65] – but a few may have worked at least a part of the property with wage labourers, some of whom travelled down the railway from the interior.[66] The same methods were also used by local property owners. An American commercial report describes the existence of large estates (*jiftliks*) in the Aidin district which were usually worked on a share-cropping basis by which the proprietor provided the working capital – including the seed and part of the expenses of reaping the cereals – in return for half the produce.[67] Extra labour was provided on a seasonal basis by peasants from outside the province, like the men who were brought over from the nearby Greek islands for the harvests or the bands of thirty or forty men who arrived from Konya or Eskişehir for the spring, summer and autumn only to return to their own fields in the winter.[68]

Other areas round the coast where there was an increase in the export of agricultural products were the districts near Bursa just across the Sea of Marmora from Istanbul, the Trabzon and Samsun/Amasya districts on the Black Sea and the plain around Mersin in the south-east (see Table 16). In the case of Bursa the main crop was silkworm eggs and cocoons, some of which were exported and some spun locally – either in simple workshops or in the increasing number of European-type reeling factories (see Table 17). Contemporary estimates of the size of the harvest vary widely but it may have been something of the order of 400,000 okes (1.4m. lbs) of cocoons in 1856 and 300,000 okes (1m. lbs) in 1862 before falling away during the rest of the 1860s and 1870s. The main period of the construction of European-type reeling factories took place during the attack of pébrine in France in the late 1850s: their numbers rising from just over 20 in 1853–5 to between 80 and 90 at the end of the decade (Table 17).[69]

Table 17 The production of silk thread in the Bursa district, 1850–69
(annual averages)

	Production		
	Vol. (,000 lb)	*Value* (£,000)	*No. of factories*
1850	961	972	18
1855–9	676	760	57
1860–4	373	737	91 (1861/2 only)
1865–9	307	561	
1870–4	276		
1875–9	187		

Sources: 'Reports . . . respecting factories for the spinning and weaving of textile fabrics abroad', *PP*, 1873, LXVIII, 187ff.

A little more is known about the development of agriculture on the lower Çukurova plain between Mersin and Adana. In spite of the general insecurity of the area some cotton was grown there at the beginning of the period, the greater part of it being sent north to Erzerum and Trabzon.[70] There was also a sufficient growth of cash crops to attract a regular inflow of seasonal wage-labour, mainly Turkoman.[71] As elsewhere, the high prices reached during the American Civil War period were sufficient to encourage a significant increase in production which was maintained until the early 1870s.[72] Gins and hydraulic presses were quickly introduced while new cultivators were attracted by the agricultural possibilities of the area from other parts of Anatolia. Further evidence of the increase in the production of cotton and other cash crops comes from the greater reliance on wage-labour: according to Davis between 50,000 and 70,000 workers arrived each summer to harvest the grain while another 12,000 to 15,000 came to pick and clean the cotton and to carry out other types of activity.[73] Another factor was the growth of exports through the local port of Mersin, a place which had developed from a small village just before the Crimean War to a thriving town of 2000 inhabitants in 1876.

The state and the Anatolian economy

Many of the leading Ottoman reformers are on record as anxious to develop the Turkish economy, demonstrating that they shared the increasingly powerful notion that the growth of productive resources was an essential ingredient of general progress.[74] The same notions are also to be found in the two general programmes of reform: the *Hatt-i Şerif* of Gulhane and the *Hatt-ı Hümayoun* of 1856. Further encouragement came from the European ambassadors and a whole host of bankers, entrepreneurs and merchants who argued over and over again that the only way out of the Empire's financial difficulties was to increase the taxable capacity of the population. Nevertheless, for all this talk the Ottoman government made very little positive effort to increase production. Limited financial resources, the lack of competent administrators, the growing technological gap between western Europe and the rest of the world, and the constraints imposed by Turkey's social structure and weakened international position all combined to set strict limits on the types of economic policies pursued. The nature of these limits can be seen with particular clarity in terms of government activity with regard to industry and trade, the agricultural sector and attempts to improve the system of transport.

To begin with industry, a number of Ottoman initiatives testify to the fact that some administrators (and perhaps the Sultan himself) were well aware of the dangers of becoming totally dependent on Europe for manufactured goods. An Industrial Reform (or Improvement) Commission was set up in the 1860s to investigate the existing state of particular industries as well as to make recommendations about how they might be improved. Trade fairs were organized at which Turkish goods were put on display. A school of industrial reform was opened in Istanbul in 1867.[75] But the effect was minimal. In the meantime, the fact that in 1861–2 the Ottomans finally obtained international consent to raise the external tariff to 8 per cent in exchange for the step-by-step reduction of duties on exports to 1 per cent did not provide a significant increase in the protection available to

local industry; while such harmful practices as taxing the internal movement of locally produced goods by Ottoman merchants were not ended
until 1874.[76] A good example of the deleterious consequences of this latter
policy concerns the many under-utilized flour mills of Istanbul which,
according to a British report, could have been kept going at something like
full capacity if only they had not had to pay a duty on the cereals they
brought into the city and on the finished product when it was sent out
again. Foreign flour, on the other hand, was only taxed once.[77] In these
circumstances the only local industries that could hope to flourish were
those that obtained some protection from European competition as a result
of high transport costs or those able to benefit from the relatively lower cost
of Anatolian agricultural produce. Manufacturing activity in the first
category included the many weavers of silk, wool and linen who continued
to exist in rural areas away from the many importing centres like those in
the Diarbekir district which, according to a British commercial report of
the early 1870s, clothed 'the greater part of the village, pastoral and town
population'.[78] The silk reeling factories of Bursa are perhaps the best
example of the successful use of a local crop. Another is the manufacture of
carpets in a number of west Anatolian towns, exports of which rose from an
annual average of £94,000 (1871–4) to £170,000 (1875–9).[79] However, in
almost all cases such activity was either begun by foreign entrepreneurs or
their local protégés, or, as in the case of the carpets, rapidly taken over by
them.[80]

But if the government was markedly unsuccessful in promoting new
industry it also paid less and less attention to the possibilities of continuing to
produce goods (and particularly military supplies) in its own factories. While
a few plants, augmented by a system of regimental workshops, continued to
manufacture uniforms, boots and some small-arms, by mid-century the pace
of European technological progress had made it increasingly difficult to
contemplate the local production of hand guns, artillery or ships.[81] In the
case of the guns it would seem likely that the major turning-point came with
the development of the rifled barrel in the 1840s, the manufacture of which
required much greater technical precision than that of the earlier smooth-
bore cannons or muskets. In the case of the navy, the need to maintain parity
with the steam-propelled iron-clads of its major European rivals meant that
few if any of the corvettes and frigates brought into service after 1850 could
be constructed in Turkish yards.[82]

Attempts to increase agricultural output took a number of forms. One
was the provision of direct assistance to cultivators, such as the distribution
of cotton seed during the American Civil War or the attempts to encourage
silk production a few years later by importing silkworm eggs from Japan to
replace those which were diseased or by ordering the planting of large
numbers of mulberry trees.[83] Another was the effort made to supply cheap

credit by establishing a network of rural, co-operative banks (*sendiks*) throughout the Empire. The aim of such banks was to obtain capital from their members and then to relend it to those in need, against the security of something of value. The scheme was first tried in the Danube Province of Tuna during the governorship of Midhat Pasha, and then extended to Anatolia and other areas from 1866 onwards. It does not seem to have been very successful in providing peasants with credit. The fact that its capital resources were limited and that the individual *sendiks* were administered by locally-elected councils must certainly have meant that most of what little cash was available was lent to the more well-to-do cultivators.[84] Given the unequal distribution of power in the rural areas and the Ottoman policy of incorporating landowners and merchants into the local administration, any scheme for assisting the local agricultural population was likely to end by benefiting only the richer strata.

The same process can be seen at work in the case of central government policies towards the land. In the Land Law of 1858 and its amendment in 1867 the Ottoman reformers returned to their twin task of trying to re-establish the state's legal right of ownership and providing each cultivator with that secure title to his fields without which, so it was thought, he would neither invest in improving production nor pay his taxes on a regular basis.[85] In the years before this legislation, according to Karpat, the government had been engaged in endless litigation in the courts with private individuals attempting to assert that the estates of *miri* and *waqf* land they controlled were really *mulk*; meanwhile large tracts of state land were kept uncultivated for fear that those who worked them might also seek to establish their own title to them.[86] Now, according to the provisions of the 1858 code, the usurpation of the state's rights was made more difficult in a number of ways, notably by reinforcing the existing prohibition against anyone putting up buildings on *miri* properties without official permission or planting them with a garden or vineyard, practices which were taken to extend ownership to the land underneath.[87] Against this, as many writers have underlined, the code can also be seen as a step in the direction of the creation of personal property. In particular, every piece of *miri* land was to be registered in the name of anyone who could prove that he had worked it continuously for a number of years; title deeds (known as *tapus*) acknowledging right of use were to be granted; communal ownership was forbidden.[88] Furthermore, other provisions confirmed and sometimes extended the rights of holders of *miri* land, allowing them to pass it on to their descendants or, in certain circumstances, to other close relatives. Those who controlled agricultural *waqfs* which had originally been converted from *miri* land, either by one of the sultans or with their permission, were also to receive *tapu* titles, after registration, and to enjoy the same rights of inheritance.[89]

Two of the consequences of this attempt to combine the provision of secure private title with the reassertion of state control are of the greatest importance. The first was that further movement towards the creation of full legal ownership was slow. Even after some further concessions in 1867 – notably an extension of the categories of relatives who could inherit registered property – it was still not possible either to mortgage land nor, until 1901, to hold it in partnership without official permission.[90] Only after the First World War were the rights regarding *miri* and *mulk* formally assimilated. Second, given the increasing value of agricultural land, the distribution of power in the rural areas, and peasant suspicion of central authority, it is not surprising that in those areas of Anatolia where a programme of registration took place title was often given not to the actual cultivator but to people with local influence.[91] In some cases claims to land were forged, a process which was greatly assisted by the poor state of the land registers; in others peasants allowed their fields to be registered in the name of powerful protectors for fear that registration might be a prelude to a demand for more taxes or for conscription. Just how widespread such practices were it is impossible to say. To begin with, at least, the process of granting *tapus* proceeded very slowly owing to difficulties with the cadastral survey with which it was supposed to be accompanied: by 1870 such surveys seem to have been confined to the areas round Bursa and Izmir in the west and the Aintab and Antakya/Antioch districts in the south-east.[92] This is one reason why the importance of land policy should not be exaggerated. Another is that the fact that while the possession of legal title was one thing, the ability to benefit from it was quite another. Thus there were probably many cases where although an estate might be registered in the name of one man, perhaps a city dweller, the peasants continued to till it in customary fashion and could only be persuaded to pay rent after a show of force. Perhaps most important of all, code or no code, control of large stretches of land would certainly have passed into the hands of wealthy merchants, tribal chieftains and others. Nevertheless, for all this, it remains true that, where it was applied, far from assisting the emergence of a class of small cultivators with clear title to the land the Ottoman system of land registration often had exactly the opposite effect.

A second significant piece of land legislation was a second law of 1867 granting foreigners the right to own landed property in the Ottoman Empire. Such a concession had long been demanded by the representatives of the European powers; it had also been promised in the *Hatt-ı Hümayoun* of 1856, and there were many who saw it as a means of encouraging the further application of foreign capital and foreign companies to Turkish agriculture. Fuad and Ali Paşas, however, were unwilling formally to concede this right until the Europeans, for their part, had agreed to forgo any of the Capitulatory privileges which might be thought to apply to lands

owned by their own nationals.[93] Once again Ottoman intentions were sub-
verted: even though the 1867 law contained a clause stating that foreigners
could only hold land on the same basis as local subjects, subject to the same
regulations and taxes, this was offset by a sentence in the protocol which
stated that the land in question 'ne porte aucune atteinte aux immunitées
consacrées par les traités et qui continueront à courier la personne et les
biens meublés des étrangers devenus proprietaires d'immeubles'.[94] In other
words, as Du Velay correctly pointed out, once it was established that the
domicile of foreign land-owners was to remain inviolable and could only be
entered by the police with the express permission of the relevant consulate it
was impossible to enforce the laws relating to land or the judgments of local
courts against European proprietors in the face of consular opposition.[95]

A third sphere of government activity was that of transport. If there was
one thing which both resident Europeans and Ottoman reformers were
agreed on it was that there would be no real economic progress without the
construction of proper roads and railways, thus reducing the cost of
carriage and allowing cultivators in the interior to start producing for the
foreign market. Consular report after consular report provided facts and
figures designed to prove this same point. Thus, according to an official at
the British Embassy at Istanbul it cost four times more to send wheat over a
given distance than it did in the United States, while another dispatch
speaks of the times when a shortage of pack animals prevented cultivators in
the interior from sending their crop to the coast at a profit.[96] As a result any
surplus generally remained locked up in the interior while towns only two or
three days ride from grain-producing districts were forced to import cereals
from abroad.[97] To remedy this situation a number of roads were begun
during the 1850s and 1860s, but with no very great success. J. L. Farley, in
his *Egypt, Cyprus, and Asiatic Turkey*, described such an attempt: the
efforts to improve the track between Trabzon and Erzerum. Work was
begun in 1852 only to be stopped after the construction of a few miles of new
road, on the grounds of expense. Nothing then happened until 1864 when,
after a survey by European experts, another 20 km or so were built before
once again construction was brought to a halt on the grounds of rising costs.
Only after operations were entrusted to an army officer using a corvée of
local labour was the whole 350 km of road finally completed.[98] But the story
did not end there: a report of 1873 complains that the surface was already in
such disrepair that it was almost impassable.[99] Few provincial administrations had money to spend on public works and the little that was achieved
was usually the work of the military, for example the Mersin/Adana road
built by the Reform Division between 1867 and 1873.[100]

In these circumstances, efforts to improve the system of internal
transport depended either on the fortuitous arrival of the Circassian
refugees with their high-wheeled ox or bullock-drawn carts (*arabas*) or the

introduction of railways. Davis mentions the amount of business carried out by Circassian drivers in the Adana district in the 1870s and it seems likely that such men were responsible for reintroducing the wheel into many parts of Anatolia (and Syria) where they were settled.[101] As for the railways, these rapidly became the chosen instrument of the Ottoman government for opening up areas round the coastal fringe and it was prepared to go to some lengths to attract the necessary European capital and expertise required. The main inducement was the offer of a guaranteed return on capital. In the case of the Izmir/Aydin line, for instance, this took the form of an agreement to guarantee interest of 6 per cent on costs of construction which were initially estimated at 30.5 million francs. Later, as the company ran into both financial and engineering difficulties, the government was twice persuaded to accept an increase in the sum guaranteed, first to 45.5 million francs (March 1861) and then to 47.5 million francs (July 1863), thus making it much easier for the entrepreneurs to raise the extra money they required.[102] The fact that the company did not begin to make a profit until 1869 must have involved the government in a considerable outlay, so much so that it only agreed to allow the further extension of the line in 1879 on condition that the sum it might be required to pay in one year did not exceed £34,000.[103] The other line (Izmir/Kasaba) was more successful. It too had received an initial guarantee of 6 per cent on costs of construction of 20 million francs, but such were the profits it made that it was soon able to renounce any government support and to make its own way.[104]

After these difficult early experiences the government turned, briefly, to an attempt to build the lines itself, using the advice and assistance of foreign engineers as well as, in some cases, European contractors. But this too presented great problems. The first stretch of line — 57 miles from Adapazari on the Asian side of the Bosphorus to Ismit — was so badly constructed that it needed constant improvement while the short stretch of track from Mudanya (on the Sea of Marmora) to Bursa, completed in 1875, could not be used as it went up a hill that was too steep for its locomotives to climb. Finally, efforts to extend the Adapazari/Ismit line in the direction of Ankara were abandoned after 6 or 7 kilometres for lack of funds.[105] The story is not without a moral: having tried — and failed — to use Turkey's own resources of money and manpower for the purposes of economic development the government was, once again, forced to rely on European assistance organized and controlled by the powerful Public Debt Administration established in 1881.

5 Egypt, 1850–1882 : from foreign borrowing to bankruptcy and occupation

In many important essentials Egypt followed the same path as Turkey via large-scale foreign borrowing to bankruptcy and increased European control. As with the Ottomans, a series of ambitious rulers began to introduce programmes of development and reform which soon required a great deal more money than could be raised from local revenue. Egypt also acquired enormous financial obligations under the disastrous agreements with De Lesseps and the company formed to construct the Suez Canal. The result was recourse to a number of temporary expedients – loans from local banks, the issue of short-term bonds – followed by continued access to the much greater source of funds to be found in the European money markets. Again as with the Ottomans, a succession of larger and larger loans led quickly to an increase in the sums required to service the debts well beyond the state's ability to manage. Egypt's official declaration of bankruptcy, in April 1876, followed Turkey's by just seven months.

If the progress of foreign borrowing was more or less the same in both Cairo and Istanbul the consequences were not. To begin with, much of the money which Egypt obtained from abroad was used not on the armed forces or on the administration of a large empire but, directly or indirectly, on the encouragement of agriculture, and in particular on the cultivation of cotton, to a point at which it would be true to say that by the late 1870s the entire Delta had been converted into an export sector devoted to the production, processing and export of two or three crops. Second, when it came to a final settlement with their creditors, Egypt was in a very much weaker position than Turkey. Its smaller size, its strategic situation across the route to the east, the ambiguity of its relations with its former Ottoman masters, all combined to encourage those who had lent it money – usually backed by their governments – to impose harsher terms on Cairo than on Istanbul; and then, when these terms seemed to be challenged by a movement of Egyptian protest against increasing foreign domination, the country was occupied by foreign troops, a fate not suffered by the Turks of Anatolia until defeat at the end of the First World War.

The growth of the public debt:
the financial policies of Abbas, Said and Ismail

The tendency, apparent throughout Muhammad Ali's reign, for expenditure to outrun revenue certainly did not come to an end with the Treaty of London (which limited the size of the Egyptian army) or the more cautious policies of his later years. Whatever savings might have come from a reduction in military spending, the closing of factories and schools and the transfer of part of the cost of rural administration to the holders of private estates were certainly balanced by the loss of income consequent on the enforced withering away of the system of state monopolies.

The same imbalance persisted through the reign of Abbas (1849–54). In spite of the fact that he too pursued a policy of financial retrenchment, closing down more schools and further reducing military expenditure, revenue was still insufficient to meet the cost of administration, of the ruler's private expenses, and of the one major public works project which Abbas found it expedient to allow – the Cairo/Alexandria railway.[1] Further pressure on receipts came from the system by which a ruler was succeeded not by his eldest son but by his oldest male relative. This led everyone from Muhammad Ali onwards to attempt to protect their offspring from financial problems after their death by encouraging them to build up large fortunes for themselves, diverting a great deal of public money for this purpose. In the case of Abbas it was estimated that his son, Ilhami, inherited estates worth £3,200,000 at a time when total government receipts were no more than £2,200,000 (see Table 18).[2] It was the need to meet the continuing gap between revenue and expenses which led Abbas to attempt to revive Muhammad Ali's monopoly over the export of agricultural goods during the last two years of his reign and which also forced him to take a loan of £400,000 from the Peninsular and Orient Steamship Company in 1852.[3]

Abbas's successor, Said (1854–62) was a great deal more ambitious. In the early years of his reign he launched a number of expensive public works, notably the repair of the Delta Barrage, the doubling of the single railway track between Cairo and Alexandria and its extension to Suez, and the excavation of the Mahmudiya Canal. He also sought to develop the country's resources by the promotion of joint Egyptian–European companies like the Nile Navigation Company, which was intended to run a steamer service on the Nile, and the Medjidiah company for trade between Suez and the Red Sea coast. All this was expensive enough, but the cost was vastly increased by the growing number of European entrepreneurs and adventurers who were able to exploit Said's friendship and the growing power of the European consuls to extract either concessions or indemnity for the alleged loss of concessions from the Egyptian government.[4] The result was disastrous. In the case of the Nile Navigation Company, for instance, which ended its short life in failure in 1858, the ruler was persuaded to compensate investors by buying up their shares at an enormous premium at a total cost to the Treasury of £340,000.[5] Far and away the most important

Table 18 Estimates of Egyptian government revenues and expenditures, 1852–79 (£Em.)*

	Revenues					Expenditure	
	Land tax	Muqabala	Railways	Customs	Total	Service on external debt	Total
1852	1.74				2.143		1.96
1853					2.19		1.91
1854	1.64				2.2		2.82
1855	1.4/2.0				2.08/2.4		2.38
1856					2.47/2.4		2.64
1857					2.21		2.13
1858	2.5				2.03		2.21
1859					2.12		2.17
1860					2.15		3.0
1861	2.76			0.45	2.15/3.58		5.18/4.75
1862	2.88			0.51	3.71/3.42	0.13	8.87/6.09
1863					6.09	0.26	14.4
1864 (1580)			0.24	1.23	7.0/4.94	0.26	13.55
1865 (1581)			0.28	1.09	5.36	0.88	10.79
1866 (1582)			0.34	0.76	5.06/5.71	1.25	10.28
1867 (1583)			0.26	0.62	4.13/5.94	1.72	10.85
1868 (1584)			0.35	0.47	5.01/6.93	1.72	16.64
1869 (1585)			0.35	0.48	5.26/7.28	3.17	10.53/6.04
1870 (1586)			0.35	0.44	5.39/7.18	3.64	12.31
1871 (1587)			0.55	0.46	5.71/7.19	3.77	15.08
1872 (1588)	4.846	5.07	0.62	0.51	7.29/12.16	3.74	6.42
1873 (1589)	3.67	3.16	0.75	0.54/0.62	9.91/10.57	3.7	8.82
1874 (1590)			0.75/0.88		9.91	6.23	8.82
1875			0.99		10.54	5.7	10.03
1876	4.2		0.97	0.62	7.65/10.77		7.84
1877					9.53		8.55
1878					7.52		7.78
1879					8.47		8.3

* Some figures are for years on the Gregorian calendar, others for the Coptic year (given in brackets) which was used for the Egyptian financial year. Note also the comment in the contemporary newspaper *Le Nil*, 7 Oct. 1873: 's'il est un pays ou un budget ne signifie absolument rien, c'est bien l'Egypte'.

Sources:
Land tax: Enclosure in Green (Alexandria), 1 May 1858, FO 78/1401; Senior, *Conversations*, I, 102, 182; Hamza, *Public Debt*, 34, 212; Cave, 'Report', 113.
Muqabala: Hamza, *Public Debt*, 209, 212.
Railways: Cave, 'Report', 116; Hamza, *Public Debt*, 213; Anon, *Finances of Egypt*.
Customs: Hamza, *Public Debt*, 36, 212; Cave, 'Report', 104; Anon, *Finances of Egypt*.
Total: Girgis Hanayn quoted in Crouchley, *Economic Development*, 274–6.
Revenue: Senior, *Conversations*, I, 102, 182; J. Cattaui, *Le Khedive Isma'il et la dette de l'Egypte* (Cairo, 1935), 18; Hamza, *Public Debt*, 212; Cave, 'Report', 111; Anon, *Finances of Egypt*.
Service on external debt: Hamza, *Public Debt*, 242.
Total Expenditure: Hanayn in Crouchley, *Economic Development*, 274–6; Hamza, *Public Debt*, 35.

example of the dangerous financial consequences of the award of a concession to a foreigner, however, was the initial agreement between Said and
his friend Ferdinand De Lesseps setting out the terms under which the Suez
Canal was to be constructed. Not only did the government stand to lose a
valuable source of income from the transit in mails and passengers crossing
Egypt from Alexandria to Suez, not only did it agree to provide a corvée of
20,000 labourers a year, not only did it abandon its rights to the land along
both the main canal and a second one to be built from the Nile to the new
city of Ismailia to provide fresh water for the workers, but it also let itself in
for a huge financial obligation involving the agreed purchase of 64,000 of
the initial issue of 400,000 (500 franc) shares.[6] If this was not enough, when
subscriptions were first opened to the public in 1858 and only just over half
were taken up – making it impossible to constitute the company under
French law – De Lesseps persuaded Said to purchase almost all the rest.[7]

Against this, Said made little attempt to improve revenues and the small
increase in the sums raised by the land tax and the even smaller profit from
the railways were nothing like sufficient to meet his needs.[8] After a short
period of borrowing from a number of the new European banks which were
then being established in Alexandria he responded eagerly to another of De
Lesseps's suggestions: the issue of Treasury Bonds.[9] These bonds were
initially personal and non-transferable, but then when it was discovered
that this allowed them to tap only a tiny part of their potential market they
were made negotiable and issued for three months or longer with an interest
of 6 per cent.[10] Later, a second type, so-called 'bons d'appointment', were
used to pay government employees.[11] By 1859 there was already £2,000,000
of government paper in circulation; the next year, after more bonds were
issued to meet a first call of 100 francs on Egypt's Suez Canal shares, there
was £3,500,000.[12]

It was at this stage that Said obtained his first foreign loan, a private one
raised for him personally by the Paris branch of Charles Lafitte et Cie and
the Comptoir d'Escompte. Although for a nominal sum of 28 million
francs, the amount actually received was only 21 million francs, the first
instalment of which was received in September 1860.[13] Under the terms of
the loan, Said agreed not to issue any more Treasury Bonds, but in spite of
some ineffectual attempts at financial retrenchment this proved impossible
and the government continued to meet its obligations with short-term
paper, though under another name.[14] Estimates of the size of the floating
debt vary widely but it may have been anywhere between £7,000,000 and
£10,000,000 by the summer of 1861 and perhaps as much as £11,000,000 at
the end of the same year.[15] Meanwhile, the budgetary deficit had reached
an estimated £3,000,000.[16] With deficits of this size another foreign loan
was almost inescapable. In 1861 Said tried the Comptoir d'Escompte again
but found its terms too onerous and in 1862 he turned to a syndicate of

English and French banks organized by the house of Oppenheim and Nephew of Alexandria, agreeing to borrow £3,292,800 to be repaid over thirty years at the rate of £262,735 per annum.[17] How much was actually received is open to question. Hamza estimates it at £2,500,000.[18] Landes, on the basis of a memoir prepared for Oppenheims in 1866, puts it at no more than £2,140,320, and probably less.[19] As most of the loan was eagerly subscribed by investors, first at 82½ then at 84½, Landes's figure would mean that the amount taken in commission and other hidden charges was enormous.[20]

It was a few months later that Said died, to be succeeded in January 1863 by his nephew Ismail. The exact financial condition of Egypt at this time is again unclear. Hamza suggests a floating debt of £E12,500,000.[21] But as most contemporary estimates almost certainly derive from the new ruler himself, and as it was clearly in his interests to blame his uncle for as much as possible, such figures must be treated with caution. What is probably more important anyway is the way in which Said's over-generous concessions imposed an immediate financial burden on his successor. Not only had he agreed to pay 34,000,000 francs to shareholders in the now defunct Medjidiah company but at the end of 1862 the government had to meet another call of 200 francs a share by De Lesseps. By a Convention of March 1863 with the Suez Canal Company, Ismail confirmed his obligations under all earlier agreements and undertook to pay the remaining 200 francs a share (or a total of 35,000,000 francs) at a rate of 1,500,000 francs a month beginning in January 1864.[22]

Nevertheless, the financial situation, though dangerous, was not yet desperate. The cotton boom induced by the American Civil War was at its height, Europeans were opening new banks and floating new companies with increasing enthusiasm and there seemed no reason to suppose that the economy would not continue to develop at a rapid rate. Thus emboldened, Ismail himself embarked on an even more expensive programme of public works projects and joint companies than his predecessor while at the same time showing himself ready to spend considerable sums of money on obtaining greater political independence from Istanbul and on regaining some of the sovereignty abandoned by Said both to the Suez Canal Company and to the European consulates – particularly in the matter of Egypt's judicial rights over foreign nationals.[23]

The bills were not slow to come in. In 1863 he began to borrow money from local banks, and early in 1864 he was already being urged by Europeans to put his financial affairs in order with the aid of a public loan. For a moment he resisted: such a loan would necessitate the undignified task of seeking formal approval from the Ottoman Sultan. What finally seems to have tipped the balance were the harsh terms of Napoleon III's arbitration in the dispute between Ismail and the Suez Canal Company over the return of some of the concessions granted by Said. According to the French Emperor's decision, Egypt would have to pay the company 38,000,000 francs for the loss of the corvée labour which it no longer wished to provide, 30,000,000 francs for the return of land, 10,000,000 francs for work already undertaken along the fresh-water canal and 6,000,000 francs for the loss of exemption from certain tolls – a grand total of 84,000,000 francs (£3,360,000) or about a whole year's revenues.[24] Ismail's first public loan followed almost immediately, in September 1864. It was floated by Oppenheims at 93 and was for £5,700,000. Of this the sum actually received was £4,864,963 or 85.33 per cent, the remainder going to the bankers and other agents as what was called 'jouissance'.[25]

Table 19   Egypt's foreign loans, 1862–73 (£m.)

	Amount of loan	Rate of issue (%)	Amount received	Nominal interest (%)	Real interest (%)
1862	3293	83	2.5[1]	7	9
1864	5704	93	4.864	7	8.2
1865	3387	90	2.750	7	8.6
1866	3000	92	2.640	7	8.0
1867	2080	90	1.700	9	11.0
1868	11,890	75	7.193	7	11.5
1870	7143	75	5.000	7	10.0
1873	32,000	70	19.974	7	11.0
Total	68,497		46.621		

Source: Hamza, *Public Debt*, 256–7.

Note: 1 According to evidence quoted by Landes, Said only received some 65 per cent of the nominal value of this loan or £2,140,000; *Bankers and Pashas*, 117n, 340.

In the years that followed, Ismail obtained a further six loans for a nominal sum of £60,000,000 of which he received £40,000,000 (see Table 19). Inevitably the terms became increasingly onerous, although never anything like as bad as those offered to the Ottomans, and the last big loan of 1873/4 could still be issued at between 70 and 82½. Meanwhile, the continued issue of Treasury Bonds and other short-term paper pushed the floating debt up to perhaps as high as £35,000,000 in 1873.[26] As in Turkey, the sums required to service borrowing of this size soon took an impossibly large proportion of the budget. In 1872/3, according to Hamza, £3,800,000 was needed for the external debt and another £3,700,000 for the internal one, or 70 per cent of estimated revenue.[27] Thus, by the early 1870s, the government was already to resort to desperate measures such as the *muqabala* law of 1872 which promised that anyone who paid six years land tax in advance would be freed from half of his future tax obligations for ever.[28] Then, in 1875, the Egyptian government's shares in the Suez Canal Company were sold to Britain for £4,000,000. But this was still not enough. Early in 1876 the Treasury was being forced to borrow short term at up to 30 per cent in order to meet its obligations and in April of that same year it announced that it was going to have to postpone payment of the interest on the debt for three months. This was taken by its creditors as a declaration of bankruptcy.[29]

The parallels with the Ottoman experience are striking; but there were also important differences. One concerned the uses to which the borrowed money was put. Taking the eight loans of the period together they jointly produced a sum of £47,000,000 (see Table 19). To this must be added the money borrowed locally but not yet repaid — perhaps as much as £28,000,000 by 1875 — and the sums realized as a result of a regular surplus of ordinary revenues over ordinary expenditures.[30] How was this money spent?

As in the case of the Ottoman Empire, there were plenty of Europeans who suggested that all, or almost all, of the sums borrowed by the government had been wasted. This was particularly the case of men like Lord Cromer, anxious to use Ismail's alleged financial incompetence as a justification for the British occupation and subsequent British control.[31] However, although it is possible to cite numerous instances of money being spent on the building of palaces or the bribing of Ottoman officials this cannot possibly be the whole picture.[32] In the first place, like Turkey, a large part of the money transferred to Egypt in loans, perhaps as much as £36,200,000 by the end of 1875, was returned to Europe in payment of the sums owed as principal and interest to the country's foreign creditors.[33] Meanwhile, of the remainder, a considerable amount was spent on works of economic improvement. This would certainly include part of the proceeds of three loans (those of 1865, 1867 and 1870), totalling £9,450,000, which were used by Ismail himself to build up his private estates and to build sugar factories on them.[34] It would also include the very much larger amounts used for railway construction or port improvement and probably the only serious argument for great waste concerns the Suez Canal which according to Hamza cost the government £16,000,000 in one way or another and for which the £4,000,000 received for the sale of the shares to Britain was obviously small recompense.[35]

Figures for the total amount of money spent on public works projects during Ismail's reign can be found in a number of sources and generally amount to between £30,000,000 and £32,000,000.[36] They must not be taken too seriously, however, as it seems likely that they were all produced specifically to impress the country's European creditors that the money borrowed had been well spent.[37] Nevertheless, there is probably no reason to quarrel with some of the details. This is certainly the case with the estimates of the sums of between £10,000,000 and £13,000,000 employed to build over 1200 miles of new railway between 1863 and 1875. Many of the large towns in the Delta, including the important cotton centre of Zagazig, were added to the system while by 1874 the track had been extended as far as Asyut in Upper Egypt. Unlike other parts of the Middle East there was little competition from other forms of land transport and the Egyptian railways were able to capture much of the traffic in bulk goods even when charging relatively high tariffs.[38] Other examples of large-scale expenditure on public works include the excavation of new canals and the dredging of old ones (which Crouchley estimates as costing £12,600,000), the construction of nearly 9500 miles of telegraph lines (anywhere between £500,000 and £1,000,000) and the building of numerous bridges across the Nile.[39] Just as important from the point of view of developing the country's trade were the much needed improvements made to the harbour at Alexandria, a port which by 1870 had become the fourth most important in the Mediterranean in terms of the tonnage of ships using it.[40] Against this the sums spent on increasing the size of the army and navy and on providing them with modern weapons did not take up anything like such a large proportion of total expenditure as in Turkey. By the mid-1870s the armed forces consisted of some 90,000 men and were costing the government just under £1,000,000 a year.[41]

Nevertheless, in spite of the sums spent on public works and the general increase in agricultural output during the 1860s and 1870s, revenues did not increase fast enough to meet the heavy obligations incurred in borrowing from abroad. If the large sums raised from the *muqabala* are excluded, total receipts grew from just under £3,500,000 in 1863 to slightly over double this amount in the mid-1870s (see Table 18). Of this increase the rise in the land tax and net profits from the railway contributed about two-thirds. Whether the government could reasonably have supposed that it would be able to recoup the money it had spent on the development of the country's infrastructure over such a short period is doubtful; but what is certainly true is that its own position was made very much worse by a system of land tax collection which was both inefficient and, in an important sense, so arbitrary that it acted to inhibit a more rapid growth in agricultural output. One of the most serious anomalies was the difference in the rates of tax applied to the category of land known as *ushuriya* (which in 1877 paid only £0.30 a feddan) and that known as *kharajiya* (which paid £1.162).[42] Not only was *ushuriya* land likely to be the most fertile — it was held almost exclusively by the richer property holders — but its area also tended to increase rapidly over time as people with power and influence managed to get their *kharajiya* land reclassified. Thus, while the amount of *kharajiya* land stayed more or less constant between 1863 and 1877, that in the *ushuriya* category nearly doubled, so that, at the end of the period, it represented about a quarter of the total cultivated area (see Table 20).

To the loss of revenue represented by the under-taxation of so much

Table 20   Estimates of the area of *kharajiya* and *ushuriya* land in Egypt, 1863—77
(millions of feddans)

	ushuriya	kharajiya	Total
1863	0.636	3.759	4.395
1588 (Coptic) 1871/2	1.156	3.467	4.624
1590 (Coptic) 1873/4	1.244	3.167	
1591 (Coptic) 1874/5	1.291	3.614	4.805
1875	1.194	3.509	4.703
1877	1.282	3.461	4.743

Source: Owen, *Cotton*, 148; Hamza, *Public Debt*, 213.

fertile land must be added a haphazard system of collection which continued to allow members of the provincial administration and their allies
among the merchants and estate holders both to extract far more than the
legal limit and to keep some of the surplus for themselves.[43] As to other
sources of revenue, efforts to raise the sums collected from the European
community continued to be thwarted by the invocation of Capitulatory
privileges. Foreigners could only with difficulty be persuaded to pay tax on
land they owned while various attempts to impose a house tax on those who
lived in Cairo and Alexandria were regularly prevented by Consular opposition.[44] In these circumstances there was little hope that enough revenue
could be raised in the short run to meet Egypt's financial obligations.

Egypt and its creditors : the financial arrangements of 1876—80 and their consequences

Between 1876 and 1880 a number of projects were devised by Egypt's
foreign creditors to regulate its financial affairs. They all had two main
characteristics. First, they combined an unwillingness to reduce the size of
the funded (public) or of the floating debts with a considerable overestimate of the annual sums which the country could afford to pay in
interest and amortization.[45] The result was the imposition of a series of
burdens greater than Egypt could bear, particularly in the depressed agricultural conditions of the late 1870s. Second, each scheme involved an increasing degree of European financial control, whether viewed in terms of
the numbers of foreign officials appointed to supervise the various arrangements or in terms of their power.

The first of the foreign plans was devised by an Englishman, Stephen
Cave, the British Government's Paymaster-General, after a visit to Egypt
early in 1876 and came to nothing.[46] It was quickly followed by a second —
devised by the representatives of a group of French creditors — which was
accepted by the Khedive Ismail in May 1876. This involved a scheme to con-
solidate the total funded and floating debt at £91,000,000 with a new loan

which would be repaid over 65 years at 7 per cent. The sum required for annual servicing came to £6,444,000, or two-thirds of that year's revenues.[47] However, the scheme was so obviously in the interests of a group of French banks which held a sizeable share of the floating debt (for which they were to receive a 25 per cent bonus on conversion) that it was unable to obtain the necessary international support.[48]

Table 21   Estimates of the amount of money spent on Egyptian public works (£,000,000)

	1863–73[1]	1863–75[2]	1863–75[3]	1863–79[4]
Railways	10.000	9.899	13.310	13.361
Canals				12.000
Bridges	0.246			2.150
Telegraphs	0.350			0.853
Alexandria harbour	2.000	1.211		2.542
Lighthouses	0.165	0.174		0.180
Cairo/Alexandria (general improvements)	1.500	3.500		
Khedive's sugar				6.100

Sources:
1 Anon, *Finances of Egypt*.
2 R. H. L., *Financial Position of Egypt*, 7–8, 25.
3 Cave, 'Report', 106.
4 Sammarco, *Histoire*, III, 288.

The third scheme, also produced in 1876, was the joint work of two representatives of the British and French bond-holders: George Goschen, a former Liberal Cabinet minister and Edmond Joubert, a director of the Banque de Paris.[49] Its principal innovation was the division of the debt into four separate categories. First, it suggested that Ismail's borrowings for his own large private estate (485,000 feddans of land known as the Daira Saniya and the Daira Khassa) should be dealt with as a special case. The unpaid balance of the 1870 loan, which was secured on these estates, together with the Dairas' own floating debt were estimated together as £8,815,000, to be repaid with an annual interest of 5 per cent out of the estates' own revenues.[50] The second category consisted of shares in three loans which were due for early repayment – those of 1864, 1866 and 1867. Their unpaid balance was placed at £5,134,110 and interest fixed at 7 per cent. Money from the *muqabala* was assigned as security. Third, a special preference debt was created for holders of a selection of some of the bonds issued for the remaining outstanding loans – those of 1862, 1868 and 1873 (the 1866 loan had already been repaid). This privileged debt was placed at £17,000,000, to be secured on the revenues of Alexandria harbour and the state railways and repayable at 5 per cent over sixty-five years. Finally, all the remainder of the debts – shares in the rest of the 1862, 1868 and 1873 loans as well as in the floating debt calculated at 10 per cent above their face value — were lumped together as a unified debt of £59,000,000 to be repaid at 6 per cent over sixty-five years. Taking the scheme as a whole, Egypt's total indebtedness was placed at £89,308,000, a tiny reduction from the earlier French scheme, carrying an annual charge of £6,000,000.[51]

The Goschen—Joubert arrangements remained in operation until 1880 but with increasing difficulties. Once again, the sum required to service the debt was too large for the country to support. The shortage of water for irrigation as a result of the low Nile of 1877 — the worst of the century — and the consequent reduction in agricultural output only made matters worse. So too did the dispatch of a contingent of 25,000 troops to assist in the Russo-Turkish War. Thus, by 1878, interest payments on the debt could only be made with the greatest difficulty, many government officials were left without salaries and the deficit on the ordinary budget had reached £3,440,000.[52] In these circumstances Egypt's foreign financial controllers decided that the only way to avoid a second bankruptcy was to set up a Commission of Inquiry to suggest ways of bridging the gap. As a temporary palliative the Commission's preliminary report in 1878 recommended that title to the private estates belonging to the rest of the royal family (the so-called Domains of 425,000 feddans) be used as security for a new loan and their income of nearly £450,000 a year used as extra budgetary support.[53] However, the first part of this plan proved largely unsuccessful as the contractors for the new loan, Rothschilds of London and Paris, refused to release more than a small fraction of what had been raised until they were satisfied that all rival claims to any part of the royal estates had been dealt with in the newly constituted Egyptian Mixed Courts. This process took a year. In the meantime the authorities only managed to maintain payment on the debt by means of a number of unofficial bank loans.[54] The second, final, report of the Commission of Inquiry followed in April 1879. Its recommendations included on the one hand a reduction in the annual service charge by means of a diminution in the rate of interest, on the other, an attempt to increase Egypt's revenue by taxing *ushuriya* land at the same rate as *kharajiya*. Opposition to this latter proposal by both the Khedive and the large landowners led quickly to the tabling of an Egyptian counter-proposal and then to the deposition of Ismail himself.[55] The ruler's final suggestion, just before he left for Istanbul, that he pay his creditors with a further issue of Treasury Bonds is a further indication of how impossible Egypt's financial situation had become.

A second commission, the Commission of Liquidation, was formed the following year and it was its report, embodied in the Law of Liquidation of July 1880, which formed the basis of the final financial settlement between Egypt and its creditors. Under this settlement the unified debt was augmented by the inclusion of the unpaid balance of the 1864, 1865 and 1867 loans while the privileged debt was expanded to include 70 per cent of the floating debt (which had still continued to accumulate since 1876) converted at £5,744,000. With the addition of the remains of the Daira debt and provision for the repayment of the loan contracted by Rothschilds in 1878, the total consolidated debt was placed at £98,378,000. On the other hand, the lowering of the rate of interest on the unified debt from 6 to 4 per cent allowed the annual service charge to be reduced to £4,243,000.[56] That this was still at the very limits of what the country could afford is shown by the difficulties experienced by Lord Cromer and the British and French officials in maintaining debt payments in the first years of the occupation even after a substantial overhaul of the system of revenue collection and financial administration.[57] Meanwhile, other features of the Law of Liquidation included the final abolition of the *muqabala*, which was now treated as a loan from cultivators to be repaid at the rate of £150,000 a year for fifty years and the amalgamation of *ushuriya* with *kharajiya* land as soon as a new cadastral survey made this possible.[58]

The second aspect of the series of financial schemes just described was the fact that they involved a steady expansion of European (mainly British and French) control over Egypt's finances. The first plan (of May 1876) was accompanied by the establishment of a Caisse de la Dette, with directors from Britain, France, Italy and Austria, and later from Russia, to receive those revenues assigned directly for debt repayment. The Goschen—Joubert scheme at the end of the same year produced two further innovations: the appointment of two Controllers-General, one (British) with overall supervision of government receipts, the other (French) to oversee expenditure, and the creation of a Commission de la Dette Publique to look after the actual collection of revenues assigned to pay the interest on the privileged debt, in particular the railways, the Post Office and the Port of Alexandria. The next stage of European involvement was reached early in 1878 with strong British and French diplomatic pressure on the Khedive to allow a 'full and complete' examination of the country's finances by a Commission of Inquiry.[59] Then, soon after the publication of its preliminary report, two of its leading members, Rivers Wilson of Britain and Ernest-Gabriel de Blignières of France, were invited to join the Khedive's Council of Ministers in an executive capacity, the former as Minister of Finance, the latter as Minister of Public Works. The movement towards greater control received a check with Ismail's dismissal of these same two ministers in April 1879, but this was quickly reversed by the deposition of the ruler himself — for daring to threaten existing financial arrangements — and the re-establishment, in November 1879, of a system of Joint Anglo-French supervision over all aspects of Egypt's economic policy by two new Controllers-General, Evelyn Baring and de Blignières, with seats in the Cabinet. Both men were nominated by their own governments and it was understood that they could not be dismissed without official consent from Paris and London.[60] Finally, with the introduction of the Law of Liquidation, the pattern of foreign control was complete. Not only did it set out precisely what the Egyptian government could and could not do in the field of finance but it was also taken by the British at least as having the status of an international treaty, any breach of which would provide a *prima facie* case for direct foreign intervention.[61]

With the increase in European control went the increase in the numbers of Europeans employed in Egyptian government service. Muhammad Ali had begun the process of recruiting foreigners, Said and Ismail had continued it. However, the majority of their appointments were of technicians of one kind or another who were used to train the army or the police or to manage such government enterprises as the railways and the special administration which, before the opening of the Suez Canal, managed the transit of foreigners across Egypt from the Mediterranean to the Red Sea. With the creation of the Commission de la Dette in 1876 the whole process entered a new phase, with Europeans being employed at the very centre of the civil administration. In that same year Ismail was persuaded to allow foreign officials, almost all British, to reorganize the Customs, the Post Office and the Office of Public Accounts on the grounds that part of the revenues they controlled had been set aside to service the Public Debt. Each foreign director then appointed more of his fellow countrymen as his assistants.[62] Later, many more Englishmen were brought to Egypt during the period when Rivers Wilson was in the Khedive's Council of Ministers. An international commission consisting of a Briton, a Frenchman and an Egyptian was set up to run the Daira Saniya and another to run the Domains. More foreigners were employed after Ismail's deposition until by 1882, according to Schölch's calculations, there were about 1300 of them, the majority receiving annual salaries of several thousand pounds.[63]

Egyptian resentment of the presence of so many highly paid foreigners, of European interference in government, and of various schemes designed to save money such as the abolition of the privileges granted to landowners who had paid the *muqabala* soon began to make itself felt. Initially, there seems little doubt that it was aroused, in part, by the Khedive himself, anxious to use popular hostility in order to limit the powers of the foreign financial controllers. But, once he had been deposed, the adverse effect of the debt settlement and the steps necessary to maintain regular payments to overseas creditors had a sufficiently adverse effect on Egyptians of all classes to account for the groundswell of anti-European feeling which lay at the root of the National movement of 1881 and 1882.[64] Those particularly hard hit were the army officers. Not only had the Nubar—Wilson government of August 1878—April 1879 reduced the number of troops from 15,000 to 7000 but it had also placed about 2500 officers on half pay.[65] It was some of the latter who took the lead in paving the way for the appointment of the governments of Sharif Pasha and his successors which, from September 1881 onwards, attempted to exercise greater supervision over Egypt's own financial affairs. While there is no evidence that any of these governments planned to try and alter the terms of the Law of Liquidation, the European controllers, and particularly Sir Aukland Colvin (who had succeeded Evelyn Baring in 1880), were sufficiently fearful of their own position to exaggerate the danger in order to persuade their home governments that the financial settlement was at risk. As Colvin himself was later to put it:

The European interests in Egypt were too various and important to permit of the engagements contracted by the Khedive being placed at the mercy of Egyptian soldiery, or of an inexperienced native administration.[66]

While it would be wrong to suppose that the British controller and his colleagues were wholly responsible for engineering the British military invasion of August 1882, their persistent hostility to the new Egyptian governments certainly played a powerful role in pushing Gladstone's Liberal administration towards armed intervention.[67]

The agricultural sector of the economy

During the period 1850 to 1882 the amount of cultivated land in Egypt grew from just under 4.2 million feddans to nearly 4.8 million. The major part of the increase came during the reign of Khedive Ismail largely as a result, it must be assumed, of the extra water brought to marginal areas as a result of his programme of canal construction, including the fresh-water canal built between the Nile and Ismailia.[68] Of the land under cultivation in the early 1880s, some 3,000,000 feddans were in the Delta and the remainder in the Upper Egyptian provinces south of Cairo. During the same period the country's agricultural population increased from just over 4,000,000 in 1846 to about 7,000,000 in 1882.[69]

The third important increase of the period was that of agricultural production itself. Table 22 provides rough figures which help to illustrate the growth both in volume and value. To generalize enormously, while the country was able to produce enough to feed an expanding population and to maintain cereal exports at a steady rate it was also able to expand the output of its two major crops – cotton (and cotton seed) and sugar – by a very large amount. In the case of the former, where so little was consumed locally that export figures are a reliable guide to total production, the harvest grew from an average of half a million cantars a year in the 1850s to a peak of two million cantars during the latter part of the American Civil War boom. There was then a brief period of decline in the later 1860s before output regained its Civil War level in the early 1870s. At the same time the area devoted to the crop increased from 250,000 feddans in the

Table 22   Export of Egypt's principal crops, 1850–79 (annual averages)[1]

	Cotton cantars		Cotton seed[2] ardabbs		Wheat[3] ardabbs		Barley[3] ardabbs		Beans[3] ardabbs	
	(£m)	(m)*	(£m)	(m)**	(£m)	(m)**	(£m)	(m)**	(£m)	(m)**
1850–4	0.918	0.467			0.741	0.932	0.044	0.100	0.281	0.369
1855–9	1.333	0.515			1.099	1.250	0.091	0.192	0.267	0.333
1860–4	6.110	0.989	0.344	0.600	0.529	0.842	0.052	0.146	0.267	0.397
1865–9	10.213	1.367	0.586	0.910	0.489	0.455	0.061	0.218	0.354	0.405
1870–4		1.892	0.940	1.229	0.512	0.441	0.008	0.015	0.479	0.554
1875–9	8.422	2.232	1.468	1.468		0.792		0.933		0.689

*   1 cantar = 98–100 lb.
** 1 *ardabb* = 180–200 litres.

Sources:
Cotton: Owen, *Cotton*, 73, 90, 123, 126.
Cotton seed: *ibid.*, 167.
Wheat, barley, beans: *ibid.*, 126, 127; *CR*s (Belgium) 1850–64 (value converted from francs at the rate of £1 = 25 francs); Egyptian statistics in *CR* (US) Egypt 1876, *Exec. Docs.*, 45, 930–3; enclosure in Vivian (Alexandria) 29 May 1879, FO 141/127; Egypt, Direction Générale des Douanes, *Le commerce exterieur de l'Egypt. Statistique comparée, 1884–1889* (Cairo, 1891), xix.

Notes:
1 The value of the official export figures for 1874–9 have been augmented by one-ninth to compensate for Customs' undervaluation. See Owen, *Cotton*, 376–7.
2 Excludes 1860, 1874 and volume 1876–9.
3 Excludes 1850–1 and 1852 (barley).

1850s to over 1,000,000 in 1864 before establishing itself at between 750,000 and 875,000 for the rest of the period.[70] Two other points are also of importance. First, in spite of a number of attempts to introduce the cultivation of long-staple cotton into Upper Egypt the area placed under cultivation there rarely exceeded 20,000 feddans, leaving the great bulk of the crop to be grown in the Delta. Second, whereas in the 1850s a substantial proportion of total output (perhaps as much as three-eighths) came from the royal estates, during the American Civil War cotton growing became the principal agricultural activity of the majority of Lower Egyptian landholders. On the assumption that most cultivators used a biennial rotation, getting on for two-thirds of the Delta fields were placed under cotton once every two years in the mid-1860s and just over a half in the mid-1870s. Sugar, on the other hand, was mainly confined to the Upper Egyptian provinces of Minya and Asyut where, by the 1870s, between 50,000 and 75,000 feddans were devoted to its cultivation, most of it on estates owned by the Khedive Ismail.[71]

The fact that agricultural output was increasing steadily during a period when there was only a small addition to the cultivated area clearly implies that the existing land was being used more intensively. According to rough estimates of land utilization in 1873/4, some 4,500,000 feddans was being placed under winter crops, 1,000,000 under summer crops and another 2,000,000 under *Nili* (or Autumn) crops – making a total cropped area of just over 7,500,000 feddans.[72] If true, these figures show that well over half of Egypt's fields carried two crops a year. Other factors were also at work. One was a small improvement in yields, partly the result of an increase in the water available for irrigation, partly the result of the introduction of new types of seed, particularly in the case of cotton.[73] A second factor was the large sums of money spent on labour-saving investment, something of vital importance at a time when the cultivation of labour-intensive crops like cotton was spreading so rapidly. The improvement in transport as a result of the extension of the state railway system and the introduction of steam tugs on the Nile, the construction of upwards of a hundred cotton ginning factories during the American Civil War boom and, above all, the increase in the supply of easily accessible water all had an important role to play.[74]

Table 22 contains figures for the value of Egypt's main agricultural exports. They show that while income from cereal exports remained steady, that from cotton (and, after 1860, cotton seed) increased from just under £1,000,000 a year in the early 1850s to £11,500,000 in the second half of the 1860s, before declining slightly, as a result of falling prices, in the 1870s. During the same period the value of the export of various types of processed sugar (mainly in the form of loaves or molasses) rose from a tiny sum in the early 1860s to over £750,000 at the end of the period. The same table also provides a very rough guide to the relative profitability of the various crops. Thus, while the value of a cantar of cotton increased from something like £2 to £4 between the 1850s and 1880, that of wheat and beans remained more or less constant at just under £1 an *ardabb*.[75] On the assumption that cotton yields averaged at least two cantars a feddan and wheat three *ardabbs* for the same area it will be seen that the gap between the gross profits to be expected from the two crops was widening. Even if the much greater cost of cultivating the former reduced the difference between net profits, cotton still produced a considerable high net income.

The fact that cotton yielded a high rate of return and that almost all the crop was exported had a number of very important consequences. First, it ensured that Lower Egypt – the cotton sector – became the focus for the creation of a large number of new institutional arrangements designed to allow this one crop to be financed, processed and marketed overseas. It also had an important effect on the system of taxation and of landholding and land management, ensuring that changes in productive relations and in the distribution of the surplus proceeded very much more rapidly in the Delta than elsewhere. This in turn accentuated the difference between Upper and Lower Egypt and ensured, among other things, that the former became a source of cheap labour power for the latter. I will examine all these issues in the context of a discussion of changes in the role of the three important groups or institutions who shared the surplus: the merchants, ginners and usurers, the landowners and the government.

The penetration of the interior of the Delta by the merchants of Alexandria and the establishment of direct contact with the cultivators which had begun during the 1840s continued to gain momentum under Muhammad Ali's successors. There was a brief setback when Abbas tried to remonopolize some of the country's crops in 1853 and 1854, as well as to expel most of the local Greek community which had already begun to provide a large number of local agents and money-lenders.[76] But all such barriers were quickly swept aside by the accession of Said and the attraction of the high profits to be made from agricultural exports during the Crimean War boom. The importance of this movement was considerable. Cultivators, particularly those who grew cotton, required to be paid in cash for their products, and the coin to do this had to be imported from abroad. In addition, cotton producers usually needed to be provided with seed and credit. Merchants and their agents either undertook both services or, more often, left the provision of working capital to village-based shop-keepers and traders. The latter provided further stimulus to the production of cash crops by retailing much sought-after consumption goods. They were also able to strike up a profitable alliance with the tax-collectors who, once the land tax began to be collected exclusively in cash — and often in advance — found it useful to have someone ready to lend the peasants what they needed to meet their obligations. Such loans could be safely made against the security of their cotton.[77] This same decade saw the construction of the first cotton ginning factories. By 1859 there were enough of them to process something like an eighth of the harvest and demand for their services was great in spite of the fact that they usually kept all of the seed as payment, cultivators thinking it worth the expense to avoid the burdensome task of cleaning their own crop and to allow them to sell it immediately after the harvest, thus avoiding the payment of extra interest on what they might have borrowed.[78]

There was a further intensification of such activity during the American Civil War boom of the early 1860s. Spurred on by prices which nearly quadrupled between 1861 and 1865, hundreds of thousands of cultivators all over the Delta began to plant cotton for the first time. For this they required the credit to buy animals, water lifting devices and seed, as well as, in some cases, to hire extra labour. Almost every village now had its shop-keeper/money-lender.[79] Meanwhile, the number of ginning factories increased rapidly: by the beginning of 1863 there were already nearly eighty, capable of processing over a third of the total crop.[80] The fall in prices at the end of the boom and the temporary reduction in output brought some retrenchment but, as in the Izmir district of Anatolia, it was almost certainly the existence of the network of merchants, agents and ginners which prevented production from being reduced further. It is true that most of the alternatives were less profitable, but they were also much more difficult to market; while none of them could be used to obtain anything like the same amount of credit as cotton. An increasing appreciation of the value of cotton seed may also have been an additional factor.[81] So too was the government's policy of continually raising the amount taken in tax.

Most contemporary writers assumed that all the people involved in the business of financing and exporting the cotton crop were foreigners or foreign-protected persons. While this is almost certainly another example of the myopia produced by the European assumption of the existence of a basic ethnic (or religious) division of labour which made all money-lenders Jews or Armenians, all village shop-keepers Greek while totally excluding any Muslim Egyptian from trade or commerce, it would seem that, as far as the cotton sector was concerned, the balance between foreigner and local resident was much more in favour of the former than, for example, in Syria. There are a number of reasons for this. Certainly the most important was the increasing advantage possessed by those with Capitulatory rights and protected by increasingly assertive consuls. It was not simply a question of paying lower duties, if they were paid at all, or of avoiding the land and property taxes. Just as significant was the fact that in Egypt, as a result of government weakness, more and more disputes between foreigners and Egyptians or between foreigners and the government or the estates of the Khedive were being settled, not in the courts, but as the result of consular intervention.[82] In these circumstances merchants were sure enough of their position to negotiate directly with cultivators or with village headmen even if they continued to use the services of brokers (*simsars*) for other types of commercial transactions.[83]

European activity in the cotton sector was further intensified after 1875. Not only did the end of government borrowing and of the huge issue of short-term paper mean that merchants, brokers and others had to find an alternative field of investment, but also the establishment of the Mixed Courts meant that transactions involving agricultural land could now be undertaken with great security. One result was the great increase in the amount of money lent to Egyptian cultivators against their property (estimated at £7,000,000 in 1882); another was the growth of foreign landownership which had reached 225,000 feddans by 1887.[84] A number of companies were also formed at this time to undertake a variety of activities to do with rural property. These included several unsuccessful enterprises founded to reclaim and then sell uncultivated land or to engage in public works activities of one kind or another. More successful were the large mortgage companies, the Crédit Foncier Egyptien founded in 1880 by a group of Alexandria and Cairo bankers in combination with French financiers and the Land and Mortgage Company established mainly with British money.[85]

But if part of the rural surplus was appropriated by merchants and bankers, the remainder continued to be shared between landholders and the government. The process by which this took place will now be examined under three heads: changes in the distribution of control over rural land, changes in the system of taxation and changes in the organization and management of agricultural enterprises.

As far as the first is concerned two generalizations are substantially true: an increasing proportion of the cultivated land was held in large estates and an increasing proportion was also held as what soon began to approximate very closely to private ownership. Thus in 1894, the year of the first reliable survey, 42.5 per cent of the registered land comprised properties of 50 feddans and over – properties which in a country of intensive cultivation like Egypt are usually categorized as 'large'.[86] Unfortunately, however, it is impossible simply to work backwards from this figure on the assumption that there was a unilinear movement towards greater and greater concentration from the 1840s onwards. Many of those given control of large properties in the last decade of Muhammad Ali's reign lost it again under Abbas.[87] Again, even more dramatically, Ismail and the royal family were stripped of over 900,000 feddans of Daira Saniya, Daira Khassa, and Domains land by Egypt's creditors in the late 1870s. Another factor was the application of the Egyptian version of the Islamic law of inheritance which acted to fragment large estates by dividing them between a number of close relatives, although the extent to which this was actually observed in practice has never satisfactorily been investigated.[88] Nevertheless, the general trend is clear. Members of the royal family and of the urban and rural administration, as well as some foreigners, used their privileged position to acquire control over large tracts of increasingly valuable agricultural land.[89] The creation of medium-size holdings (those between 5 and 50 feddans) was also part of the same process.[90] In 1894 such properties consisted of almost 38 per cent of all privately controlled land.[91]

But if more and more of Egypt's cultivated area was being held in large and medium sized properties, the obverse of the same process was that a large number of peasants must have lost their own plots or seen them greatly diminished. The point is one of the greatest importance. Unfortunately, however, there is no way of estimating how much land was lost in this way nor how many cultivators were reduced to the status of landless labourers.[92] For what it is worth the first official *Statistique de l'Egypte 1873* gives the number of the latter in nine of the country's most important provinces as 135,000, but this can only have been based on guesswork of a very unreliable kind.[93] Meanwhile Mr Cave's assertion that 'labourers are difficult to obtain in many places' must probably be reinterpreted to mean that agricultural workers were slow to come forward given the low wages and appalling conditions.[94] In these circumstances, it seems likely that labour contractors began to use the newly built railway to bring down gangs of seasonal workers from Upper Egypt.[95]

A second generalization about the period 1850 to 1882 concerns the development of legal rights over land. As always, it is necessary to be careful about the distinction between the letter of the law and actual practice. Members of the royal family could, in effect, pledge their estates as security for loans many years before the creation of proper arrangements for mortgages; others, including the Khedive Ismail himself, could lose land, however secure their title to it might seem. It is also necessary to avoid simple explanations which seek to link the growth of property rights directly with the growth of production for the market. As in the case of Turkey, the state's own need for revenue was a more important factor in extending property rights than pressure from landowning and commercial groups. And, in at least one case, in 1858, there is evidence that regulations which would, *inter alia*, have given peasant cultivators more secure title to *kharajïya* land were opposed by members of the royal family, presumably on the grounds that this would make their own efforts to build up large estates more difficult.[96]

Under Muhammad Ali the main extension of property rights concerned only *ibadïya* land: in 1836 such grants were made heritable by the holder's eldest son, in 1842 they could legally be sold or transferred.[97] But under Said and Ismail there was a substantial improvement in the status of property of all kinds. In 1858 *ushurïya* land (a new category created in 1854 to include *ibadïyas*, *jiftliks*, and what remained of the *usyas* of former *multazims*) was declared to be full private property. At the same time rights over *kharajïya* land were extended to include its pledge, mortgage, sale, exchange or transfer.[98] Later, under Ismail, the law of the *muqabala* granted full legal title to anyone who paid the new tax on land of any type. According to Artin it was collected on 3,650,000 feddans or roughly three-quarters of the total cultivated area.[99] However, when in 1880 it came to the question of verifying who had actually chosen (or been forced) to surrender the extra sum, it was discovered that many cultivators had lost their certificates of payment while others were actually forged. Thus, while those who were finally admitted to have paid the *muqabala* received an annuity as well as full legal title to their land, those who could not substantiate their claims obtained nothing and their rights continued to be defined by Said's 1858 Land Law, until new regulations were introduced in 1891.[100]

As already noted, one of the main aims of the creation of a system of regular property rights was to increase the sums raised in tax. This worked in two ways. The first involved a process of reclassification, notably the creation of the *ushuri* category in 1854 to include land which had previously been exempt from tax. When, three years later, the holdings of the village shaikhs were also taxed for the first time, all privately controlled property was subject, at least in theory, to either *ushuriya* or *kharajiya* rates. The second process, which was begun early in Muhammad Ali's rule, was the continuing effort to ensure that every piece of agricultural land was registered according to holder and given a rate of tax which bore some relationship to its productive capacity. This work was not properly completed until the British period, for it lacked the support of a comprehensive cadastral survey; but by the end of Said's reign most villages contained a register of property holdings and of the tax which each should pay.[101] It was on this basis that the rates of tax due from various categories of land were raised regularly throughout the Said and Ismail period. However, it was a rough and ready business at best. Given the fact that after the end of the monopoly system most taxes were again collected in cash and the fact that the price of the most important products could vary considerably over time, it was obviously difficult to ensure that the tax rate bore some consistent relationship to gross earnings. To make matters worse the people usually responsible for assessing the taxable capacity of the land were the village shaikhs, who had every interest in ensuring that their own property paid at as low a rate as possible.[102]

So much for the aims behind government policy; how were taxes actually collected in practice? Here perhaps the only thing which can be said with any degree of certainty is that it is almost impossible to find out. When the Commission of Inquiry of 1878 attempted to investigate this same question it was unable to decide whether the taxes were collected according to the village registers or according to a principle of division in which the government simply decided how much it wanted to raise and then apportioned this sum among the various provinces on a more or less arbitrary basis.[103] Just as significant was another of the Commission's conclusions: 'En effet, aujourd'hui il ne trouve ni dans la loi, ni dans l'organisation administrative aucune garantie contre les extorsions des agents du fisc.'[104] To complicate matters still further, the collection of taxes in cash, supported by the spread of the growth of lucrative cash crops, made it possible for the government to begin to raise taxes in advance of the harvest, relying on money-lenders and usurers to make up the difference where this was necessary. This not only increased the opportunity for arbitrary exactions but also involved another group in the actual process of collection. As Lady Lucy Duff Gordon described the process in 1864, the money-lender followed the tax-gatherer 'like a vulture after a crow'.[105] In these circumstances it would seem best to assume that the amount of tax actually raised from the cultivators was a function of government demands on the one hand and a complicated relationship between the tax-payer, the collectors, the local shaikhs, and the usurers on the other. If the tax-payer had any power he would pay little or nothing, if he had none the other group would divide most or all of his surplus between them. By the same token, what might save a peasant from utter destitution apart from his own ingenuity, was a marked difference of interest among his oppressors. Thus, while the collectors might wish, or be forced, to try and take everything a cultivator possessed, a usurer would be anxious to ensure that he was left with sufficient working capital to grow cotton the next year and so be in a position to pay his debts.[106]

The second main form of taxation was the corvée. This was widely used not only to fulfil the government's obligation to provide men for digging the Suez Canal but also to carry out most of the major public works of the period: the railways, improvements in the system of irrigation and other projects. In addition, it was necessary to recruit men to clean out the main canals to ensure that they could continue to carry water during the summer when the Nile was at its lowest. The numbers of men involved must have been very large: in 1865, for instance, Lady Duff Gordon describes how more than half the adult males in Luxor and Karnak were taken away for sixty days for corvée duty as well as 25,000 men from Qena.[107] In many cases the men were forced to work at some great distance from their homes. Disruption was further increased when, as often happened, no food was provided and the men had to take their families with them to provide them with sustenance. In addition, irregular corvée duty was often demanded by members of the royal family and by large estate holders for work on their own land.[108]

To conclude this brief examination of the system of taxation, it would certainly be true to say that the governments of Abbas, Said and Ismail were very much more successful than their seventeenth- and eighteenth-century predecessors in securing a large share of the agricultural surplus. Unlike them they had developed a machinery for collection which, though inequitable, allowed them to raise almost all of what they demanded as well as to mobilize large numbers of peasants for the construction of public works. Against this, however, the government was largely unsuccessful in its attempts to incorporate large landowners properly within the tax system in exchange for an extension of property rights. Again, to the extent that it relied on foreign merchants and money-lenders to facilitate the extension of cash crops − and so of the taxable capacity of the land − it further accelerated the growth of an increasingly unmanageable European presence within the agricultural sector. Such were the contradictions stemming from the state's attempt to play an independent role as mediator between the capitalist economies of western Europe and the partially transformed economy of Egypt.

Some of the same contradictions also helped to shape the various systems which were developed to manage the large estates created during this same period. To begin with the royal family: in the first instance at least the great majority of the *jiftliks* created by Muhammad Ali were farmed directly by their new owners, using the labour of the existing peasant population. Such estates enjoyed a particularly privileged position.[109]

In addition, the managers of the *jiftliks* were able to recruit extra workers from the surrounding villages, a practice bitterly resented by the *mutaahids* and shaikhs who were competing with the royal estates for scarce supplies of labour.[110] Nevertheless, in the case of Muhammad Ali's own estates many of the advantages of this privileged position were offset by the fact that they were run as one large enterprise by officials in Cairo who, according to the Frenchman Hamont, issued orders about what was to be planted, and when and how, which took no account of local difference.[111] For the same reason working conditions were particularly bad. Many peasant labourers fled, others had to be locked up in special barracks overnight to prevent their escape, and it may be that this forced the introduction of a number of concessions, the most important of which was to allow members of the work force to farm a few feddans on their own using animals from the estate.[112] Other royal estates, notably those belonging to Ibrahim and Said (Muhammad Ali's sons) and to Ismail (the future khedive) seem to have been better managed. Some care was taken to retain peasant labourers by paying them regular wages and providing them with small plots of land.[113] European experts were also employed, and there was a great emphasis on the use of machinery (such as pumps and steam engines) to overcome some of the problems posed by the shortages of labour and animals.[114] In addition, a number of the royal family attempted to process their own products by building their own cotton gins, flax scutching mills and, in the case of Ibrahim and his son Ismail, plant for pressing and refining sugar.[115]

However, for all the personal care and attention which was often devoted to such estates, the problems of managing enterprises of their size never seems to have been properly mastered. The attempt to introduce more capital-intensive methods based on machines also posed serious problems. As in the case of factory industry, Egypt lacked the technological capacity to maintain even quite simple equipment, while the employment of foreign technicians was very expensive. Perhaps just as important, the cultivation of cotton was particularly difficult to mechanize. The intricate system of field canals and drains makes the movement of heavy machinery troublesome and even in the southern states of America it was a very long time before it was possible to introduce equipment designed to assist labourers in the burdensome business of weeding, picking and searching leaves for signs of the boll-weevil and cotton worm. In terms of the available technology only the steam pump and the gin — and later the construction of light agricultural railways — offered any real opportunity for substituting capital for labour. In these circumstances, if some of the royal estates were run at a profit it must have been much to do with the advantages they enjoyed as a result of their close association with the state, such as the use of corvée labour or the special privileges which they enjoyed on the state railways.[116]

Many of the problems associated with the management of large agricultural enterprises can be seen with special clarity in the case of the huge properties built up by the Khedive Ismail after his accession. By the early 1870s the Daira Saniya is said to have consisted of fifty-one estates, each averaging around 10,000 feddans; half of them in Lower Egypt where the principal activity was the cultivation of cotton, half in Upper Egypt where the main crop was sugar.[117] Large sums of money were spent on providing them with canals, with railways and with machines – some of which were almost immediately abandoned.[118] In addition, an attempt was made to use the Upper Egyptian estates as the basis for a huge industry based on the construction of at least twenty-two new factories for producing molasses, and loaf and refined sugar.[119] But, in spite of all this expenditure of money and effort, by 1876 failure to find ways of managing the estates efficiently meant that it was more profitable to let a substantial portion of the cultivable land – perhaps as much as half – to tenants at rents of up to £1.50 a feddan.[120] Other members of the royal family were also beginning to make the same kind of calculation: in 1877, of 50,000 feddans of Daira Khassa land only 10,000 feddans were being farmed directly, while in the case of the Domains, of the 340,000 feddans in cultivation, nearly half was rented to tenants.[121]

Much less is known about the management of the non-royal estates during the same period. Here perhaps the best that can be done is to present a brief outline of the options open to those who controlled them. No doubt the simplest and easiest method of exploiting them was to lease them, either for a cash rent, where this was possible, or subject to some form of share-cropping system. A system of cash rents had the great advantage, from the proprietor's point of view, that he needed to exercise little or no direct supervision over how the land was actually cultivated. On the other hand, until the 1880s the only peasants able to contemplate paying rent in this way were those who grew a crop like cotton for which they not only received an assured, regular income but which also allowed them to obtain the working capital they needed without recourse to the landlord himself. For these reasons this form of land exploitation must certainly have remained the exception rather than the rule and the main method continued to be some type of métayage system by which landlord and tenant agreed to share the harvest in some proportion which related fairly directly to their own input in terms of labour and capital as well as to who was to pay the tax.[122] The main disadvantage for the landlord was the high cost of the supervision necessary to make sure that the land was properly worked and the crop properly shared.

Nevertheless, for all those who wished simply to live in Cairo and to collect their rents at a distance there were others who paid personal attention to their estates, attempting to make a high return by growing and selling their own crops. This was certainly true of some foreigners. It must also have been true of many village shaikhs, as well as officials and others who were able to use their access to the machinery of government to overcome some of the major difficulties which they faced such as shortage of capital, the lack of a well developed market in agricultural labour and the conscription of their workers. One method which continued to be widely used was that of the employment of service tenants, peasants who agreed to provide a regular amount of work on the estate in exchange for the right to rent a small plot of land for their own use. As already noted, this system had been used on the royal *jiftliks* in the 1840s; later it became institutionalized with the creation of agricultural settlements known as *izbas* in which the tenants were housed in mud dwellings grouped round the central stores and the residence of the owner and of his *nazir* or overseer.[123] Most sources agree that the word *izba* itself first had the meaning of an encampment of temporary straw huts put up for labourers working at some distance from their village.[124] But by the time of the 1882 census it had already been given its modern meaning of 'hameau, bourgade – groupe d'habitations construites pour des ouvriers agricoles sur des terres de culture', a small, artificially constructed community which, unlike a village, generally took the name of its proprietor.[125] It seems likely that, at least initially, a significant proportion of these new communities must have been founded on *ibadiyas* or other properties made out of newly reclaimed land in the north of the Delta, particularly in Buhaira, where it was necessary to bring in a labour force from outside to work the fields. But by 1882 there were already 5000 *izbas* scattered throughout the six Lower Egyptian provinces.[126]

At the basis of the *izba* as an agricultural enterprise lay the exchange of land (and usually a place to live) for labour; but within this general formula details varied widely. Speaking of the system as it existed towards the end of the nineteenth century, J. F. Nahas describes a contract by which each peasant family was required to supply an agreed number of workers for the owner's fields at a daily wage to be determined in advance.[127] Saleh Nour Ed-Din, on the other hand, writes of a system by which the labour service was discharged on a crop-sharing basis, the workers taking one fifth of the produce of the owner's land if the owner himself provided the animals.[128] Some wages might be paid, however, for extra work or for labour performed by the peasants' wives.[129] Arrangements for working the small plots assigned to the service tenants also varied considerably but generally consisted of another crop-sharing agreement in which the relative shares were determined in the usual way in proportion to input and to who paid the land tax.[130] In the case of Nubar Pasha's 200 feddan estate near Kafr El Zaiyat in the Delta in 1882, for example, the 200 labourers leased their plots for a half-share of the product.[131]

The advantages of creating an *izba* were numerous. Not only did it secure for the proprietor a permanent, readily available labour force but also one which was easy to control and which contained men with a long experience of local conditions. Furthermore, whereas it was necessary to pay ordinary day labourers, if they could be found, a living wage, it was possible to pay service tenants at a lower rate, relying on the fact that they had food from their own plots to keep them going. The estate owner could also use the labour of the tenants and children — something which was particularly useful during the cotton-picking season (or for removing leaves infected by the cotton worm) — again at low rates. The peasants' families could also be used to look after the oxen and cattle used on the estate.[132] In exchange for all these advantages all the proprietor had to forgo was a proportion of the rent he might otherwise have been able to obtain if he had leased the plots allocated to the service tenants at the ordinary, commercial rate.

Some of the important implications of this system of land management for Egyptian agriculture will be examined in Chapter 9. But, for the time being, it is necessary to stress one point. The fact that within the small world of the *ezba* the proprietor, or his *nazir*, were all powerful and able at will to interfere in every aspect of the lives of their tenants has led some writers to describe the system of relationships to be found there as 'feudal' or 'semi-feudal'.[133] This is incorrect. Although various methods of extra economic coercion certainly existed, the basis of the proprietor's ability to exploit his workers, as well as to tie them firmly to his domain, lay mainly in his control over the scarce factors of land and credit, reinforced by the fact that he was able to stand between the inhabitants of the *izba* and access to the market for labour, working capital and the sale of their products. Fortified by this power he could withhold wages on the grounds of negligence. He could lend money and food to peasants in need at rates favourable to himself. He could make it a condition of tenancy that he sold the peasants' cotton and other cash crops for them. Most importantly, he could use the practice of settling accounts with his tenants at the end of the season (when the latter were given the balance of what they were owed for wages, for the sale of their cotton and for their share of the produce of their rented land, less what they had borrowed or forfeited) to bind them further to the domain by keeping them permanently in debt. Finally, far from having an obligation to provide the *izba* tenants with land, as he would have had to do under a classical type of feudal arrangement, he could always threaten them with the prospect of taking their small plot away from them and thus reducing them to the state which all peasants were desperate to avoid: that of landless labourers dependent for their living on the vagaries of seasonal employment.[134]

For all these reasons it is proper to see the *izba* not as an example of a particular type of Middle Eastern feudalism but as an institution which owed its existence to the particular way in which rural relations were re-organized as a consequence of the transformation of the Egyptian agricultural sector by market forces. Taking advantage of the opportunities provided by the extension of cotton and other cash crops, almost all connected with the government, *izba* proprietors proceeded to create a flexible system of land management which combined the advantage of certain economies of scale, such as less costly credit and other inputs, with the ability to extract cheap labour from a well-disciplined peasant labour force. The result was a system which, though capitalist in some of its aspects, stopped short of the reorganization of production along more capital intensive lines using a combination of wage labour and machines to allow a steady increase in agricultural productivity. As elsewhere in the non-European world, the actual production of cash crops remained in the hands of peasant agriculturists and subject, largely, to the limitations imposed by peasant techniques.[135]

Industry

The creation of a government statistical service in 1873 and its first attempt to collect information about the structure of Egyptian industry during the early 1870s provides a useful insight into the extent and breadth of local manufacturing activity even after many years during which imports of European goods had been increasing at a rapid rate (see Tables 23 and 24).[136] Not surprisingly, however, the figures shown in Table 23 give rise to a number of problems. First, as far as the traditional sector was concerned, given the underdeveloped nature of the Egyptian administration it would seem almost certain that the figures given for the size of the workforce in 1873 must be incomplete, particularly with respect to craft activity carried on outside Cairo and Alexandria. To give only two examples: Kluzinger's list of village artisans at work in Upper Egypt in the late 1870s (from locksmiths to bed-cover makers, from pipe-stem turners to men who made furniture out of date palms) suggests a wider range of production for local use than the official statistics allow while Couvidou's data about the carpenters who kept the country's 13,000 *saqiyas* in good repair makes the same point.[137] Against this, the fact that so many of Egypt's artisans also retailed their own products suggests that many of those in the labour force can only be thought of as part-time producers. Second, to turn to the modern sector, the same official statistics make no mention of a number of state-owned establishments such as the railway repair workshops and almost totally ignore any privately owned factories.[138]

Nevertheless, on the basis of these partial figures it is possible to come to a few conclusions about the condition of Egyptian industry in the years before the British occupation. To begin with the traditional sector: at least 100,000

Table 23 The Egyptian industrial sector in 1873

A *The traditional sector*

	Cairo	Male labour force[1] Alexandria	Rest of Egypt	Number of establishments
Chemicals[2]	1928	311	5325	at least 208
Food	9763	5237	20,231	at least 1366
Textiles, clothing	4529	1544	22,187	518[3]
Leather	1304	280	1281	at least 186
Metal	2718	878	3231	at least 546
Wood	3821	1670	11,449	at least 120
Stone, pottery and ceramic	1547	362	3993	at least 22
Graphic art, design	439	209	14	at least 14
Total	25,149	10,491	68,711	

B *The modern sector (establishments owned by the state or the royal family)*

	Labour force	Number of establishments
Food (biscuits and bread)		2
(sugar)		22
Textiles	1617	3
Leather		at least 3
Metal (arsenals and shipyards)		7
Stone, pottery (brickworks)	62	1
Paper	218[4]	1
Graphic art, design (Imprimerie Nationale)	182[5]	1

Source: Egypt, *Statistique de l'Egypt 1873*, 204—26.

Notes:
1 In addition to the male labour force there was a female labour force of 2575.
2 Chemical products include dyes, the manufacture of candles, perfume, etc.
3 The figures for establishments include 6 oil presses and 11 ginneries. It is not clear if their workforce is contained in the figures for employment.
4 Includes 63 workers on piecework.
5 Includes 75 workers on piecework.

men (or about 6 per cent of a total male adult labour force of perhaps 1,700,000) were employed either full or part time in providing much of the clothing and most of the processed food, tools and household equipment required by the country's growing population.[139] Furthermore, it would seem that foreign competition had not, as yet, basically altered the structure of local production with the exception of textile manufacturing, glass making and one or two other activities.[140] Where foreign imports were important, however, was in catering to the completely different consumption pattern of a large foreign population and those among the local Egyptian landowners and officials who had begun to live in European types of houses in the Europeanized sections of Cairo and Alexandria where almost everything of importance was purchased from abroad — even building materials (see Table 24).[141] It was these people who continued to act as a spearhead for foreign commercial penetration, patronizing the wholesale or retail outlets for European goods and promoting the increasingly powerful notion that anything imported was bound to be of better quality than anything Egyptian-made.[142]

Table 24   Egypt's import of selected manufactured goods via Alexandria, 1866—79
(annual averages in £E*)

	1866—9	*1870—4*	*1879*[1]
'Manufactures'	1,671,344	1,939,053	
Hats and bonnets	90,017	108,090	
Candles	53,716	54,047	64,571
Crystal and glass	25,953	26,723	47,227
Cloth	65,862	42,709	
Pottery	69,702	41,189	
Marble and stone	124,250	159,652	
Furniture	40,283	47,626	
Hardware	89,389	108,726	
Silks	104,397	87,211	95,289
Shoes and leather	95,556	88,126	116,552
Total	5,213,902	6,193,700	5,700,922

* £E1 = 100 piastres; £(sterling) = 97.5 piastres.

Sources: 1866—74: Egyptian official statistics quoted in CR (US) Egypt 1876, *Exec. Docs*, 45, 926—9.
1879: Egypt, *Le commerce exterieur de l'Egypt. Statistique comparée, 1884—1889*, XV–XVI.

Note: 1 The categories of dutiable goods changed between 1874 and 1879. I have only given figures for those items which seem unchanged.

Turning to the modern, or factory, sector it is clear from Table 23 that by 1873, ten years after his accession to the throne, Ismail had already begun to do something positive to reverse the process of de-industrialization which had begun with the abandonment of Muhammad Ali's experiments. Instead of the three or four state-owned establishments mentioned by the Belgian consul in 1856 there was now quite an extensive network of plants connected with the manufacture of arms and other military and naval supplies as well as a smaller number catering to the need of an expanding administration, such as the Bulaq paper works.[143] Unfortunately for Egypt, however, the high costs associated with these plants — in terms of the high price of European administrative salaries and of imported fuel and raw materials — meant that they could only continue in existence on the basis of substantial subsidies.[144] Once these were no longer forthcoming after Egypt's bankruptcy, many state factories were forced to close down.[145] Thus, as far as the future was concerned, the most important industrial legacy of the Ismail period was the much maligned network of sugar factories constructed in the Khedive's estates in Middle and Upper Egypt, of which some ten or eleven were still at work at the end of the 1870s.[146] While it is true that they too seem to have received a number of important subsidies in terms of cheap corvée labour and the ability to sell some of their loaf sugar and molasses below cost, the enormous increase in the volume of Egypt's sugar exports and the fact that sugar imports were contained at a fairly low level (see Table 25) do suggest that they were a more viable economic enterprise than their critics allow.[147]

Table 25　Egypt's trade in sugar, 1863–80 (Alexandria only)

	Imports		Exports	
	Volume quintals (99 lbs)	Value (£E)*	Volume quintals (99 lbs)[2]	Value[1] (£E)*
1863			6041	5504
1864			11,753	16,924
1865			17,004	24,475
1866	19,808	28,524	1090	1570
1867	20,237	29,141	54,982	41,829
1868	21,427	30,855	145,212	109,526
1869	26,373	38,697	293,279	367,281
1870	25,895	38,452	283,828	299,574
1871	23,204	33,414	356,468	369,970
1872	23,212	33,425	456,851	508,948
1873	27,385	40,457	923,274	827,175
1874	23,212	99,303	986,605	924,486
1875		122,362	985,635	725,657
1876		100,633		
1877		138,563		
1878		157,810		
1879	124,006	168,352	756,251	678,693
1880	143,220	195,479	752,716	741,574

* £E1 = 100 piastres; £(sterling) = 97.5 piastres.

Sources: 1863–5: Egypt, *Statistique de l'Egypt 1873*, Table 103.
1866–74: Egyptian official statistics quoted in *CR* (US) Egypt, 1876, *Exec. Docs*, 45. 926–33.
1875–80: *Le commerce exterieur de l'Egypte*, 1884–1889, XVI–XVII.

Notes:
1 From 1873 to Aug. 1911 the Egyptian Customs officially undervalued all exports by 10 per cent, see Owen, *Cotton*, 376–7.
2 1861–5 and 1879–80 in cantars of roughly 100 lbs 1874–8 converted from okes of 2.75 lbs.

What is almost entirely missing from the figures in Table 23 is any reference to the privately owned establishments within the modern sector.[148] Not surprisingly these consisted very largely of plants associated either with the processing of local agricultural products — for example the cotton gins and presses, the steam-driven flour mills and the Alexandrian factory for extracting oil from linseed and cotton — or for providing food and simple pieces of household and other equipment for the European population.[149]

In addition, in the mid-1870s a number of Greeks from Istanbul and Izmir began to establish cigarette factories in Cairo, driven there by the difficulties imposed on them inside the Ottoman Empire proper by the newly created Ottoman Tobacco *Régie*.[150] It was industries of this type which were to provide the basis for Egypt's industrial activity throughout the remainder of the nineteenth century.

6   The provinces of Greater Syria, 1850–1880 : the economic and social tensions of the 1850s and their consequences

In Egypt and Anatolia the period of economic and social transformation inaugurated by the reforming rulers of the early nineteenth century and by the huge increase in commercial and financial links with Europe was accompanied, as elsewhere in the world, by great hardship and unhappiness among many sections of the population but by remarkably few overt signs of popular discontent – at least until the months before the Urabi revolt of 1882. In Mount Lebanon, the Syrian interior and Palestine, on the other hand, the situation was very different. There, where the power of local governments was much less strong, the series of disturbances which culminated in the inter-communal fighting in the Mountain and the Damascus riots of 1860 represent a specifically political response to the growth of European influence and to associated changes in the balance of power between various social groups. In Lebanon the further development of the money economy through the growth of trade and the production and export of silk resulted in a confrontation between the (predominantly Druze) *muqatajis* and a number of different forces anxious to put an end to their particularly privileged position. In Syria and Palestine resentment at Ottoman attempts to reimpose a tighter system of administrative control, combined with the increasing dissatisfaction of social groups which had suffered economic hardship as a result of the growth of trade with Europe, produced a number of outbursts of popular discontent.

So much can be said in general terms. It is not the purpose of this chapter to provide a detailed account of each specific outbreak of violence: at the very least such an attempt would require a lengthy examination of the complex inter-relationship between economic, political and religious factors which is far beyond the scope of the present work. Just as important, it would direct attention away from a second major theme: the way in which the response of both the Ottomans and the leading European powers to the upheavals of the 1850s and 1860 led to an effort to create a new political and administrative order such as would provide a more secure framework for the growth of trade and the extension of commercial agriculture. These themes will be examined in terms first of Mount Lebanon, then of the provinces of the Syrian interior and of Palestine.

Beirut and Mount Lebanon

Taking the period between 1850 and 1880 as a whole, undoubtedly the main development in Mount Lebanon was the establishment of silk production and silk export as the major form of economic activity. This, in turn, had important repercussions on many sectors of the local economy, notably agriculture, industry and commerce. Two more introductory points ought also to be made. First, in the context of the multiplication of links between Syria and Europe, silk was an important factor binding Mount Lebanon ever more closely with France and with the international economic system. Second, in terms of the region's own history, the middle of the nineteenth century was remarkable for the fact that, as a result of profits to be made from silk, the main focus of attention of the bankers and merchants of Beirut was directed towards the Mountain itself. Before this period, Beirut's primary importance was as an entrepôt for goods passing between Europe, Damascus and the interior of Syria; after it, as the profits to be made from silk declined, interest in the Mountain waned and the international, or extra-Lebanese, aspect of the city's financial activity was reinforced by investment in agricultural land outside the Mountain or by the establishment of branches of Beiruti businesses in Europe, West Africa and major Mediterranean ports like Alexandria.

In the form which it took in nineteenth-century Lebanon, the production, processing and export of silk involved five separate but related activities.[1] The first was the cultivation of the mulberry trees which provided the leaves used to feed the silkworms. This was basically the work of peasant agriculturalists using their own, or rented, land. Second, the silkworms themselves had to be reared from eggs until the moment when they began to spin their cocoons. As a rule the eggs were obtained from merchants or brokers who, in turn, purchased them from Lebanese or foreign sources. The business of rearing the worms was also undertaken by peasants, often women, and usually carried out in huts situated on the same land as the mulberry trees. Third, the cocoons were either exported or sold to local manufacturers. In both cases it was necessary to place them in heated ovens in order to stifle the worm (now transforming itself into a butterfly) lest, in its attempt to escape, it damage the single continuous thread out of which the cocoon was made. Fourth, the cocoons were steamed or even placed in basins of water to unseal the glue which kept them together and their thread was unwound and spun. By 1850 the greater part of Lebanese spinning was being carried out in European-style factories. Fifth, the thread was either exported or else woven into silk cloth by local weavers.

Given this multiplicity of activities, as well as the absence of reliable statistics for either Mount Lebanon or Syria as a whole, it is impossible to

Table 26   The value of silk exports from Beirut and the price of Lebanese cocoons, 1850–9

	Value of exports[1] (francs)	Price of an oke* of cocoons (piastres)
1850	2,406,250	15
1851		18
1852	2,253,120	20–24
1853	4,586,150	
1854	7,963,710	18–22
1855	7,929,617	20–22
1856	10,131,825	35
1857	9,791,157	45
1858		22–25
1859		35

* 1 oke = 1.28 gm.

Source: French consular sources in Chevalier, *Mont Liban*, 226, 230.

Note: 1 Exports include both cocoons and thread. In 1857 exports of cocoons were valued at just over £300,000 and those of thread at just over £185,000. Farley, *Two Years in Syria*, 372.

give a coherent account of the increase in silk production during the period in question. The best that can be done is to treat the whole process in a more piecemeal way, illustrating the argument where possible with what little quantitive evidence there is to be found. The problem of statistics is particularly obvious during the first decade of the period, the 1850s, when, according to most contemporary writers, there was a significant increase in the value of both the production and export of silk. According to figures from French consular sources, the value of silk (both thread and cocoons) shipped from Beirut jumped by over 400 per cent between 1850 and 1856 after having remained more or less constant during the 1840s[2] (see Table 26). The reasons for this enormous increase are not difficult to discover. On the demand side, the great drop in French cocoon production as a result of the ravages of the worm disease, pébrine, in the late 1840s and early 1850s forced the silk manufacturers of Lyons to search for alternative sources of supply.[3] This, in turn, was in large part responsible for the rapid rise in the international price of silk. In the case of Lebanon, for example, the price of an oke of new cocoons rose from an average of 12 piastres in 1848 to over 20 piastres in the early 1850s and to a high of 45 piastres in 1857[4] (see Table 26). Meanwhile, on the supply side, the establishment of more modern silk-reeling factories in the Mountain allowed the better use of local cocoons to produce a higher quality thread. What is not clear, however, is whether the increase in the value of silk exports during the 1850s was accompanied by any significant growth in either the cultivation of mulberry leaves or the production of cocoons. The fact that a British consular report of 1856 speaks of an extension of the land devoted to mulberry trees is hardly conclusive.[5] Again, the figures themselves do not allow examination of the question of whether this same increase in the value of exports involved some internal reorganization of the Lebanese silk trade by which a greater proportion of an unchanging volume of cocoons was purchased by Europeans at the expense of local spinners and weavers.[6] All that can be said is that if cocoon prices rose as high as the French figures indicate, the silk manufacturers of Mount Lebanon and the Syrian interior must certainly have experienced some difficulty in maintaining their purchases of such an increasingly expensive material.

Table 27   Syrian silk production, 1861–80

	Cocoons	Price of cocoons	Estimate of amount of factory-produced thread[1]
	(kgs)	(piastres/oke)	(kgs)
1861	960,000	22–28	
1862	1,900,000	25–35	
1863	1,500,000	24	
1864	1,200,000	25–27	
1865	2,000,000	36–48	
1866	3,400,000	32–38	
1867	2,450,000	40–44	
1868	1,700,000	33–58	
1869	1,350,000	33–42	
1870	1,152,000	33–38	
1871	2,100,000	31–42	
1872	2,000,000	29–37	
1873	2,300,000	12–20	150,000
1874	1,800,000	19–21	170,000
1875	1,795,000	15–16	135,000
1876	1,667,000	24–25	117,000
1877	1,500,000		140,000
1878	2,250,000	28.5–29	165,000
1879	2,000,000		171,000
1880	2,468,000		193,000

Sources: Ducousso, *L'industrie de la soie*, 100–1, 110–11; Chevalier, 'Lyon et la Syrie', 286, 283n.

Note: 1 The estimate is based on the number of cocoons processed in the factory basins and depends on a calculation as to how much a cocoon might yield.

The situation in the 1860s and 1870s is rather better documented. Figures for Syrian silk production and for the price of cocoons are given in Table 27. They show a rise in production during the mid-1860s followed by a sharp fall at the end of the decade, and then two smaller peaks in the 1870s. These movements seem to be related to concomitant changes in price but the figures are not certain enough to allow this hypothesis to be properly tested. They also reflect the effect of the disease which struck the local silkworms in the early 1870s.[7] There is no separate series for Mount Lebanon itself but, according to French sources quoted by Chevalier, in 1864 production in the Mountain accounted for some four-fifths of the Syrian total.[8] As to the use to which the cocoons were put, according to a French consular dispatch of 1861 a third were exported direct to France, a third spun in European-style factories and a third hand-spun for sale to Syrian and Egyptian weavers.[9] Rough figures for the output of the European-style factories in the 1870s are given in Table 27.

The figures for the value of silk exports from Beirut (Table 29) are equally unsatisfactory and relate only to value. In addition, they give no indication of the brief, but profitable, export of silkworm eggs which began in the mid-1860s after the French eggs began to suffer from a second major attack of disease, this time of muscadine. This trade reached its peak in 1875 when over 100,000 ounces of Syrian eggs were sold in France, a tenth of the country's requirements.[10] But disaster followed. In spite of assistance from France, the men who prepared the eggs for export (such as the merchant Michel Medawar) were unable to ensure that they maintained their quality over time and by 1877 French complaints about the deterioration of the Lebanese product had reached such a pitch that export came to an end.[11] Worse was to follow from a Lebanese point of view. For reasons which remain unclear, the Syrian breeders were unable to master the Pasteur system of egg selection which had been introduced in 1874 and from the 1880s onwards neither Syria nor Mount Lebanon could produce enough eggs for their own needs, let alone for sale abroad.[12]

A major factor underlying the increase in the production and export of Lebanese silk was the establishment of more and more European-style spinning factories. During the early 1850s there were nine or ten such enterprises in the Mountain, owned by foreigners, mostly French, employing some 800 to 900 workers and with a capacity of perhaps 35,000 kg a year.[13] There were also at least four or five smaller factories erected by local entrepreneurs.[14] Several more foreign establishments were put up later in the decade.[15] Some silk factories were then destroyed during the fighting in 1860 only to be rebuilt by French troops the following year.[16] Thereafter, the tremendous rise in silk prices during the early 1860s encouraged more Syrian and Lebanese merchants and bankers to invest in silk manufacture. While the number of European owned factories remained more or less constant at around ten or eleven, those established by local entrepreneurs (including members of leading commercial families like the Sursuqs and the Tuwaynis) rose from thirty-three in 1862 to forty-seven in 1867.[17] Again, while the next decade saw a reduction in European ownership as perhaps half the existing factories were sold off to local residents, the number of Syrian and Lebanese owned factories jumped to around a hundred by 1880.[18] Even though such factories were generally of a much smaller capacity with lower productivity than the European owned enterprises, an increase in numbers of this magnitude must certainly have been responsible for the considerable increase in the output of silk thread.

The reason for the increasing control of silk production by local entre-preneurs had much to do with the nature of the industry itself. In its initial years it was foreigners who enjoyed a particular advantage, for not only did the construction of a factory and its provision with a hot water boiler and reeling machines require a substantial amount of capital but it was also necessary to have access to a regular line of credit in order to finance each season's purchase of cocoons. In both cases the bulk of this capital came from the silk manufacturers of Lyons and there were close links between individual French firms and particular Mountain factories.[19] Later, how-ever, as local Beiruti banks became better established and as the mechan-ism for transferring funds from France to Lebanon improved, it became easier for local entrepreneurs to raise the initial capital themselves as well as to obtain the requisite credit. According to Chevalier, a Syrian or Lebanese factory owner who was considered a good credit risk could obtain a hundred days advance from Lyons at between 4 and 6 per cent against future deliveries of thread; while one whose prospects were less good could get a similar sum from a Beirut bank at 10 per cent.[20]

Once they found a way of obtaining such funds on a regular basis the local owners had two major advantages over their foreign rivals. The successful management of a factory required an orderly supply of both cocoons and labour at as cheap a rate as possible, and in each case a knowledge of local conditions and an ability to ensure that contracts were kept was an enormous asset in what was, inevitably, a very competitive market.[21] Cocoons were generally purchased in advance, sometimes in return for a new supply of silkworm eggs as well as cash, and it was a difficult business for the brokers employed by the various factories to make sure that deliveries were made at exactly the right time and at the right quality. Labour presented even more of a problem. Almost at once a large part of the factory workforce came to be composed of (unmarried) women employed on a seasonal basis for up to 200 days a year.[22] But it was often hard to persuade local families to allow their daughters to work in such factories.[23] It was also hard to ensure that women, once trained, would return to the same factory for the next season, the more so as agents for another owner might well try to entice them away. On occasions managers were successful in persuading the Maronite clergy to provide them with female spinners, sometimes even orphans.[24] But, for the most part, it was a question of using a combination of a kind of quasi-legal contract (in which a worker would promise to work the next season in exchange for a small advance) reinforced where possible by pressure and persuasion, and whatever kinship ties or other links the owner might have with the people of a particular district. Once again, in such conditions a local entrepreneur had an obvious advantage.[25]

Some of the consequences of this situation will be examined in Chapter 9. For the time being it is enough to make two points. First, whatever the pattern of ownership, the industry as a whole remained firmly subservient to French capital and French commercial interests. Many of the local entrepreneurs were French-protected persons. More importantly, French firms provided the bulk of the working capital, whether directly or via Beirut subsidiaries, and the manufacturers of Lyons bought the greater part of the thread. Second, French control may have been made even more easy by the multiplicity of small factories, almost all totally dependent on borrowed money, and the fact that there was no tendency towards a concentration of activity in a few large firms with a large accumulation of capital resources of their own.[26]

Looked at in slightly wider perspective it is easy to see how silk production, and especially the activities of the spinning factories, came to act as a spearhead for the further transformation of the economy of the silk districts in the centre and south of Mount Lebanon. Increased concentration on the cultivation of mulberry trees led to a greater agricultural specialization in which the peasants who tilled the mountain terraces tended to rely more and more on the sale of their crop of leaves to provide them with food and other necessities. For some, additional income was provided either by silkworm rearing or by the wages earned by members of the families employed in the spinning factories. Others began to work as day labourers outside their own districts once the silk harvest was over.[27] Meanwhile, the receipt of regular money incomes by the mulberry cultivators greatly facilitated the extension of cash rents.[28] Even where land was let on a crop-sharing basis, as in the case of the Khazin's property in the Kisrawan, the tenants were required to pay the taxes and a number of extra charges with money which they often had to borrow from merchants in Beirut.[29]

The expansion of factory production must also have had a serious impact on the local textile industry, but this is more difficult to trace. As far as can be ascertained from the limited – and rather contradictory – information available, the period under discussion witnessed a further reorganization of the Lebanese weaving industry marked by its concentration in a number of major centres such as the villages and small towns of Zuq and Dair al-Qamar and, after 1860, of Bikfaya, Shwaifat and Brumana.[30] In each case entrepreneurs were able to withstand the rising tide of foreign imports (see Table 28) by taking advantage of certain local economies of scale, by developing new products (like the special cloth called *dima*) suitable for Middle Eastern markets, by making use of imported yarn and thread and, finally, in some instances, by replacing the old putting-out system by the employment of day labourers or piece-workers in regular workshops.[31] At the same time, costs were kept down and risks reduced by continuing to work mostly on demand. Silk formed an important ingredient of many of the textiles produced and, as a rule, it was purchased as cheaply as possible either from those local spinners using traditional methods who were still able to compete with the factories for cocoons or from factory-spun thread which had been rejected by the export merchants as sub-standard.[32] In either case sudden upward movements in price presented great problems if costs were to be kept sufficiently low to maintain a competitive position against imported textiles. This can be seen with special clarity in the fierce opposition of the weavers to the attempt by the Ottoman authorities in 1859 to reimpose a duty of 12 per cent on silk cloth produced inside the Empire.[33]

Table 28   British exports of cotton goods to Syria/Palestine, 1852–72
(annual averages)

	Cotton cloth	Cotton yarn		Total cotton exports
	(£,000)	*(£,000)*	*(lbs,000)*	*(£,000)*
1852–4	318	50	1878	395
1857–9				721[1]
1860–4	751	57		903
1865–9	1079	79		1291
1870–2	982	112		1208

Source: British foreign trade figures in *PPs*.

Note: 1 The official sources give two slightly different figures for each of these years.

The increase in silk production also had an important impact on the fortunes of the bankers and merchants who provided the working capital for peasants, spinners and weavers, allowing them greatly enlarged opportunities for profit and accumulation. This money could then be used for loans to members of other groups, like the *muqatajis*, or for other types of business like the purchase and sale of foreign goods, thus encouraging the use of money and the spread of commercialization far beyond the reaches of the silk sector itself. Figures for the trade of Beirut are given in Table 29 and show that imports rose steadily during the 1850s, financed, in part, by the growing value of silk exports.

Such important developments in the mode of economic activity could not fail to have a significant impact on the pattern of relations between different social groups. It has already been noted (in Chapter 3) how, during the first half of the nineteenth century, the beginnings of sectarian politics in Mount Lebanon based on the assertion of the primacy of a religious or communal identity had become inextricably enmeshed with a growing challenge to the power and authority of the *muqatajis* by peasants and merchants.[34] What now has to be done is to trace some aspects of this process in greater detail as it continued through the 1850s. As far as the challenge to the *muqatajis* by their peasants was concerned this took the

Table 29   Estimates of the value of Beirut's sea-borne trade, 1850–78
(annual averages in millions of francs)[1]

| | Exports | | Imports |
	silk	total	
1850–4	4.58[2]	20.46	27.28
1855–8	9.27	39.87	36.83
1859		42.5	36.25
1862		31.3	46.5
1871–3	11.04[3]	15.67[4]	29.35[4]
1876			27.23
1878		32.0	

Sources: Chevalier, *Mont Liban*, 196, 226; Farley, *Massacres*, 185–6; *CR* (UK) Beirut, 1873, *PP*, 1874, LXVII, 849–50; *CR* (UK) Beirut, 1876, *PP*, 1878 LXXIII, 286–7.

Notes: 1 Figures in £ converted at £1 = 25 francs.   2 Except 1852.   3 Except 1871.   4 Trade with Europe only.

form of an intensified struggle over the ownership of land and over the pay-ment of taxes and of customary gifts and presents. One sign of this is the fact that in some districts like those round Zahle and Hasbaya the cultivators went to the lengths of petitioning the Ottoman authorities to remove their villages from the jurisdiction of the local (Druze) shaikhs.[35] But, in the event, it was in the land controlled by the Khazin family in the Kisrawan, just north of the Beirut/Damascus road, that the fiercest contest took place.[36] Taking the Mountain as a whole it could well be argued that this particular family formed the weakest link in the chain of *muqataji* rule. On the one hand, it had both grown so large and lost so many of its traditional sources of income that the only way it could survive was by demanding an increase in the payment of gifts and dues. On the other, the fact that it was Christian, that it was in opposition to the Ottoman authorities, and that it was bitterly resented by the local Maronite clergy, meant that it was dangerously isolated from any of the forces which might have given it support. Just how dangerous this isolation had become is well illustrated by the way in which a peasant movement which had begun in the spring of 1858 by demanding the abolition of some of the more irksome exactions like the corvée on Khazin land quickly grew so strong that by early 1859, under its leader Taniyus Shahin it had driven most of the family from their homes and redistributed much of its property.[37]

A second group involved in the attack on the Khazins consisted of Christian merchants who saw it as the first part of a campaign which would rid all Mount Lebanon of *muqataji* rule. Such men belonged to a class which was becoming increasingly irked by the barriers to the free play of commercial enterprise which such rule still imposed. They resented the fact that they had to rely on the *muqatajis* to enforce the contracts they had made with peasant cultivators; they disliked the arbitrary levy of fees and dues on commerce and trade; they were anxious to be able to buy and sell land without hindrance.[38] A further source of friction arose from the fact that some of the merchants had made large loans to *muqatajis* which they were having great difficulty in getting repaid.[39] For all these reasons some of their number were willing to encourage and support the peasant revolt in the Kisrawan and then, in the latter part of 1859, to take things further by organizing a committee in Beirut under Bishop Tubiyya to make preparations for the second stage of the struggle against the *muqatajis* which they believed was soon to come. To this end they purchased and distributed weapons and helped to organize peasant defence committees in the Mountain villages.[40]

If the peasant uprising in the Kisrawan, and the support it received from some of the Christian merchants, is best seen as having its origin in a direct challenge to *muqataji* rule, it soon assumed the aspect of a communal struggle between groups of Maronites and Druzes.[41] This was partly a result of a growing tendency to think and act in religious or confessional terms, partly a function of the Druze response. Worried by signs of peasant restiveness in their own villages in the south, disturbed by reports of Maronite purchases of arms, the Druze leaders did their best to protect their own class position by stressing the need for communal solidarity in the face of outside attack, thus giving the dispute a directly religious character.[42] It was in this guise that, once the fighting began in earnest in May and June 1860, Druze forces attacked and captured the predominantly Christian towns of Hasbayya, Rashayya, Dair al-Qamar and Zahle as well as driving out part of the Christian peasant population of the southern district of Jazzin. Many hundreds if not thousands of Christians were killed in these attacks and large numbers of others forced to leave their homes, many of whom took refuge either in Beirut or in the more solidly Maronite districts to the north.[43]

Druze success was only temporary, however. In spite of early Ottoman attempts to bring things under control before outside intervention, the overtly confessional character of the fighting and the fact that Druze victories in the Mountain seemed to be the trigger for yet another serious attack on a local Christian community, this time in Damascus, prompted the dispatch of a French expeditionary force and the occupation, for some months, of most of the predominantly Druze districts in south Lebanon. This was soon followed by the formation of an international commission consisting of the representatives of a number of European powers, including Britain and France, to discuss the future status of the Mountain. The result was the issue of a constitutional document – Règlement et Protocole relatifs à la reorganisation du Mont-Liban – in June 1861 which, with its amendments of 1864, provided the basis for a new political and economic order, replacing the rule of the *muqatajis* with that of a special type of administration largely independent of Ottoman control.[44] In the words of this document all 'feudal' privileges were abolished while power was transferred to a local Christian governor, known as a *mutasarrif*, assisted by an administrative council of twelve members chosen on a confessional basis. Law and order was to be maintained by a corps of Lebanese gendarmes which was also to take part in the collection of taxes. The taxes themselves were fixed at a low level which it was difficult to increase, and could only be used inside the *mutasarriflik/mutasarrifiya* itself. One result among many was that Mount Lebanon became the only place within the Empire where tax-farming was completely abolished.

The Règlement thus represented a considerable victory for those forces seeking to put an end to *muqataji* rule in the interests of a further opening up of Mount Lebanon to foreign commercial interests and to the unfettered pursuit of private profit. In spite of their community's losses in the fighting, the Christian merchants had achieved their objective – as a result of international intervention. There was also another group which had every reason to be satisfied: the European bankers and merchants of Beirut. For some years its British and French members in particular had been pressing for the jurisdiction of the Commercial Tribunal established in the town in 1850 to be extended to the Mountain. As it was, anyone who owed money to a Beirut-based firm or who was involved in any business dispute with it could simply flee to the hills from which he could only be forced to return if his creditor could persuade one of the *muqatajis* there to arrest him.[45] This the *muqatajis*, many of whom were themselves in debt to foreign merchants, were often unwilling to do.[46] From the point of view of the foreign commercial community the problem became even more pressing after business in Beirut began to be affected by the European financial crisis of 1857. As inevitably happened on such occasions, the amount of credit allowed to local concerns by the British and French banking houses was much restricted, the international price of exports declined and trade diminished. The result was a general increase in bad debts and a rash of bankruptcies which made the foreign merchants more anxious than ever to find ways of bringing their debtors to court.[47] In these circumstances it can be no coincidence that the Règlement of 1861 embodied many of the measures for which such merchants had long been pressing. Not only did it abolish the judicial powers of the *muqatajis* but it also stated specifically that any commercial or civil case involving an inhabitant of the Mountain should be tried in the Commercial Tribunal in Beirut, even though the town itself was not part of the *mutasarrifiya*.[48]

As was so clearly intended by its signatories, the Règlement of 1861 provided the framework for the future economic development of the Mountain. The establishment of better security, the institution of a regular system of tax collection, the improvements in the administrative structure – all helped to create conditions in which money wealth could be accumulated without official harassment or sudden arbitrary changes in procedures.[49] The institution of special courts to register land and to regulate its sale allowed the further purchase of *muqataji* land by merchants or rich peasant proprietors. Cultivators were relieved of the most onerous ties which had bound them to their lords and could now dispose of their labour time freely and without obstruction. In addition, Mount Lebanon's special status meant that its inhabitants were not conscripted into the Ottoman army nor liable to pay the special taxes which were levied in time of war.[50] This was of particular advantage during the Ottoman campaigns against the Russians in the late 1870s when agricultural life in the rest of Syria was very much disrupted by the call-up of peasants for military duty. The importance which Mountain merchants attached to this type of privilege can also be seen in the way in which they fought, successfully, to ensure that the *mutasarriflik* was exempt from the control exercised by the Ottoman Tobacco *Régie* and the institutions established after 1881 by the Ottoman Public Debt Administration.[51]

It would be wrong, however, to exaggerate the extent of changes produced by the new order in the Mountain. This can be clearly seen by looking at the peasants and the *muqatajis*, the two groups whose conflict had sparked off the fighting in 1858. As far as the latter were concerned, though they had lost most of their legal and administrative privileges and were forced to sell some of their land, they still remained in possession of sizeable estates which they continued to let to peasant–clients bound to them by ties of communal or family loyalty.[52] Moreover, in a significant number of cases, individual members of *muqataji* families were further able to re-establish their power as a result of their recruitment into the new central administration controlled by the *mutasarrif* at Baabda.[53] Others supplemented their income by going into business with merchants or entrepreneurs down on the coast. Hence if some continued to lose money and to be forced to sell land, the majority prospered to such an extent that their descendants were well placed to play a leading role in the new Lebanon created by the French after the First World War. Even in the Kisrawan the peasants seem to have been unable to hold on to the gains they had won from the Khazins during the early stages of their revolt. It soon became clear that neither the Maronite church, nor the merchants, nor the European powers were going to allow the fighting to develop into a general attack on property. For this reason, the leaders of the peasant movement were specifically excluded from the new system of administration instituted in 1861 while members of the Khazin family were not only allowed to regain most of their land but were also given many top posts in both the local and the central administration.[54] Thereafter, the Kisrawani peasants, like those everywhere else in the Mountain, were in the disadvantageous position of having to compete for scarce supplies of land against landowners who still possessed many means of economic and extra-economic coercion.

Partly as a result of the new order established by the Règlement, Mount Lebanon quickly recovered from the worst effects of the fighting to experience a decade of considerable economic growth. Other factors also had a role to play. One was the activity of French troops in occupation of the southern districts in rebuilding many of the Christian-owned factories and workshops which had been destroyed during the disturbances; another was the provision of some £250,000 by foreign charitable organizations, much of which was spent on the purchase of new spinning and weaving equipment.[55] But what was probably the most important single cause was the renewed increase in the international price of silk in response to the world-wide shortage of cotton produced by the American Civil War. As already noted, this stimulated a rapid recovery in silk output as well as the construction of many new silk reeling factories.[56] By 1863 the value of loans granted to peasant cultivators by Lebanese silk merchants was already four times as high as in 1858 or 1861.[57] An extra fillip was provided by the 1861 revision of the commercial conventions between the Ottomans and the major European powers which allowed a gradual reduction in the duty on the Empire's exports from 8 per cent down to 1 per cent in 1868.[58] Thus as early as 1861 a British consular report could speak of the 'surprising progress in wealth, population and general prosperity' of the Mountain and of the rise in its population.[59] And in the next few years continued high profits from silk allowed many merchants and peasants to buy land, particularly on the plain just to the south of Beirut towards Shwaifat. Higher incomes from silk also encouraged the revival of manufacturing. In Dair al-Qamar a loan from the French government was used to rehabilitate forty-two workshops in which 400 workers were employed.[60] Elsewhere, foreigners who toured the Mountain in the 1860s and 1870s wrote of considerable numbers of looms at Zuq, Bikfaya, Shwaifat and Brumana as well as fourteen soapworks and numerous workshops making shoes and other leather goods.[61]

An important role in the revival of economic activity was played by the merchants of Beirut. Even though the town was outside the official boundary of the *mutasarrifiya*, its own important facilities and the fact that its Commercial Tribunal had been given such wide powers of jurisdiction made it, *de facto*, the economic capital of the Mountain. It provided the channel for funds coming from Europe for the purchase, processing and export of silk; it generated local funds for investment in the Mountain or for loans to Mountain merchants and entrepreneurs.[62] A further link between the coast and the interior was provided by the opening in 1863 of the Beirut/Damascus private carriage road constructed by a French company.[63]

This not only provided a regular means of communication with Syria but also with a number of important Lebanese towns like Zahle which were either on or near the route. Later, after the government of the *mutasarrifiya* established its own public works department in 1867, smaller, public, roads were built running south from Aley, halfway up the first ridge of the Lebanese mountain chain, to the villages of the Shuf.[64] All this encouraged the further growth of the town of Beirut itself. From a population of some 40,000 in 1857 it grew to perhaps 65,000 in 1875 and 80,000 in 1880.[65]

If the 1860s were a decade of prosperity for Beirut and the Mountain, the 1870s saw a significant reduction in the level of economic activity. A series of bad silk harvests from 1868 was followed by a sharp fall in price. Hence, even when production recovered in the early 1870s, profits were much reduced. Later, in the mid-1870s, both Beirut and the Mountain suffered considerably from the effects of the economic depression in Syria and Anatolia which led to a falling off of trade and a drastic reduction in the market for Lebanese goods.[66] A further problem was the dramatic fall in the value of the Ottoman bonds held by many of the merchants and bankers of Beirut as bankruptcy approached.[67] Cuts in the Ottoman subsidy towards the *mutasarrifiya*'s budget only made matters worse.[68] The result was a contraction of credit, a decline in local investment and a marked increase in indebtedness.[69] Land prices which fell by 50 per cent between 1865 and 1872 fell still more, forcing many people who had purchased plots on borrowed money to sell at a loss.[70] As the recession deepened many silk factories were temporarily forced to suspend operations.[71]

Nevertheless, there were some who still prospered. One result of the decline in profit margins was the final elimination, in the early 1870s, of all but one of the British merchants established at Beirut, leaving the field clear for their local competitors to take complete control of the business of importing Manchester goods.[72] Again, there were bankers and merchants with enough capital to buy up large tracts of cheap land for themselves outside the Mountain. Some like the Eddés continued to expand their estates in the Bekaa valley, sometimes using Ottoman troops to expel the existing peasant population.[73] Others like the Sursuqs took advantage of the local Ottoman administration's perennial financial embarrassment to obtain state lands either for small amounts of money or as payment for goods and services provided.[74] This same tendency to look for investment possibilities outside the Mountain can also be seen in the case of the merchants who established branches of their firms in Alexandria, Europe and the Americas.[75] Contacts overseas were further encouraged by the increase in the numbers of Mountain Lebanese, many of them young men, leaving the country as emigrants. This movement had begun as a result of the fears aroused by the attacks on the Christian population in 1860.[76] Later, in the 1870s, it was continued as a response to the recession as well as to the fact that foreign mission schools were producing far more educated youths than the economy could absorb.[77] According to one source over 300 Ottoman subjects from Syria migrated to the United States in the 1870s.[78] The same years saw the first movement of Lebanese to Brazil, a number of whom established commercial houses in Rio.[79] This search for economic opportunity outside the Mountain was to be a recurring feature of Lebanese economic history.

The Syrian interior [80]

During the 1850s the Syrian provinces continued to suffer from all the defects in the Ottoman administrative arrangements introduced after the Egyptian withdrawal. The power of the local governors remained divided and weak. The same vicious circle continued in which low revenues prevented the recruitment of extra troops while the small size of the local garrisons did not allow any increase in the amount of taxes collected. Indeed, in some respects the situation became even worse. Although the size of the army of Arabistan (with its headquarters at Damascus) was increased from 12,000 men in 1850 to 17,000 in 1853 it then lost most of its effective strength as many of its members were withdrawn to fight in the Crimean War.[81] Even after the war was over troop levels remained low with a total of only 8000 in 1858.[82] As a result it seems likely that the Ottomans were still unable to maintain regular security outside the areas immediately surrounding the major garrison towns and it was only in a few areas, like parts of the Bekaa valley, that conditions improved enough to allow any obvious expansion of the settled area.[83] Meanwhile, little progress was made in the constant struggle to control the nomadic tribes living in close proximity to peasant populations.[84]

What effect the general lack of security may have had on the level of economic activity is impossible to say. While it is unlikely that there could have been any major increase in agricultural output in most areas there is some scattered evidence to show that Syrian cultivators were able to make an impressive response to the increased European demand for Middle Eastern cereals following the repeal of the British Corn Laws and then, even more importantly, during the Crimean War. Some rough estimates for the export of wheat from Syria and Palestine to the United Kingdom are given in Table 30. It may well be that just as large an amount was sent, either by the Ottoman government or by private merchants, to provision the allied armies fighting the Russians in the Crimea.[85] Another local crop which responded quickly to the higher prices prevailing in the mid-1850s was silk. Even though the greater part of each harvest was grown in the Lebanese Mountain, a smaller proportion was produced either in those districts of Syria adjacent to the Mountain or in the north.[86] Figures for the value of

Syrian crops exported from Beirut and other ports during this same period confirm the same impression of a general expansion of sales abroad.[87] But this still leaves the usual question of whether a rise in exports represented an increase in cultivation or simply a diversion of part of the harvest from the domestic to the foreign market.[88]

Table 30   Exports of cereals from ports on the Syria/Palestine coast

A   *United Kingdom import of wheat from Syria and Palestine, 1850–5*

	tons
1850	3300
1851	10,390
1852	3090
1853	5225
1855	c.20,000[1]

Sources: British official figures to be found in *PP*, 1854/5, LI, 569 and LII 25–34.
Note: 1 Estimate by Schölch.

B   *Exports of wheat, barley and other cereals, all ports, 1873–82 (annual averages in £)*

	1873–7	1878–82
Wheat	59,367	135,000
Barley	12,931	71,259
Other cereals	84,555	159,000
Total	156,853	365,259

Source: British *CR*s in Kalla, 'Role of Foreign Trade', 260.

If the early and middle years of the 1850s were ones of some prosperity for those engaged in the cultivation and sale of cash crops, the last three must certainly have witnessed quite a substantial contraction in economic activity. The European recession of 1857/8 brought the boom in the price of primary products to an end. As far as the provinces of Damascus and Aleppo were concerned this was accompanied (as in Mount Lebanon) by a tightening of credit, at least one very bad cereal harvest (1858) and a general reduction in local purchasing power which hit importers and local producers alike.[89] As usually happened at such times, matters were made still worse by an increase in nomadic raiding, no doubt exacerbated by the failure of the harvest along the desert fringe and the provincial administration's failure to find the funds either to increase military activity or to pay the tribes to keep quiet.[90] Attacks on the settled population increased and in 1857 one of the main Baghdad caravans was plundered of goods estimated by a British consul at the high figure of £5,000,000, forcing a great deal of the trans-desert traffic to eschew Damascus and to adopt the safer northern route to Aleppo.[91]

These economic difficulties provide some of the background to the

Damascus riots of 1860 in which some thousands of the city's Christian population were killed.[92] Not only did they lead to an obvious increase in hardship but they also acted to exacerbate the tensions which already existed between various social as well as confessional groups. One example of this is the animosity felt by Muslim textile workers towards some of their Christian competitors who, they felt, were able to capture more of a shrinking local market by using their better contacts with the European consuls and merchants to avoid local duties and to introduce cheaper methods of production based on the use of imported thread.[93] Another example concerns the measures which the provincial administration was forced to take to meet the growing financial deficit caused by the need to increase expenditure – whether on local security or on the remittances demanded by the central treasury in Istanbul – at a time of falling local revenue. It is surely no accident that it was in 1857 that an Ottoman governor, Nedım Paşa, was first forced to raise money by an issue of *serghis*, short-term bonds paying an interest of 2.5 to 3 per cent a month renewable on an annual basis.[94] But this at once raised fresh problems. Given the administration's continued shortage of funds it soon became the practice to give the holders of these bonds *havalés* or certificates entitling them to collect taxes from particular villages in lieu of interest.[95] This was disruptive enough when it concerned only Muslim holders of *serghis*. But when it was realized that many of them were owned either by Europeans or by Jewish and Christian protégés of the European consulates in Damascus there was a very real fear that such people might use their creditor position to obtain control, and perhaps even ownership, over sizeable areas of land.[96] The fact that in 1858 the administration was forced to borrow money from the same group to defray the expenses of the Hajj (pilgrimage) served to arouse Muslim susceptibilities still further.[97]

For all this, however, the links between such overlapping economic and religious tensions and the Damascus outbreak itself should not be over-stated. While it is true, for instance, that during the riots and massacres most, if not all, of the looms owned by Christians in the central part of the city were burned this still does not provide more than a part of a very much more complex total story. As most accounts show, there were a large number of other factors – the influence of the fighting in Mount Lebanon, the fears aroused by Ottoman and European promotion of Christian interests, rivalries between different groups of Damascenes, and so on – which also have to be taken into account.[98] Just as much to the point for present purposes is the fact that, for the purpose of the study of the economic history of Syria, the causes of the riots were probably less important than their consequences. It is to this aspect that I will turn next.

Not surprisingly, the short term effects of the riots on the economic life of the city of Damascus were extremely disruptive. Textile production was much reduced as a result of the wholesale destruction of Christian-owned looms. According to J. L. Farley, these had numbered nearly 3000 out of a total of 3500 in the year before the riots, the vast majority of which were smashed.[99] Meanwhile, business and commercial life was much disrupted by the punitive measures taken against many members of the city's leading families. Some were executed or sent into exile; others were only released from arrest after the payment of a large ransom; others again lost much of their land. The fines levied on the non-Christian communities and the wholesale conscription of young Muslims into the Ottoman army added further burdens.[100]

What is not clear, however, is the length of time in which economic life remained in this depressed state. For one thing, the important commercial quarter outside the city walls, the Maidan, was totally untouched by the rioting and, indeed, acted as something of a haven for Christian artisans fleeing from the mob.[101] Later, it was Maidani merchants who were active in advancing capital to a new group of weavers, mostly Muslim, anxious to revive the local textile industry, and it may be that this was one of the reasons why the city's productive capacity was so quick to return to its pre-riot volume.[102] Second, the arrival of large numbers of Ottoman troops was made the occasion for a concerted, and often successful, drive for government control over the adjacent rural areas. Beginning with the Hauran, which was subject to more rigorous taxation in 1861/2, Ottoman military expeditions began to be sent further and further afield until, by the end of the decade, the security situation in the districts to the south of the city was much improved. Lewis, who has examined this process in detail, writes of the dramatic changes which took place all along the desert fringe and in the north of what is now Jordan in the late 1860s as a result of a combination of the use of better armed troops – especially after the introduction of breech-loading rifles – better tactics, and the policy of settling hardy agricultural colonists, such as the Circassians, in exposed districts.[103] Even if it was still necessary to strike bargains with powerful local leaders like the Druze family of al-Atrash in the Hauran, the result must certainly have been an increase in rural tax revenues as well as an increase in the volume of surplus appropriated by those city-based families who gained control of land in the newly pacified districts by means of tax-farms or even outright ownership.[104] This latter trend was further intensified by the deliberate policy of Reşid Paşa, the provincial governor in the late 1860s, of auctioning off state land to members of the city's leading families as a way of winning their co-operation.[105] Although Ottoman administrators might cast envious eyes at the new order established in Mount Lebanon with its system of the direct collection of taxes on government account, their own position was too weak to follow suit and the best that they could do was to attempt to share access to the rural surplus with their Syrian allies.[106]

A similar process was also taking place in the province of Aleppo. There too Ottoman troops began to establish new posts along the desert frontier and to score a notable series of victories against the more powerful of the local tribes. As early as 1862 a permanent garrison was established at Deir Ez-Zor on the Euphrates to the east of Aleppo and this was then used as a base for operations further down the river.[107] As in the south, pacification was accompanied by beduin settlement, by increased revenues and by the award to local notables of rights to control over land.[108]

It would seem likely that one of the most obvious results of this whole process must have been an increase in agricultural production, the more so as the 1860s was a period of particularly high prices. But, once again, there is an unfortunate lack of hard evidence. While it is clear that there was a significant increase in the production of certain cash crops like cotton and tobacco during the mid-1860s, particularly in the districts round Latakia, no figures exist for the more important products like wheat and barley.[109] There is the same difficulty concerning wool, which was being exported in increasing quantities whenever conditions in the desert were peaceful enough to allow it.[110]

What is more certain, however, is that any advance which may have taken place during the 1860s was soon checked and that for almost all the inland districts of Syria the 1870s was a decade of increasing economic difficulty. One reason for this was the large number of bad harvests in one part of the region or another. In the case of Damascus, for example, there were poor crops almost every year between 1869 and 1879. Another was the impact of events elsewhere in the Empire. Ottoman bankruptcy brought ruin or great difficulty to many of the richer inhabitants of Damascus and Aleppo who had invested heavily in shares in the government's public debt.[111] This was followed by the Russian war which forced an increase in both conscription and taxation augmented by a number of forced loans.[112] Finally, there were a number of harmful changes in the international environment ranging from the depressing effects of the Franco-Prussian war to the fall in the world price of most agricultural products and the opening of the Suez Canal. Given their low quality and the high cost of internal transport, many Syrian crops, such as wheat, barley and cotton, could only occasionally be exported at a profit.[113] On top of this, the re-direction of trade via the Suez Canal reduced still further the amount of trans-desert commerce which was possible with Baghdad, Persia and the east.[114] By 1874, according to the British vice-consul, the 'former active trade' of Damascus had more or less ceased to exist.[115]

In this gloomy picture there are only two bright spots. One is the continued improvement in rural security as large-scale punitive expeditions gave way to a more positive policy of establishing regular garrisons, encouraging beduin settlement and making good use of the influx of

Circassian refugees from Russia's southern borders. In some districts like the Bekaa valley there was a steady increase in agricultural production as the population almost doubled in the ten years up to 1880.[116] In others, like the area round Kunaitra (Qunaytirah) on the Gaulan, Circassian settlers brought a return to agricultural life after years of neglect.[117] Those who were able to derive particular profit from these developments were, as always, men close to the centres of provincial administration who were able to use their connections to obtain control over wide stretches of land.[118] As elsewhere, there were great difficulties in getting land registered and thus obtaining secure title. It was also necessary to have access to the Ottoman troops necessary to coerce the agricultural population into paying their rents or taxes or meeting their debts.[119] But for those who could manage it the profits were large. As Midhat Paşa, the would-be reforming governor of Damascus at the end of the 1870s, was quick to find, there were ways of 'fixing' the bidding for government tax-farms in such a way that the revenues were reduced to perhaps only a half of what they could properly have yielded.[120]

Table 31   Estimates of the number of textile looms at work in the main Syrian towns, 1861–79

	Aleppo	Damascus	Homs/Hama
1861	10,000	550	
1864		3156	
1871	5000		
1872	6400	1300	
1874	5000		2500
1875	2400	12,000	
1876	700		
1879		4000	

Sources: Kalla, 'Role of Foreign Trade', 201–2; Farley, *Turkey*, 212; British *CRs* in *PPs* 1872, LVII and LVIII, 1874, LXVII, 1875, LXXVII, 1876, LXXXI, 1877, LXXXIII, 1880, LXXIV.

The other area of growth was that of certain sectors of local industry. Here Syrian weavers were able to take advantage of the world recession of the 1870s to expand their own production. In particular, the depression in the French textile industry at the beginning of the decade brought welcome relief from some of the worst effects of foreign competition.[121] Further stimulus came from the abolition of the internal Ottoman customs tariff in 1874 and from the fall in the cost of locally produced cotton, silk and wool.[122] Given this small degree of leeway it proved possible to produce local goods which were cheap enough to find an expanding market among the poorer classes in the towns as well as among nomads and agriculturalists living in remote areas where European goods were less well-known.[123] The result was a real revival of activity, not only in Aleppo and Damascus, but also in other centres like Homs (described by one British consul as 'the Manchester of Syria') and Hama where, according to one estimate, there were already 2500 looms in operation in 1874 (see Table 31).[124]

Palestine[125]

The economic history of Palestine between 1850 and 1880 shows certain general similarities to that of the Syrian provinces for the same period. As in Syria, the 1850s was a decade marked by great insecurity in the rural areas and growing social tensions in the towns, while the 1860s and 1870s saw a major expansion in agricultural output, first as a result of the stimulus of rising world prices, then of a determined Ottoman effort to extend their authority into areas at some distance from the major garrison towns. But as in Syria too, examination of the period presents major problems as a result of lack of reliable information and the uneven, irregular nature of many key developments. Once again, treatment will consist only of an attempt to focus on general trends.

The years immediately after 1850 saw an intensification of the struggle between the leading families in the mountains north and south of Jerusalem for control of their respective districts.[126] The impression to be gained from the reports of contemporary European observers who witnessed some of the major battles of the period is that they involved larger bodies of men and led to a much greater destruction of life and property and a much greater disruption of agricultural activity than the more ritualized confrontations of earlier times.[127] Villages were regularly destroyed. Pierotti describes a fight between supporters of the Abu Ghosh and the Laham families near Jerusalem in which many olive trees were cut down and large numbers of cattle stolen.[128] The regular use of beduin allies in the battles encouraged repeated nomadic incursions up into the hills. In part this was a further development of the process begun after the Egyptian withdrawal in which more families, with greater wealth at their disposal, struggled more intensively for control of the larger economic and political resources to be found in mid-nineteenth-century Palestine. But the immediate cause was the withdrawal of most, if not all, of the Ottoman regular garrison at the beginning of the Crimean War leaving the country to be policed by disorderly bands of locally recruited soldiers and horsemen.[129]

From a security point of view the situation began to improve with the return of a Turkish batallion to Jerusalem in late 1854 and the beginnings of a more forceful policy aimed at reasserting government authority. That this was absolutely necessary was brought home to the Ottomans not only by the immediate danger of what Hoexter has described as a 'civil war' between the leading families but also by the ever present fear that the prevailing insecurity would be used as an occasion for greater European intervention, something which became even more of a threat after the anti-Christian riots in Nablus in 1856 — yet another example of the tensions produced by the changes in the power and position of members of the various religious communities.[130] As revenues and the increase in the numbers of Ottoman troops permitted, one mountain district after another was brought under control, its inhabitants subjected to regular taxation and conscription, and the military power of its leading families broken. In the north a build-up of Turkish forces allowed an Ottoman governor to be imposed on Nablus in 1858 and Arraba, the stronghold of the most bellicose local family, the Abd al-Hadis, to be bombarded into submission in 1859. In the south a similar process led to the destruction of the power of the emirs at Hebron. Thereafter, as Porath has noted, the rivalry of the leading families was transferred from the battlefield to the chambers of the Majlis al-Idara and other local councils of which most were members.[131]

With their authority over the mountains secure, the Ottomans were then able to turn their attention to the foothills and the plains. Using the same methods as in Syria they made a concerted effort to establish new garrisons, to extend their control over the nomadic tribes and to encourage settlement of sparsely populated lands. The results were often dramatic, for example, on the fertile plain of Esdaelon (Marj Ibn Amir) which stretched north-west from Beisan and Jenin north of Nablus to Haifa on the coast. In 1870, according to C. R. Conder of the Palestine Exploration Society's survey team, only a sixth of the corn land was tilled and the plain was 'black with Arab tents'.

But the Turks wrought a great and sudden change; they armed their cavalry with the Remington breech-loading rifle, and the Bedawin disappeared as if by magic.[132]

He went on to observe, with a little exaggeration no doubt, that in 1872 nine-tenths of the plain was cultivated, half with wheat and barley, and the rest with millet, sesame, cotton, tobacco and the castor oil plant.[133] Elsewhere, for example on the inhospitable plain of Caesaria along the coast between Jaffa and Haifa, the process was much slower.[134] There were also occasional lapses, as when nomadic incursion was encouraged by the withdrawal of Ottoman troops during the campaign against the Russians in 1877. But, once begun, the general trend was irreversible.

As the land on the central and northern plains became more secure various types of people hastened to cultivate it and to assert their claims over it. One group was the inhabitants of the nearby hill villages, some of whom had traditionally tried to farm such fields whenever it seemed safe.[135] Another consisted of the families of nomads who, seeing the profits to be obtained from cereal cultivation, were soon persuaded of the advantages of settled life. Tribesmen had already made a significant contribution to Palestinian agriculture, particularly in the south round Gaza, and this was no more than a continuation of the same trend.[136] A third, quite different group, were city-based bankers who were quick to use their contacts with the Ottoman authorities to purchase large tracts of land. Certainly the best known example is that of the Sursuqs of Beirut who obtained a large part of the Marj Ibn Amir, perhaps as much as 70 square miles, in the early 1870s.[137] This they attempted to exploit in the triple role of landowners, money-lenders and tax-farmers and were soon making many thousands of pounds a year.[138] But there were also the Bergheims of Jerusalem who by the end of the 1870s were farming some 5000 acres at Abu Shasham.[139] Finally, there was a small group of religious settlers, both Christian and Jewish, who had their own special reasons for attempting to found colonies in Palestine. These included the German Templars and a number of Jewish groups like the one from Jerusalem which acquired land at Petah Tikvah near Jaffa in 1878.[140]

The impact of these first attempts to develop, or in some cases to in-tensify, the agricultural development of the foothills and plains is difficult to gauge. On the one hand security was not completely established in many areas and title to particular plots was often disputed. The fact that the Ottoman government laid claim to huge stretches of land meant that it was often reluctant to encourage the type of registration provided for by the Land Law of 1858. Even the Sursuqs had to make a number of costly visits to Istanbul before they could be sure that they had obtained sure title to what they had bought.[141] They also experienced particular difficulty in per-suading peasants to settle — and then to remain — on their estates.[142] On the other hand it would seem likely that at least part of the increase in the production and export of agricultural crops (now to be examined) was the result of an expansion of cultivation into the newly settled areas. In addition, certain of the new foreign settlements, like those of the Templars, acted as pioneers in the development of fruit farming and viticulture where it was necessary to pay particular attention to method and to the proper preparation of the crop for market.[143]

The major crops produced in Palestine during this period were cereals (mainly wheat, barley and maize), sesame, cotton, olives and oranges. Estimates of the trade of the area's principal port, Jaffa, show that all of them were exported in increasing quantities for most of the period (see Tables 32 and 33). But, as is usually the case, the figures themselves are either too fragmentary or too unreliable to allow them to be taken as more than a very rough guide to a concomitant growth of agricultural produc-tion. The best that can be done is to attempt to use them to make some general points about the development of Palestinian agriculture in the three decades under discussion.[144]

As far as the cultivation of cereals was concerned, the main focus of attention continued to be the coastal region in the south. According to an

Table 32   Estimates of the sea-borne trade of Jaffa, 1850–81 (£,000)

	Exports			Imports
	Cereals (wheat, barley, maize)	Oranges	Total	Total
1850–3			24[1]	
1857			156	
1858			122	
1859		12	74	
1860		10	150	
1862			224	
1863			260	
1873	84	36	314	
1874	120		266	146
1875	147		331	142
1876	102		563	298
1877	27	12	157	262
1878	15			
1879	2	34	253	316
1880		58	307	325
1881	156	68	336	370

Sources: British *CR*s in FO 78/839, 78/874, 78/963; Foreign consular figures in Schölch, 'Aspekte der Wirtschaftlichen', Table I (converted from piastres at the rate of £1 = 100 piastres); *CR* (US) 'Cereal Production of Turkey–2', VII, 25½ (Nov. 1882), 281 (converted at the rate £1 = $5).

Note: 1 Exports to UK only.

estimate made in an American consular report for 1882, some 150,000 to 200,000 acres in the districts of Jerusalem, Hebron, Jaffa and Gaza had been placed under such crops during the previous ten years.[145] But as the first two districts were in the hill country and the third was said to have contained no more than between 20,000 and 25,000 acres of cereal land, the bulk of the production must have been in Gaza. Being so close to the coast there can have been no great problem about transport; while the fact that neither Jaffa nor Gaza yet possessed quays at which ships could be loaded directly from the land does not seem to have been a major obstacle to cereal export.[146] There is also no evidence that, in spite of their low average rainfall, the southern districts of Palestine were any more vulnerable to climatic factors than elsewhere. The peasants and semi-settled nomads of the coastal regions were thus well placed to respond to the increased European demand for cereals from the late 1840s onwards and the assumption must certainly be that production expanded considerably between the late 1850s and the late 1870s. Estimates of the growth in exports from Jaffa are given in Table 33; similar figures for Gaza, if they existed, would no doubt show an even more significant advance. The problem of finding usable statistical sources is just as apparent in the north. It can be assumed that the extension of cereal cultivation mentioned by Conder must certainly have been reflected in an increase in the amounts exported from the two nearest ports, Haifa and Acre.[147] Unfortunately, however, it is difficult to distinguish between the export of grain produced locally and the much larger quantities sent across northern Palestine from the Hauran. For what it is worth, the local German consular authorities calculated that Syrian wheat accounted for 1m. out of the 1.5m. *kilé* exported from Acre in 1876 and 1m. out of the 1.75m. exported in 1879, but this can only have been the very roughest of guesses.[148]

Table 33   Estimates of the volume of agricultural exports from Jaffa, Haifa and Acre, 1857–80[1]

	Oranges (thousands)	Wheat (kilé,000)*	Barley (kilé,000)*	Durra (kilé,000)*	Sesame (oke,000)**	Olive oil (oke,000)**
1857	6000	45	245	39	503	20
1858	3000	18	143	167	820	100
1859	6000	30	30	25	400	100
1862	8000	80	118	58	1856	1674
1863	8300	177	192	114	2893	300
1873	27,750	1110	260	25	4000	250
1874	25,500	3012	770	2715	5000	480
1875	10,200	4948	1088	3271	7800	1630
1876	14,000	2030	50	250	2900	3850
1877	14,200	580	120	566	2370	1350
1878		1950[3]	100[3]	–[3]	–[3]	–[3]
1879	26,250	293	–	5	1100	2040
1880		850	281	275	4000	800

* 1 *kilé* = 36.1 kgs.
** 1 *oke* = 1.28 kgs.

Source: Foreign consular sources in Schölch, 'Aspekte der Wirtschaftlichen', Tables 3, 5 and 6.

Notes:
1 Figures for 1857–9 are for Jaffa only.
2 Figures for oranges are for Jaffa only.
3 Excludes any exports from Jaffa.

After cereals the next two most valuable export crops (at least as far as Jaffa was concerned) were sesame seed and olive oil. Olives were grown in the hills and much of their oil was used locally, either for food or for the soap made in the factories at Nablus, Jerusalem, Ramle and Jaffa.[149] But increasing amounts were sold abroad, particularly during the two periods when there was a significant rise in price: the early 1860s and the mid-1870s (see Table 33). Sesame, which was increasingly used by European soap makers, was grown on the plains and exported in large amounts from all three of the principal ports (Table 33).[150]

Another crop which certainly experienced a similar increase in output was that of the orange, grown mostly in the gardens round Jaffa. According to a British trade report for 1873 a sixth of the crop (estimated at over

33,000,000 oranges worth about £25,000) was consumed locally and the rest exported to Egypt and Turkey.[151] The same report also mentions that there were then 420 orchards around the town and that there was a 'continuous planting' of new trees. Production was further encouraged by the first exports to Europe at about the same time. The fact that one of the larger varieties had a particularly thick skin which prevented bruising and the drying up of its rich juice during transit allowed it to be packed and sent off on long sea journeys without any danger to its taste.[152] By the early 1880s the American consular authorities estimated that Jaffa then possessed about 500 gardens, each of between two and six acres, with a total of some 800,000 trees.[153] Figures for the increase in exports are given in Tables 32 and 33.

The last major crop was cotton. This had been grown in small quantities in various parts of Palestine during the first half of the nineteenth century but, as elsewhere, it was the large rise in price first during the Crimean War then during the American Civil War boom which encouraged peasants to grow it over a wide area. The centre of production was in the Nablus district where several million lbs may have been produced for export in the early 1860s and perhaps four million (the equivalent of 40,000 cantars) in 1869.[154] However, the sharp fall in price in the early 1870s brought an equally dramatic reduction in cultivation so that by 1875 exports had dropped away to no more than 30,000 okes.* [155]

Scattered pieces of evidence of this kind about an increase in the production of a number of different Palestinian crops pose more questions than they can possibly answer. They show that, given the opportunity to sell his produce for cash, the local peasants were as quick to respond to market advantage as those anywhere else in the Middle East, even – to James Finn's surprise – at times of great insecurity.[156] But what they do not show is how this response was actually engineered. Was it largely self-financed, from the peasants' point of view, or did it rely on the creation of an extensive system of credit? What was the role of the local merchants? Who was responsible for organizing the transport, or the processing, of the quite large quantities of agricultural produce brought to the coastal ports? Every now and again there is an occasional glimpse of the development of new mechanisms for facilitating trade – for example Firestone's evidence about the new use of contracts validated by the local religious authorities during the Crimean War – but this is hardly sufficient to allow the construction of a general argument.[157]

It is equally impossible to gauge the effects of what, in the first instance at least, must have been a significant increase in the cultivators' incomes. Even though much of the money they obtained for their crops was undoubtedly

* 1 oke = 1.28 kgs.

taken from them in taxes and dues, local consular officials observed that enough remained to allow a considerable increase in consumption.[158] Others to profit were obviously the village merchants, the men with camels and donkeys who transported the produce to the coast, and the people engaged in ancillary activities like cotton ginning, olive oil pressing and the construction of orange boxes. In these circumstances it is not surprising to find an increase in imports like coffee, sugar and rice.[159] There must also have been a considerable fillip to local manufacturers. But, as always, the greater part of the rural surplus must certainly have passed to the merchants, tax-collectors and controllers of land living in the towns. Part of it was used to buy Ottoman bonds. More surprisingly, in a Middle Eastern context, another part of it was apparently reinvested in the agricultural sector itself, in this case in the planting of orange trees in the gardens around Jaffa.[160] The remainder, as always, was used in the struggle for wealth and power, now based almost exclusively on the purchase or control of agricultural lands.

7 The Iraqi provinces, 1850–1880

As far as the provinces of Mosul, Baghdad and Basra were concerned the period 1850 to 1880 was one in which the influence of Ottoman reform and the growth of commercial relations with Europe finally began to have a discernible effect on the local economy. In both cases 1869 is a date of great importance: this was the year in which the opening of the Suez Canal permitted the establishment of a regular steamship service between Basra and a number of Europe's major ports. It was also the year in which Midhat Paşa arrived in Baghdad at the start of what was to be the first serious attempt to extend government influence into the rural areas along the lines long established in Egypt and western Anatolia. Just as in Syria, he failed to achieve almost all his stated objectives. But, just as in Syria, this failure provided an opportunity for shaikhs and others with rural power to take maximum advantage of the new possibilities provided by the increase in commercial agriculture made possible by the opening up of new markets both in Iraq itself and in Europe.

The development of Iraq's sea-borne trade

At mid-century the main characteristics of Iraqi trade remained more or less the same as they had been fifty years earlier. Then, as in 1800, a large part of this trade consisted of goods in transit. As in 1800, too, Basra's major exports consisted of horses destined for India, dates for the ports of the Arabian peninsula and the Red Sea, and small quantities of wool, rice and grain. Meanwhile, the goods received in return continued to be dominated by coffee from Yeman and a variety of Indian goods including indigo, sugar and textiles.[1] In spite of the occasional sailing ship which arrived direct from Britain with cargoes for the few English merchant houses established in Basra and Baghdad, the bulk of British imports still came by way of either Aleppo or Bombay.[2] Contemporary consular reports put the value of Iraq's sea-borne trade at this time at about £280,000, consisting equally of imports and exports.[3]

The major obstacles to any increase in trade also remained more or less the same. Goods traffic along both the Tigris and the Euphrates remained difficult, slow and subject to heavy duties imposed by both the government and the tribes which controlled strategic points along the river banks.[4] The cargoes of the small boats engaged in this traffic were still held to ransom or plundered at regular intervals.[5] Sea-going ships faced other problems, notably the monsoons which made it hard for a sailing vessel to make more than one trip to India a year.[6] With access to external markets so difficult there was little incentive to increase production and the captains of the few British ships which reached Basra with goods from England generally complained of being unable to find a return cargo.[7]

There was some small improvement in this situation in the two decades before the opening of the Suez Canal. As far as internal transport was concerned some of the work of the Chesney expedition began to bear fruit in the establishment first of an Ottoman, then of a British, service of river steamers on the Tigris between Basra and Baghdad. The former was started in 1855 and soon had four ships on the river.[8] While it was badly managed, irregular in service, and carried no cargo, it did allow a safer passage of merchants and money up and down the river while providing the Ottoman administration with a better means of preventing attacks on vessels of all kinds.[9] A few years later, the British merchant firm of Lynch decided to augment its fleet of sailing boats with a number of specially constructed river steamers. In 1861 with the support of the British government it established the Euphrates and Tigris Steam Navigation Company with permission to operate two such steamers, the *City of London* which was placed on the Tigris in 1862 and the *Diyala* in 1865 — both of 100 tons.[10] The result was the creation of a regular secure cargo service which reduced the round trip from Baghdad to Basra from between three and four weeks to ten days.[11] The success of this venture then encouraged the Ottoman authorities to try to compete and in 1867 Namık Pasa, the governor of Baghdad, began the reorganization of the Turkish river fleet as the Oman–Ottoman line with two steamers, soon increased to five, and a number of towing barges.[12] Even though the new company often experienced great difficulty in keeping its service going — boats sometimes broke down or ran out of fuel or were diverted for use by soldiers or pilgrims — it provided a great increase in cargo carrying capacity.[13] While communications along the Tigris were being improved so too were those in and out of Basra. In 1862 the Indian government began to subsidize a regular steamship service from Bombay. At first boats arrived at Basra every six weeks but by 1866 this had been reduced to once a fortnight.[14]

The result was a small but steady increase in the provinces' sea-borne trade. In spite of an Ottoman ban on the export of horses (from 1864 to 1867) the value of goods shipped out of Basra on which duty was paid rose from between £80,000 and 90,000 in the mid-1860s to an average of £200,000 in 1869 and 1870 (see Table 34). In addition the Ottoman authorities had begun to export several thousands of tons of cereals, mostly

wheat and barley, to provision their garrisons along the Red Sea.[15] Meanwhile, as far as imports were concerned, there was a sudden and temporary
increase during the mid-1860s, some of them probably destined for the
Persian market (see Table 34). As elsewhere in the Middle East, textiles
formed a significant proportion of this trade, perhaps as much as a fifth to a
quarter (Table 34). The increase in commercial activity during the 1860s
can also be seen from the growth in the volume of shipping passing in and
out of Basra. During the five years 1864/5 to 1868/9 the number of
Ottoman vessels doubled from 552 (50,000 tons) to 1105 (28,000 tons) while
the number of British ones went up from 27 (12,000 tons) to 52 (28,000
tons).[16] Of these latter 3 came direct from England in 1864/5 and 10 in
1868/9 − all of them under sail.[17]

Table 34   The growth in Iraq's foreign trade 1864−80 (£,000)[1]

	Exports					Imports	
	Dates	Wool	Wheat and barley	Animals	Total	Textiles	Total
1864	78	2			89	60	294
1865	74	11	3		99	83	344
1866					90		358
1867					104		256
1868	67	12	16	3	117	26	154
1869	126		57		240	21	199
1870	167	15	12		206	4	314
1871					231		406
1872					231		406
1873					123		406
1874					366		515
1875					357		276
1876					677		341
1877					573		517
1878	35	199	12[2]	122	1176		533
1879	34				1164		722
1880					1275		722

Sources: M. S. Hasan, 'Foreign trade in the economic development of Iraq, 1869−1939',
D. Phil., Oxford (1958), 304−11, 317−18, 321−3, 336−8, 351−4, and his *al-Tatawwur al-
Iqtisadi fi-l-'Iraq* (Said, 1965), 506−7. *CR* (UK) Basra 1869−70, *PP*, 1872, LVII, 300.
Notes:
1 Sea-borne trade. Overland trade is excluded except for the transit trade with Persia. Figures
up to 1874 have been converted from Turkish Grand Senior Piastres.
2 Wheat only.

Nevertheless, in spite of such signs it seems likely that Iraq's foreign trade
would have remained of only modest proportions if the opening of the Suez
Canal in 1869 had not also opened up the possibility of direct and cheap
access to European, mainly British, markets. In this context it is significant
that in spite of official efforts to increase the cultivation of cotton even the

high prices of the American Civil War period produced only a minute increase in its export.[18] It is equally significant that the crop which emerged as the major export crop in the late 1860s – dates – was one which not only had a large local Middle Eastern market but which also posed no particular problems of transport given the fact that it was grown so close to Basra.[19] The arrival in the Gulf of the first British steamer direct from England via the Suez Canal in June 1870, however, ushered in a new era in which many of the major restraints in the way of an increase in Iraqi exports, and thus of Iraqi agriculture, were swept away.[20] Within a few years there was an enormous growth of trade with the value of exports increasing from an annual average of £230,000 during the first five years of the 1870s to nearly £800,000 in the second (Table 34). Unlike the 1860s, it was not dates which contributed a large share of this increase but bulk goods like wool and cereals from districts many miles to the north of Basra. Wool, for instance, provided a major cargo for the Lynch steamers and it was probably because of this that they increased their capacity still further at the end of the 1870s, first by replacing the sunken *Diyala* with the larger *Blosse Lynch*, then by importing a third steamer, the *Khalifa*.[21] Although the company was still only allowed to run two steamers at any one time the fact that it always had one in reserve meant that, during the busy season, it was able to work non-stop.[22] Meanwhile, the Ottomans also put more boats on the river, making ten in all. But they continued to experience considerable difficulty in keeping them all in regular service.[23]

Even during the first ten years the short-term effects of the increase in trade with Europe made possible by the Suez Canal were considerable. One was the stimulus given to agricultural production even during years of tribal unrest when river communications were often interrupted. A second was the replacement of India as Iraq's major trading partner by the United Kingdom. A third, already mentioned in connection with the Syrian provinces, was the reduction in the import of European goods along the desert route from Damascus and Aleppo to Mosul. This had the further consequence of drawing Mosul itself more firmly into the economic sphere of Basra and Baghdad, which now provided the major source of its imports of manufactured goods and its exports of wool and nuts.[24] Once again, it is significant that the Ottomans sought to encourage such trade by opening up a steamship service on the Tigris between Mosul and Baghdad – where the Lynchs had not been given permission to operate – but without immediate success.[25]

Ottoman policy towards the agricultural sector

As in Syria, Midhat Paşa's few years in Iraq (1869–71) are usually seen as something of a watershed in the provinces' history – mostly for the wrong reasons.[26] While it is true that he instituted a more comprehensive series of reforms than any of his predecessors it is equally true that he failed in almost everything he tried. Thus, again as in Syria, his Iraqi period is significant mainly as a demonstration of the difficulties which still stood in the way of efforts to strengthen the powers of the central government, particularly in the rural areas. As a corollary, the failure of these policies not only provides yet another indication of the strength of the local social forces which opposed them but also, in some ways, actually acted to reinforce their position.

Another way in which the importance of Midhat's policies is usually exaggerated is to contrast them with the lacklustre performance of earlier provincial governors. But this too is to overstate the case. In the 1850s and 1860s there were at least two administrators, Mehmed Reşid (1852–7) and Namık (1861–8), who attempted to use their relatively long tenures as governors of Baghdad to increase revenues and to extend government control. To do this they derived some measure of advantage from the fact that, compared with the Syrian provincial governors to the west, they were already in a position to pay for the upkeep of a substantial armed force. In the early 1850s, for instance, annual revenues were estimated at £350,000 (plus an extra £50,000 which was sent to Istanbul as a subsidy) which was more than enough to maintain a Baghdad garrison of 16,000 men.[27] In this situation they were quite well placed to extend the area of relative security round both Mosul and Baghdad. As already stated, they also paid attention to the improvement of river traffic along the Tigris and to the export of local cereals.[28]

Mehmed Reşid and Namık experienced major problems, however, in the riverain districts south of Baghdad.[29] There, tribal power remained too strong and the terrain too difficult to allow them to establish a permanent Ottoman presence. As always, the only method of raising any revenue or of maintaining any sort of order was by dealing directly with the leading shaikhs. While the less important could often be overawed by the threat of force, success with the stronger ones depended on a complex system of bargaining and manoeuvring in which the cost of mounting a military expedition had to be balanced against the possibility of either bribing the shaikh in question or reducing his power by setting up rivals against him. The pashas of the 1850s and 1860s attempted to introduce new elements into this equation with their more forceful attempts to incorporate some of the tribal leaders, notably the shaikhs of the Muntafiq on the lower Euphrates, more closely into the system of provincial government by making them responsible for certain newly created administrative sub-units (known as *cazas*). Such was the policy of Namık Paşa in the early 1860s when he was able briefly to coerce the Emir or current head of the Sadun family to accept the post of *qaimmaqam* of one of these new units established in Muntafiq territory. Even if the post soon had to be abolished as a result of intense opposition from the rest of the Saduns, the idea itself remained very much alive and was re-used by Midhat himself. Another tactic was to encourage the shaikhs to bid against one another in the annual auctions for the tax-farms over their tribal areas. This was tried by Namık at Amarah on the Tigris and, in spite of the hostility which it promoted, may well have led to an increase in government revenues.[30]

A second area in which Mehmed Reşid and Namık both encouraged new methods was that of irrigation. Both seem to have recognized the importance of trying to improve agricultural production by clearing old canals and digging new ones. In each case the initial spur to action may well have been provided by the need to tackle the dangerous situation which had developed along the middle Euphrates where increasing volumes of flood water were able to escape down the Hindiyah Canal to the west of the river's two main channels.[31] This had the double effect of encouraging the over-flooding of the rich rice-growing land controlled by the Kazail Arabs near Babylon while reducing the water passing through the eastern channel past Hilla, something which was harmful to agriculture and shipping alike.[32] To make matters worse, frequent military expeditions against the Kazail only aggravated the situation by encouraging them to flood their own fields as a protection against the advancing troops.[33] One possible solution attempted by an earlier governor was to block off the mouth of the Hindiyah with dams of earth and stones; but in spite of repeated efforts such structures were usually washed away by the next spring flood and the problem was not properly solved until just before the First World War.[34] Meanwhile, the temptation to use the canals and the provision of water as a way of encouraging the payment of taxes or of disciplining recalcitrant tribes must also have reduced the effect of the two pashas' improvements in the system of irrigation.[35]

With the arrival of Midhat in Baghdad the whole problem of the relationship between land, water, taxes and tribal policy was looked at anew. After a brief preliminary examination of Iraqi conditions he decided to replace the piecemeal policies of his predecessors with a programme of land registration and tax reform which, so he hoped, would increase production, encourage nomadic settlement, raise revenues and destroy the power of the tax-farmers and tribal shaikhs all in one go. Such, after all, was the main purpose of the Ottoman Land Code of 1858 and Midhat seems to have believed that by using its provisions to encourage the registration of agricultural land in the name of its actual cultivators he could achieve the same goal.[36] To this end he secured the appointment of a land commission which was soon set to work in the Hillah–Diwaniyah districts, now cowed as a result of his comprehensive defeat of the Kazail in 1869, issuing *tapu sanads* or titles after a cursory examination.[37] Later, more titles seem to have been issued in the Muntafiq districts on the southern Euphrates, in the lands around Basra and Baghdad, and, perhaps, in the area of Mosul as well; although how much of this was actually accomplished before Midhat left the Iraqi provinces in 1872 is less clear.[38] What is more certain is that the issue of *tapu sanads* more or less came to an end in 1881 as a result of a new Ottoman ordinance which tightened up administrative procedures to such an extent that further registration was made extremely difficult.[39]

The results of this policy were little different from anywhere else in the Arab provinces. The Land Commission was understaffed and its members inexperienced.[40] Again, registration was generally undertaken without any initial survey and often resulted in the issue of titles which provided only the vaguest indication of the extent of the plot in question. An extreme example of this can be found in the two *sanads* examined by a British administrator referring to date groves on the Shatt al-Arab near Basra, one with a western boundary described as the 'Red Sea', the second with northern, southern, eastern and western boundaries given as *al-hur* (the marsh).[41] Lastly, with the exception of some of the date groves where Midhat's Commission took special care to award ownership to those who actually owned the trees, it seems unlikely that more than a very few titles passed directly into the hands of the real cultivators.[42] As is often pointed out, the Land Code itself took no recognizance of the fact that much of the land in Syria and Iraq was held in some form of communal ownership by peasants who attached no importance to the idea of individual private property.[43] There was also a general and no doubt real fear that registration was going to be a preliminary to conscription or increased taxation. In these circumstances Midhat's promise that cultivators who settled down on a particular plot, built a house on it, and then allowed it to be registered would pay lower taxes cannot possibly have had much effect.[44]

Even without such peasant reluctance it would seem likely that a large proportion of the land would have ended up in the hands of those with local power. This was certainly the case in the Muntafiq districts where the Sadun family began to accumulate titles once Midhat had returned to Namık's policy of appointing the senior shaikhs to important posts within the administration.[45] Later, after 1871, many more *sanads* were accumulated as the Ottoman authorities began to auction them with the assistance of Nasir Sadun, the new governor of Basra.[46] Meanwhile, in the north, round Mosul, there is no reason to suppose that Midhat's policies had any other effect than to continue the already existing trend by which much of the fertile land was passing steadily into the control of members of the city's *majlis*.[47]

Conditions on the middle Euphrates were more complicated, for there the issue of titles soon got mixed up with the perennial struggle between government and tribal shaikhs for control of the rural surplus. A number of Midhat's successors began a deliberate policy of using the *sanads* themselves as instruments of policy, cancelling those belonging to groups they wished to discipline and granting them to those they wished to reward.[48] To make matters more complicated this whole process took place against a considerable disturbance in agricultural life brought about by further changes in the system of irrigation and flood control.

Midhat's own contribution to this situation was considerable and stands in marked contrast to his usual efforts to treat the rural problems in their entirety. Three acts combined to alter the balance of water in the various branches of the Euphrates south of Baghdad. The first was the closing of Saklawiya escape channel north-west of Baghdad in order to prevent flood waters travelling eastwards towards the capital and thus exacerbating the effects of the disastrous Tigris flood of 1867.[49] This action greatly increased the amount of water passing down the Hindiyah Canal – once again unprotected by any dam at its northern end – and the western branch of the Euphrates.[50] Meanwhile, the other two acts had served to reduce the water available to cultivators along the eastern branch of the same river. One was the blocking off of the Dhaghghara Canal as a preliminary to Midhat's military assault on the Kazail in 1869. Until then this canal had been used as a regular store of summer water trapped there at flood time by temporary dams of rushes and mud.[51] The second was the construction of the Kananiya Canal to take off water eastward from the eastern branch of the Euphrates to irrigate potential fertile land just south of Baghdad. Due to its faulty construction this new canal soon began to act as yet another drain reducing the already low levels in its parent branch.[52] The result of all three acts was to encourage a movement of cultivators away from the eastern districts along the Hillah where water was scarce to those in the west, particularly the Samiyya south of Najaf, where water was now more plentiful. This move was also encouraged by the Ottoman authorities as a way of further reducing the power of the Kazail along the Dhaghgharah.[53] Migrations of such a kind were seldom without widespread ramifications, however. Groups in the western districts resented the arrival of the newcomers and fought to keep them out; other groups filtered into the deserted parts of the eastern districts to the great resentment of their former cultivators. To make matters still more complicated, about 1880 some of the remaining Kazail succeeded in unblocking the Dhaghgharah Canal again and filling it with what little water they could take out of the eastern Euphrates.[54] The result of this and all the other changes in the system of irrigation was to inaugurate a period of violent strife between different groups of cultivators which lasted on and off until the First World War.[55]

It can be seen from this brief discussion that the immediate result of Midhat's policies in the south of the country was an increase in instability triggered off by a struggle between various tribal groups, as well as inside various tribal groups, for land. In the long run this was to have the effect of altering the nature of the relationship between tribesmen and shaikhs by converting the latter into landlords and tax-farmers concerned only to maximize their share of the rural surplus. But, as Chapter 12 will show, this process was infinitely more complex and more varied than most previous accounts have allowed. Meanwhile, its effect on agricultural production is also difficult to gauge. On the one hand the increase in exports in the 1870s certainly demonstrates that production could be expanded in certain parts of the country, even at a time of great social disruption. The systems of irrigation and bulk transport still operated with little need of assistance from the government.[56] Groups like the Muntafiq habitually postponed battles until after the harvest.[57] On the other hand, the situation in districts like those along the middle Euphrates must certainly have acted to discourage agricultural expansion. This too is a major theme which will be dealt with further in Chapter 12.

8 Anatolia and Istanbul, 1881–1914

At the time of the First World War the population of the districts which were later to form Republican Turkey was something of the order of 14,000,000. This consisted of the more than 12,000,000 people who according to the 1906 census lived in the thirteen Anatolian provinces and the *mutasarriflik* of Izmir, the 1,000,000 inhabitants of Istanbul, and the 600,000 or so people living in that part of the European province of Edirne which remained in Ottoman hands after the end of the Balkan wars.[1] The vast majority of this population lived in the rural areas with perhaps no more than 10 per cent in towns and cities of 10,000 and over.[2] According to the information in earlier censuses, numbers had been growing at a rate of nearly 1 per cent a year since 1885 when the population of Anatolia had been calculated at 9,750,000.[3] This was largely due to natural increase but also owed something to the arrival of several hundreds of thousands of Muslim refugees from southern Russia and from the lost provinces in the Balkans.[4]

As elsewhere in the Middle East, the vast majority of Anatolia's population was employed in the agricultural sector. Government figures suggest that something like 5,500,000 hectares (13,585,000 acres) of land was sown with crops in 1909/10.[5] But given the fact of an almost total dependence on good winter rains, the areas cultivated each year were subject to very large variations, with that of a good year being almost double that of a bad.[6] Up to 90 per cent of the land was sown with cereals, mostly wheat and barley, under a system of a biennial rotation.[7] The total value of field crops just before the First World War has been estimated at about £T20,000,000.

The second most important economic activity was industry. According to the first (partial) industrial census of 1913 there were then some 270 plants defined as factories in western Anatolia employing some 17,000 workers and producing goods worth £T6,300,000 a year.[8] To this must be added the value of the articles produced by the several hundreds of thousands of craftsmen in the craft-industrial sector for whom no reliable figures can possibly exist. In these circumstances any attempt to try to estimate the size and sectoral breakdown of the national product must be a particularly hazardous enterprise. For what it is worth, Eldem has calculated that in 1914 agriculture contributed 56 per cent of national income and a mixed

189

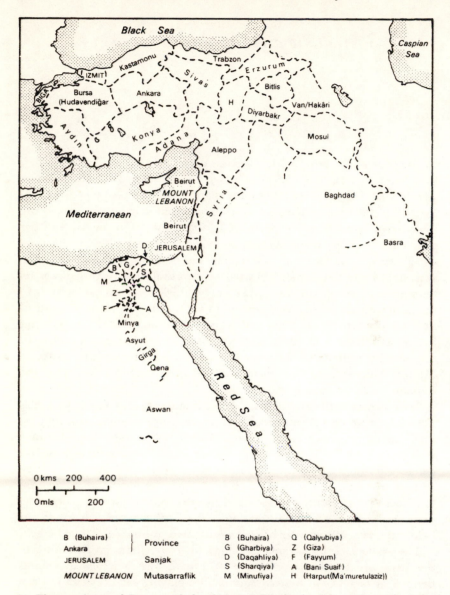

3   The provinces of Egypt and the Ottoman Empire in Asia at the end of the
nineteenth century

bag of manufacturing, mining, electricity, gas and water, construction,
transport and communications another 17 per cent.[9] A little more
credibility can be attached to a second estimate for the early Republican
period which indicates that in the mid-1920s agriculture contributed

Table 35   Turkey's foreign trade, 1880–1913 (annual averages)

| | Ottoman Empire | | Exports from Izmir, Adana/Mersin, |
	Imports (£Tm.)	Exports (£Tm.)	Samsun and Trabzon (£m.)
1880–4	19.58	11.19	5.56[1]
1885–9	20.26	12.96	5.84[2]
1889–94	24.01	14.16	6.14[3]
1895–9	23.30	14.95	5.56[4]
1900–4	24.75	16.08	7.14
1905–9	32.89	18.84	8.10[5]
1910–13	43.03	26.28	

Sources: Ottoman Empire – Turkey, La Direction Générale de la Presse, *La Turquie en chiffres* (Ankara, 1937).
4 Anatolian ports – British consular figures in Quataert, *Ottoman Reform*, 361.

Notes: 1 Excludes 1884.   2 Excludes 1885, 1887.   3 Excludes 1893.   4 Excludes 1896, 1897.
5 1906, 1907 only.

between 40 to 50 per cent of net national product and industry (widely interpreted) some 17 or 18 per cent.[10]

Attempts to calculate the value of Anatolia's foreign trade run into other kinds of difficulties. The only continuous series (Table 35) refers to the Ottoman Empire as a whole. Among many other shortcomings it almost certainly underestimates the value of Ottoman exports. As many contemporary observers noted, figures for the foreign sales of tobacco (worth £T3,000,000 a year just before 1914) and a number of other products controlled by foreign agencies are excluded.[11] Recent studies also suggest that the apparently very unfavourable balance of trade must have been very much less than the official figures would seem to indicate.[12] Table 35 also gives estimates of the exports from four of Anatolia's main ports – Izmir, Adana/Mersin, Trabzon and Samsun – derived from British consular reports. While they almost certainly include the export of crops like tobacco they have the disadvantage of excluding the trade of a whole host of minor ports as well as that which passed into southern Europe overland.

Given this lack of reliable data, it is almost as difficult to attempt to assess Anatolia's economic performance during this period as it was for earlier periods in the nineteenth century. In what follows I will seek only to trace the main outlines of a complex process by which progress in certain areas has to be fitted into the wider story of the further restructuring of the economy under the influence of Europe.

The pattern of foreign financial control

Unlike the cases of Egypt and Tunis, Ottoman bankruptcy in the 1870s did not lead to foreign occupation. But it did produce a system of international financial control which, in a number of ways, led to an equivalent loss of sovereignty. The main instrument of this control was the Ottoman Public Debt Administration (PDA) established by the Decree of Muharram (October 1881), assisted by the three major foreign-controlled banks − the Imperial Ottoman, the Deutsche Bank and the National Bank of Turkey − as well as, on numerous occasions, by the diplomatic support offered by the most important European embassies in Istanbul. Initially, the two powers most interested in the management of Turkey's finances were Britain and France; but they were soon joined by Germany in a triple alliance which, though often split at the political level by intra-imperialist rivalries, continued to co-operate well enough inside the Empire itself for the whole system to be described as a single international regime.[13] The primary aim of this regime was to safeguard the position of those who held shares in the Ottoman public debt, but in time a second aim came to assume increasing importance: that of opening up the Turkish economy to further European economic penetration. Here, the development of the Turkish railway system was seen as the principal instrument, although attention was also paid to the award of concessions for the production and export of mineral products like coal and chrome and for important public works in and around the major towns. All this was done with the co-operation of the Ottoman government, if possible. However, it was also made repeatedly clear that the Sultan and his government were expected to go along with European plans and that they would only receive further financial support if they did so. As time went on, the sheer blatancy of this method of economic control became ever more galling to a number of Turks and was subject to increasing verbal attack.[14] But even the Young Turk reformers of the years just before the First World War were too weak and too dependent on European loans to challenge it to any real degree.

As already indicated, the main agency of European financial control was the PDA. This consisted of a seven-man council composed of the representatives of the main groups of bondholders (British, Dutch, French, German, Austro-Hungarian, Italian and local Ottoman) plus a member nominated by the Imperial Ottoman Bank, assisted by a large staff of permanent administrators and officials.[15] Presidency of the council alternated between a Frenchman and a Briton, on the grounds that these were the countries with the greatest interest in the proper management of the debt.[16] Its semi-official role as an agency of European control was further reinforced by the fact that most members of the council were appointed with the active, though usually covert, support of their respective national governments.[17] As for the Ottoman government itself, it was given only a watching brief through the right to send a commissioner to attend meetings of the council but with no vote.

The initial aim of the PDA was to collect the revenues allocated to it under the Decree of Muharram and to use them to meet the interest and to repay some of the principal on the external debt. These revenues included the salt monopoly, the stamp and spirits duties, the fish tax and the silk tithe for a number of districts, as well as the part of the Annual Tribute from several provinces which was paid to it directly (see Table 36).[18] Initially, the PDA also collected the tobacco tax. But in May 1883 it farmed this out to a newly created foreign agency, La Société de la Régie Cointeressé des Tabacs de l'Empire Ottomane (the *Régie* for short) for an annual sum of £T750,000 and a share of the profits.[19] Within a few years, the PDA had either gained or been given a wide variety of other duties.[20] One was the collection of a number of revenues set aside specifically for the servicing of new foreign loans or of financial guarantees given to foreign railway promoters. Another was the direct collection of certain duties (notably the customs surcharge of 3 per cent imposed in 1907) on behalf of the Ottoman Ministry of Finance itself. Third, the PDA played an active role in assisting the Ottoman government in obtaining a whole series of new foreign loans. Finally, in concert with the major foreign banks and a number of foreign companies, the Administration encouraged the promotion of a variety of schemes for railway construction, mineral extraction and the provision of public works.

Table 36   Revenues ceded to the PDA, 1882–1913 (5 year averages, £T,000)

	1882/3–1886/7	1887/8–1891/2	1892/3–1896/7	1897/8–1901/2	1902/3–1906/7	1908/9–1912/13
Six indirect contributions:						
Tobacco[1]	823	755	788	726	816	899
Salt	651	702	756	861	987	1124
Stamps	147	186	213	222	321	366
Spirits	198	229	259	269	274	283
Fisheries	34	44	44	47	53	70
Silk	24	39	56	69	99	131
Total	1867	1956	2117	2197	2576	2873
Other Revenues	402	372	387	341	385	
Gross Revenue	2350	2328	2503	2538	3061	
Expenses	388	392	346	419	523	
Net Revenue	1952	1936	2157	2120	2538	

Sources: 1882/3–1906/7, Caillard, 'Turkey', 438.
1908/9–1912/13, Ottoman PDA, *Rapport sur la question des dîmes, agnam et revenues divers par la Conseil d'Administration de la Dette Publique Ottomane, année 1912/13 (1328) comparée avec l'année 1911/12* (Constantinople, 1914).

Note: 1 The tobacco monopoly was farmed to the Tobacco *Régie* for £T750,000 and a share of the profits.

From the point of view of the European investor the activities of the PDA were undoubtedly a great success.[21] Its council soon proved itself to be a powerful and ever-watchful protector of their interests. Its prompt and regular payment of the moneys owed to the bondholders produced a steady increase in the value of shares in the public debt as quoted in the major financial markets.[22] From an Ottoman point of view, however, the situation was obviously much more ambiguous. On the one hand, the PDA was certainly instrumental in underwriting the government's credit and ensuring that it obtained loans on very much more favourable terms than in the days before bankruptcy.[23] Of the £T166,000,000 borrowed during the period 1881 to 1914, the government itself received £T147,000,000 or 89 per cent.[24] On the other hand, the very size of the PDA's staff, the independence of its operations and the increasing limitations its presence imposed on Ottoman fiscal sovereignty were bound to create great resentment. In 1886 it employed a staff of 3040 (of whom fifty-five were Europeans and the rest Ottoman subjects); by 1912/13 this had increased to over 5500 full-time officials, a few more than in the Ottoman Ministry of Finance itself.[25] Another aspect of its large size was the fact that, by the turn of the century, it had spread itself out into 720 separate tax-collecting offices all over the Empire, as well as the management of over 100 salt works.[26]

The entrenched position of the PDA at the heart of the control of Ottoman financial affairs was even more galling. Until its amendment in September 1903 the Decree of Muharram effectively prevented the government from obtaining any share of the revenues collected by the Administration, however much they might be increased.[27] To make matters worse, the Decree also required the authorities to co-operate with the PDA in a number of costly measures from which they themselves derived no profit, for example the maintenance of an expensive system of cordons and patrols aimed at preventing contraband traffic in goods like salt over which the Administration had a monopoly.[28] It is little wonder that they set about such tasks with so little enthusiasm that a great deal of potential revenue was lost.[29] Concessions were required from both sides in order to allow the amendment of the Decree of Muharram in such a way that the maximum sum permitted for repayment of the pre-1881 debt was fixed at £T2,157,000, leaving any surplus to be divided between government and PDA in the ratio 75 : 25.[30]

A second dispute which broke out two years later concerned an Ottoman attempt to extend a new scheme for the direct collection of the agricultural tithe to certain districts where the PDA was already active in supervising the auction of those tax-farms set aside to provide the guarantees necessary to meet any shortfalls in the profits of several foreign railway companies. On this occasion, however, there was no room for compromise and the PDA's claim that the proposed change might be detrimental to the interests of foreign holders of shares in these same railway companies was allowed to carry the day.[31]

The main auxiliaries of the PDA were the two (and, after the creation of the National Bank in 1909, the three) major foreign banks. Of these the Imperial Ottoman was the oldest and, by the 1880s, had become largely a French concern.[32] Its main official function was to act as banker to the Ottoman government, issuing banknotes and providing short-term credit when necessary. But it combined this duty, somewhat ambiguously, with active support for French companies anxious to sell goods in the Empire or to promote railways or other large schemes. The Deutsche Bank, established at Istanbul in 1888, was the main instrument of German financial penetration.[33] Like the Imperial Ottoman, its main profits came from the provision of short-term credit to the government and from the commissions it received for floating large public loans. It too also acted powerfully in support of the interests of a large number of German concerns – ranging from railway companies to armaments manufacturers such as Krupp – with which it was closely associated. In spite of the rivalries which existed between their different national governments both banks maintained a considerable degree of co-operation both with each other and with the council of the PDA. A good example of this is provided by one of the promoters of the largely British National Bank of Turkey, Sir Adam Block, as he described the mechanism by which the Ottomans were faced with a common European front when they were short of money:

Both parties [i.e., both major banks] made advances at high rates of interest, and when it was desired to force the government to accept the terms of a loan operation by either party, the doors of both German and French establishments were closed to further temporary accommodation. The Ottoman government is therefore obliged, in its present penurious condition, to accept the usurious terms which are offered.[34]

It was in the hope of breaking this common front that the Young Turk government was willing to countenance the establishment of the new National Bank in 1909, albeit under strong British pressure.[35] But as events were to prove, the British financiers were just as anxious as everyone else to combine with the PDA and their competitors in order to gain from the rich profits which access to the Empire's economic resources continued to provide.

Further light can be thrown on the nature of such European financial co-operation by an examination of the three principal areas of activity: government loans, railway promotion and the exploitation of various concessions. According to Suvla's figures, Abdul-Hamid's governments borrowed £T120,000,000 in seventeen separate loans between 1886 and 1906, of which they actually received £T108,000,000, and the Young Turk governments another £T46,000,000 in nine loans between 1908 and 1914, of which they received £T39,000,000.[36] As in the days before the Decree of Muharram, the main reason for this large-scale foreign borrowing was a combination of a continued imbalance between revenue and expenditure and an easy access to European credit. As before, this was a situation which gave the foreign bankers at Istanbul considerable power. There were, how-ever, two new elements. One was the presence of the PDA which acted both as a general guarantor of Ottoman credit and, on at least ten occasions, as an active participant in the arrangements made for servicing new debts.[37] The second was the way in which the whole process of borrowing was used directly as a means of pressuring the Ottoman government into accepting a variety of related financial projects. Thus in some cases a bank's agreement to float a loan was only given in return for the grant of a certain concession to one of its own nationals. In others, the proceeds of the loan itself were used to pay for the construction of a railway or for the purchase of specific foreign imports like military equipment.[38]

A related aspect of this co-ordinated foreign financial activity was the promotion of railway concessions. The further development of the rail system was regarded both by the Ottoman government and by most foreign observers as the key to the Empire's economic progress, but in only a few in-stances did the Turks possess either the financial or the technical resources to undertake the work themselves. After the two remaining government-owned lines were sold off to European companies in the early 1890s the only major enterprise undertaken by the government itself was the construction of the Hijaz railway from Damascus to Medina, and even this required an extraordinary and very special effort to find the money required.[39] In these circumstances there was nothing for it but to allow foreign companies to build the new lines themselves. For their part, the PDA council and the major banks were only too happy to oblige and co-operated together to launch a number of large schemes, notably the German-built Anatolian and Baghdad railways and the French-built Smyrne-Cassaba et Prolonge-ments in north-western Anatolia and the Chemin de Fer Damas-Hamah et Prolongements connecting Beirut and the Hauran with the principal cities of the Syrian interior.[40] The reasons for such extensive co-operation are sometimes explained simply in terms of the overlap of interests between members of the same small group of financiers which sat on the boards of a number of banks and railways and even on the PDA council itself.[41] But even more important was the fact that the success of the institutions them-selves so obviously depended on a system of mutual co-operation in support of certain common goals. Once again they have to be seen as part of a wider system of financial exploitation in which the questions of repaying old loans, raising new ones and promoting foreign enterprise were inextricably intermixed.

The fact that the council and the banks were able to act in concert with the foreign railway promoters as well as providing the Ottoman government with financial and technical assistance placed them in a strong position to obtain favourable terms for their protégés. Two subjects in particular became the subjects of fierce bargaining and later controversy. One was the award of a great number of ancillary rights to the main foreign railway companies, for example the ownership of any mineral deposits, including oil, which might be found within 20 km on either side of the Baghdad railway's line from Konya, in central Anatolia, to the Iraqi provinces.[42] Even though such awards meant little in real terms before 1914, they were often the basis of huge claims for concessions presented to the successor states of the Ottoman Empire after the First World War.[43] The second subject was the so-called kilometric guarantee obtained by a number of companies for lines built both in European and Asiatic Turkey. Although the actual terms varied, the principle remained the same: provided the company in question ran a certain number of trains over a particular piece of track the government promised to make up any shortfall in gross receipts up to a certain amount, usually somewhere between 13,000 and 18,000 francs per kilometre.[44] What was more, as additional security, the revenues set aside to meet this guarantee were to come from tithes or sheep tax collected from the districts along the new line under the supervision of the PDA. Whether it was the government itself or a foreign institution which first suggested this arrangement is less important than the fact that its introduction in the concession for the Anatolian railway in 1888 provided yet another area of co-operation between the council, the banks and the European promoters.

The further question of whether the system of guarantees was actually necessary and of its effect on the management of the new lines cannot be answered satisfactorily on the basis of current knowledge. Nevertheless there is some evidence to suggest that where the lines passed through wide tracts of cultivated land the guarantees were higher than necessary and that where they passed through empty areas of country the guarantees tended both to encourage wasteful expenditure on construction and to discourage the proper development of goods traffic (see Table 46).[45]

Table 37 The Ottoman Empire's revenues and expenditures, 1887/8–1911/12
(annual averages in £Tm.)

	Revenues		Expenditures			
	Total	External debt	Mins. of Army and Navy	Education	Public Works	Total
1887/8–1889/90	16,148	2151	7822			18,517
1890/1–1894/5	16,693	2733	7176			17,871
1895/6–1899/1900	16,657	3575	7285			18,563
1900/1–1904/5	18,212[1]	3726	6596[1]			20,127[1]
1905/6–1909/10	26,962[2]	5593	9651[3]			27,753[3]
1910/11–1911/12	28,630	9924	12,617	0.85	1011	35,244

Source: Shaw, 'Ottoman Expenditure and Budgets', 373–8.
Notes: 1 1900/1–1903/4 only.   2 1908/9–1909/10 only.   3 1909/10 only.

A third area of joint co-operation involved the award of a wide variety of public works and other concessions. These included the tramways and telephones at Istanbul and the docks and the water, gas and electricity supplies at both Istanbul and Izmir. In addition, by 1910 foreign companies had obtained possession of over two-thirds of the Empire's production of coal, chrome, copper and a number of other minerals.[46] Figures for total foreign investment and for the profits paid by most foreign-owned companies testify to the success of this drive for favoured access to Ottoman resources. According to calculations quoted by the French writer Y. Guyot, total French investments in the whole Ottoman Empire stood at 2,500,000,000 francs in 1912, including 1,500,000,000 francs which was placed in the public debt, 400,000,000 in railways, 62,500,000 in mining and manufacturing and 50,000,000 in shipping.[47] The equivalent figures for German and British investment (including the public debt) were 900,000,000 francs and 750,000,000 francs respectively.[48] As for the profits obtained in return, Tezel estimates that the foreign railway companies made some £T26,000,000 (1899–1909), the public utilities in Istanbul, Izmir, Beirut and Salonica £T3,100,000 (1891–1909), and five mining concerns £T1,500,000 (1898–1909).[49] To this might be added the Imperial Ottoman Bank which distributed around £T30,000,000 in dividends between 1863 and 1909 and the Tobacco *Régie* which made the same amount in profits between 1884 and 1914.[50]

Behind the PDA, the big banks and the foreign concessionaires stood the governments of the major European powers, often ready to act forcefully in support of enterprises managed by their fellow-countrymen. This could take the form of direct pressure at Istanbul. Just as often it involved a refusal to permit the flotation of a particular loan until some claim had been met or a further concession granted. To give only one example out of many, in 1903 the French government delayed the progress of an attempt to convert part of the Ottoman debt until the Turkish authorities had met the claims of one of the French railway companies, agreed to leave control of the Istanbul docks in French hands and given orders for the supply of military equipment to French factories.[51] Furthermore, for all the growing political preoccupation in London, Paris and Berlin with threats from foreign rivals, there were only a few occasions on which national considerations were allowed to get in the way of the normal course of economic and financial co-operation. The Baghdad railway project is a good example of this. Much is often made of the British and French governments' attempts to scupper the scheme in 1903, either by instructing their nationals to withdraw or, in the French case, by refusing to allow the necessary loan to be quoted on the Paris Bourse.[52] On the other hand, given the fact that the German promoters did not have large enough funds of their own it was inevitable that they would continue to try and obtain the participation of French and, later, British capital — with some success.[53] In truth, given the absence of any alternative strategy, the different European governments had little alternative but to support their own national entrepreneurs in whatever scheme they happened to be engaged in and it was only in the few years immediately before the First World War that a more purely national approach began to emerge with the tentative division of the Empire into separate spheres of economic interest.[54]

A last, and very vital, factor in the growth of European financial control was the role of the Ottoman government itself and, in particular, its inability to balance its own budget (see Table 37). In essence, the problem remained unchanged from the pre-1881 period. On the revenue side there were still considerable barriers in the way of any rapid increase in tax receipts, including continued reliance on the farming of agricultural taxes (exacerbated by the PDA's opposition to plans to introduce direct collection in certain parts of Anatolia), European resistance to the taxation of their own nationals, and the loss of many of the most profitable sources of income to the PDA and the *Régie*.[55] The situation only began to improve a little after the turn of the century with the growth in taxable rural incomes and permission to raise the customs duty from 8 to 11 per cent in 1907.[56] Meanwhile, on the expenditure side the cost of maintaining the multi-purpose army required both to protect the Empire from external attack and to put down internal insurrections continued to rise. In particular, such close geographical proximity to so many major European states made it difficult to avoid entanglement in an arms race in which, like most of their neighbours, the Ottomans were regularly coerced or seduced into buying the latest weapon from the factories of Vickers or Krupp. Thus by 1904 the Ottomans already possessed an army of over 1,000,000 men armed with German artillery and Mauser and Martini–Henry rifles, and a fleet containing several iron-clad ships as well as torpedo boats and two submarines.[57]

After the military, the next largest item of expenditure was the servicing of the external debt. As always, it was easier for the government to borrow rather than to put its own financial house in order. As always, pressure to service old debts with new loans meant that there was little money left over for revenue-producing investments in public works. Just how difficult it was to redress the situation is shown by the experience of the Young Turk governments after 1908. Greatly anxious to reduce their dependence on European financiers, they instituted a number of reforms aimed at increasing revenues by the more efficient auctioning of tax-farms and by the promotion of new schemes of economic development.[58] But the small successes they achieved were largely neutralized by the pressures of almost continuous military campaigning. In the six years before 1914, expenditures on armaments rose dramatically while the loss of more of the Empire's rich European provinces meant a reduction of several million pounds in revenues.[59] In these circumstances, early efforts to find ways of reducing the financial power of the PDA had quickly to be abandoned and by 1914 Turkey's new rulers were as dependent on the services of European financiers as their predecessors had ever been.

The agricultural sector

On the basis of the available evidence there are two general statements which can safely be made about Anatolian agriculture during the period 1881 to 1913: the first is that there was a significant increase in agricultural production, the second that this was accompanied by a considerable extension of the area subject to a commercial agriculture based largely on the cultivation and export of a variety of cash crops. What is more difficult, however, is to chart the movement of this process in any detail. For reasons which have already been set out earlier in this chapter, there is great difficulty in finding reliable figures which relate to agricultural practice either in Anatolia or in the slightly larger area of what, in 1923, was to become Republican Turkey. Given these constraints, the only practicable method is to begin by looking at the situation as it existed at the very end of the period and then to try to work backwards.

Table 38 The proportion of land devoted to crops of various types in the provinces and sanjaks of Anatolia, 1909/10 (%)

	Cereals	Vegetables	Industrial/ oleaginous	Vines
Adana	63.89	1.03	32.45	2.63
Aidin	72.81	4.03	5.77	17.39
Harput	73.58	2.83	9.03	14.56
Bursa	79.47	1.89	2.79	15.85
Diyarbakir	81.08	3.55	2.86	12.51
Trabzon	89.49	7.27	3.24	–
Ankara	90.45	1.18	0.25	8.12
Konya	90.50	1.74	1.64	6.12
Sivas	92.53	2.13	1.26	4.08
Kastamonu	94.85	1.64	0.93	2.58
Van	95.37	0.42	2.72	1.49
Erzerum	98.99	0.90	0.04	0.07
Izmir	74.79	2.66	6.63	15.92
Biga	83.67	7.35	0.36	8.62

Source: Government figures in Nickoley, 'Agriculture', 284–5.

Table 38 gives the official Ottoman government estimates of the allocation of land to various types of crops in the fifteen main Anatolian administrative regions in 1325 AH (1909–10). These highlight the importance of cereals which occupied some 80 to 90 per cent of the cultivated area in most provinces. They also point to the four provinces or sanjaks where more than a fifth of the land was devoted to vegetables, industrial crops and vines. Of these Adana (with 36 per cent of its land under crops other than cereals), Aidin (with 27 per cent) and Izmir (with 25 per cent) were on the coast and produced a large share of Anatolia's agricultural exports. Figures to indicate the relative value and importance of such exports are impossible to find and the best that can be done is to refer to statistics for trade at Izmir, Anatolia's major port (Table 39) which show that grapes and raisins were the most valuable exports, followed − in the early twentieth century − by cereals, figs, valonia and cotton.[60]

Table 39 The value and volume of some of Izmir's major agricultural exports, 1880–1912 (annual averages)

A *The value of major exports (£m.)*

	1880–4	1885–9	1890–4	1894–9	1900–4	1905–8	1910
Grapes/raisins	1.023	1.294[1]	0.747[2]	0.935[3]	1.057	1.478[4]	
Figs	0.480	0.341[1]	0.649[2]	0.294[3]	0.504	0.660[3]	0.591
Valonia	0.572	0.755[1]	0.649[2]	0.448[3]	0.415	0.421[4]	0.476
Olive oil	0.070	0.058[1]	0.081[2]	0.031[3]	0.033	0.096	0.074
Tobacco	0.086	0.055[5]	0.062[2]	0.056[3]	0.203	0.201[4]	0.210
Cotton	0.229	0.281[1]	0.192[2]	0.089[3]	0.253	0.228[4]	0.244
Opium	0.355	0.296[1]	0.202[2]	0.305[3]	0.288	0.137[4]	0.415
Cereals	0.361	0.252[1]	0.530[2]	0.344[3]	0.652	0.650	0.267

B *The volume of major exports (cwts,m.)*

	1880–4	1885–9	1890–4	1895–9	1900–4	1905–9	1910–12
Grapes/raisins	0.899	1.323[1]	0.997[6]	0.922[7]	0.897	1.045	0.772
Figs	0.237	0.247[8]		0.259[7]	0.367	0.471	0.464
Valonia	0.809	0.950[1]	0.884[2]	1.116[7]	1.173	1.090	1.036
Olive oil					0.020	0.078	

Sources: CRs (UK) in Quataert, 'Turkish Reform', 381, 391, 398, 400, 402, 404–6 and PP 1914, xcv, 107–8

Notes: 1 Excludes 1887. 2 Excludes 1893. 3 Excludes 1895/7. 4 Excludes 1906. 5 Excludes 1886/7. 6 Excludes 1893/4. 7 Excludes 1895/6. 8 Excludes 1887/9.

To turn to the individual crops, the official figures given in Table 38 indicate that in 1909/10 cereals were grown over an area of some 4,300,000 hectares.[61] Of this, just under two-thirds was planted with wheat, the major food crop, and nearly another third with barley, which was used either for animal fodder or sent to the coast for export.[62] Most of the remaining cereal land was devoted to small quantities of maize and oats. Assuming a good average yield of about a ton per hectare, such figures suggest a possible average cereal harvest of between 4,000,000 and 4,500,000 tons.[63] It has already been noted, however, that the size of the harvest varied enormously according to rainfall. Such variations meant, among other things, that cultivators were forced to keep quite large stocks of grain in store as a guard against crop failure.[64] As for exports, even in a good year only a small part of the total harvest was sent out of Anatolia for foreign sale. Figures in Table 40 show that in 1911 perhaps 600,000 tons of cereals were either exported from the region's four major ports or shipped to Istanbul along the Anatolian railway, some 15 per cent of a possible harvest of 4,000,000 tons.[65]

Table 40   Exports of cereals from Anatolia, 1881–1911 (annual averages in cwts m.)

	Exports from Izmir, Adana/Mersin, Trabzon and Samsun	Cereals carried on Anatolian Railway	
		Uskudar/Ankara	Eskişehir/Konya
1881–5	2.561		
1886–90	3.482		
1891–5	5.737	0.681	0.245[3]
1896–1900	3.864	2.665	1.072
1901–5	4.064	4.281	2.003
1906–7	3.572[1]	3.376	1.591
1911	2.557[2]	5.243	2.934

Sources: 1881–1907, Quataert, 'Ottoman Reform', 387–8.
1911, *CR* (UK) Smyrna, *PP*, 1912/13, c, 631–3: Rey, *Statistique 1911*, 'Chemin de Fer Ottoman d'Anatolie'.

Notes: 1 1906 only.   2 Izmir only.   3 1895 only.

There seems little doubt that there was a regular increase in cereal production throughout the period in spite of dramatic fluctuations in world prices. The sharp increase in grain exports from the major Anatolian ports between 1881–5 and 1891–5 (Table 40) would seem to testify to an ability to respond forcefully to increased opportunities for foreign sales, at least in areas where transport to the coast was not prohibitively expensive. Later, during the next two decades, a number of estimates suggest that there was a further expansion of output.[66] On the supply side there was certainly a steady increase in the area of cultivated land as a result both of population growth and of the government's policy of settling nomads and Muslim immigrants from the Balkans and Russia in little-populated districts on the central plateau and in the east.[67] A second factor was the reduction in transport rates as a result of the extension of the railway system into the rich cereal-growing lands in the provinces of Ankara and Konya.[68] As a result, for the first time it became profitable to export grain grown near the new lines to the coast, even at the low world prices which prevailed during the 1890s. What is less easy to prove, however, is the extent to which the increasing shipments along the Anatolian railway (Table 40) represented extra production or simply the diversion of part of the regular harvest towards an external market. As far as the Ankara district is concerned, evidence of an increase in harvest size during the 1890s would seem to support Quataert's assertion that all the grain which can be shown to have

Table 41   The production and export of tobacco, silk and cotton from certain districts of Anatolia, 1881–1914 (annual averages)

A   *Production of tobacco and silk*

	Tobacco*		Silk (fresh cocoons)
	Production (kgs m.)	Area (hectares)	Production (kgs m.)
1884	22.48	17,675	
1885–9	19.44	22,833	2.57[1]
1890–4	24.94	29,884	4.18
1895–9	28.54	34,665	4.82
1900–4	33.34	41,073	5.83
1905–9	35.71	45,470	7.44[2]
1910–13	53.56	63,595	7.50[3]

B   *Production and export of cotton from Izmir and Adana (bales**)*

	Izmir		Adana	
	Production	Export	Production	Export
1881–5		30,534	42,000[6]	
1886–90		26,850		
1891–5		22,076		
1896–1900		20,421	2000[7]	
1901–5	38,333	27,439	45,367[8]	42,333
1906–10	41,666	33,476	65,000[9]	58,200
1911–13	55,000[4]	36,147[5]		105,000
1914				150,000

* Refers only to tobacco licensed by the Tobacco *Régie*.
** The weight of a bale varied over time. Quataert gives an average of 5.09 bales/ton, 'Turkish Reform', 401.

Sources: Tobacco: Turkey, *Annuaire Statistique 1936/7*, 169.
Silk: Quataert, 'Turkish Reform', 394; *CR* (UK) Turkey 1919, 918–19.
Cotton: Quataert, 'Turkish Reform', 290–1; Turkey, *Annuaire Statistique 1936/7*, 171; *CRs* (UK), *PP*, 1912/13, c, 63 and 1914, xcv, 107; Nickoley, 'Agriculture', 288.

Notes: 1 1888–9 only.   2 1905 only.   3 1912 only.   4 1911 only.   5 1911–12 only.   6 1884 only.   7 1896 only.   8 1905 only.   9 1906–8 only.

been shipped by rail was indeed a net addition to local output.[69] Unfortunately the figures for the Konya districts are much less conclusive and, for what they are worth, do not indicate any significant rise in production in the years after the arrival of the railway.[70]

Passing to an examination of the remainder of Anatolia's agricultural output, the official figures for 1909/10 show that just over 250,000 hectares were devoted to industrial and oleaginous crops, and a slightly larger area to vines. Products in the first category included tobacco, which was grown over some 80,000 hectares, and cotton which may have been cultivated on another 50,000.[71] What is not clear is whether the official figures also include other important bush or tree crops like mulberries (which were planted over at least 55,000 hectares), figs and olives.[72] In addition, beyond the cultivated area, valuable export products were gathered from the groves of oak and hazel (valonia and oil), from fields of wild poppies (opium) and from the sheep and goats which grazed on the inland pastures (mohair, wool and skins). Figures for the production and export of some of these crops will be found in Tables 39 and 41. The fact that all these heterogeneous activities were devoted largely to the production of goods for export, had three very important consequences. The first was the influence exercised by international prices. Figures in Table 42 show that the Istanbul price of most of the major Anatolian agricultural commodities fell throughout the 1880s and 1890s before rising rapidly again in the years just after the turn of the century. Figures in Tables 39 and 41 suggest that, as far as tobacco, cotton, silk, figs and grapes were concerned, such price movements had a considerable influence, depressing exports in the 1890s and then stimulating a major revival of foreign sales during the next decade. In every case, by 1905–9, the volume exported had reached, or even exceeded, the level attained during the early 1880s, while the total value was a good deal higher. Only with the disturbed conditions of the later Young Turk period did this trend begin to weaken. Further encouragement to Anatolian exports came from the reduction of transport costs due to an increasing use of the railways. In the case of Izmir, for example, over half the total exports of valonia and dried raisins were carried to the port along the Izmir/Kassaba line in 1911.[73]

Table 42 Changes in the average annual price of major Anatolian crops at Istanbul, 1881–1908 (1901–5 = 100)

	Raw cotton (Adana)	Figs	Grapes (Red)	Soft wheat (Anatolia)	Maize (Anatolia)	Barley	Mohair (Ankara)	Tobacco
1881–5	116	69				82	127	
1886–90	118	90				85	96	
1891–5	86	75		106	78	86	110	
1896–1900	79	78	95	87	67	67	127	59
1901–5	100	100	100	100	100	100	100	100
1906–8	108	100	100	119	111	131	114	158

Source: Quataert, 'Turkish Reform', 22, 396.

The second feature shared by most export crops was the way in which their links with the international market came more and more to be mediated by a variety of official, semi-official or commercial organizations specifically created to organize and control their production, processing and foreign sale. The most extreme example of such an organization was the Tobacco *Régie* which, by law, had the sole right to license cultivation and to provide credit.[74] It also had an obligation to purchase all leaves grown for local consumption.[75] Only with the tobacco grown specifically for sale abroad did it share its duties with individual exporters or commercial organizations like the American tobacco company established at Izmir.[76] Silk was subject to an almost equally tight control, this time by the PDA which, after 1888, was given responsibility for taxing production throughout the Empire.[77] In an effort to increase its revenues it joined with the government in an active programme designed both to raise output and to improve quality. To this end, free mulberry grafts were widely distributed to would-be planters, particularly in Bursa province, while the PDA exercised a tight control over the methods employed to raise worms and over the sale of eggs and cocoons.[78] In the case of other crops, it was foreign companies which took a direct role in providing credit and in controlling purchase of the finished product. Thus in the Adana region it was the German Levantische Baumwolle Gesellschaft established in 1904 which provided cultivators with seed and low interest loans, while at Izmir the commercial association known as Smyrna Fig Packers established a near monopoly over the local sale of figs and sultanas.[79] The result of such activity certainly had many positive features. The production and the quality of many primary products was increased, providing more raw materials both for local industry and for foreign sale. In the case of silk, too, there was a notable reduction in the need to import foreign eggs as improved local strains began to be developed to take their place.[80] Against this, however, the control exercised either by law or by means of the provision of credit and the monopoly of purchase meant that the terms on which such crops were produced were largely determined by foreign agencies and that a sizeable share of the profits found its way abroad.

The third feature which Anatolia's cash crops had in common was their involvement in government-inspired schemes to encourage their production. This is a subject which has been exhaustively studied by Quataert. As he is able to demonstrate, the government played an important role in assisting the PDA to promote the revival of the Anatolian silk industry.[81] It played an even more important role in supporting the grape producers in their efforts to survive the dangerous problems posed first by the revival of the vine disease phylloxera in the 1880s, then by the Méline tariff of 1892 which practically barred the French market to Turkish products.[82] As a result of concerted efforts to encourage methods known to protect vineyards against the disease and by distributing over a million free shoots of disease-free vines, the government had much to do with preventing the collapse of Anatolia's most important crop.[83] Another method of encouraging the production of cash crops was the use of the Agricultural Bank founded in 1888 to provide cheap credit to cultivators. Between 1889 and 1903, the Bank was providing loans averaging just over £T8 at the rate of some 40,000 a year, half of which were concentrated on two of the provinces where commercial agriculture was most advanced – Aidin and Bursa.[84] As Quataert rightly points out, it is unlikely that many such loans were obtained by the smaller farmers nor that they had much impact on Anatolian agriculture as a whole with its million or so peasant families.[85] Nevertheless, they must certainly have provided some assistance for those growing the more commercially successful crops.

The more difficult problem is how to assess the total impact on the agricultural sector of government activity which consisted not only of specific efforts to encourage production but also of a whole set of practices and regulations many of which had exactly the opposite effect. To take only one of the most obvious examples, the method of tax collection was obviously seriously detrimental to the activities of most rural producers. In the case of the duties on the Angora goat, for instance, they were usually collected in March, that is before the mohair wool had been clipped and before the death of many animals during the last few winter months, a practice which gave the peasant herdsmen little option but to borrow unnecessarily large sums to meet their obligations.[86]

The production and export of a variety of cash crops in the districts around the major port-cities and, to some extent, along the new railways, produced areas with many of the characteristics of so-called export sectors, where economic relations based on the use of money were highly developed.[87] It was here that the system of cash rents and of the use of wage labour was most advanced; here, as Rougon notes of the Izmir district, that the price of land most directly reflected the profitability of the crops which could be grown on it.[88] Another example of this same phenomenon was the creation of new methods of giving credit, in which the role of landlord and tax-farmer was, to some extent, bypassed by organizations like the Tobacco *Régie* or by specialist merchants and exporters dealing in specific crops for which they were willing to advance money in exchange for future delivery. In other cases it was peddlers or shop-keepers who stepped in to act as the last link in the chain connecting such areas with the banks and merchant houses of Europe, providing not only credit but the incentive to earn enough to buy foreign imports in exchange for cash crops and, in many cases, perpetual indebtedness. As in the Egypt of the cotton boom, wherever new lines of communications like railways were introduced, the opening of a village shop was almost sure to follow.[89]

Beyond all this, the increasing value of agricultural land in the export-oriented enclaves provided a powerful stimulus towards the creation of large estates. According to government figures provided by Mears, the two Anatolian provinces with the highest proportion of medium and large rural properties (defined as being of 5 hectares and over) were Aidin and Anana, major centres of export production, where nearly half the land was held in this way (Table 43). As earlier in the century, such properties could be created either by purchase, by seizure for debt or, in some cases, by having them registered in the name of a local protector or tribal chief. Unfortunately, however, Mears's statistics give no indication either of the average size of these medium and large estates or of the total amount of land they contained. To obtain some impression of these proportions it is necessary to have recourse to figures collected in the early Republican period when, according to a Turkish economic geographer, some 35 per cent of the cultivated land was contained in 33,000 large estates of over 1250 hectares each.[90] But some of these at least must have consisted of properties taken from fleeing Greeks or dead Armenians and there is no way of knowing how many of them had been created before 1914.

Table 43   The proportion of agricultural land in Anatolia held in properties of various sizes, 1909/10

	under 1 hectare	*1–5 hectares*	*over 5 hectares*
Diyarbakir	17	36	47
Aidin	18	36	46
Adana	18	36	46
Bitlis	21	41	38
Konya	23	46	31
Ankara	13	58	29
Harput	27	45	28
Van	36	37	27
Bursa	15	60	25
Sivas	32	46	22
Trabzon	38	46	16
Erzerum	45	40	15
Kastamonu	28	58	14
Izmir		67	33
Biga	21	49	30

Source: Government figures in Nickoley, 'Agriculture', 296.

It is also possible to make a distinction between export-oriented and other regions in terms of the way in which the medium and large estates were exploited. Whereas the usual method was to let them out to share-croppers according to a variety of arrangements based on the relative share of imputs, the crops to be produced and so on, there is much evidence to show that, in districts where cash crops were grown, at least part of a number of estates was exploited by the proprietors themselves. This practice may well have begun on the British-owned properties near Izmir in the 1860s and 1870s, but by the end of the century it was to be found on *jiftliks* in the provinces of Ankara, Bursa and Adana as well as in Aidin itself.[91] On the Çukurova Plain in the south-east, for example, parts of some estates were farmed directly using peasant labourers from central Anatolia who were given lodgings and wages in exchange for six or seven months' work picking cotton and planting wheat.[92] Further evidence of the same process is provided by the increasing import of agricultural machinery which must certainly have been intended for use on the larger properties under the personal supervision of the landlord or his agent.[93] Figures in the British consular reports show that by 1908/9, agricultural equipment worth over £10,000 was being imported duty-free at Izmir, including over 500 ploughs and their accessories.[94] The owners of the great estates around Adana were also anxious to compensate for a shortage of seasonal labour by employing steam-threshers and steam-ploughs.[95] Meanwhile, in the interior, considerable quantities of machinery were sold at certain points along the Anatolian railway, sometimes through the agency of the railway company itself.[96]

Important though the spread of commercial farming was, its significance as far as the whole agricultural sector was concerned should not be exaggerated. At the end of the Ottoman period, Anatolia remained predominantly a place of peasant farmers, either working their own plots or those of richer and more powerful neighbours. Mears's figures (Table 43) show that the majority of private plots were of less than 5 hectares. Later studies indicate that even such small plots were likely to be greatly fragmented into tiny parcels of land in a number of different places around the village.[97] Techniques were also little changed: for most of the peasants of Anatolia, animal manure was used for fuel rather than fertilizer; cereals were harvested with a simple sickle or even pulled out by hand; thrashing was still by an ox- or horse-drawn sledge.[98] In many cases the only noticeable improvement in methods during the later Ottoman period was the substitution of an iron for a wooden spike on the traditional scratch plough.[99]

To make matters worse, the centralizing policies of the government did little to affect the domination of the local protector or tax-farmer. In some ways it may even have increased it by policies which, whether directly assisting the larger proprietors (for example, by providing them with loans from the Agricultural Bank) or by increasing the need for small cultivators to borrow money, added new methods of economic control to the more traditional ones of extra-economic coercion. If there was anything to counter this from the peasants' own side it can only have been that, in most areas, a continued shortage of agricultural workers gave them a small amount of bargaining power. Quataert suggests that there is evidence of a small rise in agricultural wages in central Anatolia during the early years of the twentieth century, possibly because of the fact that labour had been attracted out of the area and down to the estates on the coast.[100] But, for the most part, conditions must have been closer to those described by a candidate for the 1908 parliament for Ayancık on the Black Sea coast, a village controlled by the Sukru family:

The Sukru family is rich. They call them bet or aga. The peasants from the neighbourhood bring the lumber they cut from the forests close-by, their cereals and their fruits to these landings [at the village] and sell it to the agas. They get in exchange cloth, petrol, coffee, sugar and enough cash to pay their taxes. These Turkish peasants have no other needs. What primitiveness!

The villages are poor, miserable villages. Even in winter they wear a cloth shirt that they make themselves. Their chest is bare and they wear tattered cloth pants. The hair on their chests become icicles. They mostly produce apples. The apples that go as far as Egypt as 'Inebolu apples' originate here.

The agas gather these, send them to Inebolu by rowboat and sell them on their backs from the village. I once asked such a group, 'How many hours is your village from here?' They said, 'Eight hours.' Every one of the apple baskets carried by the men weigh six to eight okes [80–100 lbs]. And the cost [is] three to four kuruş.

Imagine this exertion and this misery. Probably nothing has changed since Noah's time. What primitiveness and what poverty. But there is more.

The peasant keeps bringing these and the aga places them in his depot [and] gives the peasant in exchange one or two things that he wants. And then the peasant keeps bringing in more to pay his debt. But the debt never ends . . . This simplicity of heart is inequalled. And then there is also the following: if he [the peasant] complains a little he is insulted, beaten and can't get what he needs. From whom is he going to get the sugar and the petrol. In particular if the tax collector is after him from whom is he going to get the cash to pay his taxes? If one thinks of it, despite all, the peasant has indeed reason to be grateful to the aga.[101]

Industry and mining

Anatolia's first industrial census was taken in 1913, followed by a second in 1915.[102] Both were confined exclusively to two large areas in the west centred on Istanbul and Izmir. Both adopted a rather limited definition of what constituted an industrial enterprise: a factory with capital assets worth at least £T1000, paying 750 days' wages or more a year, and employing motive power of 5 hp or upwards.[103] As a result, a number of plants in central and eastern Anatolia (notably those round Ankara and Adana) were excluded as were some large enterprises which used hand-powered machinery.[104] In addition, many of the so-called factories which were listed scarcely deserved the name, being little more than small workshops. And, as Kurmuş notes, only a third of the enterprises on the list employed even a minimal form of book-keeping.[105]

The main findings of the 1915 census are set out in Table 44. They show that in terms of numbers of workers, of the value of output or of the motive power employed, western Anatolian industry was dominated by two major types of activity: the preparation of foodstuffs and the manufacture of textiles. The further breakdown of the census figures by different types of activity not surprisingly reveals enormous variations in the size of the workforce and of the capacity of installed machinery. In the case of the latter, the situation was dominated by the two cement factories with a joint motive power of 3192 hp or 15.2 per cent of the census total.[106] In the case of the former, the plants with the largest workforce were the five cotton spinning and weaving mills with an average of 325 workers each.[107] To these might be added the two cotton mills at Adana, outside the census area, with their 15,000 spindles and 230 power-driven looms.[108]

Table 44   The Turkish industrial censuses of 1915 and 1921

A   *Census of 1915 (western Anatolia)**

	No. of establishments in operation	Nos of workers	Installed hp	Value of product (kuruş m.)
Agricultural products	75	3916	7893	531.9
Building materials	17	336	3837	2.7
Leather goods	13	1270	961	62.6
Wood	24	377	513	5.9
Textiles	73	6763	6247	90.8
Paper	51	1267	705	46.2
Chemicals	11	131	821	17.0
Total	264	14,060	20,977	757.0

* Information about employment, installed hp and value of the product was not provided by all of the establishments enumerated.

Source: Ankara University, *Osmanli Sanayïi, 1913, 1915*, Tables IV, VI, IX.

B   *Census of 1921 (areas under Republican control)*

	No. of establishments	Nos of workers
Textiles, clothing	20,957	35,300
Leather, shoes	5347	18,000
Metal goods	3273	8000
Wood	2067	6000
Food, tobacco	1273	4500
Bricks, earthenware	704	3600
Chemicals	337	800
Total	33,058	76,200

Source: Teẓel, 'Turkish Economic Development', 56.

The information contained in the two censuses also allows some more general conclusions about the development of industry in western Anatolia before the First World War. In terms of ownership, it was dominated by members of local minorities, mostly Greeks and Armenians, although it is also true that the very largest plants tended to be owned by foreigners.[109] Again, it was mainly concerned with the processing of locally-produced primary products for the domestic market. In the absence of any real protection from a low external tariff (8 per cent until 1907, 11 per cent thereafter) it was necessarily forced to concentrate on those products where the raw materials needed were relatively cheap and where foreign competition either was not very strong or where there was some indirect protection to be derived from the high cost of transporting imported foreign products.

Cement is a good example of a product of which transport costs provided a high proportion of its final price. The cheap woollen cloth produced by the Ottoman Cloth Company founded by five British merchants at Izmir in 1910 is an example of a product at the lower end of the market for which there was a local demand not met by the factories of Europe.

It must go without saying that the boundary between what was defined for census purposes as an industrial establishment and what was not was very hazy and will always be the subject of much debate. In particular, at the bottom end of the scale there were a large number of workshops and ateliers which might be placed either just one side of the border or the other. Some idea of the extent of this problem comes from the 1921 census of industrial activity carried out in those parts of Anatolia, mostly in the centre and east, then under the direct control of the Ankara government. This lists over 33,000 establishments with 76,200 workers or an average of two men per plant (Table 44). In addition, in the western part of Anatolia there were a number of industries either organized on a putting-out system or employing hand-driven machinery which do not seem to have shown up in the 1913/15 census at all. Of these, certainly the most important was that of carpet manufacture which according to one estimate employed some 60,000 people in and around Izmir to spin and dye the wool and to weave the actual carpets.[110] Another very large category consisted of the tailors, shoemakers and others who worked in their own shops.[111]

If it is difficult to establish the structure and composition of Turkish industry just before the First World War it is a virtually impossible task to chart its progress in the three preceding decades. As far as the factories listed in the 1913/15 censuses are concerned, the best that can be said is that only a few existed before 1880 and that the vast majority were established during the Hamidian and Young Turk periods.[112] For the rest, reliable information is so scarce that comprehensive analysis has to give way to a more impressionistic survey of some of the leading sectors. To begin with textiles. Here the weaving of the cheaper types of cotton and woollen cloth was able to continue, and even to expand, towards the end of the century for the same two reasons as elsewhere in the Ottoman Empire: first, the exploitation of a growing local market based on an increasing, and in some cases an increasingly prosperous, urban and agricultural population; second, the skilful use of imported threads and dyes.[113] A good example of this is the production of the clothing material known as *adjala* which, according to Rougon, was woven in all the towns and villages of the Izmir district in the 1890s.[114] In addition, two types of activity were revived in new form during the same period: silk production and the manufacture of carpets. In the first instance the stimulus came from the increasing supplies of good quality silk, particularly in the districts round Bursa. While the thread was spun in the forty-one small factories in Bursa listed in the 1913/15 industrial censuses, weaving was generally organized on a domestic basis in homes throughout the district.[115] By 1905–9, output of silk thread was averaging some 580,000,000 kgs a year, equal to that of Syria/Lebanon, the Middle East's other major producer.[116]

The development of the organization of carpet manufacture was different again. Here, according to Kurmuş, production throughout western Anatolia was very nearly the monopoly of six British merchant houses at Izmir supported by a large network of brokers, dyers and spinners by whom the necessary wool was bought, spun, dyed and then distributed to local weavers along with instructions about size, colour and pattern.[117] By the early 1890s there were already at least 1000 looms and 2500 weavers at work in the Izmir *caza* itself, with another 1000 or so looms further inland.[118] Later, by energetic use of the railway systems and other new means of transport, operations were gradually extended until by 1900 they had come to embrace small workshops as far away from the coast as Konya.[119] However, increasing profits and increasing European and American demand encouraged competition from local rivals and in 1908 there was a complete reorganization of operations with the British merchants forming the Amalgamated Oriental Carpet Manufacturers Ltd, with a capital of £300,000, to centralize the process of dying and spinning yarn in a single building.[120] Shortly afterwards, a further increase in capital to £1,000,000 allowed the construction of at least seventeen workshops in which a large part of the carpet-weaving was relocated under closer supervision.[121] The result was not only to drive out most of the local competition but also to permit a further growth of production and export.[122] In the case of the former, the company was manufacturing at least 1,000,000 square metres of carpets by 1913, compared with a total western Anatolian output of 150,000 square metres in 1884 and 367,000 in 1893, and a total Turkish production of 668,000 square metres in 1909.[123] Meanwhile, however much connoisseurs might bemoan the replacement of traditional patterns by those specifically designed to cater to the west's idea of Oriental taste, the value of exports from Izmir rose dramatically, from £284,000 in 1901 to £735,000 in 1920.[124]

If the figures given in the 1921 census are any sort of indication, about half the workforce in the craft-industrial sector was engaged in textile production, with the remainder distributed in a huge variety of activities based on the use of local raw materials like wood, leather, metals and a large number of agricultural crops (Table 42).[125] As in the case of factory industry, new activities could be begun and old ones expanded, but only in terms of the increasingly tight constraints imposed by forces emanating from the most advanced sectors of the world economy. In some cases, as with carpets, an increase in foreign demand opened up new markets for a reorganized local industry; in others, the further penetration of European products (for example, along the railways) or a reduction in their price due to technological change exposed old activities to a competition with which they could not cope. Another aspect of the same process was the way in which local raw materials might suddenly become very much more expensive or even disappear entirely as a result of the pull of foreign demand. To make matters more difficult, Anatolian producers could rely very little on help from the Ottoman government. In spite of a few tentative efforts to encourage certain types of local activity like flour milling, the general situation was one in which Turkish products were usually burdened with extra taxes and duties as compared with their foreign competitors as well as suffering from the government's neglect of technical education and of institutions for providing industrial credit.[126] The Young Turk governments' laws for the encouragement of industry in 1909 and in 1913 were a small and very belated effort to make up for long years of neglect.[127]

Table 45 The production of minerals in Anatolia, 1909/10

	Output (metric tons)	Value (£s)
Coal	766,393	354,001
Lignite	41,226	14,385
Chromium	16,604	33,995
Emery	27,656	90,516
Meerschaum	115	61,306
Pandermite	11,362	75,636

Source: FO (UK), *Anatolia*, 94.

The last important activity to be found in the Turkish industrial sector was that of mining. This, too, increased rapidly in size during the period as foreign firms began to invest large sums in the production of coal, emery and other minerals. Table 45 gives figures for the volume and value of output in 1910–11. It shows the overwhelming importance of coal which, itself, was dominated by the French-owned Société Minérale d'Heraclée with its mines, light railway and port of Zongulduk. The Black Sea Company output increased from 61,000 tons in 1865 to 827,000 in 1913, a large part of which was either sold to passing steamships or sent to Istanbul.[128] Foreign firms also dominated the rest of the industry, controlling over two-thirds of production in 1910.[129] In the case of most minerals, some 90 to 100 per cent of output was exported; only coal and lignite could find a domestic market of any size.[130]

Trade and payments

As already noted, the figures concerning Ottoman foreign trade (to be found in Table 35) are too inexact and unreliable to allow any detailed

Table 46   The amount paid by the Ottoman government in kilometric guarantees to foreign
railway companies

A   *Total payments of guarantee to all railway companies in the Ottoman Empire*

	Length of lines subject to guarantees (kms)	Guarantees paid (£T)	Total government expenditure (£T m.)
1899/1900	2271	900,081	18.225
1900/1	2271	883,489	18.685
1901/2	2271	684,302	19.008
1902/3	2459	678,769	20.155
1903/4	2459	793,639	22.658
1904/5	2559	779,707	
1905/6	2659	722,264	
1906/7	2802	691,101	
1907/8	2802	753,191	
1908/9	2802	771,504	
1909/10	2802	748,910	27.753
1910/11	2802	528,918	33.783
1911/12	2840	406,318	36.704
1912/13	3211	341,388	

Sources: Ottoman, PDA *Rapport . . . année 1912/13 comparée avec l'année 1911/12*, 122–3;
Shaw, 'Ottoman Expenditure and Budgets', 374.

B   *Kilometric guarantees paid on particular Anatolian lines (francs, m.)*

	1898	1910	1911
Anatolian railway:			
Uskudar/Ankara	1.6	0.6	− [1]
Eskişehir/Konya	2.9	2.4	1.1
Baghdad railway		2.6	2.7
Izmir/Kassaba and extension	4.9	3.3	2.8

Source: Rey, *Statistique 1898* and *Statistique 1911*.

Note: 1 In 1911 the Anatolian railway paid the government 300,000 francs as a result of the
fact that profits exceeded the guaranteed minimum.

analysis. They certainly testify to a sizeable increase in the value of both
imports and exports, particularly in the last decade before the First World
War. But the fact that they have been shown to underestimate the sales of
Turkish goods abroad means that they are of limited use either as a guide to
the growth of local production or to the possible extent of the Empire's
trade deficit.

Much the same problem can be found when it comes to an examination
of the balance of payments as a whole. While Teẓel's careful calculations
show that the Ottomans experienced a net outflow of funds of some
£T69,000,000 during the period 1882 to 1913, as a result of the excess of
money paid out in debt servicing over new money borrowed from abroad,
too little is known about the flow of private foreign capital to permit any
general statement about the final balance and thus about whether or not

there was a substantial transfer of the Turkish economic surplus to Europe.[131] The point is an important one. Clearly, any large drain of capital abroad must have had serious repercussions on the Empire's ability to develop its own resources. I would not want to argue, however, as many writers have done, that such a drain — if it existed — could have been the sole or even the major cause of Turkey's economic backwardness.[132] It is not the loss of capital itself which was the key to the situation but rather the way in which the whole economic system was restructured during the process of its incorporation with the international economy. Only with the development of the 'statist' policies of the Republican Peoples Party after 1923 was it possible to establish some limited control over the way Turkey was forced to do business with the rest of the world.[133]

9 *The Egyptian economy, 1882–1914*

According to the first official census taken in May 1882 just before the British occupation, the population of Egypt then numbered 6,831,131, of whom just over 90,000 were Europeans.[1] While a number of writers have pointed out that this figure is certainly too low (perhaps by as much as 1,000,000) the fact that any census at all was held at such a time represented a remarkable achievement on the part of the government's embryonic statistical service and provided a useful basis for further developments during the British period when an improved administrative system was used to generate a wealth of data of a scope and quality far in excess of that to be found anywhere else in the Middle East.[2] Excellent figures for foreign trade and for the production and export of cotton were soon complemented by the first regular calculations of the area placed under different crops (1894), the distribution of landed property into holdings of various sizes (1894) and the first reliable census of population (1897). While some of these figures pose difficult problems, there is no doubt that they have enabled economic historians to create useful new indices and to conduct analyses of a sophistication which would be impossible in most other countries of the non-European world.[3] If a few of these same economic historians seem sometimes to have ignored the fact that there is no way in which even the most elaborate mathematical techniques can be used to improve the truth or the unrepresentativeness of unreliable or partial figures, it remains a fact that their work, collectively, provides information about most of the major processes at work within the Egyptian economy during the period.

Baer's upward reworking of Egypt's 1882 population is given in Table 47, together with his calculation of the distribution between urban and rural segments based on the 1882, 1897 and 1907 censuses.[4] To complete the picture, I have added information from the 1917 (wartime) census together with an estimate of the number of rural families and of the ratio of men to land as a way of illustrating change in one of the basic relationships in what was still fundamentally an agricultural economy. Taken together the figures in Table 47 make a number of important points: they show a population growing at an average of between 1.33 and 1.5 per cent a year; they show that the increase in the rural segment of this population was a

216

good deal faster than the increase in the supply of cultivable land; and they show that between 1897 and 1917 the proportion of the total population living in large towns remained more or less constant at between 14 and 15 per cent, suggesting that there was as yet no substantial urban migration in spite of some evidence of intense pressure for land in certain areas.[5]

Table 47   Egypt's population and cultivated land, 1882–1917

	Total population (th'000s)	Population of 23 major towns ('000s)	Rural* population ('000s)	Rural families ('000s)**	Cultivated area (feddans) (m.)	Amount of land per rural family (feddans)
1882	7930	1015	6915	1153	4.957[2]	4.3
1897	9734[1]	1454	8263	1377	5.048	3.67
1907	11,287	1596	9691	1615	5.403	3.35
1917	12,751	1994	10,757	1793	5.232	2.92

* Rural population equals total population minus inhabitants of 23 major towns.
** Based on the assumption of an average family size of 6.

Sources: Baer, 'Urbanization', 158; Egypt, Ministry of Finance, *The Census of Egypt Taken in 1917*, 1 (Cairo, 1920), and sources in Owen, *Cotton*, Table 43.

Notes:
1 Includes an extra 17,177 people living in areas along the Sudanese border and the Oasis of Siwa which were incorporated into Egypt between the censuses of 1897 and 1907.
2 Figure for 1886.

Two other points ought also to be mentioned by way of further clarification. First, although the increase in the rural population was certainly encouraged by rising incomes, better nutrition and the temporary cessation of serious epidemics, it was also accompanied by a tremendous expansion of the water-borne disease bilharzia which, as a result of the further expansion of perennial irrigation, may well have come to affect something like half of the peasants of Lower Egypt during the early twentieth century.[6] Second, as far as the large towns were concerned, numbers were augmented by the immigration of perhaps 200,000 foreigners between 1882 and 1914, about half of whom were Europeans.[7]

More information about conditions in the rural sector is provided in Tables 48 and 49 which show changes in the way Egypt's agricultural land was owned and in the way it was used. Table 48 gives figures for the division of this land into properties of various sizes: 50 feddans and over (large), 5 to 50 feddans (medium) and 5 and under (small).[8] The most obvious trend over time was one in which an already unequal distribution of ownership became still more unequal, with the proportion of land held in large properties increasing from 42.5 per cent in 1894 to 44.2 per cent in 1913.[9] At the other end of the scale, the growth of rural population ensured that although the total amount of land held in small properties expanded slightly (mostly at the expense of medium holdings) the average size of such

Table 48   The distribution of Egypt's agricultural land in properties of various sizes, 1897–1913

	1897		1901		1913	
	No. of props	Total area (feddans)	No. of props	Total area (feddans)	No. of props	Total area (feddans)
Less than 1 feddan	644,066	1,020,463	815,950	1,145,978	942,530	405,595
1–5 feddans					468,628	1,013,364
5–50 feddans	144,532	1,813,868	139,393	1,735,571	132,594	1,633,413
More than 50 feddans	12,184	2,227,740	11,952	2,215,882	12,558	2,420,558

Sources: Egypt, Ministry of Finance, Dept. of General Statistics, Annuaire Statistique de l'Egypte, 1910 (Cairo, 1910), 234–5; Annuaire Statistique, 1914, 320–1.

plots fell from just under 1.5 feddans in 1900 to only 1 feddan in 1913.[10] There was also a significant increase in the number of families without any land at all. In 1907, just before the end of the period, the position relating to rural property was as follows: three-quarters of the land was held in 147,000 large and medium properties while the remaining quarter was held in small, usually fragmented, plots by the remaining 1,120,000 land-owners.[11] Another way of looking at the same situation is in terms of family units of an average of six people.[12] In 1907, of Egypt's 1,600,000 rural families, no more than 9 per cent at most owned at least 5 feddans – or roughly what British officials calculated was necessary to provide them with adequate sustenance – another 70 per cent or so possessed some property but not enough to satisfy all their immediate needs, while the remaining 21 per cent owned no land at all.[13]

Figures for the amount of land devoted to seven major crops are given in Table 49. Here the most important development was the rapid expansion of cotton cultivation from the early 1890s onwards, particularly in Lower Egypt. This was partly the result of its cultivation on new land, partly the

Table 49   Areas devoted to seven major Egyptian crops, 1886/7 and 1893/4–1912/13 (annual averages in ,000 feddans)

	Cotton	Maize	Wheat	Beans	Barley	Rice	Sugar
1886/7	866	1125	1241	756	520	150	71
1893/4	966	1476	1296	689	460	181	72
1894/5–1898/9	1090	1474	1214	651	499	199	79
1899/1900–1903/4	1305	1727	1270	647	537	164	79
1904/5–1908/9	1583	1782	1207	574	448	249	47
1909/10–1912/13	1700	1838	1270	525	373	246	48

Sources: 1886/7: Boinet, official figures in Eid (Cairo), 15 Nov. 1892, RC (Belgium), 78 (1893), 86–7.
1893/4: Egypt, Ministry of Finances, Department of General Statistics, Annuaire Statistique de l'Egypte, 1909 (Cairo, 1909), 268–9.
1894/5–1912/13: Annuaire Statistique 1910, 238–41 and Annuaire Statistique 1914, 322–5.

result of a more intensive use of existing land through a major switch from a triennial to a biennial cotton rotation.[14] Changes in the system of rotation also favoured the production of maize and clover – figures for which are too unreliable to include – but led to a reduction in the area placed under important food crops like beans and barley.[15] Given the fact that there was a concomitant rise in yields, especially of cotton, there was a considerable expansion of agricultural output during the period. This will be further discussed later in the chapter.

The fact that most of the new cotton was grown in the Delta further emphasized the different pattern of rural development between Lower and Upper Egypt. In spite of a serious effort to convert large areas of the latter from basin to perennial irrigation by the construction of new canals, there was still insufficient summer water to allow more than a small number of its peasants to benefit from the second cotton boom.[16] Thus in 1912/13, for instance, only 22 per cent of Egypt's cotton was grown south of Cairo, and even then most of it was of the lower-yielding Ashmouni variety.[17] The result, according to one calculation, was that the average net value of output per feddan was nearly twice as much in Lower as in Upper Egypt.[18] No doubt for the same reason there were fewer large properties in the south (only 30 per cent of the privately-owned land being held in this way as against 55 per cent in the Delta) while the lack of summer employment there meant that it continued to act as a huge reservoir of seasonal labour for work in the cotton fields of the north.[19] The fact that southerners had not yet begun to suffer from bilharzia to any appreciable extent made their contribution even more welcome.

Cotton also had an increasingly important role to play in Egypt's foreign trade. Whereas in 1880–4 it contributed 75 per cent to the total value of exports, by 1910–13 this proportion had reached just over 92 per cent. Another result of the growth in cotton income was a strong upward movement in what might be called the 'cotton terms of trade' (that is, the value of cotton exports expressed in terms of the price of British manufactured goods) allowing Egypt to increase its purchase of foreign imports by nearly 350 per cent during the same three decades.[20] A good way of bringing out the underlying significance of the same development is to look at changes in the value of imports per head of population. Not only did this increase from an average of just under £1 in the early 1880s to over £2 in 1913 but also, at the latter date, it was well in excess of such countries as Greece and Japan and at more or less the same level as Spain.[21]

In spite of the increase in local purchasing power, the development of Egyptian factory industry proceeded only slowly. According to information provided by the British Chamber of Commerce of Egypt, in 1901 there were then twenty-three companies engaged in some type of manufacture, with paid up capital and debentures worth nearly £E3,500,000.[22] Of these, all but three had been founded in the 1890s, although a few of the remaining – notably the giant Société Générale de Sucreries et de la Raffinerie d'Egypte with capital and debentures of 42,500,000 francs (£1,700,000) – employed plant and machinery which had first been installed in the 1870s and 1880s.[23] By 1911, government records show that the number of such companies had increased to thirty-seven with total capital of just under £E8,500,000.[24] Information about the craft-industrial sector is very much more difficult to obtain, but some information as to its size can be obtained from the figures for industrial employment of all kinds to be found in the 1907 census: nearly 500,000 workers, out of a total Egyptian labour force of 5,800,000.[25] It is also impossible to do more than guess at the value of manufacturing output. The government's Commission on Commerce and Industry estimated that the country's national income was £E120,000,000 in 1913 but did not attempt to give a figure for its industrial component.[26] A second, and much criticized, attempt to calculate national income for 1921–2 estimated manufacturing income at £E56.8m. or 18.9 per cent of the whole.[27]

The pattern of British control over the Egyptian economy

For some years the British occupation of Egypt was regarded in London as a temporary affair designed simply to re-establish the mechanisms of foreign financial control which it was thought had been seriously threatened by the Urabi movement. But as the decision to withdraw was delayed and delayed, these mechanisms themselves became subject to a number of important amendments in the interests of strengthening Britain's own power to manage Egyptian finances. The first to go was the Dual Control exercised by the British and French Controllers: in 1883 this was replaced by the appointment of a single British financial adviser empowered to attend all meetings of the Khedive's Council of Ministers and to supervise all important decisions affecting revenue and expenditure.[28] Then, two years later, an international conference in London produced a major amendment to the Law of Liquidation, raising the ceiling established for the government's administrative expenditure (to £E5,237,000) and providing that any of the revenues assigned to the Caisse de la Dette over and above what was needed to meet annual payments of interest and amortization should not simply be put in a reserve fund but shared with the government in the ratio 50 : 50. The conference also authorized the floating of one last public loan of £E9,000,000, of which £E8,000,000 was to be used to fund the new floating debt which had been created during the first years of the occupation and £1,000,000 was assigned to works of economic development.[29] Finally, in 1904, as part of the general settlement of Anglo-French differences round the world, the French government agreed to remove the ceiling on Egyptian administrative expenditure and to allow the abolition of the mixed international agencies which had been set up in the late 1870s to run those organizations like the railways, the telegraphs, the port of Alexandria and the former Royal estates whose revenues had been specifically allocated to the Caisse de la Dette.[30] With this agreement the British-controlled Egyptian government regained a large measure of day-to-day control over local finances, but still remained subject to a variety of international obligations of which the requirement to maintain the regular servicing of the debt was certainly the most onerous.

The prolonged and sometimes acrimonious negotiations which led to these agreements are sometimes portrayed in British sources in terms of an enlightened defence of Egyptian interests against the more narrow, selfish concerns of the French and other bond-holders.[31] But it is an obvious strategy of any colonial power to seek to appear as a champion of the rights of those it rules and this should not be allowed to obscure the central features of the whole process: the progressive recognition by most Europeans that with a European power in actual physical control of Egypt there was no longer such pressing need for an elaborate set of safeguards to ensure proper management of the debt or the protection of a host of related interests. Again, there is little evidence that any of these international arrangements seriously interfered with the ability of British officials to manage the economy as they thought fit. Indeed, it could easily be argued that in some cases they might even have been quite welcome; for example to the extent that they provided a reason for keeping expenditure on something like public education to a minimum, thus reducing what in British eyes was seen as the possible threat posed to their position by the growth of an educated urban intelligentsia.[32] Once the occupation became permanent, the formation of economic policy on Egypt has to be seen less in terms of the force of international constraints and more in terms of the ordinary needs of a colonial power anxious to maintain its hold over a subject people at least cost to itself. The result, as in India and elsewhere in the Empire, was not so much the formulation of a consistent programme but more the establishment of guidelines balancing economic with political considerations so as to ensure that the economy itself grew in such a way that it supported certain important imperial interests without damaging others.[33]

The first concern of the British administrators, both chronologically and in terms of importance, was the Egyptian agricultural sector. During the early years of the occupation it was here that most efforts were concentrated in a successful effort to generate revenues large enough to avoid a second bankruptcy. The key to the whole process was seen as the improvement of the system of irrigation and the provision of larger supplies of summer water, particularly in Lower Egypt where the bulk of the cotton crop was grown. To this end the Delta Barrage (first begun in the days of Muhammad

Ali) was entirely reconstructed and then connected to the Lower Egyptian canals by two high-level feeder canals, the re-excavated Buhaira Canal in the west, and the Sharqiya (renamed the Taufiqiya) in the east.[34] Once the new system was at work in 1890 it not only provided more water all the year round but provided it at a higher level, thus allowing fields to be irrigated by the simple method of opening sluices rather than by using man and animal power to lift it from low-lying channels. The next stage in the programme was to build a new dam at Aswan in Upper Egypt (completed in 1902 and further heightened between 1907 and 1912) designed to hold up a significant part of the Nile's autumn flood rather than leaving it to run to waste in the Mediterranean.[35] Some of the extra water was then used to allow the conversion of much of the northerly part of Upper Egypt (known also as Middle Egypt) from basin to perennial irrigation via the construction of yet more subsidiary canals.[36]

The result, almost everywhere, was a sudden and dramatic increase in the output of every major Egyptian crop (to be analysed later in the chapter). But it soon became clear that this improvement had brought quite new and unanticipated problems of its own and that the care taken to provide all the extra water had not been matched by steps taken to ensure its efficient use or to build the drains needed to allow it to flow away properly. The first and most dangerous sign was the steady decline in cotton yields from the turn of the century onwards, culminating in the disastrous harvest of 1909. Although expert opinion took some time to establish a consensus as to the exact causes, it was generally recognized that the deterioration had something to do with a profligate over-watering of the Delta fields which produced an alarming rise in the underground water-table and a more intensive use of agricultural land which not only reduced the annual fallow period but also multiplied the number of host plants on which cotton's main predators, the worm and weevil, could feed.[37] Early efforts to remedy the situation were not pursued with sufficient energy and it was only just before the First World War that Kitchener's programme of constructing huge new Delta drains and the increased use of chemical fertilizer promised to do something to restore part of the soil's lost fertility.[38]

Irrigation apart, other types of government activity also contributed to the increase in agricultural output. One was the final abolition of the corvée between 1885 and 1889 which provided a sizeable increase in the supply of rural labour.[39] Another was the attention paid to improvements in the system of transport, first by the construction of over 2400 km of agricultural roads, then by the encouragement of the development of privately-owned light agricultural railways.[40] By 1912/13 three railway companies had built up networks of lines with a total length of over 1200 km which were used to carry at least half of that year's cotton harvest.[41] Improvements in the method of rural tax collection and the final establishment of full property rights in land were also an important incentive behind increased agricultural output.[42]

It was policies of this kind which allowed production and tax receipts to increase just fast enough during the 1880s to win what Lord 'Cromer later dramatized as a 'race against bankruptcy'.[43] Figures in Table 50 show that there was then a period of stagnant revenues during the 1890s as the fall in the price of Egypt's major crops prevented any significant rise in rural incomes.[44] Finally, the agricultural-led economic advance of the years after 1900 produced enough growth in receipts from indirect taxes and dues and from state undertakings like the railways to allow the government to take advantage of the removal of the ceiling on official expenditure as a result of the Anglo-French accord of 1904. Money spent on administrative services and on the army was increased at a rapid rate while, for the first time, there was a real reduction in the proportion of government revenues spent on servicing the public debt – from 33 per cent in 1895–9 to 23 per cent in 1910–13.[45]

Table 50   Egyptian government revenues and expenditures, 1881–1913
(annual averages in £E,000)

	Revenues				Expenditures			
	Direct taxes	Indirect taxes	Railways, Ports, etc.	Total	Public debt	Adminis- tration/ collection	Military	Total
1881–4	5335	1994	1518	9945	3936	2228	638	9448
1885–9	5393	2410	1618	11,488	4316	2471	480	11,230
1890–4	5155	2985	1902	10,975	3995	2550	574	10,335
1895–9	4952	3497	2167	11,482	3740	2692	695	10,711
1900–4	4826	4488	2530	13,205	3756	2737	720	12,232
1905–9	5232	5632	3684	16,612	3916	4209	873	17,335
1910–13	5549	5860	4188	17,267	3924	5234	1072	17,314

Source: Annuaire Statistique, 1914, 405–8, 410–11, 413, 418–19.

British concern with the Egyptian agricultural sector was not based solely on financial considerations, however; there were also important political factors involved. It was an article of faith shared by most officials with Indian experience that the basis of imperial rule over non-European peoples was to be found in an alliance with the supposedly conservative landlord and peasant classes.[46] In an Egyptian context, belief in the importance of such an alliance was further accentuated by worries about what was seen as a dangerous rise in rural crime (or 'brigandage') in the 1880s, by periodic increases in the level of agricultural indebtedness (notably in the mid-1890s and after the financial crisis of 1907) and by fears that high rents and loss of peasant land would exacerbate social tensions in the countryside.[47] As always, the first concern was with security; but when this seemed to have been established, as a result, in part, of giving greater authority to landowners and village officials, attention was turned to other matters such as the reduction of the level of direct taxation, the provision of cheap credit and efforts to increase the supply of land available to the poorer peasants.[48] Thus, after a number of experiments, the policy of providing low-interest loans was institutionalized by the establishment of the Agricultural Bank in 1902, while some effort was made to try to ensure that the decision to allow a private company to sell off the remainder of the Daira Saniya estates (between 1899 and 1906) was done in such a way as to benefit small purchasers.[49]

From an official point of view, however, the problem was that such policies ran counter to important economic as well as institutional constraints. Poor peasants had neither the resources nor the credit-worthiness either to buy much land for themselves or to borrow money on the security of their own plots. Meanwhile, institutions like the Daira Saniya Company and the Agricultural Bank found it easier and more profitable to do business with medium and large proprietors rather than with the owners of small plots whose requests for loans or land were as costly to process as those of the rich and much more costly to renegotiate if something went wrong. All the available evidence points to the fact that the bulk of the Daira Saniya land was sold as large or medium-sized properties.[50] Figures from the Agricultural Bank indicate that the bulk of its loans went not to small peasants, who were fearful of its links with the government and the fact that repayments were collected by the official tax-gatherers, but to the owners of larger properties.[51] Reports by Bank officials in the aftermath of Egypt's 1907 financial crisis indicate that they were well aware that something had gone wrong.[52] But before matters could be remedied Lord Kitchener introduced a new method of safeguarding small property holders – the Law of Five Feddans of 1912 preventing the seizure of plots of under 5 feddans for debt – which, whatever its own merits, removed the one resource which a peasant could offer as security for a loan, thus bringing the Bank's business virtually to an end.[53] In these circumstances, the major beneficiaries of British policies were the large landowners who saw a huge increase in the value of their properties, in their ability to borrow money and in their incomes after 1882. Here, if anywhere, was the alliance which safeguarded imperial interests in the countryside and which was a vital factor in permitting the restoration of order there during the widespread rural revolt which broke out in the first months of 1919.[54]

British policy towards other sectors of the economy was very much less interventionist, very much more in line with the conventional laissez-faire economic thinking of the day. Private enterprise was encouraged, particularly by the award of a string of lucrative concessions to establish such organizations as the National Bank of Egypt, the Agricultural Bank and the light agricultural railways.[55] Laws affecting business activity were as un-restrictive as possible, and even then not always applied to foreign-owned enterprises covered by Capitulatory privileges. The urban population largely escaped direct taxation once it was decided that the general collection of the 'professional' (or rudimentary income) tax would create too many difficulties with the international community.[56] The National Bank, in spite of its name, was given no power to control the money supply, to determine the rate of interest, or to act as lender of last resort for other financial institutions. Proof of the rigidity with which such policies were pursued came after the 1907 financial depression when the administration refused to heed the pleas of the country's largest mortgage company, the Crédit Foncier Egyptien, for a loan of £E2,000,000 which, so it was argued, was necessary to prevent a complete loss of commercial confidence.[57] In the event, all that the government would agree to do was somewhat belatedly to exercise a greater degree of control over the operations of the Cairo and Alexandria stock exchanges.[58]

The only sector where the British-controlled administration was pre-pared to intervene with any greater purpose was that of industry. Here it had a very mixed record. On the one hand, it insisted that the two new cotton spinning and weaving factories established at the turn of the century pay a countervailing duty of 8 per cent on all their products, thus depriving them of even the small degree of protection afforded by the external tariff.[59] Just how much this contributed to their lack of success, it is impossible to say with precision.[60] But there is no doubt that the decision gave the general impression among entrepreneurs that the government was ambivalent, to say the least, about Egypt's industrial development. On the other hand, the administration was prepared to come to the aid of the main sugar producer, the S.G. des Sucreries et de la Raffinerie, in 1906 when it was just able to save itself from liquidation by, among other things, selling off its network of unprofitable light railways to the government.[61] Again, there were a number of occasions on which local industrial concerns were given a small amount of (usually temporary) tariff advantage, notably the sugar company in 1906 and the one surviving cotton mill, owned by the Anglo-Egyptian Spinning and Weaving Company, in 1908.[62] Probably the answer to this apparently contradictory attitude to modern industry is to be seen less as an attachment to the conventional economic wisdom of the day and more as consideration of imperial interest in which fears about Lancashire's reaction to a successful Egyptian cotton spinning and weaving enterprise – the dominant factor underlying Cromer's decision to impose a counter-vailing duty in 1901 – might at other times be balanced by worries as to local nationalist reaction if this or that enterprise was seen to fail with the British standing idly by.[63]

The last point is important in another way as well. Cromer and other

British officials were very much preoccupied with what was then the quite new idea of using economic advance as a justification for imperial control. It was for this reason that Cromer himself was so concerned to stress the contrast between the spendthrift Ismail and his own, more sound, financial practices. The initial success of British irrigation policy was put to the same use, while each of his annual reports on Egypt was used to instruct both his British and his local audience as to the economic benefits of his programmes.[64] The result, not surprisingly, was to project the question of the proper management of the Egyptian economy right to the centre of the developing political debate between Britons and nationalists. If Cromer based an important part of his case for continued British control on an appeal to Egypt's current prosperity, events like the 1907 financial crisis and the disastrous 1909 cotton harvest could be used to make almost the opposite point: that under the British the country had become dangerously dependent on one single crop, that it had lost any control that it might have had over its own economic destiny, and that the main hope for the future lay in a programme of industrialization, increased government intervention, and the development of genuinely Egyptian financial institutions such as a locally controlled National Bank. Ideas of this kind were widely expounded in the years just before the First World War.[65] By the time the official Commission on Commerce and Industry presented its report in 1917 they had had a major influence on the economic thinking of the majority of the country's businessmen, financiers and bankers.[66]

The agricultural sector

The years of the British occupation saw a large and unprecedented increase in Egyptian agricultural output. Unfortunately, however, there are no official figures to illustrate this progress before 1909, and even then they are based on what must certainly have been a very inexact calculation of the average national yield of the major field crops.[67] Only in the case of cotton are there reasonably accurate estimates of harvest size going back to 1885/6.[68] In recent years, however, there have been a number of useful attempts by economic historians to fill the gap. Of these I have chosen two series produced by Hansen and Wattleworth as likely to be the most reliable (see Table 51).[69] The first is for the output of seven important crops — cotton, cotton seed, wheat, barley, beans, maize, rice and their straw and stalks; the second seeks to provide a more comprehensive picture of Egyptian agricultural production by imputing figures for the cultivation of *birsim*, vegetables and fruit. Both series depend heavily on the presumed accuracy of a government statistician's single attempt to estimate crop areas for 1886/7 and on the use of figures for yields on the State Domains as proxy for national yields before 1913.[70] In addition, they exclude sugar, one of

Egypt's most valuable crops, and farm animals.[71] For all these reasons they must certainly be used with great caution. Nevertheless, they do provide some general indication of the very marked rise in agricultural output during the 1890s, followed by a period of uneven and less rapid growth as yields (particularly of cotton) began to fall away towards the First World War.

Table 51 Egyptian agricultural production: quantity indexes of major field crops and all field crops, 1887–1914 (1887 base)

	Major field crops	*All field crops*
1887	100.0	100.0
1894	129.1	128.3
1895	138.3	133.9
1896	146.5	139.5
1897	156.5	147.0
1898	152.4	143.3
1899	161.7	153.0
1900	145.5	137.7
1901	159.1	152.4
1902	154.3	147.1
1903	162.1	155.6
1904	160.6	153.8
1905	156.5	149.4
1906	166.4	159.4
1907	172.0	165.3
1908	164.3	157.3
1909	145.1	139.1
1910	172.7	166.5
1911	172.2	166.5
1912	173.0	166.7
1913	179.2	172.7
1914	162.1	151.5

Source: Wattleworth, 'Report on the construction of agricultural indexes', Tables XLIV, XLIX.

The same series can also be decomposed – as Hansen and Wattleworth have done – to give some idea of the relative importance of the various factors underlying the general upward trend.[72] Here they are able to demonstrate that the major role was played by an expansion of the land devoted to Egypt's main crops, whether by the more intensive use of existing plots or the reclamation of new areas. A lesser contribution was made by the overall increase in yields and by a change in the mix of crops in the direction of high value products like cotton. A graphic method of illustrating the first of these factors is provided by El-Imam. Using his concept of something he calls the 'exploitation rate', that is the number of months during which the average acre was placed under some kind of cultivation, it can be shown that land use increased from 6.37 months a year in 1886/7 to 7.94 months in 1912/13; and this excludes reference to an important fodder crop like *birsim*, figures for which are too inaccurate to be of any use in such calculations.[73]

The next task is to attempt to measure the concomitant increase in the value of Egyptian agricultural output, both in current and in real terms. A first effort in this direction was made in 1895 by Sir William Willcocks who produced a figure of just over £39,000,000 for all field crops.[74] But this was a year in which the price of most Egyptian crops was at its lowest. Later estimates, for 1908 and 1913, show that the current value of Egypt's harvest had then increased to at least £65,000,000 to £70,000,000.[75] As for the increase in the value of output in real terms, calculations by Hansen and Wattleworth suggest that this rose by nearly 200 per cent between 1886/7 and 1912/13.[76]

Finally, if this increase in output and income is to be seen in its proper perspective it is necessary to examine it in relation to the accompanying growth in Egypt's rural population. Looked at in these terms it is not surprising to find that much of the gain in harvest size was lost as a result of the accelerating increase in the number of mouths to feed. As far as production *per capita* was concerned, Hansen and Wattleworth's calculations indicate that this showed a rise of over 35 per cent during the period 1886/7 to 1898 only to fall away in the first years of the twentieth century, leaving the overall increase between 1886/7 and 1914 at about 20 per cent.[77] The same authors' estimate of the real value added *per capita* in the agricultural sector shows the same kind of trajectory, with an increase of over 38 per cent between 1886/7 and 1898 and a subsequent fall to about 25 per cent overall by 1912.[78] From a purely statistical point of view, therefore, it would seem that there was a substantial rise in the gross income of the average Egyptian rural family (if such an entity can be said actually to exist) during the 1890s, and very little progress after that.

As always, such very general statements have to be qualified by the fact that the distribution of wealth and resources in the agricultural sector was very uneven. To make only the obvious points, it would seem clear that more of the initial rise in income must have gone to families in the Delta (where the bulk of the cotton, the highest value crop, was grown) rather than in Middle or Upper Egypt. It would seem equally clear that the small number of families which owned over half of Lower Egypt's cultivable land in large estates must have received a disproportionate share of the increase compared with those who owned the tiniest plots or no land at all. An examination of the pattern of economic relations in the agricultural sector will help to make this point more clear.

It has already been noted that in the early twentieth century about 45 per cent of Egypt's cultivated land was owned in nearly 12,500 properties of 50 feddans and over (see Table 52). At the same time it would seem likely that the majority of such properties contained an *ezba*, or agricultural village, providing houses for a permanent labour force.[79] The advantages of such a system in terms of certain economies of scale when it came to lowering the

Table 52 The distribution of Egyptian medium and small landed property into plots of various sizes in 1913

Size of plot	Number of properties			Area owned
(feddans)	Egyptian owned	Foreigner owned	Total	(feddans)
under 1	940,501	1167	942,530	405,595
1–5	466,603	2887	468,628	1,013,364
5–10	75,513	824	76,337	528,706
10–20	36,022	601	36,623	505,344
20–30	10,810	345	11,155	271,385
30–50	8098	381	8479	327,978
Total	1,537,547	6205	1,543,752	3,052,372

Source: Annuaire Statistique, 1914, 320–1.

cost of certain key inputs and of the ability to meet a fluctuating demand for labour throughout the agricultural year have already been outlined in Chapter 5.[80] What cannot be discovered with any degree of certainty, however, is the way in which the actual practice of estate management developed over time. There is some evidence of a substantial move towards the replacement of crop-sharing (métayage) agreements between landlords and tenants by the payment of a substantial part of the rent in cash (*fermage*) and it is not difficult to see why.[81] On the one hand, the further spread of cotton cultivation meant that more and more peasants were producing a crop for which they were paid in cash and against which they could secure ample credit. On the other, the *fermage* system required less costly supervision, allowed landlords to put up rents quickly in order to be able to profit from periods of rising prices and, perhaps most important of all, enabled them to shift all the burdens and uncertainties of agricultural life – shared under the métayage system – fairly and squarely on to their tenants' shoulders.

What is not clear, however, is whether the shift to cash rents was accompanied by a second shift in the direction of reducing the area of large properties farmed and managed by the owner himself. Some evidence that this might have taken place is provided by the often-repeated assertion of agricultural experts that it was always more profitable for large proprietors to let out their land to tenants rather than to attempt to exploit it on their own account.[82] In Egypt, as in many other areas of the non-European world where cash crops were grown, small landowners were usually able to obtain a higher net income per acre by exploiting all the resources of their family labour and by placing their fields under a more intensive system of rotation. That some landowners were prepared to take advantage of this situation there is no doubt; but the question is: how many? Reports of a series of visits paid by members of the Union Syndicale des Agriculteurs d'Egypte to various Delta estates in 1901 reveal evidence of both practices. The land owned by E. Zervudachi at Kafr el Dawwar was almost entirely rented out with the central farm buildings and an attached field used only for experiments with fertilizers and live-stock breeding, the results of which were made available to the tenants.[83] Against this, Riaz Pasha preferred to farm his 530 feddan estate at Mahallat Ruh using the labour of 100 families of service tenants (*tamaliyya*) each of whom received nearly a feddan of land at a much reduced rent in exchange for their services.[84] Mustafa Manzalawi employed the same system at his *izba* at Abu Sir (Gharbiya), leasing nearly half his land to tenants and farming the remainder himself, a third of which he placed under cotton. Labour was provided by his own tenants and augmented, at harvest time, by day workers (*tarahil*) supplied by contractors.[85] On balance it would seem that exploitation by the owner was the more usual practice. According to information contained in the 1939 agricultural census, only 20 per cent of Egypt's land held in estates of over 50 feddans was then being rented rather than worked by its proprietor, and this after two decades during which the area subject to rent is said to have been increasing.[86]

The point is an important one. If it could be established that the majority of Egypt's large estates were indeed farmed according to some version of the *izba* system before 1914, then the pattern of land management and of rural economic relationships would become much more clear. It could then be stated with confidence that the *izba* was the dominant form of agricultural enterprise on up to half Egypt's cultivated land. Other assumptions follow. The typical *izba* would have been run as a single unit, whether it was a matter of obtaining cheap inputs or of allocating different uses for different parts of the enterprise. In most cases part of the land would have been cultivated with cotton by the owner himself, using a rotation of three rather than two years to preserve the fertility of the soil. The rest of the land was then assigned to the service tenants to grow their own food crops and the fodder necessary to support the *izba*'s work animals. Such tenants would have no permanent rights to their plots and were further tied to the proprietor by their need for credit and, in those cases where they were also allowed to grow cotton, by the fact that he might insist on selling it for them. Finally, the assumption must be that the bulk of the profits from Egypt's *izbas* were used outside the agricultural sector and not reinvested in capital improvement. Such figures as exist indicate that only relatively small sums were used in this way. For example, the value of imported agricultural machinery averaged less than £E200,000 a year in the ten years before 1914.[87] Other figures show that even in the case of chemical fertilizers only some 15 to 20 per cent of the cultivated land was being treated in this way before 1914.[88]

Information about the management of properties of under 50 feddans is much more fragmentary. Figures for the division of such properties into plots of different sizes are given in Table 52 and show that about half the land was in parcels of over 5 feddans, that is, in units which if cultivated with cotton or rice or some other labour-intensive crop would have required more agricultural workers than could be provided by the owner's own immediate family. Some would have been required on a purely seasonal basis; others, on the larger properties, would have been needed all the year round. Where such labour was unavailable or considered too expensive, the owner would have the option of renting some of his land, perhaps on a crop-sharing basis. Further down the scale, some of the plots of 5 feddans and under would have been sufficient to provide a living for the average peasant but the majority were certainly too tiny and, in such cases, the owners would have had to hire out their labour for part of the year. As far as the exploitation of the small and medium size properties is concerned, two generalizations are certainly possible. First, although the owners of these properties derived great benefit from the provision of extra water for irrigation, particularly in the Delta, some of this advantage was soon lost as a result of the tendency to cultivate the land more intensively than on the larger estates, both for the purposes of raising income and to provide the extra cuttings of *birsim* needed as fodder for their animals.[89] The result was that soil fertility declined more rapidly than on the big properties producing a drop in yields which the peasants were too poor to compensate for by the use of expensive imported chemical fertilizer.[90] In the case of cotton, yields were further reduced in the years before the First World War by the fact that extra crops of *birsim* planted in the spring provided a very convenient host for the cotton pests and prevented the early planting of the cotton itself which was recommended as one of the most important ways of reducing infestation.[91]

The second generalization concerns the provision of credit and working capital. It has already been suggested that government efforts to provide the small cultivator with low interest loans was largely ineffectual. This can be seen with some clarity in figures provided by an Agricultural Bank investigation into rural indebtedness in 1913 (see Table 53). Of the total debt owed by over 600,000 owners of small plots of five feddans and under, more than 75 per cent was owed to usurers and other creditors and only just under 25 per cent to the Bank itself. Given the fact that the sums owed to usurers are likely to have been underestimated in such a survey, total indebtedness was probably even worse than these figures show. Meanwhile, statistics from an earlier survey of the Agricultural Bank's lending in September to November 1908 suggest that much of the debt owed to the Bank itself was the result of money lent not for working expenses or improvements in the capital stock but for the purchase of land or for meeting old debts.[92] The picture is clear. For the great bulk of their working expenses, Egypt's small peasants continued to rely on usurers and other private sources, the majority

Table 53   The state of indebtedness of Egyptian owners of 5 feddans or less, by province, 1913

	Total no. of owners of 5 feddans or less*	Area of land owned	Total no. of debtors	Area owned by debtors	Outstanding debt		Total
					Owed to Agr. Bank	Owed to other creditors	
		(feddans)		(feddans)	(£E)	(£E)	(£E)
Lower Egypt							
Buhaira	102,419	91,609	44,178	48,729	393,706	751,533	1,145,239
Sharqiya	130,491	113,727	58,615	62,494	502,148	1,099,066	1,601,214
Daqahliya	151,230	116,445	70,731	71,480	599,902	1,559,677	2,159,579
Gharbiya	235,180	180,024	100,635	101,702	685,508	2,390,647	3,076,055
Minufiya	253,442	166,882	105,934	92,578	863,697	2,273,511	3,137,208
Qalyubiya	84,926	61,714	33,389	29,111	257,262	839,729	1,096,991
Total	957,688	730,401	413,482	406,094	3,302,223	8,914,163	12,216,286
Upper Egypt							
Giza	63,483	55,726	16,594	17,151	33,815	457,430	491,245
Fayyum	80,602	58,950	23,139	24,754	45,951	270,722	316,673
Bani Suaif	58,980	46,822	15,861	16,386	68,732	315,062	383,794
Minya	56,570	52,275	15,171	15,617	50,402	265,288	315,690
Asyut	131,919	118,043	33,619	37,977	76,626	593,561	669,187
Girga	142,359	123,629	48,822	50,404	86,096	833,677	919,773
Qena	147,619	119,760	47,780	46,020	187,965	433,547	621,512
Total	681,532	575,205	200,986	208,309	549,587	3,169,287	3,717,874

* No explanation is given for the fact that the total number of owners of small properties is indicated as being over 200,000 higher than the number to be found in the government figures for the distribution of land into properties of various sizes to be found in *Annuaire Statistique, 1914*, 320–1 and reproduced in Table 51.

Source: Annuaire Statistique, 1914, 509.

of whom must certainly have provided money at rates much higher than the legal minimum of 9 per cent laid down by the Mixed Courts.[93] Just how easily this might be done is revealed in the following quotation from an official of the National Bank of Egypt:

We are the bankers' bank, in other words we are the usurers' bank. Go to the usurer, pay him from 36 to 60% and he will supply you. Next day the Bank takes over the bill or note of the native with, of course, the signature of the usurer or so-called banker on it, and gives him very extensive credit of 5½ to 6½% and this is shown in the accounts as 'Bankers' accounts . . . Twelve of those local usurers are the relations of one of the Directors of the National Bank.[94]

Quite a different structure of credit was developed for owners of large estates. Here the basic institution was the mortgage company, the first and largest of which was the French-owned Crédit Foncier Egyptien set up in 1880 shortly after the legal status of mortgage transactions had been established under Egypt's Mixed Code. Business was slow in the 1880s and early 1890s and actions for foreclosure numerous.[95] .But with the enormous increase in value of agricultural production which began in the 1890s and with the security for foreign investment established by the British, the amount of European money available for loans on land multiplied rapidly. According to Crouchley's figures there were two mortgage companies with a capital of just over £6,000,000 in 1897, three with £10,500,000 in 1902 and five with £40,000,000 in 1907.[96] Meanwhile, Egypt's total mortgage debt had risen to an estimated £60,000,000 or about £24 for each feddan of cultivated land owned in estates of more than fifty feddans.[97] A small part of this money must have been used for purposes of agricultural investment, land reclamation and, as already noted, loans to small cultivators; but there seems little doubt that the overwhelming bulk was devoted to the purchase of land and the expansion of existing estates.[98] And it was to this purpose that much of the money raised by a host of newly-established land companies was devoted as well as significant funds lent on the security of agricultural property by banks, insurance companies and private individuals.[99]

The result of the creation of this ocean of cheap credit, as Crouchley notes, was to help to push up the price of land at a rapid rate.[100] In 1901, the Belgian Consul-General reported that he knew of estates which had risen 100 per cent in value over the past seven or eight years.[101] In 1904, Delta fields were being sold at between £E60 and £E80 a feddan, while just before the boom broke in 1907 some fields had reached £E160 a feddan.[102] A second result was to create a structure of debt which was too large for the country to bear. Once credit became more difficult to obtain after 1907 and the price of land began to level off or even to fall, many proprietors found it difficult to maintain interest payments on the money they had borrowed. Some were forced to sell up; others struggled on by means of fresh loans.[103] That the situation did not become worse was due to the fact that the existing mortgage companies soon found new sources of European funds with which they were able to allow their creditors a little greater latitude.[104] In spite of an increasing number of foreclosures and forced sales, land prices managed to regain their former high level and by 1913 averaged well over £E100 a feddan throughout most of Egypt.[105] The whole episode is an instructive one and provides yet another example of the way in which part of Egypt's agricultural surplus was sucked abroad with very little benefit to the country itself.

Industry, commerce and banking

During the twenty years before the First World War huge sums of money were invested in a wide variety of Egyptian banks, land companies and other enterprises. Crouchley's estimates of the amounts involved are given

Table 54   Paid-up capital and debentures of companies operating in Egypt showing amount held abroad and amount held in Egypt, 1883–1914* (£E,000) (after Crouchley)

Type of company	1883			1892			1897		
	Held abroad	Held in Egypt	Total	Held abroad	Held in Egypt	Total	Held abroad	Held in Egypt	Total
Mortgage	3401	425	3826	4122	425	4547	5543	425	5968
Banking/financial	1843		1843	681	93	774	681	93	774
Agricultural/urban land		180	180	221	368	589	360	982	1342
Transport/canals	62		62	145		145	1851	367	2218
Industrial/mining/commercial	669		669	915	356	1271	2974	609	3583
Total	5975	605	6580	6085	1242	7326	11,409	2476	13,885

Type of company	1902			1907			1914		
	Held abroad	Held in Egypt	Total	Held abroad	Held in Egypt	Total	Held abroad	Held in Egypt	Total
Mortgage	9601	924	10,525	34,090	5590	39,680	48,369	6200	54,569
Banking/financial	1770	522	2292	4895	3200	8095	3229	2498	5727
Agricultural/urban land	2096	878	2974	7135	12,221	19,356	7261	11,312	18,573
Transport/canals	3245	725	3970	3620	2327	5947	3988	2088	6076
Industrial/mining/commercial	5418	1101	6159	7170	6928	14,098	8406	6801	15,207
Total	22,130	4150	26,280	56,910	30,266	87,176	71,253	28,899	100,152

* The figures given show only the net changes in capital between the years given: that is, gross additions to capital less the capital in liquidated companies. The Suez Canal Company is not included.

Source: Crouchley, *Investment*, 148, 154–6.

in Table 54. They show that such investments doubled between 1892 and 1897, doubled again between 1897 and 1902, and then exhibited an enormous advance during the boom years before the financial crisis of 1907. There was then a period of less rapid advance when a large number of companies went into liquidation, either as a result of bankruptcy or as a result of the 1908 change in Egypt's company law which forced foreign-registered concerns to re-register in Egypt if they wished to continue in business. Previously many firms operating in the country had preferred to evade Egyptian regulations by establishing themselves in London or elsewhere in Europe and a number chose to close down entirely rather than to allow themselves to become subject to closer scrutiny.[106] Many more banks, land companies and industrial enterprises closed down between 1907 and 1914 than were created, and the only major source of capital growth was in the mortgage sector where capital assets were increased by some £E15,000,000 during the same period.[107] Crouchley's figures in Table 54 also illustrate the importance of companies connected with the sale, reclamation or mortgage of rural and urban land, such companies providing two-thirds of total Egyptian capital in 1907 and over 70 per cent in 1914.

Crouchley's calculations also give some indication of the source of the money invested in Egyptian enterprises during this period. The greater part of it came from abroad, but there was also a short period, between 1897 and 1907, when local residents in Egypt (both native Egyptians and foreigners living in the country) made a significant contribution to the total. Roughly half of these local funds were placed in land companies which were either the creation of local residents or else contained a number of Egyptian-based directors, while the remainder were spread over a wide variety of enterprises, both new and old. The establishment of a stock exchange in Cairo in 1903 must certainly have made it much easier for Egyptians to purchase shares.[108] The main reason for this great upsurge in investment, however, was a combination of a large increase in incomes derived from agriculture and the promise of high profits from companies which were involved in any kind of business connected with either rural land or the boom in urban property. The shock administered by the crisis of 1907 brought this type of local investment almost to a complete halt.

During the 1870s the Egyptian banking sector had made its profits mainly from loans to the government. With the end of such business a period or reorganization was necessary and it was not until the turn of the century that new banks began to be created in any significant number.[109] Capital came largely from abroad as it was difficult to obtain deposits from local residents other than official organizations like government departments, the railways or the Caisse de la Dette.[110] This provided a considerable source of weakness as foreign funds were always in danger of being cut off or much reduced at times when there was a credit squeeze in Europe and interest rates rose high in London and Paris. The primary business of Egypt's banks – including the National Bank – was financing trade (particularly cotton exports) and lending money to local residents on a variety of securities. As a rule, each bank would deal with members of a particular local community. The government exercised little control over these activities, something which was illustrated in a spectacular way by the collapse of the Bank of Egypt in 1911, when it was revealed that the manager had tied up much of the bank's capital in unsafe medium- or long-term loans to rural landowners.[111]

Another sector to attract foreign, and some local, capital between 1897 and 1907 was that of industry and mining (see Table 54). The question of Egypt's industrial development, or lack of it, has always aroused controversy; but before dealing with the wider question of the degree of British or other blame for slow progress it would be useful to attempt to look at what actually happened during the period and at the difficulties which faced those factories and other plant actually in existence. To begin with the modern sector where European techniques and methods of manage-ment were employed: in the absence of a proper census, Table 55 gives two separate estimates of both the numbers of industrial enterprises of various kinds in 1901 and 1911 and of their capital assets. These lists are certainly not complete. There are also problems of definition.[112] However, they un-doubtedly contain all the larger manufacturing or processing plants with the bulk of the financial resources.

Table 55 Companies in the Egyptian modern industrial sector, 1901 and 1911

	1901		1911	
	No. of cos	Paid-up capital & debentures	No. of cos	Paid-up capital & debentures
Cotton ginning and pressing	5	358,140	5	1,063,884
Sugar refining	2	1,895,000	1	3,609,441
Food and drink	6	579,000	6	1,382,368
Oil and soap	3	123,000		
Tobacco and cigarettes	3	165,000	4	1,060,363
Building and construction	1	60,000	10	523,628
Textiles	2	285,000	1	146,250
Fertilizers	1	15,500	1	30,000
Total	23	3,480,640	37	8,438,780

Sources: **British Chamber of Commerce,** *List of . . . Companies Established in Egypt* (1901); *Annuaire Statistique, 1914,* 526–7.

Three points can be made about these estimates at once. First, there was a considerable investment in industry in the years before the First World War, leading to the creation of firms which, by 1911, contained nearly 10 per cent of all funds placed in Egyptian public companies. According to Radwan's calculations, the new fixed capital stock in Egyptian industry (at constant prices) increased from £E89,000,000 in 1899 to £E143,900,000 in 1907 and £E154,500,000 in 1913.[113] Second, industry was dominated by firms which processed local raw materials for the local market. The only major exceptions to this were the cotton ginning and pressing companies and the cigarette factories, which not only imported the tobacco they used from abroad but also exported a significant amount of the finished product. Apart from the output of these latter enterprises, Egypt's exports of manufactured goods were virtually non-existent.[114] Third, the majority of firms produced products which obtained protection not from the low external tariff of 8 per cent but from such factors as the high cost of transport involved in the import of bulk goods like building materials or the deterioration in the quality of foreign goods like foodstuffs which took days if not weeks to reach the country by sea.

Nevertheless, this is certainly not the whole story. In order to look at some of the problems and constraints facing those anxious to develop a modern manufacturing sector it will be useful to examine the history of three types of industrial enterprise in somewhat greater detail. These are cotton spinning and weaving, sugar refining and cement production, all activities which, historically, have formed the basis for the introduction and expansion of factory industry in a large number of non-European countries.

Attempts to establish textile factories in Egypt began just before the turn of the century, culminating in the founding of the Egyptian Cotton Mills Ltd in 1899 with a plant in Cairo and the Anglo-Egyptian Spinning and Weaving Company, also in 1899, with a mill at Alexandria. Both companies were founded on the assumption that they would not be required to pay any local tax and it came as a considerable shock when Lord Cromer's decision to deprive them of tariff protection by imposing a so-called countervailing duty of 8 per cent was upheld in a case brought by one of the companies before the Mixed Courts.[115] Nevertheless, both decided to continue operations, although with no great success. The Cotton Mills Company was rarely able to make a profit, paid no dividends to its shareholders, and went out of business in 1907. Without a detailed analysis of its records it is impossible to assign the blame for this unhappy event but it can be noted that it was the opinion of at least one contemporary observer that both bad management and the increase in price as a result of the countervailing duty played an important role.[116] In addition, the company claimed to suffer from many of the problems which usually face any infant industrial enterprise: lack of skilled labour, shortage of working capital and difficulties in finding a retail outlet for its goods.[117] This last complaint was particularly important in an Egyptian context where the wholesale trade was controlled by merchants with close links with importers who were not anxious to lose their existing market to local competition.[118]

The Anglo-Egyptian Spinning and Weaving Company was only a little more successful. It too was never able to pay a dividend and only managed to survive after 1908 by persuading the government to lift the countervailing duty for five years. In 1912 it was reorganized, with reduced capital, by a group of German businessmen and renamed the Filature Nationale d'Egypte. In these circumstances the contribution of the Anglo-Egyptian mill to the economy is unlikely to have been large. When working to capacity, its 20,000 spindles and 400 looms were able to produce cotton thread and cloth worth £E50,000 a year, compared with imports of these same products to the value of £E2,703,000 1900–4 and £E4,085,000

1910–13.[119] At the same time it utilized some 25,000 to 30,000 cantars of locally-produced low quality cotton a year at a time when total Egyptian output was growing from an annual average of 6,000,000 to 7,500,000 cantars.[120]

A second, and more important, industry was that of sugar refining. During the first two decades of the British occupation the Daira Saniya continued to be far and away the largest producer of juice and cane but almost all of it was sent abroad for refining, only a minute quantity being processed at a small privately-owned plant at Hawamdiya near Cairo established in 1881.[121] In the 1890s, however, the rising price of sugar attracted the attention of a number of entrepreneurs, both local and foreign, and at least seven new companies were formed to refine Egypt's crop locally.[122] Only two, funded by French capital, survived more than a few seasons and, in 1897, these latter joined together to form the Société Générale des Sucreries et de la Raffinerie d'Egypte working a new factory built at Nag Hammadi in Upper Egypt.[123] Five years later, the company expanded its operations enormously by purchasing the remaining nine cane processing factories and a network of light agricultural railways from the Daira Saniya. But the problems of administering this enlarged enterprise were too much and in 1905/6 the company was only saved as a result of government intervention.[124] In the course of the inquiry surrounding this event a number of reasons were put forward to explain the failure, ranging from bad management to the heavy burden of debt incurred in the Daira Saniya purchase and difficulties of obtaining an assured supply of cane at a time when many peasants were beginning to cultivate cotton rather than sugar.[125] Under new management the company was able to increase its annual production of refined sugar and molasses from 58,000 tons, 1904/5 to 1908/9 to 84,000 tons, 1909/10 to 1912/13.[126] According to calculations made by the Commission on Commerce and Industry, this was certainly sufficient to supply all Egypt's domestic needs.[127] But it would seem from the foreign trade statistics that, before the outbreak of war in 1914, there were still substantial imports of foreign produced sugar, presumably of a higher quality than the Sugar Company itself was able to produce.[128]

The third important new industry was that of producing cement. The main producers were the S.A. des Ciments d'Egypte, a Belgian firm established in 1900, and the Alexandria Cement Company.[129] In spite of the fact that both enterprises experienced no difficulty in obtaining contracts to supply the government's Public Works Department and other agencies, neither proved to be a particularly profitable enterprise. Coal had to be imported from abroad to run the machines; the Alexandria Cement Company was also forced to bring in lime and clay from Dalmatia when unable to find local products of a high enough standard.[130] As a result neither firm was able to expand its capacity beyond a joint total of some 45 to 50,000 tons a year, leaving a gap of anything up to 100,000 tons to be filled by imports from Europe.[131]

Even such a brief survey of these three important industries is sufficient to show that an attempt to pass judgement on what ought to have been the proper pace of Egyptian industrial advance is no easy matter. By the standards of most countries in the non-European world, Egypt had substantial advantages in terms of a well-developed infrastructure, a sizeable market for a whole range of manufactured goods and, at least in the period up to 1907, large amounts of capital available for investment in the industrial sector. Against this there were important structural features of the economy – notably the enormous concentration of effort and resources on the production and export of cotton, a credit system geared to the needs of merchants and large landowners and a well-entrenched foreign community – which imposed quite severe constraints on the way in which industry was able to develop. In addition, the country was deficient in certain basic resources such as coal for energy, wood and metals, and even a low quality cotton suitable for producing cheap cloth, all of which had to be imported at some cost.

It was just because of these constraints and problems that the role of government became so important. As the members of the Commission on Commerce and Industry were quick to point out, Egyptian industry could only surmount the obstacles it faced with a considerable degree of official support, which in the period up to 1914 was almost entirely lacking. For all Lord Cromer's repeated assertions that the development of factory industry was an essential feature of future progress, British refusal to countenance any rise in the external tariff and, more important, the impression given during the dispute with the cotton mills over the countervailing duty that the administration would go to great lengths to prevent the establishment of firms which might compete with British imports, meant that the main weight of government policy was seen to be on the side of deterrence rather than encouragement.[132] It is no wonder that the subject has rapidly become one over which there is much dispute.[133]

Without a proper census it is impossible to form any very accurate idea about the basic structure of the remainder of Egypt's industrial sector in the years before 1914. The best that can be done is to take the findings of a later census, that of 1927, as a rough guide to its major characteristics. According to the very loose definitions adopted by the census enumerators, there were then 70,314 manufacturing establishments in Egypt of which 39 per cent consisted of a single worker and another 49 per cent possessed a labour force of between one and four. This left only 8 per cent of establishments with between five and nine workers and a final 4 per cent with more than nine.[134] As for the type of goods produced, just over 32 per cent of all enterprises were concerned with clothing and 12 per cent with the spinning and weaving of textiles.[135]

Table 56   Workers in the Egyptian industrial and craft-industrial sector 1897, 1907 and
1917*

	1897	1907	1917
Textiles	50,644	65,529	72,778
Leather	16,551	22,692	27,387
Wood and basket work	39,468	61,585	12,237
Metals	33,618	48,547	48,445
Pottery and glass	8957	10,202	9941
Chemical products	247	690	1958
Food products	114,616	140,999	238,744
Clothing	61,803	97,583	146,282
Construction	24,606	43,391	66,093
Printing	1675	2521	3591
Total	352,185	493,739	627,456

* Methods of defining particular categories of occupation changed from one census to another.

Source: Figures from the censuses of 1897, 1907 and 1917 in Lévi, 'Recensement de 1917', 506.

Direct comparison with the pre-First World War period is dangerous as the industrial sector experienced a great expansion during the war years; but figures for the population censuses of 1897, 1907 and 1917 (Table 56) would seem to suggest that in these decades, too, clothing and textiles were the dominant form of activity (providing about a third of employment) followed closely by food products. It would also seem that it was these same activities that, together with construction, experienced the biggest growth between 1897 and 1917.

Comparison between the firms in the modern sector and the more heterogeneous group of enterprises (usually lumped together under the heading of 'traditional' or 'small-scale') which possessed little capital, used few machines and employed only small amounts of motive power is also interesting. Given Egypt's low external tariff and the particular pattern of local demand, enterprises in both sectors generally made their profits from products which derived some protection from transport costs, problems of long-distance shipping or the social character of local tastes. Again, many workshops in the traditional sector were just as dependent on imported raw materials as modern factories such as those producing cigarettes. In 1912, for instance, thread to the value of £E650,000 was bought from abroad, mostly for use by Egypt's weavers, while much of the large volume of foreign flour was purchased by local bakers and confectioners catering to the European community.[136] Clearly the ability of its craft industry to survive, and even to prosper, in the face of foreign competition in no way reduced the country's dependence on imports from abroad.

Trade and payments

As a result of the increase in the volume and value of cotton production and

Table 57   Egypt's foreign trade, 1885–1913 (annual averages, £E,000)*

	Imports				Exports**	
	Textiles: cloth and thread	Cereals, flour and vegetables	Coffee, sugar	Total	Cotton and cotton seed	Total
1885–9	2586	720	309	7947	9874	12,548
1890–4	2981	736	323	8872	11,322	14,494
1895–9	3161	1112	257	10,249	12,338	14,963
1900–4	4898	1672	318	16,297	17,779	20,583
1905–9	6296	3260	765	23,805	24,412	27,161
1910–13	7178	3321	838	26,238	29,675	32,652

* Excludes specie.
** Export values have been increased by one-ninth to 1911. I have used Crouchley's calculations for total exports, *Investment*, 173–4.

Sources: Annuaire Statistique, 1914, 300–7; Crouchley, *Investment*, 173–4.

a favourable movement in its terms of trade, Egypt experienced a period of rapidly increasing imports and exports in the two decades before 1914. Unfortunately the government's figures (given in Table 57) are not entirely satisfactory. As already noted, all exports except tobacco were officially undervalued by 10 per cent before 1911.[137] I have compensated for this by raising them the appropriate amount. In addition, as Crouchley is able to demonstrate, there is good reason to suppose that the value of cotton sold abroad was further undervalued, perhaps by as much as 8 per cent between 1906 and 1910 and 16 per cent between 1911 and 1915.[138] If this is taken into account Egypt's trade performance is even better than it would seem, with the substantial increase in exports from the late 1890s onwards providing a larger favourable balance on visible account than the present figures indicate. Another way of looking at this performance is in terms of volume and value *per capita*. According to Hansen and Lucas's reworking of Egypt's foreign trade statistics, *per capita* export volumes increased steadily until the end of the nineteenth century and then maintained a high constant plateau until 1913.[139] This was accompanied by a favourable movement in the net barter terms of trade as the prices of agricultural exports rose faster than those of imported manufactured goods from the late 1890s to about 1910, producing, in turn, a considerable rise in the income terms of trade – that is, in Egypt's ability to pay for imports.[140] The result, as far as Egyptian welfare was concerned, was a strong upswing in import volumes *per capita* until about 1907. After that there was a downturn to 1913 as population continued to grow and the influence of rising exports and favourable international price movements weakened.

Table 57 also gives some indication of the composition of Egypt's foreign trade. On the export side the dominance of cotton is easy to see, with sales of this commodity contributing nearly 90 per cent to total foreign earnings at the end of the period. Imports, on the other hand, were more various. In value terms, textiles, both cloth and thread, were the most important followed by food products like cereals, flour and vegetables. Somewhere about the turn of the century Egypt turned into a net importer of food as its own production of wheat, barley, beans and maize became only just sufficient for local needs while increasing quantities of high quality foreign flour were required to provide its European community and the well-to-do Egyptian with bread.[141] Changes in the proportion of imports of consumption goods, raw materials for local working and investment goods for industry and agriculture were also important. According to what is, admittedly, a very rough distribution of imports between these three categories, the proportion of investment goods increased from 12 to 14 per cent between 1885–9 and 1910–13 while that of consumption goods declined from 61 per cent between 1885 and 1889 to 56 per cent between 1900 and 1904, before rising again to 58 per cent between 1910 and 1913. Meanwhile, in absolute terms, the value of goods imported for investment in industry and agriculture grew from an annual average of just under £E1,000,000 to £E3,500,000 during the same period.[142]

Table 58   Egypt's balance of payments, 1884–1914 (annual averages, £E,000)

	Visible account balance (+ or −)	Invisible account balance (+ or −)	Overall balance of payments (+ or −)	Net inflow of private foreign capital
1884–92	+4422	−4841	− 419	12
1893–7	+4162	−5430	−1268	1065
1898–1902	+2650	−5373	−2723	2144
1903–7	− 354	−8718	−9072	8616
1908–14	+4473	−7033	−2550	3150

Source: Crouchley, *Investment*, 193, 195–6.

Finally, figures to illustrate changes in the main items in Egypt's balance of payments are given in Table 58. As far as visible trade is concerned the favourable balance is reduced quite considerably when movements of specie are included. As far as the account for invisibles is concerned, the most important features were the net outflows of interest and dividends to private foreign investors and to holders of shares in the public debt. If the two accounts are then combined, it can be seen that Egypt's trade surplus was not large enough to cover interest payments abroad but that this gap was met in the short run by new inflows of private foreign capital. On the face of it, it would seem that, during this period at least, there was no substantial drain of the Egyptian surplus abroad.

The pattern just described could be taken as typical of a 'colonial' economy: on the one hand, the maintenance of a small budgetary surplus, with the limited amounts of public investment financed largely out of revenues, and a favourable balance of trade; on the other, conditions which encouraged the inflow of considerable amounts of private foreign capital. The result would certainly have been a sizeable addition to Egypt's financial resources had it not been for the need to continue to service the public debt.

Once again it is necessary to be clear as to the exact nature of the argument. Clearly it cannot be maintained that Egypt suffered from a shortage of investment capital in the two decades before 1914, nor, by extension, that this was the prime cause of the country's lack of development. But what can be suggested is that the inflow of funds on private account was of a different quality from that of the outflow of public funds required to service the debt. Given the fact that the national propensity to save and invest seems to have been very low, and that most of the productive investment which did take place was undertaken by the government, any reduction in the sums available to the state for public works and other similar activities deprived Egypt of a possible addition to its capital assets.[143]

10 Mount Lebanon, Syria and Palestine, 1880–1914

Just before the First World War the population of Greater Syria is variously estimated to have been between 3,500,000 and 4,000,000, of whom some 500,000 were nomads.[1] Nearly a million or so of these people lived in each of the provinces of Aleppo, Damascus and Beirut, with perhaps another 400,000 or so each in the *mutasarrifliks* of Mount Lebanon and of Jerusalem.[2] In terms of the distribution between rural and urban areas, about a million people lived in towns of over 10,000 inhabitants, the great majority in the four major cities of Damascus (about 250,000), Aleppo (200,000), Beirut (150,000) and Jerusalem (80,000).[3] Most of the remainder of the population can reasonably be assumed to have worked in the agricultural sector.

Table 59 Ottoman census figures for the populations of the three provinces of Aleppo, Beirut and Damascus and the *mutasarriflik* of Jerusalem, 1885–1914*

	1885	1897	1906	1914
Aleppo	787,714	623,505	877,682	617,790
Beirut	568,014	921,345	561,619	824,873
Damascus	400,748	701,134	478,775	918,409
Jerusalem	234,774	264,317	231,209	328,168
Total	1,991,250	2,429,301	2,149,285	2,689,240

* Excludes *mutasarriflik* of Mount Lebanon.

Source: Shaw, 'Ottoman Census System', Appendix 2.

There seems to have been general agreement among contemporaries that this population had been growing quite fast in the years before 1914.[4] Such a view is certainly supported by the Ottoman census figures (see Table 59), even though their overall reliability is open to much doubt.[5] What makes the rise in Syria's population more noteworthy is that it took place at a time when there was a considerable loss of people through migration. According to a variety of estimates, 5000 to 10,000 Lebanese and Syrians as well as some Palestinians were leaving the region each year during the 1890s, rising to perhaps as many as 15,000 to 20,000 just before the First World War.[6] In global terms this loss of population has been calculated at 120,000 between 1860 and 1900 and 210,000 between 1900 and 1914.[7] What proportion of these migrants actually settled permanently abroad is unclear.[8] But it must certainly have been in excess of a net inward migration of perhaps 50,000 Jews, 30,000 Circassians, and smaller numbers of other people from other parts of the Middle East, North Africa and the Balkans.[9]

The result of demographic increase coupled with such a large movement of migrants in and out of the Syrian provinces was a significant redistribution of the local population. Because of over-population, many males and some families were now beginning to leave the crowded hillside terraces of Mount Lebanon, Syria and Palestine, either for emptier lands on the plains or for a new life in a new land overseas. Meanwhile, a few of the Jewish, and almost all the Circassian, settlers were being directed to districts where cultivation was sparse. In all this, the continued improvement in rural security had an important role to play. The establishment of permanent Ottoman garrisons — to the east along the desert frontier, to the south-east around Amman and Karak, to the south at Beersheba — greatly expanded the area in which settled agricultural life could be carried on in reasonable safety.[10] The construction of the Hijaz railway with its regular system of fortified blockhouses set a final seal on this process, forcing most of the remaining nomads further eastwards into the desert.[11]

Areas of insecurity remained; but the result was certainly another great increase in the amount of permanently cultivated land. Contemporary European travellers were unanimous on this point. When Sir Mark Sykes travelled from Aleppo towards the Euphrates in 1906 he found evidence of large-scale beduin settlement and 'stretches of glorious corn-bearing land, spotted with brown mud villages where once all had been waste'.[12] When Kelman rode north-east of Damascus at the same time, he said that for a long time the 'circles of ploughed land' around each hamlet almost touched one another.[13] There are no reliable figures by which to chart this process but some post-First World War estimates suggest that there may have been some 2,000,000 hectares (4,940,000 acres) of cultivated land in Syria and Lebanon at the beginning of the twentieth century — of which perhaps 5 per cent was under irrigation.[14] Most of it, perhaps as much as three-quarters, was sown with cereals every second year, while there were small pockets of more intensive agriculture based on vines, mulberries, olives and fruit.[15] As for Palestine, Cuinet suggests that, at the end of the nineteenth century, there may have been 220,000 hectares (540,000 acres) of cultivated land in the southern districts round Hebron, Jerusalem, Jaffa and Gaza.[16]

A second factor encouraging the development of inland agriculture was the rapid improvement in the system of transport as a result of the construction of the first Syrian railways. At the beginning of the period, in 1880, there were only a few metalled roads, many of them in bad repair and most either charging high tolls or, like the Beirut/Damascus carriageways, run by a company with a monopoly over the wheeled vehicles allowed to use it.[17] Thus, in spite of the growing use of carts, notably among the Jewish, Circassian and other new agricultural settlers, the great bulk of the region's agricultural produce continued to be carried by animals, mostly camels, at rates which might be as much as half of the value of an individual load.[18] Thirty years later, however, the Syrian provinces contained nearly 1400 km of railways, grouped in three systems.[19] The first to be built was the French-owned line between Jaffa and Jerusalem, opened in 1888. This was followed by the lines from Damascus to Muzerib in the Hauran (1894) and to Beirut (1895), later connecting at Rayak with a northern extension to Hama (1903), Aleppo (1906) and the coastal town of Tripoli (1911). Finally, there was the Ottoman-built Hijaz railway which linked Damascus with Deraa (1903) and Haifa (1906). Rivalry between the different railway promoters, and between their different governments, ensured that the system was far from perfect: the northern and southern sections of the lines owned by the French Chemin de Fer Damas-Hamah et Prolongements were of different gauges and goods passing between them had to be trans-shipped at Rayak; for some years the line to Beirut did not run as far as the French-built port opened in 1893; the French and Ottoman lines from Damascus to the Hauran were usually operated in open competition with one another.[20] The DHP (as the Chemin de Fer Damas-Hamah became known) also created a great deal of early difficulty for itself by pitching freight rates too high.[21] Nevertheless, by the early 1900s all three systems began to make considerable inroads into animal and carriage transport.[22] By the First World War they were certainly conveying enough goods (Table 60) to suggest that not only were they generating a great deal of extra trade but also that they were carrying as much as 50 per cent of Syria's internal goods traffic.[23] In 1911, for instance, the railways conveyed some 500,000 metric tons, at rates much lower than their animal-powered competitors.[24]

Table 60 Tonnage of goods traffic carried on the Syrian railways, 1899–1911 (metric tons)

	Beirut/Damascus/ Hauran	Rayak/Homs/ Aleppo	Homs/Tripoli	Total
1899	90,908			
1900	92,527			
1902	100,181	10,557		110,738
1903	156,840	39,760		196,600
1904	128,872	30,096		158,968
1905	155,291	71,680		226,971
1906	233,214	89,277		322,491
1907	218,540	76,020		294,560
1908	251,211	86,094		337,305
1909	218,104	81,775		299,879
1910	214,538	94,242		308,780
1911	198,392	103,643	75,054	377,089

Source: CRs (UK) and Kanzadian and de Bertalot, *Atlas*, 78–9.

Table 61   Estimates of the trade at Syria/Palestine's seven principal ports (Iskanderun, Latakia, Tripoli, Beirut, Acre/Haifa, Jaffa and Gaza*) 1883 to 1913 (annual averages, £,000)

	Exports	Imports
1883–7	2300	4012
1888–92	2360	4515
1893–7	2926	4261
1898–1902	2962	4824
1908–12	3591	5920
1913	3649	6942

Table 62   Estimates of the composition of exports at Syria/Palestine's seven principal ports,* 1883 to 1913 (annual averages, £,000)

	1883–7	1888–92	1893–7	1898–1902	1903–7	1908–12	1913
Animal products	729	415	395	511	633	743	565
Fruits	66	99	196	225	253	363	483
Pastoral products	210	395	406	442	617	627	611
Uncultivated or wild products**	167	82	107	135	113	135	72
Cocoons and raw silk	433	679	792	915	1083	891	735
Processed and manufactured products	207	367	486	516	567	606	528

*   Excludes Gaza until 1898–1902.
**   Wild products include gall nuts, yellow berries, etc.

Source: Kalla, 'Role of Foreign Trade', Table I and II (Kalla's estimates are based on figures from British commercial reports but also include his own imputed figures for trade at Beirut and Jaffa in some years).

Such an improvement in the system of transport, allied to the increase in population and the probable increase in agricultural production, was certainly enough to encourage a sizeable increase in Syria's sea-borne trade. Figures taken from British trade reports for the total value of imports and exports at the seven most important ports on the Mediterranean coast (Table 61) show a rise of 50 per cent between 1883/4 and 1913. As far as exports were concerned, this upward movement reflected a growth in foreign sales of three categories of produce: silk, fruits (mostly oranges) and pastoral products (mostly wool) (Table 62). This was more than matched by an increase in the import of textiles, certain intermediary articles like cotton yarns, leather, metal and wood, and agricultural goods like tobacco, sugar and flour, leading to a persistent and growing adverse balance of trade.

How the Syrian provinces could sustain a persistent imbalance of this kind for so many years has long been a subject of considerable debate. Some economic historians argue that it must, inevitably, have produced a continuous loss or drain of specie.[25] Against this it is possible to suggest that part of the answer can be found in the counter movement of a net inflow of foreign capital. French investments have been estimated at 200,000,000 francs (£25,000,000) in the years leading up to 1914.[26] There was also significant Ottoman investment in the construction of the Hijaz railway. Finally, Ruppin calculated that just before the First World War the provinces had invisible earnings of some 60,000,000 francs (£2,400,000) a year, consisting of 30,000,000 francs from the remittances of migrants overseas and 10,000,000 francs each from tourists and pilgrims, funds sent to foreign religious and missionary enterprises and money devoted to the support of the Jewish community in Palestine.[27] It can also be suggested that another part of the answer may well relate to profits earned as a result of Syria's role in a complex pattern of economic relationships with its Middle Eastern neighbours, either exporting its own products to Egypt and the adjacent Ottoman provinces or re-exporting goods from Europe.[28] In the case of the three ports of Iskanderun, Beirut and Jaffa, for example, there was a large favourable balance with Egypt in the years 1910 to 1912 (see Table 63). It may well be that the provinces' overland trade showed a similar profit, but apart from the rough estimate that the total value of such trade was about a quarter to a third that of sea-borne commerce, too little is known about this subject to push the argument any farther.[29]

Table 63   Eastern Mediterranean sea-borne trade: the trade of Iskanderun, Beirut and Jaffa with Egypt and Turkey, 1910–12 (£,000)

Imports from:	Egypt	Turkish Ports	Total Imports
1910	118	724	2292
1911	123	704	1939
1912	141	618	1621
Exports to:	Egypt	Turkish Ports	Total Exports
1910	367	636	2759
1911	501	494	2305
1912	572	413	2402

Source: Kanzadian and de Bertalot, *Atlas*, 70–1.

So much can be said in general terms. It is also important to note that the pattern of intra-regional economic relations within Syria was changing throughout the period, making any definitive summing-up impossible. One of the main reasons for this was the impact of the railways on the existing system of transport. As in any region where new lines were being built

rapidly, often in competition with one another, the relative importance of
the various commercial centres altered dramatically over quite a short time.
In the north, the arrival of the line at Aleppo, coupled with the fact that
communications with the port of Iskanderun remained difficult, served to
divert a substantial portion of the province's foreign trade (one report
suggested as much as half) to the south to the profit of Beirut.[30] Before this,
however, some of the advantages which the latter city might have been expected to enjoy from its earlier rail link with the interior were lost as a result
of high freight rates – which made it cheaper to send Haurani grain to
Haifa – and big harbour charges which encouraged the use of other
ports.[31] For these and other reasons no one port on the coast achieved a
complete ascendancy over its rivals before 1914 (as Beirut was to do later)
while the relative importance of the major cities of the interior which they
served also changed a number of times. It will now be useful to examine this
process in some greater detail.

Mount Lebanon and Beirut

For the inhabitants of Mount Lebanon and for a section of Beirut's commercial community the production, processing and export of silk continued
to act as the major focus for economic activity after 1880. Something of its
importance can be seen from a few figures. By the 1890s mulberry trees
were planted on about half of the cultivated land in the Mountain and its
adjacent slopes.[32] During the same decade nearly 50 per cent of Beirut's
exports (by value) consisted of silk thread.[33] Finally, if the total factory
workforce of some 14,000 is added to the 165,000 or so people who were said
to be employed in the care of the mulberry trees and the raising of the
cocoons, it is easy to see how Naccache could assert that something like
50,000 Mountain families (perhaps half of the total) owed their livelihood
directly to this one product.[34] For all these reasons the central role of silk in
the economic and social life of the Mountain is difficult to exaggerate. By
the same token, the weaknesses in the structure and organization of the
industry revealed in the years just before the First World War were of the
greatest consequence.

The figures in Table 64 show that there was a great increase in silk production throughout almost all the period, the manufacture of cocoons and
raw silk almost doubling before falling prices and falling profits led to a
decline in output in the last few years before the First World War. As far as
cocoons were concerned, the years of most rapid growth were in the early
1890s when, it has been estimated, the number of mulberry trees was
doubled.[35] There was then a period of slower increase until production
reached its peak in 1910. The manufacture and export of raw silk followed
a roughly similar pattern (Tables 64 and 65). So too did the numbers of silk

factories, which rose from just over 100 in the early 1880s to nearly 200 in the first decade of the twentieth century, until a sharp fall in price put thirty to forty out of business.[36]

Table 64   Production of Syrian silk, 1880–1913 (annual averages in kgs 000,000)

	Cocoons	Raw silk	Total value (francs, 000)
1880–4	2940	268	
1885–9	3450	431	
1890–4	4680	394[1]	
1895–9	4950	445[2]	
1900–4	5130	468	26,700
1905–9	5320	445	30,100
1910–13	5620		26,900

Sources: Ducousso, *L'industrie de la soie*, 100–1, 142; Saba, 'Development and Decline', 60–1; Verney and Dambmann, *Puissances étrangères*, 649; Samné, *La Syrie*, 123.

Notes: 1 1895–7 only.   2 1901–4 only.

Table 65   Volume and price of Beirut's exports of silk thread and value of Syria/Palestine's silk exports, 1881–1913 (annual averages)

	Bales	Beirut's export of silk thread. Price of bale (£)	Total value of Syrian silk exports* (£,000)
1881–2	1350	204	
1883–7	2165	193	433
1888–92	3040	190	679
1893–7	3571	152	792
1898–1902	2880	185	915
1903–7	3792	201	1083
1908–12	3175	155	891
1913	2800	155	735

* Includes exports of cocoons and silk waste.

Source: Figures from *CR*s (UK) in Kalla, 'Role of Foreign Trade', Tables I and II.

Further difficulties followed. It is a well-known fact that the Lebanese silk industry was virtually wiped out in the First World War, then experienced a brief revival in the 1920s only to be destroyed for good during the Great Depression of the early 1930s. A close examination of the state of the industry shows, however, that it was already facing serious problems even before 1914 as a result of falling world prices and an inability to compete internationally – especially with Japanese producers who managed an enormous expansion in silk production from the late nineteenth century onwards.[37] Contemporary observers close to the industry were well aware of what was happening. Thus a British commercial report of as early as 1910 noted that in some districts mulberry trees were being uprooted and replaced by oranges while a year later James Elroy Flecker, the acting Vice-Consul in Beirut, made the prescient remark that Lebanese silk production was 'probably doomed'.[38]

Gaston Ducousso, an official at the French Consulate in Beirut, wrote his comprehensive study, *l'Industrie de la soie en Syrie* (Paris, 1913) in the same pessimistic vein. As his analysis amply illustrates, there were signs of backwardness and inefficiency at every stage in the industrial process. Problems began with the production of cocoons. Even after nearly three-quarters of a century this remained almost exclusively the work of the individual peasants who either owned the mulberry trees or rented the land on which they grew. The cocoons themselves were produced in small sheds, a process characterized by a great lack of care in raising and feeding the eggs and great difficulties in maintaining them at a constant temperature during the late spring. The result, according to Ducousso, was one of the lowest yields – in terms of the ratio of the weight of cocoons to the number of eggs – among the silk-producing countries of the world.[39] This unhappy situation was further compounded by the fact that the cocoons were then spun into raw silk in a large number of small, technologically inefficient factories, the overwhelming majority of them still using the machines and the system of organization with which they had first begun. With few exceptions there was an almost total reliance on manual techniques based on a system of spinning from 'two ends' which had long since been superseded in France and Italy. According to Ducousso, there was only one properly modern factory in the Mountain, that owned by Veuve Guerin at Krey, which had installed new machinery allowing it to spin from four to six ends.[40] This may have been a bit of an exaggeration – other writers speak of a larger number of establishments with such equipment – but the general point about a widespread failure to invest in up-to-date equipment is certainly well made.[41]

The exact reasons for this state of affairs are more difficult to discover, but it would seem probable that they stem from the same set of circumstances which, on the one hand, permitted local entrepreneurs to take over the silk-spinning industry from its first European founders – leaving only three French-owned factories by the early 1900s – and, on the other, encouraged the multiplication of a large number of small, Mountain-based establishments. In both cases, it might well be argued that the root cause lay in a situation in which the chief concern of new entrants into the industry was not access to working capital, which was available at a price, but the ability to secure both a regular supply of cocoons from a large number of individual peasant proprietors, and a stable, seasonal, labour force. In either case, entrepreneurs with good local connections had many advantages, as has already been argued.[42] An additional reason for the proliferation of a large number of small widely-dispersed factories might well have been the use of large quantities of cheap local wood for fuel for their boilers — until this was made illegal by the *mutasarrifiya* government in the 1880s, forcing everyone to turn to imported coal instead.[43]

If this line of argument is correct, the presence of so many small factories — each with an average of some fifty or so basins manned by 75 to 80 workers — is more easy to explain. So too is the absence of any movement towards a concentration of effort in just a few larger concerns, a process which would have required not only a change in the system of cocoon production but also a labour force of the size which only a large town would possess. The consequences are equally clear: an industry constrained within the limits imposed by a scattered, badly trained labour force, by poor control over quality and by small profit margins. Such a structure could only be maintained when the international price was high and when Lebanese silk had a more or less protected share of the French market. Once other producers like the Chinese and the Japanese were able to manufacture a cheaper, better quality thread the industry was immediately put under great pressure.

Two other results of the Lebanese silk industry's weak position ought also to be mentioned. One is the fact that it remained firmly under the control of French capital. Not only did at least half of each season's working capital come from France but a small number of French houses — no more than five — were responsible for purchasing two-thirds of Beirut's silk exports.[44] Second, there was its continued reliance on imported eggs once efforts to maintain a local breed had failed in the late 1870s. As the efforts of the Pasteur Institute established by the Ottoman Public Debt Administration at Bursa clearly show, domestic production had great advantages over foreign imports in terms both of cost and of a higher yield as a result of better acclimatization to local conditions. In this context it is certainly significant that Beiruti merchants (including, almost certainly, importers of foreign silkworm eggs) were instrumental in preventing an attempt to establish a second Pasteur Institute in Mount Lebanon itself in the late 1880s on the grounds that it would introduce a tight system of rules and regulations governing egg sales which, so they argued, would clearly act as a restraint on trade.[45] Only when the industry's profit margins were severely squeezed just before the First World War did it become possible to break the monopoly of imported eggs with a significant number of locally produced ones.[46] But these, though cheap, were not subject to the system of quality control on which a Pasteur Institute would certainly have insisted.

For all these reasons the Lebanese silk industry is a good example of a type of industrialization which is called forth by a special interaction of international market forces and local comparative advantage, only to be decimated when these same conditions no longer obtain. It is also important to note that, even at its height, the profits to be derived from silk were not large. At no time did the value of exports from Beirut exceed 20,000,000 francs; and this, divided among 150 factories, could have meant an average gross profit per establishment of no more than £40,000 to £50,000, out of which it was necessary to pay the wages, the cost of the raw material and fuel and a high rate of interest (at least 10 per cent) on borrowed working capital.[47] In these circumstances, silk production itself must certainly have ceased to be an attractive proposition for the more wide-awake entre-preneurs and merchants of Beirut. Those who remained associated with the industry at all almost certainly did so only as egg merchants, bankers or exporters. Those who left were able to find better fields for speculation in land (mostly outside the Mountain), in foreign trade, in public utility con-cessions like the railways, and in the establishment of branches in countries like Egypt where the agricultural surplus was many times larger and the prospect of profit correspondingly more great.

Another source of income for many of the inhabitants of Beirut and the Mountain was the remittances from relatives who had migrated overseas. Even if Ruppin's estimate for these funds in the years just before the First World War is too high it would seem reasonable to assume that they pro-vided at least as great a source of income as silk, and probably greater. It was this money that was responsible for the building or rebuilding of so many of the characteristically red-roofed village houses from the 1890s onwards, this money, too, that allowed the construction of the first Mountain hotels in summer resorts like Aley.[48] Sadly, however, there is too little data to carry this examination further or even to speculate on the changes which the growth in the size of remittances must have produced in the economic and social relations of different groups. Probably only two points can be made with any degree of certainty. One is that, in some districts, profits from silk and money from relatives overseas allowed individual peasants to purchase large quantities of village land either from the Maronite church or from the old *muqataji* families.[49] It is significant that much of the land in the north, where there were fewer silk factories and perhaps less migration, remained in ecclesiastical hands.[50] Second, the combination of population growth, money from abroad and silk pro-duction must certainly have widened the market for Lebanese industrial products such as woven cotton and the lower quality factory silk known as 'scandaroun' — for which there were said to be 2000 looms just before the First World War — tobacco, olive oil and soap.[51]

The Syrian interior

The Syrian provinces of Damascus and Aleppo experienced a period of economic revival in the years after 1880, but how far and how fast it is impossible to say. While it is certain that a growth in population, improvements in rural security and a better system of transport allowed a considerable increase in agricultural production, there are no figures which would satisfactorily illustrate the extent of this progress. It is also true that the continued dependence of most sections of Syrian society on the proceeds from animal husbandry and a rain-fed agriculture meant that a cycle of a few bad years could still produce a major down-turn in production which would affect the whole economy. The intrusion of political factors often made matters worse: such was the case in the province of Aleppo from 1909 onwards when the effects of a series of bad winters leading to the loss of perhaps 80 per cent of the sheep population was exacerbated by the popular disturbances (including attacks on Armenians) which marked the early stages of the Young Turk Revolution and the conscription of many young men (including, for the first time, Christians) into the Ottoman army.[52] The result was a period of serious economic hardship highlighted by a dramatic falling off in both imports and exports.[53]

As far as the agricultural sector was concerned, the main developments stemmed directly from continuation and intensification of that process of repopulating new areas of cultivable land which had already been discussed many times. As elsewhere, this process gave particular opportunities to those with power and influence to obtain either title to the new land or at least access to its surplus. Apart from the usual combination of city merchants, local notables and nomad shaikhs, one person to derive great benefit from these opportunities was Sultan Abdul-Hamid who in the 1880s began to buy up large estates for himself in the districts around Aleppo and Homs.[54] Again, as elsewhere, title to land had to be supplemented by an ability, first to build up a stable labour force, then to be able to collect both taxes and rent. Something of the variety of response to these opportunities and problems can be seen from a number of fragmentary pieces of information about conditions in various parts of the Aleppo province.

To begin in the north, the period before the First World War was one of a continuous extension of the agricultural frontier eastwards along the Euphrates towards Raqqa. In some cases the new land was controlled by beduin shaikhs who were able to have it registered in their name and then to work it with peasants who had been encouraged to migrate there or with men from local semi-independent tribes.[55] Elsewhere the new imperial estates were farmed either by peasants or, in the case of those at Membij and Raqqa, by Circassian colonists.[56] Such estates enjoyed considerable advantages in that their cultivators paid no land tax while enjoying a relatively high level of services in the shape of the provision of roads and markets.[57] There were more imperial estates farmed by Circassians around Hama but here the main beneficiaries of the improvement in rural security were the major urban families like the Kilanis, Baraziz and Azms who bought or simply appropriated large tracts of land from nomadic tribes, sometimes bringing in poor Alawite peasants from the hills to put them into cultivation.[58]

Apart from the creation of large estates out of new land there was also a second process by which more and more of the already existing cultivated land passed out of peasant hands as a result of the familiar combination of coercion, sale for debt, and simple chicanery when it came to land registration. Thus the landlords of Hama were able to buy up a number of Alawite villages at the fringes of their district.[59] Thus too, in the Hauran, Druze chiefs like Ibrahim al-Atrash were so active in seizing land and evicting its previous cultivators that they precipitated a number of peasant revolts in the 1880s.[60] Figures to illustrate the extent of this process are naturally suspect, the more so as almost all of Syria's local land records were lost or destroyed during the First World War. Perhaps the best estimates are those concerned with the size of the Sultan's estates, for these were taken over by the Ottoman government after 1908 and came to form the bulk of the state domains in the Mandate period. According to Moutran they amounted to some 1,250,000 hectares (3,088,000 acres).[61] For the rest, Granott quotes an estimate for 1907 to the effect that only 20 to 30 per cent of the land in Syria (presumably this refers to the province of Damascus) remained in peasant hands.[62] Later, during the 1920s, another rough calculation puts the proportion of land in Mandatory Syria in large and medium sized properties as 75 per cent.[63]

The next question to ask is how these estates were worked. Where clear title existed and the proprietor was in obvious control the almost invariable practice seems to have been to let (and in some cases to sub-let) the land according to some form of métayage or share-cropping contract. To judge from evidence from the inter-war period such contracts were annual, usually verbal and revocable at will by the owner.[64] The terms themselves varied greatly according to a number of factors, mostly obviously the type of crop to be grown. On cereal land there was likely to be a simple 50/50 sharing of the harvest after the tenant had paid the tithe. Such was the case on the imperial estates near Aleppo at the end of the century where the produce was equally divided between tenant and the domain's administration after the former had repaid any money and seed which may have been lent him.[65] On land which was irrigated or where trees were planted the arrangements were generally more complex.[66] In addition, the tenant may have been expected to supply various labour services to the estate, although the only evidence for this comes from the inter-war period.[67]

The situation with regard to land which remained in peasant hands is much more difficult to discover. To begin with it is necessary to make the distinction between fields held in individual title and those subject to some form of communal ownership. As far as the former was concerned such land was most usually found in the older established villages in the hills or near major urban centres. Elsewhere, and particularly on newly reclaimed land, it seems likely that the communal or *mushaa* system was more the rule; but there is no way in which this can be proved. To take the land in individual title first: here peasant proprietors either worked their fields on their own account or in uneasy partnership with a usurer or powerful protector, or both. As a British consular report from Aleppo in 1890 described the situation, only 10 to 15 per cent of the cultivators could manage to work the land using their own resources while the remainder, 'through poverty', allied themselves with a usurer or an 'influential man' of the nearest town. The latter provided money and seed. In return, in spite of the existence of a nominal crop-sharing arrangement, he took as much of the harvest as he was able, subject only to the peasant's ability to resist.[68]

The other major type of peasant ownership, the *mushaa*, presents a very much more difficult problem of analysis. Apart from its intrinsic complexity, it seems to have been regularly misunderstood or misrepresented by the colonial officials who became the main source of information about it, most of whom saw it as an archaic system destined soon to wither away. The unsatisfactory nature of their treatment provides few clues to such central questions as where did it begin, what were its major forms and how did it develop or mutate over time? It is only with the work of later researchers like Weulersse and Firestone that any of these problems began to be examined seriously, and I will draw heavily on their analysis in what follows.[69]

According to both Weulersse and Firestone there were two basic types of *mushaa* system in the Mandatory period in Syria and Palestine. In each, the village land subject to collective ownership (excluding orchards and gardens) was divided into sections of relatively homogeneous quality – usually three or four – and then periodically redistributed in such a way that every person or group of persons entitled to a share obtained a parcel or plot in every section. The principle according to which the land was allocated varied, however. According to the first system (which Weulersse calls the 'old' and Firestone, the 'open-ended') plots were distributed to each family on the basis of the number of males or the number of ploughs it possessed – in other words according to some local definition of agricultural input, whether in terms of labour power, or tools, or both. Any increase or decrease in the number of such units meant a corresponding increase or decrease in the number of shares.

On the second system (which Firestone calls 'quantified shares') access to the land was not dependent on units of input but, rather, was divided into a fixed number of shares which did not vary over time. As in the first system, each share entitled its owner (or owners) to plots in each of the village's three or four sections, but in this case future distribution of land took place only between share-holders so that newcomers could no longer be accommodated.

In addition, the shares themselves rapidly developed into something much more like a fixed title and could be bought and sold or transferred, either among the villagers themselves or in transactions with outsiders. They could also be subdivided as a result of sale or inheritance.

Lastly, to complete the list of major variations, it was possible for redistribution under either system to come to an end, leaving the actual plots of land, or title to them, in the hands of whoever possessed them at that particular moment.

According to Weulersse the second system, just described, was a natural development of the first; and it is easy to see why he should assert this. To a European observer, change to a fixed or quantified method of sharing (to use Firestone's word) might well seem to have been a response both to growing commercialization and to those changes in local power relationships which tended to increase the role of merchants and notables. As already noted, his second system allowed the sale and purchase of title as a way of valorizing an individual's or family's share in the communal land. It also permitted non-labouring outsiders, excluded under the first system, to obtain access to village land, something usurers, protectors and local strongmen must obviously have been anxious to do. To this list of factors Firestone himself could add the growth of population pressure: as he rightly points out, the 'quantified share' system allowed out-migrants from over-populated villages to continue to hold either a title share or part of one without actually being physically present.

However, against this, it is important to note that Firestone himself, unlike Weulersse, is unwilling to allow that all villages passed inevitably from one system to the other and this is certainly a useful caveat. Given the paucity of information, the enormous variation in local conditions and the different historical experience of different villages in different districts, it would be wise not to be too categoric. To make only a few of the most obvious points: although it is known that collective ownership was common in Syria and Palestine in the late nineteenth century almost all the data concerning it comes from a later period. Again, there is the obvious distinction to be made between those villages which may have held their fields in common for many decades and those new settlements established on recently secured land which chose to begin the practice *de novo*. To make matters even more complex, the number of variables which have to be taken into account when seeking to explain changes within the system are very large. The role of increasing monetization and of rural power relationships have already been mentioned. To these should be added the question of the availability of labour, something which, when scarce, might well have encouraged a system in which newcomers, especially those with ploughs, were rapidly given access to village land (the 'open-ended') and, when plentiful, one in which surplus labourers could more easily be exported (the 'quantified share').

Lastly, there is the vital question of the incidence of taxation and the way in which the tithe was actually collected. In Firestone's valuable argument, the open-ended system, with its built-in mechanism for dividing the available land into equal shares among all producers, can readily be seen as a natural response on the part of both cultivator and collector to a situation in which taxes were collected in one lump sum from whole villages at the highest possible rate. It follows logically that communities in which the burden of both agricultural production and tax payments were equally divided could manage to deliver a larger volume over a longer period than those in which an unequal distribution of land must inevitably mean that the weaker units are soon driven to the wall leaving an ever smaller number of cultivators to shoulder the total burden on their own. There is Weulersse's observation that the *mushaa* system seems, historically, to have been closely associated with the dominant type of agricultural practice: that of the dry-farming of cereals.[70]

Sadly, however, such an argument can only remain a useful hypothesis so long as the data to prove it is unobtainable. The actual correlation between high taxes and redistribution of land in equal shares remains to be demonstrated. If and when it can be managed it will have to be done with reference to the fact that, in many districts, the tax-farmer and the man who controlled the land were either the same person – or else closely in league – and that their joint interest in maximum taxes might well have been in conflict with their wider concern to appropriate more of the surplus via their additional roles of usurer, protector or even, if they could break into the village monopoly of land, owner.

When so little is known about the origins, development and geographical spread of the *mushaa* system in any of its variations, it is naturally just as difficult to say anything very much in general about its economic and social consequences. It has long been a commonplace among economists that systems of communal landownership inhibit investment and changes in agricultural practice. This is certainly true, and was one of the reasons why the Ottoman government, through its Land Code, attempted to put an end to it.[71] But the argument is not as simple as it may first seem. For one thing the *mushaa* system, with its emphasis on communal solidarity, was almost certainly a useful mechanism for facilitating the colonization of newly secured land. For another, if Weulersse is right about its connection with dry-farming, it was associated with a type of agriculture for which no great improvement in productivity was possible anyway, short of large-scale mechanization. Meanwhile, those key activities in the rural economy where improvement was possible – notably the cultivation of fruit, vines and vegetables – were carried out on privately-owned land.

Having said all this it also remains a fact that the *mushaa* system – as well as any decision to stop the regular redistribution of village land – was a major contributor to that minute and inefficient sub-division, or parcelization, of agricultural properties which was so widely remarked during the inter-war period. According to one survey of the Bekaa, carried out in 1932, the number of separate parcels of land owned by each proprietor varied between fourteen and fifty-six.[72] One village alone, Bar Elias, contained 32,648 tiny plots.[73] Given the existence of over-population and a law of inheritance which, when enforced, also contributed to the continual break-up of larger plots, it is obvious that the *mushaa* system itself cannot be attacked as the only major cause of the phenomenon, but it was certainly an important one. Once the redistribution of land under the open-ended system came to an end, those in possession of what were already three or four separate parcels in the various sections of village land were left free to dispose of them as they wished or as the law and economic circumstances dictated. Parcelization was the obvious consequence. By the same token it may well have been that one of the major reasons for switching to a quantified share system was just to prevent the possibility of such a damaging sub-division. Under this latter system, while the shares themselves could be endlessly subdivided, it was still possible, at least in theory, to keep the land to which they referred intact and to farm it as one unit.[74]

As already noted, the bulk of Syria's cultivated land, both old and new, was devoted to cereal cultivation. The result was certainly an increase in the volume of cereal production but one that was constrained by such factors as the enforced use of lower-yielding, marginal land and the problems involved in transporting significant quantities of grain from the newly-opened districts in the east. In the province of Aleppo this produced a situation in which almost all of the increase went to feed the growing population, leaving a smaller and smaller amount over for export. In the case of Iskanderun, the main entrepôt for the northern districts, cereal exports dropped from a high of some 30 to 35,000 tons in 1885 to an average of only 5600 tons, between 1899 and 1903, before ceasing almost entirely just before the First World War.[75] As the foreign consuls were only too anxious to point out, the process was certainly accelerated by the fact that, given the rudimentary system of transport and the fall in the international price of grain towards the end of the nineteenth century, the newly developed cereal lands along the Euphrates were too far from the coast to allow cultivators there to grow much of a surplus for sale overseas.[76] Only to the south, and especially in the Hauran, did the construction of railways permit an increase of cultivation for export. Even there the response was not as great as might have been supposed, with the result that, taking the Syrian interior as a whole, the ratio of exports to production must certainly have declined during the period bringing the region dangerously close to a position where it could only just about feed itself in an average year.[77]

Figures for the export of various categories of Syrian and Palestinian agricultural products are given in Table 62. They show that the main foreign currency earners were silk, certain pastoral or field crops like cereals, tobacco and cotton, certain animal products like wool and hides, and citrus fruits. In every case there was a large increase in the value of exports during the 1890s and the first years of the twentieth century, before adverse movement in the international price and a return to relatively more insecure conditions in part of the Aleppo province just before the First World War acted to reduce the returns from important crops like silk, cereals and wool.

Table 66　Estimates of the volume of exports of certain important agricultural products from Syrian/Palestinian ports, 1881 to 1913 (annual averages)

	Aleppo/Alexandretta				Jaffa		Gaza
	Cereals	Cotton	Wool	Hides/ leather	Sesame	Oranges	Barley
	(tons)	(tons)	(tons)	(tons)	(tons)	(cases)	(tons)
1881–2	27,742	782	1988	256			
1883–7	26,156	386	2756	236	2104	107,577	
1888–92	12,799	149	3063	399	3272	236,000	
1893–7	11,594	251	2709	647	3908	270,000	19,603
1898–1902	5366	255	1923	898	1784	311,323	32,000
1903–7	11,760	1005	2226	860	2268	509,911	35,000
1908–12	1771	602	519	510	2624	912,401	12,103
1913	753	603	42	307	1535	1,608,570	19,055

Source: CRs (UK) in Kalla, 'Role of Foreign Trade', Table III.

Cotton, which as far as the Syrian provinces were concerned was grown mainly in the hill country between Aleppo and the coast, produced a harvest of about 1000 tons in 1885 before almost going out of cultivation when the international price tumbled in the 1890s.[78] There was then a revival during the early years of the twentieth century taking production to a total of some 2000 tons, grown over perhaps 20,000 acres.[79] Of this harvest, a third was exported from Iskanderun.[80] Tobacco was also grown in the coastal districts, notably those around Latakia. Like cotton, the area subject to its cultivation was greatly influenced by changes in the international price, falling in the 1890s only to revive once again at the turn of the century. But, unlike cotton, its cultivation was only legally possible with a licence from the French-controlled *Régie*, a constraint which may account for the fact that, even when demand was good, its growth was never extended over an area of more than 4000 to 5000 acres.[81] A large part of the crop was exported, mainly to England and Egypt.[82] The last of the important field crops, sesame, was grown mainly for its oil and could be found in the Homs and Hama districts. In the years just before the First World War perhaps a third of its crop of 30,000 tons was exported.[83] Animals and animal products continued to remain the prerogative of nomadic or semi-nomadic groups, most of them living at the edge of the desert. The increase in the export of such products (Tables 62, 66) for most of the period would seem to indicate a substantial growth in the region's animal population.

Table 67   Estimates of the numbers of looms and textile workers in Syria's major towns, 1890–1912

	Damascus		Homs		Hama		Aleppo
	looms	*workers*	*looms*	*workers*	*looms*	*workers*	*looms*
1890							3135
1891	3000		4000		700		5884
1892	2000						
1899	5000						
1900		21,000		28,000		4900	
1902	5000	10,000	5000		1000		
1908		10,000	8500	10,000			
1909	2500		10,000		1000		10,000
1912							7650

*Sources: CR*s (UK) and Hakim, 'Industry', 124.

As elsewhere, the link between agricultural and industrial progress was an important one. In the Syrian case there would seem much to support the view that the continued revival of the region's handicrafts was a direct result of the market provided by an increasing, and in some districts increasingly prosperous, agricultural population. This link can be seen with some clarity in the case of the textile weaving industry. The figures for the number of looms to be found in the four major centres (Table 67) suggest a regular increase in industrial capacity for most of the period. Another index of this same increase comes from the figures for the imports of the cotton and silk thread on which the local industry relied. These show a rise in the former from an annual average of between £60,000 and £70,000 in the 1890s to £400,000 (1903–7) and a peak of £650,000 (1908–12).[84] Meanwhile, imports of silk thread increased from an annual average of just under £100,000 at the turn of the century to £250,000 in the years just before the First World War.[85] Something of the nature of this revival of local industrial activity can also be seen from what is admittedly a very rough calculation for Aleppo to the effect that the city produced at least twice as much cloth in 1906 in terms of value (£500,000) as it imported.[86]

Although there were a number of factors which underlay its revival, certainly the most important would seem to be the industry's ability to find new markets among Syria's urban and rural population as well as to recapture old ones previously lost to foreign competition. To do this it concentrated on producing cotton and woollen cloths at the cheaper ends of these markets and silk and cotton cloths at the most expensive. Contemporary consular reports abound with examples. In the case of the former activity the main type of product remained the *dima*, made of pure cotton.[87] But to this can be added, among others, the woollen *abas* which were much in demand among the nomads and the *izar* or long veil of local cloth which women of Damascus began to wear in preference to English white calico.[88] A clue to the success of this counter-attack against the purchase of British products can be seen from a consular report of 1897 urging the Lancashire manufacturers to obtain samples of Syrian cloth in order to copy them.[89] Meanwhile, at the other end of the market, there was a concentration on the more intricate, finely-woven cloths which foreigners simply could not copy, such as the fabrics specially woven for the embroidered dresses and head-dresses worn by the women of Palestine.[90] And in both cases, whether with the cheaper or the more expensive products, there is a possibility, supported by hints here and there in commercial reports, that the further deepening of a local market might have been attempted, by the conscious manipulation of fashion.[91] This process of constant change, well-known to the couturiers of Paris and elsewhere, would have had the double advantage of inhibiting foreign imitation (by the time a particular design was copied in Manchester it would no longer be in vogue in Damascus) and, at the same time, ensuring that some at least of the consumers felt obliged to replace old styles with new at regular intervals.

As to the structure of the industry, it remained largely organized on a householder workshop basis with a maximum of a dozen to fifteen looms in any one establishment.[92] For the most part the looms themselves were of a simple wooden construction costing no more than £0.30 to £0.50, but in a few cases, richer weavers were able to buy Jacquard models (for £5 to £7), some made in Beirut, some driven by electricity. Estimates of their number vary but do not suggest that there were more than a hundred at most in the years just before the First World War, of which perhaps half were power driven. Other reports suggest that keeping the new looms running was only just within the technical capacity of the local mechanics. This was one of the many reasons why the few attempts to introduce factories along European lines all came to nothing. In addition to the weaving industry itself there were also some dozen related activities of which one of the most important was dyeing. By 1909 there were at least 130 dye houses in Aleppo alone. According to contemporary accounts, this activity had run the interesting, and significant, path from the use of local vegetable dyes to the import of European ones, and then on to the manufacture of chemical dyes in Syria itself.

Most other Syrian industries depended more directly on the use of agricultural raw materials. These included the few silk factories outside Mount Lebanon and other factories for making cigarettes, licorice, shoes and wines and spirits. In addition, there were upwards of a hundred soap plants, many steam mills and between 600 and 800 olive oil presses.[93] As elsewhere in the Middle East, few of these concerns employed either modern machinery or modern European methods of organization. Indeed it could well be argued that there were more failures than successes when it came to trying to set up establishments of this latter kind.[94] For the rest the majority of plants employed only a small number of men and the most rudimentary equipment. The majority of the soap-making plants, for example, had only a single boiler while very few had iron pans to serve as receptacles for the boiling oil.[95] For all these reasons such concerns were only able to exist, and partially to flourish, either because they could exercise some local monopoly or because no foreign competitor had, as yet, attempted to penetrate their markets. Like the Lebanese silk industry, many of them were to prove incapable of surviving the harsher conditions of the post-First World War period.[96]

Apart from the general improvements in security and a few minor concessions such as the reduction of certain internal tariffs, the role of the Ottoman state in the development of Syrian agriculture and industry was minimal.[97] In this respect the Syrian provinces were in a similar position to those in Anatolia itself where an impoverished and indebted central government was able to release little money for infrastructural and other investment and where the construction of major public works — the Hijaz railway apart — was left almost entirely to foreign enterprise. Again, as in Anatolia, provincial funds were perennially squeezed, on the one hand by the need to surrender large sums to the Central Treasury, and on the other by the continuing failure to reform the system of tithe collection on which perhaps a third of Syria's revenues depended.[98]

Of the three Syrian provinces, that of Damascus experienced the greatest financial difficulty. As already noted, Midhat's brief period of reforms at the end of the 1870s left little substantial legacy.[99] As before, the power of the local governor was severely circumscribed both by pressures from Istanbul and by the constraints imposed by the local councils. As before, the province's financial problems were exacerbated by the extra demands imposed by the cost of the pilgrimage and the army of Arabistan as well as the much larger demands imposed by the Central Treasury in Istanbul. To make matters worse it was still Ottoman policy to attempt to keep on good terms with recalcitrant social groups by granting them large tax-concessions, for example, the Druze inhabitants of the Hauran and Jabal Druze.[100] The Young Turk Revolution of 1908 briefly promised a more efficient approach to provincial reform; but in spite of the decision to try and improve the system of tax-collection and to inaugurate a number of public works, efforts in this direction were continually hampered by lack of funds.[101]

In these circumstances only a tiny part of the rural surplus was directed towards productive investment. Much of it was simply exported either in the form of support for the central Ottoman budget or as profits made by foreign companies, augmented in the case of the Rayak—Aleppo railway line by a substantial kilometric guarantee.[102] Meanwhile, the part which remained in Syria accrued mostly to the large landowners and merchants and was used by them in part either for the purchase of imported goods or the construction of urban houses. On his visit to Aleppo in 1906 Sir Mark Sykes noted that 'beyond the walls houses of great beauty and originality are springing up in every direction' and that 'many of the brakes and gardens which surrounded the place have vanished and been replaced by whole new quarters of the growing city'.[103] He also came across a master mason who employed some 80 to 100 workmen in building houses in a combination of European and local Syrian style.[104] In Damascus, two years later, the British consul noted that there were already 750 shops and houses lit with electricity. Compared with this, the sums available for investment in local industry were so tiny that in 1909 a Damascus glass factory with plant worth only £16,000 failed for want of working capital.[105]

Palestine

In Palestine the period 1880—1913 was one of steady economic growth if measured by the conventional indices. To begin with demography: the population increased from half a million to nearly 750,000 during these three decades.[106] As elsewhere in the Middle East this was partly the result of better security and better nutrition as well as of some improvements in public health, but in this particular case it was augmented by quite substantial inward migration. In addition to some 50,000 Jews there were smaller numbers of Trans-Jordanians, Druzes, and a variety of agricultural colonists such as Circassians, Sudanese, Persians and others.[107]

At the same time there was also a significant change in the distribution of this population. On the one hand there was an acceleration of that process of filling in the empty or sparsely occupied areas on the coastal plains to the north of Jaffa which has already been described in Chapter 6: according to the first official census of 1922, some 200,000 people, or nearly a quarter of the total population, were then settled on the Maritime Plain.[108] On the other, there was also a substantial growth in the size of the larger towns. According to one calculation, the population of the twelve largest urban areas (Jerusalem, Acre, Haifa, Jaffa, Ramle, Gaza, Hebron, Bethlehem, Nablus, Nazareth, Tiberias and Safad) may almost have doubled between 1880 and 1920, from 120,000 to 230,000.[109]

As elsewhere, too, the increase in numbers and improvements in security allowed a marked expansion of the cultivated area. Hill villages threw off satellite settlements (known as *khirbas*) down on the plain; nomads began to live permanently on the land; large landowners brought in farm workers from neighbouring areas.[110] The result was a considerable increase in agricultural output. In the hills this was represented by a widespread planting of olive trees.[111] Meanwhile, down on the plains, the most important crops were cereals and sesame. Barley, for example, was grown over ever larger areas in the district round Gaza, stimulating a substantial export until just before the First World War.[112] Lastly, there was a big extension of the citrus groves to be found round the major towns. In the case of Jaffa, the major centre, the areas of its orchards increased from some 4000 *dunums* (1000 acres) in the early 1880s to about 30,000 *dunums* (7500 acres) thirty years later.[113] Meanwhile, the export of oranges, mostly to Britain, nearly quintupled by volume during the same period.[114]

Table 68   The foreign trade of Palestine, 1883–1913 (annual averages, £,000)

	Jaffa			Haifa/Acre		Gaza
	Imports total	*Exports*		*Imports total*	*Exports total*	*Exports total*
		Oranges	*total*			
1883–7	264		135		237	
1888–92	290	84[1]	277		267	
1893–7	292	86	317		108	
1898–1902	385	94[2]	274	80*	200*	100*
1903–7	569	127	394	199	273	107
1908–12	1008	217	648	368	220	82
1913	1313	298	745			

* Kalla's own estimate.

Sources: CRs (UK) in Kalla, 'Role of Foreign Trade', Appendix Table I; Tolkowsky, *Gateway of Palestine*, 183–4.

Notes: 1 Excludes 1888–9.   2 Excludes 1901–2.

Evidence for the increase in agricultural production can be found in the figures for the value of exports from Jaffa and Gaza – the main centre for the foreign sale of the barley grown in the southern districts. As far as Jaffa was concerned these show an overall rise from just over £250,000 a year (1888–92) to nearly £750,000 in the years just before the First World War (Table 68). Table 68 also shows the growing importance of Jaffa oranges which, by the years 1908–13 were providing something like 40 per cent of total foreign sales. Figures for Gaza's exports are more fragmentary but would seem to reveal a steady sale of cereals worth round about £100,000 a year. Meanwhile, the increase in agricultural exports combined with the growth of population in general – and a growing number of people of European origin in particular – to encourage a concomitant rise in the value of imports. These advanced from an annual average of £260,000 (1883–7) to over £1,000,000 (1908–13) (Table 68). As already noted, a growing trade deficit was paid for by a combination of remittances, invisible earnings (mainly from foreign pilgrims) and straightforward capital transfers to missionary establishments and to the Jewish settlers.[115]

A final index of economic growth is presented by the increase in industrial and craft-industrial production. According to the first Industrial Census of 1927/8 there were 1236 factories and workshops with a capital investment of over £P1,000,000 which had been established before the First World War.[116] Of these, according to Himadeh, about 925 were Arab-owned and 300 Jewish.[117] As always there are great difficulties in defining what exactly constituted a factory.[118] But in this case these figures would seem to indicate that industry in Palestine was quite as well developed as its Syrian neighbours. Clearly one reason for this situation was the resources of capital and skill available to the Jewish colonists. According to the Jewish Agency's own Agricultural and Industrial Census of 1930 there were then 341 establishments in existence which had been set up before 1920 representing a capital investment of nearly £P400,000.[119] Of these, 102 were classified as proper industries (as opposed to 'handicrafts') with capital of just over £P375,000 and a labour force of 1322.[120] Such factories must certainly have included a large number producing olive and sesame oil, wine and soap, as well as several flour mills.[121] It is also possible to assume that, in almost every case, the Jewish use of power and machinery was in advance of their local counterparts. According to Himadeh the only soap plants with motors and the only sesame oil plants with hydraulic presses were Jewish-owned.[122]

Nevertheless, the growth and development of indigenous production was also impressive. Two activities stand out. One was that of soap making, mainly concentrated at Nablus where there were already 30 small plants in the early 1880s.[123] The other was spinning and weaving. This too had begun to be concentrated in a number of major centres like Safad and Nazareth in the north, Nablus, Beit Jala and Hebron in the hills and Gaza and Majdal on the southern plains. In 1908 Nazareth alone is said to have contained 300 looms.[124] At the same time nearly every family in Majdal is also supposed to have owned one.[125] While some of the finer stuffs continued to be imported from Syria, local weavers must have provided a large proportion of the cheaper materials, both for the settled population and for the nomads.[126] Other industrial activity involved the manufacture of carpets, leather goods and glass.

As elsewhere in Syria, economic growth owed much to the greater security which the Ottomans were able to provide and to the construction of the Hijaz railway with its Haifa branch. For the rest, however, local tax revenues were too small to permit the execution of any public works. The roads remained in bad repair.[127] At Jaffa there were still no quays and ships continued to be loaded and offloaded offshore, while at Gaza, as a British captain noted, the only way to discover what was supposed to be the harbour was to look for the mounds of barley on the beach.[128] In these circumstances it was necessary to rely heavily on European capital for projects like the Jaffa/Jerusalem railway even though it was clearly so profitable that no kilometric guarantee was required. An equally important role was played by members of the European community, whether members of the many foreign consulates, the missionary and other ecclesiastical establishments, or the Jewish settlers. As in other non-European countries they acted as a powerful incentive for the creation and expansion of European quarters in the major towns and for the promotion of a European pattern of import-dependent consumption. In addition, they were responsible for a number of important technical innovations, whether it was the carts and the new ploughs of the Jewish agricultural settlers, the new methods of cultivating high value cash crops like grapes introduced by the German Templars and the Jews, or some of the machinery to be found in the new European-owned factories.

That the spread effect of these innovations on the Arab inhabitants of Palestine was as great as is sometimes asserted is more debatable. While there were certainly some cases in which, for example, Jewish/European methods of improving the productivity of the orange trees near Jaffa were important, the system of share-cropping and the fact that so few Palestinian landlords actually farmed their own fields must certainly have stood as a substantial barrier to any improvement in most agricultural practices. Meanwhile, the almost complete absence of power-driven machinery in the Arab industrial sector would seem to argue against any significant influence from the European or Jewish factories.

Just as significant as the general increase in the volume of economic activity was the associated change in certain key economic relationships. Among these the changes in the pattern of control over agricultural land were certainly the most important. As far as the newly secured land was concerned it would seem that a relatively small number of individuals were able to take advantage of the Ottoman programme of land registration and of the Ottoman desire to encourage settlement of sparsely populated areas to acquire large estates. In the north, on the Marj Ibn Amir, control of some 500,000 *dunums* was almost entirely divided between the Sursuqs of Beirut and the Sultan.[129] Elsewhere title was obtained by local magnates like the Abd al-Hadis of Jenin or urban-based merchants, usurers and others like the Mudawwars and the Tuwaynis of Beirut or the notables of Nablus and Jerusalem.[130] In some cases this process involved previously empty lands, in others it meant the takeover of fields at least nominally owned by villages in the adjacent hills.[131] What, though, is less clear is the extent to which this led to a loss of land actually under cultivation by peasants, either on the plains or in the more densely populated districts to the east. In such circumstances all attempts to calculate the areas in question must be treated with great caution; but for what it is worth, one estimate mentioned by Granott is that in the early twentieth century something like a third of Palestine's cultivable land − 3,000,000 *dunums* (750,000 acres) − was held by only 144 families.[132] However, of this, 2,000,000 *dunums* consisted of the tribal grain-growing lands round Beersheba and Gaza, leaving only 1,000,000 for the Sultan, the Sirsuqs and the rest. If this estimate is to be trusted it would seem unlikely that much of the hill country had, as yet, been incorporated into large estates.

Where control over large areas of land had been obtained there were the usual problems first of obtaining a secure title, then of finding a labour force to work it. In the case of the Sirsuqs for instance, there is the story of how, having obtained control of the land belonging to the village of Soulam on the Marj Ibn Amir, they then attempted to find labour either from the village itself or by attracting migrants down from the hills. But, although they were ready to provide animals and seed on credit and a free house, the terms of the actual crop-sharing arrangement − in which the tenant only received a fifth of the produce after he himself had paid the tithe − were so onerous and protection against nomadic incursion so insubstantial that the cultivators regularly fled their fields. Only some years later, about 1900, when the Sirsuqs' local agent awarded several hundred acres to a tough family from Arabeh was permanent cultivation possible.[133] The rewards were then great. A large landowner like the Sirsuq family who was also able to obtain tax-farming rights was in a very good position to appropriate the bulk of the agricultural surplus. In terms of the advantages which a landlord like this enjoyed, it would seem that Bergheim's calculation that, on the Plain of Sharon, a third of the crop was collected as tithe and rent was probably too low.[134]

In more populated areas methods of letting estate land to tenants varied greatly. Firestone suggests four basic systems involving different combinations of the three primary inputs − land, labour and capital − and different degrees of landlord participation in the actual process of production. They begin with the landlord − present in the village − providing land, tools and working capital and the tenant only his labour; and end with the landlord − absent − doing no more than collect his rent in cash.[135] This provides a useful way of classifying different aspects of the economic component of the relationship between landlord and share-cropping peasant. It also suggests a way of looking at the various stages by which rural-based families, like the Abd al-Hadis, might gradually dissociate themselves from the active day-to-day management of their fields to take up the larger opportunities for acquiring power and wealth opened up by joining the Ottoman local administration first in Nablus, then in the more important centre of Jerusalem.[136] Only the first system just mentioned required the active presence of the landlord or a close relative in the village to ensure that the capital input was properly employed and the full return from its use collected. After that the gradual process of disengagement simply required the maintenance of a system of local control sufficient to ensure that the owner's interests were not disregarded. Such a system had the additional advantage that it ensured absentee landlords of a local power base which added greatly to the weight they could exercise at Jerusalem, whether in terms of obtaining tax-farming rights or deriving other forms of pecuniary advantage. Just how many families chose to take this route is unclear. The only rough guide is a calculation made by the Johnson–Crosbie Commission's examination of 104 Palestinian villages in 1930 in which it was found that 21 per cent of the village land was owned by absentee landlords.[137]

What of the land which remained in peasant hands? Granott provides figures taken from a Turkish census of 1909 to the effect that peasant land in the three sanjaks of Jerusalem, Nablus and Acre was owned by 17,000 families, each with an average of some 50 *dunums*.[138] In terms of Palestinian conditions a plot of this size was no more than a smallholding. To make matters worse such plots were often greatly fragmented. In what is admittedly a much later period, a survey of five Palestinian villages in 1944 showed that the total number of separate parcels of land varied from 265 to 828 a village or an average of nine parcels per individual landholding.[139]

Most writers, following the observations of nineteenth-century observers, tend to assume that collective ownership was mainly to be found down on the plains where it might be supposed to have the obvious advantage of encouraging communal solidarity in an inhospitable terrain.[140] Firestone, on the other hand, can find no reason why geographical location should be the determining factor and suggests instead that its spread was a function of the system of taxation and of a particular village's ability to resist heavy demands imposed on the community as a whole.[141] It follows, for him, that the kind of village likely to employ a system of regular redistribution of communal lands on an equalizing basis must have been one inhabited by weak clans or splinter groups of newly settled nomads or migrant cultivators which lacked the power or the presence of a local protector necessary to resist heavy demands. In nineteenth-century Palestine such villages were more likely to be found on the plains; but not necessarily so. As for the principle upon which regular redistribution of the communal land took place, contemporary observers write of it being based either on units of input – according to the number of animals or ploughs a family possessed or the amount of land (measured in feddans) which it might be supposed to be able to plough – or units of consumption – families or clans.[142] The first case clearly corresponds to Firestone's 'open-ended share'; the second suggests his 'quantified share' system.

Information from the Mandate period suggests that many Palestinian villages were subject to a complex process of social differentiation as a result of over-population, of increasing inequalities in land-holding and of a greater reliance on off-farm occupations, either in the village itself or outside.[143] Given the fact that so little is known about the last Ottoman decades the temptation to assume that this process began much earlier is great, but has to be resisted. The most that can be suggested is that many of the same factors were also present in the pre-First World War period, although certainly not in anything like so extended a form. Post's remark in the 1890s that villagers were already losing land as a result of accumulated debt suggests the beginning of a process of the creation of a strata of landless labourers.[144] Robinson Lees's observation, from the same period, about the inhabitants of particular villages who supplemented their agricultural income with particular off-farm skills — for example, masons, building labourers, or camel men — indicates that opportunities already existed for some families in some places to reduce their dependence on the inevitable risks involved in agricultural life.[145] But how far or how fast such developments had proceeded by 1914 it is impossible to say.

Any complete account of the economic history of Palestine at the end of the nineteenth century must also involve an examination of the agricultural activity of the Jewish population from 1882 onwards.[146] While the bulk of the new immigrants went straight to the towns, an important section began to establish themselves on the land in a variety of different kinds of colonies. By 1908 there were twenty-six such colonies with 10,000 members and 400,000 *dunums* (100,000 acres) of land; six years later the number of colonists had risen to 12,000 (of which about 7500 were actually involved in the process of cultivation) and the amount of land to 450,000 *dunums*.[147] Most of this land was obtained either from the Ottoman government or from large estate owners.[148] In only a very few instances was it bought from peasant cultivators.[149] On the other hand, whatever its legal ownership, the land in question had almost invariably been cultivated by peasants or semi-nomads who had either to be evicted or to be employed by the new colonists as labourers.[150]

Once purchased there was then the problem of how to work the new land. From the point of view of the colonists themselves the question was one of finding a method of farming it in such a way as to support the European standard of living necessary to attract new immigrants with only limited capital and without, for both political and ideological reasons, relying over much on cheap local labour. It took nearly three decades of experiment to find a suitable answer. To begin with, the settlements established in the early 1880s tried, in the main, to grow field crops using a combination of European techniques and those employed by their Arab neighbours. But they soon found that it was virtually impossible to produce cereals in the quantities required.[151] At Ekron, an early colony established between Jaffa and Jerusalem, it was calculated that it was necessary to allocate up to 400 *dunums* (100 acres) a family simply to provide them with food.[152] Meanwhile, those few settlements which attempted more intensive methods based on the planting of vines or olives were equally unsuccessful. The result was that, for most colonies, survival was only possible as a result of their being rescued by the Paris banker, Edmund de Rothschild, who, from 1887 to 1900, not only provided them with regular subsidies but also attempted to direct them towards a more specialized form of agriculture concentrated on plantation crops like grapes, almonds and fruit.[153] This policy, too, ran into serious difficulties: as Schama notes, the fact that such a mix of crops was widely practised in the south of France was no guarantee that it would succeed in the very different conditions of Ottoman Palestine.[154] The collapse of the world price for many of these products and the repeated attacks of diseases like phylloxera only made matters worse.[155] The result was yet another period of organizational and financial crisis resulting in 1900 in Rothschild's activities being taken over by the newly formed Jewish Colonisation Association.

From then on the situation of the colonies began to improve, at least from a purely economic point of view. In the southern settlements around Caesaria and Jaffa which specialized in plantation crops, better methods, the introduction of marketing co-operatives and the continued use of cheap labour allowed a large increase in the production of crops like oranges and grapes with a ready European or Middle Eastern sale. For example, in the case of Petah Tikvah, just outside Jaffa, the area devoted to orange trees had reached 400 *dunums* by 1909 and output 236,000 boxes (15 per cent of that year's Palestinian exports) by 1913.[156] Meanwhile, in the northern colonies a new attempt was made to concentrate attention once again on cereals, but with an important admixture of horticulture and dairy farming. This too led to a considerable growth of incomes over the years 1907 to 1911 as yields increased and grain prices improved.[157]

Other problems still remained, however. Whatever the crop mix there was a continuing reliance on Arab labour while some Zionists were beginning to object to the proliferation in the settlements of non-agricultural workers like teachers, craftsmen and merchants performing the kind of tasks which immigrant Jews were supposed to have left behind.[158] Moreover, the cereal farming attempted in the north was regarded by many as monotonous and unrewarding, leading a number of settlers either to cultivate their land in association with Arab share-croppers or to rent it out entirely. Such developments proved deeply shocking to many of the more ideologically motivated Zionists who entered the country after the turn of the century, among them David Ben Gurion who was to write later of his experience in those years:

Among the early disappointments was the spectacle of Jews of the First Aliya (of 1882 and afterwards), now living as efendis, drawing their income from groves and fields worked by hired workmen or from occupations imposed on our people in their exile. It was clear that we could never achieve national rehabilitation that way.[159]

It was for this reason, among others, that the final mutation took place in 1909: the establishment of the first kibbutz at Deganiya, a co-operative enterprise based on mixed farming with limited use of Arab labour.[160] With this the Jewish settlers had finally developed the ideal instrument for colonizing a harsh and to some extent hostile terrain.[161] In the comparison between the well-organized kibbutz and the increasingly fragmented Arab village lies an important clue to the history of Arab/Jewish relations in the inter-war period.

11 The Iraqi provinces, 1880–1913

According to Hasan's calculations, the population of the Iraqi provinces rose from just over 1,250,000 in 1867 to 1,825,000 in 1890 and 2,500,000 in 1905.[1] Such figures must be treated with more than usual caution: they are based for the most part on estimates made by British consular officials who, for all their knowledge of the country, could not be expected to do more than guess at the size of the many nomadic and semi-nomadic groups often living in inaccessible mountain or marshy districts. There is a little more reason to trust the first rough census of the British period taken in 1919 which gave the total population as 2,694,282, consisting of 1,360,304 in the province of Baghdad (including 250,000 in the capital city itself), 785,600 in Basra province and 548,378 in the districts of Mosul then under British control.[2] A second, marginally more reliable, calculation made by Sir Ernest Dowson from local estimates in 1930 gives the slightly larger total figure of 2,824,000, of which only 900,000 of the rural population were described as 'settled' and the rest as nomads or semi-nomads.[3]

Given their origin, there is little point in trying to use such estimates to even hazard a guess at the possible rate of population increase in the period before 1914. The best that can be done is simply to suggest that, on the evidence, there was likely to have been some growth; and that, as elsewhere, this was probably due to a combination of greater security and a better supply of food. In addition, in the Iraqi case, there may well have been some extra advantage from the ending of attacks of plague – the last serious outbreak was in 1876/7 – and from the serious efforts to contain epidemics of cholera by the imposition of strict quarantine on river traffic.[4]

Another reason for suggesting a rising population at the end of the nineteenth century is the evidence of a substantial expansion of the cultivated area during the same period. Hasan suggests that this may have risen from something like 100,000 to 150,000 *dunums* in the 1860s to some 1,600,000 *dunums* (988,800 acres) in 1913.[5] Other sources give similar figures for the decade just before the First World War.[6] Further confirmation comes from a British estimate that total cereal production may have reached 250,000 tons during the same years, a harvest which, if true, would have required an area of some 500,000 acres.[7] Given the usual practice of a biennial rotation this figure would then have to be doubled to obtain an estimate of the total

cereal-producing acreage. A further, well-justified, assumption is that most
of the expansion in grain cultivation must have taken place in those
northern rain-fed districts of the country (notably the land around Mosul)
where transport was easiest.[8] But there was undoubtedly some expansion
along the Tigris, just south-east of Baghdad, as well.[9]

Transport and trade

An examination of the Iraqi experience during the years 1880–1914 reveals
yet another Middle Eastern example of export-led growth. Figures to
illustrate the increase in the value of trade are given in Table 69. They show
that sea-borne exports (including a small quantity of Persian goods in
transit) tripled between 1880–4 and 1910–13.[10] As elsewhere in the region
there was an initial period of growth in the 1880s, a fallback as the price of
most exported commodities tumbled in the 1890s, and then a decade of
very rapid increase just after the turn of the century. Table 69 also reveals
that half the total value of the provinces' exports were made up of four particular products — dates, wool, wheat and barley. Just how important was
the role played by the opening up of new foreign markets for these products
can be seen by the rough calculations about the cereal harvest made by the
Imperial Ottoman Bank for the years 1911 to 1913. These show that while
local consumption was estimated at 20,000 tons of wheat and barley exports
in a few good years reached 200,000 tons or ten times that amount.[11] Other
products which provided a significant portion of foreign sales included rice
(in years of good harvest), gall nuts from the north and horses, hides and
skins from the desert areas. As the export figures for the years 1880 to 1913
show (Table 69), Iraq was far from being a one-crop economy and derived
considerable advantage from the fact that if the supply of some products
failed or prices declined there were always others to take their place. This
was certainly some compensation for all the disadvantages which the
provinces faced in terms of unruly rivers, uncertain systems of transport and
general rural insecurity.

The value of imports rose a little faster than exports throughout the
period (for prices of exports see Table 70). But it was only in the last few
years before 1914 that a serious deficit on current account developed,
largely as a result of the arrival of large quantities of rails and other equipment for the proposed Iraqi sections of the Baghdad railway.[12] In most
years textiles provided between 33 and 40 per cent of purchases from
abroad. After that a second product which was also imported in increasing
quantities was sugar (see Table 69). What is less clear is the proportion of
goods arriving at Basra which were then trans-shipped on towards western
Persia. According to Curzon, writing in the early 1890s, about 20,000 to
25,000 mules a year were being sent from Baghdad to Khanaqin on the

Table 69   The value of Iraq's sea-borne trade, 1880–1913 (annual averages, £,000)*

	Imports			Exports				
	Sugar	Textiles	Total	Dates	Wool	Wheat	Barley	Total
1880–4			788[4]					940
1885–90			988	292[5]	268[5]	72[5]	22[5]	1208
1890–4	60[1]		1523	336	240	165	89	1453
1895–9	86[2]	451[2]	1222	257	321	64	77	1259
1900–4	91[3]	512[3]	1373	317	188	30	216	1536
1905–9	87	839	2019	402	222	129	260	1959
1910–13	256	1002	3170	487	273	151	619	2700

* Includes Persian transit trade.

Source: Hasan, 'Foreign Trade in the Economic Development of Iraq', 304–11, 317–18, 323, 334–8, 351–4.

Notes: 1 Excludes 1891.   2 Excludes 1896.   3 Excludes 1900.   4 1884 only.   5 1888–9 only.

Persian frontier, of which 7500 were loaded with manufactured goods 'mainly from Manchester'.[13] Later, in 1908, an official statement in London put a rough figure of £1,000,000 on the value of this overland trade with the east.[14] Unfortunately the British commercial reports from Baghdad provide no estimates of their own which could be used as a check.

Another feature of the provinces' sea-borne trade was its further re-direction towards Europe (notably Britain) and North America as a result of the ever increasing use of the Suez Canal. According to rough estimates of the value of Baghdad's foreign commerce (excluding the transit trade with Persia) for the years 1901 to 1904, goods worth an annual average of £1,600,000 were then being imported from Europe and North America as against only £250,000 from India.[15] The decline in India's share of Iraq's exports was slightly less important. By 1910/12, 23 per cent of Iraqi products were being sent to Indian ports compared with 29 per cent shipped to Britain.[16]

Table 70   The volume and price of Iraq's principal sea-borne exports, 1880–1913 (annual averages)

	Dates		Wool		Wheat		Barley	
	(long tons)	(£/ton)	(tons)	(£/ton)	(tons)	(£/ton)	(tons)	(£/ton)
1880–3	12,200	5.0						
1888–9	39,800	7.3	10,100	25.4	11,500	6.5	10,800	2.1
1890–4	55,700	6.1	10,000	24.2	33,200	4.8	34,300	2.4
1895–9	46,800	5.6	14,700	20.2	29,200	2.4	29,700	3.0
1900–4	63,500	5.1	11,700	16.3	9600	3.3	48,800	4.7
1905–9	67,900	5.4	9900	27.0	20,200	6.8	43,500	6.1
1910–13	67,800[1]	7.4	4200	64.0	17,700	8.7	66,900	9.1

Sources: CRs (UK) and Hasan, 'Foreign Trade in the Economic Development of Iraq', 304–18, 323.

Notes: 1 Excludes 1910.

It will now be clear that it was Britain which dominated the provinces' trade with the west. In the years between 1900 and 1913, it was the United Kingdom which provided nearly half of Iraq's imports and was the market for over a quarter of its exports. If India is included then the figures for Britain's share of trade in certain years (for example 1912–13) rise to two-thirds of imports and nearly half of exports.[17] In spite of Foreign Office fears of increasing European, and particularly German, competition in the years just before the First World War there is no sign that this British predominance was being seriously challenged.[18] In the three years 1911–13 for example, the United Kingdom provided an average of 45 per cent of Baghdad's imports as opposed to Belgium's 11 per cent, Austria–Hungary's 9 per cent and Germany's 5 per cent.[19]

Figures for the tonnage of shipping passing in and out of Basra make the same point. Not only did British vessels dominate the transport of goods between both Europe and India and Iraq but they also came to capture most of the local carrying trade around the coasts of the Arabian peninsula as well. Thus, whereas in the three years 1864/5 to 1866/7 Ottoman shipping dominated Basra's commerce with a total volume of nearly 75,000 tons (both steam and sail) as compared with a British tonnage of 21,000 tons, by 1896 the British volume had reached 137,000 tons while what was then called 'Arab and Turkish shipping' had fallen back to only 12,500 tons.[20] The inequality between the importance of British carriers and their major continental rivals was nearly as marked. In the years 1910–13, for instance, British shipping at Basra averaged nearly 240,000 tons a year as against Germany's 38,000.[21] Again, to look only at 1913, while twenty ships of the German Hamburg America Line called at the port, this was only a small number when compared with the 163 British steamers arriving there in the same year.[22]

Turning to the provinces' overland trade with their Middle Eastern neighbours the picture is much less clear. Apart from the rough estimates of the value of the transit trade with Persia, already given, there are no figures which would even begin to suggest an order of magnitude. The problem is further compounded by the fact that this type of commerce was so various and conducted in so many different districts. At the very least it has to be divided into two main categories. The first is one in which foreign products entering Iraq were redistributed to neighbouring areas: apart from the export of British goods to Iran in exchange for carpets and opium, European manufactures were sent west into the Syrian desert and south towards the Najd while the Persian goods, notably tobacco, continued to be sent along the northern caravan route to Aleppo.[23] Second, products of local origin were exported in all directions. These included the many thousands of camels driven westward to the Syrian provinces and then on to Egypt and the tens of thousands of sheep sold in Aleppo, Anatolia and

southern Russia.[24] Other local products sent to neighbouring countries
included hides and skins and small quantities of silk thread, grain and gall
nuts.[25] Given the complete lack of quantitive information there is no way of
comparing the rival importance of land as opposed to sea-borne trade.
There is also no way of discovering whether the value of overland transactions was growing over time. The best that can be done is to suggest that,
given the nature of this trade, it may well have responded fairly directly to
changes in the income of the agricultural population in the surrounding
areas, increasing in the 1880s, falling off in the 1890s, and then rising quite
rapidly during the first decade of the twentieth century.

A major role in the increase of Iraq's sea-borne and transit trade was
played by improvement in the cargo-carrying capacity of the steamers and
other craft at work on the river Tigris. As far as the Lynch line (The
Euphrates and Tigris Steam Navigation Co.) was concerned, it tried consistently, with the support of the Foreign Office and the Baghdad
Residency, to obtain permission to increase the size of its fleet. The
Ottoman authorities, rightly fearful that the Lynchs were being used as a
spearhead for the further extension of British commercial influence, just as
consistently tried to oppose such demands.[26] Given the imbalance of power
between the two contestants, however, the Turks were sometimes forced to
give way, notably in 1899 when Lynch's were finally given the right to tow
cargo barges and in 1907 when they were allowed to put a third steamer in
regular service on the river.[27] The result was to increase the capacity of each
vessel (with its associated barges) to at least 400 tons in the flood season,
when the river was at its highest, and 280 tons at low water.[28] During the
1880s the diaries of J. M. Svoboda, one of the Lynchs' clerks, reveal that the
major cargoes carried down river were wool, dates and a little rice according to season.[29] In the case of the wool, the bales were sometimes piled so
high that they almost completely surrounded the captain's bridge.[30] Lynch's
main competition came from the Turkish river line which in 1904 was
bought and then reorganized by the Sultan's Daira al-Saniya. It continued
to purchase steamers with barges, but because of technical difficulties
seldom managed to keep more than about five or six in regular service.[31] A
third competitor to appear just before the First World War was the locally-
owned Arab Steamship Company with three small vessels.[32]

In spite of all that has been written about the Lynch line, its exact role in
the increase in Iraq's river-borne traffic remains something of a mystery.
On the one hand, both the British Residence in Baghdad and the Lynchs
themselves had every reason to exaggerate the importance of the British line
and to play down the value of its Ottoman competitor. On the other,
relations between the company and the Residence were not always smooth,
with the latter often accusing it of charging monopoly prices and
obstructing wider British commercial interests.[33] In the middle of all this,

hard facts are few and far between. To take only one example, British
residency figures for 1899 and 1900 would seem to suggest that the British
company carried almost all goods reaching Baghdad from Basra by river.[34]
But as the Lynchs themselves may well have supplied the information for
both the value of their own cargo and that of total trade, the correspondence is probably not surprising. To make matters even more complicated, the Ottoman steamers must certainly have carried large quantities of
goods which, because they were owned either by the government or the
sultan, paid no duty and thus did not show up in the foreign trade statistics
at all. In these circumstances it is probably safe to say that the Lynch
monopoly, if it existed, was confined to goods arriving at Basra on private
account and could not possibly have extended to all agricultural goods
shipped to Basra for export. Such a finding relates directly to a second
problem area: that of the Lynchs' own charges. Figures from a number of
British trade reports suggest that in some years in the early 1900s it cost as
much, or nearly as much, to ship goods from Basra to Baghdad by Lynch
steamer as it did to send them out to Basra from Britain.[35] If true this must
certainly be taken as further evidence of the strength of the Lynchs' position
as far as the carriage of imported European goods was concerned. On the
other hand, the fact that the Residence itself was clearly so anxious to
publicize such charges and to indicate that it thought them too high could
also be taken as evidence of considerable pressure to get them reduced.[36] By
1909 Lynch's charges had been reduced to only two-thirds of the sea rates to
Europe.[37]

Elsewhere in the three provinces the growth in trade depended on an
expansion in more traditional means of transport. On the Tigris, north of
Baghdad, most goods continued to be moved by *kalak*, the large, open rafts
with a capacity of some 20 to 30 tons.[38] Local craft were also used on the
Euphrates and its branch canals, although with increasing difficulty as a
result of the very low levels of water to be found in certain sections during
summer.[39] At Basra too, such craft were necessary to load and unload the
cargo from ocean-going steamers forced to anchor in mid-river in the
absence of docks or quays.[40] Meanwhile, on land there were still considerable obstacles to the use of wheeled vehicles, and pack animals
remained the usual method of transport. In 1914, with the exception of a
short length of the Aleppo caravan route, there were no metalled roads
outside the major towns.[41] Again, most of the provinces' bridges were impassable to carts, consisting as they did of narrow plank walks supported on
a line of boats.[42] Only on the road between Baghdad and Khanaqin on the
Persian frontier were horse- or bullock-drawn vehicles used in any
quantity.[43] Lastly, there was as yet no help from the Iraqi section of the
Baghdad railway: by November 1914 only the short stretch from Baghdad
itself to Samarra had been completed.[44]

Agriculture and government policy towards the land

The almost total absence of reliable information and the enormous difference in agricultural practice between one part of the three provinces and another make analysis of developments in the rural sector difficult. As elsewhere there must be a general assumption that the growth in population and the expansion of the cultivated area was responsible for a steady increase in production. But, once again, the only figures which can be used to give any indication of changes in output are those for the sea-borne export of certain major crops (Table 70). If compared with figures for the 1870s in Table 34, these show a large rise in the volume of dates and cereals shipped abroad during the 1880s, followed by a period of much slower, more irregular advance, to 1910–13. However, in both cases there is some reason to suppose that total production may have increased faster than these figures indicate. Calculations by two European observers who visited Basra twenty years apart suggest that there was a widespread planting of new palm trees between 1901 and 1921.[45] As for cereals, it would seem likely that these same years witnessed a considerable expansion in the harvest in the districts around Mosul, only a portion of which was sent to Basra for export and the rest disposed of in Syria, Anatolia and Persia.[46] To the south, as already noted, there may also have been an increase in production in the land along the Tigris; but this has to be balanced against the evidence of diminished output in the Hillah–Diwaniyah area as a result of the further fall in the level of the Hillah branch of the Euphrates.[47] All efforts to create a viable system of water management in this district came to nothing as the Hindiyah barrage, built in 1890, began to give way after only a few years of service.[48] It was not replaced by a sounder structure until 1913.[49]

As for the crops grown, one change in practice came to assume an increasing importance: the substitution of barley for wheat. While the latter enjoyed no special advantage on world markets, particularly during the years of falling international prices in the 1890s, Iraqi barley was of a high quality and suffered only from the fact that its cultivators were accustomed to add quantities of dirt to it in an effort to increase its weight.[50] Other crops to experience an expansion in output during this period were rice and the leaves from the mulberry trees planted near Baghdad from 1906 onwards.[51]

With the spread of commercial agriculture, land itself became more valuable and was subject to an intensified struggle for control. As in the Syrian provinces to the west, the main contestants were the Ottoman authorities, anxious as always to increase tax revenues, the urban merchants and officials who controlled the local councils, and the tribal shaikhs and others who possessed actual rural power. As in the Syrian provinces, too, attempts to unravel this process are subject to a number of nearly insurmountable difficulties. Not only was the pattern of land holding and the system of land rights of enormous complexity but information about it is fragmentary. Such records as did exist were mostly destroyed by both the Turks and the British during the First World War.[52] In the years which followed, the efforts of the early foreign administrators to understand and to manage the system were no more successful than in Syria and Palestine.[53] In this difficult situation only a few generalizations are possible. The first concerns government policy: on the evidence of two decrees issued in 1881 there seems no doubt that the authorities deliberately put a stop to the issue of any more *tapu sanads*, having come to the belief, as Haidar suggests, that the state had already given away too much of its rights.[54] An obvious corollary to this belief would have been the introduction of a new policy aimed at the deliberate reassertion of the government legal ownership.

What happened in actual practice was somewhat different: on the one hand, an endless process of bargaining about taxes with those who actually controlled the land, on the other, the build up of huge royal estates consisting of areas either seized or simply reclassified as belonging to the Sultan in all parts of the three provinces but concentrated mainly in the Hillah–Diwaniyah area on the Tigris, the banks of the Tigris round Amara and the southern districts near Basra.[55] According to Cuinet's rough calculation, the Sultan already owned some 30 per cent of the cultivated land in Baghdad province by the early 1890s, compared with another 30 per cent belonging to the state, 20 per cent (some of it registered as *tapu*) to private individuals, with the remaining 20 per cent classified as *waqf*.[56]

When it comes to trying to discover how the various types of land were taxed or exploited the only certain evidence comes from the royal estates themselves. These were administered on the Sultan's behalf by the local officials of the Daira al-Saniya responsible directly to Istanbul. Such a close link with the ruler gave the estate managers numerous advantages: they were able to manipulate the provinces' system of irrigation as it suited them; they could attract labour by offering interest-free loans and the promise of exemption from military conscription; they had direct access to the boats of the Oman–Ottoman line which, anyway, the Daira began to administer in 1904. Perhaps most important of all they could call upon all the resources of the Ottoman Sixth Army which had its headquarters at Baghdad, using its engineers and surveyors to direct the construction of many new canals, drains, bridges and storehouses and its soldiers to collect rent and taxes from any recalcitrant tenants.[57] There is no reason to suppose that these same advantages did not continue after 1908 when the estates were transferred to a new administration, the Amlak al-Madawwara, under the control of the Turkish Ministry of Finance.[58]

For all the size of this administrative superstructure it does not seem that much of the royal land was exploited directly by the Daira authorities. In the case of the estates on the Tigris, for example, rights of control and revenue collection were auctioned at regular intervals (usually every five years) to the shaikhs of the tribes there.[59] Such a practice had the double advantage of releasing the Saniya officials from the expensive and onerous task of disciplining a semi-nomadic tribal workforce which still regarded the land as its own, while at the same time encouraging the breakdown of tribal solidarity by substituting monetary relationships for the older ties of kinship or protection. It also reproduced the situation to be found on the Egyptian *izba* and other large Middle Eastern estates in which the economies of scale to be obtained with respect to certain inputs like capital and technical expertise were combined with the possibilities of profit to be derived from the surplus produced by the peasant family farm.[60] Just how all this worked out in practice is less clear. Who, for example, decided what crop was to be grown and how? Given the important role played by the Saniya administration itself in providing credit and in bringing new land into cultivation for crops like rice it would seem likely that there was a con-siderable degree of central direction – but there is no clear evidence to support this.[61]

Elsewhere the pattern of ownership and control and the method of exploitation varied enormously, influenced by a great number of factors, among them the degree of government control, the nature of tribal power, the system of irrigation and many others. Probably the simplest division to make is that between the cultivated areas close to the main towns or along major trade routes or certain canals where there was reasonable security, a settled population and weak tribal power and the less secure, less settled, tribal districts beyond. In the first case there was considerable individual ownership and control, either by the peasant cultivators or by a growing class of largely urban-based landlords who were often able to use their official connections to build up large estates.[62] No contemporary figures exist for the division of such land into large or small properties but a British survey in 1930 reveals a considerable variation from district to district. Whereas in the Baghdad *liwa* only 162 of the 862 properties surveyed could be classified as small (i.e., from 1 to 64 acres) and 360 of them were very large (over 640 acres) the reverse was true in the neighbouring *liwa* of Dullaim where 2344 out of 2577 properties were in the first category and only three in the second.[63] As far as the large holdings were concerned the majority were rarely visited by their owners who preferred to leave the business of management to middlemen with share-cropping tenants.[64] But there were a few in which the proprietor took a more active interest in the land, perhaps like the Wali of Mosul, who owned land on the Tigris, in-vesting in a motor pump or some other work of agricultural improvement.[65] Meanwhile, taxes could be collected with a degree of certainty; and in some districts like the cereal-growing lands of Diyala the authorities even felt secure enough to award the tax farm to the peasants themselves.[66]

Beyond this first area was a second in which the government's authority was more tenuous but where it still tried to establish a system of individual ownership when conditions allowed. Just how this might be done is well illustrated in the following extract from a letter written by one of the first British administrators posted to the Middle Euphrates after the First World War. It concerns the history of a dispute over some property near Ghammas:

The land . . . is about 1,500 acres and nearly thirty years ago it belonged to a great tribe called the Khazal, who took no notice of the Turkish Government and did not pay any taxes. In 1889 the Turkish Government decided to do something so they sold the land, with an enormous amount besides − probably 30,000 acres in all − for a nominal sum to a rich man called Saiyid Hasan who stood well with them, on his promising to pay the necessary taxes. The whole business was accompanied by amazing bribery and fraud and the deeds of sale are so fatuous as to be entirely invalid. But the Turks provided troops to push out the tribes, and Saiyid Hasan managed to get possession and to cultivate the greater part of the land.[67]

However, as the letter goes on, the new owner was never able to obtain regular control of the particular piece of land in question − in spite of two military expeditions the tribesmen kept coming back − and, like so many others of his kind, he had to wait until the Mandatory period to assert his legal rights.[68] In the interim such men had to make whatever arrangements they could with the cultivators actually in possession.[69]

Finally, in the tribal areas proper the Ottoman authorities had no alternative but to deal with those who possessed local power. This might be the shaikh or *agha* himself; it might be some intermediary − like a *sirkal* − more closely connected with the cultivators themselves.[70] To make analysis more difficult, changes in the balance of power within a particular tribal group could happen very quickly as the Ottomans changed allies or fighting broke out within the group itself. Nevertheless, on the whole it seems safe to assert that, in the southern half of the country at least, this was a period in which the authority of most shaikhs was under increasing pressure.[71] On the one hand, some of their traditional functions of leading tribal self-defence against outsiders were no long required or, like the organization of a sparse, still semi-nomadic labour force, or the management of the irrigation system, better performed by men who lived closer to the land. On the other, they themselves were often quick to take advantage of the opportunities available to develop a new role as landlord and tax-collector, thus substantially altering their relationship with their former followers. In either case they came to distance themselves more and more from the day-to-day management of tribal affairs, sometimes to the extent of leaving the land entirely, and to rely more and more on intermediaries like the *sirkals* or their *hashiya* (private armed guards) to manage their property and to collect their rents and taxes.[72]

So much can be said in general terms. For the rest it is necessary to examine specific practices in specific parts of the country. In the present case it is hoped that two examples will be enough to give some indication of the complexities of the situation and of the large number of possible permutations. The first concerns the Kurdish mountains in the north-west where many of the *aghas* had managed to build up sizeable holdings of land, sometimes with the aid of *tapu sanads*, sometimes without.[73] These they exploited either by letting them out to share-croppers or by farming them themselves. On the whole, it seems to have been the irrigated land (usually watered by underground chain wells) which they preferred to keep under their own control, paying labourers to cultivate it with rice, tobacco or vegetables.[74]

The second example involves the arrangements developed in the south where title to large areas of tribal land was claimed by members of shaikhly families. What happened next depended on the balance of power between these new owners, the government authorities and the various strata of cultivators. In the case of the Sadun shaikhs of the Muntafiq, for instance, many of them experienced great difficulty in profiting from their parade of legal ownership, particularly after the turn of the century.[75] For one thing, their transformation from leaders to landlords not only destroyed their cohesion as a ruling family but also deprived them of much of their customary authority as warlords and protectors. For another, the Ottoman authorities made matters worse for them, first by deliberately forcing them to compete with one another for tax farms, then by withdrawing most of their troops from the Muntafiq region during the Balkan wars of the Young Turk period.[76] The result was a growing reliance by both the government and the absentee Saduns on the *sirkals* – the men who actually organized agricultural activity in the tribal areas – to forward as much of what was owed as they could be persuaded to.[77] In these complex circumstances the way in which the agricultural surplus was divided between the contending parties cannot possibly be spelled out with any degree of accuracy. While the Turkish Commission of Inquiry of 1911 into tribal disorder was certainly right to attribute part of the blame to the fact that the tribal lands were in the hands of a few powerful shaikhs who oppressed their fellow tribesmen, it is also true that these same shaikhs could only maintain their position with the help of a second group lower down in the Muntafiq hierarchy with their own links with both government authority and the commercial world of the exporters and merchants.[78] Such was the outcome of a process by which, in Batatu's analysis, the existing social cleavages within the tribal structure were given a new and specifically economic form.[79]

Any attempt at a short summary of the complex arrangements relating to the different types of land in the three Iraqi provinces is clearly impossible.

What can be done, however, is to make a few general comments about the effect of these, first on agricultural production, second on the distribution of the agricultural surplus. As far as the former is concerned it seems true to say that, as elsewhere in the Middle East, there were few medium or large estates in which the owners were willing to take an active interest in their land or to invest more than tiny sums of money in its improvement. One index of this is the small number of motor-driven pumps erected in the irrigation zone: only 143 by 1921, of which 103 were in the immediate vicinity of Baghdad.[80] The only major exception to this general rule were the Saniya estates which were certainly well managed by contemporary standards and which undoubtedly played a major role in increasing the output of field crops, particularly rice, during the period.[81] On the other hand, if the export figures are anything to go by, the existing pattern of land ownership and control, with all its obvious imperfections, was such as to permit a substantial growth in production. In the north and east the large proprietors continued to provide their tenants with the security and, via a system of crop-sharing, the credit which the Ottoman authorities were not able to give. In the south, including the Daira Saniya estates, a system by which decisions over production, irrigation and the day-to-day control of a highly mobile and often elusive labour force were left to local agents was probably the most efficient form of management in very difficult circumstances.

As for the distribution of the surplus, two points can be made. The first is that, for all its lack of overall authority, the central government seems to have been remarkably successful in appropriating a substantial share of total output. According to Haidar and Himadeh, basing themselves on British figures, the tithe on agricultural produce in the three provinces rose from just over £300,000 in 1890 to £527,000 in 1911.[82] To this latter figure should be added some thousands of pounds from silk and tobacco and a few other smaller taxes, as well as the much larger sum of £180,000 from the animal tax (levied on goats, sheep, camels and water buffaloes).[83] Taken together these figures indicate a level of taxation, about £0.33 per head of the rural and desert population, which is roughly in line with that of Egypt. What cannot be calculated, however, is the ratio of tax to total output. In the absence of any reliable figures, Haidar's attempt to estimate such a ratio for field crops based on the value of exports of dates and cereals has the obvious disadvantage that it neglects other exports like rice and would seem to exclude almost all the produce of the northern rain-fed zone.[84] That the Ottoman authorities were relatively assiduous in trying to maximize tax returns — at least until the last few years before the First World War — is shown by a variety of evidence. In 1911, for example, Gertrude Bell came across Turkish troops collecting the animal tax at the Shammar tribe's summer capital at Hatra, many miles into the western desert.[85] But, given the general weakness of its authority and the continued reliance on the farming of taxes through powerful intermediaries, it is impossible to agree with Haidar's final conclusion that nowhere in the world was agricultural production taxed so heavily as in Iraq's irrigated zone.[86]

The second point concerns the other division of the surplus, that between the actual cultivator and the man or men who controlled or even owned the land. While in many parts of the country, particularly in the north or round the major towns, it would seem likely that the superior economic and political power of the proprietor ensured him a substantial proportion of agricultural profits, in the south there is some evidence that a greater part of the surplus accrued to both middlemen or *sirkals* and cultivators. In the case of the former the reasons for this were obvious and stemmed directly from their direct control over production and over the working lives of their subordinates. In the case of the latter, the situation is less clear but it would seem that they derived some advantage from the fact that, given the general shortage of labour compared with the amount of cultivable land, members of semi-nomadic tribal groups required a special incentive to settle down. This at least was the case in the Muntafiq lands where it was sometimes necessary to offer tenants a much more favourable share of the final crop than peasants could obtain elsewhere in the interests of tying them more closely to the land.[87]

Industry

Factories with power-driven machinery hardly existed in the Iraqi provinces before 1914. Such as they were they were confined to a number of steam-powered woollen presses, two Ottoman military factories in Baghdad for making flour and cloth for uniforms and two ice plants.[88] Apart from the usual problems which faced would-be entrepreneurs everywhere in the Middle East in the shape of low tariffs, few credit facilities and a largely illiterate labour force, Iraqi industry faced the additional disadvantage of a particularly under-developed infrastructure in which, for example, Baghdad was the only town with regular supplies of pumped water and electricity.[89]

Workshop industry using man or animal power was very much more widespread. As in the Syrian provinces, the most important activity was the manufacture of textile goods of silk, cotton and wool. Here again, local artisans were able to benefit from an expanding internal market not only to compete with foreign manufactures in a large number of products but also, in the case of some Indian goods, almost to drive them out completely.[90] While producers in the larger cities like Baghdad and Mosul concentrated on more specialized items, like turbans and tablecloths often patterned with gold and silver, those in smaller centres tended to make rougher materials like sail-cloth, rugs and blankets.[91] In Baghdad, just before the First World War, there were at least 312 weaving shops, each with an average of two or three looms, 68 dye shops, 22 silk manufacturies and 7 textile printing works.[92] Of the raw materials used, most of the wool and, after 1906, the silk came from the provinces themselves, but a substantial proportion of the cotton had to be imported, usually as thread.[93]

Much of the remaining manufacturing activity concerned either the processing of food and other agricultural products or, of the greatest importance in an Iraqi context, the building of boats. In the case of Baghdad itself, the city possessed 116 flour mills in 1911, 24 sugar refineries, 35 tanneries and 2 plants for making sesame oil.[94] Arak, distilled from either grapes or dates, was made in Baghdad, Basra and Mosul; soap in Mosul.[95] Boats of all types were made at various places along the rivers, often with great skill. McNie mentions a Baghdadi blacksmith/mechanic, Joseph Haluka, who opened a yard in 1890 in which he built the hulls (and in one case the engine) of five steamers for the Lynch and Ottoman river lines. Though illiterate and unable to make a drawing or a plan he seems to have managed to lay out the frames and plates by eye.[96] Similar skills were to be found in Sulaymania where, according to Mark Sykes, other local craftsmen were able to make 10 to 20 breech-loading rifles a year modelled on the Martini–Peabody.[97] If nothing else, such activities are a powerful reminder of the talents possessed by populations in provinces so often condemned as sleepy and backward.

12 A century of economic growth and transformation : conclusion

During the nineteenth century the population of that part of the Middle East covered by this survey increased by roughly 300 per cent, from somewhere between 11 to 12 million to approximately 32 to 33 million. During the same period the value of the region's foreign trade increased even more rapidly, from under £10,000,000 a year (at current prices) to well over £100,000,000. Taken together, both sets of figures provide a good index of the growth experienced by the Middle Eastern economy between 1800 and 1914, whether this is measured in terms of the expansion of the cultivated area, the growth of agricultural output, or the increase in income generated by the sale of primary products to Europe. They also provide an insight into some of the major historical forces which lay behind this process of economic growth. One was the rapid expansion of the European market for a variety of Middle Eastern agricultural products, an expansion which, as elsewhere in the non-European world, allowed the region's agriculture to overcome the constraints imposed by limited facilities for the transport of bulk goods and the low level of local demand. A second was the establishment – in response to European political and military pressure – of strong, centralizing regimes in Istanbul and Cairo whose concern with security and more efficient methods of tax collection provided the framework in which population could grow and agricultural output expand. Third, demographic increase was further encouraged by the sudden, and so far inexplicable, disappearance of the plague as a major cause of death at the beginning of the nineteenth century as well as, later, by governmental efforts to reduce the impact of other serious diseases like cholera.

The result was a process which was infinitely more complex than most economic models either of growth through trade or of the consequences of links with European markets allow. It is certainly true that in certain areas (notably the cereal-growing lands of the Syrian and Iraqi provinces and districts producing pastoral products like wool and hides) growth was much as Myint and others have suggested: that is, output was expanded relatively easily in response to European demand on the basis of existing tools and techniques and with little resource to outside capital.[1] But there were many other areas like Lower Egypt and Mount Lebanon or like the citrus groves around certain major towns where the introduction of new crops or the

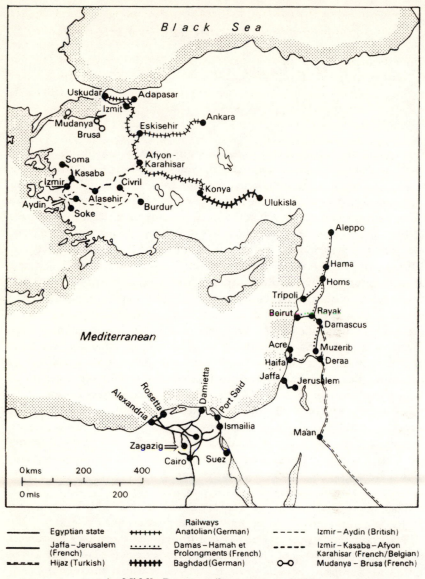

B l a c k   S e a

Uskudar
Adapasar
Izmit
Mudanya
Brusa
Soma
Kasaba
Izmir
Civril
Alasehir
Aydin
Soke
Burdur
Eskisehir
Ankara
Afyon-
Karahisar
Konya
Ulukisla

Aleppo
Hama
Homs
Tripoli
Beirut
Rayak
Damascus
Acre
Muzerib
Haifa
Deraa
Jaffa
Jerusalem
Ma'an

Mediterranean

Rosetta
Damietta
Port Said
Alexandria
Zagazig
Cairo
Ismailia
Suez

0 kms   200   400
0 mls   200

Railways		
——— Egyptian state	+++++ Anatolian (German)	- - - - - Izmir – Aydin (British)
——— Jaffa – Jerusalem (French)	.... Damas – Hamah et Prolongments (French)	- - - - Izmir – Kasaba – Afyon Karahisar (French/Belgian)
-●-●-●- Hijaz (Turkish)	++++++ Baghdad (German)	o─o Mudanya – Brusa (French)

4   Middle Eastern railway systems, *c.*1914

expansion of old ones required new methods, a substantial injection of capital and the creation of facilities for processing the raw product. Later, governments or official agencies like the Ottoman Tobacco *Régie* or the PDA intervened actively to raise productivity and quality still further through the introduction of improved seed and more efficient systems of control.

Models based on the assumption that the growth of agricultural exports to Europe was accompanied by the decimation of local handicrafts as a way of creating an expanded market for European manufactured goods are similarly over-simple.[2] In most parts of the Middle East artisans showed themselves to be remarkably tenacious, adopting new techniques when necessary and discovering or even creating new markets for their products. They were also helped by the steady rise in population which continued to provide new opportunities for Middle Eastern producers. For all these reasons there were certainly more textile weavers in the major Syrian towns at the end of the nineteenth century than there were at the beginning, and this pattern may well have been repeated in many other areas as well. By the same token, the presence of active foreign competition provided no absolute barrier to the creation of local factory industries, whether it was the silk mills of Mount Lebanon or the tobacco, cement or food processing plants of Egypt. Moreover, the commercial future of such enterprises was controlled by a multitude of factors − for example, access to raw materials, expertise and working capital − and not simply by forces emanating directly from the international economy.

A third model which, again, illustrates only a part of a wider truth is that of the importance for trade expansion of the establishment of an 'open economy' under colonial control.[3] In the case of the Middle East it was the local states themselves which performed certain key roles such as the introduction and enforcement of low tariffs and new systems of commercial law long before European political intervention was organized on a regular basis. The rulers of such states were also easily persuaded of the need to borrow large sums of money to improve infrastructures or simply to purchase expensive European goods like weapons and machines. It was only when foreign-imposed economic arrangements seemed directly threatened by the movement of popular revolt − as in Egypt − that there was a direct imposition of colonial control. Elsewhere, in Mount Lebanon after 1860 or in Istanbul after 1881, European interests were thought better protected by the imposition of an international economic order which fell short of systematic political regulation.

The application of simple generalizations to other aspects of Middle East economic transformation can be equally misleading. While it is true that peasant cultivators remained in control of the means of production in most parts of the region, this single fact disguises a multitude of different types of rural relationships and the development of a variety of different types of agricultural enterprise. The majority of peasants may also have been free, at least in theory, to grow what crops they chose without direct interference by merchant or landowner. But in practice the ability to expand production of many of the more lucrative crops was tied very closely to access to the seed, working capital and credit which only men like landowners and merchants could provide. The agricultural history of the Middle East in the nineteenth century is, of necessity, the history of the particular arrangements surrounding the cultivation of particular crops in particular areas.

In these circumstances what generalizations can be made? One concerns the growth in Middle East income during the century. While it is demonstrably impossible to calculate the gains from trade made by any one country or group of provinces other than Egypt — and then only for a few decades before the First World War — the fact that the value of exports clearly increased more rapidly than population suggests that such an increase must certainly have taken place. I have also tried to argue that the impact of this increase cannot have been more than marginally affected by the drain of part of the local surplus to Europe via the payment of interest on borrowed money or profits on capital invested nor, if it can be shown to have existed, via a persistently unfavourable balance of trade. On the other hand, a general rise in income must not automatically be assumed to have produced a rise in general well-being, as E. P. Thompson has pointed out forcefully in the context of the British Industrial Revolution, particularly when it was accompanied by a radical restructuring of existing social relationships and such a challenge to existing values and life styles.[4] It was also deeply influenced by geography and by the distribution of economic and political power. In the first instance the main gains from trade must have accrued to those involved in the production of export crops even if there was then some spread effect to other districts by means of the extra consumption of urban-produced goods or the wages paid to migrant labour. Again, I have argued that in most parts of the Middle East the bulk of the agricultural surplus accrued to the small number of families that managed to obtain control over a considerable proportion of the cultivated land.

Second, given the fact that so much of the surplus accrued via tax and rent to such a small class of landowners or land controllers, it is also possible to argue that little of it was reinvested in capital works or agricultural improvement. The greater part of it was either simply consumed — and consumed mostly in the towns in pursuit of an increasingly European style of life — or used as a basis for urban political activity. In the Syrian and Iraqi provinces it was those with money from land who were most likely to obtain official positions or, latterly, to obtain election to the Ottoman Parliament. In Egypt it was the large landowners who provided the colonial power with its most important local ally and who used this position to assert an increasingly important influence over local politics. Only in Anatolia itself was there a somewhat different process as a result of the fact that power there was seized, after 1908, by soldiers and bureaucrats who owed their position more to their official connections than their landed wealth. Meanwhile, most of what investment there was in the agricultural sector was the work of governments or, in a few cases, of foreign enterprises.

Third, the great increase in sea-borne trade with Europe involved a fundamental restructuring of many parts of the Middle East economy. In some cases such a restructuring was necessary if the area devoted to the production of cash crops was to expand in the first place. Lines of credit had to be established to provide producers with working capital, methods of transport improved and new systems of irrigation introduced where necessary. Later, the growth in trade itself began to produce important effects in many areas, leading to an intensification of monetary relations, an increase in agricultural specialization, and important changes in the relations between producers and those who controlled the cultivated land. Another series of effects involved the pattern of Middle Eastern trade. Even though it seems likely that the volume and value of commercial exchanges within the region may have increased in absolute terms over the century, the sector which enjoyed the most rapid growth and which tended to act as a focus for entrepreneurial efforts and local capital resources was that of trade with Europe and associated activities like infrastructural development and the construction of buildings in the major port cities.

The result was a significant geographical shift in economic power as the towns on the coast increased in size and prosperity much faster than most of those in the interior. There was also an equally significant socio-economic shift giving greater importance to the members of those local communities able to insert themselves into the chain of commerce and credit which linked Middle Eastern peasant with European manufacturer and consumer. In many cases a key role was played by merchants and bankers belonging to minority groups like the Christians of Beirut and Mount Lebanon and the Jews of Baghdad, leaving Muslim traders to deal with the less lucrative business in areas where foreigners or their local protégés could not maintain themselves. But it would be wrong to lay too much emphasis on this point. On the one hand, the relative importance of Europeans and local entrepreneurs varied greatly from one part of the Middle East to another depending on a number of variables including the ability of foreigners to deal directly with peasant producers, small retailers and others. As a rule it would seem from the economic history of Lower Egypt and the Anatolian coast that where such direct dealing was possible local middlemen were soon squeezed out. But where political circumstances were difficult — as in the cities of the Syrian interior — or where it was a question of ensuring a steady supply of raw material in a very competitive situation — as with the silk producers of Mount Lebanon — local expertise and local social commercial contacts were indispensable. On the other hand, there were certainly some important Muslim merchants in every Middle Eastern port city, even if their presence often seems to have been systematically ignored by the European consuls or by writers committed to the mistaken notion that there was a purely ethnic or religious division of labour.

Fourth, the major force or group of forces behind the restructuring of Middle Eastern economic life can be shown to have come from Europe and from the world economy. Bearing in mind the warning that these forces affected different parts of the region in different ways at different times, I have suggested that their impact could be analysed in terms of a three-stage process: first commercial, then financial and commercial, and finally political, financial and commercial. The purely commercial stage was the product of the early decades of the European Industrial Revolution and largely involved the expansion of trade and the type of political pressure necessary to eliminate monopolies, reduce tariffs and, in general, remove any obstacles to the free flow of goods. The second stage, the financial, began (at least as far as Egypt and the core of the Ottoman Empire was concerned) in the 1840s, a period when the inability of these two regimes to finance further reform out of tax revenues coincided with the establishment of the first European credit institutions designed to mobilize funds for large-scale lending to foreign governments. The fact that both regimes became increasingly dependent on foreign loans made it easier for European states and European banks and public works companies to put pressure on them to grant larger and larger concessions. Equally important, the situation was one which could be put to good use to engineer a further expansion of European trade once local governments themselves became important purchasers of European goods. Finally, in the period of competitive European imperialisms which began during the last quarter of the nineteenth century, Egyptian and Ottoman bankruptcy was used to establish international financial regimes in both capitals within which economic dependence was further reinforced by the systematic employment of political persuasion and, in the case of Egypt, by direct political control. The result of the whole process was the creation of a pattern of dependence in which the rate of growth of the Middle Eastern economy and the income generated in its various sectors was largely determined by outside forces like the price of exports, the availability of credit and pressures on the distribution of public revenues.

Fifth, it has been stressed repeatedly that both Ottoman and Egyptian governments played an important, if subordinate, role in the process of Middle Eastern economic transformation. The attempt to reform administrative structures, to strengthen armies and to bring distant provinces under central control was an authentic local response to fears of further European political and military encroachment into Muslim lands. But, in the event, such policies only exposed new weaknesses which increased dependence rather than reduced it. In these circumstances it proved difficult to resist foreign pressure for economic and financial concessions, the more so as they could often be presented in terms of the wide area in which the interests of Europe and local rulers seemed to coincide, whether in terms of improving security, increasing agricultural production or placing entire populations within the domain of a single system of commercial and criminal law. What it would be wrong to suggest, however, is that either the Ottoman or the Egyptian regimes always acted directly in terms of European economic interest or that they possessed the power to enforce particular policies in every part of their territories. Control over agricultural land in the Ottoman Empire is a case in point. Whatever pressure there might have been to introduce a proper system of registration, taxation or private rights of property, the actual result of policy was generally a bargain between the central government, local councils and men of rural power which was clearly neither in the interests of efficient administration nor the most profitable development of the region's agricultural resources.

Sixth, and finally, in the years just before the First World War a growing local awareness of this role of local government in the creation of a system of economic dependence produced the beginnings of a 'national' reaction among certain sections of the local élites, whether army officers and officials in Istanbul, bankers and merchants in Beirut, or entrepreneurs and professional men in Cairo. By 1914 there was fairly general agreement in such circles that political weakness was reinforced by economic weakness, that this weakness was partly the result of over-dependence on agriculture (to the exclusion of industry) and on foreign financial institutions, and that the only satisfactory way ahead was to use the state apparatus to intervene more directly in pursuit of a more 'national' economic policy. However, as developments after the First World War were to prove, such a programme was easier to articulate than to implement. In Egypt the embryonic National Bourgeoisie was so weak that it had to rely for political support on more powerful groups like the large landowners and the foreign business community with often quite different economic interests. In post-war Turkey, the regime established by Atatürk and the Republican People's Party remained embarrassingly dependent on foreign capital and on foreign enterprise even during the period of étatist policies in the 1930s. Nevertheless, by 1914, the beginnings of a movement directed against the structure of dependence established in the nineteenth century can dimly be discerned. On this subject let Charles Issawi have the last word. Writing in 1961 he noted:

In the last forty years, and more particularly in the last ten, three main shifts of power have taken place in the Middle East: from foreigners to nationals; from the landed interest to the industrial, financial, commercial and managerial interests; and from the private sector to the state.[5]

Notes

Preface

1 Quoted in C. M. Cipolla, *Before the Industrial Revolution: European Society and Economy, 1000–1700* (London, 1976), 119n.

Introduction: The Middle East economy in the period of so-called 'decline', 1500–1800

1 H. A. R. Gibb and H. Bowen, *Islamic Society and the West*, I, 1 (London, 1950), I, 2 (London, 1957). For other expositions of the 'decline' thesis see B. L. Lewis, *The Emergence of Modern Turkey* (London, 1961) and 'Some reflections on the decline of the Ottoman Empire' in C. M. Cipolla (ed.), *The Economic Decline of Empires* (London, 1970); P. M. Holt, *Egypt and the Fertile Crescent 1516–1922* (London, 1966), pt 2; C. Issawi, *The Economic History of the Middle East 1800–1914* (Chicago, 1966), 3–13. For a critique of this concept see R. Owen, 'The Middle East in the eighteenth century – an "Islamic" society in decline: a critique of Gibb and Bowen's *Islamic Society and the West*', *ROMES*, I (London, 1975).

2 For contemporary accounts of the alleged 'decline' see C. Volney, *Travels Through Syria and Egypt in the Years 1783, 1784 and 1785* (trans.), 2 vols (London, 1787), for example, II, 147 or 426, or Koçi Bey's analysis in N. Steensgaard, *The Asian Trade Revolution of the Seventeenth Century* (Chicago and London, 1974), 76–8.

3 See the widely differing estimates of Egypt's population between 1000 and 1800 in T. H. Hollingsworth, *Historical Demography* (London, 1969), 311 and J. C. Russell, 'The population of mediaeval Egypt', *Journal of the American Research Center in Egypt*, V (Cairo, 1966), 69–82.

4 For examples of the few works which try to find quantitative data on these relationships: O. L. Barkan, 'Essai sur les données statistiques des registres de recensement dans l'Empire ottoman au XVe et XVIe siècles', *JESHO*, I (1958), 20–31 and M. A. Cook, *Population Pressure in Rural Anatolia 1450–1600* (London, 1972); B. L. Lewis, 'Studies in the Ottoman Archives – I', *BSOAS*, XVI, 3 (1954), 'Nazareth in the sixteenth century according to the Ottoman *tapu* registers' in G. Makdisi (ed.), *Arabic and Islamic Studies in Honor of Sir Hamilton A. R. Gibb* (Leiden, 1965), and 'Jaffa in the sixteenth century according to the Ottoman *tahrir* registers', *Turk Tarih Kurumu Basımevi* (Ankara, 1969); and S. J. Shaw, *The Financial and Administrative Organization and Development of Ottoman Egypt 1517–1798* (Princeton, 1958).

5 See M. Weber, *Economy and Society* (trans.), 3 vols (New York, 1968); M. Rodinson, *Islam and Capitalism* (trans.) (London, 1974), chs 1–4; B. Turner, *Marx and the End of Orientalism* (London, 1978), ch. 3 and 'Islam, capitalism and the Weber thesis', *BJS*, XXV (1974).

6 For a critique of this view, S. Zubaida, 'Economic and political activism in Islam', *ES*, I, 3 (August 1972).

7 See the works reviewed in A. H. Hourani, 'The Islamic city in the light of recent research' in A. H. Hourani and S. M. Stern (eds), *The Islamic City* (Oxford, 1970); A. al-Azmeh, 'What is the Islamic city?', *ROMES*, II (1976).

8 See Lewis, *Emergence*, 28.

9   See F. Braudel, *Le Méditerranée et le monde méditerranéen à l'époque de Philippe II*, I (Paris, 1966), 493–7.

10 See R. Lopez, H. Miskimin and A. Udovitch, 'England to Egypt, 1350–1500: Long-term trends and long-distance trade' in M. A. Cook (ed.), *Studies in the Economic History of the Middle East* (London, 1970); M. Dols, *The Black Death in the Middle East* (Princeton, 1977), and his 'The second plague and its recurrence in the Middle East', *JESHO*, XXII, 2 (May, 1979); I. M. Lapidus, *Muslim Cities in the Later Middle Ages* (Cambridge, Mass., 1967), 39–40.

11 See H. Inalcik, *The Ottoman Empire* (London, 1973), pt 3 and 'Bursa and the commerce of the Levant', *JESHO*, III (1960), 141–5; G. W. Stripling, 'The Ottoman Turks and the Arabs, 1511–1574', *University of Illinois Studies in the Social Sciences*, XXVI (1940–2); A. H. Lybyer, 'The Ottoman Turks and the routes of Oriental trade', *EHR*, CXX (Oct. 1915), 586.

12 H. Inalcik, *The Ottoman Empire* (London, 1973), pt 3.

13 Barkan, 'Essai', 20–31; Cook, *Population Pressure*, 10–12.

14 Cook, *Population Pressure*, 10–12. See also, H. Islamöglu and S. Faroqhi, 'Crop patterns and agricultural trends in sixteenth-century Anatolia', *Review*, II (Winter 1979), 407.

15 L. Gücer, 'Le commerce interieur des céréales dans l'Empire Ottoman pendant le second moitié du XVIe siècle', *Revue de la Faculté des Sciences Economiques de l'Université d'Istanbul*, XI, 1–4 (Oct. 1949–July 1950), 169–70; F. W. Carter, 'The commerce of the Dubrovnik republic, 1500–1700', *EHR*, 2nd ser., XXIV, 3 (Aug. 1971), 388; O. L. Barkan, 'The price revolution of the sixteenth century: a turning point in the economic history of the Middle East' (trans.), *IJMES*, VI (1975), 6–7, 26; M. Aymard, *Venise, Raguse et le commerce du blé pendant le seconde moitié du XVIe siècle* (Paris, 1966); H. Inalcik, 'Quelques remarques sur la formation de capital dans l'Empire Ottoman' in *Mélanges en l'honneur de Fernand Braudel: histoire économique du monde méditerranéen, 1450–1600* (Toulouse, 1973), 236–7.

16 Lewis, 'Studies', 469–501 and 'Nazareth', 42, 423; W. D. Hütteröth and K. Abdul-Fattah, *Historical Geography of Palestine, Transjordan and Southern Syria in the Late Sixteenth Century* (Erlangen, 1977), 54–5.

17 Shaw, *Organization*, 12–19.

18 F. C. Lane, 'The Mediterranean spice trade: its revival in the sixteenth century' in his *Venice and its History* (Baltimore, 1966), 25–33 and 'The Mediterranean spice trade: further evidence for its revival in the sixteenth century' in B. Pullen (ed.), *Crisis and Change in the Venetian Economy* (London, 1973), 52–3.

19 See K. S. Salibi, 'Northern Lebanon under the dominance of Gazir (1517–1591)', *Arabica*, XIV, 2 (June 1967), 149–50.

20 See S. H. Longrigg, *Four Centuries of Modern Iraq* (Oxford, 1925), 10, 25, 40; Stripling 81–2; H. Inalcik, 'The Heyday of the Ottoman Empire' in *CHI*, 1, 330; Holt, *Fertile Crescent*, 56–67; R. Mantran, 'Règlements fiscaux ottomans. Le province de Bassora (2e moitié du XVIe s.)', *JESHO*, X (1967), 253–60.

21 A. Raymond, 'Les grandes épidémies de peste au Caire aux XVIIe et XVIIIe siècles', *BEO*, XXV (1972).

22 Shaw, *Organization*, 80.

23 See J. Bertin, J-J. Hémardinquer, M. Keul and W. G. L. Randles, *Atlas des cultures vivières/Atlas of Food Crops* (Paris, The Hague, 1971), map 9; F. Braudel, *Capitalism and Material Life 1400–1800* (trans.) (London, 1973), 112–13.

24 P. S. Girard, 'Mémoire sur l'agriculture et le commerce de la haute Egypte', *La Décade Egyptienne*, III (Cairo, An VIII/1800), 45.

25 See A. A. ʿAbd al-Rahim, *Al-Rif al-Misri fi al-Qarn al-Thaman ʿAshr* (ʿAyn Shams, 1974). Also references to al-Jabarti's descriptions in my 'Al-Jabarti and the economic history of eighteenth century Egypt – some introductory remarks' in A. A. ʿAbd al-Karim (ed.), *ʿAbd al-Rahman al-Jabarti* (Cairo, 1976), 21–8.

26 A. Raymond, *Artisans et commerçants au Caire au XVIIIe siècle*, I (Damascus, 1973), chs 4, 5 and 7.

27 Ibid., 182–4, 229, 231.

28 W. Hütteroth, 'The pattern of settlement in Palestine in the sixteenth century.

Geographical research on Turkish *defter-i Mufassal'*, in M. Ma'oz (ed.), *Studies on Palestine during the Ottoman Period* (Jerusalem, 1975).

29 Ibid., 6–9.

30 D. H. K. Amiran, 'The pattern of settlement in Palestine', *IEJ*, III, 2 (1953), 72–3 and III, 3 (1953), 197–9.

31 Gibb and Bowen, I, 1, 266–7.

32 See J. Poncet, 'Le mythe de la catastrophe hilalienne', *Annales*, XXII (1967), 390–6; C. Cahen, 'Quelques mots sur les Hilaliens et le nomadisme', *JESHO*, XI (1968), 130–3; T. Asad, 'The Beduin as a military force: notes on some aspects of power relations between nomads and sedentaries in historical perspective', in C. Nelson (ed.), *The Desert and the Sown: Nomads in a Wider Society* (Berkeley, 1973).

33 A. Cohen, *Palestine in the Eighteenth Century* (Jerusalem, 1973), 184–8. Also, Abbé Mariti, *Travels through Cyprus, Syria and Palestine* (trans.), II (London, 1791), 157–61.

34 See R. Davis, 'English imports from the Middle East, 1580–1780' in Cook, *Studies*, 196–9.

35 A. Russell, *The Natural History of Aleppo*, II (London, 1974), 335–6; H. Laoust, *Les gouverneurs de Damas sous les Mamlouks et les premiers Ottomans* (Damascus, 1952), 225, 230, 236, 243. See also D. Panzac, 'Le peste à Smyrne au XVIIIe siècle', *Annales*, XXVIII, 4 (July–Aug. 1973).

36 See Barkan, 'Price Revolution', 27–8; Cook, *Population Pressure*, 43–4; Inalcik, *Ottoman Empire*, 50–1.

37 H. Inalcik, 'Centralization and decentralization in the Ottoman administration' in T. Naff and R. Owen (eds), *Studies in Eighteenth Century Islamic History* (Carbondale and Edwardsville, Ill., 1977).

38 Barkan, 'Price Revolution', 7–8.

39 J. Carswell, 'From the tulip to the rose' in Naff and Owen, *Studies*, 353–4.

40 M. Genç, 'A comparative study of the life-term tax farming data and the volume of commercial and industrial activities in the Ottoman Empire during the second half of the eighteenth century' (trans.), *mimeo* of paper delivered to Symposium on South Eastern European and Balkan Cities and the Industrial Revolution in Western Europe, Hamburg, March 1976.

41 See R. Davis, 'English Imports' and *English Overseas Trade 1500–1700* (London, 1973), chs 2–4; Steensgaard, *Asian Trade*, ch. 2; A. C. Wood, *A History of the Levant Company* (Oxford, 1935).

42 Volney, *Travels*, II, 172–3.

43 P. Masson, *Histoire du commerce français dans le Levant au XVIIIe siècle* (Paris, 1911), 446.

44 F. Hasselquist, *Voyages and Travels in the Levant in the Years 1749, 1750, 1751, 1752* (trans.) (London, 1766), 397.

45 'Report on the commerce of Arabia and Persia' in 'Report on British trade with Persia and Arabia' by S. Manesty and H. Jones, Basra, 18 Dec. 1790, Factory Records – Persia and the Persian Gulf, *IO* G 29/21.

46 K. Hetteb, 'Influences orientales sur le verre de Bohème du XVIIIe au XIXe siècles' in *Journées Internationales de Verre: Annales du 3e Congrés Internationale d'Etude Historique du Verre* (Damascus, 1964); Baron de Tott, *Memoirs of Baron de Tott* (trans.), I (London, 1786), pt 1, 222.

47 Raymond, *Artisans et commerçants*, I, ch. 1.

48 See Inalcik, *Ottoman Empire*, 109–10; Gibb and Bowen, I, 2, ch. 7.

49 For some of the difficulties with the concept of 'surplus' see C. Keydar, 'Surplus', *JPS*, II, 2 (1975), 221–4.

50 See Inalcik, *Ottoman Empire*, 107–18; for details of the award of a particular *timar* see I. Beldiceaunu-Steinherr, M. Berindei and G. Veinstein, 'Attribution de timar dans le province de Trebizonde (fin de XVe siècle)', *Turcica*, VIII, 1 (1976), 279–90. For data about the proportion of land held in *timars* see O. L. Barkan, 'Feodal Duzen ve Osmanli Timari' in O. Okyer (ed.), *Turkiye Iktisat Tarihi Semineri* (1975).

51 See H. Inalcik, 'Capital formation in the Ottoman Empire', *JEH*, XXIX, 1 (1969), 127–30 and *Ottoman Empire*, 112; Islamöglu and Faroqhi, 'Crop patterns', 404–5.

52 Gibb and Bowen, I, 1, 1–26; Inalcik, *Ottoman Empire*, pp. 116–18.

53   O. L. Barkan, 'The social consequences of the economic crisis in later fifteenth century Turkey', Turkey, Economic and Social Studies Conference Board, *Social Aspects of Economic Development* (Istanbul, n.d.), 27–8; Inalcik, *Ottoman Empire*, 47, 49.

54   Gibb and Bowen, I, 1, 52n.

55   Shaw, *Organization*, 26, 31.

56   Holt, *Fertile Crescent*, 42.

57   According to the records for the four Palestinian sanjaks of Safad, Gaza, Jerusalem and Nablus for the 1530s studied by Lewis, 343 villages were registered as Imperial *khass* as against over 800 awarded as *timars* and *ziamets*; 'Studies', 473, Table 1.

58   See K. H. Karpat (ed.), *Social Change and Politics in Turkey: a Structural–Historical Analysis* (Leiden, 1973), 35; Barkan, 'Price revolution', 24–6; Inalcik, *Ottoman Empire*, 48.

59   Barkan, 'Price revolution', 26–7; H. Islamöglu, 'M. A. Cook's *Population Pressure in Rural Anatolia 1450–1600*: a critique of the present paradigm in Ottoman history', *ROMES*, III (1978), 130–1.

60   See Shaw, *Organization*, 32–3; Cohen, *Palestine*, 179.

61   See Inalcik, *Ottoman Empire*, 49 and 'Capital formation', 136; Holt, *Fertile Crescent*, 66–7.

62   Barkan, 'Price revolution', 24–5; Islamöglu, 'Critique', 130–1.

63   D. Urquhart, *Turkey and its Resources* (London, 1833), 107.

64   Inalcik, *Ottoman Empire*, 112; S. Faroqhi, 'Sixteenth century periodic markets in various Anatolian *sancaks*: Içel, Hamid, Karahisavi Sahib, Kutäya, Aydin and Menteşr', *JESHO*, XXII, 1 (Jan. 1979), 41.

65   Shaw, *Organization*, 22, 57–8. The *usya* might comprise as much as 50 per cent of an *iltizam*, A. A. ʿAbd al-Rahim, *Al-Rif al-Misri* (Cairo, 1975), 80.

66   Ibid., 56–7.

67   For example the peasant poems discussed in A. A. ʿAbd al-Rahim, 'Hazz al-Quhuf, a new source for the study of the fallahin of Egypt in the seventeenth and eighteenth centuries', *JESHO*, XVIII, 3. Also, Inalcik, *Ottoman Empire*, 112.

68   The best description of these changes is in Inalcik's 'Centralization and decentralization', *passim*.

69   Ibid., 33–4.

70   Ibid., 32.

71   See S. Mardin, 'Power, civil society and culture in the Ottoman Empire', *CSSH*, II, 3 (June 1969), 267; Inalcik, *Ottoman Empire*, 87.

72   Inalcik, 'Centralization and decentralization', 30; Gibb and Bowen, I, 1, 225–6; B. A. Cvetkova, 'L'évolution du régime féodal Turc de la fin du XVIe jusqu'au milieu du XVIIIe siècle', *Etudes Historiques à l'occasion du XIe Congrès International des Sciences Historiques*, Stockholm, Aug. 1960 (Sofia, 1960).

73   Inalcik, 'Capital formation', 129–30.

74   Quoted in Mardin, 'Power', 260.

75   For example, Holt, *Egypt and the Fertile Crescent*, 77–101; Raymond, *Artisans et Commerçants*, I, 4–16; D. Ayalon, 'Studies in Al-Jabarti: Notes on the transformation of Mamluk society in Egypt under the Ottomans', pt 2, *BSOAS*, III (1960), 291–5.

76   A. Raymond, 'Essai de géographie des quartiers de residence aristocratiques au Caire au XVIIIe siècle', *JESHO*, VI (1963), 84–95 and *Artisans et commerçants*, II (Damascus, 1974), chs 14 and 16; D. Ayalon, 'Studies in al-Jabarti', 1, *JESHO*, III (1960), 291.

77   Ayalon, op. cit., 291.

78   'Studies in al-Jabarti', 3, *JESHO*, III (1960), 310.

79   S. J. Shaw, 'Landholding and land-tax revenues in Ottoman Egypt' in P. N. Holt (ed.), *Political and Social Change in Modern Egypt* (London, 1968), 100 and *Organization*, 8–9; Gibb and Bowen, I, 1, 230–1.

80   ʿAbd al-Rahim has a useful table in which he provides dates of the first occasion on which members of different groups of native-born Egyptians obtained rural *iltizams*, e.g. merchants in 1728, women in 1732, *Al-Rif al-Misri*, 88. For the holdings of members of the *Ulama* see A. L. al-Sayyid Marsot, 'The wealth of the ulama in late eighteenth century Egypt', in Naff and Owen, *Studies*, 205–9.

81   The entry of native-born Egyptians into the ranks of tax-farmers and the intensified
     competition for tax-farms which this must have produced may well account for the fact
     that the numbers of *multazims* increased rapidly during the eighteenth century from just
     over 1700 in 1658—60 to over 4400 at the time of the French Expedition – with a
     consequent decline in the average size of *iltizams*: 'Abd al-Rahim, *Al-Rif al-Misri*, 88.
82   P. S. Girard, 'Mémoire sur l'agriculture, l'industrie et le commerce de l'Egypt', in
     Description de l'Egypte, II (Paris, 1809), 589; Comte Esteve, 'Mémoire sur les finances de
     l'Egypte', in *Description de l'Egypte*, I (Paris, 1809), 319—20.
83   Shaw, *Organization*, 22—3, 57.
84   'Abd al-Rahman al-Jabarti, *'Aja'ib al-Athar*, II (Bulaq, 1297 A.H.), 274. See also A. A.
     'Abd al-Rahim, 'Financial burdens on the peasants under the aegis of the iltizam system
     in Egypt', to be published in A. L. Udovitch (ed.), *Land, Population and Society:
     Studies in the Economic History of the Middle East from the Rise of Islam to the Nine-
     teenth Century* (forthcoming).
85   For a further expansion of this point see my 'Al-Jabarti and the economic history of late
     eighteenth century Egypt'.
86   A. K. Rafeq, 'Local forces in Syria in the seventeenth and eighteenth centuries' in V. J.
     Parry and M. E. Yapp (eds) *War, Technology and Society in the Middle East* (London,
     1975), 282—3.
87   Cohen, *Palestine*, 179—84; A. K. Rafeq, *al-'Arab wa-al-'uthmaniyyun 1517—1917*
     (Damascus, 1974), 120.
88   A-K. Rafeq, *The Province of Damascus, 1723—1783* (London, 1966), 91—2.
89   H. L. Bodman, *Political Factions in Aleppo, 1760—1826* (Chapel Hill, 1963) 93ff.; A-K.
     Rafeq, 'Changes in the relationship between the Ottoman central administration and
     the Syrian provinces from the sixteenth to the eighteenth century', in Naff and Owen,
     Studies, 65—6.
90   See Rafeq, *Province*, chs 3—4.
91   See Rafeq, 'Changes', 60.
92   See A-K. Rafeq, 'Economic relations between Damascus and the dependent countryside,
     1743—1771', in Udovitch, *Land, Population and Society*.
93   Ibid.
94   See I. F. Harik, *Politics and Change in a Traditional Society: Lebanon 1711—1845*
     (Princeton, 1968), 21—69.
95   Ibid., 21.
96   D. Urquhart, *The Lebanon: A History and a Diary*, I (London, 1860), 183—4.
97   Cohen, *Palestine*, 179—81.
98   Ibid., 9—10.
99   Ibid., 87.
100 Ibid., 11—17.
101 Ibid., 39—40, 71.
102 Ibid., 21—3.
103 See U. Heyd, *Ottoman Documents on Palestine 1552—1615* (Oxford, 1960), 45—89;
     Volney, *Travels*, II, 328ff.
104 Inalcik, *Ottoman Empire*, 105. Also Gibb and Bowen, I, 1, 202—3.
105 Holt, *Fertile Crescent*, ch. 19 ; Longrigg, *Modern Iraq*, chs 6—8. Also Sir H. Jones
     Brydges' comments about the relatively high revenues obtained from the province of
     Baghdad, *An Account of the Transactions of H.M.'s Mission to the Court of Persia in the
     years 1807—1811, and a Brief History of the Wahauby*, II (London, 1834), 17—18.
106 Holt, *Fertile Crescent*, 148.
107 A. H. Hourani, 'The Fertile Crescent in the 18th century' in his *A Vision of History*
     (Beirut, 1961).
108 The major study of this relationship is Raymond's *Artisans and commerçants*, especially,
     II, chs 9, 10, 13, 14. But also, Bodman, *Aleppo*, 55—64; Rafeq, 'Economic relations'.
109 See G. Baer, 'Monopolies and restrictive practices of Turkish guilds', *JESHO*, XIII, 2
     (April 1970); H. Gerber, 'Guilds in seventeenth century Anatolian Bursa', *AAS*, XI, 1
     (Summer 1976), Inalcik, *Ottoman Empire*, 150—62; Raymond, *Artisans and
     commerçants*, II, ch. 12.

110 Raymond, op. cit., 650, 652.
111 See J. W. Livingstone, 'Ali Bey Al-Kabir and the Jews', *MES*, VII, 2 (May 1971), 221–5.
112 Inalcik, *Ottoman Empire*, 156.
113 See al-Sayyid Marsot, 'Wealth of the ulama', 212–16.
114 See, for example, A. Raymond, 'Quartiers et mouvements populaires au Caire au XVIIIe siècle' in Holt, *Political and Social Change*; G. Baer, 'Popular revolt in Ottoman Cairo', *Der Islam*, LIV, 2 (1977); R. W. Olson, 'The Esnaf and the Patrona Halil rebellion of 1730: a realignment of Ottoman politics?', *JESHO*, XVII, 3 (Sept. 1974) and 'Jews, Janissaries, Esnaf and the revolt of 1740 in Istanbul. Social upheaval and political realignment in the Ottoman Empire', *JESHO*, XX, 2 (May 1977).
115 For useful introductions to the voluminous literature on this subject see E. J. Hobsbawm's introduction to K. Marx, *Pre-capitalist Economic Formations* (trans.) (London, 1964) and Turner, *Orientalism*, chs 1 and 2. See also P. Anderson, *Passages from Antiquity to Feudalism* (London, 1974) and *Lineages of the Absolutist State* (London, 1974); T. Asad and H. Volpe, 'Concepts of Modes of Production', *ES*, V (1976); S. Avineri (ed.) *Karl Marx on Colonialism and Modernization* (New York, 1968); C. Keydar, 'The dissolution of the Asiatic mode of production', *ES*, V (1976).

1: The Middle East economy in 1800

1   See C. Issawi, 'Population and resources in the Ottoman Empire and Iran' in Naff and Owen, 'Studies', 152–4; W. Eton, *A Survey of the Turkish Empire* (London, 1798), 266–83.
2   The exact population of the empire at this period will probably never be known. I have taken C. Issawi's 'guesstimate' for Anatolia based on the 1831 and later censuses ('Population', 157) and J. A. McCarthy's 'guesstimate' for Egypt based on a reworking of the data from the French Expedition and the 1846 census ('Nineteenth-century Egyptian population', *MES*, XII, 3 (Oct. 1976), 16). The figure for Mount Lebanon is based on reports of a census taken in 1851 which gave the total male population as just under 100,000, details of which can be found in 'Survey of the population of Lebanon and Syria' (Beirut, 1861), FO 226/158. The general estimates for the total population of Syria are based on figures to be found in Issawi, *Economic History*, 209. That of Iraq is based on M. S. Hasan's estimate of the population in 1867, 'Growth and structure of Iraq's population, 1867–1947' parts of which are reproduced in Issawi, *Economic History*, 155–62.
3   See C. Issawi, 'Economic change and urbanization in the Middle East' in I. M. Lapidus (ed.), *Middle Eastern Cities* (Berkeley and Los Angeles, 1969), 102–8.
4   Ibid., 103.
5   Ibid., 105–6; J. Abu-Lughod, 'Varieties of urban experience: contrast, coexistence, and coalescence in Cairo', in Lapidus, *Middle Eastern Cities*, 167–8.
6   See M. M. Alexandrescu-Dersca, 'Contribution à l'étude de l'approvisionnement en blé de Constantinople au XVIIIe siècle', *Studia e Acta Orientalia* (Bucharest), I (1957), 15.
7   See Issawi, 'Economic change', 105–6; Abu-Lughod, 'Urban experience', 164.
8   See Issawi, 'Economic change', 105–6; Abu-Lughod, 'Urban experience', 167–8; Panzac, 'La peste', 1085.
9   (Citizen) Renati, 'Topographie physique et medicale du Vieux-Kaire', *La Décade Egyptienne*, II (An VIII), 187.
10 Abu-Lughod, 'Urban experience', 167–8; A. N. Groves, *Journal of a Residence at Baghdad during the Years 1830 and 1831* (London, 1832). For a contemporary European equivalent see R. Cobb, *The Police and the People: French Popular Protest 1789–1820* (Oxford, 1970), 230–4.
11 'La peste', 1085, 1092–3.
12 M. Jomard, 'Description de la ville et de la citadelle du Caire', *DE*², XVIII (Paris, 1829), 370.
13 A. Katznelson, 'Vital statistics in Palestine', in Congrès International de Medécine Tropicale et d'Hygiène, *Comptes Rendus* (Cairo, 1932), 900–1.
14 M. R. El-Shanawany, 'The first national life tables for Egypt', *EC*, 162 (March 1936). See also W. Cleland, 'A population plan for Egypt', *EC*, 185 (May 1939), 463, who gives

the life expectancy in 1927 as about 30. For thirteenth-century England see J. C. Russell, 'Population in Europe 500–1500' in C. M. Cipolla (ed.) *The Fontana Economic History of Europe*, I, *The Middle Ages* (London, 1972), 47.

15 Katznelson, 'Vital statistics', 900–1.

16 For useful general studies of Middle Eastern geography, see W. B. Fisher, *The Middle East*, 7th edn (London, 1978); D. G. Hogarth, *The Nearer East* (London, 1902); W. C. Brice, *South-West Asia* (London, 1966); E. Wirth, *Agrargeographie der Irak* (Hamburg, 1962); and *Syrien: Eine Geographische Landeskunde* (Darmstadt, 1971).

17 E. Hirsch, *Poverty and Plenty on the Turkish Farm* (New York, 1970), 2.

18 Y. Asfour provides such a table for 1948–56, *Syria: Development and Monetary Policy* (Cambridge, Mass., 1959), 22.

19 J. S. Fraser saw carts in northern Iraq, *Travels in Koordistan, Mesopotamia*, I (London, 1840), 94. Volney mentions that there were no wheeled vehicles in Syria, *Travels*, II, 419. A. Granott maintains that the first carts brought into Palestine in the modern period were those introduced during the Egyptian occupation in the 1830s, *The Land System in Palestine* (trans.) (London, 1952), 71. C. Fellows states that the only transport in Izmir was by camel, *A Journal Written during an Excursion in Asia Minor*, 1838 (London, 1839), 9.

20 R. W. Bulliet, *The Camel and the Wheel* (Cambridge, Mass., 1975).

21 See Hütteroth, 'Pattern of settlement', 5–9; H. Margalit, 'Some aspects of the cultural landscape during the first half of the nineteenth century', *IEJ*, XIII, 3 (1963), 212–15. For an interesting discussion of the differences between mountain and plain later in the nineteenth century by the British Consul, Jago, see *CR* (UK) Beirut 1874, *PP*, 1875, LXXV, 372–5.

22 In the mid-twentieth century a third of Anatolia's cultivated land was in the coastal plain and the remaining two-thirds on the central plateau, Hirsch, *Poverty and Plenty*, 1. At the beginning of the nineteenth century the proportion of cultivated land along the coast is likely to have been considerably higher.

23 See Urquhart, *Turkey and its Resources*, ch. 7; F. E. Bailey, *British Policy and the Turkish Reform Movement* (Cambridge, Mass., 1942), 77–8.

24 M. A. Ubicini, *Letters on Turkey* (trans.), I (London, 1856), 318–20.

25 *Richard Wood Papers* (St Antony's College, Oxford), Notebook, 'Route from Konieh to Kutaya'.

26 M. E. Meeker, 'The great family aghas of Turkey: a study of changing political culture' in R. Antoun and I. Harik (eds), *Rural Politics and Social Change in the Middle East* (Bloomington, 1972), 240; P. de Tchihatcheff, *Le Bosphore et Constantinople* (Paris, 1864), 110.

27 For the crops grown in Syria at this period see Volney, *Travels*, I, 318–25.

28 See T. Tresse, 'L'irrigation dans le Ghota de Damas', *REI* (1929).

29 According to Volney the cereals grown in Mount Lebanon were only sufficient to feed its population for three months a year, *Travels*, II, 72. See also E. Blondel, *Deux ans en Syrie et en Palestine* (Paris, 1840), 29; D. Chevalier, 'Les cadres sociaux de l'économie agraire dans le Proche-Orient au début du XIXe siècle: le cas de Mont Liban', in Cook, *Studies*, 334.

30 C. Audebeau, 'Le region de Rosette et l'irrigation perenne avant le XIXe siècle', *BIE*, X (1927/8), 97–8.

31 For detailed studies of Egyptian crops and Egyptian agricultural practice at this time, see Girard, 'Mémoire', DE^1, *passim*. L. Reynier, 'Considérations générales sur l'agriculture de l'Egypte et sur les améliorations dont elle est susceptible', *Mémoires du l'Egypte publiés pendant les campagnes du General Bonaparte*, IV (Paris, An x), 41–65. Also H. A. B. Rivlin, *The Agricultural Policy of Muhammad ʿAli in Egypt* (Cambridge, Mass., 1961), ch. 8.

32 Girard, 'Mémoire', DE^1, 583–4.

33 Ibid., 564ff.

34 J. Mazuel, *L'Oeuvre géographique de Linant de Bellefonds* (Cairo, 1937), 131. Girard, 'Mémoire', 557, 564.

35 For conditions in the north see C. J. Rich, *Narrative of a Residence in Koordistan*, I

(London, 1836), 133–4. Also J-B. L. J. Rousseau, *Description de la Pachalik de Bagdad* (Paris, 1809), 82, 100.

36　See J. Batatu, 'The shaikh and the peasant in Iraq, 1917–1958', Ph.D. (Harvard, 1960), 5; Wirth, *Irak*, map 11; Rousseau, *Description*, 61, 80.

37　For a general discussion of the two rivers see, M. G. Ionides, *The Regime of the Rivers Euphrates and Tigris* (London, 1937); Sir W. Willcocks, *The Irrigation of Mesopotamia* (London, 1911), 8–9.

38　Calculations made during the years 1939–41 show that in any one year there could be up to ten times as much water in the rivers at flood time as at low water. In addition, the volume of water in both rivers could vary as much as 400 per cent from year to year. Ionides, *Regime*, 3.

39　R. A. Fernea, *Shaykh and Effendi* (Cambridge, Mass., 1970), 9.

40　IBRD, *The Economic Development of Iraq* (Baltimore, 1957), 4.

41　For a fuller treatment of Ottoman land law see Gibb and Bowen, I, 1, ch. 5, and the sources quoted there.

42　Ibid., 147–8, 151, 255–6; M. D'Ohsson, *Tableau général de l'Empire Ottoman*, III (Paris, 1820), 368–9; A. du. Velay, *Essai sur l'histoire financière de la Turquie* (Paris, 1903), 46–50; Rafeq, 'Economic relations'; Shaw, *Organization*, 37–8.

43　See H. Cattan, 'The Islamic Law of Waqf', in M. Khadduri and A. J. Keibesny (eds), *Law in the Middle East*, I (Washington DC, 1955), 209–10; Y. Artin, *Propriété foncière en Egypt* (Cairo, 1883), 82–90; Rivlin, *Agricultural Policy*, 32–6.

44　For a discussion of this point see ibid., 33–4. For other views see Estève, 'Mémoire sur les finances', 332; Al-Sayyid Marsot, 'Wealth', 208–9.

45　Al-Jabarti, *ʿAjaʾib al-Athar*, IV, 93–4, 141. For a figure for the whole Ottoman Empire in the mid-nineteenth century see R. H. Davison, *Reform in the Ottoman Empire 1856–1876* (Princeton, 1963), 257.

46　I. F. Harik, 'The Impact of the domestic market on rural–urban relations in the Middle East', in Antoun and Harik, *Rural Politics*, 345, and *Politics and Change*, 27–8.

47　For example, Girard, 'Mémoire', *DE*[1], 580.

48　M-A. Lancret, 'Mémoire sur le systeme d'imposition teritoriale et sur l'administration des provinces de l'Egypt', in *Description de l'Egypt*, I (Paris, 1809), 235; Rafeq, 'Economic relations'.

49　Harik, *Politics and Change*, 27–8.

50　Gibb and Bowen, I, 1, 240–2.

51　Batatu, 'The shaikh and the peasant', 17.

52　See Issawi, *Economic History*, 163; S. Haidar, 'Land problems of Iraq' in Issawi, *Economic History*, 164–6.

53　On the *mushaa* system and its possible origins see Y. Firestone, 'Faddan and musha: land population and the burden of impositions in the lowlands of Palestine in late Ottoman times', to be published in Udovitch, *Land, Population and Society*; A. Latron, *La vie rurale en Syrie et au Liban* (Beirut, 1936), 14–18, 182–203; J. Weulersse, *Paysans de Syrie et du Proche-Orient* (Paris, 1946), 99–109; Granott, *Land Systems*, 174–9.

54　For such speculation about its origins see Weulersse, *Paysans*, 107–9.

55　Lancret, 'Mémoire', 246–7.

56　Gibb and Bowen, I, 1, 240.

57　See Shaw, *Organization*, 64, 97; ʿAbd al-Rahim, *al-Rif al-Misri*, 65–124.

58　Quoted in Gibb and Bowen, I, 1, 269n–70n; for Syria see G. Douin (ed.), *Le mission de Baron de Boislecomte: L'Egypte et la Syrie en 1833* (Cairo, 1927), 226.

59　L. Tallien, 'Mémoire sur l'administration de l'Egypte à l'époque de l'arrivé des Français', *La Decade Egyptienne*, III, 218.

60　Rich, *Koordistan*, I, 96.

61　*Richard Wood Papers*, Notebook, 'Memorandum and notes', Baghdad, Aug. 1836.

62　S. N. Spyridon, 'Annals of Palestine, 1821–1841', *JPOS*, XVIII (1936), 74; J. S. Buckingham, *Travels among the Arab Tribes Inhabiting the Countries of Syria and Palestine* (London, 1825), 180.

63　(Citizen) Shulkowski, 'Description de la route du Kaire à Salehyeh', *La Décade Egyptienne*, I (An VII), 27–8.

64 M. Otter, *Voyage en Turquie et en Perse*, II (Paris, 1748), 197.
65 For example, Spyridon, 'Annals', 74; Volney, *Travels*, II, 64.
66 Al-Jabarti in Gibb and Bowen, I, 1, 269n–70n; G. Baer, 'Fellah and townsman in Ottoman Egypt', *AAS*, VIII, 3 (1972), 226–7.
67 H. Inalcik, verbal contribution to discussions during the Colloquium on the Middle East in the Eighteenth Century, University of Pennsylvania, 1971.
68 Tallien, 'Mémoire', 211; Shaw, *Organization*, 74–85; J. L. Burckhardt, *Travels in Syria and the Holy Land* (London, 1822), 187–8, 300.
69 Shaw, *Organization*, 80–5.
70 See for example, the comments of the British Ambassador at Istanbul; H. Granville, *Observations sur l'état actuel de l'Empire Ottoman*, ed. A. S. Ehrenkreutz (Ann Arbor, 1965), 26.
71 Shaw, *Organization*, 307.
72 J. L. T. Reynier, *State of Egypt after the Battle of Heliopolis* (trans.) (London, 1802), 66; W. F. Lynch, *Narrative of the U.S. Expedition to the River Jordan and the Dead Sea* (Philadelphia, 1849), 149.
73 J. F. Jones, 'Journal of a steam-trip to the north of Baghdad, 5 Nov. 1846', in *Selections from the Records of the Bombay Government*, XLIII (Bombay, 1857), 4.
74 C. Neibuhr, *Travels through Arabia and other Countries in the East* (trans.), I (Edinburgh, 1792), 37; Burckhardt, *Travels*, 301–2.
75 See Burckhardt, *Travels*, 299.
76 See, for example, 'Abd al-Rahim's gloomy conclusion, *al-Rif al-Misri*, 249–54.
77 See T. Shanin, 'Introduction' in Shanin (ed.), *Peasants and Peasant Societies* (Harmondsworth, 1971) and 'The nature and logic of the peasant economy' 1–3, *JPS*, I, 1 and 2 (Oct. 1973, Jan. 1974); K. Post, 'Peasantisation and rural class differentiation in western Africa', *ISS Occasional Papers* (The Hague, Sept. 1970).
78 On the problem of maintaining a stable labour force see A. S. Barnett, 'A sociological study of the Gezira scheme, Sudan', Ph.D. (Manchester, 1968).
79 Lancret, 'Mémoire', 244.
80 C. Audebeau and V. Mosséri, 'Le labourage en Egypte', *BIE*, 5th ser. x (1916), 125–6; CR (UK) Beirut 1873, *PP*, 1874, LXVII, 862–3; Gibb and Bowen, I, 1, 264n.
81 See G. Robinson, *Three Years in the East* (London/Paris, 1837), 194.
82 P. Stirling, 'The domestic cycle and the distribution of power in Turkish villages' in J. Pitt-Rivers (ed.), *Mediterranean Countrymen* (Paris, The Hague, 1963), 207.
83 For Anatolia see Levant Herald, *The Famine in Asia Minor* (Constantinople, 1875), 133.
84 For example, H. Couvidou, *Etude sur l'Egypte contemporaine* (Cairo, 1873), 208.
85 Gibb and Bowen, I, 1, 242. Also, Ubicini, *Letters*, I, 323.
86 Rich, *Narrative*, 134.
87 G. A. Olivier, *Voyage dans l'Empire Ottoman, l'Egypte et la Perse*, III (Paris, An 12), 287–90.
88 Shaw, *Organization*, 56–9; Burckhardt, *Travels*, 297.
89 Burckhardt, *Travels*, 297.
90 See Girard, 'Mémoire', *DE¹*, 583–4; Volney, *Travels*, II, 318–25.
91 (Citizen) Girard, 'Notice sur l'aménagement et le produit des terres de la province de Damiette', *La Décade Egyptienne*, I, 232–3, 243.
92 Girard, 'Mémoire', *Decade*, 73.
93 Cohen, *Palestine*, 13, 21.
94 For the view of the village as an independent and self-sufficient unit see Gibb and Bowen, I, 1, 159–60, 211, 213. I have attempted to criticize this view in my 'The Middle East in the eighteenth century'.
95 See Russell's description of some of the villages near Aleppo, *Natural History*, I, 39–40. For a description of the wide range of village specialization in late nineteenth-century Egypt see references to 'Ali Pasha Mubarak, *al-Khitat al-Taufiqiya al-Jadida*, 20 vols (Cairo, 1887–9) in J. Berque, *Egypt: Imperialism and Revolution* (trans.) (London, 1972), 56–8. For village specialization in general see T. Shanin, 'Peasant economy', 2, 186–92.

96   Shanin, op. cit., 186–92.
97   See A. G. Hopkins, *An Economic History of West Africa* (London, 1973), 51–77, and the sources cited there.
98   J-P. Labat (pseud.), *Mémoires du Chavalier d'Arvieux*, III (Paris, 1735), 343.
99   Hopkins, *West Africa*, 52–3. See also R. Grey and D. Birmingham, 'Some economic and political consequences of trade in central and eastern Africa in the pre-colonial period', in their *Pre-Colonial African Trade: Essays on Trade in Central and Eastern Africa before 1900* (Birmingham, 1970), 3–6.
100 Girard, 'Memoire', *DE*¹, 621–2.
101 Raymond, *Artisans et commerçants*, I, 184–91.
102 Girard, 'Mémoire', *DE*², XVII (Paris, 1824), 145–6.
103 See C. P. Grant, *The Syrian Desert* (London, 1937), 22–3. Also, B. Spooner, 'Desert and sown: a new look at an old relationship', in Naff and Owen, *Studies*.
104 Naff and Owen, *Studies*, 138; Buckingham, *Travels among the Arabs*, 179.
105 Olivier, *Voyage*, IV (Paris, An 12), 275.
106 Burckhardt, *Travels*, 26.
107 Bodman, *Aleppo*, 5.
108 Bodman, *Aleppo*, 5–10.
109 F. Barth, *Nomads of South Persia* (Oslo, London, 1961), 9–10, 98–9.
110 This point is made forcefully by T. Asad in his 'Equality in nomad social systems?', *Critique of Anthropology*, III, 11 (Spring 1978), 57–64.
111 See I. M. Lapidus, 'Muslim cities and Islamic societies' in his *Middle Eastern Cities*, 47–74; Hourani, 'The Islamic city', 16–20.
112 See J. Gulick, 'Village and city: cultural continuities in twentieth century Middle Eastern cultures', in Lapidus, *Middle Eastern Cities*, 137–8.
113 Olivier, *Voyage*, IV, 26, 47, 181, etc.; *Richard Wood Papers*, Notebook, 'Route from Konieh to Kutaya', 'Note and commonplace book on Syria, Palestine, Lebanon'; Burckhardt, *Travels*, 6–7, 15, 147, etc.; Buckingham, *Travels among the Arabs*, 334, 497, etc.
114 Girard, 'Mémoire', *DE*¹, *passim.*
115 See Hasselquist, *Voyages*, 109.
116 Cited in A. Raymond, 'Les sources de la richesse urbaine au Caire au dix-huitième siècle' in Naff and Owen, *Studies*, 192–3, and in *Artisans et commerçants*, I, 222.
117 Girard, 'Mémoire', *DE*¹, 574ff.
118 *Natural History*, I, 101–2.
119 See L. Valensi, 'Islam et capitalisme: production et commerce de chechias en Tunisie et en France au XVIIIe et XIXe siècles', *Revue d'Histoire Moderne et Contemporaine*, XVI (1969).
120 This system is described by R. Joseph, 'The material origins of the Lebanese conflict of 1860', B. Litt. (Oxford, 1977), 17–26.
121 See Raymond, *Artisans et commerçants*, I, 206–12, 218–21.
122 S. J. Shaw, 'Selim III and the Ottoman navy', *Turcica*, I (1969), 221–6.
123 *Natural History*, I, 161.
124 Cited in M. Clerget, *Le Caire*, II (Cairo, 1934), 228–9.
125 Gibb and Bowen, I, 1, 278, 281–7; Raymond, *Artisans et commerçants*, II, ch. 12; G. Baer, *Egyptian Guilds in Modern Times* (Jerusalem, 1964), 57–65 and 'Monopolies and restrictive practices', 146ff.; Gerber, 'Guilds', *passim.*
126 See Gibb and Bowen, I, 1, 282–3; 'Report on the Financial conditions of Turkey by Mr Foster and Lord Hobart', 7 Dec. 1861, *PP*, 1862, LXIV, 509; Olson, 'Esnaf', 334–6.
127 *Capital* (London, 1970), I, 358.
128 This argument is based on A. L. al-Sayyid Marsot's study of the wills of leading *alims*, 'Wealth of the ulama', in Naff and Owen, *Studies*, 212–16, and his article 'The political and economic functions of the ulama in the eighteenth century', *JESHO*, XVI (1973), 153–6.
129 Raymond, *Artisans et commerçants*, I, 214.
130 *Voyages*, 397.
131 Eton, *Survey*, 482.

132   Raymond, *Artisans et commerçants*, I, 203–6.
133   Ibid., ch. 8.
134   Ibid., 204.
135   Raymond, 'Le richesse urbaine', 193–4.
136   *Artisans et commerçants*, I, 220.
137   Ibid., 277–8.
138   Ibid., 237–9.
139   Ibid., 291–4.
140   *Artisans et commerçants*, II, 507–14.
141   Ibid., 517–19.
142   For the situation in Istanbul see Olsen, 'Esnaf', 336–8.
143   *Artisans et commerçants*, II, 588–96.
144   Ibid., 589–90.
145   Al-Jabarti, ʿAjaʾib al-Athar, II, 116. For the same practice in other parts of the Ottoman
       Empire see Bodman, *Aleppo*, 55–64; Rafeq, 'Local Forces', 302–7.
146   Raymond, 'Mouvements populaires', 115; N. Tomiche, 'Notes sur la hiérarchie sociale
       en Egypte à l'époche de Muhammad ʿAli', in Holt, *Political and Social Change*, 256–8.
147   For Middle East trade in general at this time see Gibb and Bowen, I, 1, 299–313; Davis
       'English imports', 196–206; Paris, *Le Levant*, 372ff.; C. Issawi, 'The decline of Middle
       Eastern trade, 1100–1850', in D. S. Richards (ed.), *Islam and the Trade of Asia*
       (Oxford, 1970); T. Walz, *Trade between Egypt and Bilad as-Sudan 1700–1820* (Cairo,
       1978), chs 1 and 2.
148   UK IO 'Report on British trade with Persia and Arabia'.
149   See J. S. Buckingham, *Travels in Mesopotamia*, II (London, 1827), 205.
150   Raymond, *Artisans et commerçants*, I, ch. 4.
151   See 'Remarks on the Turkey trade' (n.d.), *SRO*, GD 51/424; J. Morrison, 'A concise
       account of the trade carried on by the European nations to the Levant', 16 Aug. 1788,
       Liverpool Papers, XXXIV, British Museum, Add MS. 38, 233, 139–40; C. Issawi, 'The
       Tabriz–Trabzond Trade, 1830–1900', *IJMES*, I, 1 (1970), 18–19.
152   For example, Gücer, 'L'Approvisionnement', 158–69.
153   Raymond, *Artisans et commerçants*, I, 189–91.
154   Ibid., 185–9; Grenville, *Observations*, 54–7; W. Beawes, *Lex Mercatoria Rediviva: or
       the Merchant's Dictionary* (London, 1752), 734–5.
155   Paris, *Le Levant*, 370, 383; Beawes, *Merchant's Dictionary*, 735.
156   Quoted in Paris, *Le Levant*, 382.
157   Quoted in Raymond, *Artisans et commerçants*, I, 136, 149, 193.
158   Ibid., 167–71.
159   Masson, *Commerce*, 103, 401.
160   Girard, 'Mémoire', DE^2, XVII, 366.
161   V. Fontanier, *Narrative of a Mission to India and the Countries Bordering on the Persian
       Gulf* (trans.), I (London, 1844), 120.
162   Buckingham, *Travels in Mesopotamia*, II (London, 1827), 203; Fontanier, *Narrative*, II
       (London, 1844), 265.
163   Rich, *Narrative*, II (London, 1836), 128n.
164   Ibid.
165   For example, Beawes, *Merchant's Dictionary*, 725.
166   J-G. Barbie de Bocage, 'Notice sur le carte des Pachaliks de Bagdad, Orfa et Alep . . .',
       Receuil de voyages et de mémoires publiés par la Société de Géographie, II (Paris, 1825),
       241.
167   C. P. Grant, *The Syrian Desert* (London, 1937), 144–5.
168   Ibid., 137; UK IO 'Report on the Commerce of Arabia and Persia'; Douin, *Mission*,
       254–5.
169   Grant, *Syrian Desert*, 143, 146.
170   P. Masson, *Histoire de commerce français dans le Levant au XVIIe siècle* (Paris, 1896),
       419.
171   Douin, *Mission*, 255–6; Rafeq, *Province*, pp. 73–4; Raymond, *Artisans et
       commerçants*, I, 126–9; G. Baldwin, *Memorial Relating to the Trade in Slaves*

(Alexandria, 1789), 2; Hasselquist, *Voyages*, 77–83.

172   Gibb and Bowen, I, 1, 301–2.

173   See Volney, *Travels*, II, 160.

174   Enclosure in Wood (Damascus), 26 July 1848, FO 78/761.

175   Gibb and Bowen, I, 1, 309.

176   Wood, *Levant Company*, 49, 181.

177   Raymond, *Artisans et commerçants*, I, 154–5, II, ch. 11; A. H. Hourani, 'The Syrians in Egypt in the eighteenth and nineteenth centuries', *Colloque Internationale sur l'Histoire du Caire* (Cairo, 1972), 222–4. For the economic role of the Syrian merchants in general see R. Haddad, *Syrian Christians in Muslim Society* (Princeton, 1970).

178   See W. G. Browne, *Travels in Africa, Egypt and Syria, from the Year 1792 to 1798* (London, 1799), x–xi; Russell, *Natural History*, II, 2, 11; Wood, *Levant Company*, 232–6.

179   See Paris, *Le Levant*, 374–6; Volney, *Travels*, I, 230.

180   Wood, *Levant Company*, 234.

181   Volney, *Travels*, II, 427–8; Hourani, 'Fertile Crescent', 68.

182   Hourani, op. cit., 69.

183   Fontanier, *Narrative*, II, 269.

184   UK IO 'Report on the Commerce of Arabia and Persia'.

2: The economic consequences of the age of reforms, 1800–1850

1   S. J. Shaw, 'The origins of Ottoman military reform: the Nizam-i Cedid army of Sultan Selim III', *JMH*, XXXVII, 3 (Sept. 1965), 292, 300; M. E. Yapp, 'The modernization of Middle Eastern armies in the nineteenth century: a comparative view', in Parry and Yapp, *War*, 344–5.

2   Shaw, 'Selim III and the Ottoman navy', 217–26.

3   S. H. Shaw, *History of the Ottoman Empire and Modern Turkey*, II (Cambridge, Mass., 1977), 1–22. Shaw cites evidence of progress relating to other parts of the army such as the artillery corps before 1826, ibid., 6–7.

4   Ibid., 29.

5   Davison, *Reform in the Ottoman Empire*, ch. 1; S. Mardin, *The Genesis of Young Ottoman Thought* (Princeton, 1962), Ubicini, *Letters*, I, 259–81.

6   For example, H. Inalcik, 'Application of the Tanzimat and its social effects', *AO*, V (1973), 102–3; Shaw, *History*, II, 59–61.

7   For example, Davison, *Reform*, ch. 1; Shaw, *History*, II, ch. 2; Lewis, *Emergence*, ch. 3.

8   Shaw, 'Origins', 294–9.

9   Ibid., 300.

10   Canning (Istanbul), 25 March 1809, FO 78/63; T. Thornton, *The Present State of Turkey* (London, 1807), 248. For the British figures, see B. R. Mitchell, *Abstract of British Historical Statistics* (Cambridge, 1962), 388.

11   For a rough estimate of the proportion of government revenues coming from various sources see Ubicini, *Letters*, I, 266.

12   Thornton, *Present State*, 223.

13   Mardin, *Genesis*, 148; E. S. Creasy, *History of the Ottoman Turks* (London, 1877), 529–30.

14   Shaw, *History*, II, 40.

15   Lewis, *Emergence*, 91–2; K. H. Karpat, 'The land regime, social structure, and modernization in the Ottoman Empire' in Polk and Chambers, *Beginnings of Modernization*, 80–1; Ubicini, *Letters*, I, 296–7.

16   Inalcik, 'Application', 107–14; E. Engelhardt, *La Turquie et le Tanzimat*, I (Paris, 1882), 40–50.

17   A. Gould, 'Pashas and brigands: Ottoman provincial reform and its impact on the nomadic tribes of southern Anatolia 1840–1885', Ph.D. (UCLA, 1973), 34–7 and 'Lords or bandits? The derebeys of Cilicia', *IJMES*, VII, 4 (1976), 487–8.

18   Quoted in Inalcik, 'Application', 108–9.

19 Davison, *Reform*, 111; Ubicini, *Letters*, I, 295; S. Lane Poole (ed.), *The People of Turkey*, I (London, 1878), 175.
20 V. J. Puryear, *International Economics and Diplomacy in the Near East* (Stanford, 1935), 120–1
21 Engelhardt, *La Turquie*, I, 101; P. de Tchihatcheff, 'L'Asie Mineure et l'empire ottoman', 2, 'Situation politique, militaire et financière de la Turquie', *RDM*, new ser., VI (1 June 1850), 849.
22 Puryear, *International Economics*, 123–5.
23 Ibid., 195–6.
24 Davison, *Reform*, 111–12; Ubicini, *Letters*, I, 298–9.
25 Shaw, *History*, II, 43.
26 Yapp, 'Modernization', 346–7; Shaw, *History*, II, 41–5, 85–6.
27 Shaw, op. cit., 44–5; E. C. Clark, 'The Ottoman Industrial Revolution', *IJMES*, V (1974), 66–9.
28 Clark, op. cit., 67–73; O. C. Sarç, 'Ottoman industrial policy' in Issawi, *Economic History*, 55–7.
29 Shaw, *History*, II, 122–3; Clark, 'Industrial Revolution', 72–5.
30 See, for example, the title of Clark's article.
31 Ubicini, *Letters*, I, 208; D. Quartaert, 'Ottoman reform and Agriculture in Anatolia 1876–1908', Ph.D. (UCLA, 1973), 92–3.
32 G. Baer, 'The development of private ownership in land', in his *Studies in the Social History of Modern Egypt* (Chicago, 1969), 67–8.
33 For example, Gould, 'Pashas and brigands', 12, 14; W. B. Barker, *Lares et Penates: or Cilicia and its Governors*, ed. W. F. Aynsworth (London, 1853), 104–8; P. Dumont, 'La pacification du sud-est Anatolieh en 1865', *Turcica*, V (1975), 110.
34 There are many statements to this effect in the British consular correspondence, for example, Suter (Kaissariah), 2 Apr. 1851, FO 78/870.
35 Gibb and Bowen, I, 1, 228–31; Volney, *Travels*, I, 143–4; A. G. Politis, *L'Hellènisme et l'Egypte modern*, I (Paris, 1929), 92–4.
36 Raymond, *Artisans et commerçants*, II, 772–5; Gibb and Bowen, I, 2, 63, 66–7.
37 Gibb and Bowen, I, 66.
38 Estève, 'Memoire', 317; Shaw, *Organization*, 182–3.
39 S. J. Shaw, *Ottoman Egypt in the Age of the French Revolution* (Cambridge, Mass., 1964), 124, 142–3; Rivlin, *Agricultural Policy*, 40, 43–6.
40 Rivlin, *Agricultural Policy*, 53–60; G. Baer, *A History of Landownership in Modern Egypt, 1800–1950* (London, 1962), 2–6. See also A. A. al-Hitta, *Tarikh al-Zira'a al-Misriya fi 'Asr Muhammad 'Ali al-Kabir* (Cairo, 1950), 34–5.
41 G. Baer, 'The village shaykh, 1800–1950', in his *Studies*, 37–40, 46–8, 53–4, 63; 'Abd al-Rahim, *al-Rif al-Misri*, 18; E. de Cadalvène and J. de Breuvery, *L'Egypte et la Turquie de 1829 à 1836*, I (Paris, 1836), 108.
42 Owen, *Cotton*, 19.
43 Ibid., 20–1.
44 For example, *'Aja'ib al-Athar*, IV, 52.
45 For example, G. Guemard, *Les Réformes en Egypt*, II (Cairo, 1936), 310–14; J. Mazuel, *L'Oeuvre géographique de Linant de Bellefonds* (Cairo, 1937), 130–2; al-Hitta, *Tarikh*, 51–60.
46 Rivlin, *Agricultural Policy*, 164–5.
47 Owen, *Cotton*, 28–9 and sources there. See also F. Charles Roux, *Le production du coton en Egypte* (Paris, 1908), 22–4; G. R. Gliddon, *A Memoir on the Cotton of Egypt* (London, 1841), 13–14; H. Sidqi, *al-Qutn al-Misri* (Cairo, 1950), 32–89.
48 Owen, *Cotton*, 29–30.
49 Ibid., 36–40.
50 Ibid., 31–2.
51 For example, J. Bowring, 'Report on Egypt and Candia', *PP*, 1840, XXI, 19.
52 For example, G. S. Saab, *The Egyptian Agrarian Reform 1952–1962* (London, 1967), 4–5.
53 As one of the simple roller gins then employed could only process 12–15 lb of cotton a

day, the time taken to clean two cantars − the average yield of an acre − must have been in the region of 45−55 days. See Owen, *Cotton*, 31.

54 For example, Rivlin, *Agricultural Policy*, 116−18. For the social impact of these policies see J. Tucker, 'Decline of the family economy in mid-nineteenth century Egypt', *ASO*, I, 3 (1979), 249−63.

55 Quoted in Guemard, *Réformes*, II, 458.

56 Owen, *Cotton*, 382−3.

57 See, for example, the extract from A. al-Giritli's *Tarikh al-sina'a fi misr* in Issawi, *Economic History*, 39−40, 398−9. Also Douin, *Mission*, 90−9; A. Silvera, 'Edmé-François Jomard and the Egyptian reforms of 1839', *MES*, VII, 3 (Oct. 1971), 309−10, al-Hitta, *Tarikh*, 159−60.

58 Rivlin, *Agricultural Policy*, 194; 'Bulletin du mois de Mars 1814' in E. Driault (ed.), *Mohamed Aly et Napoleon (1807−1814)* (Cairo, 1925), 242.

59 *'Aja'ib al-Athar*, IV, 255, 282−3. See also, M. Fahmy, *Le révolution de l'industrie en Egypte et ses conséquences sociales au 19e siècle* (Leiben, 1954), 9−10, 13−15; V. Schoelcher, *L'Egypte en 1845* (Paris, 1846), 54−5.

60 Fahmy, *Révolution de l'industrie*, 13; J. A. St John, *Egypt and Mohammed Ali*, II (London, 1834), 408−9.

61 These are Fahmy's figures, *Révolution de l'industrie*, 23−4. Other sources give slightly different numbers. For example Bowring cites a report by the British Consul-General in 1829 which states that there were then seventeen factories with machinery and seven without, 'Report', 31−5.

62 For the full list of factories see Fahmy, *Révolution de l'industrie*, 24. Boislecomte agreed that there were thirty factories, Douin, *Mission*, 92. But the British Consul-General asserted that there were only twenty-four, Bowring, 'Report', 35.

63 Fahmy, *Révolution de l'industrie*, 12; Bowring, 'Report', 139; St John, *Egypt*, II, 411.

64 Fahmy, *Révolution de l'industrie*, 24. Again, Bowring cites a report by the British Consul-General that gives slightly different figures, 'Report', 35.

65 On a visit to one of the factories in 1831 Hekekyan found thirty 'spinning machines' in a storehouse, not yet assembled, *HP*, XIV, 41.

66 Fahmy, *Révolution de l'industrie*, 50−3. See also, *HP*, IV, 30−41.

67 The figures for the factory average can be found in Duhamel (Alexandria) 6 July 1837 in R. Cattaui, *Le règne de Mohamed Aly d'après les archives russes en Egypt*, II (Rome, 1834), 124ff. St John's assertion that the workforce was reduced to 6000 in 1833 probably refers to a temporary measure during the early part of the occupation of Syria, *Egypt*, II, 417.

68 Ibid., 433. See also Fahmy, *Révolution de l'industrie*, 25 and al-Giritli, *Tarikh*, in Issawi, *Economic History*, 398−402.

69 Estimates of the amount of Egyptian cotton consumed in the factories vary widely. St John put it at 70,000 cantars a year, *Egypt*, II, 418. But Bowring gives a much lower figure of 30,000 cantars, 'Report', 41.

70 Fahmy, *Révolution de l'industrie*, 26.

71 Ibid., 26.

72 *HP*, II, 105. Fahmy's list of factories gives only eight with looms, *Révolution de l'industrie*, 24.

73 Mimaut (Cairo), 1 Mar. 1831 in G. Douin (ed.), *Le première guerre de Syria*, I (Cairo, 1931), 488ff.; E.-F. Jomard, *Coup d'oeil impartial sur l'état de l'Egypte* (Paris, 1836), 18; A. Colin, 'Lettres sur l'Egypt' − 'Commerce', *RDM*, 4th ser. XVII (1 Jan. 1839), 67.

74 Fahmy, *Révolution de l'industrie*, 27.

75 Quoted by Bowring, 'Report', 187.

76 According to the British Consul-General, Muhammad Ali calculated the cost of his cloth simply on the basis of the price of the raw materials used, neglecting to include the cost of wages, power, etc., quoted in Bowring, 'Report', 186.

77 Bowring, 'Report', 145; T. Boaz, *Egypt* (London, 1850), 42; Fahmy, *Révolution de l'industrie*, 37−8.

78 Ibid.

79 Guemard, *Réformes*, II, 365.

80 Fahmy, *Révolution de l'industrie*, 39–43; D. Farhi, 'Nizam-i Cedid: military reform in Egypt under Mehmed 'Ali', *AAS*, VIII, 2 (1972), 170.
81 Bowring, 'Report', 93, 95.
82 Viesse de Marmont, *Voyage de Marechal Duc de Raguse en Hongrie, en Transylvanie . . . à Constantinople . . . et en Egypt*, II (Paris, 1837), 225; see also Fahmy, *Révolution de l'industrie*, 79.
83 A. Colin, 'Lettres sur l'Egypt' – 'L'industrie manufacturière', *RDM*, 4th ser., IV, 15 May 1838, 518, 522.
84 Bowring, 'Report', 35. Colin, 'Industrie manufacturière', 521.
85 For example, A. Abel-Malek, *Idéologie et renaissance nationale: l'Egypte moderne* (Paris, 1969), 24–33 and sources cited there. For support for my argument see R. Mabro and S. Radwan, *The Industrialization of Egypt 1939–1973* (Oxford, 1976), 16–18.
86 In England in 1822 there were at least 10,000 steam engines and some 2000 power looms, *Quarterly Review*, XXXII (June 1825), 171.
87 *HP*, II, 116; Colin, 'Industrie manufacturière', 522–4. The French novelist, Flaubert, came across an interesting example of Muhammad Ali's failure to use trained men in the right post, F. Steegmuller (ed.), *Flaubert in Egypt* (London, 1972), 60–1.
88 *HP*, II, 101.
89 Ibid., 123–4.
90 For a good account of Muhammad Ali's administration see R. B. Hunter, 'Bureaucratic politics and the passing of Viceregal absolutism: the origins of modern government in Egypt, 1805–1879', Ph.D. (Harvard, 1979), ch. 1.
91 Owen, *Cotton*, 40.
92 Rivlin, *Agricultural Policy*, 64–6; Owen, *Cotton*, 58–61 and 'The development of agricultural production in 19th century Egypt – Capitalism of what type?', in Udovitch, *Land, Population and Society*; A. Sami, *Taqwim al-Nil was 'Asr Muhammad 'Ali Pasha*, II (Cairo, 1928), 490–1. See also, A.-B. Clot-Bey, *Aperçu général sur l'Egypte*, II (Brussels, 1840), 185.
93 P. N. Hamont, 'De l'Egypte depuis la paix de 1841', *RO*, I (1843), 40–1. See also the same author's *L'Egypte sous Méhémet-Ali*, I (Paris, 1843), 26, 131.
94 *HP*, III, 68.
95 Rivlin, *Agricultural Policy*, 72.
96 For example, Baer, 'Village Shaykh', 48–9, 54–5. See also, N. W. Senior, *Conversations and Journals in Egypt and Malta*, I (London, 1882), 279.
97 For example, *HP*, II, 112, III, 63.
98 *HP*, III, 12, 153.
99 For example, *The Times*, 11 Feb. 1842, Hekekyan, III, 36.
100 A. Sami, *Taqwim al-Nil*, III (Cairo, 1936), 1, 10.
101 Baer, *Landownership*, 14–15.
102 For the terms of the Convention and the Treaty see J. C. Hurewitz (ed.), *Diplomacy in the Near and Middle East*, I (Princeton, 1956), 110–11, 116–19.
103 *HP*, II, 66–7, 149.
104 Ibid., III, 42–3.
105 De Leon, 'Answers to queries on cotton culture in Egypt' (Alexandria), 21 July 1856, *US, Egypt*, II; T. K. Fowler, *Report on the Cotton Cultivation in Egypt* (Manchester, 1861), 10.
106 For example, Schoelcher, *L'Egypte en 1845*, 52–3.
107 For example, Hekekyan's many reports, *HP*, II, ff. 66, 123–4, etc.
108 This was certainly Hekekyan's opinion in 1843, *HP*, II, ff. 123–4. It was shared by the Austrian Consular officials, 'Egypten in jahre 1844' (Vienna), 24 Mar. 1845, *AA*, F.3, Box 21, 17.
109 For example, F. Mengin, *Histoire de l'Egypte sous le gouvernement de Mohammed-Aly*, II (Paris, 1823), 375; A. Sami, *Taqwim al-Nil*, II, 290.
110 For example, Owen, *Cotton*, 83.
111 For example, Issawi, *Economic History*, 389.
112 Egypt, Ministère de l'Interieur, *Statistique de l'Egypte*, 1873 (Cairo, 1873), 211–12; Raymond, *Artisans et commerçants*, 204, 229.

113 M. Ma'oz, *Ottoman Reform in Syria and Palestine 1840–1861* (Oxford, 1968), 4–11; see also M. Abir, 'Local leadership and early reforms in Palestine 1800–1834' in Ma'oz, *Studies on Palestine*, 295–8.
114 For example, A. Cohen, 'The Army in Palestine in the eighteenth century: sources of its weakness and strength', *BSOAS*, xxxiv, 1 (1971), 47–51.
115 For example, Gibb and Bowen, i, 1, 224.
116 Ma'oz, *Ottoman Reform*, 13–15; Y. Hofman, 'The administration of Syria and Palestine under Egyptian rule (1831–1840) in Ma'oz, *Studies on Palestine*, 311–15; Y. Ben-Ariah, 'The changing landscape of the Central Jordan Valley', *SH*, xv, Pamphlet No. 3 (1968), 36–8; Anon., *Rambles in the Deserts of Syria* (London, 1864), 2.
117 Ma'oz, *Ottoman Reform*, 13.
118 For a detailed description of the system of taxation under the Egyptians see enclosures in Campbell (Alexandria), 31 July 1836, FO 78/283. See also, Campbell's 'Report on Syria' in Campbell (Alexandria), 23 Aug. 1836, FO 78/283.
119 For example, Harik, *Politics and Change*, 239–40.
120 See Farren's answer to Campbell's question 19 in Campbell, 31 July 1836.
121 G. Baer, 'Village shaykh' and 'The Economic and social position of the village-mukhtar in Palestine' in G. Ben-Dor (ed.), *The Palestinians and the Middle East Conflict* (Haifa, 1978), 101–4.
122 W. R. Polk, *The Opening of South Lebanon 1788–1840* (Cambridge, Mass., 1963), 170–1; Puryear, *International Economics*, 38–41.
123 Wood, 'Summary Report on Syria', Aug. 1834 in A. B. Cunningham (ed.), *The Early Correspondence of Richard Wood 1831–1841* (London, 1966), 49–50; Rose (Beirut), 5 March 1843, FO 195/221.
124 For example, Farren, Moore and Werry's answers to Campbell's question 14 in Campbell, 31 July 1836.
125 Boislecomte, 1 Sept. 1833 in Douin, *Mission*, 257.
126 For example, Werry's answer to Campbell's question 28 in Campbell, 31 July 1836.
127 F. Charles Roux, 'La domination égyptienne en Syrie', *RHC*, xxi (July/Oct. 1933), 194; A. J. Rustum, 'Syria under Mehemet Ali', *AJSLL*, xli, 1 (Oct. 1924), 41.
128 For example, M. Sabry, *L'empire égyptienne sous Mohamed-Ali et la question d'Orient 1811–1849* (Paris, 1930), 353–5.
129 See Werry's answer to Campbell's question 8 in Campbell, 31 July 1836.
130 A. Naff, 'A Social History of Zahle. The Principal Market Town in Nineteenth Century Lebanon', Ph.D. (UCLA, 1972), 43, 243; Polk, *Opening of South Lebanon*, 167. But also, D. Chevalier, *La Société du Mont Liban à l'époque de la revolution industrielle en Europe* (Paris, 1971), 113–14.
131 For example, answers to Campbell's questions 13 and 16 in Campbell, 31 July 1836.
132 J. Bowring, 'Report on the commercial statistics of Syria', *PP*, 1840, xxi, 250.
133 Ibid., 294.
134 Quoted in Charles Roux, 'La domination egyptienne', 194.
135 Werry (Aleppo), 17 Feb. 1845, a copy of which can be found in W. R. Polk, 'Rural Syria in 1845', *MEJ*, xvi, 4 (Autumn 1962), 508ff.
136 Boislecomte, 1 Sept. 1833, in Douin, *Mission*, 259.
137 See figures in D. Chevalier, 'Western development and Eastern crisis in the mid-nineteenth century: Syria confronted with the European economy' in Polk and Chambers, *Beginnings of Modernization*, 214.
138 Bowring, 'Report on the commercial statistics of Syria', 296. See also, Werry, 'Gross returns of British and foreign trade at the Port of Alexandretta during the year ended 31st December 1841', in (Aleppo) 1 June 1842, FO 78/497.
139 Ma'oz, *Ottoman Reform*, chs 4 and 6.
140 See J. P. Spagnolo, *France and Ottoman Lebanon: 1861–1914* (London, 1977), 15–16.
141 Ma'oz, *Ottoman Reform*, 69–72, 78–81.
142 For example, Werry (Aleppo), 22 Apr. 1842, FO 78/497.
143 Ma'oz, *Ottoman Reform*, 78–81, 93, 98.
144 Ibid., 69–72.
145 For example, I. al-Nimr, *Tarikh Jabal Nablus wa'l-Balqa*, i, (Damascus, 1938), 274ff.

146   For example, M. Hoexter, 'The role of the Qays and Yaman factions in local political divisions: Jabal Nablus compared with the Judean Hills in the first half of the nineteenth century', *AAS*, IX 3 (1973), 266–74.

147   For example, Ma'oz, *Ottoman Reforms*, ch. 9. See also N. H. Lewis, 'The frontier of settlement in Syria, 1800–1950' in Issawi, *Economic History*, 259–62.

148   Werry (Aleppo), 22 Sept. 1842, FO 78/497, 3 Sept. 1845, FO 78/621.

149   Wood (Damascus), 30 July 1843, FO 78/538.

150   Werry, 17 Feb. 1845 in Polk, 'Rural Syria', 509; Ben-Ariah, 'Changing landscape', 36.

151   For example, the British Consul-General's complaint that the Ottomans could not even protect cultivators near the great towns of Aleppo, Homs, Hama, Damascus and Jerusalem (Beirut), Aug. 1848, FO 78/760.

152   For example, S. H. Longrigg, *Four Centuries of Modern Iraq* (London, 1925), 255–6, 261; Fontanier, *Narrative*, I, 192, 323, 325, 338–9.

153   Longrigg, *Four Centuries*, 284–8.

3: The expansion of trade with Europe, 1800–1850

1   Douin, *Mission*, 252.

2   Wood, *Levant Company*, 140–2. See also R. T. Rapp, 'The unmaking of the Mediterranean trade hegemony: international trade rivalry and the commercial revolution', *JEH*, XXXV, 3 (Sept. 1975), 501–20.

3   Davis, 'English imports from the Middle East', 203–4.

4   Douin, *Mission*, 252.

5   Hurewitz, *Diplomacy*, I, 67–9; Bailey, *British Policy and the Turkish Reform Movement*, 81; Wood, *Levant Company*, 49.

6   Review of Mengin's Histoire de l'Egypte, *Quarterly Review*, XXX (Jan. 1824), 485.

7   P. Deane and W. A. Cole, *British Economic Growth 1688–1959: Trend and Structure*, 2nd edn (Cambridge, 1967), 187.

8   Wood, *Levant Company*, 194.

9   C. P. Kindleberger, *Economic Growth in France and Britain, 1851–1950* (Cambridge, Mass., 1964), 273.

10   Bowring, 'Report on Syria', 266, 313, 324; answers to question 19, in Campbell, 31 July 1836.

11   The first British ships appeared off the Palestinian coast in 1848, Finn (Jerusalem), 14 Jan. 1847, FO 78/705; Kayat (Jaffa) 12 May and 20 Dec. 1848, FO 78/755. See also Finn (Jerusalem), 26 Apr. 1853, FO 78/963.

12   *PP*, 1844, XLVI, 650, 670; A. Ubicini, *La Turquie actuelle* (Paris, 1855), trans. as *Letters on Turkey*, I (London, 1856), 351–8.

13   *PP*, 1844, XLVI, 650; Ubicini, *Letters*, I, 355.

14   P. J. Puryear, *France and the Levant* (Berkeley and Los Angeles 1941), 1–9; H. Salvador, *L'Orient, Marseille et la Mediterranée. Histoire des échelles du Levant et des colonies* (Paris, 1854), 373–6.

15   M. Block, *Statistique de la France*, 2nd edn, II (Paris, 1875), 291–2.

16   J. Macgregor, *Commercial Statistics*, V (London, 1850), 12–13.

17   Owen, *Cotton*, 161.

18   Clot, *Aperçu général*, II, 307.

19   C. Issawi, 'British trade and the rise of Beirut, 1830–1860', *IJMES*, VIII (1977), 98–9. See also, Rose (Beirut), 5 Mar. 1843, FO 195/221 and Moore (Beirut), 26 Aug. 1848, FO 78/754.

20   J. R. McCulloch, *A Dictionary . . . of Commerce and Navigation* (London, 1844), 1158.

21   Guys (Beirut), 15 Nov. 1833, quoted in Joseph, 'Material origins of the Lebanese conflict', 1–2.

22   McCulloch, *Dictionary*, 1158.

23   For example, C. MacFarlane, *Constantinople in 1828*, 2nd edn, I (London, 1829), 65–7.

24   Bowring, 'Report on Syria', 313–17, 328–30.

25   Moore (Beirut), 10 Jan. 1849, FO 78/802; Rose (Damascus), 17 May 1849, FO 78/760. There were, however, six merchants (probably Indian) under British protection.

26 D. Chevalier, 'De la production lente à l'économie dynamique en Syrie', *Annales*, XXI (1966), 67.

27 For an interesting account of the business activities of one such merchant money-lender, see A. J. Kayat, *A Voice from Lebanon* (London, 1847). For a more general account, P. Saba, 'The development and decline of the Lebanese silk industry', B. Litt. (Oxford, 1977), 17–32.

28 Wood, *Levant Company*, 198–202; D. C. M. Platt, *The Cinderella Service: British Consuls since 1825* (London, 1971), 125–31; 'Memoire on the political and commercial relations of Great Britain with Asia Minor' (1820?), FO 78/96. For criticism of the Company's monopoly, see A. Redford *et al.*, *Manchester Merchants and Foreign Trade 1794–1854* (Manchester, 1934), 90.

29 Platt, *Cinderella Service*, 16, 126.

30 Puryear, *France and the Levant*, 10–14.

31 Chevalier, 'Western development and Eastern crisis in Polk and Chambers, *Beginnings of Modernization in the Middle East: the nineteenth century* (Chicago, 1968), 206–7. Once established, some lines developed their activities, others were forced to give up their service, see for example, Wood (Damascus), 26 July 1848, FO 78/761.

32 For the figures for Beirut see Moore (Beirut), 30 Apr. 1855, FO 78/117. For those of Izmir, G. Rolleston, *Report on Smyrna* (London, 1856), 86.

33 C. R. Low, *History of the Indian Navy 1613–1863*, II (London, 1877), 37–50, 50n.

34 M. S. Kalla, 'Role of Foreign Trade in the Economic Development of Syria 1831–1914', Ph.D. (American University, Washington, 1969), 52n. See also Wood (Damascus), 26 Jul. 1848, FO 78/761.

35 For a general account of this process see Baily, *Turkish Reform Movement*, 43–8.

36 For example, Werry (Aleppo), 24 Apr. 1842, FO 78/497; Rose (Beirut), 17 May 1849, FO 78/802.

37 Rolleston, *Report on Smyrna*, 27–30; Colin, 'Commerce', 66; D. Urquhart, *The Lebanon: A History and a Diary*, II (London, 1860), 354.

38 Bowring, 'Report on Syria', 329; Ma'oz, *Ottoman Reform*, 174–5; Guemard, *Réformes*, II, 261–2.

39 Ubicini, *Letters*, I, 166, 173–4, 349; Shaw, *History of the Ottoman Empire*, II, 118–19.

40 Ubicini, *Letters*, I, 344; Puryear, *International Economics*, 119–21; Macgregor, *Commercial Statistics*, II (London, 1844), 14; Kalla, 'Role of foreign trade', 93.

41 Douin, *Mission*, 258.

42 Bowring, 'Report on Syria', 300.

43 For the Treaty, see Hurewitz, *Diplomacy*, I, 110–11. See also, Puryear, *International Economics*, 117–25.

44 Ibid., 199.

45 For example, Charnaud (Izmir), 22 Feb. 1839 and Brant (Izmir), 25 Oct. 1839, FO 195/128. For Egypt, see Rivlin, *Agricultural Policy*, 185–90.

46 For some examples of later, and not very important, attempts to reactivate certain monopolies, see O. Kurmus, 'The role of British capital in the economic development of Western Anatolia 1850–1913', Ph.D. (London, 1974), 30–2.

47 See for example the impact in Egypt of the European commercial crisis of 1836, Owen, *Cotton*, 40, or the impact in Beirut of the 1847 crisis, Moore (Beirut), 9 Feb. 1848, FO 78/754.

48 An example of the way in which developments taking place over many decades can be 'telescoped' can be found in I. M. Smilianskaya, 'The distintegration of feudal relations in Syria and Lebanon in the middle of the nineteenth century' in Issawi, *Economic History*, 227–47.

49 For example, in the case of Lower Egypt, see Owen, *Cotton*, 71–4.

50 For example, Barker's information about seasonal wage labour in Cilicia, *Lares et Penates*, 120; or Chevalier's data about money rents, *Mont Liban*, 136–43.

51 *PP*, 1844, XLVI, 125.

52 Issawi, *Economic History*, 208; Anon., *Rambles*, 149; Joseph, 'Material origins', 68.

53 J. R. McCulloch, *A Dictionary . . . of Commerce and Navigation*, 2nd edn (London, 1844), 375.

54 Moore (Beirut), 2 Feb. 1846, FO 78/661.
55 D. Chevalier, 'Un example de resistance technique de l'artisinat Syrien aux XIXe et XXe siècles. Les tissus Ikatés d'Alep et de Damas', *Syria*, xxxix, 3–4 (1962), 300.
56 Ibid., 301ff.
57 *CR* (Aleppo, 1855), *PP*, 1856, LVII, 266.
58 For Egypt, Issawi, *Economic History*, 389; for Mount Lebanon, Chevalier, 'Production lente', 61.
59 For example, Sarc, 'The Tanzimat and our industry', 50.
60 Chevalier, 'Un example de resistance', 301–2.
61 Quoted ibid., 301n.
62 For example, Eyres (Beirut), 4 Nov. 1886, FO 78/3911.
63 Joseph, 'Material origins', 190n.
64 For example, Macgregor, *Commercial Statistics*, II, 107; Bowring, 'Report on Syria', 318.
65 *PP*, 1862, LI, 490–2.
66 *Commercial Statistics*, II, 107.
67 For example, Rassam (Mosul), 26 July 1844, FO 195/228. For figures for the export of British 'white cloth' to the Middle East, see *PP*, 1842, xxxix, 135; *PP*, 1852, LI, 490–3.
68 Urquhart, *Turkey and Its Resources*, 149. See also, Moore (Beirut), 1 Feb. 1845, FO 78/621.
69 G. Ducousso, *L'industrie de la soie en Syrie et au Liban* (Beirut/Paris, 1913), 145–50; Polk, *Opening*, 78.
70 A. E. Crouchley, *The Economic Development of Modern Egypt* (London, 1938), 266; Table 9.
71 For example, Finn (Jerusalem), 14 Jan. 1847, FO 78/705.
72 For lower dues, see Bailey, *British Policy*, 79n. In 1845 large quantities of grain were sent to Beirut in Turkish and Greek ships to meet a local shortage, Moore (Beirut), 10 Nov. 1845, FO 78/660.
73 F. W. Kinglake reports on this practice in *Eothen* (Paris, 1846), 66.
74 Douin, *Mission*, 254.
75 For Anatolia, see Ubicini, *Letters*, I, 301; for Syria see Chevalier, 'Western development', 213–15.
76 For example in *Mont Liban*, ch. ix.
77 I am indebted to Dr N. Gross for this point.
78 G. Le Père, 'Mémoire sur la ville d'Alexandie', *DE*², XVIII, 402; H. Thuile, *Commentaires sur l'atlas historique de l'Alexandrie* (Cairo, 1822), 47–51.
79 H. Guys, *Beyrout et le Liban*, I (Paris, 1850), 9–10.
80 D. Chevalier, 'Signes de Beyrouth en 1834', *Bull. d'Etudes Orientales*, xxv (1972), 211n; Ma'oz, *Ottoman Reform*, 180–1.
81 For estimates of Izmir's population, see Rolleston, *Report on Smyrna*, 20 and A. de Besse, *l'Empire Turc* (Paris and Leipzig, 1854), 97.
82 *HP*, II, 94.
83 P. A. Baran, *The Political Economy of Growth*, pb edn (New York, 1968), 194.
84 G. Wiet, *Mohammed Ali et les beaux-arts* (Cairo, n.d. (1949?)), 53–5; Schoelcher, *L'Egypte en 1845*, 103.
85 Rose (Beirut), 15 May 1849, FO 78/802.
86 'Report on Syria', 292. See also Joseph, 'Material origins', 9.
87 Joseph, op. cit., 1–8; Moore (Beirut), 27 Dec. 1848, FO 78/754.
88 For example, Colin, 'Commerce', 65–6.

4: The Ottoman road to bankruptcy and the Anatolian economy, 1850–1881

1 O. Anderson, 'Great Britain and the beginnings of the Ottoman public debt, 1854–55', *HJ*, VII, 1 (1964), 47–8. See also R-S. Suvla, 'Debts during the Tanzimat period', in Issawi, *Economic History*, 98–9, who gives the date of Reşid's contract as 1850.
2 For a general description of the Ottoman financial situation at this period see D. C. Blaisdell, *European Financial Control in the Ottoman Empire* (New York, 1929), ch. 2

and A. Du Velay, *Essai sur l'histoire financière de la Turquie* (Paris, 1903), 24–69. Tentative efforts to raise a foreign loan had been made as early as 1839–41, Anderson, 'Beginnings', 47.

3 For example, E. Engelhardt, *La Turquie et le Tanzimat*, i (Paris, 1882), 101.

4 Quoted in Davison, *Reform*, 112n.

5 D. C. M. Platt, *Finance, Trade and Politics: British Foreign Policy 1815–1914* (London, 1968), 200–5; Anderson, 'Beginnings', 52–3. Figures for the sums borrowed and for the sums actually realized in Ottoman loans from Y. S. Tezel, 'Notes on the consolidated foreign debt of the Ottoman Empire: The servicing of the loans', *The Turkish Yearbook of International Relations* (1972), Table 1. Additional information about the Ottoman debt from Suvla, 'Debts', 100–1 and J. Ducruet, *Les capitaux européens au Proche-Orient* (Paris, 1964), ch. 2.

6 Anderson, 'Beginnings', 55; Tezel, 'Notes', Table 1; Suvla, 'Debts', 100.

7 Du Velay, *Essai*, 1410.

8 Platt, *Finance*, 200–2; Tezel, 'Notes', Table 1.

9 Tezel, 'Notes', Table 1. Suvla, 'Debts', 101–2 gives a slightly higher figure.

10 For estimates of the size of the floating debt see A. Ubicini and P. de Courteille, *Etat présent de l'empire ottoman* (Paris, 1876), 136ff. and Du Velay, *Histoire*, 318, 324.

11 This is Blaisdell's calculation (*European Financial Control*, 76–7). According to Shaw's figures in Table 12 the proportion of revenue taken up with debt servicing was only one-third.

12 J. R. T. Hughes, *Fluctuations in Trade, Industry and Finance: A Study of British Economic Development 1850–1960* (Oxford, 1960), 40. R. E. Cameron, *France and the Economic Development of Europe 1800–1914* (Princeton, 1961), 523.

13 Hughes, *Fluctuations*, 44–5.

14 Cameron, *France*, 88.

15 R. Cameron 'France' in R. Cameron (ed.), *Banking in the Early Stages of Industrialization* (London etc., 1967), 107–9; D. S. Landes, *Bankers and Pashas; International Finance and Economic Imperialism in Egypt* (London etc., 1958), 47–52. The quotation is from Landes, 56n.

16 For example, Blaisdell, *European Financial Control*, 20.

17 Landes, *Bankers and Pashas*, 57–8.

18 J. Bouvier, 'Les interets financiers et la question d'Egypte (1875–76)', *RH*, ccxxiv (July–Sept. 1960), 76–8.

19 A. Baster, 'The origins of British banking expansion in the Near East', *EHR*, v, 1 (Oct. 1934), 76–86; Landes, *Bankers and Pashas*, 62–7. For a history of the Imperial Ottoman see A. Biliotti, *La Banque impériale ottomane* (Paris, 1909).

20 Ibid., 319; Tezel assumes that commissions and expenses accruing to the banks from the issue of state loans represented 2 per cent of the nominal value of the loan, 'Notes', 92n. But he also cites a reference which suggests that they were often much higher. See also, Blaisdell, *European Financial Control*, 39–40.

21 Biliotti, *Banque impériale*, 319–22.

22 For example, Blaisdell, *European Financial Control*, 31–5.

23 Ibid., 39; Du Velay, *Essai*, 265, 276.

24 Tezel, 'Notes', Table 1; Suvla, 'Debts', 101. Tezel asserts that the 'average' issue price was '40'.

25 Once again I have taken Tezel's figures, 'Notes', Table 1.

26 Ibid., 95 and Table 2.

27 For an example of a common criticism of Ottoman extravagance, see P. de Tchihatcheff, *Lettres sur la Turquie* (Brussels/Leipzig, 1859), 42.

28 Davison, *Reform*, 264–6; Ubicini and Courteille, *Etat présent*, 177–82. For figures for military expenditure, see S. J. Shaw, 'Ottoman expenditures and budgets in the late nineteenth and early twentieth centuries', *IJMES*, ix (1978), 376.

29 Shaw, *Ottoman Empire*, ii, 115–18. Also Gould, 'Pashas and brigands', 74–118, and 'Lords or bandits?', 497–9.

30 For example, 'Report by Mr Barron . . . on the taxation in Turkey', *PP* (1870), lxv, 575–6. Also Gould 'Pashas and brigands', 125–6, 138.

31 'Report by Mr Barron', 589–603.
32 Davison, *Reform*, 73; 'Report on the financial condition of Turkey by Mr Foster and Lord Hobart', 509–11.
33 Du Velay, *Essai*, 276.
34 Ibid., 264–5, 269–70.
35 UK IO 'Report on the Financial Condition of Turkey', 498.
36 Ibid., 503.
37 UK IO 'Report by Mr Barron', 565–76, 582–3.
38 Ibid., 591–603.
39 Quoted in Davison, *Reform*, 251.
40 *European Financial Control*, 38–9.
41 Quoted in K. Bell, 'The Constantinople Embassy of Sir Henry Bulwer 1858–65', Ph.D. (London, 1961), 88.
42 Blaisdell, *European Financial Control*, 80.
43 M. Winkler, *Foreign Bonds: An Autopsy* (Philadelphia, 1933), 34–5.
44 For references see Table 12.
45 For estimates of the financial losses suffered as a result of the weather see F. Burnaby, *On Horseback through Asia Minor*, I (London, 1877), 133. Also, Davison, *Reform*, 301–6.
46 Du Velay, *Essai*, 381, 397; D. C. M. Platt, *Finance, Trade and Politics: British Foreign Policy 1815–1914* (Oxford, 1968), 201–2; Blaisdell, *European Financial Control*, 81–2.
47 Du Velay, *Essai*, 371.
48 Du Velay estimates that as a result of the loss of these provinces total government revenues were reduced to £14,000,000 a year; *Essai*, 386–7.
49 Ibid., 354–5, 371. As part of the government governing this loan the Ottomans started to repay the interest due on the 1854 and 1871 loans which they had previously suspended. In return they were allowed to withdraw the Egyptian tribute as security for those loans and to pledge it to the new (1877) loan instead, ibid., 371.
50 Ibid., 397–405. Blaisdell, *European Financial Control*, 88.
51 Blaisdell, op. cit., 84–5.
52 Ibid., 89–99.
53 Ubicini and De Courteille, *Etat présent*, 178–85.
54 Apart from the usual warning regarding the reliability of such figures it should be noted that they certainly include some commodities which were grown elsewhere in Anatolia. In the 1870s, for example, E. J. Davis pointed out that half the Adana cotton crop was exported via Izmir, *Life in Asiatic Turkey* (London, 1879), 188.
55 D'Egremont (Smyrne), 14 Jan. 1863, *RC* (Belgium), IX, 1863, 476 and 30 June 1866, *RC* (Belgium), XII, 1866, 565. Salvati (Aidin), 31 Dec. 1863, *RC* (Belgium), X, 1864, 132.
56 'Circular to H.M.'s Consuls in the Ottoman Dominions regarding cotton cultivation together with a summary of their replies', *PP*, 1865, LVII, 800–8.
57 For example, D'Egremont, 14 Jan. 1863, 476 and 25 July 1864, *RC* (Belgium), X, 1864, 578–9. Also Quataert, 'Ottoman reform', 278–9.
58 D'Egremont, 25 July 1864, 580.
59 R. Rougon, *Smyrne: situation commerciale et économique* (Paris/Nancy, 1892), 145–50; O. Conker, *Les chemins de fer en Turquie et la politique ferroviaire Turque* (Paris, 1935), 17–18; 'Report by Major Law on railways in Asiatic Turkey', *PP*, 1896, XCVI, 770–4.
60 *CR* (UK) Smyrna, 1866, *PP*, 1867–8, LXVIII, 231.
61 O. Kurmuş, 'Role of British capital', 97.
62 Ibid., 35.
63 Ibid., 17–18, 42–3.
64 Ibid., 138.
65 Ibid., 142–4.
66 Ibid., 146.
67 Stevens (Smyrna), July 1884, *CR* (US), XI, No. 48 (Dec. 1884), 707.
68 'Reports . . . respecting the condition of the industrial classes in other countries', *PP*, 1870, LXVI, 577; A. Choisy, *L'Asie Mineure et les Turcs en 1875* (Paris, 1876), 266–7.
69 'Reports . . . respecting factories for the spinning and weaving of textile fabrics abroad',

PP, 1873, LXVIII, 187; J. L. Farley, *Banking in Turkey* (London, 1863), 26–30 and *Turkey*, 205; *CR* (Brussa), 1854, *PP*, LV, 583–7 and 1856, *PP*, 1857, XXXVIII, 781.
70 Barker, *Lares et Penates*, 119.
71 Ibid., 120.
72 Gould, 'Pashas and brigands', 68, 196; D'Egremont, 30 Nov. 1864, *RC* (Belgium), XI, 166; Davis, *Life*, 188.
73 Ibid., 172. See also Gould, 'Pashas and brigands', 196.
74 For example, Lewis, *Emergence*, 132–3; E. Kuran, 'Küçük Said Paşa (1840–1914) as a Turkish Modernist', *IJMES*, I, 2 (April 1970), 126; Sarç, 'Tanzimat', 52–3.
75 Ibid., 53.
76 Ibid., 54–5; 'Report by Mr Barron', 628; O. Köymen, 'The advent and consequences of free trade in the Ottoman Empire', *Etudes Balkaniques*, VII, 2 (1971), 48ff. The fact that in the case of the great majority of foreign goods on which duty was charged according to the 1861 tariff their price was specified in the tariff and never altered meant that, when international prices rose, the actual protective value of the *ad valorem* duty was reduced, Kurmuş, 'Role of British capital', 264–5. On the abolition of internal duties see Ubicini and Courteille, *Etat présent*, 130–1.
77 *CR* (UK) Constantinople, 1873, *PP*, 1874, LXVII, 885.
78 *CR* (UK) Erzerum, 14 Nov. 1872, *PP*, 1873, LXVII, 695.
79 Kurmuş, 'Role of British capital', 180–2; Rougon, *Smyrne*, 247–51.
80 Kurmuş, 'Role of British capital', 180–2. For a comparison with what the Japanese were able to achieve in the field of military technology at this time see K. Yamamura, 'Success illgotten? The role of Meiji militarism on Japan's technological progress', *JEH*, XXXVII, 1 (March 1977).
81 *CR* (UK) Constantinople, 1873, 884.
82 'Report by Mr Rumbold . . . on the Turkish budget for the year 1871/72', *PP*, 1872, LIX, 596–7; Ubicini and Courteille, *Etat présent*, 182ff. See also the information about ships in the Turkish fleet contained in C. Hecquard, *L'Empire Ottoman: La Turquie sous Abdel-Hamid II* (Brussels etc., 1901), 347–52; *The Army and Navy Illustrated*, III, 12 March 1897, 186.
83 D'Egremont (Smyrne), 8 July 1865, *RC* (Belgium), XI, 663n.
84 Davison, *Reform*, 152; Quataert, 'Ottoman reform', 130.
85 Karpat, 'Land regime', in Polk and Chambers, *Beginnings of Modernization*, 85–90; Davison, *Reform*, 99–100. For the land laws themselves see F. Ongley, *The Ottoman Land Code* (London, 1892).
86 'Land regime', 85.
87 Baer, 'Development of private ownership of land', 57–9.
88 For example, Karpat, 'Land regime', 86, 88–9, Shaw, *Ottoman Empire*, II. 114–15, and H. Inalcik, 'Land problems in Turkish government', *Muslim World*, XLV, 3 (July 1955), 226–7.
89 Quataert, 'Ottoman reform', 38–9; Davison, *Reform*, 258–60; Du Velay, *Essai*, 235–8. See also Inalcik, 'Land problems', 227.
90 Baer, 'Development of private ownership of land', 70–1.
91 Karpat, 'Land regime', 88–89; Quataert, 'Ottoman reform', 42–4.
92 'Report by Mr Barron', 598–603; Baer, 'Development of private ownership of land', 73.
93 Davison, *Reform*, 260–1.
94 Quoted in Du Velay, *Essai*, 241.
95 Ibid.
96 *CR* (UK) Turkey, 1856, *PP*, 1857–8, LV, 166–175; Salvati (Aidin), 31 Dec. 1862, *CR* (Belgium) IX, 1863, 55.
97 *CR* (UK) Erzerum, 1865, *PP*, 1866, LXX, 230.
98 (London, 1878), 125. J. L. Farley made the same point in his *Modern Turkey* (London, 1872), 284–5.
99 *CR* (UK) Trebizond, 1872, *PP*, 1873, LXIV, 835.
100 Gould, 'Pashas and brigands', 143–4; Davis, *Life*, 28–9.
101 For example, ibid., 187. See also M. Hecker, 'Die Eisenbahnen der Asiatischen Turkei', *Archiv für Eisenbahnwesen* (1914), 753, 779–84.

102 Ibid., 779–80; Kurmuş, 'Role of British capital', 42–58; D'Egremont (Smyrne), 25 July 1864, 582.

103 *CR* (Smyrna), 1869, *PP*, 1871, LXV, 550; Rougon, *Smyrne*, 145–6.

104 Hecker ('Die Eisenbhanen', 787) maintains that the government's payment of the guarantee, while it lasted, was 'irregular'.

105 Ibid., 781–4. See also W. von Pressel, 'Principal routes' in Issawi, *Economic History*, 92–3.

5: Egypt, 1850–1882: from foreign borrowing to bankruptcy and occupation

1   For an account of the diplomatic pressures which encouraged Abbas to allow the construction of the first railway line, see H. A. B. Rivlin, 'The railway question in the Ottoman–Egyptian crisis of 1850–1852', *MEJ*, xv, 4 (Autumn 1961), 365–97.

2   J. C. (J. Claudy), *Histoire financière de l'Egypte depuis Said Pasha, 1854–1876* (Paris, 1878), 2; Landes, *Bankers and Pashas*, 112–15 and Appendix D.

3   A-M. Hamza, *The Public Debt of Egypt, 1854–1876* (Cairo, 1944), 6, 34; L. H. Jenks, *The Migration of British Capital to 1875* (London, 1938), 302.

4   Hamza, *Public Debt*, 14–16; Landes, *Bankers and Pashas*, 91–101; J. Marlowe, *Spoiling the Egyptians* (New York, 1975), 84–91. Between 1857 and 1861 an average of 30,000 foreigners entered Egypt each year, Landes, *Bankers and Pashas*, 87. It is not certain how many of them stayed for more than a few months. There are no proper figures for the numbers of permanent foreign residents at this period. According to D. Panzac ('Alexandrie: Evolution d'une ville cosmopolite', *Annales Islamologiques*, xIV (1978), 197) there were 25,000 'foreigners' living in Alexandria in 1846 but it seems unlikely that more than 10,000 or so of these were Europeans. However, by 1871 it has been estimated that there were 80,000 Europeans in the country (Egypt, *Statistique de l'Egypte 1873*, 13) and there may well have been many more during the cotton boom. See also François-Levernay, *Guide-Annuaire d'Egypt: Année 1872–1873* (Cairo, n.d.), 10–11, for an assertion that the official figures given by the consulates underestimate the foreign population by about half.

5   Hamza, *Public Debt*, 12; Marlowe, *Spoiling the Egyptians*, 88; *The Times*, 20 Nov. 1858.

6   D. A. Farnie, *East and West of Suez: The Suez Canal in History, 1854–1956* (Oxford, 1969), 40; Marlowe, *Spoiling the Egyptians*, 58–9; A. Sammarco, *Histoire de l'Egypte moderne*, III, *Le règne du Khédive Ismaïl de 1863 à 1875* (Cairo, 1937), ch. 3.

7   Landes, *Bankers and Pashas*, 176–7; Hamza, *Public Debt*, 27.

8   See Table 17.

9   J. C., *Histoire financière*, 5–6, 15; Hamza, *Public Debt*, 41.

10 Marlowe, *Spoiling the Egyptians*, 93; Hamza, *Public Debt*, 43–4; *The Times*, 9 Sept. 1859; J. C., *Histoire financière*, 4.

11 Hamza, *Public Debt*, 44; J. C., *Histoire financière*, 5–6.

12 Marlowe, *Spoiling the Egyptians*, 93; Landes, *Bankers and Pashas*, 106, 106n–107n.

13 For a study of Egypt's loans during this period see Hamza, *Public Debt* and Ducruet, *Les capitaux européens*, ch. 1. For Said's first loan see also Marlowe, *Spoiling the Egyptians*, 94–7 and Landes, *Bankers and Pashas*, 107–8.

14 Ibid., 108.

15 These are Landes's figures, ibid., 108–10. Hamza gives a figure of £10,000,000 for May 1861, *Public Debt*, 48.

16 Landes, *Bankers and Pashas*, 109.

17 Hamza, *Public Debt*, 53–60; Ducruet, *Les capitaux européens*, 22–3.

18 *Public Debt*, 256–7.

19 *Bankers and Pashas*, 117.

20 Ibid., 117 and 117n.

21 See Hamza's discussion of this point in *Public Debt*, 60–4.

22 For the terms of this Convention see Sammarco, *Règne du Khédive Ismaïl*, 371–3.

23 For Ismail's efforts to secure greater independence from the Ottoman Empire see ibid., ch. 6. For the extension of European Capitulatory rights see Marlowe, *Spoiling the Egyptians*, ch. 3.

24 For the terms of Napoleon III's arbitration see Sammarco, *Règne du Khédive Ismaïl*, 373–88. See also, Landes, *Bankers and Pashas*, 160, 187–8; Hamza, *Public Debt*, 77–8.

25 Ibid., 79–81; Marlowe, *Spoiling the Egyptians*, 164–5; Landes, *Bankers and Pashas*, 220.

26 This estimate is taken from the official report of a former official at the Egyptian Ministry of Finance. It includes the government's floating debt of £28,500,000 and Ismail's private floating debt of £6,500,000, Hamza, *Public Debt*, 210–12.

27 Ibid., 210–13.

28 Ibid., 186–90; Marlowe, *Spoiling the Egyptians*, 172–3.

29 Landes, *Bankers and Pashas*, 317–18; Marlowe, *Spoiling the Egyptians*, 214.

30 Hamza, *Public Debt*, 232. This includes Ismail's private debts. The English financial expert, Stephen Cave, estimated the Egyptian floating debt (official and private to Ismail) at just over £21,000,000 in 1875 ('Report by Mr Cave on the financial condition of Egypt', *PP*, 1876, LXXXIII, 108–10). Lord Cromer gives an estimate of £26,000,000 for 1876, *Modern Egypt*, I (New York, 1908), 13. Other estimates given by Ismail himself (Marlowe, *Spoiling the Egyptians*, 254n) or referred to by Hamza (*Public Debt*, 225) would seem to be too low. One of the problems is to estimate how much of the 1873 loan was used to reduce the floating debt. According to Hamza 'by far the larger part' of the nearly £20,000,000 which the Egyptian government actually received was paid in Egyptian government bonds. This would have reduced the estimate of the debt in 1872/3 (see above, n. 26) by at least £10,000,000, if not more. However, new debts were certainly created in the meantime. For the surplus of revenue over expenditure see ibid., 236–7.

31 *Modern Egypt*, I, 11. Lord Milner is concerned to make the same point, *England in Egypt*, 11th edn (London, 1904), 176–80.

32 For example, it has been estimated that the bribes required to obtain the 1873 firman granting Egypt almost full autonomy cost £1,000,000, Marlowe, *Spoiling the Egyptians*, 161.

33 Hamza, *Public Debt*, 274–5. I have subtracted the payments for 1876 from Hamza's total. His calculations assume that the Egyptian government was scrupulous in meeting its obligations on time according to the schedules set out in the original loan agreements.

34 Ibid., 256–7.

35 Ibid., 236–7.

36 For example, 'Report by Mr Cave' (108) puts the money spent on works of utility at £30,240,058.

37 Two pamphlets which appeared in London in 1874 give almost identical figures for expenditure on public works to those given to Cave by Ismail and his advisers two years later. It would appear that these were an attempt to impress would-be investors. See Anon., *The Finances of Egypt* (London, 1874) and R. H. L., *The Financial Position of Egypt* (London, 1874). Also Hunter, 'Bureaucratic politics', 224.

38 For Egyptian railway development at this time see L. Wiener, *L'Egypte et ses chemins de fer* (Brussels, 1932) and C. Issawi, 'Asymmetrical development and transport in Egypt 1800–1914' in Polk and Chambers, *Beginnings of Modernization*, 394–7. For the cost see 'Report by Mr Cave', 116.

39 Crouchley, *Economic Development*, 117.

40 *Cambridge Modern History*, X (Cambridge, 1960), 419–20.

41 For the size of the army see the document quoted in G. Guindi and J. Tagher, *Ismail d'après les documents officiels* (Cairo, 1946), 173. For the money allocated to the army and navy see Hamza, *Public Debt*, 282–4.

42 Baer, *Landownership*, 31.

43 See, for example, 'Memorandum by Capt. Baring of interview with a native as to the collection of taxes, Feb. 1878' in *Revenue Survey of Egypt* (1879?) a copy of which can be found in the Library of the Royal Geographical Society, London, LBR, MSS, AR/116.

44 See, for example, 'Report of the International Commission upon Consular Jurisdiction', *PP*, 1870, LVI, 637–50. Also Nubar's dispatch of 10 Aug. 1867 quoted in Guindi and Tagher, *Ismail*, 71–4.

45 For an example of such an exaggeration see the estimate of Egypt's revenues prepared by a committee of Europeans in Alexandria, 1878, B. Jerrold, *Egypt under Ismail Pasha*

(London, 1879), 114–31. The willingness of the representatives of foreign creditors to exaggerate in this way was further increased by the fact that Ismail himself and his officials used to make the same kind of overestimate in order to try to convince potential investors of the country's financial good health. See for example, Cave, 17 Jan. 1876, FO 78/2538. See also Hunter, 'Bureaucratic politics', 266–82.

46   Marlowe, *Spoiling the Egyptians*, 214–17; Platt, *Finance, Trade and Politics*, 157–8.
47   Marlowe, *Spoiling the Egyptians*, 216–21; Platt, *Finance, Trade and Politics*, 158.
48   Bouvier, 'Les intérêts financiers', 94–5.
49   English writers like Platt (*Finance, Trade and Politics*, 158–60) often underline the fact that Goschen was officially a representative of the British bond holders not of the British government. This is not a point which Ismail himself is likely to have appreciated. Whether or not Goschen had the total support of his own government, the power he possessed to propose and execute his financial scheme in conjunction with Joubert was enormous. See, for example, R. A. Atkins, 'The origins of the Anglo-French condominium in Egypt, 1875–1876', *The Historian*, xxxvi, 2 (Feb. 1974), 278.
50   Two other loans (those of 1865 and 1867) were secured wholly or partially against the Daira estates. But they were of short maturity and thus placed in the same category as the loans of 1864, 1866 and 1867.
51   For details of the scheme as a whole see Marlowe, *Spoiling the Egyptians*, 222–5; Hunter, 'Bureaucratic politics', 277–8.
52   Marlowe, *Spoiling the Egyptians*, 227–31.
53   Ibid., 232–4, 237–40.
54   Ibid., 241–2.
55   Ibid., 246–52; Cromer, *Modern Egypt*, i, ch. 7; Hunter, 'Bureaucratic politics', 330–1, 343–60.
56   Marlowe, *Spoiling the Egyptians*, 261–2.
57   For example, Cromer, *Modern Egypt*, ii (New York, 1908), ch. 53.
58   Cromer, *Modern Egypt*, i, 117–22, 168. The complete amalgamation of *ushuriya* and *kharajiya* land had to wait for the completion of the cadastral survey conducted between 1898 and 1907, Baer, *Landownership*, 12; R. L. Tignor, *Modernization and British Colonial Rule in Egypt, 1882–1914* (Princeton, 1966), 246–7.
59   Cromer, *Modern Egypt*, i, 44–5.
60   Marlowe, *Spoiling the Egyptians*, 260.
61   Platt, *Finance, Trade and Policy*, 170.
62   Marlowe, *Spoiling the Egyptians*, 225, 228.
63   A. Schölch, *Agypten den Agyptern! Die Politische und gesellschaftliche Krise der Jahre 1878–1882 in Agypten* (Zurich and Frieburg, n.d.), 339–40.
64   Ibid., 177–90.
65   Marlowe, *Spoiling the Egyptians*, 242–4; Schölch, *Agypten den Agyptern*, 127–9; Cromer, *Modern Egypt*, i, 74.
66   Sir A. Colvin, *Making of Modern Egypt* (London, n.d.), 25.
67   This is the argument of A. Schölch, 'The "Men on the spot" and the English occupation of Egypt in 1882', *HJ*, xix, 3 (1976), 773–85. I have followed it in my own, 'Robinson and Gallagher and Middle Eastern nationalism: the Egyptian argument' in Wm R. Louis (ed.), *Imperialism; The Robinson and Gallagher Controversy* (New York, London, 1976), 212–16. But it should also be noted that the reasons for the British occupation of Egypt have never ceased to be a source of controversy, beginning with the men who were actually involved at the time. The events of 1882 have also often been used to attempt to prove or disprove one or other theory of imperialism. For some recent contributions to this debate see R. Robinson and J. Gallagher with Alice Denny, *Africa and the Victorians* (London, 1970), ch. 4; Platt, *Finance, Trade and Politics*, 154–80; and my own 'Egypt and Europe; from French Expedition to British Occupation' in R. Owen and B. Sutcliffe (eds), *Studies in the Theory of Imperialism* (London, 1972), 195–209.
68   Owen, *Cotton*, 148; *Statistique de l'Egypte 1873*, ix.
69   I have used the figures for Egypt's population in 1846 and 1882 to be found in McCarthy, 'Nineteenth century Egyptian population', 1–42. This involves accepting McCarthy's argument about the accuracy of the 1846 census and the underestimate involved in the

1882 census. I have then subtracted the population of Cairo and Alexandria and other large towns.

70 Owen, *Cotton*, 89, 95, 102–4, 130.
71 *Statistique de l'Egypte* 1873, 288–9; Farman (Alexandria), 1 Nov. 1876, *CR* (US) 1876, *Exec. Docs*, 1877, 903–37.
72 Ibid.
73 Owen, *Cotton*, 129–30.
74 Ibid., 106, 128, 140–3.
75 The *ardabb* was a unit of volume and varied between 180 and 200 litres.
76 D. R. Serpell, 'American consular activities in Egypt, 1849–1863', *JMH*, x, 3 (Sept. 1938).
77 T. K. Fowler, *Report on the Cultivation of Cotton in Egypt* (Manchester, 1861), 18.
78 Owen, *Cotton*, 77–8.
79 For example, D. M. Wallace, *Egypt and the Egyptian Question* (London, 1883), 269–70.
80 Owen, *Cotton*, 106.
81 Ibid., 122–6.
82 J. H. Scott, *The Law Affecting Foreigners in Egypt* (Edinburgh, 1907), 192–204; 'Un Ancien Juge Mixte', *L'Egypte et l'Europe*, I (Leiden, n.d. – preface written in 1881), 118–19n, 129–30; Marlowe, *Spoiling the Egyptians*, ch. 3.
83 Owen, *Cotton*, 130–1; François-Leverney, *Guide-Annuaire*, 261ff.
84 Baer, *Landownership*, 37.
85 Ibid., 69–70.
86 Figures from ibid., 224–5. 'Registered land' contained a small amount of uncultivated land and was thus slightly larger than the cultivated area. I have accepted Baer's definition of 'large' properties as being over 50 feddans. However, this view has often been challenged by those who believe that a better definition of 'large' would be 100 feddans and over. For example, A. al-Disuqi, *Kibar mullak al-aradi al-ziraiyya wa dawruhum fi'l mujtama al-misri, 1914–1952* (Cairo, 1975), 24–6.
87 Baer, *Landownership*, 14–15.
88 Ibid., 38–9.
89 *HP*, III, f68; Baer, *Landownership*, 13–19, 40–3. See also, Huber (Cairo), 3 May 1852, AA Box 24, for information about the agricultural properties left by Muhammad Ali at his death, and the following sources for Ismail's acquisitions: G. Douin, *Histoire du regue du Khedive Ismail*, I (Rome, 1933), 261; J. C. M'Coan, *Egypt as It Is* (London, 1877), 150. For non-royal acquisitions, see Baer, *Landownership*, 26–7, 45–60; A. Abdel-Malek, *Idéologie et renaissance nationale: L'Egypte moderne* (Paris, 1969), 81–8.
90 Ibid., 50–6. See also Baer's, 'The village shaykh 1800–1950' in *Studies*, 37–60; Abel-Malek, *Idéologie et renaissance nationale*, 87–8; Wallace, *Egypt and the Egyptian Question*, 198.
91 Baer, *Landownership*, 224.
92 For information about the 'flight' of the peasants from the land see Baer, *Landownership*, 38; Wallace, *Egypt and the Egyptian Question*, 232; and I. ʿAmr, *al-Ard wal-Fallah* (Cairo, 1958), 81–2. See also my own calculation that the loss of peasant land was probably in excess of 300,000 feddans, *Cotton*, 147–8.
93 *Statistique de l'Egypt 1873*, 269. This figure would, of course, be in line with the loss of 300,000 feddans of peasant land (see note 92 above) given the very small size of the average Egyptian plot.
94 UK IO 'Report by Mr Cave', 102–3.
95 For information about this practice as it had developed by the 1880s see Y. Artin, 'Essai sur les causes du renchérissement de la vie matérielle au Caire au courant du XIXe siècle (1800 à 1907)', *MIE*, v (Cairo, 1907), 87.
96 Huber (Alexandria), 17 July 1857, AA Box 31.
97 Baer, *Landownership*, 16–17.
98 Ibid., 7–10.
99 Y. Artin, *The Right of Landed Property in Egypt* (trans.) (London, 1885), 67–9.

100   Baer, *Landownership*, 11–12; Cromer, *Modern Egypt*, I, 117–22.
101   P. Merruau, 'L Egypt sous le gouvernement de Said-Pasha', *RDM*, XI, 2nd period, 15 Sept. 1857, 328.
102   Artin, *Right of Landed Property*, 92.
103   Egypt, Commission Supérieure d'Enquête, *Rapport préliminaire adressé à S.A. le Khédive* (Cairo, 1878), 27–8. For another detailed description of the system of tax collection at this time see 'Memorandum by Captain Baring'.
104   Commission Supérieure d'Enquête, *Rapport*, 30.
105   *Letters from Egypt* (London, 1902), 191.
106   Owen, *Cotton*, 150–1. The relationship is well described by 'Un ancient juge mixte', *L'Egypte*, I, 131–4.
107   *Letters from Egypt*, 243, 257.
108   For example, Commission Supérieure d'Enquête, *Rapport*, 33; M'Coan, *Egypt as It Is*, 117; Jerrold, *Egypt under Ismail Pasha*, 294–99; Dr E. Rossi, *La population et les finances: Quéstion égyptienne* (Paris, 1878), 55.
109   For example, W. H. Yates, *The Modern History and Conditions of Egypt*, I (London, 1843), 133.
110   *HP*, III, 63; see also, Hamont, *L'Egypte*, 126–7.
111   Hamont, op. cit., 69. See also, Rivlin, *Agricultural Policy*, 69–70.
112   Rivlin, op. cit., 77.
113   Hamont, *L'Egypte*, I, 77; Giddon, *Memoir*, 26.
114   See for example Abbas Pasha's comments to Hekekyan, *HP*, II, 39.
115   J. Mazuel, *Le sucre en Egypte* (Cairo, 1937), 33–4.
116   M'Coan, *Egypt as It Is*, 117 and J. C. McCoan, *Egypt under Ismail* (London, 1889), 55; enclosure in Malet (Alexandria), 2 June 1880, *PP*, 1880, LXXV, 757.
117   *Statistique de l'Egypte 1873*, 289; Owen, *Cotton*, 129; Wallace, *Egypt and the Egyptian Question*, 343.
118   M'Coan, *Egypt as It Is*, 151–2; 'Report by Mr Cave', 103; Wallace, *Egypt and the Egyptian Question*, 344; Mazuel, *Le sucre en Egypte*, 35–7.
119   UK IO 'Report by Mr Cave', 103.
120   M'Coan, *Egypt as It Is*, 151.
121   Ibid.
122   *CR* (UK) Alexandria 1872/3, *PP*, 1874, LXVII, 54.
123   For a description of an early *izba* see Villiers Stuart, *Egypt after the War* (London, 1883), 27–9. See also, J. Lozarch and G. Hug, *L'habitat rural en Egypte* (Cairo, 1930), 158; Hunter, 'Bureaucratic politics', 182–3.
124   Lozarch and Hug, *L'habitat rural*, 156.
125   Egypt, *Recensement général de l'Egypte 1882*, I (Cairo, 1884), xxxi.
126   Ibid., 203.
127   J. F. Nahas, *Situation économique et sociale du fellah égyptien* (Paris, 1901), 141, 143.
128   S. Nour Ed-Din, 'Conditions des fellahs en Egypte', *RI*, III (1898), 5–6.
129   R. de Chamberet, *Enquête sur la condition du fellah égyptien* (Dijon, 1909), 19.
130   Nour Ed-Din, 'Conditions', 6; Nahas, *Situation*, 134–5.
131   Stuart, *Egypt after the War*, 144–5.
132   J. B. Piot Bey, 'Coup d'oeil sur l'économie actuelle du betail en Egypte', *EC*, VI (March 1911), 201–2.
133   For example, ʿAmr in his *al-Ard wal-Fallah*, 81–2.
134   Ibid., 124.
135   For a more general account of this phenomenon see my 'Development of agricultural production'. For the use of the *izba* as a rural political base see Hunter, 'Bureaucratic politics', 182–4.
136   For the decree creating the government statistical service see Gundi and Tagher, *Ismail*, 95.
137   C. B. Kluzinger, *Upper Egypt: Its People and Its Products* (London, 1878), 11–15; Couvidou, *Etude sur l'Egypte contemporaine*, 208–9.
138   For an account of the railway repair workshops see A. I. Garwood, *Forty Years in an Engineer's Life at Home and Abroad* (Newport, Mon., n.d.), 98–9.

139 I have used McCarthy's population figures ('Nineteenth century population', Table 12) and assumed that half the male population was over 15.

140 For the impact of foreign glass see Kluzinger, *Upper Egypt*, 14. To judge from the figures for the import of certain manufactured goods contained in Table 23 it would seem that some local products like candles may well have been under pressure from foreign competition.

141 For the paving of the streets of Alexandria with imported stone see François-Levernay, *Guide-Annuaire*, 113.

142 See, for example, Kluzinger's remarks on the subject, *Upper Egypt*, 16.

143 Zinzinia (Alexandria), 29 Feb. 1856, *RC* (Belgium) II (1856), 335. For a statement of Ismail's industrial strategy see his speech to the opening of the 1869 session of the Egyptian Assembly of Notables, a translation of which can be found in Hale (Alexandria), 13 Feb. 1869, US (Egypt), v (13 Jan. 1868–28 May 1870).

144 For one of the many contemporary criticisms of the Khedive's factories see *CR* (US) Egypt 1876, *Exec. Docs*, 45, 903–37.

145 For example, ibid.

146 Mazuel, *Sucre*, 35–7; *CR* (US) Egypt 1878, *Exec. Docs*, 1878/9, 1116–30.

147 For the suggestion that Egypt's sugar exports were subsidized see UK IO, 'Report by Mr Cave', 103.

148 A few such factories may be contained in the official statistics relating to cotton ginning and pressing.

149 For information about the private sector see, *inter alia*, François-Levernay, *Guide-Annuaire*, 20–1, 170–3; C. Edmond (pseud.), *L'Egypte à l'exposition universelle de 1867* (Paris, 1867), 250ff.

150 Owen, *Cotton*, 158; A. Wright (ed.), *Twentieth-Century Impressions of Egypt* (London, 1909), 487–95.

6: The provinces of Greater Syria, 1850–1880: the economic and social tensions of the 1850s and their consequences

1 For detailed accounts of this process see Ducousso, *L'industrie de la soie*, 85–9, 105–7, 116, 129, 136; Chevalier, *Mont Liban*, ch. 14; Saba, 'Development and decline', 48–59.

2 Chevalier, *Mont Liban*, 226.

3 Ibid., 231–3; J. Laffey, 'Roots of French imperialism in the nineteenth century: the case of Lyon', *French Historical Studies*, VI, 1 (Spring 1969), 81n; M. Emerit, 'La crise syrienne et l'expansion économique française en 1860', *RH*, CCVII (1952), 211–32. See also, D. Chevalier, 'Lyon et Syrie en 1919. Les bases d'une intervention', *RH*, CCXXIV (Oct./Dec. 1960), 276–7.

4 Chevalier, *Mont Liban*, 230.

5 *CR* (UK) Beirut 1856, *PP*, 1857, XXXVIII, 783. The fact that, according to the French figures, both the *price* and the *value* of silk exports rose by about 400 per cent between 1850 and 1856 could be taken as evidence to support the argument that there had been no increase in the *volume* of Lebanese silk production during this same period. On the other hand, the figures themselves pose many problems: they may not be accurate, they include the value of the export of cocoons as well as thread, they exclude exports from Tripoli and Saida, and they probably exclude the export of non-factory thread to other parts of the Middle East. In these circumstances there seems little point in pursuing the argument further.

6 Joseph, 'Material origins', 68, 111.

7 V. Cuinet, *Turquie d'Asie*, V., *Syrie, Liban et Palestine* (Paris, 1896), 218.

8 *Mont Liban*, 232n.

9 Ibid.

10 Ducousso, *L'industrie de la soie*, 66–9.

11 Ibid., 69. See also, G. Ducousso, 'Le grainage au Liban' in Comité Executif du Ier Congrès Libannais de la sériculture, *Rapport du Ier Congrès Libanais de la sériculture* (Beirut, n.d. (1930?)), 80.

12 It is possible that a disruptive role may have been played by those merchants with an

interest in maintaining the continued import of foreign eggs. This was certainly the case in the next decade when such men were instrumental in preventing the Ottoman Public Debt Administration from setting up a Pasteur Institute for egg selection in the Mountain. Saba, 'Development and decline', 68–9.

13 Chevalier, *Mont Liban*, 219; Ducousso, *L'industrie de la soie*, 125.
14 Chevalier, *Mont Liban*, 220.
15 Emerit, 'Crise syrienne', 226.
16 Kalla, 'Role of foreign trade', 209–10.
17 Ducousso, *L'industrie de la soie*, 125.
18 Ibid., 127.
19 D. Chevalier, 'Aux origines des troubles agraires libanais en 1858', *Annales*, XIV, 1 (Jan.–Mar. 1959), 52–3; *Mont Liban*, 214–16, 218.
20 Chevalier, 'Lyon et Syrie', 294.
21 Chevalier, *Mont Liban*, 234–6; Emerit, 'Crise syrienne', 225–6; Ducousso, *L'industrie de la soie*, 126–7.
22 A. Gaudry, *Recherches scientifique en Orient . . . 1853–1854, Partie Agricole* (Paris, 1855), 293.
23 For a good description of some of these problems see A. I. Tannous, 'Social change in an Arab village', *American Sociological Review*, VI, 5 (Oct. 1941), 655–6.
24 Emerit, 'Crise syrienne', 227; Ducousso, *L'industrie de la soie*, 134.
25 For example, Tannous, 'Social change', 654–5.
26 See pp. 251–2.
27 Smilianskaya, 'Disintegration of feudal relations', 234–5.
28 Ibid., 235.
29 Chevalier, 'Aux origines', 51.
30 Smilianskaya, 'Disintegration of feudal relations', 242; Ducousso, *L'industrie de la soie*, 180; *CR* (UK) Beirut 1850 in Moore (Beirut), 1 Mar. 1851, FO 78/873.
31 Joseph, 'Material origins', 63–5; Kalla, 'Role of foreign trade', 202–3; Saba, 'Development and decline', 33–4.
32 Ducousso, *L'industrie de la soie*, 145–7.
33 Chevalier, *Mont Liban*, 201–2.
34 See pp. 98–9.
35 Saba, 'Development and decline', 41.
36 Events in the Kisrawan have been endlessly written about, almost to the exclusion of other places. For the situation there see Chevalier, 'Aux originies', 37–63; A. D. Al-'Aqiqi, *Lebanon in the last years of feudalism*, trans. and ed. M. H. Kerr (Beirut, 1959); Y. Porath, 'The peasant revolt of 1858–61 in Kisrawan', *AAS*, II (1966), 77–157. See also T. Touma, *Paysans et institutions féodales chez les Druses et les Maronites du Liban du XVIIe siècle à 1914* (Beirut, 1971), 246–71.
37 M. J. Deeb, 'The Khazin family: a case study of the effect of social change on traditional roles', M.A. (American University of Beirut, 1972), 56; K. S. Salibi, *The Modern History of Lebanon* (London, 1965), 86–7.
38 For a good description of their mood see Joseph, 'Material origins', 157–8.
39 For example, enclosure in Moore (Beirut), 4 Jan. 1863, FO 78/1752. See also P. Saba, 'The creation of the Lebanese economy: economic growth in the nineteenth and early twentieth centuries' in R. Owen (ed.), *Essays on the Crisis in Lebanon* (London, 1976), 10.
40 'Correspondence relating to the affairs of Syria', *PP*, 1861, LXVIII, 482; R. de Witte (ed.), *The Massacres in Syria* (New York, 1860), 56; R. Edwards, *La Syrie 1840–1862* (Paris, 1862), 133–4; Joseph, 'Material origins', 157–62. See also F. Steppat, 'Some Arabic manuscript sources on the Syrian crisis of 1860', in J. Berque and D. Chevalier (eds), *Les Arabes par leurs archives* (Paris, 1876), 186.
41 Interesting support for the view that the fighting had its origin in an attack on *muqataji* (or, in his parlance, 'feudal') rule comes from Lord Dufferin, the British Commissioner sent to report on events in Lebanon. As he argued in a dispatch he sent from Beirut on 25 April 1861: 'If we had paused to observe that the first invader of the Druze Kaimcam-ship has been the leader of a successful agrarian revolt in his own district (Yusuf

Karam); that the original instigators of the hostile movement against the Druzes were this man's partisans; that the priesthood to whom public repute assigned a principal share in preparing the events that followed had extended their patronage to the revolted peasants; and that numerous members of the Maronite landed aristocracy were accused of sympathising with the Druze nation, it would be difficult to avoid arriving at the opinion that the contest was to be regarded rather as a demonstration against feudalism and the community which is regarded *par excellence* the representative of the feudal principle, than a contest of race or religion', FO 195/659.

42   Salibi, *Modern History*, 87–8.
43   Not surprisingly there is considerable disagreement about the numbers actually killed. Salibi (*Modern History*, 106) gives a figure of 11,000 with 4000 more who died of destitution. J. P. Spagnolo speaks only of 'hundreds' dead, *France and Ottoman Lebanon: 1861–1914* (London, 1977), 31. There is no dispute about the vast destruction of property.
44   Ibid., 41–5. For a copy of the document itself see Hurewitz, *Diplomacy*, I, 166ff.
45   This is what the British silk factory owner, Scott, tried to do. See enclosure in Moore (Beirut), 5 Nov. 1858, FO 195/587.
46   See for example, 'Memorial from British merchants . . . on various grievances' in Moore (Beirut), 4 Nov. 1858, FO 226/126.
47   *CR* (UK) Beirut 1859 in Moore (Beirut), 7 Feb. 1860, FO 78/1539. Also 'Sketches of cases requiring settlement at Beyrout' in Calvert (Beirut), 10 Sept. 1869, FO 195/648. According to J. L. Farley, the manager of the newly-opened branch of the Ottoman Bank in Beirut, the bank had bad debts worth £100,000 in 1858, *Two Years in Syria* (London, 1858), Appendix II.
48   Article 10, Hurewitz, *Diplomacy*, I, 167.
49   There was a short period when the writ of the *mutassarif* hardly ran in any of the Mountain's northern districts but matters improved with the exile of Yusuf Karam in 1867, J. P. Spagnolo, 'Mount Lebanon, France and Daud Pasha: a study of some aspects of political habituation', *IJMES*, II (1971), 149–58.
50   'Report on the financial state of Mount Lebanon', 16 Mar. 1878, FO 226/198.
51   'Report on the present state of Mount Lebanon', 24 Nov. 1875, FO 226/184.
52   For information concerning the reduced size of the former *muqatajis'* estates see Saba, 'Creation of the Lebanese economy', 13.
53   Salibi, *Modern History*, 111–12.
54   Deeb, 'The Khazin family', 89–96; M. Fevret, 'Un village du Liban', *Revue de Géographie du Lyon*, XXV (1950), 279; Al-'Aqiqi, *Lebanon*, 25.
55   Emerit, 'Crise syrienne', 226.
56   See p. 157.
57   Spagnolo, *France and Ottoman Lebanon*, 94n.
58   For the terms of this convention see E. Hertslet, *Treaties and Tariffs Regulating Trade between Great Britain and Foreign Nations: Turkey* (London, 1875), 54–70.
59   *CR* (UK) Beirut 1861, *PP*, 1863, LXX, 448.
60   Ducousso, *L'industrie de la soie*, 180.
61   Saba, 'Creation of the Lebanese economy', 15.
62   Smilianskaya, 'Disintegration of feudal relations', 231–2.
63   E. Eléfteriadès, *Les chemins de fer en Syrie et au Liban* (Beirut, 1944), 39–44. A copy of the concession can be found in Alison (Beirut), 26 Feb. 1858, FO 226/124.
64   Cuinet, *Syrie, Liban et Palestine*, 225–8.
65   Kalla, 'Role of foreign trade', Table VI; *CR* (UK) Beirut 1880, *PP*, 1881, XC, 651.
66   *CR* (UK) Syria 1875, *PP*, 1876, LXXV, 282–4.
67   Ibid.
68   Spagnolo, *France and Ottoman Lebanon*, 143.
69   'Report on the present state of Mount Lebanon', 24 Nov. 1875 and *CR* (UK) Syria 1875, 284.
70   *CR* (Beirut) 1873, *PP*, 1874, LXVII, 863; 'Report on the present state of Mount Lebanon', 25 Nov. 1875.
71   'Report . . . upon revenues and taxation . . . in Syria', *PP*, 1877, LXXXI, 607.

72   *CR* (UK) Beirut 1873, 849.

73   Information from Mr Fawwaz Trabulsi.

74   For sources see below, note 137.

75   For information about this migration see A. H. Hourani, *Syria and Lebanon* (London, 1946), 34–5.

76   For example, section on 'Emigration', in R. Widmer, 'Population', in S. B. Himadeh, *Economic Organization of Syria* (Beirut, 1936), 13–15.

77   See 'Report on "Education" in Mount Lebanon', *PP*, 1875, LXXVII, 1722–3.

78   'La question syrienne', *RMM*, II (June/July 1907), 520–1.

79   Ibid., 521–2.

80   The area covered by this survey is roughly that of the Ottoman pashalics of Damascus and Aleppo as reorganized after 1840. For further details of the boundaries of these pashalics see Ma'oz, *Ottoman Reform*, 31–4.

81   Ibid., 49–51.

82   Ibid., 51–2.

83   Ibid., 112–13, 165; Naff, 'A social history of Zahle', 332ff. For a description of the Bekaa in the 1840s see Guys, *Beyrout et le Liban*, II (Paris, 1850), 37.

84   Ma'oz, *Ottoman Reform*, ch. 9; Lewis, 'The frontier of settlement in Syria', 262–3. See also Skene (Aleppo), 25 Aug. 1858 in file on 'Turbulence and banditry in Aleppo District', FO 226/129. Anon., *Rambles*, 27–34 contains a very good contemporary account of Ottoman tribal policy.

85   Kalla, 'Role of foreign trade', 15.

86   For example, Skene (Aleppo), 20 Feb. 1858, FO 226/121.

87   Kalla, 'Role of foreign trade', Appendix, Table 1; J. L. Farley, *Two Years in Syria*, 370–1 and *Massacres in Syria* (London, 1861), 185–6.

88   Some evidence for an increase in the size of the harvest comes from the report that there was a 100 per cent increase in the sum for which the rural tithe in the Aleppo district was farmed between 1846 and 1856, *CR* (UK) Aleppo 1857, *PP*, 1859, 2, XXX, 809.

89   *CR* (UK) Damascus 1858, *PP*, 1859, XXX, 854–5 and Damascus 1859, *PP*, 1862, LVIII, 596.

90   For example, Skene (Aleppo), 25 Aug. 1858.

91   Sandwith (Damascus), 25 Feb. 1862, FO 195/724.

92   There is the usual doubt as to the exact number killed. Steppat quotes an anonymous Christian writer who gives a figure of 6000, 'Some Arabic manuscript sources', 189. L. Schatkowski-Schilcher mentions 8000, 'The decline of Syrian localism: the Damascene notables 1785–1870', D. Phil. (Oxford, 1978), 150. K. S. Salibi asserts that there were 5500 killed on the first day, 'The 1860 upheaval in Damascus' in Polk and Chambers, *Beginnings of Modernization*, 200n.

93   For example, Joseph, 'Material origins', 54–8.

94   *CR* (UK) Damascus 1872, *PP*, 1873, LXIV, 372–3.

95   Ma'oz, *Ottoman Reform*, 73; Schatkowski-Schilcher, 'Decline of Syrian localism', 125–6.

96   Rogers (Damascus), 5 Feb. 1863, FO 195/760; Schatkowski-Schilcher, 'Decline of Syrian localism', 126, 129.

97   Rogers (Damascus), 31 Dec. 1862, FO 195/727.

98   For general accounts of the Damascus riots see Ma'oz, *Ottoman Reform*, 231–40; Salibi, 'The 1860 upheaval in Damascus'; Steppat, 'Some Arabic manuscript sources'. See also A. K. Rafiq (Rafeq), *al-'Arab waal-'Uthmaniyun*, 1516–1916 (Damascus, 1974), 424–5. For an interesting survey of the various types of argument put forward to explain these events see Schatkowski-Schilcher, 'Decline of Syrian localism', 149–56.

99   *Turkey*, 212. See also Table 8.

100 Salibi, 'The 1860 upheaval in Damascus', 198–200; Jago (Beirut), 12 Dec. 1873, FO 225/177; Schatkowski-Schilcher, 'Decline of Syrian localism', 156–8.

101 Schatkowski-Schilcher, 'Decline of Syrian localism', 152.

102 See Table 31. See also Rogers (Damascus), 26 Jan. 1865, FO 195/806.

103 Lewis, 'Frontiers of settlement', 262–6. For the early use of Circassian colonists see *CR* (UK) Damascus 1872, *PP*, 1873, LXIV, 377 and G. Schumaker, *The Jaulan* (trans.)

(London, 1888), 57–8. For the Hauran see R. F. Burton and C. F. Tyrwhitt-Drake, *Unexplored Syria*, I (London, 1872), 178–80.

104 For example, Rogers (Damascus), 7 May 1867, FO 195/806 and Eldridge (Beirut), 30 Sept. 1868, FO 195/903. For relations with the al-Atrash see D. McDowell, 'The Druze revolt, 1925–7, and its background in the late Ottoman period', B. Litt. (Oxford, 1972), 35–6, 42–9.

105 Schatkowski-Schilcher, 'Decline of Syrian localism', 187–8. Some of the land in the newly pacified districts was previously cultivated by peasants who had been forced to flee in recent times as a result of the renewed rural insecurity in the 1840s and 1850s. The state was quick to assert its legal right to ownership of this land, *CR* (UK) Damascus 1879, *PP*, 1880, LXXIV, 247.

106 For a detailed description of the system of tax-farming see *CR* (UK) Damascus 1880, *PP*, 1881, XC, 1087–90.

107 Lewis, 'Frontiers of settlement', 262; H. S. Cowper, *Through Turkish Arabia* (London, 1894), 166–7.

108 For a good account of this process see *CR* (UK) Aleppo, June 1890, FO 861/22.

109 For conditions round Latakia see Anon., 'La province turque de Latakie, son étendue, ses habitants, son importance commerciale', *Annales des Voyages*, I (Feb. 1867), 241–5.

110 *CR* (UK) North Syria 1871, *PP*, 1872, LVII, 275–6.

111 *CR* (UK) Damascus, 1877, *PP*, 1878, LXXIII, 519; Jago (Aleppo), 29 Apr. 1877, FO 226/191.

112 Some 115,000 men were conscripted from the Syrian provinces, S. Shamir, 'The modernization of Syria: problems and solutions in the early period of Abdulhamid', in Polk and Chambers, *Beginnings of Modernization*, 379. See also Jago (Aleppo), 21 Jan. and 29 Apr. 1877, FO 226/191; *CR* (UK) Damascus 1879, *PP*, 1880, LXXIV, 237.

113 For example, *CR* (UK) North Syria 1871, 282 and *CR* (UK) Aleppo 1873, *PP*, 1874, LXVII, 275.

114 Farnie, *East and West*, 145–7. In 1870 Richard Burton, the British consul in Damascus, examined a newly arrived desert caravan with 4000 camels from Baghdad. It contained 2500 loads of Persian tobacco and 700 loads of dates. However, he doubted whether it would find more than 200 loads of merchandise for its return journey, Burton (Damascus), 20 Jan. 1870, *PP*, 1871, LXV, 664–5. In the early 1880s the average number of loads from Baghdad was estimated at 2000 a year and the loads sent to Baghdad from Damascus at 1000 a year. *CR* (UK) Damascus 1882, *PP*, 1883, LXXII, 551–2.

115 *CR* (UK) Damascus 1874, *PP*, 1874, LXVII, 978. Also Damascus 1877, *PP*, 1878, LXXIII, 518–19.

116 *CR* (UK) Damascus 1882, 549.

117 For sources see note 103.

118 Shamir, 'Modernization of Syria', 365–6.

119 For example, *CR* (UK) Damascus 1872, *PP*, 1873, LXIV, 372 and Damascus 1879, *PP*, 1880, LXXIV, 243.

120 Shamir, 'Modernization of Syria', 365–7.

121 *CR* (UK) Damascus 1873, *PP*, 1874, LXVII, 305–7.

122 Kalla, 'Role of foreign trade', 202–3.

123 *CR* (Damascus) 1879, *PP*, 1880, LXXIV, 236; Chevalier, 'Lyon et Syrie', 290.

124 *CR* (UK) Tripoli 1874, *PP*, 1875, LXXVII, 471.

125 This survey concerns itself with the districts within the independent *vilayet* of Jerusalem (created in 1854) and the *sanjak* of Acre. See Ma'oz, *Ottoman Reform*, 32–4.

126 For a fuller account of this struggle see ibid., 113–23; Hoexter, 'The role of the Qays and Yaman factions', 266–74; J. Finn, *Stirring Times: Or Records from the Jerusalem Consular Chronicles of 1853 to 1856*, 2 vols (London, 1878), I and II, *passim*.

127 For example, E. Finn, 'The fellaheen of Palestine', in *Palestine Exploration Fund, The Survey of Palestine: Special Papers* (London, 1881), 339–41.

128 E. Pierotti, *Customs and Traditions of Palestine* (trans.) (Cambridge/London, 1864), 273–4.

129 For example, Finn, *Stirring Times*, I, 327–30, 350–5; Ma'oz, *Ottoman Reform*, 121.

130 Ibid., ch. 16 and 226–30.

131 Y. Porath, *The Emergence of the Palestine–Arab National Movement 1918–1929* (London, 1974), 11–15 and 'The political awakening of the Palestinian arabs and their leadership towards the end of the Ottoman period' in Ma'oz, *Studies on Palestine*, 364–5.

132 C. R. Conder, *Tent Work in Palestine*, i (London, 1878), 112–13.

133 Ibid.

134 Ibid., 211–12.

135 For example, Y. Firestone, 'Crop-sharing economics in Mandatory Palestine – 1', *MES*, xi (1975), 3–4.

136 For example, D. K. Amiran and Y. Ben-Ariah, 'Sedentarization of beduin in Israel', *IEJ*, xiii, 3 (1963), 166–7.

137 There is some dispute in the sources about how many villages the Sursuqs obtained and for how much. See Conder, i, 165–6; sources quoted in A. Bonné, *State and Economics in the Middle East*, 2nd edn (London, 1955), 189, and 'Report upon revenues and taxation in Syria' (1876), 608.

138 L. Oliphant, *The Land of Gilead: with Excursion in the Lebanon* (Edinburgh, 1880), 329.

139 Conder, *Tent Work*, ii, 328–9.

140 Ibid., 305–27; A. Carmel, 'The German settlers in Palestine and their relations with the local Arab population and the Jewish community 1858–1918' in Ma'oz, *Studies on Palestine*, 443–4. As a rule the first Jewish agricultural settlements were founded very close to a major town. In the 1870s there were two just outside the walls of Jaffa and another near Haifa. There was also an agricultural school near Jaffa. The first attempt to found a settlement in a rural area, that by thirty Moroccan Jewish families at Shafr Amir near Nazareth, was soon abandoned. Conder, *Tent Work*, ii, 305–7, 326–7; A. Ruppin, *The Agricultural Colonisation of the Zionist Organisation in Palestine* (trans.) (London, 1926), 3.

141 FO 'Report upon revenues and taxation in Syria' (1876), 608.

142 Firestone, 'Crop-sharing economics', 1, 12–13.

143 Carmel, 'German settlers', 445–6.

144 For a more extensive discussion of the state of Palestinian agriculture at this time see A. Schölch, 'European penetration and the economic development of Palestine, 1856–82' in R. Owen (ed.), *Studies in the Political Economy of Palestine in the Nineteenth and Twentieth Centuries* (forthcoming).

145 *CR* (US), 'Cereal production of Turkey – 2', viii, No. 25½ (Nov. 1882), 280.

146 On the difficulties at Jaffa see Conder, *Tent Work*, i, 3–4 and A. Robin, *De la Palestine: ses resources agricoles et industrielles* (Paris, 1880), 4–5.

147 See note 133.

148 A. Schölch, 'Aspekte der Wirtschaftlichen Entwicklung Pälastinas in Der 2. Halfte des 19. Jahrhunderts' (*mimeo*), 4.

149 Robin, *De la Palestine*, 5.

150 Kalla, 'Role of foreign trade', 164.

151 *CR* (UK) Jaffa 1873, *PP*, 1874, lxvii, 318.

152 See 'The origin of the Jaffa orange', in S. Tolkowsky, *The Gateway of Palestine: A History of Jaffa* (London, 1924), Appendix III.

153 *CR* (US) 'Fruit culture in Palestine', xii 45 (Sept. 1884), 53–4.

154 *CR* (UK) Syria 1871, *PP*, 1872, lviii, 234–5.

155 Schölch, 'Aspekte', Table 3.

156 *Stirring Times*, i, 437.

157 Y. Firestone, 'Production and trade in an Islamic context: Sharika contracts in the transitional economy of northern Samaria, 1853–1943 – I', *IJMES*, vi (1975), 192–201.

158 For example, Finn and Kayat quoted in Schölch, 'European penetration'.

159 Ibid.

160 For example, *CR* (UK) Jaffa 1873, 318.

7: The Iraqi provinces, 1850–1880

1 For detailed reports on Iraq's trade at mid-century see report and enclosure in Rawlinson

(Baghdad), 5 Aug. 1846, FO 78/656 and enclosure in Rawlinson (Baghdad), 1 May 1852, FO 78/870. The first of these enclosures estimated that a third to a half of Baghdad's imports were re-exported to Persia. For figures for trade at the beginning of the century see J. Batatu, *The Old Social Classes and the Revolutionary Movements of Iraq* (Princeton, 1978), 234–5.

2 Ibid.
3 For example, *CRs* (UK) Basra 1845 and 1846 in Rawlinson (Baghdad), 27 Apr. 1846, FO 78/656.
4 W. K. Loftus, *Travels and Researches in Chaldea and Susiana* (London, 1857), 104.
5 For example, enclosure in Rawlinson (Baghdad), 2 Dec. 1854, FO 78/1018.
6 Fontanier, *Narrative*, I, 264–5.
7 Ibid., 266; enclosure in Rawlinson (Baghdad), 5 Aug. 1846.
8 T. G. McNie, 'History of steam navigation in the Middle East', *SAPP*, 4; Longrigg, *Four Centuries*, 293–4; J. M. Svoboda, 'Tigris and Euphrates Co.' (unpublished private paper in possession of Mrs M. Makiya), 5–6. McNie says that the company was started in 1850–1, Longrigg that it was formed in 1855. Svoboda says that the first two steam tugs were not imported until 1855.
9 McNie, 'History of steam navigation', 4.
10 Ibid., 5; Svoboda, 'Tigris and Euphrates, Co.', 6–7; Anon., 'The story of the Euphrates Company' in Issawi, *Economic History*, 147–8. S. A. Cohen suggests that the Lynch's concession was based on earlier rights to run steamers on the Euphrates, not the Tigris, *British Policy in Mesopotamia 1903–1910* (London, 1976), 8–9. For government pressure see Z. Saleh, *Mesopotamia (Iraq) 1600–1914; A Study in British Foreign Affairs* (Baghdad, 1957), 183–4.
11 Svoboda, 'Tigris and Euphrates Co.', 8.
12 Ibid., 7; McNie, 'History of steam navigation', 5, Longrigg, *Four Centuries*, 294.
13 McNie, 'History of steam navigation', 4–5.
14 *CR* (UK) Basra 1864–6, *PP*, 1867, LXVII, 266.
15 Ibid.; *CR* (UK) Baghdad 1866, *PP*, 1867/8, LXVIII, 397.
16 *CR* (UK) Basra 1864–6, 266–7; *CR* (UK) Basra 1868–9, *PP*, 1870, LIV, 391.
17 Ibid.
18 *CR* (UK) Basra 1864–6, 271.
19 *CRs* (UK) Baghdad 1866, 396 and Basra 1870, *PP*, 1873, LXVII, 992.
20 Farnie, *East and West*, 146; *CR* (UK) Baghdad 1870–1, *PP*, 1872, LVII, 293..
21 McNie, 'History of steam navigation', 6; Svoboda, 'Tigris and Euphrates Co.', 9–13. A renewed effort to get permission to be allowed to put towed barges on the river failed at about this time, ibid., 13. Svoboda's diaries (also in the possession of Mrs Makiya) have graphic accounts of the Lynch steamers piled so high with wool that the bridge was entirely surrounded with bales.
22 Saleh maintains that by running the three steamers in rotation the Lynchs were able to increase their carrying capacity by 50 per cent, *Mesopotamia*, 217.
23 McNie, 'History of steam navigation', 7; Svoboda gives a list of the Turkish steamers on the river in March 1881 and the repairs which some of them required, *Svoboda Diaries*, 23, Jan.–Nov. 1881, 39. See also Saleh, op. cit., 75, 222.
24 Farnie, *East and West*, 147.
25 Longrigg, *Four Centuries*, 318; *CR* (UK) Baghdad 1877–8, *PP*, 1878, LXXIV, 223–4.
26 For an exaggerated view of Midhat as a reformer see Davison, *Reform*, 160–4.
27 Rawlinson (Baghdad), 14 June 1853, FO 78/957.
28 Longrigg, *Four Centuries*, 283–4, 291; Rawlinson (Baghdad), 15 Apr. 1854, FO 78/1018.
29 Longrigg, *Four Centuries*, 291–2. See also Batatu, *Old Social Classes*, 74–5. A. Jwaideh, 'Midhat Pasha and the land system of Lower Iraq', *St Antony's Papers*, XVI (London, 1963), 114.
30 Ibid.
31 For a general description of the irrigation system in this area see Fernea, *Shaykh and Effendi*, 33; Loftus, *Travels*, 43–6.
32 Ibid., 43–4, 73.

33 For example, ibid., 10, 39.
34 Ibid., 45, 106, 112. For later efforts to solve this problem, see ch. 11, p. 279.
35 Ibid., p. 111; Jwaideh, 'Midhat Pasha', 113—14.
36 The main source for this policy is Jwaideh, 'Midhat Pasha', 115—26. But see also S. Haider, 'Land problems in Iraq' in Issawi, *Economic History*, 166—9 and Batatu, *Old Social Classes*, 74—6.
37 Jwaideh, 'Midhat Pasha', 115, 118—22.
38 Ibid., 124—6; Haider, 167—9. No *sanads* were issued on the Tigris round the rich lands at Amara, P. Sluglett, *Britain and Iraq 1914—1932* (London, 1976), 237.
39 There is some difference of agreement on exactly when registration came to an end. I have followed Jwaideh. See her 'Midhat Pasha', 25—6, where she takes issue with Sir Ernest Dowson's assertions contained in his *Enquiry into Land Tenure* (Letchworth, n.d. (?1931)), 21.
40 Jwaideh, 'Midhat Pasha', 124—6; Haider, 'Land problems in Iraq', 169.
41 E. B. Howell, 'The Qanun al-Aradhi', *JCAS*, IX, 1 (1922), 32.
42 Jwaideh, 'Midhat Pasha', 121—2, 129, 133.
43 See ch. 4, note 85.
44 For Midhat's promise, Jwaideh, 'Midhat Pasha', 119—20.
45 Ibid., 121; Batatu, *Old Social Classes*, 74—5.
46 Jwaideh, 'Midhat Pasha', 130—1.
47 For example, Rassam (Mosul), 12 Feb. 1855, FO 78/1115.
48 Jwaideh, 'Midhat Pasha', 128—9.
49 Loftus, *Travels*, 126; M. G. Ionides, *The Regime of the Rivers Euphrates and Tigris* (London, 1937), 67, 74—5.
50 W. Willcocks asserts that the Saklawiya escape channel was 'permanently' blocked by Midhat's action (*The Irrigation of Mesopotamia* (London, 1911), 15) but he may have been referring to the 'weir' which Ionides says was built in the 1880s (*Regime*, 75—6). Certainly the British consular reports mention several occasions on which the channel was 'unblocked' in the 1870s, for example, *CR* (UK) Baghdad 1877—8, *PP*, 1878, LXXIV, 708.
51 Fernea, *Shaykh and Effendi*, 32—3.
52 Jwaideh, 'Midhat Pasha', 127; *CR* (UK) Baghdad 1878/9, *PP*, 1878/9, LXXII, 226.
53 Fernea, *Shaykh and Effendi*, 34; Jwaideh, 'Midhat Pasha', 127.
54 Fernea, *Shaykh and Effendi*, 33.
55 This is certainly Jwaideh's opinion, 'Midhat Pasha', 128—30.
56 This is one of Fernea's major points, *Shaykh and Effendi*, 9.
57 For example, *Svoboda Diaries*, 23 (Jan.—Nov. 1881), 103.

8: *Anatolia and Istanbul, 1881—1914*

1 Figures from S. J. Shaw, 'The Ottoman census system and population, 1831—1914', *IJMES*, IX (1918), 338. Eldem gives the higher estimate of 15,800,000 (in Teẓel, 'Turkish economic development', 59). The first census taken in Republican Turkey gave a population of 13,700,000, but this was after all the death, destruction and large-scale movements of population during the First World War, the War of Independence and after.
2 According to the 1927 census, there were then only fifty-two towns and five cities with a population of more than 10,000 each, R. D. Robinson, *The First Turkish Republic* (Cambridge, Mass., 1963), 59.
3 Shaw, 'Ottoman census system', 338.
4 K. H. Karpat gives a rough estimate of 200,000 Circassian refugees who entered the Ottoman Empire after 1880, 'Migration and its effects', *mimeo* of paper presented to 1974 Middle East Economic History Conference at Princeton. A similar estimate has been given for the numbers of Muslims who fled into Anatolia from the Balkans during this same period, E. C. Eran quoted in Quataert, 'Ottoman reform', 410n.
5 The figures are quoted in E. F. Nickoley, 'Agriculture' in E. G. Mears (ed.), *Modern Turkey* (New York, 1924), 284—5.

6 In the early Republican period the size of the cultivated area varied from 7,000,000 hectares in 1926 to 4,000,000 in 1927, Teẓel, 'Turkish economic development', 66n.

7 Nickoley, 'Agriculture', 284–5, 291. See also I. A. Waismann, 'L'economie rurale de la Turquie', *REI*, II, iv (1928), 537.

8 Ankara University, Siyasal Bilgiler Fakültesi Yayine, no. 29, *Osmalı Sanayii 1913, 1915 yılları sanayi istatistiki* (Ankara, 1970), Tables I, VI, IX. Of the 269 plants enumerated in the census, 17 were not at work.

9 Quoted in Teẓel, 'Turkish economic development', 67. See also idem, 373.

10 T. Bulutay, Y. S. Teẓel and N. Yıldırım, *Türkiye Milli Geliri (1923–1948), Tabolar* (Ankara, 1974), Table 120/B.

11 For example, the study undertaken by the French Chamber of Commerce at Istanbul in 1905, quoted in Teẓel, 'Notes on the consolidated debt', 97–8.

12 This subject is treated in Teẓel, 'Notes on the consolidated debt', 96–8. See also the sources quoted there.

13 See, for example, Blaisdell, *European Financial Control*, chs 6 and 7; A Fleury, *La pénétration allemande au Moyen-Orient 1919–1939: Le cas de la Turquie, de l'Iran et de l'Afghanistan* (Leiden/Geneva, 1977), ch. 1; U. Trumpner, *Germany and the Ottoman Empire 1914–1918* (Princeton, 1968), ch. 1; W. Shorrock, *French Imperialism in the Middle East: The Failure of Policy in Syria and Lebanon, 1900–1914* (Madison, Wisc., 1976); J. Thobie, 'Les intérêts français dans l'Empire ottoman au debut du XXe siècle: étude des sources', *RH*, CCXXXV (April/June 1966); D. McLean, 'Finance and "Informal Empire" before the First World War', *EHR* (2nd ser.), XXIX, 2 (May 1972); H. S. W. Corrigan, 'British, French and German interests in Asiatic Turkey, 1881–1914', Ph.D. (London, 1954), etc., etc.

14 See, for example, U. Heyd, *Foundations of Turkish Nationalism: The Life and Teachings of Ziya Gokalp* (London, 1950), 146–7; K. H. Karpat, *Turkey's Politics* (Princeton, 1959), 23, 83.

15 Blaisdell, *European Financial Control*, 94–7; Ducruet, *Les capitaux européens*, 101–2.

16 Ducruet, op. cit., 102.

17 Blaisdell, *European Financial Control*, 94–5; Platt, *Finance, Trade and Politics*, 198–9.

18 For a fuller account of the revenues assigned to the PDA, see Blaisdell, *European Financial Control*, 108–20.

19 Ibid., 113–14.

20 Ibid., ch. 6.

21 For contemporary European praise of the activities of the PDA, see C. Morawitz, *Les finances de la Turquie* (Paris, 1902), 419 and Sir Vincent Caillard's article 'Turkey' in *Encyclopaedia Britannica* (11th edn), XXVII, 436–8.

22 Blaisdell, *European Financial Control*, 119–20.

23 Ibid., 152.

24 These are Suvla's figures, 'Ottoman debt', 104–6. Some of the money borrowed was used immediately to service previous loans. According to Teẓel the net addition to the Ottoman debt between 1886 and 1914 was a nominal £T83,288,000 of which the government actually received £T83,288,000, 'Notes on the consolidated foreign debt', Table 1.

25 Blaisdell, *European Financial Control*, 118n; Mears, 'Levantine concession-hunting', in his *Modern Turkey*, 356; O. Conker and E. Witmeur, *Redressement économique et industrialisation de la nouvelle Turquie* (Paris, 1937), 46.

26 Morawitz, *Finances*, 235, 273.

27 Blaisdell, *European Financial Control*, 97–9; Ducruet, *Les capitaux européens*, 104.

28 Morawitz, *Finances*, 273–5.

29 Ibid., 275.

30 Blaisdell, *European Financial Control*, 97–9, 119.

31 Ibid., 129–32.

32 For the history of the Imperial Ottoman, see Biliotti, *La Banque Imperiale Ottomane*; Baster, *International Banks*, 97–109.

33 For the Deutsche Bank see Baster, op. cit., 100–1.

34 Quoted in Baster, *International Banks*, 100–1.

35 For the National Bank, see ibid., 107. Also K. Grunwald, ' "Windsor-Cassel" — the last court Jew', *Year Book of Leo Beck Institute*, xiv (London/Jerusalem, 1969), 144–6; M. Kent, 'Agent of empire? The National Bank of Turkey and British foreign policy', *HJ*, xviii, 2 (1975).

36 'Ottoman debt', 104–6.

37 Ducruet, *Les capitaux européens*, 109.

38 For examples see H. Feis, *Europe the World's Banker 1870–1914* (New Haven, 1930), 322–5 and Shorrock, *French Imperialism*, 147–8, 150–1.

39 See J. M. Landau, *The Hejaz Railway and the Muslim Pilgrimage* (Detroit, 1971) and W. L. Ochsenwald, 'The financing of the Hijaz railroad', *WI*, N.S. xiv, 1–4 (1973).

40 Blaisdell, *European Financial Control*, 124, 46.

41 For examples of this overlap of interests see ibid., 133–4.

42 For example, E. M. Earle, *Turkey, the Great Powers and the Baghdad Railway* (New York, 1924), 77–8, 81.

43 For a treatment of this subject as it related to Mesopotamia see M. Kent, *Oil and Empire* (London, 1976), 15–30; P. Sluglett, *Britain in Iraq 1914–1932* (London, 1976), 104–10; H. Mejcher, *Imperial Quest for Oil 1910–1928* (London, 1976), chs 1 and 4–7.

44 For information about the kilometric guarantee system, see Blaisdell, *European Financial Control*, 127–9; A. Rey, *Statistique des principaux résultats de l'exploitation des chemins de fer de l'Empire ottoman pendant l'exercise 1911* (Constantinople, 1913); O. Conker, *Les chemins de fer en Turquie et la politique ferroviaire Turque* (Paris, 1935), 19–24, 80–2. For the sums disbursed as kilometric guarantee, see Table 46.

45 For support for this argument see Caillard, 'Turkey', 439; 'Report by Major Law', 779–80; General Sir O. Mance, 'Note on the railways in Asia Minor', 18 May 1924 (to be found in Mance Papers, *SAPP*).

46 Conker and Witmeur, *Redressement économique*, 51; Teẓel, 'Turkish economic development', 65; M. Housepian, *Smyrne 1922* (London, 1972), 66, 84. See also FO (UK), *Anatolia* (April 1919), 85–94.

47 'The amount, direction and nature of French investments', *Annals of the American Academy of Political and Social Science*, lxviii (Nov. 1916), 51. Feis, using a study made by the Commission pour la defense des porteurs de valeurs et de fonds ottomans in 1914, gives a total of 2,600,000,000 francs, *Europe the World's Banker*, 320n. Yet another French estimate for 1914 can be found in Mears, 'Levantine concession-hunting', 356–7, which gives the total French investment in the Ottoman public debt as 2,454,000,000 francs and in private companies as 900,000,000 francs.

48 Guyot, 'French investments', 51. Once again Feis and Mears give slightly different figures, *Europe the World's Banker*, 320n, and 'Levantine concession-hunting', 346–57.

49 Teẓel, 'Turkish economic development', 65–6.

50 Ibid., 64.

51 Feis, *Europe the World's Banker*, 322; Fleury, *Pénétration allemande*, 20.

52 For example, R. M. Frances, 'The British withdrawal from the Baghdad railway project in April 1903', *HJ*, xvi, 1 (1973).

53 Fleury makes this point well, *Pénétration allemande*, 20–1.

54 This subject is well treated in R. Khalidi, *British Policy towards Syria and Palestine, 1906–1914* (London, 1980), ch. 3.

55 For example, Caillard, 'Turkey', 432–6 and W. W. Cumberland, 'The Public Treasury' in Mears, *Modern Turkey*, 390–9.

56 See figures in Table 36.

57 Caillard, 'Turkey', 428–9; Hecquard, *L'Empire ottoman*, i, 347–54; Yapp, 'Middle Eastern army modernization', 348–56.

58 Caillard, 'Turkey', 432–3; Lowther (Constantinople), 29 March 1910, FO 371/1007; F. Ahmed, *The Young Turks* (Oxford, 1969), 69–74, 76. For the Young Turks' ambitious ideas about developing the economy, see Empire Ottoman (Turkey), *Programme du Ministere des Travalux Publics* (Constantinople, 1909), 7–11.

59 For example, figures in Mallet (Constantinople), 18 May 1914, FO 371/2114.

60 The value of Izmir's exports was roughly the same as that of the three other main

Anatolian ports (Adana/Mersin, Samsun and Trabzon) combined, Quataert, 'Ottoman reform', 361.

61   Compare this with A. D. Novichev's estimate of 4,700,000 hectares in 1899, 'The development of commodity-money and capitalist relations in agriculture . . .', in Issawi, *Economic History*, 66 and a British estimate of 4,006,000 for 1919, *CR* (UK) Turkey, 1919, *PP*, 1920, XLII, 915.

62   Waisman, 'L'économie rurale', 537–9.

63   For estimates of average yields, see Nickoley, 'Agriculture', 291.

64   Hirsch, *Poverty and Plenty*, 2–3.

65   Quataert argues that all the cereals sent along the Anatolian railway were destined either for export or for the provisioning of Istanbul or the Ottoman army, 'Limited revolution', 149–50.

66   For example, Eldem's estimate that Turkish cereal production increased by just over 50 per cent (1888–1911), Tezel, 'Turkish economic development', 57, or the Istanbul Chamber of Commerce's calculation that Anatolian wheat production rose from 13,000,000 hectolitres (1889–91) to 15,600,000 (1900–3), Quataert, 'Ottoman reform', 456n.

67   J. Hinderink and M. B. Kiray, *Social Stratification as an Obstacle to Development* (New York, Washington, London, 1970), 12–13; D. Kandiyoti, 'Social change and social stratification in a Turkish village', *JPS*, II, 2 (Jan. 1975), 207. For some of the problems experienced by the new immigrants, see G. L. Bell, 'Asiatic Turkey' in Anon., *The Arabs of Mesopotamia* (Basra, 1917), 179.

68   D. Quataert, 'Limited revolution: the impact of the Anatolian Railway on Turkish transportation and the provisioning of Istanbul, 1890–1908', *Business History Review*, LI, 2 (Summer 1977), 144–8.

69   Ibid., 148.

70   The figures are in Quataert, 'Ottoman reform', 208.

71   For tobacco, see Turkey, *Annuaire Statistique*, Baskakanlik Istatistik/Office Central de Statistique, Istatistik Villigi, *1936/7* (Ankara, n.d.), 169. For cotton I have used Quataert's figures for exports from Izmir and Adana ('Turkish reform', 289–90) and assumed an average yield of one bale per hectare, Nickoley, 'Agriculture', 291.

72   Figures for mulberry area in Caillard, 'Turkey', 437.

73   Rey, *Statistique 1911*, 'Graphique des recettes brutes kilometriques' de Chemin de Fer Smyrne-Cassaba et Prolongements.

74   Quataert, 'Turkish reform', 261–74; Issawi, 'The expansion of tobacco growing in the nineteenth century', in Issawi, *Economic History*, 60–1.

75   Quataert, 'Turkish reform', 265.

76   Ibid.; *CR* (UK) Smyrna, 1912–13, *PP*, 1912–13, C, 621.

77   Quataert, 'Turkish reform', 245–61.

78   Ibid., 247–9; Morawitz, *Finances*, 319–20.

79   Quataert, 'Turkish reform', 292–5; Kurmuş 'Role of British capital', 162; *CRs* (UK) Smyrna 1912–13, *PP*, 1912–13, C, 621 and 1914, *PP*, 1914, XCV, 101.

80   Quataert, 'Turkish reform', 258–9.

81   Ibid., 245–61.

82   Ibid., 217–44.

83   This is Quataert's conclusion, ibid., 243–4.

84   Ibid., 104–2 and Appendix I, Table D, 375.

85   Quataert points out that it was difficult for poor peasants to obtain loans. On the other hand, he seems to exaggerate the Bank's effectiveness by assuming that the 800,000 loans made during the Hamidian period went to almost as many cultivators. It would seem more likely that it was mainly the same group of borrowers which kept coming back for more, ibid., 139–40.

86   *CR* (US), 'The Angora goat', April 1883, X, No. 31 (July 1883), 3–4.

87   For a discussion of the concept of an 'export sector', see J. V. Levin, *The Export Economies* (Cambridge, Mass., 1960).

88   *Smyrne*, 74.

89   In a Turkish context see, for example, I. Yasa, *Hasanöglan: Socio-economic Structure of a Turkish Village* (Ankara, 1957), 56, 177–9.

90   Quoted in Teẓel, 'Turkish economic development', 251.
91   Kurmuş 'Role of British capital', 136–8, 140–50; Nickoley, 'Agriculture', 294–5;
     Hinderink and Kiray, *Social Stratification*, 14–16.
92   Ibid., 15–16.
93   For example, Quataert, 'Turkish reform', 155–85.
94   *CR* (UK) Smyrna, 1909, *PP*, 1910, CIII, 372.
95   Quataert, 'Turkish reform', 165–9.
96   Ibid., 172–4. See also C. Mühlmann, 'Die Deutschen Baunternenmungen in der
     Asiatischen Türkei, 1888–1914', *Weltwirtschaftliches Archiv*, XXIV (1926), 111–37,
     365–99.
97   Teẓel, 'Turkish economic development', 260; Kurmuş, 'Role of British capital', 153. See
     also Kandiyoti, 'Social Change', 207–8.
98   For example, G. E. White, 'Agriculture and industries in Turkey' in W. H. Hall (ed.),
     Reconstruction in Turkey (New York?, 1918), 140–1.
99   Ibid., 140.
100 Hirsch notes that in the 1920s peasants got a larger share of the cereal crops under a crop-
     sharing agreement in areas where there was a relative scarcity of labour, *Poverty and
     Plenty*, 39–40.
101 Quoted in S. Mardin, 'Center-periphery relations. A key to Turkish politics', *mimeo*
     (March 1972), 31–2.
102 The censuses were originally published in Turkish and French by the Ministry of
     Commerce and Agriculture as *1329, 1331 Seneleri Istatistiki* (Istanbul, 1333/1917) and
     Statistique industrielle des années 1913 et 1915 (Constantinople, 1917). The same
     information can be found in *Osmanli Sanayii: 1913, 1915* and page references are cited
     from this latter work.
103 Ibid., 4.
104 For the districts excluded see ibid., 2.
105 Kurmuş, 'Role of British capital', 175.
106 *Osmanli Sanayii: 1913, 1915*, Tables XXI and XXII.
107 Ibid., 148–53.
108 FO (UK) *Anatolia*, 99.
109 *Osmanli Sanayii: 1913, 1915*, 14–16.
110 FO (UK) *Anatolia*, 97.
111 Kurmuş, 'Role of British capital', 179.
112 Unfortunately *Osmanli Sanayii: 1913, 1915* lists the dates of only the thirty-three flour
     mills, twenty-five of which were established after 1880 (Table XIV).
113 For example, Rougon, *Smyrne*, 258–9.
114 Ibid., 258.
115 *Osmanli Sanayii: 1913, 1915*, 161–3; FO (UK) *Anatolia*, 95–6.
116 *Correspondance d'Orient*, III 1 (1 Jan. 1910).
117 'Role of British capital', 180–6.
118 Rougon, *Smyrne*, 248.
119 For example, Earl Percy found three carpet-weaving workshops in the neighbourhood of
     Konya employing Armenian and Greek girls to work on patterns supplied from Istanbul,
     Highlands of Asiatic Turkey (London, 1901), 34–5.
120 For the extent of local competition and for details of the proposed new company, see
     RMM, III, 10 (Oct. 1907), 279–81 and III, 7 (May 1907), 53–4, 386. Kurmuş gives the
     capital of the company as £400,000, 'Role of British capital', 183–4.
121 Ibid., 184–5.
122 Ibid., 184.
123 Ibid., 185–6; Z. Y. Hershlag, *Introduction to the Modern Economic History of the
     Middle East* (Leiden, 1964), 141.
124 For the collectors' reaction, see Arts Council (UK), *Carpets from the Collection of Joseph
     V. McMullen* (London, 1972), 4–5 and sources cited there. For export figures see *CR*
     (UK) Turkey, 1919, 928.
125 For a list of Anatolia's varied craft activities, see White, 'Agriculture and industries',
     151–7.

126 For example, Marowitz, *Finances*, 12. For a more general criticism of industrial policy, Tezel, 'Turkish economic development', 56, 66–8.
127 Z. Y. Hershlag, *Turkey: An Economy in Transition* (The Hague, 1958?), 61.
128 FO (UK) *Anatolia*, 86.
129 Tezel, 'Turkish economic development', 66.
130 Ibid. See also FO (UK) *Anatolia*, 86–94.
131 'Notes on the consolidated debt', 87.
132 For an argument which depends very largely on a 'drain' or transfer of surplus, see Baran, *Political Economy*, ch. 5.
133 This argument is well developed by C. Keydar, 'The political economy of Turkish democracy', *NLR*, 115 (May/June 1979), 4–13.

9: The Egyptian economy, 1882–1914

1 *Recensement général de l'Egypt, 1882*, II (Cairo, 1885), x–xi.
2 Doubts about the reliability of the 1882 census were first widely publicized by the Director General of the Census Department in 1907, Egypt, Ministry of Finance, *The Census of Egypt taken in 1907* (Cairo, 1909), 24–5. Among others to make the same point have been W. Cleland, *The Population Problem in Egypt* (Lancaster, Pa., 1936), 9 and G. Baer, 'Urbanization in Egypt, 1820–1907' in Polk and Chambers, *Beginnings of Modernization*, 133–6. For a history of the government's statistical service see J. Fresco, 'Histoire et organisation de le statistique offiale de l'Egypt', *EC*, 191–2 (April/May 1940).
3 For example, S. Radwan's indices for capital formation in his *Capital Formation in Egyptian Industry and Agriculture 1882–1967* (London, 1974) or the various estimates of agricultural output to be found in P. K. O'Brien, 'The long-term growth of agricultural production in Egypt: 1821–1962' in Holt, *Political and Social Change*, and B. Hansen and M. Wattleworth, 'Agricultural output and consumption of basic foods in Egypt, 1886/87–1967/68', *IJMES*, IX (1978).
4 'Urbanization in Egypt', 156–7. Some doubts have been thrown on the accuracy of the 1897 and 1907 census figures for the populations of Cairo and Alexandria, with the suggestion that they were too low, A. Eid, *La propriété urbaine en Egypt* (Brussels, 1907), 14–19. It should also be noted that not all the rural population were engaged directly in agriculture. On the other hand, some town dwellers worked fields in the surrounding countryside, Abu-Lughod, 'Varieties of urban experience', 164–5.
5 For one of the first warnings of the existence of over-population on the land in certain areas see Lord Cromer, 'Reports . . . on the condition of Egypt and the Soudan in 1903', *PP*, 1904, CXI, 14–15.
6 For example, A. R. Ferguson, 'Bilharzis', *CSJ*, IV, 45 (June 1910), 129.
7 I. Lévi, 'Le recensement de la population de l'Egypte de 1917', *EC*, 67 (Nov. 1922), 503–4; Egypt, Dept of General Statistics, *Annuaire Statistique 1914* (Cairo, 1914), 35.
8 See ch. 5, note 86.
9 Baer, *History of Landownership*, 224–5.
10 *Annuaire Statistique 1914*, 320–1.
11 Ibid. As Baer notes, it would be wrong to equate the figures for the numbers of properties with those for the number of landowners. Many of the latter owned several properties: *History of Landownership*, 71–2.
12 For evidence on the average size of the Egyptian family see Lévi, 'Le recensement', 489.
13 Figures from Baer's calculation of rural population in Table 45 and *Annuaire Statistique 1914*, 320–1. My own calculations certainly underestimate the numbers of landless families as they have to be based on the assumption that each property was owned by a separate family. For a higher estimate of the number of landless families, see Sir O. Thomas, 'Agricultural and economic position of Egypt', *Milner Papers* (Bodleian Library) Box 164.
14 Owen, *Cotton*, 185–7.
15 One of the advantages of maize and *birsim* was that they did not take as many months to grow as most of the other food crops, W. L. Balls, *Egypt of the Egyptians* (London, 1915), 184–8.

16 By 1912, 1,032,000 feddans of Upper Egypt's 2,250,000 feddans of cultivated land had been converted to perennial irrigation. But only half of the converted land was planted with summer crops, Lord Kitchener, 'Reports . . . on the condition of Egypt and the Soudan in 1912', *PP*, 1913, cxxxi, 212; *Annuaire Statistique 1914*, 322–3.

17 Ibid., 322–3, 352–3; Egypt, Ministry of Agriculture, *The Pink Boll-worm in Egypt in 1916–1917*, by H. A. Ballou (Cairo, 1920), 59.

18 See, for example, the calculations by Verschoyle reported in the *Egyptian Gazette*, 29 Oct. 1906.

19 For the distribution of large properties, see Baer, *History of Landownership*, 226–7. I have used the government's definition of Upper Egypt as consisting of the province of Giza and all other provinces to the south.

20 Radwan, *Capital Formation*, 243.

21 *Annuaire Statistique 1914*, 295; Issawi, 'Assymetrical development and transport in Egypt', 384.

22 *List of Financial, Manufacturing, Transport and Other Companies Established in Egypt*, 3rd edn (Alexandria, June 1901). I have included the five cotton ginning and pressing establishments to be found in the same source.

23 Mazuel, *Sucre*, 47.

24 *Annuaire Statistique 1914*, 524–9. The official classification of 'industrial' companies includes three electricity companies and one telephone company.

25 Ibid., 34.

26 Egypt, *Rapport de la Commission du Commerce et de l'Industrie* (Cairo, 1918), 54.

27 I. Lévi, 'L'augmentation des revenus de l'état: possibilités et moyens d'y parvenir', *EC*, 68 (Dec. 1922), 596–624. See also the criticism of Lévi's calculations in J. Baxter, 'Notes on the estimate of the national income of Egypt for 1921–1922', *EC*, 72 (May 1923) and in M. A. Anis, 'A study of the national income of Egypt', *EC*, 261–2 (Nov./Dec. 1950), 849–58.

28 Tignor, *Modernization*, 50–1, 51n; Cromer, *Modern Egypt*, ii, 286–7.

29 Tignor, *Modernization*, 76–9.

30 Ibid., 214–15; Cromer, *Modern Egypt*, ii, ch. 48.

31 For example, Cromer, *Modern Egypt*, ii, ch. 41.

32 See, for example, my 'The influence of Lord Cromer's Indian experience on British policy in Egypt, 1883–1907', *St Antony's Papers*, xvii (Oxford, 1965), 126–8, 132–4. See also Cromer's rather disingenuous defence of British educational policy in *Modern Egypt*, ii, ch. 54.

33 This is a major argument of Owen, 'Influence of Lord Cromer's Indian experience', 112ff.

34 R. L. Tignor, 'British agricultural and hydraulic policy in Egypt, 1882–1892', *Agricultural History*, xxxvii, 2 (April 1963), 4–6; R. H. Brown, *History of the Barrage at the Head of the Delta of Egypt* (Cairo, 1896).

35 W. Willcocks and J. I. Craig, *Egyptian Irrigation*, 3rd edn, ii (London, 1913), chs 12 and 13.

36 Ibid., i (London, 1913), ch. 7; E. Bechara, *Irrigation perenne des bassins de la Moyenne Egypte* (Lausanne, 1905).

37 Owen, *Cotton*, 190–6. For a useful summary of the findings of the government's Cotton Commission established to investigate the situation, see L. Jullien, 'Chronique agricole de l'année 1920', *EC*, xii, 55 (Jan. 1921), 48ff.

38 For an analysis of the long-term effects of British agricultural policy, see my 'Agricultural production in historical perspective: a case study of the period 1890–1939' in P. J. Vatikiotis (ed.), *Egypt Since the Revolution* (London, 1968).

39 Tignor, *Modernization*, 120–3; Cromer, *Modern Egypt*, ii, ch. 50.

40 Owen, *Cotton*, 213–15; *Annuaire Statistique 1914*, 363.

41 *Annuaire Statistique 1914*, 178–207. See also L. Wiener, *L'Egypte et ses chemins de fer* (Brussels, 1932), ch. 12.

42 Baer, *Landownership*, 11–12, 31; Cromer, *Modern Egypt*, ii, 447–53.

43 Ibid., 443–4.

44 See Table 50.

45 See Table 49.

46 Owen, 'Influence of Lord Cromer's Indian experience', 113–14, 123–6.

47 These ideas are spelled out explicitly in, for example, Lord Cromer, 'Reports . . . on the condition of Egypt and the Soudan in 1903', *PP*, 1904, CXI, 220–1, and Sir E. Gorst's, 'Reports . . . on the condition of Egypt and the Soudan in 1909', *PP*, 1910, CXII, 364–5.

48 Tignor, *Modernization*, 132–8; Berque, *Egypt: Imperialism and Revolution*, 133–5.

49 Baer, *Landownership*, 95–6; Tignor, *Modernization*, 237–8; Cromer, 'Reports . . . on the condition of Egypt and the Soudan in 1902', 972–5.

50 These views are supported by Baer, *Landownership*, 82–90 and Tignor, *Modernization*, 238–9.

51 The Agricultural Bank gave two types of loans, 'A' loans of £E120 repayable in one sum and 'B' loans of £E10–300, then £E500, repayable in instalments over 5½, then 10½, and finally 20½ years. It is generally assumed that small cultivators anxious to borrow working capital or money for capital improvement would only have been able to afford the 'A' loans. Between 1902 and 1908 the total amount lent in 'A' loans was £E2,110,000 and in 'B' loans, £E13,030,000, P. Harvey, 'Memorandum regarding the Agricultural Bank of Egypt' (1909), a copy of which can be found in FO 368/284; 'Memorandum on the proposed land legislation in Egypt and its effect on the Agricultural Bank of Egypt', 14 Aug. 1912, in FO 141/531/439.

52 For example, Harvey, 'Memorandum regarding the Agricultural Bank'.

53 A. E. Crouchley, *The Investment of Foreign Capital in Egyptian Companies and Public Debt* (Cairo, 1936), 68.

54 On this general subject, see Disuqi, *Kibar*, ch. 4 and W. Kazziha, 'The evolution of the Egyptian political elite, 1907–1921: a case study of the role of large landowners in politics', Ph.D. (London, 1970), chs 1 and 5.

55 Crouchley, *Investment*, 32–3, 38–40, 54–5.

56 J. H. Scott, 'The Capitulations' in A. Wright (ed.), *Twentieth-Century Impressions of Egypt* (London, 1909), 113.

57 Crouchley, *Investment of Foreign Capital*, 69.

58 Tignor, *Modernization*, 370–1.

59 For a general discussion of this incident, see my 'Lord Cromer and the development of Egyptian industry 1883–1907', *MES*, II, 4 (July 1966), 283–301.

60 A contemporary Belgian writer assigns the blame for failure equally between the government action and bad management of the companies themselves, H. de Saint-Omer, *Les entreprises belges en Egypte* (Brussels, 1907), 17–18. See also F. Charles Roux's comments along the same lines, *La production du coton en Egypte* (Paris, 1908), 296–7.

61 P. Arminjon, *La situation économique et financière de l'Egypte* (Paris, 1911), 242.

62 For example, Mazuel, *Le sucre*, 172; Owen, 'Lord Cromer and the development of Egyptian industry', 292–3.

63 Evidence for this can be found in Cromer's and Gorst's statements to be found in Owen, 'Lord Cromer and the development of Egyptian industry', 290, 292–3.

64 For an interesting analysis of this type of policy see Berque, *Egypte*, 175–82, 230–1.

65 See, for example, Owen, *Cotton*, 244–349.

66 For the general approach of the Commission, see *Rapport*, 43–5, 53–60. See also M. Deeb, 'Bank Misr and the emergence of the local bourgeoisie in Egypt', *MES*, XII, 3 (Oct. 1976); R. L. Tignor, 'The Egyptian Revolution of 1919: new directions in the Egyptian Economy', *MES*, XII, 3 (Oct. 1976).

67 See, for example, information provided by the new Department of Agriculture in 1911, Lord Kitchener, 'Reports . . . on the condition of Egypt and the Soudan in 1911', *PP*, 1912/13, CXXI, 652–6.

68 *Annuaire Statistique 1914*, 357.

69 'Agricultural output and consumption', Tables 3 and 4.

70 For a defence of both assumptions, see Hansen and Wattleworth, ibid., 450–2.

71 Some very tentative figures for changes in Egypt's animal population can be found in *Annuaire Statistique 1914*, 366.

72 'Agricultural output and consumption', Table 2.

73 For more information about these calculations, see Owen, *Cotton*, 249.

74 W. Willcocks, *Egyptian Irrigation*, 2nd edn (London, 1899), 17–18.
75 Comte Cressaty, *L'Egypte d'aujourd'hui* (Paris, 1912), 178–9; Egypt, Institute of National Planning, Memo. No. 259, *A Production Function for Egyptian Agriculture* by Dr M. El-Imam (Cairo, 31 Dec. 1962), 16, 38–41.
76 M. Wattleworth and B. Hansen, 'Report on the construction of agricultural indexes for Egypt, 1887–1968', *mimeo*, 15 Sept. 1975 (Inst. of International Studies, University of California, Berkeley), Table XLI.
77 'Agricultural output and consumption', 462.
78 B. Hansen, 'Income and consumption in Egypt 1886/1887 to 1937', *IJMES*, x (1979), 28–30.
79 Just after the First World War the Ministry of the Interior put the number of Egyptian *izbas* at 17,302 or several thousand more than the number of properties over 50 feddans, E. Minost, 'Essai sur le revenue agricole de l'Egypte', *EC*, 123 (Nov. 1930), 709. See also, S. Nour Ed-din's observation in the late 1890s that anyone owning property of over 100 feddans 'necessarily' had an *izba*, 'Conditions des fellahs en Egypte', 5.
80 See p. 146–8.
81 See, for example, W. Cartwright, 'Notes on rent, labour and joint-ownership in Egyptian agriculture', *CSJ*, IV, 41 (Feb. 1910), 30; J. A. Todd, *Political Economy* (Edinburgh/Glasgow, 1911), 52–3.
82 For example, C. Pensa, *Les cultures de l'Egypte* (Paris, 1897), 77; M. Schanz, *Cotton in Egypt and the Anglo-Egyptian Sudan* (Manchester, 1913), 44–5.
83 M. Poilay Bey, 'Excursions dans les grands domaines d'Egypte-Daira Draneth Pacha', *BUSAE*, I, 2 (Aug. 1901), 9–17.
84 Y. Aghion and M. Poilay, 'Excursions dans les grands domaines – propriété de S. E. Riaz Pacha', *BUSAE*, I, 5 (Nov. 1901), 164–70.
85 Information from the copy-books of the Manzalawi estate in the possession of Professor Mahmoud Manzaloui who has kindly allowed me to use them. Further information about these estates can be found in Owen, 'Development of agricultural production'.
86 Egypt, Ministry of Agriculture, *Agricultural Census of Egypt, 1939* (Cairo, 1946), 10–18. I have included land which was rented under some type of 'mixed' arrangement.
87 *Annuaire Statistique 1914*, 302–3. See also Radwan's calculation of total private capital formation, *Capital Formation*, Table 4.1.
88 Schanz quotes an estimate that in 1909–10 some 5 per cent of the cultivated land was being treated with chemical fertilizer, *Cotton in Egypt*, 36. Between 1909 and 1914 imports of such fertilizers increased by about 200 per cent, *Annuaire Statistique 1914*, 302–3.
89 Balls, *Egypt of the Egyptians*, 185; J. B. Piot Bey, 'Coup d'oeil sur l'économie actuelle du betail en Egypte', *EC*, 6 (March 1911), 201–2.
90 For example, J. Anhoury, 'Le blé en Egypte', *EC*, 85 (March 1925), 197; V. Mosséri, 'Le sol egyptien sous le régime de l'arrosage par inondation', *BIE*, v (1923), 21ff.
91 For example, H. K. Selim, *Twenty Years of Agricultural Development in Egypt (1919–1939)* (Cairo, 1940), 118; G. P. Foaden and F. Fletcher (eds), *Textbook of Egyptian Agriculture*, II (Cairo, 1910), 383–5.
92 Harvey, 'Memorandum regarding the Agricultural Bank of Egypt'.
93 J. Zannis, *Le crédit agricole en Egypte* (Paris, 1937), 35–6. It has been asserted that foreign usurers were not punished for charging more than the legal rate of interest established under the Mixed Courts, K. A. Greiss, 'De l'usure en Egypte', *EC*, XII, 56 (Feb. 1921), 102.
94 Quoted in Kazziha, 'Evolution', 171–2.
95 Crédit Foncier Egyptien, *Crédit Foncier Egyptien 1880–1930* (n.p., n.d.), 14–16; E. Papasian, *L'Egypte économique et financière* (Cairo, 1926), 238–9.
96 *Investment*, 70, 105–7.
97 Ibid., 58.
98 See p. 231.
99 Crouchley, *Investment*, 57–9.
100 Ibid., 58–9.
101 (Ramleh) 15 June 1901, *RC* (Belgium), 113 (1901), 330.

102 *Egyptian Gazette*, 6 Jan. 1904; *The Times*, 1 Jan. 1906.
103 Crouchley, *Investment*, 65, 67–9.
104 Ibid., 69–70.
105 For an official estimate of the average value of land in Egypt's different provinces, see *Annuaire Statistique 1914*, 509.
106 Crouchley, *Investment*, 65–7.
107 See Crouchley's figures in Table 53.
108 M. Z. 'Abd El-Motaal, *Les bourses en Egypte* (Paris, 1930), 94ff.
109 Crouchley, *Investment*, 31–2.
110 Ibid., 32. For the balance sheet of the National Bank showing the various sources of its funds, see *Annuaire Statistique 1914*, 500–1.
111 For an account of these practices, see *The Times*, 19 Oct. 1911.
112 For example, according to G. Socolis there were thirty soap factories in Egypt at the turn of the century, of which only two are in the British Chamber of Commerce's List, *L'Egypte et son histoire économique depuis 30 ans* (Paris, 1903), 58, 72.
113 *Capital Formation in Egyptian Industry and Agriculture*, 98–9.
114 For a detailed breakdown of Egypt's exports in 1912–13, see *Annuaire Statistique 1914*, 284–8.
115 Owen, 'Lord Cromer and the development of Egyptian industry', 289–91.
116 See p. 225.
117 Owen, 'Lord Cromer and the development of Egyptian industry', 291–2.
118 See, for example, A. A. I. El-Gritly, 'The structure of modern industry in Egypt', *EC*, 241–2 (Nov./Dec. 1947), 365.
119 Owen, 'Lord Cromer and the development of Egyptian Industry', 290; *Annuaire Statistique 1914*, 302–3.
120 B. Hansen and K. Nashashibi, *Foreign Trade, Regimes and Economic Development: Egypt* (New York, 1975), 208; M. Casoria, 'Chronique agricole de l'année 1922', *EC*, XIV, 70 (Feb. 1923), 152; *Annuaire Statistique 1914*, 356.
121 Mazuel, *Sucre*, 37, 185–6.
122 Ibid., 42; Egypt, *Rapport de la Commission du Commerce et de l'Industrie*, 148.
123 E.g. *Annuaire Statistique 1914*, 362.
124 Mazuel, *Sucre*, 43–7; Williams, De Broe and Co., *Sugar in Egypt and Elsewhere* (London, 1903), 58, 106.
125 Mazuel, *Sucre*, 45–6.
126 For example, *Annuaire Statistique 1914*, 362.
127 Egypt, *Rapport de la Commission du Commerce et de l'Industrie*, 148.
128 *Annuaire Statistique 1914*, 288.
129 See Saint-Omer, *Entreprises belges*, 105–10; *Rapport de la Commission du Commerce et de l'Industrie*, 154–5; R. Owen, 'The Cairo building industry and the building boom of 1897 to 1907', *Colloque International sur l'Histoire du Caire* (Cairo, 1972), 346–7.
130 Owen, 'Cairo Building Industry', 346; Saint-Omer, *Entreprises belges*, 106–7.
131 Owen, 'Cairo building industry', 346–7; Saint-Omer, *Entreprises belges*, 106–7; *Annuaire Statistique 1914*, 284.
132 For a more detailed examination of Cromer's views about industry see E. R. J. Owen, 'The attitude of British officials to the development of the Egyptian economy, 1882–1922', in Cook, *Studies*, 490–2 and 'Lord Cromer and the development of Egyptian industry', 282ff.
133 For an early criticism of British policy, see ibid., 291. For more detailed attacks on British policy towards Egyptian industry, see T. Rothstein, *Egypt's Ruin* (London, 1910), and Congrès National Egyptien, *Oeuvres du Congrès National Egyptien ténu à Bruxelles le 22, 23, 24 Septembre 1910* (n.p., n.d.), 231–4.
134 Egypt, *Industrial and Commercial Census, 1927* (Cairo, 1931), x–xi.
135 Ibid.
136 For the volume and value of such imports in 1912/13, see *Annuaire Statistique 1914*, 284–8.
137 See note in Table 22.
138 *Investment*, 176–84.

139 B. Hansen and E. Lucas, 'A new set of foreign trade indices for Egypt', Working Papers in Economics, No. 4, Oct. 1976, Institute of International Studies, University of California at Berkeley (quoted by kind permission of the authors).
140 Ibid., 17–22.
141 Owen, *Cotton*, 307–9.
142 I have used the detailed trade figures to be found in Egypt, Direction Générale des Douanes, *Commerce extérieur de l'Egypte. Statistique comparé, 1884–1903* (Cairo, 1904), Table II. For figures after that I have had to rely on the global figures to be found in *Annuaire Statistique 1914*, 300–3.
143 Radwan estimates Egypt's gross fixed capital formation at 10–15 per cent for the period 1880–1914 (*Capital Formation*, 235). However, Professor Bent Hansen calculates that, for the decade just before the First World War, the ration was perhaps only half this and may only have been enough to create an annual growth of 1 per cent/per capita domestic product (private communication).

10: *Mount Lebanon, Syria and Palestine, 1880–1914*

1 A. Ruppin gives a figure of 3,040,000 excluding nomads, *Syria: An Economic Survey* (trans.) (New York, 1918), 6. The Ottoman census for 1914 shows 2,700,000 excluding Mount Lebanon, S. J. Shaw, 'The Ottoman census system and population, 1931–1914', *IJMES*, X, 3 (Aug. 1978), 338. After the First World War (and a general decline in population) the first calculations of the colonial period give 2,140,000 for Syria and Lebanon, R. Widmer, 'Population' in S. B. Himadeh (ed.), *Economic Organization of Syria* (Beirut, 1936), 5, and 750,000 for Palestine, H. C. Luke and E. Keith-Roach, *The Handbook of Palestine* (London, 1922), 33, L. G. Hopkins, 'Population' in S. B. Himadeh (ed.), *Economic Organization of Palestine* (Beirut, 1938), 6.
2 For the distribution of population by provinces see the Ottoman census in Shaw, 'Ottoman census system', 338. See also *CR* (UK) Aleppo 1906, *PP*, 1907, XCIII, 12 and Widmer, 'Population', 5.
3 Kalla, 'Role of foreign trade', Tables VI, VII. Other, slightly different, estimates can be found in Dr G. Samné, *La Syrie* (Paris, 1921), 110–16 and P. Huvelin (ed.), *Que vaut la Syrie?* (Paris/Marseille, 1919), 23.
4 For contemporary estimates of population growth, see Kalla, 'Role of foreign trade', Table I.
5 Shaw, 'Ottoman census system', 336.
6 A. Ruppin, extract from *Syrien als Wirschaftsgebiet*, in Issawi, *Economic History*, 270–1. See also estimates in 'La question syrienne', *RMM*, II (June/July 1907), 520–1.
7 Lebanon, Ministère du Plan, *Besoins et possibilités de developpement du Liban: Etude préliminaire* (Mission IRFED, Liban, 1960–1961), I, 47; Issawi, *Economic History*, 269; Widmer, 'Population', 16.
8 Widmer suggests that in the early stages, emigration was mainly temporary and that most male migrants expected to return to Lebanon, ibid., 17. On the other hand, P. M. and J. M. Kayal suggest that few actually did return on a permanent basis, *The Syrian–Lebanese in America* (Boston, 1975), 68–72.
9 Issawi, *Economic History*, 270. Ruppin (in Issawi, ibid.) gives a figure of 40,000 for net Jewish migration to Palestine. Other writers give the higher estimate of 50,000, e.g., N. Mandel, 'Turks, Arabs and Jewish immigration into Palestine, 1882–1914', *St Antony's Papers*, XVII (Oxford, 1965), 17, 80. This is supported by the figures in Luke and Keith-Roach, *Handbook*, 52.
10 Lewis, 'Frontiers of settlement', 265–6; FO (UK), *Syria and Palestine* (April 1919), 42–3.
11 Lewis, 'Frontiers of settlement', 263.
12 *The Caliph's Last Heritage* (London, 1915), 301.
13 J. Kelman, *From Damascus to Palmyra* (London, 1908), 175.
14 For example, Z. Kanzadian and L. de Bertalot, *Atlas de géographie économique de Syrie et du Liban* (Paris, 1926), 57. They give a figure for the area cultivated in any one year. I have doubled this to allow for a system of rotation by which fields were only planted every other year.

15 Ibid., maps, 56–8.
16 Quoted in Granott, *Land System*, 36–7.
17 For example, Eleftériadès, *Les chimins de fer en Syrie*, 39–42.
18 For example, G. Schumaker, *Across the Jordan* (London, 1886), 23–4, 267–8; Jago (Aleppo) 'Detailed report on the Vilayet', June 1890, FO 861/22.
19 For a general survey of Syrian railways see Eleftériadès, *Chemins de fer en Syrie*, 37–78.
20 Shorrock, *French Imperialism*, 147–9; E. F. Nickoley, 'Transportation and communications' in Himadeh, *Economic Organization of Syria*, 180–4; Kalla, 'Role of foreign trade', 136–40.
21 For example, *CR* (UK), Damascus, 1901, *PP*, 1902 cx.
22 *CR* (UK) Damascus, 1902, *PP*, 1903, LXXIX, 263–5; N. Verney and G. Dambmann, *Les puissances étrangères dans le Levant, en Syrie et en Palestine* (Paris/Lyons, 1900), 250–1; Kalla, 'Role of foreign trade', 138.
23 See Huvelin's estimate in Kalla, 'Role of foreign trade', 140.
24 Figures from Table 59 and Kanzadian and de Bertalot, *Atlas*, 78–9. In addition to the three lines about which information is given in Table 59, the Hijaz railway carried 77,523 tons in 1911/12 and the Jerusalem/Jaffa 46,000 in 1911.
25 See sources quoted in pp. 97–8. Also, Kalla, 'Role of foreign trade', 31; N. Burns and A. D. Edwards, 'Foreign trade' in Himadeh, *Economic Organization of Syria*, 229–30.
26 Speech by Jacques Doriot in French National Assembly, 20 Dec. 1925, quoted in M. Daher, *Tarikh Lubnan al-Ijtima'i* (Beirut, 1974), 22; Huvelin, *Que vaut la Syrie?* 45–8.
27 Ruppin, *Syria*, 12.
28 For example, Kalla, 'Role of foreign trade', 31–2.
29 Huvelin, *Que vaut la Syrie?*, 46.
30 *CR* (UK), Aleppo, 1911, *PP*, 1912/13, c, 539. See also Kalla, 'Role of foreign trade', 137.
31 For example, *CRs* (UK), Beirut, 1895, *PP*, 1897, XCIV, 75–7, Beirut, 1908, *PP*, 1909, XCVIII, 897–8.
32 Saba, 'Development and decline', 6–62; Ducousso, *L'industrie de la soie*, 117–18.
33 Cuinet, V, *Syrie, Liban et Palestine*, 67.
34 A. Naccache, 'Moriculture, grainage, sericiculture et filature au Liban', *Actes de la Conference technique Sericicole Internationale* (Ales, France, 1955), 38. See also Ducousso, *L'industrie de la soie*, 155–6; J. Couland, *Le mouvement syndical au Liban (1919–1946)* (Paris, 1970), 42.
35 Ducousso, *L'industrie de la soie*, 117.
36 Ibid., 125 and Annexes I, II, III.
37 Chevalier, 'Lyon et la Syrie', 291; Saba, 'Development and decline', 72n; G. C. Allen, 'Industrialization in the Far East' in M. Postan and H. J. Habakkuk (eds), *The Cambridge Economic History*, VI, 2 (Cambridge, 1965), 878–9.
38 *CRs* (UK) Beirut, 1910, *PP*, 1911, XCVI, 809–10, Beirut, 1911, *PP*, 1912/13, c, 487.
39 *L'industrie de la soie*, 85–9, 91.
40 Ibid., 133–5.
41 For example, Nacacche maintains that about 30 per cent of Lebanon's factories spun to '4 ends' before 1914, 'Moriculture . . . au Liban', 39. See also Saba, 'Development and decline', 58–60.
42 See p. 158.
43 Ducousso, *L'industrie de la soie*, 151–2.
44 Saba, 'Development and decline', 74–7.
45 Ibid., 68–9; Ducousso, *L'industrie de la soie*, 71.
46 Ducousso, op. cit., 76.
47 Saba, 'Development and decline', 85; Ducousso, *L'industrie de la soie*, 151–2.
48 For example, *CRs* (UK), Beirut, 1890, *PP*, 1890/1, LXXXVIII, 306–7 and Beirut, 1891–2, *PP*, 1893/4, XCVII, 400–1. For the first hotels see Cuinet, V, *Syrie, Liban et Palestine*, 241.
49 Saba, 'Creation of the Lebanese economy', 13; P. Klat, 'Land tenure in Syria and Lebanon and its economic and social effects with some suggestions for reform', B. Litt. (Oxford, 1948), 58–9.

50   F. Jouplain (P. Noujaim), *La Question du Liban* (Paris, 1908), 564.
51   FO (UK), *Syria and Palestine*, 118–25; Huvelin, *Que vaut la Syrie?*, 28–9.
52   For example, *CRs* (UK), Aleppo, 1909, *PP*, 1910, CIII, 207; Aleppo, 1913, *PP*, 1914,
     XCV, 285. See also T. E. A. M. Harran, 'Turkish–Syrian relations in the Ottoman con-
     stitutional period (1908–1914)', Ph.D. (London, 1969), 107.
53   Trade figures quoted in Kalla, 'Role of foreign trade', Tables III, V.
54   Granott, *Land System*, 52–3; Jago (Aleppo), 'Detailed report on the Vilayet'; M. Kurd
     Ali, *Khitat al-Sham*, IV (Damascus, 1926), 214–15.
55   Lewis, 'Frontier of settlement', 266; see also 'Notes sur la propriété foncière dans la Syrie
     Centrale' AF, 309 (1933), 133–4.
56   Jago (Aleppo), 'Detailed report on the Vilayet'.
57   For example, Sykes, *The Caliph's Last Heritage*, 449.
58   'Notes sur la propriété foncière', 132–5.
59   Ibid., 132.
60   Klat, 'Land tenure', 54; McDowell, 'Druze revolt', 61–2.
61   N. Moutran, *La Syrie de demain* (Paris, 1916), 304.
62   Granott, *Land System*, 38.
63   Khanzadian and de Bertalot, *Atlas*, 56.
64   'Notes sur la propriété foncière', 135–6.
65   Jago (Aleppo), 'Detailed report on the Vilayet'.
66   Weulersse, *Paysans*, 122–3.
67   Ibid., 124–5.
68   For example, Jago (Aleppo), 'Detailed report on the Vilayet'.
69   Weulersse, *Paysans*, 99–109; Y. Firestone, 'The land equalizing institution and the
     economic transformation of the Levant', *mimeo* of paper presented to Middle East
     Studies Association Conference, Boston, 1974, and 'Faddan and Musha: land,
     population and the burden of impositions in the lowlands of Palestine in the late
     Ottoman period', *mimeo* of paper presented to the Middle East Economic History
     Conference, Princeton, 1974.
70   D. Warriner, 'The real meaning of the Ottoman land code', in Issawi, *Economic
     History*, 73–4.
71   Ibid., 73–7.
72   Klat, 'Land tenure', 67.
73   Ibid., 68–9.
74   Firestone, 'Land equalizing institution', 4–5.
75   British consular figures in Kalla, 'Role of foreign trade', Table III.
76   For example, *CR* (UK), Aleppo, 1899, *PP*, 1900, XCVI, 471.
77   This assertion is based on the comparison between estimates of harvest size and cereal
     exports in Khanzadian and de Bertalot, *Atlas*, 58–9. See also Ruppin, *Syria*, 18.
78   See for example the survey of Syrian agriculture in FO (UK) *Syria and Palestine*,
     93–8.
79   Ibid., 97; *CR* (UK), Aleppo, 1899, 473.
80   Khanzadian and de Bertalot, *Atlas*, 60–1. I have assumed an average yield of 2 ginned
     quintals/acre.
81   Kalla, 'Role of foreign trade', 164. See also A. Khuri, 'Agriculture' in Himadeh,
     Economic Organization of Syria, 81–3.
82   FO (UK), *Syria and Palestine*, 97.
83   Ibid., 95–6; Khuri, 'Agriculture', 82–3.
84   British consular figures in Kalla, 'Role of foreign trade', Tables IV, V.
85   Ibid., Table IV.
86   Quoted ibid., 227n.
87   For example, *CR* (UK), Damascus 1898, *PP*, 1899, CIII, 243.
88   Moore (Jerusalem), 27 Nov. 1886, FO 78/3911.
89   Quoted in Kalla, 'Role of foreign trade', 225n. See also Eyres (Beirut), 4 Nov. 1886, FO
     78/3911.
90   Chevalier, 'Un example de resistance technique', 301–2; S. Weir, *Spinning and
     Weaving in Palestine* (British Museum, London, 1970), 5.

91 Eyres mentions 'changes of fashion' in his report of 4 Nov. 1886.
92 Information about Syrian industry in this paragraph comes from Kalla, 'Role of foreign trade', 204–5, 226–7n. See also, G. Hakim, 'Industry' in Himadeh, *Economic Organization of Syria*, 119–22 and K. Grunwald and J. O. Ronall, *Industrialization in the Middle East* (New York, 1960), 297–8.
93 Hakim, 'Industry', 120–1; FO (UK), *Syria and Palestine*, 120–1; R. Hilan, *Culture et developpement en Syrie* (Paris, 1969), 93.
94 Examples of industrial failures can be found in various British commercial reports, for example Damascus, 1909, *PP*, 1910, cIII, 192–3.
95 For example, Père J.-A. Jaussen, *Coutumes Palestiniennes*, I, *Naplouse et son district* (Paris, 1927), 288–90; Hakim, 'Industry', 166.
96 Hakim, 'Industry', 122–30.
97 Kalla, 'Role of foreign trade', 100–2, 107–11.
98 Samné, *Syrie*, 302–3, 325–7; Jago (Aleppo), 'Detailed report of the Vilayet'; Moutran, *La Syrie de demain*, 302.
99 See p. 172.
100 Shamir, 'Modernization', 364; McDowell, 'Druze revolt', 94ff.
101 Harran, 'Turkish–Syrian relations', 106.
102 Moutran, *La Syrie de demain*, 269; Rey, *Statistique 1911*, 'Chemin de fer Damas-Hameh et prolongements'.
103 *Caliph's Last Heritage*, 298.
104 Ibid., 299.
105 *CRs* (UK), Damascus, 1908, *PP*, 1909, xcVIII, 857, Damascus, 1909, *PP*, 1910, cIII, 192–3, Damascus, 1911, *PP*, 1912/13, c, 690.
106 Cuinet, v, *Syrie, Liban et Palestine*, 93, 179, 493, 520, where he gives figures of 341, 638 for the *mutasarrifiya* of Jerusalem and 245,259 for the Sanjaks of Acre, Balqa and Maan, parts of which fell outside the boundaries of twentieth-century Palestine.
107 For example, Ben-Arieh, 'Changing landscape', 37–40, 42.
108 Hopkins, 'Population', 6.
109 Y. Ben-Arieh, 'The population of the large towns in Palestine during the first eighty years and the nineteenth century, according to western sources', in Ma'oz, *Studies*, 49–69.
110 A. Cohen, *Arab Border Villages in Israel* (Manchester, 1965), 10–11; Firestone, 'Crop-sharing economics – 1', 12.
111 Firestone, 'Production and trade in an Islamic context', 2, 309–10.
112 Kalla, 'Role of foreign trade', Table III.
113 M. Brown, 'Agriculture', in Himadeh, *Economic Organization of Palestine*, 138.
114 Kalla, 'Role of foreign trade', Table III.
115 See p. 248. In 1899, for example, there were 2300 tourists and 13,400 pilgrims, *CR* (UK), Palestine, 1899, *PP*, 1900, xcVI, 493. A later report estimates the total amount of cash brought into the country by such visitors as £60,000–80,000, *CR* (UK), Palestine, 1907, *PP*, 1908, cxVI, 873.
116 Palestine, *First Palestine Census of Industries 1928* (Jerusalem, 1929), 8.
117 S. B. Himadeh, 'Industry', in Himadeh, *Economic Organization of Palestine*, 221.
118 The Census itself uses an extremely wide definition: 'all factories and workshops producing any article either by hand or power, with or without paid labour, ready for sale', *First Palestine Census*, 5–6.
119 Jewish Agency, *Report and General Abstracts of the Censuses of Jewish Agriculture, Industry and Handicrafts and Labour, Taken in 1930* (Jerusalem, 1931), 43.
120 Ibid.
121 Cuinet, v, *Syrie, Liban et Palestine*, 182, 616–18; Himadeh, 'Industry', 216–22.
122 Himadeh, 'Industry', 217–18.
123 Sources in Schölch, 'European penetration'; also Himadeh, 'Industry', 217.
124 Himadeh, 'Industry,' 218–19.
125 Weir, *Spinning and Weaving*, 5.
126 Himadeh, 'Industry', 218–19.
127 For example, Verney and Dambmann, *Puissance étrangères*, 253, 397.

128 *CR* (UK), Palestine, 1907, *PP*, 1908, CXVI, 871.
129 Granott, *Land System*, 80–1, 95, 337n.
130 Ibid., 81–4. See also the 1911 list of large landowners who had sold land to the Jewish colonists in A·W. S. Kayyali, 'The Palestinian Arab reaction to Zionism and the British Mandate, 1908–1939', Ph.D. (London, 1970), 25–7.
131 Granott, *Land System*, 82–3; Firestone, 'Crop-sharing economics – 1', 3–4; P. Baldensperger, 'The Immovable East', PEF, *Quarterly* (1906), 192–3.
132 *Land System*, 38–9.
133 Firestone, 'Crop-sharing economics – 1', 12.
134 S. Bergheim, 'Land tenure in Palestine', PEF, *Quarterly* (1894), 197–9.
135 Firestone, 'Crop-sharing economics – 1', 4–7.
136 See, for example, Porath, *Emergence of the Palestinian–Arab National Movement*, 11–16.
137 Quoted in Granott, *Land System*, 40.
138 Ibid., 38–9.
139 Ibid., 2–5.
140 For example, ibid., 179. See also Baldensperger, 'The Immovable East', 192.
141 'Faddan and Musha', 13–16.
142 For example, Bergheim, 'Land tenure', 192–5; G. Robinson Lees, *Village Life in Palestine* (London, 1905), 137–8.
143 For example, Firestone's data in 'Crop-sharing economics – 1', 7. G. E. Post, 'Essays on the sects and nationalities of Syria and Palestine', 2, PEF, *Quarterly* (April 1891), 105.
144 PEF, *Quarterly* (April 1891), 105.
145 *Village Life*, 161–95.
146 Information taken from D. Giladi, 'The agromic development of the old colonies in Palestine (1882–1914)' in Ma'oz, *Studies*; A. Ruppin, *The Agricultural Colonization of the Zionist Organisation in Palestine* (trans.) (London, 1926), 3–6, 78, and S. Schama, *The Two Rothschilds and the Land of Israel* (London, 1978) chs 3–5.
147 Ruppin, *Agricultural Colonization*, 6, 78; N. J. Mandel, 'Ottoman practice with regards to Jewish settlement in Palestine, 1881–1908', MES, XI, 1 (Jan. 1975), 42.
148 Kayyali, 'Palestinian–Arab reaction', 25–7.
149 Ibid., 27.
150 Mandel, 'Turks, Arabs and Jewish immigration', 85–6.
151 Giladi, 'Agronomic development', 176.
152 Schama, *The Two Rothschilds*, 73–4.
153 Ibid., ch. 4.
154 Ibid., 110.
155 Ibid., 109–10, 121–4, 127.
156 Ibid., 156. But Schama gives a mistaken figure for Palestinian orange exports: see Tolkowsky, *Gateway of Palestine*, 184.
157 Schama, *The Two Rothschilds*, 164–6.
158 Ibid., 128–9; Giladi, 'Agronomic development', 178–80. In 1914, Petah Tikvah had a population of some 2600 Jewish settlers, many of whom worked in Tel Aviv and Jaffa, 600 resident Palestinian Arab workers, in addition to employing 1100 more Palestinians on a casual basis, Schama, *The Two Rothschilds*, 156.
159 D. Ben Gurion, *Israel: Years of Challenge* (London, 1964), 7.
160 Ruppin, *Agricultural Colonization*, 4; V. D. Segré, *Israel: A Society in Transition* (London, 1971), 68.
161 Segré, *Israel*, 68–78.

11: The Iraqi provinces, 1880–1914

1 'Growth and structure of Iraq's population', 155–7.
2 A. T. Wilson, 'Mesopotamia, 1914–1921', *JCAS*, VIII, 3 (1921), 146–7.
3 Dowson, *Inquiry into Land Tenure*, 12.
4 For example, J. J. Malone, 'Surgeon Colvill's fight against plague and cholera in Iraq 1868–1878', in F. Sarruf and S. Tamim (eds), *American University of Beirut Festival Book*

(Beirut, 1967), 167–77. See also Svoboda's description of the quarantine system operated on the rivers, for example Diary 23 (Jan.–Nov. 188), 82, Diary 33 (Dec. 1888–Sept. 1889), 172–6.

5   'The role of foreign trade in the economic development of Iraq', 349–50.

6   For example, Anon., 'Turkish rule and British administration in Mesopotamia', *QR*, CCXXXI, 491 (Oct. 1919), 422: Wilson, 'Mesopotamia', 150.

7   Figures in *CR* (UK) Basra, 1913, *PP*, 1914, XCV, 212. Yield estimate for the 1920s in Hasan, 'The role of foreign trade in the economic development of Iraq', 352. The Ottoman tax collectors assumed an average yield of half a ton of cereals per *dunum*, Howell, 'Qanun al-Aradhi', 37.

8   For example, Sykes's findings, *Caliph's Last Heritage*, 338, 340. Also (UK) Admiralty War Staff, Intelligence Division, *A Handbook of Mesopotamia* (Aug. 1916), I, 132.

9   (UK), *Handbook of Mesopotamia*, 131–2.

10 The main Persian goods were opium and carpets, with smaller quantities of wool, gall nuts, etc., (UK) *Handbook of Mesopotamia*, I, 145.

11 *CR* (UK), Basra, 1913, 212.

12 See ibid., 221–3. There are no calculations of invisible earnings but they must have been considerable. For example some 150,000 Shia pilgrims are said to have visited the holy cities of Najaf and Karbala each year, F. Lemoine, 'En Mésopotamie', *Correspondence d'Orient*, II, 21 (1 Aug. 1909), 702.

13 G. N. Curzon, *Persia and the Persian Question*, II (London, 1892), 577–8. See also estimates in I. L. Bird (Mrs Bishop), *Journeys in Persia and Kurdistan*, I (London, 1891), 43.

14 Figures in *PP*, 1908, CXXV, 5, quoted in Salih, *Mesopotamia*, 226. A few years later, however, the value of the two main Persian exports passing through Basra only came to £150,000 (UK) *Handbook of Mesopotamia*, I, 146.

15 *CRs* (UK), Baghdad, 1900, *PP*, 1902, CX, 457–8; Baghdad, 1902, *PP*, 1903, LXXIX, 228–9; Baghdad, 1904, *PP*, 1906, XCCVIII, 870–3.

16 British consular figures quoted in Salih, *Mesopotamia*, 259–60.

17 Figures quoted ibid., 223–5, 258–61.

18 These fears are well dealt with ibid., ch. 7 and by Cohen, *British Policy in Mesopotamia*, ch. 2.

19 Figures quoted in Salih, *Mesopotamia*, 261.

20 *CRs* (UK), Basra, 1864–6, *PP*, 1867, LXVII, 266–7; Basra, 1866/7, *PP*, 1866/7, LXVIII, 395–6; Salih, *Mesopotamia*, 220.

21 Salih, *Mesopotamia*, 259–61.

22 Ibid., 260.

23 (UK) *Handbook of Mesopotamia*, I, 145; *CR* (UK), Basra, 1902, *PP*, 1903, LXXIX, 207.

24 (UK) *Handbook of Mesopotamia*, I, 145.

25 Ibid.; *CR* (UK), Baghdad, 1904, *PP*, 1906, CXXVIII, 866.

26 For the complicated history of these negotiations see Salih, *Mesopotamia*, 212–18.

27 McNie, 'History of steam navigation', 8; *CR* (UK), Basra, 1906, *PP*, 1907, XCIII, 50–1.

28 (UK) *Handbook of Mesopotamia*, I, 170.

29 For example, Diary 33, ff. 28, 35, 37, 41, 44.

30 Ibid., ff. 124.

31 *CRs* (UK), Baghdad 1908, *PP*, 1901, XCVIII, 941; Basra, 1908, *PP*, 1909, XCVIII, 841; Basra 1913, *PP*, 1914, XCV, 216–17; L. Bouvat, 'Le Vilayet de Bagdad et son organisation administrative', *RMM*, XXIII (June 1913), 249.

32 *CR* (UK), Baghdad 1912, *PP*, 1914, XCV, 42.

33 For example, Cohen, *British Policy in Mesopotamia*, 54–5, 155.

34 *CR* (UK), Baghdad, 1900, *PP*, 1902, CX, 459.

35 For example, *CR* (UK), Baghdad, 1904, *PP*, 1907, XCIII, 29. See also Batatu, *Old Social Classes*, 238–9.

36 For example, British sources quoted in Cohen, *British Policy in Mesopotamia*, 54.

37 Batatu, *Old Social Classes*, 239.

38 (UK) *Handbook of Mesopotamia*, I, 166–8; Lt Col. L. J. Hall, *The Inland Water Transport in Mesopotamia* (London, 1921), 93; P. Vaucelles, *La vie en Irak il y a un siècle* (Paris, 1963), 16.

39 For example, *CR* (UK), Basra, 1902, *PP*, 1903, LXXIX, 205.
40 India, General Staff, *Field Notes: Mesopotamia* (Calcutta, 1917), 25.
41 Ibid., 112; (UK) *Handbook of Mesopotamia*, I, 163–6.
42 (UK) *Handbook of Mesopotamia*, 162–3.
43 Ibid., 163–4.
44 Ibid., 160.
45 Quoted in V. H. W. Dowson, *Dates and Date Cultivation in Iraq*, I (Cambridge, 1921), 4–5.
46 (UK) *Handbook of Mesopotamia*, I, 131–2.
47 *Field Notes: Mesopotamia*, 35; Bell, 'Asiatic Turkey', 128.
48 Ionides, *Regime*, 75–6; (UK) *Handbook of Mesopotamia*, I, 120–1.
49 (UK) *Handbook of Mesopotamia*, 120.
50 Ibid., 131–2.
51 Ibid., 132–3, 142.
52 Dowson, *Inquiry into Land Tenure*, 20–1.
53 Sluglett, *Britain in Iraq*, 238–9; Dowson, *Inquiry into Land Tenure*, 7; G. A. K. Rasheed, 'Development of land taxation in modern Iraq', *BSOAS*, XXV, 2 (1962), 262.
54 'Land problems in Iraq', 169.
55 Ibid., 168, Batatu, *Old Social Classes*, 169–70; A. Jwaideh, 'The Saniya lands of Abdul Hamid II in Iraq', in G. Makdisi (ed.), *Arabic and Islamic Studies* (Leiden, 1965), 327–8.
56 *Turquie d'Asia*, III, *Vilayet de Baghdad* (Paris, 1894), 44.
57 Jwaideh, 'Saniya lands', 332–5.
58 Ibid., 335.
59 Ibid., 33–4; Anon., *Arabs of Mesopotamia*, 57, 87.
60 See pp. 228–9.
61 Jwaiden, 'Saniya lands', 332.
62 Batatu, *Old Social Classes*, 160–5, 289–93; Haidaer, 'Land problems in Iraq', 168.
63 Figures in Sluglett, *Britain in Iraq*, 317.
64 Howell, 'Qanun al-Aradhi', 31.
65 J. G. Lorimer, 'Tour Journal No. 1 of 1910' in Lowther (Constantinople), 23 Mar. 1910, FO 371/1007.
66 Howell, 'Qanun al-Aradhi', 38.
67 J. S. Mann, *An Administrator in the Making* (London, 1921), 185.
68 Ibid. For British land policy see Batatu, *Old Social Classes*, 86–99, Sluglett, *Britain in Iraq*, ch. 6.
69 Howell, 'Qanun al-Aradhi', 30–1.
70 *Arabs of Mesopotamia*, 55; Sluglett, *Britain in Iraq*, 233–4; Batatu, *Old Social Classes*, 86.
71 Ibid., 73–8, 83–4.
72 Ibid., 83–4; Jwaideh, 'Midhat Pasha', 132–3.
73 W. R. Hay, *Two Years in Kurdistan* (London, 1921), 95–6.
74 Ibid., 103–4.
75 Jwaideh, 'Midhat Pasha', 132–3; Batatu, *Old Social Classes*, 74–5.
76 For example, Crow (Basra), 31 Mar. 1910 in Lowther (Constantinople), 9 May 1910, and 25 June 1910 in Lowther (Constantinople) 19 July 1910, FO 371/1007.
77 *Arabs of Mesopotamia*, 6–7. Jwaideh, 'Midhat Pasha', 132–3.
78 Quoted in Iraq, 'Administrative report on the revenue dept. for the year 1919', CO 696/2, 24.
79 *Old Social Classes*, 77–8.
80 Dowson, *Inquiry into Land Tenure*, 27–9.
81 'Turkish rule and British administration', 407.
82 'Land problems in Iraq', 170–1; S. Himadeh, extract from *Al-nizam al-iqtisadi fi al-'Iraq* (trans.) in Issawi, *Economic History*, 187.
83 Ibid., 187–90.
84 'Land problems in Iraq', 170–1.
85 'Asiatic Turkey', 141.

86 'Land problems in Iraq', 171.
87 Iraq, Administrative Report, Muntafiq Division, 1919, 7, CO 696/2.
88 On industry in general see A. Lanzoni, 'La Mesopotamia economica' (trans.) in Issawi, *Economic History*, 180—1; (UK) *Handbook of Mesopotamia*, I, 141—3; Cuinet, III, *Vilayet de Bagdad*, 64—9.
89 F. Jalal, *The Role of Government in the Industrialization of Iraq, 1950—1965* (London, 1972), 141.
90 Cuinet, III, *Vilayet de Bagdad*, 65—7.
91 H. S. Cowper, *Through Turkish Arabia* (London, 1894), 253; (UK) *Handbook of Mesopotamia*, I, 142.
92 Official figures for 1911 quoted in Bouvat, 'Vilayet de Bagdad', 255—6.
93 (UK) *Handbook of Mesopotamia*, I, 142, 146—7.
94 Bouvat, 'Vilayet de Bagdad', 255—6.
95 Dowson, *Dates and Date Cultivation*, 58; (UK) *Handbook of Mesopotamia*, I, 143; 'Turkish rule and British administration', 409.
96 'History of steam navigation', 7—8.
97 M. Sykes, *Through Five Turkish Provinces* (London, 1900), 56—7.

12: *A century of economic growth and transformation: conclusion*

1 For example, H. Myint, *The Economics of the Developing Countries*, 3rd edn (London, 1967), chs 2 and 3.
2 For example, Baran, *Political Economy of Growth*, 173—4.
3 For a discussion of this concept see Hopkins, *Economic History*, 168—71.
4 *The Making of the English Working Class* (Harmondsworth, 1968), 226—32.
5 'Shifts in economic power' in *Economic History*, 505.

Bibliography of references cited*

1. Unpublished sources

(a) Private papers

Austria, Consul Reports from Egypt, 1841–60 (copies found in Abdin Palace, Cairo).

General Mance Papers, St Antony's Private Papers, Oxford.

Hekekyan Papers, British Museum, London.

Liverpool Papers, Scottish Record Office, Edinburgh.

Manzaloui Family Records (in possession of Professor Mahmoud Manzaloui).

McNie, T. G. 'History of steam navigation in the East', St Antony's Private Papers, Oxford.

Richard Wood Papers, St Antony's Private Papers, Oxford.

Svoboda, J. M. 'Tigris and Euphrates Co.' (in possession of Mrs M. Makiya).

Svoboda Diaries (in possession of Mrs M. Makiya).

Thomas, Sir O. 'Agricultural and economic position of Egypt' Milner Papers, Bodleian Library, Oxford.

(b) Unpublished government papers

Memorandum by Capt. Baring of interview with native as to the collection of taxes', Feb. 1878 in *Revenue Survey of Egypt* (1879?) a copy of which can be found in the Library of the Royal Geographical Society, London.

'Report on the commerce of Arabia and Persia' in 'Report on British trade with Persia and Arabia' by S. Manesty and H. Jones, Basra 18 Dec. 1790, Factory Records – Persia and the Persian Gulf, India Office, London.

(c) Theses and mimeographed papers

Barnett, A. 'A sociological study of the Gezira scheme Sudan', Ph.D. (Manchester, 1973).

Batatu, J. 'The shaikh and peasant in Iraq 1917–1958', Ph.D. (Harvard, 1960).

Bell, K. 'The Constantinople Embassy of Sir Henry Bulwer 1858–65', Ph.D. (London, 1961).

Corrigan, H. S. W. 'British, French and German interests in Asiatic Turkey, 1881–1914', Ph.D. (London, 1954).

* This bibliography only includes works cited in the text. For two useful general bibliographies see, E. R. J. Owen, 'The recent economic history of the Middle East 1800–1967' in D. Grimwood-Jones, ed., *Middle East and Islam; a Biographical Introduction* (Zug, Switzerland, 1979) and Issawi, *Economic History*, 527–37.

Deeb, M. J. 'The Khazin family: a case study of the effect of social change on traditional roles', M.A. (American University of Beirut, 1972).

Firestone, Y. 'The land equalizing institution and the economic transformation of the Levant', *mimeo* of paper presented to Middle East Studies Association Conference, Boston, 1974.

'Faddan and musha: land, population and the burden of impositions in the lowlands of Palestine in the late Ottoman period', *mimeo* of paper presented to the Middle East Economic History Conference, Princeton University, 1974.

Genç, M. 'A comparative study of the life-term tax farming data and the volume of commercial and industrial activities in the Ottoman Empire during the second half of the eighteenth century (trans.), *mimeo* of paper delivered to symposium on South-Eastern European and Balkan cities and the Industrial Revolution in western Europe', Hamburg, March 1976.

Gould, A. 'Pashas and brigands: Ottoman provincial reform and its impact on the nomadic tribes of southern Anatolia 1840–1885', Ph.D. (UCLA, 1973).

Hansen, B. and Lucas, E. 'A new set of foreign trade indices for Egypt', Working Papers in Economics, No. 4, Oct. 1974 (University of California, Berkeley).

Harran, T. E. A. M. 'Turkish–Syrian relations in the Ottoman constitutional period (1908–1914)', Ph.D. (London, 1969).

Hasan, M. S. 'Foreign trade and the economic development of Iraq, 1869–1939', D. Phil. (Oxford, 1958).

Hunter, R. B. 'Bureaucratic politics and passing of viceregal absolutism: the origins of modern government in Egypt, 1805–1879', Ph.D. (Harvard, 1979).

Joseph, R. 'The material origins of the Lebanese conflict of 1860', B. Litt. (Oxford, 1977).

Kalla, M. S. 'Role of foreign trade in the economic development of Syria 1831–1914', Ph.D. (American University, Washington, 1969).

Karpat, K. H. 'Migration and its effects', *mimeo* of paper presented to the Middle East Economic History Conference, Princeton University, 1974.

Kayyali, A.-W. S. 'The Palestinian Arab reaction to Zionism and the British Mandate, 1908–1939', Ph.D. (London, 1970).

Kazziha, W. 'The evolution of the Egyptian political elite, 1907–1921: a case study of the role of large landowners in politics', Ph.D. (London, 1970).

Klat, P. 'Land tenure in Syria and Lebanon and its economic and social effects with some suggestions for reform', B. Litt. (Oxford, 1948).

Kurmuş, O. 'The role of British capital in the economic development of western Anatolia 1850–1913', Ph.D. (London, 1974).

McDowell, D. 'The Druze revolt, 1925–27 and its background in the late Ottoman period', B. Litt. (Oxford, 1972).

Mardin, S. 'Center-periphery relations. A key to Turkish politics', *mimeo* (March 1972).

Naff, A. 'A social history of Zahle. The principal market town in nineteenth century Lebanon', Ph.D. (UCLA, 1972).

Quataert, D. 'Ottoman reform and agriculture in Anatolia 1876–1908', Ph.D. (UCLA, 1973)

Saba, P. 'The development and decline of the Lebanese silk industry', B. Litt. (Oxford, 1977).

Schatkowski-Schilcher, L. 'The decline of Syrian localism: the Damascene notables 1785–1870', D. Phil. (Oxford, 1978).

Schölch, A. 'Aspekte der Wirtschaftlichen Entwicklung Palastinas in Der 2. Halfte des 19. Jahrhunderts', *mimeo* (Essen, n.d.).

Wattleworth, M. and Hansen, B. 'Report on the construction of agricultural indexes for Egypt, 1887–1968', *mimeo*, 15 Sept. 1975 (Inst. of International Studies, University of California, Berkeley).

2. Government publications

Belgium

Ministère des Affaires Etrangères, *Recueil Consulaire* (Brussels, 1850).

Egypt

Commission Supérieure d'Enquête, *Rapport préliminaire addressé à S.A. le Khédive* (Cairo, 1878).

Industrial and Commercial Census, 1927 (Cairo, 1931).

Rapport de la Commission du Commerce et de l'Industrie (Cairo, 1918).

Recensement général de l'Egypte, 1882, I (Cairo, 1884), II (Cairo, 1885).

Direction Général des Douanes, *Le commerce extérieur de l'Egypte. Statistique comparée 1884–1889* (Cairo, 1891).

Ministère de l'Interieur, *Statistique de l'Egypte 1873* (Cairo, 1873).

Ministry of Agriculture, *Agricultural Census of Egypt, 1939* (Cairo, 1946).

Ministry of Agriculture, *The Pink Boll Worm in Egypt in 1916–1917* by H. A. Ballou (Cairo, 1920).

Ministry of Finance, *The Census of Egypt Taken in 1917*, I (Cairo, 1920).

Ministry of Finance, Department of General Statistics, *Annuaires Statistiques, 1910* (Cairo, 1910) and *1914* (Cairo, 1914).

India

General Staff, *Field Notes: Mesopotamia* (Calcutta, 1917).

Lebanon

Ministère du Plan, *Besoins et possibilités de developpement du Liban: Etude préliminaire*, Mission IRFED (Liban, 1960–1).

Palestine

First Palestine Census of Industries 1928 (Jerusalem, 1929).

Turkey (Ottoman Empire)

Baskakanlik Istatistik/Office Centrale de Statistique, *Istatistik Yilligi/Annuaire Statistique* 1936/7 (Ankara, n.d.).

Ministry of Commerce and Agriculture, *1329, 1331 Seneleri Istatistiki* (Istanbul, 1333/1917). Published in French as *Statistique industrielle des années 1913 et 1915* (Constantinople, 1917).

Programme du Ministère des Travaux Publics (Constantinople, 1909).

United Kingdom

Admiralty War Staff, Intelligence Division, *A Handbook of Mesopotamia* (Aug. 1916), I.
Foreign Office (London), *Anatolia* (April 1919).
Foreign Office (London), *Syria and Palestine* (1919).

United States

Annual reports on the commercial relations of the United States with foreign countries: executive documents published by the House of Representatives, Washington DC.

3. Books and articles

ʿAbd al-Rahim, A. A. 'Financial burdens on the peasants under the aegis of the iltizam system in Egypt' in A. L. Udovitch (ed.), *Land, Population and Society: Studies in the Economic History of the Middle East from the Rise of Islam to the Nineteenth century* (forthcoming).
   'Hazz al-Quhuf, a new source for the study of the fallahin of Egypt in the seventeenth and eighteenth centuries', *JESHO*, XVIII, 3 (1975).
   Al-Rif al-Misri fi al-Qarn al-Thaman ʿAshr (ʿAyn Shams, 1974).
Abdel-Malek, A. *Idéologie et renaissance nationale: l'Egypte moderne* (Paris, 1969).
Abd El-Motaal, M. Z. *Les bourses en Egypte* (Paris, 1930).
Abir, M. 'Local leadership and early reforms in Palestine 1800–1834' in M. Maʿoz (ed.), *Studies on Palestine during the Ottoman Period* (Jerusalem, 1975).
Abu-Lughod, J. 'Varieties of urban experience: contrast, coexistence and coalescence in Cairo' in I. M. Lapidus (ed.), *Middle Eastern Cities* (Berkeley and Los Angeles, 1969).
Aghion, Y. and Poilay, M. 'Excursions dans le grands domains – propriété de S. E. Riaz Pacha', *BUSAE*, I, 5 (Nov. 1901).
Ahmed, F. *The Young Turks* (Oxford, 1969).
Alexandrescu-Dersca, M. M. 'Contribution à l'étude de l'approvisionnement en blé de Constantinople au XVIIIe siècle', *Studia e Acta Orientalia*, I (Bucharest, 1957).
Allen, G. C. 'Industrialization in the Far East' in M. Postan and H. J. Habakkuk, (eds), *The Cambridge Economic History*, VI, 2, pt 2 (Cambridge, 1965).
Amiran, D. H. K., 'The pattern of settlement in Palestine', pts 1 and 2, *IEJ*, III, 2 and 3 (1953).
Amiran, D. K. and Ben-Ariah, Y. 'Sedentarization of beduin in Israel', *IEJ*, XIII, 3 (1963).
ʿAmr, I. *Al-Ard wa al-fallah* (Cairo, 1958).
Un Ancien Juge Mixte *L'Egypte et Europe*, 2 vols (Leiden, n.d. (1881?)).
Anderson, O. 'Great Britain and the beginnings of the Ottoman public debt, 1854–55', *HJ*, VII, 1 (1964).
Anderson, P. *Lineages of the Absolutist State* (London, 1974).
Anderson, P. *Passages from Antiquity to Feudalism* (London, 1974).
Anhoury, J. 'Le blé en Egypte', *EC*, 85 (March 1925).

Anis, M. A.   'A study of the national income of Egypt', *EC*, 261–2 (Nov.–Dec. 1950).

Ankara University   Siyasal Bilgiler Fakültesi Yayine, no. 29, *Osmanlı Sanayii 1913, 1915 yılları sanayi istatistiki* (Ankara, 1970).

Anon.   'La province turque de Latakie, son étendue, ses habitants, son importance commerciale', *Annales des Voyages*, I (Feb. 1867).

Anon.   *Rambles in the Deserts of Syria* (London, 1864).

Anon.   *The Finances of Egypt* (London, 1874).

Anon.   'The story of the Euphrates Company' in C. Issawi (ed.), *The Economic History of the Middle East 1900–1914* (Chicago, 1966).

Anon.   'Turkish rule and British administration in Mesopotamia', *QR*, CCXXXI (Oct. 1919).

Al-ʿAqiqi, A. D.   *Lebanon in the Last Years of Feudalism 1840–68*, trans. and ed. M. H. Kerr (Beirut, 1959).

Arminjon, P.   *La situation économique et financière de l'Egypte* (Paris, 1911).

Artin, Y.   'Essai sur les causes du renchérissement de la vie materielle au Caire au courant du XIXe siècle (1800 à 1907)', *MIE*, V (Cairo, 1907).

Artin, Y.   *Propriété foncier en Egypt* (Cairo, 1883) trans. as *The Right of Landed Property in Egypt* (London, 1885).

Arts Council (UK)   *Carpets from the Collection of Joseph V. McMullen* (London, 1972).

Asad, T.   'Equality in nomad social systems?', *Critique of Anthropology*, II, 11 (Spring 1978).
'The beduin as a military force: notes on some aspects of power relations between nomads and sedentaries in historical perspective', in C. Nelson (ed.), *The Desert and the Sown: Nomads in a Wider Society* (Berkeley, 1973).

Asad, T. and Volpe, H.   'Concepts of modes of production', *ES*, V (1976).

Asfour, Y.   *Syria: Development and Monetary Policy* (Cambridge, Mass., 1959).

Atkins, R. A.   'The origins of the Anglo-French condominium in Egypt, 1875–1876', *The Historian*, XXXVI, 2 (Feb. 1974).

Audebeau, C.   'Le région de Rosette et l'irrigation perenne avant le XIXe siècle', *BIE*, X (1927/7).

Audebeau, C. and Mosséri, V.   'Le labourage en Egypte', *BIE*, 5th ser., X (1916).

Avineri, S. (ed.)   *Karl Marx by Colonialism and Modernization* (New York, 1968).

Ayalon, D.   'Studies in al-Jabarti: notes on the transformation of Mamluk society in Egypt under the Ottomans', pt 2, *BSOAS*, III (1960).

Ayalon, D.   'Studies in al-Jabarti', pts 1–3, *JESHO*, III (1960).

Aymard, M.   *Venise, Raguse et le commerce du blé pendant le seconde moitié du XVIe siècle* (Paris, 1966).

Al-Azmeh, A.   'What is the Islamic City', *ROMES*, II (1976).

Baer, G.   'The development of private ownership in land', in G. Baer, *Studies in the Social History of Modern Egypt* (Chicago, 1969).

Baer, G.   'The economic and social position of the village-mukhtar in Palestine' in G. Ben-Dor (ed.), *The Palestinians and the Middle East* (Haifa, 1978).

Baer, G.   *Egyptian Guilds in Modern Times* (Jerusalem, 1964).

Baer, G.   'Fellah and townsman in Ottoman Egypt', *AAS*, VIII, 3 (1972).

Baer, G.   *A History of Landownership in Modern Egypt 1800–1950* (London, 1962).

Baer, G.   'Monopolies and restrictive practices of Turkish guilds', *JESHO*, XIII, 2 (April 1970).

Baer, G. 'Popular revolt in Ottoman Cairo', *Der Islam*, LIV, 2 (1977).

Baer, G. 'Urbanization in Egypt, 1820–1907' in W. R. Polk and R. L. Chambers (eds), *Beginnings of Modernization in the Middle East* (Chicago, 1968).

Bailey, F. E. *British Policy and the Turkish Reform Movement* (Cambridge, Mass., 1942).

Baldensperger, P. 'The immovable East', *PEF Quarterly* (1906).

Baldwin, G. *Memorial Relating to the Trade in Slaves* (Alexandria, 1789).

Balls, W. L. *Egypt of the Egyptians* (London, 1915).

Ballou, H. A. *The Pink Boll-worm in Egypt in 1916–1917* (Cairo, 1920).

Baran, P. A. *The Political Economy of Growth*, pb edn (New York, 1968).

Barbie de Bocage, J.-G. 'Notice sur le carte des Pachaliks de Bagdad, Orfa et Alep . . .', *Receuil de voyages et de mémoires publiés par la Société de Géographie*, II (Paris, 1825).

Barkan, O. L. 'Essai sur les données statistiques des registres de recensement dans l'Empire ottoman au XVe et XVIe siècles', *JESHO*, I (1958).

Barkan, O. L. 'Feodal Duzen ve Osmanli Timari' in O. Okyer (ed.), *Turkiye Iktisat Tarihi Semineri* (1975).

Barkan, O. L. 'The price revolution of the sixteenth century: a turning point in the economic history of the Middle East' (trans.), *IJMES*, VI (1975).

Barkan, O. L. 'The social consequences of the economic crisis in later fifteenth-century Turkey', Turkey, Economic and Social Studies Conference Board, *Social Aspects of Economic Development* (Istanbul, n.d.).

Barker, W. B. *Lares et Penates: or Cilicia and its Governors*, ed. W. F. Aynsworth (London, 1853).

Barth, F. *Nomads of South Persia* (Oslo and London, 1961).

Baster, A. 'The origins of British banking expansion in the Near East', *EHR*, I (Oct. 1934).

Batatu, J. *The Old Social Classes and the Revolutionary Movements of Iraq* (Princeton, 1978).

Baxter, J. 'Notes on the estimate of the national income of Egypt for 1921–1922', *EC*, 72 (May 1923).

Beawes, W. *Lex Mercatoria Rediviva: or the Merchant's Dictionary* (London, 1752).

Bechara, E. Irrigation perenne des bassins de la Moyenne Egypte (Lausanne, 1905).

Beldiceaunu-Steinherr, Berindei, M. and Vernstein, G. 'Attribution de timar dans le province de Trebizonde (fin de XVe siècle)', *Turcica*, VIII, 1 (1976).

Bell, G. L. 'Asiatic Turkey' in Anon., *The Arabs of Mesopotamia* (Basra, 1917).

Ben-Ariah, Y. 'The changing landscape of the Central Jordan Valley', *SH*, XV, 3 (1968).

Ben-Ariah, Y. 'The population of the large towns in Palestine during the first eighty years of the nineteenth century according to Western sources', in N. Ma'oz (ed.), *Studies on Palestine during the Ottoman Period* (Jerusalem, 1975).

Ben-Gurion, D. *Israel: Years of Challenge* (London, 1964).

Bergheim, S. 'Land tenure in Palestine', *PEF Quarterly* (1894).

Berque, J. *Egypt: Imperialism and Revolution* (trans.) (London, 1972).

Bertin, J., Hémardinquer, J.-J., Keul, M. and Randles, W. G. L. *Atlas des culture vivières/Atlas of Food Crops* (Paris/The Hague, 1971).

De Besse, A.   *L'Empire Turc* (Paris and Leipzig, 1854).

Biliotti, A.   *La Banque impériale ottomane* (Paris, 1909).

Bird, I. L. (Mrs Bishop)   *Journeys in Persia and Kurdistan*, I (London, 1891).

Blaisdell, D. C.   *European Financial Control in the Ottoman Empire* (New York, 1929).

Block, M.   *Statistique de la France*, 2nd edn, II (Paris, 1875).

Blondel, E.   *Deux ans en Syrie et en Palestine* (Paris, 1840).

Boaz, T.   *Egypt* (London, 1950).

Bodman, H. L.   *Political Factions in Aleppo, 1760–1826* (Chapel Hill, 1963).

Bonné, A.   *State and Economics in the Middle East*, 2nd edn (London, 1955).

Bouvat, L.   'Le vilayet de Bagdad et son organisation administrative', *RMM*, XXIII (June 1913).

Bouvier, J.   'Les interêts financiers et la question d'Egypte (1875–76)', *RH*, CCXXIV (July–Sept. 1960).

Braudel, F.   *Capitalism and Material Life 1400–1800* (trans.) (London, 1973).

Braudel, F.   *Le Méditerrannée et le monde méditerranéen à l'époque de Philippe II*, 2 vols (Paris, 1966).

Brice, W. C.   *South-West Asia* (London, 1966).

British Chamber of Commerce of Egypt   *List of Financial, Manufacturing and Transport Companies Established in Egypt*, 3rd edn (Alexandria, 1901).

Brown, M.   'Agriculture', in S. B. Himadeh (ed.), *Economic Organization of Palestine* (Beirut, 1939).

Brown, R. H.   *History of the Barrage at the Head of the Delta of Egypt* (Cairo, 1896).

Browne, W. G.   *Travels in Africa, Egypt and Syria from the Year 1792 to 1798* (London, 1799).

Buckingham, J. S.   *Travels among the Arab Tribes Inhabiting the Countries of Syria and Palestine* (London, 1825).

Buckingham, J. S.   *Travels in Mesopotamia*, II (London, 1827).

Bulliet, R. W.   *The Camel and the Wheel* (Cambridge, Mass., 1975).

Bulutay, T., Tezel, Y. S. and Yıldırım, N.   *Turkiye Milli Geliri (1923–1948)*, and *Tabolar* (Ankara, 1974).

Burckhardt, J. L.   *Travels in Syria and the Holy Land* (London, 1822).

Burnaby, F.   *On Horseback through Asia Minor*, I (London, 1877).

Burton, R. F. and Tyrwhitt-Drake, C. F.   *Unexplored Syria*, I (London, 1872).

de Cadalvène, E. and de Breuvery, J.   *L'Egypte et la Turquie de 1829 à 1836*, I (Paris, 1836).

Cahen, C.   'Quelques mots sur les Hilaliens et la nomadisme', *JESHO*, XI (1968).

Caillard, Sir V.   'Turkey' in *Encyclopaedia Britannica* (11th edn), XXVII (1911).

Cambridge Modern History, 2nd edn, X (Cambridge, 1960).

Cameron, R. E. or R.   'France' in R. Cameron (ed.), *Banking in the Early Stages of Industrialization* (London, New York and Toronto, 1967).

Cameron, R. E. or R.   *France and the Economic Development of Europe 1800–1914* (Princeton, 1961).

Carmel, A.   'The German Settlers in Palestine and their relations with the local Arab population and the Jewish community 1858–1918' in M. Ma'oz (ed.), *Studies on Palestine during the Ottoman Period* (Jerusalem, 1975).

Carswell, J.   'From the tulip to the rose' in T. Naff and R. Owen (eds), *Studies in Eighteenth Century Islamic History* (Carbondale and Edwardsville, Illinois, 1977).

Carter, F. W. 'The commerce of the Dubrovnik Republic, 1500–1700', *EHR*, 2nd ser., XXIV, 3 (Aug. 1971).

Cartwright, W. 'Notes on rent, labour and joint-ownership in Egyptian agriculture', *CSJ*, IV, 41 (Feb. 1910).

Casoria, M. 'Chronique agricole de l'année 1922', *EC*, XIV, 70 (Feb. 1923).

Cattan, H. 'The Islamic law of waqf', in M. Khadduri and A. J. Keibesny (eds), *Law in the Middle East*, I (Washington D.C., 1955).

Cattaui, J. *Le Khédive Isma'il et la dette de l'Egypte* (Cairo, 1935).

Cattaui, R. *Le Règne de Mohammed Aly d'après les archives russes en Egypte*, II (Rome, 1934).

de Chamberêt, R. *Enquête sur la condition du fellah égyptien* (Dijon, 1909).

Chevalier, D. 'Les cadres sociaux de l'économie agraire dans le Proche-Orient au début de XIXe siècle: le cas de Mont Liban' in M. Cook (ed.), *Studies in the Economic History of the Middle East* (London, 1970).

Chevalier, D. 'Un example de résistance technique de l'artisinat Syrien aux XIXe et XXe siècles. Les tissus Ikatés d'Alep et de Damas', *Syria*, XXXIX, 3–4 (1962).

Chevalier, D. 'Lyon et Syrie en 1919. Les bases d'une intervention', *RH*, CCXIV (Oct./Dec. 1960).

Chevalier, D. 'Aux origines des troubles agraires libanais en 1858', *Annales*, XIV, 1 (Jan.–Mar. 1959).

Chevalier, D. 'De la production lente à l'économie dynamique en Syrie', *Annales*, XXI (1966).

Chevalier, D. 'Signes de Beyrouth en 1834', *Bull. d'Etudes Orientales*, XXV (1972).

Chevalier, D. *La Société du Mont Liban à l'époque de la revolution industrielle en Europe* (Paris, 1971).

'Western development and Eastern crisis in the mid-nineteenth century' in W. R. Polk and R. L. Chambers (eds), *Beginnings of Modernization in the Middle East* (Chicago, 1968).

Choisy, A. *L'Asie Mineure et les Turcs en 1875* (Paris, 1876).

Clark, E. C. 'The Ottoman Industrial Revolution', *IJMES*, V (1974).

(J. Claudy), J. C. *Histoire financière de l'Egypte depuis Said Pasha, 1854–1876* (Paris, 1878).

Cleland, W. 'A population plan for Egypt', *EC*, 185 (May 1939).

Cleland, W. *The Population Problem in Egypt* (Lancaster, Pa., 1936).

Clerget, M. *Le Caire*, II (Cairo, 1934).

Clot, A. B. *Aperçu général sur l'Egypte*, II (Paris, 1840).

Cobb, R. *The Police and the People: French Popular Protest 1789–1820* (Oxford, 1970).

Cohen, A. *Arab Border Villages in Israel* (Manchester, 1965).

Cohen, A. 'The army in Palestine in the eighteenth century: sources of its weakness and strength', *BSOAS*, XXXIV, 1 (1971).

Cohen, S. A. *British Policy in Mesopotamia 1903–1910* (London, 1976).

Collin, A. 'Lettres sur l'Egypte – Commerce', *RDM*, 4th ser., XVII (1 Jan. 1839).

Collin, A. 'Lettres sur l'Egypte – L'industrie manufacturiere', *RDM*, 4th ser., IV, 15 (May 1838).

Colvin, Sir A. *Making of Modern Egypt* (London, n.d.).

Conder, C. R.   *Tent Work in Palestine*, I (London, 1878).

Congrès National Egyptien   *Oeuvres du Congrès National Egyptien ténu à Bruxelles le 22, 23, 24 Septembre 1910*.

Conker, O.   *Les chemins de fer en Turquie et la politique ferroviaire Turque* (Paris, 1935).

Conker, O. and Witmeur, E.   *Redressement économique et industrialisation de la nouvelle Turquie* (Paris, 1937).

Cook, M. A.   *Population Pressure in Rural Anatolia 1450–1600* (London, 1972).

Couland, J.   *Le mouvement syndical au Liban (1919–1946)* (Paris, 1970).

Couvidou, H.   *Etude sur l'Egypte Contemporaine* (Cairo, 1873).

Cowper, H. S.   *Through Turkish Arabia* (London, 1894).

Creasy, E. S.   *History of the Ottoman Turks* (London, 1877).

Crédit Foncier Egyptien   *Crédit Foncier Egyptien 1880–1930* (n.p., n.d.).

Cressaty, Comte   *L'Egypte d'aujourd'hui* (Paris, 1912).

Cromer, Lord   *Modern Egypt*, 2 vols (New York, 1908).

Crouchley, A. E.   *The Economic Development of Modern Egypt* (London, 1938).

Crouchley, A. E.   *The Investment of Foreign Capital in Egyptian Companies and Public Debt* (Cairo, 1936).

Cuinet, V.   *Turquie d'Asie*, III (Paris, 1894), V, *Syria, Liban et Palestine* (Paris, 1896).

Cunningham, A. B. (ed.)   *The Early Correspondence of Richard Wood 1831–1841* (London, 1966).

Curzon, G.   *Persia and the Persian Question*, II (London, 1892).

Cvetkova, B. A.   'L'évolution de régime féodal Turc de la fin du XVIe jusqu'au milieu de XVIIIe siècle', *Etudes Historiques à l'occasion du XIe Congrès International des Sciences Historiques*, Stockholm, Aug. 1960 (Sofia, 1960).

Daher, M.   *Tarikh Luban al-ijtima'i* (Beirut, 1974).

Davis, E. J.   *Life in Asiatic Turkey* (London, 1879).

Davis, R.   'English imports from the Middle East, 1580–1780' in M. Cook (ed.), *Studies in the Economic History of the Middle East* (London, 1970).

Davis, R.   *English Overseas Trade, 1500–1700* (London, 1973).

Davison, R. H.   *Reform in the Ottoman Empire 1856–1876* (Princeton, 1963).

Deane, P. and Cole, W. A.   *British Economic Growth 1688–1959: Trend and Structure*, 2nd edn (Cambridge, 1967).

Deeb, M.   'Bank Misr and the emergence of the local bourgeoisie in Egypt', *MES*, XII, 3 (Oct. 1976).

al-Disuqi, A.   *Kibar mullak al-aradi al-zira'iya wa dauruhum fi al-mujtama al-misri, 1914–1952* (Cairo, 1975).

Dols, M.   *The Black Death in the Middle East* (Princeton, 1977).

'The second plague pandemic and its recurrence in the Middle East', *JESHO*, XXII, 2 (May 1979).

Douin, G.   *L'Egype de 1828 à 1830* (Rome, 1935).

Douin, G., (ed.)   *Le mission de Baron de Boislecomte: L'Egypte et la Syrie en 1833* (Cairo, 1927).

Douin, G.   *Le première guerre de Syria*, I (Cairo, 1931).

Dowson, Sir E.   *Enquiry into Land Tenure* (Letchworth, n.d. (1931?)).

Dowson, V. H. W.   *Dates and Date Cultivation in 'Iraq*, I (Cambridge, 1921).

Driault, E. (ed.)   *Mohamed Aly et Napoleon (1807–1814)* (Cairo, 1925).

Ducousso, G.   'Le grainage au Liban' in Comité Executif du Ier Congrès Libannais de la sericulture, *Rapport de ler Congrès Libanais de la sericulture* (Beirut, n.d. (1930?)).

Ducousso, G. *L'industrie de la soie en Syrie et au Liban* (Beirut/Paris, 1913).

Ducruet, J. *Les capitaux européens au Proche-Orient* (Paris, 1964).

Dumond, P. 'La pacification du sud-est Anatolieh en 1865', *Turcica*, v (1975).

Earle, E. M. *Turkey, the Great Powers and the Baghdad Railway* (New York, 1924).

Edmond, C. (pseud.) *L'Egypte à l'exposition universelle de 1867* (Paris, 1867).

Edwards, A. B. 'Foreign trade' in S. B. Himadeh (ed.), *The Economic Organization of Syria* (Beirut, 1936).

Edwards, R. *La Syria 1840–1862* (Paris, 1862).

Eid, A. *La propriété urbaine en Egypte* (Brussels, 1907).

Eléfteriadès, E. *Les chemins der fer en Syrie et au Liban* (Beirut, 1944).

Emerit, M. 'La crise syrienne et l'expansion économique française en 1860', *RH*, CCVII (1952).

Englehardt, E. *La Turquie et le Tanzimat*, I (Paris, 1882).

Estève, Comte 'Mémoire sur les finances de l'Egypte', *Description de l'Egypte*, I (Paris, 1809).

Eton, W. *A Survey of the Turkish Empire* (London, 1798).

Fahmy, M. *Le révolution de l'industrie en Egypte et ses conséquences sociales au 19e siècle* (Leiden, 1954).

Farhi, D. 'Nizam-i Cedid: military reform in Egypt under Mehmed 'Ali', *AAS*, VIII, 2 (1972).

Farley, J. L. *Banking in Turkey* (London, 1863).

Farley, J. L. *The Massacres in Syria* (London, 1861).

Farley, J. L. *Modern Turkey* (London, 1872).

Farley, J. L. *The Resources of Turkey* (London, 1862).

Farley, J. L. *Turkey* (London, 1866).

Farley, J. L. *Two Years in Syria* (London, 1858).

Farnie, D. A. *East and West of Suez: The Suez Canal in History, 1854–1956* (Oxford, 1969).

Faroqhi, S. 'Sixteenth-century periodic markets in various Anatolian *sancaks*: Içel, Hamid, Karahisaví, Sahib, Kutäya, Aydin and Menteşe', *JESHO*, XXII, 1 (Jan. 1979).

Feis, H. *Europe the World's Banker 1870–1914* (New Haven, 1930).

Fellows, C. *A Journal Written During an Excursion in Asia Minor, 1838* (London, 1839).

Ferguson, A. R. 'Bilharzis', *CSJ*, IV, 45 (June 1910).

Fernea, R. A. *Shaykh and Effendi* (Cambridge, Mass., 1970).

Fevret, M. 'Un village du Liban', *Revue de Géographie du Lyon*, XXV (1950).

Finn, E. 'The fellaheen of Palestine', in PEF, *The Survey of Palestine*, Special Papers (London, 1881).

Finn, J. *Stirring Times: Or Records from the Jerusalem Consular Chronicles of 1853 to 1856*, 2 vols (London, 1878).

Firestone, Y. 'Crop-sharing Economics in Mandatory Palestine – 1', *MES*, XI (1975).

Firestone, Y. 'Production and trade in an Islamic context: Sharika contracts in the transitional economy of northern Samaria, 1853–1943 – 1', *IJMES*, VI (1975).

Fisher, W. B. *The Middle East*, 7th edn (London, 1978).

Fleury, A.   *La pénétration allemande au Moyen-Orient 1919–1939: Le cas de la Turquie, de l'Iran et de l'Afghanistan* (Leiden/Geneva, 1977).

Foaden, G. P. and Fletcher. F. (eds)   *Textbook of Egyptian Agriculture*, II (Cairo, 1910).

Fontanier, V.   *Narrative of a Mission to India and the Countries Bordering on the Persian Gulf* (trans.) I (London, 1844).

Fowler, T. K.   *Report on the Cotton Cultivation in Egypt* (Manchester, 1861).

Frances, R. M.   'The British withdrawal from the Baghdad Railway project in April 1903', *HJ*, XVI, 1 (1973).

François-Levernay, *Guide-Annuaire d'Egypte: Année 1872–1873* (Cairo, n.d.).

Fraser, J. S.   *Travels in Koordistan, Mesopotamia*, I (London, 1840).

Fresco, J.   'Histoire et organisation de la statistique officielle de l'Egypte', *EC*, 191–2 (April/May 1940).

Garwood, A. I.   *Forty Years in an Engineer's Life at Home and Abroad* (Newport, Mon., n.d.).

Gaudry, A.   *Recherches scientifique en Orient . . . 1853–1854, Partie Agricole* (Paris, 1855).

Georgiades, D.   *Smyrne et l'Asie Mineure au point de vue économique et commerciale* (Paris, 1885).

Gerber, H.   'Guilds in seventeenth-century Anatolian Bursa', *AAS*, XI, 1 (Summer 1976).

Gibb, H. A. R. and Bowen, H.   *Islamic Society and the West*, I, pt 1 (London, 1950), I, pt 2 (London, 1957).

Giladi, D.   'The agronomic development of the old colonies in Palestine (1882–1914)' in M. Ma'oz (ed.), *Studies on Palestine during the Ottoman Period* (Jerusalem, 1975).

Girard, P. S.   'Mémoire sur l'agriculture, l'industrie et le commerce de l'Egypte', in *Description de l'Egypte*, II (Paris, 1809) and *Description de l'Egypte* (2), XVII (Paris, 1824).

Girard, P. S.   'Mémoire sur l'agriculture et le commerce de la haute Egypte', *La Décade Egyptienne*, III (Cairo, An VIII/1800).

Gliddon, G. R.   *A Memoir on the Cotton of Egypt* (London, 1841).

Gould, A.   'Lords or Bandits? The Derebeys of Cilicia', *IJMES*, VII, 4 (1976).

Granott, A.   *The Land System in Palestine* (trans.) (London, 1952).

Grant, C. P.   *The Syrian Desert* (London, 1937).

Granville, H.   *Observations sur l'état actuel de l'Empire Ottoman*, ed. A. S. Ehrenkreutz (Ann Arbor, Mich., 1965).

Greiss, K. A.   'De l'usure en Egypte', *EC*, XII, 56 (Feb. 1921).

Grey, R. and Birmingham, D.   'Some economic and political consequences of trade in central and eastern Africa in the pre-colonial period', in R. Grey and D. Birmingham, *Pre-Colonial African Trade: Essays on Trade in Central and Eastern Africa before 1900* (Birmingham, 1970).

El-Gritly, A. A.   'The structure of modern industry in Egypt', *EC*, 241–2 (Nov./Dec. 1947).

El-Gritly, A. A.   'Tarikh al-sina'a fi Misr' trans. in C. Issawi (ed.), *The Economic History of the Middle East 1800–1914* (Chicago, 1966).

Groves, A. N.   *Journal of a Residence at Baghdad During the Years 1830 and 1831* (London, 1832).

Grunwald, K.   '"Windsor-Cassel" – the last Court Jew', *Year Book of Leo Beck*

Institute, XIV (London/Jerusalem, 1969).

Grunwald, K. and Ronall, J. O. *Industrialization in the Middle East* (New York, 1960).

Gücer, L. 'Le commerce interieur des céréales dans l'Empire Ottoman pendent le second moitié du XVIème siècle', *Revue de la Faculté des Sciences Economiques de l'Université d'Istanbul*, XI, 1–4 (Oct. 1949–July 1950).

Guémard, G. *Les Réformes en Egypte*, II (Cairo, 1936).

Guindi, G. and Tagher, J. *Ismail d'après les documents officiels* (Cairo, 1946).

Gulick J. 'Village and city: cultural continuities in twentieth-century Middle Eastern cultures' in I. M. Lapidus (ed.), *Middle Eastern Cities* (Berkeley and Los Angeles, 1969).

Guyot, Y. 'The amount, direction and nature of French investments', *Annals of the American Academy of Political Science*, LXVIII (Nov. 1916).

Guys, H. *Beyrout et le Liban*, 2 vols (Paris, 1850).

Haider, S. 'Land problems in Iraq' in C. Issawi (ed.), *The Economic History of the Middle East 1800–1914* (Chicago, 1966).

Hall, Lt. Col. L. J. *The Inland Water Transport in Mesopotamia* (London, 1921).

Hamont, P. N. 'De l'Egypte depuis la paix de 1841', *RO*, I (1843).

Hamont, P. N. *L'Egypte sous Mehémét-Ali*, I (Paris, 1843).

Hamza, A.-M. *The Public Debt of Egypt, 1854–1876* (Cairo, 1944).

Hansen, B. 'Income and consumption in Egypt 1886/1887 to 1937', *IJMES*, X (1979).

Hansen, B. and Nashashibi, K. *Foreign Trade, Regimes and Economic Development: Egypt* (New York, 1975).

Hansen, B. and Wattleworth, M. 'Agricultural output and consumption of basic foods in Egypt, 1886/87–1967/68', *IJMES*, IX (1978).

Harik, I. F. 'The impact of the domestic market on rural–urban relations in the Middle East' in R. Antoun and I. F. Harik (eds), *Rural Politics and Social Change in the Middle East* (Bloomington, Ind., 1972).

Harik, I. F. *Politics and Change in a Traditional Society: Lebanon 1711–1845* (Princeton, 1968).

Hasan, M. S. 'Growth and structure of Iraq's population, 1867–1947' in C. Issawi (ed.), *The Economic History of the Middle East 1800–1914* (Chicago, 1966).

Hasan, M. S. *Al-Tatauwur al-iqtisadi fi al-'Iraq. Al-tijara al-kharijiyya wa al-tatauwur al-iqtisadi, 1864–1958* (Saida, 1965).

Hasselquist, F. *Voyages and Travels in the Levant in the Years 1749, 1750, 1751, 1752* (trans.) (London, 1766).

Hay, W. R. *Two Years in Kurdistan* (London, 1921).

Hecker, M. 'Die Eisenbahnen der Asiatischen Turkei', *Archiv für Eisenbahnwesen* (1914).

Hecquard, C. *L'Empire Ottoman: La Turquie sous Abdel-Hamid II* (Brussels etc., 1901).

Hershlag, Z. Y. *Introduction to the Modern Economic History of the Middle East* (Leiden, 1964).

Hershlag, Z. Y. *Turkey: An Economy in Transition* (The Hague, 1958).

Hertslet, E. *Treaties and Tariffs Regulating Trade between Great Britain and Foreign Nations: Turkey* (London, 1875).

Hetteb, K. 'Influences orientales sur le verre de Bohème du XVIIIe au XIXe siècles' in *Journées Internationales de Verre: Annales du 3e Congrès Internationale d'Etude Historique du Verre* (Damascus, 1964).

Heyd, U.   *Foundations of Turkish Nationalism: The Life and Teachings of Ziya Gokalp* (London, 1950).
Heyd, U.   *Ottoman Documents on Palestine 1552–1615* (Oxford, 1960).
Hilan, R.   *Culture et developpement en Syrie* (Paris, 1969).
Himadeh, S. B.   'Industrie', in S. B. Himadeh (ed.), *Economic Organization of Palestine* (Beirut, 1939).
Himadeh, S. B.   'Al-Nizam al-iqtisadi fi al-'Iraq', trans. in C. Issawi (ed.), *The Economic History of the Middle East 1800–1914* (Chicago, 1966).
Hinderink, J. and Kiray, M. B.   *Social Stratification as an Obstacle to Development* (New York, Washington and London, 1970).
Hirsch, E.   *Poverty and Plenty on the Turkish Farm* (New York, 1970).
al-Hitta, A. A.   *Tarikh al-Zira'a al-Misriya fi 'Asr Muhammad 'Ali al-Kabir* (Cairo, 1950).
Hoexter, M.   'The role of the Qays and Yaman factions in local political divisions: Jabal Nablus compared with the Judean Hills in the first half of the nineteenth century', *AAS*, IX, 3 (1973).
Hofman, Y.   'The administration of Syria and Palestine under Egyptian rule (1831–1840)' in M. Ma'oz (ed.), *Studies on Palestine during the Ottoman Period* (Jerusalem, 1975).
Hogarth, D. G.   *The Nearer East* (London, 1902).
Hollingsworth, T. H.   *Historical Demography* (London, 1969).
Holt, P. M.   *Egypt and the Fertile Crescent 1516–1922* (London, 1966).
Hopkins, A. G.   *An Economic History of West Africa* (London, 1973).
Hopkins, L. G.   'Population' in S. B. Himadeh (ed.), *Economic Organization of Palestine* (Beirut, 1938).
Hourani, A. H.   'The Fertile Crescent in the eighteenth century' in A. H. Hourani, *A Vision of History* (Beirut, 1961).
Hourani, A. H.   'The Islamic city in the light of recent research' in A. H. Hourani and S. M. Stern (eds), *The Islamic City* (Oxford, 1970).
Hourani, A. H.   *Syria and Lebanon* (London, 1946).
Hourani, A. H.   'The Syrians in Egypt in the eighteenth and nineteenth centuries', *Colloque Internationale sur l'Histoire du Caire* (Cairo, 1972).
Housepian, M.   *Smyrne 1922* (London, 1972).
Howell, E. B.   'The Qanun al-Aradhi', *JCAS*, IX, 1 (1922).
Hughes, J. R. T.   *Fluctuations in Trade, Industry and Finance: A Study of British Economic Development 1850–1960* (Oxford, 1960).
Hurewitz, J. C. (ed.)   *Diplomacy in the Near and Middle East*, I (Princeton, 1956).
Hütteroth, W.   'The pattern of settlement in Palestine in the sixteenth century. Geographical research on Turkish defter-i Mufassal' in M. Ma oz (ed.), *Studies on Palestine during the Ottoman Period* (Jerusalem, 1975).
Hütteroth, W. D. and Abdul-Fattah, K.   *Historical Geography of Palestine, Transjordan and Southern Syria in the Late Sixteenth Century* (Erlangen, 1977).
Huvelin, P. (ed.)   *Que vaut le Syrie?* (Paris/Marseille, 1919).
IBRD (World Bank)   *The Economic Development of Iraq* (Baltimore, 1957).
El-Imam, Dr M.   *A Production Function for Egyptian Agriculture*. Egypt, Institute of National Planning, memo 259 (Cairo, 31 Dec. 1962).
Inalcik, H.   'Application of the Tanzimat and its social effects', *AO*, V (1973).
Inalcik, H.   'Bursa and the Commerce of the Levant', *JESHO*, III (1960).

Inalcik, H. 'Centralization and decentralization in the Ottoman administration' in T. Naff and R. Owen (eds), *Studies in Eighteenth Century Islamic History* (Carbondale and Edwardsville, Illinois, 1977).

Inalcik, H. 'The heyday of the Ottoman Empire', *CHI*, I (1970).

Inalcik, H. 'Land problems in Turkish government', *Muslim World*, XLV, 3 (July 1955).

Inalcik, H. *The Ottoman Empire* (London, 1973).

Inalcik, H. 'Quelques remarques sur la formation de capital dans l'Empire Ottoman' in *Mélanges et l'honneur de Fernand Braudel: histoire économique du monde mediterranéen, 1450–1600* (Toulouse, 1973).

Ionides, M. G. *The Regime of the Rivers Euphrates and Tigris* (London, 1937).

Islamöglu, H. 'M. A. Cook's *Population Pressure in Rural Anatolia 1450–1600*: a critique of the present paradigm in Ottoman history', *ROMES*, III (1978).

Islamöglu, H. and Faroqhi, S. 'Crop patterns and agricultural trends in sixteenth-century Anatolia', *Review*, II (Winter 1979).

Issawi, C. 'Assymetrical development and transport in Egypt, 1800–1914' in W. R. Polk and R. L. Chambers (eds), *Beginnings of Modernization in the Middle East* (Chicago, 1968).

Issawi, C. 'British trade and the rise of Beirut, 1830–1860', *IJMES*, VIII (1977).

Issawi, C. 'The decline of Middle Eastern trade, 1100–1850' in D. S. Richards (ed.), *Islam and the Trade of Asia* (Oxford, 1970).

Issawi, C. 'Economic change and urbanization in the Middle East' in I. M. Lapidus (ed.), *Middle Eastern Cities* (Berkeley and Los Angeles, 1969).

Issawi, C. *The Economic History of the Middle East 1800–1914* (Chicago, 1966).

Issawi, C. 'The expansion of tobacco growing in the nineteenth century' in C. Issawi (ed.), *The Economic History of the Middle East 1800–1914* (Chicago, 1966).

Issawi, C. 'Population and resources in the Ottoman Empire and Iran' in T. Naff and R. Owen (eds), *Studies in Eighteenth-Century Islamic History* (Carbondale and Edwardsville, Illinois, 1977).

Issawi, C. 'The Tabriz–Trabzond trade, 1830–1900', *IJMES*, I, 1 (1970).

Al-Jabarti ʿAbd al-Rahman, *ʿAjaʾib al-Athar*, 4 vols (Bulaq, 1297 AH).

Jalal, F. *The Role of Government in the Industrialization of Iraq, 1950–1965* (London, 1972).

Jaussen, Père J.-A. *Coutumes Palestiniennes*, I, *Naplouse et son district* (Paris, 1927).

Jenks, L. H. *The Migration of British Capital to 1875* (London, 1938).

Jerrold, B. *Egypt under Ismail Pasha* (London, 1879).

Jewish Agency *Report and General Abstracts of the Censuses of Jewish Agriculture, Industry and Handicrafts and Labour, Taken in 1930* (Jerusalem, 1931).

Jomard, E.-F. *Coup d'oeil impartial sur l'état de l'Egypte* (Paris, 1836).

Jomard, M. 'Description de la ville et de la citadelle du Caire', *Description de l'Egypte*, II, XVIII (Paris, 1829).

Jones, J. F. 'Journal of a steam-trip to the north of Baghdad, 5 Nov. 1846', in *Selections from the Records of the Bombay Government*, XLIII (Bombay, 1857).

Jouplain, F. (P. Noujaim), *La Question du Liban* (Paris, 1908).

Jullien, L. 'Chronique agricole de l'année 1920', *EC*, XII, 55 (Jan. 1921).

Jwaideh, A. 'Midhat Pasha and the land system of Lower Iraq', *St Antony's Papers*, XVI (London, 1963).

Jwaideh, A.   'The Saniya lands of Abdul Hamid II in Iraq' in G. Makdisi (ed.), *Arabic and Islamic Studies in Honor of Hamilton A. R. Gibb* (Leiden, 1965).

Kandiyoti, D.   'Social change and social stratification in a Turkish village', *JPS*, II, 2 (Jan. 1975).

Kanzadian, Z. and de Bertalot, L.   *Atlas de géographie économique de Syrie et du Liban* (Paris, 1926).

Karpat, K. H.   'The land regime, social structure and modernization in the Ottoman Empire' in W. R. Polk and R. L. Chambers (eds), *Beginnings of Modernization of the Middle East* (Chicago, 1968).

Karpat, K. H.   *Turkey's Politics* (Princeton, 1959).

Karpat, K. H. (ed.)   *Social Change and Politics in Turkey: A Structural–Historical Analysis* (Leiden, 1973).

Katznelson, A.   'Vital statistics in Palestine', in Congrès International de Medecine Tropicale et d'Hygene, *Comptes Rendus* (Cairo, 1932).

Kayal, P. M. and J. M.   *The Syrian–Lebanese in America* (Boston, 1975).

Kayat, A. J.   *A Voice from Lebanon* (London, 1847).

Kelman, J.   *From Damascus to Palmyra* (London, 1908).

Kent, M.   'Agent of Empire? The National Bank of Turkey and British foreign policy', *HJ*, XVIII, 2 (1975).

Kent, M.   *Oil and Empire* (London, 1976).

Keydar, C.   'The dissolution of the Asiatic mode of production', *ES*, V (1976).

Keydar, C.   'The political economy of Turkish democracy', *NLR*, 115 (May/June 1979).

Keydar, C.   'Surplus', *JPS*, II, 2 (1975).

Khalidi, R.   *British Policy towards Syria and Palestine, 1906–1914* (London, 1980).

Khuri, A.   'Agriculture' in S. B. Himadeh (ed.), *Economic Organization of Syria* (Beirut, 1936).

Kindleberger, C. P.   *Economic Growth in France and Britain, 1851–1950* (Cambridge, Mass., 1964).

Kinglake, A. W.   *Eothen* (Paris, 1846).

Kluzinger, C. B.   *Upper Egypt: Its People and Its Products* (London, 1878).

Köymen, O.   'The advent and consequences of free trade in the Ottoman Empire', *Etudes Balkaniques*, VII, 2 (1971).

Kuran, E.   'Küçük Said Pasa (1840–1914) as a Turkish modernist', *IJMES*, I, 2 (April 1970).

Kurd Ali, M.   *Khitat al-Sham*, IV (Damascus, 1926).

R. H. L\   *The Financial Position of Egypt* (London, 1874).

Labat, J.-P. (pseud.)   *Mémoires du Chevalier d'Arvieux*, III (Paris, 1735).

Laffey, J.   'Roots of French imperialism in the nineteenth century: the case of Lyon', *French Historical Studies*, VI, 1 (Spring 1969).

Lancret, M.-A.   'Mémoire sur le systeme d'imposition teritoriale et sur l'administration des provinces de l'Egypte', in *Description de l'Egypte*, I (Paris, 1809).

Landau, J. M.   *The Hejaz Railway and the Muslim Pilgrimage* (Detroit, 1971).

Landes, D. S.   *Bankers and Pashas; International Finance and Economic Imperialism in Egypt* (London, Melbourne and Toronto, 1958).

Lane, F. C.   'The Mediterranean spice trade: further evidence for its revival in the sixteenth century' in B. Pullen (ed.), *Crisis and Change in the Venetian Economy* (London, 1973).

Lane, F. C. 'The mediterranean spice trade: its revival in the sixteenth century' in F. C. Lane, *Venice and its History* (Baltimore, 1966).

Lane Poole, S. (ed.) *The People of Turkey*, I (London, 1878).

Lanzoni, A. 'La Mesopotamia economica', trans. in C. Issawi (ed.), *The Economic History of the Middle East 1800–1914* (Chicago, 1966).

Laoust, H. *Les gouverneurs de Damas sous les Mamlouks et les prèmiers Ottomans* (Damascus, 1952).

Lapidus, I. M. 'Muslim cities and Islamic societies' in I. M. Lapidus (ed.), *Middle Eastern Cities* (Berkeley and Los Angeles, 1969).

Lapidus, I. M. *Muslim Cities in the Later Middle Ages* (Cambridge, Mass., 1967).

Latron, A. *La vie rurale en Syrie et au Liban* (Beirut, 1936).

Lemoine, F. 'En Mesopotamie', *Correspondence d'Orient*, II, 21 (Aug. 1909).

Levant Herald, *The Famine in Asia Minor* (Constantinople, 1875).

Levi, I. 'L'augmentation des revenues de l'état: possibilités et moyens d'y parvenir', *EC*, 68 (Dec. 1922).

Levi, I. 'Le recensement de la population de l'Egypte de 1917', *EC*, 67 (Nov. 1922).

Levin, J. V. *The Export Economies* (Cambridge, Mass., 1960).

Lewis, B. L. *The Emergence of Modern Turkey* (London, 1961).

Lewis, B. L. 'Jaffa in the sixteenth century according to the Ottoman *tahrir* registers', *Turk Tarih Kurumu Basımevi* (Ankara, 1969).

Lewis, B. L. 'Nazareth in the sixteenth century according to the Ottoman *tapu* registers' in G. Makdisi (ed.), *Arabic and Islamic Studies in Honor of Sir Hamilton A. R. Gibb* (Leiden, 1965).

Lewis, B. L. 'Some reflections on the decline of the Ottoman Empire' in C. M. Cipolla (ed.), *The Economic Decline of Empires* (London, 1970).

Lewis, B. L. 'Studies in the Ottoman Archives – 1', *BSOAS*, XVI, 3 (1954).

Lewis, N. H. 'The frontier of settlement in Syria, 1800–1950' in C. Issawi (ed.), *The Economic History of the Middle East 1800–1914* (Chicago, 1966).

Livingstone, J. W. ''Ali Bey al-Kabir and the Jews', *MES*, VII, 2 (May 1971).

Loftus, W. K. *Travels and Researches in Chaldea and Susiana* (London, 1857).

Longrigg, S. H. *Four Centuries of Modern Iraq* (Oxford, 1925).

Lopez, R., Miskimin, H. and Udovitch, A. 'England to Egypt, 1350–1500: long-term trends and long-distance trade' in M. A. Cook (ed.), *Studies in the Economic History of the Middle East* (London, 1970).

Low, C. R. *History of the Indian Navy 1613–1863*, II (London, 1877).

Lozarch, J. and Hug, G. *L'habitat rural en Egypt* (Cairo, 1930).

Luke, H. C. and Keith-Roach, E. *The Handbook of Palestine* (London, 1922).

Lybyer, A. H. 'The Ottoman Turks and the routes of Oriental trade', *EHR*, CXX (Oct. 1915).

Lynch, W. F. *Narrative of the U.S. Expedition to the River Jordan and the Dead Sea* (Philadelphia, 1849).

Mabro, R. and Radwan, S. *The Industrialization of Egypt 1930–1973* (Oxford, 1976).

MacFarlane, C. *Constantinople in 1828*, 2nd edn, I (London, 1829).

Macgregor, J. *Commercial Statistics: A Digest of the Productive Resources, Commercial Legislation, Customs, Tariffs . . . of the Nations*, II (London, 1844), V (London, 1850).

Madden, R. R. *The Turkish Empire and its Relations with Christianity and Civilization*, I (London, 1862).

Malone, J. J. 'Surgeon Colvill's Fight against Plague and Cholera in Iraq 1868–1878', in F. Sarruf and S. Tamim (eds), *American University of Beirut Festival Book* (Beirut, 1967).

Mandel, N. 'Ottoman practice with regards to Jewish settlement in Palestine, 1881–1908', *MES*, XI, 1 (Jan. 1975).

Mandel, N. 'Turks, Arabs and Jewish immigration into Palestine, 1882–1914', *St Antony's Papers*, XVII (Oxford, 1965).

Mann, J. S. *An Administrator in the Making* (London, 1921).

Mantran, R. 'Règlements fiscaux ottomans. Le province de Bassors (2e moitié du XVIe s.)', *JESHO*, X (1967).

Ma'oz, M. *Ottoman Reform in Syria and Palestine 1840–1861* (Oxford, 1968).

Mardin, S. *The Genesis of Young Ottoman Thought* (Princeton, 1962).

Mardin, S. 'Power, civil society and culture in the Ottoman Empire', *CSSH*, II, 3 (June 1969).

Margalit, H. 'Some aspects of the cultural landscape during the first half of the nineteenth century', *IEJ*, XIII, 3 (1963).

Mariti, Abbé *Travels through Cyprus, Syria and Palestine* (trans.) II (London, 1791).

Marlowe, J. *Spoiling the Egyptians* (New York, 1975).

Marshall, J. *A Digest of all the Accounts Relating to the Population, Production, Revenues . . . of the United Kingdom and Ireland* (London, 1833).

Marx, K. *Capital* (trans.) I (London, 1970).

Marx, K. *Pre-Capitalist Economic Formations*, trans. and ed. by E. J. Hobsbawm (London, 1964).

Masson, P. *Histoire de commerce français dans le Levant au XVIIe siècle* (Paris, 1896).

Masson, P. *Histoire du commerce français dans le Levant au XVIIIe siècle* (Paris, 1911).

Mazuel, J. *L'Oeuvre géographique de Linant de Bellefonds* (Cairo, 1937).

Mazuel, J. *Le sucre en Egypte* (Cairo, 1937).

McCarthy, J. A. 'Nineteenth-century Egyptian population', *MES*, XII, 3 (Oct. 1976).

McCoan, J. C. *Egypt under Ismail* (London, 1889).

McCulloch, J. R. *A Dictionary . . . of Commerce and Navigation*, 2nd edn (London, 1844).

McLean, D. 'Finance and "Informal Empire" before the First World War', *EHR*, 2nd ser., XXIX, 2 (May 1972).

Mears, E. G. 'Levantine concession-hunting' in E. G. Mears (ed.), *Modern Turkey* (New York, 1924).

Meeker, M. E. 'The great family Aghas of Turkey; a study of changing political culture' in R. Antoun and I. Harid (eds), *Rural Politics and Social Change in the Middle East* (Bloomington, 1972).

Mejcher, H. *Imperial Quest for Oil 1910–1928* (London, 1976).

Mengin, F. *Histoire de l'Egypte sous le gouvernement de Mohammed-Aly*, II (Paris, 1823).

Merruau, P. 'L'Egypte sous le gouvernement de Said-Pasha', *RDM*, XI, 2nd ser. (15 Sept. 1857).

Milner, Lord, *England in Egypt*, 11th edn (London, 1904).

Minost, E. 'Essai sur le revenu agricole de l'Egypte', *EC*, 123 (Nov. 1930).

Mitchell, B. R. *Abstract of British Historical Statistics* (Cambridge, 1962).

Morawitz, C. *Les finances de la Turquie* (Paris, 1902).

Mosseri, V. 'Le sol égyptien sous le régime de l'arrosage par inondation', *BIE*, V (1923).

Moutran, N. *La Syrie de demain* (Paris, 1916).

Mubarak, 'Ali Pasha *Al-Khitat al-Taufiqiya al-Jadida*, 20 vols (Cairo, 1887–9).

Muhlmann, C. 'Die Deutschen Baunternenmungen in der Asiatischen Türkei, 1888–1914', *Welwirtschaftliches Archiv*, XXIV (1926).

Myint, H. *The Economics of the Developing Countries*, 3rd edn (London, 1967).

Naccache, A. 'Moriculture, grainage, sericiculture et filature au Liban', *Actes de la Conference technique Sericicole International* (Ales, 1955).

Nahas, J. F. *Situation économique et sociale du fellah égyptien* (Paris, 1901).

Neibuhr, C. *Travels through Arabia and other Countries in the East* (trans.) I (Edinburgh, 1792).

Nickoley, E. F. 'Agriculture' in E. G. Mears (ed.), *Modern Turkey* (New York, 1924).

Nickoley, E. F. 'Transportation and communications' in S. B. Himadeh (ed.), *Economic Organization of Syria* (Beirut, 1936).

Al-Nimr, I. *Ta'rikh Jabal Nabulus wa al-Balqa'*, I (Damascus, 1938).

Nour Ed-Din, S. 'Conditions des fellahs en Egypte', *RI*, III (1898).

Novichev, A. D. 'The development of commodity-money and capitalist relations in agriculture . . .' in C. Issawi (ed.), *The Economic History of the Middle East 1800–1914* (Chicago, 1966).

O'Brien, P. K. 'The long-term growth of agricultural production in Egypt: 1821–1962' in P. M. Holt (ed.), *Political and Social Change in Modern Egypt* (London, 1968).

Ochsenwald, W. L. 'The financing of the Hijaz Railroad', *WI*, new ser., XIV, 1–4 (1973).

D'Ohsson, M. *Tableau général de l'Empire Ottoman*, III (Paris, 1820).

Oliphant, L. *The Land of Gilead: with Excursion in the Lebanon* (Edinburgh, 1880).

Olson, R. W. 'The Esnaf and the Patrona Halil rebellion of 1730: a realignment of Ottoman politics?', *JESHO*, XVII, 3 (Sept. 1974).

Olson, R. W. 'Jews, Janissaries, Esnaf and the revolt of 1740 in Istanbul. Social upheaval and political realignment in the Ottoman Empire', *JESHO*, XX, 2 (May 1977).

Ongley, F. *The Ottoman Land Code* (London, 1892).

Otter, M. *Voyage en Turquie et en Perse*, II (Paris, 1748).

Ottoman Public Debt Administration *Rapport sur la question des dimes agnam et revenues divers par la Conseil d'Administration de la Dette Publique Ottomane, année 1912/13 (1328 AH) comparée avec l'année 1911/12* (Constantinople, 1914).

Owen, R. 'Agricultural production in historical perspective: a case study of the period 1890–1939' in P. J. Vatikiotis (ed.), *Egypt since the Revolution* (London, 1968).

Owen, R. 'Al-Jabarti and the economic history of eighteenth-century Egypt – some introductory remarks' in A. A. 'Abd al-Karim (ed.), *'Abd al-Rahman al-Jabarti* (Cairo, 1976).

Owen, R. 'The attitude of British officials to the development of the Egyptian economy, 1882–1922' in M. A. Cook (ed.), *Studies in the Economic History of the Middle East* (London, 1970).

Owen, R.　'The Cairo building industry and the building boom of 1897 to 1907', *Colloque International sur l'Histoire du Caire* (Cairo, 1972).

Owen, R.　*Cotton and the Egyptian Economy 1820–1914* (Oxford, 1969).

Owen, R.　'The development of agricultural production in nineteenth- century Egypt – capitalism of what type?' in A. L. Udovitch (ed.), *Land, Population and Society* (forthcoming).

Owen, R.　'Egypt and Europe: from French expedition to British Occupation' in R. Owen and B. Sutcliffe (eds), *Studies in the Theory of Imperialism* (London, 1972).

Owen, R.　'The influence of Lord Cromer's Indian experience on British policy in Egypt, 1883–1907', *St Antony's Papers*, XVII (Oxford, 1965).

Owen, R.　'Lord Cromer and the development of Egyptian industry, 1883–1907', *MES*, II, 4 (July 1966).

Owen, R.　'The Middle East in the eighteenth century – an "Islamic" society in decline: a critique of Gibb and Bowen's *Islamic Society and the West*', *ROMES*, I (1975).

Owen, R.　'Robinson and Gallagher and Middle Eastern nationalism: the Egyptian argument' in Wm R. Louis (ed.), *Imperialism: the Robinson and Gallagher Controversy* (New York, London, 1976).

Panzac, D.　'Alexandrie: Evolution d'une ville cosmopolite', *Annales Isamolgiques*, XIV (1978).

Panzac, D.　'La peste à Smyrne au XVIIIe siècle', *Annales*, XXVIII, 4 (July–Aug. 1973).

Papasian, E.　*L'Egypte économique et financier* (Cairo, 1926).

Pensa, C.　*Les cultures de l'Egypte* (Paris, 1897).

Percy, Earl, *Highlands of Asiatic Turkey* (London, 1901).

Le Père, G.　'Mémoire sur la ville d'Alexandrie', DE^2, XVIII (Paris, 1824).

Pierotti, E.　*Customs and Traditions of Palestine* (trans.) (Cambridge/London, 1864).

Piot Bey, J. B.　'Coup d'oeil sur l'économie actuelle du bétail en Egypte', *EC*, VI (Mar. 1911).

Platt, D. C. M.　*Finance, Trade and Politics: British Foreign Policy 1815–1914* (London, 1968).

Platt, D. C. M.　*The Cinderella Service: British Consuls since 1825* (London, 1971).

Poilay Bey, M.　'Excursions dans le grands domains d'Egypte-Daira Draneth Pacha', *BUSAE*, I, 2 (Aug. 1901).

Politis, A. G.　*L'Hellenisme et l'Egypte modern*, I (Paris, 1929).

Polk, W. R.　*The Opening of South Lebanon 1788–1840* (Cambridge, Mass., 1963).

Polk, W. R.　'Rural Syria in 1845', *MEJ*, XVI, 4 (Autumn 1962).

Poncet, J.　'La mythe de la Catastrophe hilalienne', *Annales*, XXII (1967).

Porath, Y.　*The Emergence of the Palestine–Arab National Movement 1918–1929* (London, 1974).

Porath, Y.　'The Peasant Revolt of 1858–61 in Kisrawan', *AAS*, II (1966).

Porath, Y.　'The political awakening of the Palestinian Arabs and their leadership towards the end of the Ottoman period' in M. Ma'oz (ed.), *Studies on Palestine during the Ottoman Period* (Jerusalem, 1975).

Porter, G. R.　*The Progress of the Nation* (London, 1847).

Post, G. E. 'Essays on the sects and nationalities of Syria and Palestine', pt 2, 'Land tenure, agriculture . . . in Palestine', PEF, *Quarterly* (Apr. 1891).

Post, K. 'Peasantisation and rural class differentiation in Western Africa', *I.S.S. Occasional Papers* (The Hague, Sept. 1970).

Von Pressel, W. 'Principal routes' in C. Issawi (ed.), *The Economic History of the Middle East 1800–1914* (Chicago, 1966).

Puryear, V. J. *France and the Levant* (Berkeley and Los Angeles, 1941).

Puryear, V. J. *International Economics and Diplomacy in the Near East* (Stanford, 1935).

Quataert, D. 'Limited Revolution: the impact of the Anatolian Railway on Turkish transportation and the provisioning of Istanbul, 1890–1908', *Business History Review*, LI, 2 (Summer 1977).

Radwan, S. *Capital Formation in Egyptian Industry and Agriculture 1882–1967* (London, 1974).

Rafeq (Rafiq), A. K. *Al-'Arab wa al-'uthmaniyyun 1516–1916* (Damascus, 1974).

Rafeq (Rafiq), A. K. 'Changes in the relationship between the Ottoman central administration and the Syrian provinces from the sixteenth to the eighteenth centuries' in T. Naff and R. Owen (eds), *Studies in Eighteenth Century Islamic History* (Carbondale and Edwardsville, Illinois, 1977).

Rafeq (Rafiq), A. K. 'Local forces in Syria in the seventeenth and eighteenth centuries' in V. J. Parry and M. E. Yapp (eds), *War, Technology and Society in the Middle East* (London, 1975).

Rafeq (Rafiq), A. K. *The Province of Damascus, 1723–1783* (London, 1966).

Rambert, G. (ed.) *Histoire du commerce de Marseilles*, V, *Le Levant* by R. Paris (Paris, 1957).

Rapp, R. T. 'The unmaking of the Mediterranean trade hegemony: international trade rivalry and the commercial revolution', *JEH*, XXXV, 3 (Sept. 1975).

Rasheed, G. A. K. 'Development of land taxation in Modern Iraq', *BSOAS*, XXV, 2 (1962).

Raymond, A. *Artisans et commerçants au Caire au XVIIIe siècle*, I (Damascus, 1973) II (Damascus, 1974).

Raymond, A. 'Essai de géographie des quartiers de residence aristocratiques au Caire au XVIIIème siècle', *JESHO*, VI (1963).

Raymond, A. 'Les grandes épidémies de peste au Caire au XVIIe et XVIIIe siècles', *BEO*, XXV (1972).

Raymond, A. 'Quartiers et mouvements populaires au Caire au XVIIIème siècle' in P. M. Holt (ed.), *Political and Social Change in Modern Egypt* (London, 1968).

Raymond, A. 'Les sources de la richesse urbaine au Caire au dix-huitieme siècle' in T. Naff and R. Owen (eds), *Studies in Eighteenth-Century Islamic History* (Carbondale and Edwardsville, Illinois, 1977).

Redford, A. *et al.*, *Manchester Merchants and Foreign Trade 1794–1854* (Manchester, 1934).

(Citizen) Renati 'Topographie physique et medicale du Vieux-Caire', *La Décade Egyptienne*, II (Cairo, An VIII/1800).

Renier, J. L. T. *State of Egypt after the Battle of Heliopolis* (trans.) (London, 1802).

Rey, A. *Statistique des principaux résultats de l'exploitation des chemins de fer de l'Empire ottoman pendant l'exercice 1898* (Constantinople, 1899).

Rey, A. *Statistique des principaux résultats de l'exploitation des chemins de fer de l'Empire ottoman pendant l'exercice 1911* (Constantinople, 1913).

Reynier, L. 'Considerations générales sur l'agriculture de l'Egypte et sur les ameliorations dont elle est susceptible', *Mémoires dur l'Egypte publiés pendent les campagnes du Général Bonaparte*, IV (Paris, An X).

Rich, C. J. *Narrative of a Residence in Koordistan*, I (London, 1836).

Richards, D. S. (ed.) *Islam and the Trade of Asia* (Oxford, 1970).

Rivlin, H. A. B. *The Agricultural Policy of Muhammad 'Ali in Egypt* (Cambridge, Mass., 1969).

Rivlin, H. A. B. 'The railway question in the Ottoman–Egyptian crisis of 1850–1852', *MEJ*, XV, 4 (Autumn 1961).

Robin, A. *De la Palestine: Ses resources agricoles et industrialies* (Paris, 1880).

Robinson, G. *Three Years in the East* (London/Paris, 1837).

Robinson, R. and Gallagher, J., with Denny, Alice *Africa and the Victorians* (London, 1961).

Robinson, R. D. *The First Turkish Republic* (Cambridge, Mass., 1963).

Robinson Lees, G. *Village Life in Palestine* (London, 1905).

Rodinson, M. *Islam and Capitalism* (trans.) (London, 1974).

Rolleston, G. *Report on Smyrna* (London, 1856).

Rossi, Dr E. *La population et les finances; Question égyptienne* (Paris, 1878).

Rothstein, T. *Egypt's Ruin: A Financial and Administrative Record* (London, 1910).

Rougon, F. *Smyrne: situation commerciale et économique* (Paris/Nancy, 1892).

Rousseau, J.-B. L. J. *Description de la Pachalik de Bagdad* (Paris, 1809).

Roux, F. Charles, 'La domination égyptienne en Syrie', *RHC*, XXI (July/Oct. 1933).

Roux, F. Charles, *La production du coton en Egypte* (Paris, 1908).

Ruppin, A. *The Agricultural Colonisation of the Zionist Organisation in Palestine* (trans.) (London, 1926).

Ruppin, A. *Syria: An Economic Survey* (trans.) (New York, 1918).

Ruppin, A. 'Syrien als Wirtschaftsgebiet' trans. in C. Issawi (ed.), *The Economic History of the Middle East 1800–1914* (Chicago, 1966).

Russell, A. *The Natural History of Aleppo*, II (London, 1794).

Russell, J. C. 'Population in Europe 500–1500' in C. M. Cipolla (ed.), *The Fontana Economic History of Europe*, I, *The Middle Ages* (London, 1972).

Russell, J. C. 'The population of medieval Egypt', *The Journal of the American Research Center in Egypt*, V (1966).

Rustum, A. J. 'Syria under Mehemet Ali', *AJSLL*, XLI, 1 (Oct. 1924).

Saab, G. S. *The Egyptian Agrarian Reform 1952–1962* (London, 1967).

Saba, P. 'The creation of the Lebanese economy: economic growth in the nineteenth and early twentieth centuries' in R. Owen (ed.), *Essays on the Crisis in Lebanon* (London, 1976).

Sabry, M. *L'empire égyptienne sous Mohamel-Ali et la question d'Orient 1811–1849* (Paris, 1930).

De Saint-Omer, H. *Les entreprises belges en Egypte* (Brussels, 1907).

St John, J. A. *Egypt and Mohammed Ali*, II (London, 1834).

Saleh, Z. *Mesopotamia (Iraq) 1600–1914; A Study in British Foreign Affairs* (Baghdad, 1957).

Salibi, K. S. *The Modern History of Lebanon* (London, 1965).

Salibi, K. S. 'Northern Lebanon under the dominance of Gazir (1517–1591)', *Arabica*, XIV, 2 (June 1967).

Salvador, H.   *L'Orient, Marseille et la Mediterranée. Histoire des échelles du Levant et des colonies* (Paris, 1854).

Sami, A.   *Taqwim al-Nil wa ʿAsr Muhammad ʿAli Pasha*, II (Cairo, 1928), pt 3, I (Cairo, 1936).

Sammarco, A.   *Histoire de l'Egypte moderne*, III, *Le règne du Khédive Ismail de 1863 à 1875* (Cairo, 1937).

Samné, Dr G.   *La Syrie* (Paris, 1921).

Sarç, O. C.   'Ottoman Industrial Policy' in C. Issawi (ed.), *The Economic History of the Middle East 1800–1914* (Chicago, 1966).

Al-Sayyid Marsot, A. L.   'The political and economic functions of the ulama in the 18th century', *JESHO*, XVI (1973).

Al-Sayyid Marsot, A. L.   'The wealth of the *Ulama* in late eighteenth century Egypt', in T. Naff and R. Owen (eds), *Studies in Eighteenth Century Islamic History* (Carbondale and Edwardsville, Illinois, 1977).

Schama, S.   *The Two Rothschilds and the Land of Israel* (London, 1978).

Schanz, M.   *Cotton in Egypt and the Anglo-Egyptian Sudan* (Manchester, 1913).

Schoelcher, V.   *L'Egypte en 1845* (Paris, 1846).

Schölch, A.   *Ägypten den Ägyptern! Die Politische und gesellschaftliche Krise der 1878–1882 in Ägypten* (Zurich and Frieburg, n.d.).

Schölch, A.   'European penetration and the economic development of Palestine, 1856–82' in R. Owen, *Studies in the Political Economy of Palestine in the 19th and 20th Centuries* (forthcoming).

Schölch, A.   'The "Men on the Spot" and the English occupation of Egypt in 1882', *HJ*, XIX, 3 (1976).

Schumaker, G.   *Across the Jordan* (trans.) (London, 1886).

Schumaker, G.   *The Jaulan* (trans.) (London, 1888).

Scott, J. H.   'The Capitulations' in A. Wright (ed.), *Twentieth-Century Impressions of Egypt* (London, 1909).

Scott, J. H.   *The Law Affecting Foreigners in Egypt* (Edinburgh, 1907).

Segre, V. D.   *Israel: A Society in Transition* (London, 1971).

Selim, H. K.   *Twenty Years of Agricultural Development in Egypt (1919–1939)* (Cairo, 1940).

Senior, N. W.   *Conversations and Journals in Egypt and Malta*, I (London, 1882).

Serpell, D. R.   'American consular activities in Egypt, 1849–1863', *JMH*, X, 3 (Sept. 1938).

Shamir, S.   'The modernization of Syria: problems and solutions in the early period of Abdul-Hamid' in W. R. Polk and R. L. Chambers (eds), *Beginnings of Modernization in the Middle East* (Chicago, 1968).

Shanin, T.   'Introduction' in Shanin (ed.), *Peasants and Peasant Societies* (Harmondsworth, 1971).

Shanin, T.   'The nature and logic of the peasant economy', pts 1–2, *JPS*, I, 1 (Oct. 1973), 2 (Jan. 1974).

Shaw, S. H.   *History of the Ottoman Empire and Modern Turkey*, II (Cambridge, Mass., 1977).

Shaw, S. J.   *The Financial and Administrative Organization and Development of Ottoman Egypt 1517–1798* (Princeton, 1958).

Shaw, S. J.   'Landholding and land-tax revenues in Ottoman Egypt' in P. N. Holt (ed.), *Political and Social Change in Modern Egypt* (London, 1968).

Shaw, S. J.   'The origins of Ottoman military reform: the Nizam-i Cedid Army of

Sultan Selim III', *JMH*, XXXVII, 3 (Sept. 1965).

Shaw, S. J. 'The Ottoman census system and population, 1831–1914', *IJMES*, X, 3 (Aug. 1978).

Shaw, S. J. *Ottoman Egypt in the Age of the French Revolution* (Cambridge, Mass., 1964).

Shaw, S. J. 'Ottoman expenditures and budgets in the late nineteenth and early twentieth centuries', *IJMES*, IX (1978).

Shaw, S. J. 'Selim III and the Ottoman Navy', *Turcica*, I (1969).

El-Shawany, M. R. 'The first national life tables for Egypt', *EC* (Mar. 1936).

Shorrock, W. *French Imperialism in the Middle East: The Failure of Policy in Syria and Lebanon, 1900–1914* (Madison, Wisc., 1976).

(Citizen) Shulkowski 'Description de la route du Caire à Salehyeh', *La Décade Egyptienne*, I (An VII).

Sidqi, H. *Al-Qutn al-Misri* (Cairo, 1950).

Silvera, A. 'Edmé-François Jomard and the Egyptian Reforms of 1839', *MES*, VII, 3 (Oct. 1971).

Smilianskaya, I. M. 'The disintegration of feudal relations in Syria and Lebanon in the middle of the nineteenth century' in C. Issawi (ed.), *The Economic History of the Middle East 1800–1914* (Chicago, 1966).

Socolis, G. *L'Egypte et son histoire économique depuis 30 ans* (Paris, 1903).

Spagnolo, J. P. *France and Ottoman Lebanon: 1861–1914* (London, 1977).

Spagnolo, J. P. 'Mount Lebanon, France and Daud Pasha: a study of some aspects of political habituation', *IJMES*, II (1971).

Spooner, B. 'Desert and sown: a new look at an old relationship' in T. Naff and R. Owen (eds), *Studies in Eighteenth Century Islamic History* (Carbondale and Edwardsville, Illinois, 1977).

Spyridon, S. N. 'Annals of Palestine, 1821–1841', *JPOS*, XVIII (1936).

Steegmuller, F. (ed.) *Flaubert in Egypt* (London, 1972).

Steensgaard, N. *The Asian Trade Revolution of the Seventeenth Century* (Chicago and London, 1974).

Stephenson, Sir M. *Railways in Turkey* (London, 1859).

Steppat, F. 'Some Arabic manuscript sources on the Syrian crisis of 1860', in J. Berque and D. Chevalier (eds), *Les Arabes par leur archives* (Paris, 1976).

Stirling, P. 'The domestic cycle and the distribution of power in Turkish villages' in J. Pitt-Rivers (ed.), *Mediterranean Countrymen* (Paris/The Hague, 1963).

Stripling, G. W. 'The Ottoman Turks and the Arabs, 1511–1574', *University of Illinois Studies in the Social Sciences*, XXVI (1940–2).

Stuart, Villiers, *Egypt after the War* (London, 1883).

Suvla, R.-S. 'Debts during the Tanzimat period' in C. Issawi (ed.), *The Economic History of the Middle East 1800–1914* (Chicago, 1966).

Sykes, M. *The Caliph's Last Heritage* (London, 1915).

Sykes, M. *Through Five Turkish Provinces* (London, 1900).

Tallien, L. 'Mémoire sur l'administration de l'Egypte à l'époque de l'arrivé des Français', *La Décade Egyptienne*, III.

Tannous, A. I. 'Social change in an Arab village', *American Sociological Review*, VI, 5 (Oct. 1941).

de Tchihatcheff, P. 'L'Asie Mineure et l'empire ottoman', pt 2, 'Situation politique, militaire et financière de la Turquie', *RDM*, new ser., VI (1 June 1850).

de Tchihatcheff, P. *Le Bosphor et Constantinople* (Paris, 1864).

de Tchihatcheff, P.   *Lettres sur la Turquie* (Brussels/Leipzig, 1859).

Teẓel, Y. S.   'Notes on the Consolidated Foreign Debt of the Ottoman Empire: the servicing of the loans', *The Turkish Yearbook of International Relations* (1972).

Thobie, J.   'Les intérêts français, dans l'empire ottoman au debut de XXe siècle: étude des sources', *RH*, CCXXXV (April/June 1966).

Thompson, E. P.   *The Making of the English Working Class* (Harmondsworth, 1968).

Thornton, T.   *The Present State of Turkey* (London, 1807).

Thuile, H.   *Commentaires sur l'atlas historique de l'Alexandrie* (Cairo, 1822).

Tignor, R. L.   'British agricultural and hydraulic policy in Egypt, 1882–1892', *Agricultural History*, XXXVII, 2 (Mar. 1963).

Tignor, R. L.   'The Egyptian Revolution of 1919: new directions in the Egyptian economy', *MES*, XII 3 (Oct. 1976).

Tignor, R. L.   *Modernization and British Colonial Rule in Egypt, 1882–1914* (Princeton, 1966).

Todd, J. A.   *Political Economy* (Edinburgh/Glasgow, 1911).

Tolkowsky, S.   *The Gateway of Palestine: A History of Jaffa* (London, 1924).

Tomiche, N.   'Notes sur la hiérarchie sociale en Egypt a l'époque de Muhammad ʿAli' in P. M. Holt (ed.), *Political and Social Change in Modern Egypt* (London, 1968).

Tott, Baron de, *Memoirs of Baron de Tott* (trans.), I (London, 1786).

Touma, T.   *Paysans et institutions féodales chez les Druses et les Maronites du Liban du XVIIe siècle à 1914* (Beirut, 1971).

Tresse, T.   'L'irrigation dans le Ghota de Damas', *REI* (1929).

Trumpner, U.   *Germany and the Ottoman Empire 1914–1918* (Princeton, 1968).

Tucker, J.   'Decline of the family economy in mid-nineteenth century Egypt', *ASQ*, I, 3 (1979).

Turner, B.   'Islam, capitalism and the Weber thesis', *BJS*, XXV (1974).

Turner, B.   *Marx and the End of Orientalism* (London, 1978).

Ubicini, M. A.   *La Turquie actuelle* (Paris, 1855) trans. as *Letters from Turkey*, 2 vols (London, 1856).

Ubicini, A. and de Courteille, P.   *Etat present de l'empire ottoman* (Paris, 1876).

Urquhart, D.   *The Lebanon: A History and a Diary*, II (London, 1860).

Urquhart, D.   *Turkey and Its Resources* (London, 1833).

Valensi, L.   'Islam et capitalisme: production et commerce de chechias en Tunisie et en France au XVIIIe et XIXe siècles', *Revue d'Histoire Moderne et Contemporaine*, XVI (1969).

Vatikiotis, P. J. (ed.)   *Egypt since the Revolution* (London, 1968).

Vaucelles, P.   *La vue en Irak il y a un siècle* (Paris, 1963).

Velay, A. Du   *Essai sur l'histoire financière de la Turquie* (Paris, 1903).

Verney, N. and Dambmann, G.   *Les puissances étrangères dans le Levant, en Syrie et en Palestine* (Paris/Lyons, 1900).

Viesse, de Marmont   *Voyage de Maréchal Duc de Rague en Hongrie, en Transylvanie . . . et en Egypte*, II (Paris, 1837).

Volney, C.   *Travels through Syria and Egypt in the Years 1783, 1784 and 1785* (trans.), 2 vols. (London, 1787).

Waismann, I. A.   'L'économie rurale de la Turquie', *REI*, II, 4 (1928).

Wallace, D. M.   *Egypt and the Egyptian Question* (London, 1883).

Walz, T.   *Trade between Egypt and Bilad as-Sudan 1700–1820* (Cairo, 1978).

Warriner, D.   'The real meaning of the Ottoman Land Code' in C. Issawi (ed.), *The Economic History of the Middle East, 1890–1914* (Chicago, 1966).

Wattleworth, M.   'Agricultural output and consumption of basic foods in Egypt, 1886/87–1967/68', *IJMES*, IX (1978).

Weber, M.   *Economy and Society* (trans.), 3 vols (New York, 1968).

Weir, S.   *Spinning and Weaving in Palestine* (London, 1970).

Weulersse, J.   *Paysans de Syrie et du Proche-Orient* (Paris, 1946).

White, G. E.   'Agriculture and industries in Turkey' in W. H. Hall (ed.), *Reconstruction in Turkey* (New York, 1918).

Widmer, R.   'Population' in S. B. Himadeh, *Economic Organization of Syria* (Beirut, 1936).

Wiener, L.   *L'Egypte et ses chemins de fer* (Brussels, 1932).

Viet, G.   *Mohammed Ali et les beaux-arts* (Cairo, n.d. (1949?)).

Willcocks, W.   *Egyptian Irrigation*, 2nd edn (London, 1899).

Willcocks, W.   *The Irrigation of Mesopotamia* (London, 1911).

Willcocks, W. and Craig, J. I.   *Egyptian Irrigation*, 3rd edn, II (London, 1913).

Williams, De Broe & Co.   *Sugar in Egypt and Elsewhere* (London, 1903).

Wilson, A. T.   'Mesopotamia, 1914–1921', *JCAS*, VIII, 3 (1921).

Winkler, M.   *Foreign Bonds: An Autopsy* (Philadelphia, 1933).

Wirth, E.   *Agrargeographie der Irak* (Hamburg, 1962).

Wirth, E.   *Syrien: Eine Geographische Landeskunde* (Darmstadt, 1971).

de Witte, R. (ed.)   *The Massacres in Syria* (New York, 1860).

Wood, A. G.   *A History of the Levant Company* (Oxford, 1935).

Wright, A. (ed.)   *Twentieth Century Impressions of Egypt* (London, 1909).

Yamamura, K.   'Success illgotten? The role of Meiji militarism on Japan's technological progress', *JEH*, XXXVII, 1 (March 1977).

Yapp, M. E.   'The modernization of Middle Eastern armies in the nineteenth century: a comparative view' in V. J. Parry and M. E. Yapp (eds), *War, Technology and Society in the Middle East* (London, 1975).

Yasa, I.   *Hasanoglan: Socio-economic Structure of a Turkish Village* (Ankara, 1957).

Yates, W. H.   *The Modern History and Conditions of Egypt*, I (London, 1843).

Zannis, J.   *Le crédit agricole en Egypte* (Paris, 1937).

Zubaida, S.   'Economic and political activism in Islam', *ES*, I, 3 (Aug. 1972).

Index

aba 262
Abbas Pasha (of Egypt) 74, 123, 138
Abd al-Hadi (family) 81, 267−8
Abdul-Aziz (Sultan) 105
Abdul-Hamid II (Sultan) 195, 254−5,
  267−8, 280−1
Abdullah Pasha (of Palestine) 77
Abu Gosh (family) 173
Acre 19−20, 51
Adana 60
adjala 211(def.)
agha 282
Agricultural Bank: Egyptian 224, 231−2;
  Ottoman 205−6, 208
agricultural output: (to 1800) 4−8, 17;
  (1850−80) 167−8, 171, 175−8, 183, 188;
  (1880−1914) 200−9, 218−19, 221−2,
  226−8, 259, 265−6, 274−5, 279
agricultural techniques 39−40, 66−9, 144,
  208, 222, 230−1, 267, 284
Ahmad Jazzar-Pasha (of Palestine) 7, 20, 77
Aleppo (city, district, province): (to 1800)
  7, 18, 24, 46−8, 54; (1800−50) 77,
  79−81, 88, 90, 93; (1850−80) 168,
  171−3; (1880−1914) 244, 249, 254
Alexandria: (to 1800) 24, 51, 53; (1800−50)
  71, 84, 86−8, 92, 98−9; (1850−82)
  129−30, 149−50
Alexandria Stock Exchange 225
Alexandria Cement Company 238−9
Alexandretta *see* Iskanderun
Aley (Mount Lebanon) 166, 253
Ali Bey al-Kabir (of Egypt) 64
Ali Paşa (Ottoman) 108, 119
alim (pl. *ulama*) 13(def.), 14, 17, 49, 57,
  61, 81
Amalgamated Oriental Carpet
  Manufacturers Ltd (Izmir) 212
Amir (family) 174
Amlak al-Mudawwara (Iraq) 280(def.)
Amman 245
Anaza (tribe) 6
Anglo-Egyptian Spinning and Weaving
  Company (later Filature Nationale) 225,
  237−8

animal husbandry 26, 29, 44−5, 204, 254,
  260−1, 276−7
Ankara 24
Antalya 29
Arab Steamship Company (Iraq) 277
araba 120(def.)
ardabb xiii(def.)
armies, armaments 57, 62, 67, 73, 77,
  79; Egyptian 129; Ottoman 105, 110,
  167, 170−1, 173−4, 199−200
Arraba (Palestine) 174, 268
Artin, Y. 73, 141
d'Arvieux (J-P. Labat) 42
Ashraf 18(def.)
Asiatic Mode of Production 23
Aswan Dam 222
Asyut 24
al-Atrash (family) 170, 255
avanias 21(def.), 55
Ayalon, D. 16
ayan 14(def.), 15, 63
Ayançık (Anatolia) 208−9
Azm (family) 18, 254

Baabda (Mount Lebanon) 164
Baer, G. 216
Baghdad (city, district, province): (to 1800)
  4, 20−1, 24, 48, 51, 53−4, 56; (1800−50)
  82; (1850−80) 180, 184; (1880−1914)
  273, 285−6
Bairam 48
bait (Mamluk household) 16
bales 112(def.), 203(def.)
Bani Lam (tribe) 32
Bank of Egypt 235
bankruptcy: Egyptian government 127−8,
  130−5, 220−1; Ottoman government
  108−10, 166, 171, 191−2; private 90,
  163, 234−5
banks, bankers: European 98, 102−3, 116,
  163; Middle Eastern 13, 158, 160, 223−5
banks, banking 98, 102−3, 122, 125;
  agricultural 117−18, 224, 231−3
Baran, P. 98
barat 55(def.)

Baraziz (family) 254
Barkan, O. L. 3, 8
Barrage, Delta 123, 221–2
barrani 35(def.)
Barth, K. 45
Basra (city, district, province): (to 1800) 4, 20–1, 24, 48, 51, 53, 56; (1850–80) 180; (1880–1914) 273, 278, 286
Batatu, J. 283
beans 40
beduin (nomads) 5–7, 38, 44–5, 54, 79, 171–2, 173–4
Beersheba 245
Beirut: (1800–50) 51, 54, 79–80, 86–7, 90, 98–9; (1850–80) 154, 162–3, 165–6; (1880–1914) 244, 249, 253
Beirut/Damascus Carriage Road 165–6, 245–6
Beit Jala (Palestine) 266
Bekaa (valley) 79, 166–7, 172, 259
Bell, G. L. 284
Ben Gurion, D. 271–2
Bergheim (family) 175, 268
beylerbey 11(def.)
Bikfaya (Mount Lebanon) 159, 165
bilharzia 217, 219
birsim (clover) 30, 231
Black Death (1347–9) 3
Blaisdell, D. C. 108
de Blignières, E-G. 133
Block, Sir A. 195
bonds, government: Egyptian 122, 125, 127, 132; Ottoman 100, 107, 166; Syrian 169; *see also havalé, kaimé, serghi*
Boislecomte, Baron de 91, 97
Bowring, J. 79, 88, 91, 99
British Chamber of Commerce of Egypt 219
Brumana (Mount Lebanon) 159, 165
Buhaira canal (Egypt) 222
Buckingham, J. S. 46
Bulaq (Cairo) 53, 69, 71
Burckhardt, J. L. 40, 45–6
Bursa (Brussa) 8, 23–4, 115, 117, 211–12

Cadastral Survey (Ottoman) 119
Caisse de la Dette (Egypt) 133, 220–1, 235
Caesaria, Plain of (Palestine) 174
Cairo: (to 1800) 4–5, 9, 21, 23, 47–51; (1800–50) 64, 69–71; (1850–82) 130, 149–50
Cairo Stock Exchange 225, 235
camels 54, 179, 276–7
Campbell, Col. 71
Canning, Stratford 59
cantar 69n(def.), 136n(def.)
Capitulations, capitulatory treaties 55, 60, 106–7, 113–14, 119–20, 139, 225

caravan 48, 50–6, 78, 168; pilgrimage 13, 54
carpet manufacture 117, 211–12, 266
Carswell, J. 8
Cave, S. 130, 140
caza 184(def.)
Celali (revolt, rebels) 7, 14
Celebi, E. 47
cement manufacture 211, 238–9
cereals 12, 30, 40, 52, 65–6, 92; in Anatolia 11, 189, 200–2, 208; in Egypt 135; in Iraq 181–2, 273–4, 279; in Syria/Palestine 167, 171, 175–7, 259, 265; wheat and barley 28–32, 274, 279
Charles Lafutte et Cie (Paris) 125
Chesney Expedition 90, 181
Chevalier, D. 88, 92, 97–8, 156–8
cholera 273
cigarette manufacture 152, 240, 262–3
Circassian immigrants and settlers 113, 120–1, 170–2, 202, 245–6, 254–5, 264
Civil List (Ottoman) 107
cloth (silk, linen, wool), cloth weaving 8–9, 46, 71–2, 94–5, 117, 211, 261–2
coffee 5, 9–10
Cohen, A. 7, 21
Colvin, A. 135
Commercial Courts, Tribunals 90, 163, 165
coins, coinage 10, 50, 56, 89
Commercial Conventions 116; Anglo-Turkish (1820) 61, (1838) 61, 75, 91 (1861) 116, 165
Commission de la Dette Publique (Egypt) 133–4
Commission of Inquiry (Egypt) 132, 142
Commission of Liquidation (Egypt) 132–3
Commission on Commerce and Industry (Egypt) 220, 226, 238
Comptior de'Escompte (Paris) 102–3, 125–6
Conder, C. R. 174, 176–7
Congress of Berlin (1878) 109–10
Cook, M. A. 3
corvée (tax) 143, 222
cotton (and seed) 7–9, 20, 28–32, 41, 44, 52, 79, 86; in Anatolia 86, 111–12, 115–17, 203–8; in Egypt (long-staple) 66–9, 86–7, 92, 135–8, 144, 218–19, 222; in Palestine 175, 178; in Syria 92, 171–2, 260
cotton (cloth): Egyptian 70–1, 75, 237–8; European 75, 84–7, 93–5
cotton (thread) 9, 70–1, 93–5
Cotton Boom (Egyptian) 126–7, 135–9
council, urban (*majlis*) 60, 81, 118, 279
Couvidou, H. 148
credit, commercial 88–9, 98, 158, 165, 252

Crédit Foncier Egyptien 139, 225, 232
Crédit Mobilier (Paris) 102
Cromer, Lord (Sir E. Baring) 128, 133–4, 223, 225–6
Crouchley, A. E. 233–6, 241
Cuinet, V. 245, 280
Çukurova Plain 115–16, 207
Curzon, Lord 274–5

Dadian, Ohannes 62
Dair al-Qamar (Mount Lebanon) 94, 159, 162, 165
Daira Khassa (Egypt) 131, 133, 140, 145
Daira Saniya (Egypt) 131, 133–4, 140, 145, 224, 238
Daira Saniya Company (Egypt) 224
Daira al-Saniya (Iraq) 277, 280–1, 284
Damascus (city, district, province): (to 1800) 7, 12, 17–18, 29, 46, 48, 53–4, 56; (1800–50) 77–8, 80, 88–9, 93, 97; (1850–80) 168, 171–3; (1880–1914) 244, 264
Damietta 24, 46–7, 55
Daud Pasha (Iraq) 82
dates, date palms 32, 183, 274, 279
daura 36(def.)
Davis, E. J. 116, 121
debt, indebtedness, agricultural 119, 223–4
debt, national: Egyptian 127–8, 130–5; Ottoman 108–10
debt, national, floating: Egyptian 125, 131–2, 139, 231–5; Ottoman 107
Deganiya (Palestine) 272
Deir Ez-Zor (Syria) 171
Dent, Palmer and Co. (London) 101
derebey 15(def.), 57
Deutsche Bank (Istanbul) 192–9
Daghghara Canal (Iraq) 187
dima 159(def.), 262
dira 35(def.)
Diyarbakir 48, 54, 56, 117
Dolmabahce (musket works) 62
Domains (Egyptian estates) 132, 134, 140, 145
Dowson, Sir E. 273
drains, drainage 222
Drovetti (French Consul) 69
Ducousso, G. 251
Duff Gordon, Lady L. 142–3
dunum xiii(def.)
durra (maize or sorghum) 4, 29, 40

East India Company 82
Eddé (family) 166
Egyptian Cotton Mills Company 237
Ekron (Palestine) 270–1
Eldem, V. 189–90

emigration (Syrian/Lebanese) 166–7, 244–5
emin 11(def.), 12
Emir, Amir, 19
engines (steam) 72, 76
Erzerum (town and province) 24, 60
esnaf/asnaf (guilds) 21, 47–8, 50
estates, agricultural 73–4, 92, 140–8, 206–8, 217–18, 228–30, 254–6, 267–9; methods of management 114–16, 143–8, 207–8, 255–6, 268–9, 282–4
Euphrates river 32, 53, 180–1, 185, 187, 254, 259, 278–9
Euphrates and Tigris Steam Navigation Company 181, 183, 277–8, 286

Fahmy, M. 70
faiz 35(def.)
Farley, J. L. 120, 170
feddan xiii(def.)
fellaheen 83n(def.)
ferdé 77(def.)
Fernea, R. A. 32
Flecker, J. E. 251
figs 28, 203–5
Finn, J. 178
Firestone, Y. 178, 256–8, 268–9
flax 30, 44
Fontanier, V. 56
French Expedition (1798–1801) 23, 25, 31, 43, 64–5
fruits (citrus) 28–9
Fuad Paşa (Ottoman) 108, 119

Galata, Bankers of 103, 107
Gaza 86, 176, 266
ghuta (Damascus) 29
Gibb, H. A. R. and H. Bowen 5–6, 11, 54
gins, ginning 67–8, 112, 116, 137–8, 151
Girard, P. S. 4, 40, 44, 47, 53
Girga (Egypt) 17
Gladstone, W. E. 135
gold, specie 89, 97–8
Goschen, G. 131–2
Goschen–Joubert settlement (Egypt) 132–3
Granott, A. 255, 267–9
grapes, raisins 28, 30, 111, 113, 204–5, 267, 271
Guyot, Y. 198
Guys, H. 98

Haider, S. 280, 284–5
Haifa 249
Hajj (pilgrimage) 13, 54, 159, 263
Haluka, Joseph 286
Hama 18, 24, 172–3, 255
Hamont, P. N. 73

Hamza, A-M. 126–8
Hansen B. and E. Lucas 241; and
    M. Wattleworth 226–8
hara (quarter) 49
has/khass 11(def.)
Hasan, M. S. 273
Hasbaya (Mount Lebanon) 161–2
hushiya 282(def.)
Hasselquist, F. 9, 48
Hatra 284
Hatt-ı Şerif of Gulhane 58–60, 62, 80, 116
Hatt-ı Hümayoun (1856) 116, 119
Hauran (plain) 18, 81, 90, 170, 177, 255,
    259, 263
havalé 169(def.)
Hebron 174, 266
Hekekyan, Y. 70–5
Heroditus 30, 53
hilali 95(def.)
Hillah (town and branch of Euphrates)
    24, 53, 185, 187, 279
Himadeh, S. B. 266, 285
himaya (enforced protection) 21, 50
Hindiyah Barrage and Canal 185, 187, 279
Hirsch, Baron 105
Hirsch, E. 26
hisba 50(def.)
Hoexter, M. 173
Homs 18, 24, 172–3
Hopkins, A. G. 42
hotels 253
al-hur (the marsh) 186
Hütteroth, W. D. 5

ibadiya (estates) 141, 145
Ibrahim Pasha (of Egypt) 74, 77–81, 98,
    144
Ilhami Pasha (of Egypt) 123
iltizam (tax farm) 12–13, 15, 17, 19–20,
    65, 80–1
El-Imam, Dr M. 227
Inalçik, H. 15, 22, 37
indigo, indigo works 30, 71
Industrial Reform Commission (Ottoman)
    116
industrial census: in Anatolia (1913, 1915,
    1921) 209–11; in Egypt (1927) 239–40;
    in Palestine (1927/8, 1930) 266
industry: craft 5, 8–9, 21–2, 46–8, 76,
    93–4, 117, 148–50, 159–60, 165, 172–3,
    177, 189–90, 211–13, 239–40, 261–3,
    266, 285–6; factory 69–76, 115, 117, 145,
    150–2, 157–9, 165, 189–90, 209–11,
    219–20, 235–9, 263–4, 266–7, 285;
    government policy towards 62–3, 69–73,
    75–6, 116–17, 148–51, 213, 235–9, 263;
    military 62–3, 69, 71, 75, 117, 150, 285

iqta 34(def.)
Irad-ı Cedid 59(def.)
irrigation systems 26–32, 38, 40–1, 66, 68,
    129, 143, 185, 221–2, 279
Isfahan 53, 55
Iskanderun (Alexandretta) 48, 51, 80, 98,
    249
Ismail Pasha (Khedive of Egypt) 134, 226;
    and foreign borrowing 126–9, 130–2;
    and industry 150–1; and private estates
    128, 131, 136, 140–1, 144–5, 150–1
Issawi, C. 293
Istanbul: (to 1800) 3, 23–4, 46, 48–9,
    51–2, 54, 56; (1800–50) 62, 83–7;
    (1850–81) 107
izar 262(def.)
izba (Egyptian estate) 146–8, 228–30, 281
Izmir (Smyrna): (to 1800) 8, 15, 24–5, 48,
    51, 53, 55; (1800–50) 83–6, 92, 98;
    (1881–1914) 212
Iznik (Anatolia) 8

Jabal Ansariyeh (Syria) 77
Jabal Druze 263
Jabal Nablus 5, 81
al-Jabarti, A. 16–17, 34, 36, 66, 69
Jaffa 86, 98, 176–8, 266
Jalili (family) 21, 82
Janissaries 12, 17–18, 21, 58, 77, 82
Jerusalem 177, 244, 268–9
Jewish Agency 266
Jewish Colonisation Association 271
Jewish settlers, settlements in Palestine 175,
    245–6, 248, 264, 267, 270–2
jiftlik: in Anatolia 114(def.), 207; in Egypt
    73–5(def.), 141, 143, 146
Johnson–Crosbie Commission (Palestine)
    269
Joubert, E. 131–2
Jumel, F. 67, 70

kaimé 61(def.), 238
kalak 53(def.), 278
Kananiya Canal (Iraq) 187
Kapıkullu 10(def.), 18
Karak (Jordan) 245
Karpat, K. H. 118
Kazail (tribe) 185, 187
Kelman, J. 245
Khazin (family) 159, 161–2, 164
khirbas 264–5(def.)
kibbutz 272
Kilani (family) 254
kilé xiii, 177n(def.)
kilometric guarantee 121, 197, 264

Kisrawan (Mount Lebanon) 159, 161–2, 164–5
Kitchener, Lord 222, 224
Kluzinger, C. B. 148
Konya 24
Krey (Mount Lebanon) 251
Krupp Company (Germany) 195, 199
kum 40(def.)
Kunaitra (Qunaytirah) 172
Kurmuş, O. 209
Kurunfish (Cairo) 69–70
kuruş/piastres xiii(def.)
kushufiyah 35(def.)
Kütahya (Anatolia) 8

Laham (family) 173
land: communal ownership 34–5, 186, 255–9, 269; laws 63, 114, 118–20, 141, 175, 279–81; Ottoman Land Code (1858) 185, 258; ownership and control 10–21, 33–5, 58–62, 64–5, 73–5, 79, 118–20, 140–2, 174–5, 217–18, 253–5, 267–9; prices 233
Land and Mortgage Company (Egypt) 139
Landes, D. S. 126
Latakia 48, 51, 54, 79, 98
Latif Bey of Egypt 72
lazma 35(def.)
Lees, R. 270
de Lesseps, F. 94, 122, 125
Levant Company (UK) 55, 89
Lewis B. L. 2–3
Lewis, N. H. 170
livres (French) 6n(def.), 52n(def.)
Lynch (family) *see* Euphrates and Tigris Steam Navigation Company
Lyons 158–9
Law of Five Feddans (Egypt) 224
Law of Liquidation (Egypt) 132–5, 220
Levantische Baumwolle Company (Anatolia) 205
life expectancy 25
looms 47, 93–4, 165, 169–70, 172–3, 212, 253, 262, 266; Jacquard 94, 262

McNie, T. G. 286
MacGregor, J. 95
machinery, agricultural 208, 230, 284
Mahalla (Egypt) 24
Mahmoud II (Sultan) 58, 60–4, 77, 90
Maidan (Damascus) 18, 170
Mahmudiya Canal (Egypt) 66
Majdal (Palestine) 46, 266
Majlis al-Idara (Jerusalem) 174
Mako/Jumel (cotton) 67–8
malikanes 15(def.), 17, 19

Mamluks 10, 16–17, 49–50, 57, 64–5
Mansura 47
Manzalawi, Mustafa 230
Ma'oz, M. 81
Mardin (Anatolia) 56
Marj Ibn Amir (Plain of Esdraelon) 79, 174–5, 267–8
markets 42–6
Marx, K. 23, 48
Masson, P. 54
McCulloch, J. R. 88, 93
Mears, E. G. 206–7
Mecca 12, 54
Medawar, Michael 157
medin 31n(def.)
Medjediah Company (Egypt) 123
Méline Tariff (French) 205
Membij (Syria) 254
Mersin 116
merchants 7, 9–10, 12, 17–18, 22–3, 36–7, 40, 42, 44, 46, 90, 98–9; Armenian 54–5; British 9, 20, 84, 166, 211–12; Egyptian 5, 22–3, 49–50, 138–9, 237; European 55, 67, 74, 78, 88–9, 93–5, 98–9; French 7, 9, 20, 41, 83–4, 86; Iraqi 279; Palestinian 163, 179; Syrian/Lebanese 55, 154, 157–62, 164–6, 264
Midhat Paşa 118, 172, 185–6, 263
mining 213, 235–6
Ministry of Finance (Ottoman) 107, 193–4
miri 11–12(def.), 33, 36, 63, 65, 118–19
Mixed Courts (Egypt) 132, 139, 232
mohair 9, 29, 204, 206
monopolies, agricultural 20, 65–6, 74–5, 77–8, 86, 89, 91, 123, 139
Moore (UK Consul) 93
Mosul (town, district and province): (to 1800) 20–1, 24, 46, 53, 56; (1800–50) 82; (1850–80) 183–4; (1880–1914) 273, 285–6
Moutran, N. 255
Mubayyida/Mabyadea (Cairo) 70
mudaf 36(def.)
Mudawwar (family) 267
mudif 35(def.)
Muhammad Agha (Iraq) 36
Muhammad Ali Pasha (of Egypt) 58, 77–8, 86, 89–91, 123, 134; agricultural reforms 65–9, 73–5; commercial policy 65–9; estates 144; industrial policy 69–72, 75–6
Muhammad Reşid (Ottoman) 184–5
Muharram, Decree of (1881) 110, 192–200
muhtasib 22(def.), 50
mukataa/muqataa 12(def.), 19
mukataçi/muqataji 8(def.), 19, 34, 78, 80, 153, 160–4

mulberry tree, leaves 30, 79, 117, 154–5,
   159, 203–4, 249, 251, 279
mulk 33(def.), 118–19
multezim/multazim 11–14(def.), 16–18,
   34–7, 46, 64–5, 141
Muntafiq (tribe) 32, 184–6, 188, 283
muqabala (Egyptian law) 125(def.), 129,
   131, 133–4, 141
Murad and Ibrahim Beys (of Egypt) 64
muscadine (silkworm disease) 157
mushaa 35(def.), 256–9
mutaahid 73–4(def.), 144
mutasarrif 163–4(def.)
Mutasaraflik/Mutasarrifiya: of Mount
   Lebanon 163–6, 244, 251–2; of
   Jerusalem 244
Myint, H. 287

Nablus 46, 174, 178, 266, 268
Nazareth 266
Nahas, J. F. 146
Namık Paşa 184–6
Napoleon I, Napoleonic Wars 83–4, 86–7
Napoleon III 126–7
National Bank of Egypt 224–5, 232, 235
National Bank of Turkey 192–200
national income: in Egypt 220; in Turkey
   189–90
nauraj 39(def.)
navy 58, 199
nazir 147(def.)
Nedım Paşa 169
Nile (river) 26–7, 30–1
Nile Navigation Company (Egypt) 123
nili (crop) 137(def.)
Nizam-ı Cedid 58–9(def.)
Nour El-Din, S. 146
Nubar Pasha (of Egypt) 134, 146

ojak 11(def.), 15–16, 49–50
oke xiii, 155n(def.), 177n(def.)
olives, olive oil/trees 29–30, 40, 79, 175,
   177, 203–4, 253, 263, 271
Olivier, G. A. 46
Oman–Ottoman Steamship Line (Iraq)
   181, 280, 286
opium 28–30, 113, 204
Oppenheim and Nephew (Alexandria)
   125–7
opthalma 25
oranges 175, 177–8, 265, 267, 271
Ottoman Bank (later Imperial Ottoman)
   103, 192–6, 274
Ottoman Cloth Company (Izmir) 211
Ottoman Commercial Code (1850) 90

Palestine Exploration Fund (PEF) 5

Palmerston, Lord 90–1
Panzac, D. 25
para 22n(def.)
Pasteur system 157
Pastré and Tozzizza (Alexandria Bank) 98
pataque 31n(def.)
pébrine (silkworm disease) 111, 115
Peninsula and Oriental Steamship
   Company 123
Petah Tikvah (Palestine) 175, 271
phylloxera (vine disease) 113, 205, 271
piastre xiii(def.), 67(def.)
Pierotti, E. 173
plague 4, 7, 25, 94, 273
plough 39–40, 208
population 2–3, 7–8, 24–5, 287; of
   Anatolia 189; of Egypt 135, 216–17; of
   Iraq 273; of Palestine 264; of
   Syria/Mount Lebanon 166, 244–5
Porath, Y. 174
Post, G. E. 270
pound (£E, £T) xiii(def.), 67n(def.),
   151n(def.)
Public Debt Administration (PDA) 121,
   164, 192, 200; Pasteur Institute 252

qadi (cadi) 14(def.), 56
qaimmaqam 184(def.)
Qena (Egypt) 53
Quateart, D. 202–3, 205–6, 208
quintal 7n(def.)
Quseir (Egypt) 53

Radwan, S. 236
railways 120–1, 128–9, 196–7, 238, 246,
   248–9, 259; Adapazari–Izmit 121;
   Anatolian 196, 202–3, 208; Baghdad
   196, 202–3, 208; Damas–Hamah et
   Prolongements 196, 246, 264; Egyptian
   State 123, 245–6, 266; Hijaz 196, 245–6,
   266; Jaffa–Jerusalem 246, 267;
   Izmir–Aydin 113, 121; Izmir–Kasaba
   113, 121, 196, 204
Ramle (Palestine) 179
Raqqa (Syria) 254
Rashaya (Mount Lebanon) 162
Raymond, A. 5, 10, 22, 49–51
Reform Division (Ottoman) 120
Règlement et Protocole relatifs à la
   reorganisation du Mont–Liban (1861)
   162–4
rent, systems of 34, 92, 114–15, 145–8,
   159; crop-sharing (metayage) 19, 34–5,
   40, 114, 145, 159, 207–8, 229, 255; cash
   (fermage) 206, 209
Reşid Paşa (Ottoman) 100, 170
Reynal, Abbé 52

Riaz Pasha (of Egypt) 230
rice 30–2, 40, 44, 274, 279
rice mills 71
Rosetta 24, 52–3, 71
Rothschilds (London and Paris) 101, 132–3; Edmund de 271
Rougon, F. 206, 211
Ruppin, A. 248, 253
Russell, A. 47

S.A. des Ciments d'Egypte 238–9
St John, J. A. 70
Sadun (family) 184–6, 283
Safad (Palestine) 266
Said Pasha (of Egypt): award of concessions 123–6; foreign borrowing 125–6; estates 144
salyane (province) 21(def.)
Samannud (Egypt) 47
sandik 118(def.)
sanjakbey 11(def.)
saqiya 30(def.), 39, 148
Schama, S. 271
Schölch, A. 134
Schulkowski (Citizen) 36
security, insecurity, rural 3, 5–6, 78–9, 81, 94, 167, 171–4, 184–8, 245, 254–5, 266, 281
Selim III (Sultan) 58–60, 65
serghi 169(def.)
service tenants 146–8
sesame 40, 177, 260, 265
shaikh: nomadic 10, 17, 20–1, 36, 38, 80, 184, 187–8, 254, 279–83; urban 22; village 10, 36, 38, 41, 65, 74, 78, 141–2, 146
Shahin, Taniyus (Mount Lebanon) 161
Shanin, T. 41
Sharif Pasha (of Egypt) 135
al-Sharkawi, Shaikh 17
Sharon, Plain of (Palestine) 268
Sharqiya Canal (Egypt) 222
shaduf 30(def.)
shashiya 47(def.)
Shaw, S. J. 3–4, 49
Shihab (family) 19
Shwaifat (Mount Lebanon) 159, 165
sickle 39–40
Sidon (Saida) 51, 54, 79, 98
silk (raw and thread) 9, 78–9, 86, 286; Persian 7, 9, 53; Syrian/Mount Lebanese 92, 154–60, 165–8, 249–53; Turkish 86, 111, 115, 117, 205, 211–12
silk factories: in Anatolia 115, 211–12; in Syria/Mount Lebanon 155–60, 165, 172, 249–53, 262

silkworms, silkworm eggs 30, 154–8, 205, 251–2
simsar 139(def.)
sipahi 11–13(def.), 17
sirkal 35(def.), 282–3
slaves 52
Smyrna Fig Packers (Izmir) 205
soap, soap-making 177, 253, 263, 266
Société Générale des Sucreries et de la Raffinerie d'Egypte 220, 225, 238
Société Minérale d'Heraclée (Anatolia) 213
spices, pepper 3, 5, 8–10
Suez Canal 122, 125–8, 171, 180–1, 183, 275
sugar 40–1, 135–6, 145
sugar refineries, refining 17, 41, 71, 128, 144, 150–1, 238, 286
Sukru (family) 208–9
Sulaymania (Iraq) 286
suq (bazaar) 46
Sursuq (family) 157, 166, 175, 267–8
Suvla, R. S. 195
Svoboda, J. M. 277
Sykes, Sir M. 245, 264, 286

Tallien, L. 36
tamaliyya 230(def.)
tanning, tanneries 49, 71, 286
tapu (*sanads*) 118–19(def.), 185–6(def.), 280, 283
Tanta 24
tarahil 230(def.)
tariffs 61, 75, 91, 116–17, 263; external 199, 225, 236–7; internal 54, 91, 116–17
tassaruf 34(def.)
taxes: house 130; land 4, 10–21, 35–7, 59–62, 77–8, 105–6, 126, 129–30, 138, 141–3; urban 21–2, 50, 106–7
tax farmers, farming 9; land 12–21, 33–4, 58–62, 77–8, 80–1, 105–6, 108, 163, 172, 194, 199, 206, 280–1; urban 21–3, 50
Templars (German) 175, 267
textiles 261, 274; European 51, 75–6, 83–7, 93–5, 159–60, 182, 261, 274; Middle Eastern 51, 62–3, 69–76, 159–60, 165, 169–70, 172, 211–12, 237–8, 261–2, 266, 285–6
Tezel, Y. S. 104–5, 198, 214–15
tezkere 21(def.)
Thompson, E. P. 290
Thornton, T. 59–60
Tigris (river) 32, 53, 180–1, 278
timar 11–12(def.), 19–20, 59–60, 77
tobacco 28–32, 40, 111, 171, 203–8, 253, 260

Tobacco Régie (Société de la Régie
    Cointeressé des Tabacs) 152, 164, 193,
    260
Tophane (cannon foundry, Istanbul) 62
de Tott, Baron 9–10, 15
Trabzon (town and province) 29, 60, 86,
    89, 108
trade: local 42–4; intra-regional 48–56,
    95–6, 248, 276–7; international 48–56,
    67, 80–99, 110–13, 155–7, 167–8,
    180–3, 213–5, 219, 248, 265–6, 274–5;
    with Britain 75, 83–7, 101–2; with
    France 83, 86–7, 101–2; with Austria
    86–7
transport: animal 28, 53–4, 90, 170, 246,
    278; boat 28, 32, 53, 89–90, 96, 137,
    181–2, 277–8; railway 113, 120, 128–9,
    137, 202, 204, 212, 222, 238, 259; road
    120, 222, 245–6; wheeled vehicles, carts
    28, 90, 120–1, 245–8
Treaty of London (1840) 75, 123
Trécourt 52
Tripoli (Mount Lebanon) 51, 79
Tubiyya, Bishop 162
tujjar 22–3(def.)
Tuwayni (family) 157, 267

uhda: in Egypt 73–5(def.), 168; in Mount
    Lebanon 34(def.)
ulama see alim
Union Syndicale des Agriculteurs d'Egypte
    229–30
Urabi revolt (Egypt) 153
Urquhart, D. 13, 19
Urfa (Anatolia) 56
Uşak (Anatolia) 113
ushr (tithe) 59, 194, 263, 284
ushuri, ushuriya 129, 132–3, 141–2
usury, money-lending 13–14, 18, 22, 37,
    40–1, 46, 75; in Anatolia 112–14, 206,
    208; in Egypt 138–9, 142–3, 231–2; in
    Syria/Palestine 256, 268–9

usya 17(def.), 141

vakf/waqf 11(def.), 13, 33–4, 39n, 57, 61,
    65, 118, 280
valonia 29, 86, 113, 204
Van (Anatolia) 60
vegetables 29
Du Velay, A. 101, 110, 120
verghi 106(def.), 108
Veuve Guerin (silk factory, Mount
    Lebanon) 251
Vickers Armstrong Company (UK) 199
villages (as communities) 41–2, 269–70
vines 79, 203, 271
Volney, C. 47

Wadi Tumilat (Egypt) 66
wage labour 92, 114–16, 206–8, 218,
    240–1
wali (governor) 21
water melons 40
Weulersse, J. 256–8
Wilson, Rivers 133–4
Willcocks, Sir W. 228
women labourers 147, 158
Wood, R. 28–9, 36, 46, 81
wool 171–2, 183, 274
World Bank (Mission to Iraq) 32

Yerliyya 18(def.)
Young Turks 192, 199, 213, 263

Zahir al-Umar (Palestine) 7, 19–20
Zahle (Mount Lebanon) 30, 161–2, 165
Zervudachi, E. (Egypt) 230
ziamet (fief) 11–12, 19–20
Zaidani (family) 19
Ziya Paşa (Ottoman) 60
Zonguldak (Anatolia) 213
Zuq (Mount Lebanon) 159, 165

DATE DUE
